JY 20

ALL AGAINST ALL

ALL AGAINST ALL

*The Long Winter of 1933 and the Origins
of the Second World War*

PAUL

JANKOWSKI

HARPER

An Imprint of HarperCollinsPublishers

HarperCollins books may be purchased for educational, business, or sales promotional use. For information, please email the Special Markets Department at SPsales@harpercollins.com.

FIRST EDITION

Library of Congress Cataloging-in-Publication Data has been applied for.

ISBN 978-0-06-243352-7

20 21 22 23 24   LSC   10 9 8 7 6 5 4 3 2 1

Contents

———❖———

Preface

———◆·◆———

Occasionally, people ask me what I am working on. The moment in the 1930s, I reply, when the world's greater powers and some of its lesser ones turned their backs on whatever "world order" still existed and on each other. "Sounds just like today," they often say.

I wonder about that. Between the autumn of 1932 and the early summer of 1933, Hitler came to power, Japan sent troops across the Great Wall of China and left the League of Nations, Mussolini looked southward toward the Horn of Africa; Roosevelt, the new American president, deepened American isolation from Europe, Britain withdrew into the safe zones of empire, and France watched three prime ministers try and fail to bring its two former allies back into the charmed circle of the victors of 1918. Instead the three fell out acrimoniously over war debts, arms, currency, tariffs, and Germany. They had done so before, but now two world conferences that they and the League of Nations had been planning for years, about disarmament and global economic recovery, failed abjectly. The walls were going up, everywhere. In that long winter the world finally changed, from postwar to prewar. Does that sound much like the scene today? I am not sure.

The belief in global fragmentation runs strong. It supposes a resurgence of centrifugal nationalist forces, conspiring against the mirage of global integration that turned naive heads after the Cold War ended. The dark parable of the 1930s evokes as well the rise of authoritarian movements and their demagogic leaders, together with the economic discontents thought to sustain them. The certitudes attach themselves to each other, almost like rules of deduction. Nationalism, authoritarianism, social resentment—such is today's demonic triad, sighted around the globe, signaled to all, and reflected in the distant mirror of W. H. Auden's "low, dishonest decade."

Historical analogies are easy to debunk. This one rests on muddled assumptions about the world then and now. It is true, for example, that the economic catastrophe of the early 1930s helped turn minor Fascist parties in a few countries into mass movements. But in the United States and France it brought center-left, social democratic governments to power. And until recently, "national populists" deemed blood relatives of those of the 1930s often succeeded in the most prosperous economies while struggling to break through where growth was slowest and unemployment highest. Most of the authoritarian governments of the 1930s were already in place when the Depression hit, and then, rather than bring the fractious Fascists in, contrived to keep them out, at least for a while. Some of the loudest cries of ethnic and racial panic came from the most democratic of cultures. The model falls of its own sweep. It sets off the eternal strife between the historian, who sees the trees but no forest, and the political scientist, who sees the forest but no trees.

If a historical analogy were needed to illuminate our current predicaments, the world of 1900 would probably serve more usefully than that of 1930. In the early twentieth century, transnational flows of people, goods, and capital yielded not only global integration but protectionist enthusiasms, the Yellow Peril, White Australia and *France d'abord*, exclusion acts in America and pan-Germanic fantasies in Berlin and Vienna. The great powers fretted over their world position in the coming century. The new school of geopolitics was born. Nationalism had much to thank globalization for. It still does.[1]

Still, no one reading the newspapers today can escape at times a frisson of recognition on opening those of the 1930s. Demagogues exploited national or ethnic animosities to win or keep power; internationalism, variously expressed as world bodies, transnational associations and civil society, world revolution, free trade, open borders, collective security, or the earnest repudiation of any and all great power rivalry, fell prey to strident calls for national primacy. Sometimes but not always such calls accompanied attacks on democracy; sometimes but not always they served the demagogues. Diverse governments and regimes, from Moscow to Washington and Tokyo, heeded the calls in diverse ways. Authoritarians, who bridle at multilateral constraints abroad as well as constitutions and dissent at home, might more readily take up the cry of the 1930s—"Every man for himself"—but they were not the only ones.

To some observers, in particular those called realists, the sixty or seventy years of relative peace and prosperity that elapsed under the American aegis since 1945 seem aberrant, a historical accident unlikely to recur.[2] Nothing in the scenery of the 1930s would surprise the realists among the international relations theorists now, other perhaps than the ink wasted on lamenting it. In its most elemental form, realism paints the world that way anyway—as an anarchic menagerie of states, each jostling for power, security, or advantage.[3] However differently they treat their compatriots, however foreign to each other their ways at home, they obey the same logic once they step outside and eye one another. There the world imposes on them its sovereign indifference to rules. It condemns them to compete but not necessarily to fight, for they can resort to instruments that neutralize the threat of subversion or subjection. They can, for example, restore equilibrium by manipulating the balance of power, in which smaller states typically coalesce to arrest the emergence of a hegemon in their midst, or they can deter by manifest pugnacity their greedier neighbors, or collude to eliminate or partition an inveterate troublemaker. But these tools provide no guarantees. In its different versions and manifestations, realism—still the dominant notion of explaining why nation-states behave toward one another the way they do—presents a world both anarchic and predictable, in which fitful events can reveal the recurrent sequence of threat and response to chroniclers astute enough to discern it.

Many were unwittingly doing so before realism, neorealism, and their variants elevated premise into ever more sophisticated theory. Celebrated works of traditional diplomatic history presented war, peace, and conditions in between as outcomes in the struggle between modern states for survival, expansion, or tranquility. "In the state of nature which Hobbes imagined," one of them began, "violence was the only law, and life was 'nasty, brutish and short.' Though individuals never lived in this state of nature, the Great Powers of Europe have always done so."⁴ Two and a half millennia earlier, Thucydides had assumed much the same of the powers of his own day.⁵ Neither he nor his successors knew anything of realist thought in international relations, let alone the rational choice or game theories into which some of it more recently has devolved; but they shared with it a Hobbesian premise about primitive anarchy in the world, one that had somehow to be contained lest the war of all against all reclaim its ways.

Just such a prospect haunted the interwar years. Minds that in the 1920s looked back on the Great War as a descent into primeval strife looked ahead in the 1930s to an even more calamitous relapse, the shedding of all lingering restraints on human savagery. Public figures routinely warned of the end of civilization. Genocide they did not foresee, oddly, but chemical warfare and skies dark with bombers—two other innovations from the previous conflict—they did. The threat of renewed international anarchy seemed somehow to lie at the heart of the matter. Arnold Toynbee, scrutinizing public opinion in 1936, found resignation as well as dismay—the gloomy prognosis that a condition that had lasted four centuries might last for another four. In the short term, "the new international era (if new it was) was likely to end in the catastrophic fashion of its nineteenth-century predecessor."⁶

Whether preaching the virtues of necessity like its classical ancestors or revealing the inexorable constraints of an anarchic world like its structural exponents, realism both recommended and predicted balancing.⁷ It envisaged the ceaseless creation and re-creation of equilibriums in a multipolar and even, for some, a bipolar world order, without troubling to explain how they flourished or withered, or whether conflicts erupted from their formation or from their dis-integration. All, in a pattern taken from organization theory, would conform to the unwritten rules, as the weaker states emulated the most successful ones. But nothing of the sort happened in the inter-war years. The alliances that had held together throughout the Great War vanished with the peace, and none emerged to take their place. Even while Britain sought to foster the rehabilitation of Germany, and France with increasing desperation to contain it, a balance of power, a will-o'-the-wisp that found no artisans, never materialized. The Soviet Union, which sought in the morning to prevent any coalition of European powers from taking shape, at midday to turn one against Germany, and at nightfall to join the Reich itself, appeared most faithful to realist logic; but these were tactical devices to allow its own militarization, which had begun before any of the others. The United States was not interested in balances of any kind.

Later, realists would try to attribute the instabilities of the inter-war world to structural flaws—by explaining, for example, that no Concert system emerged to keep the peace as it had after 1815, or that no global hegemon filled the place that Britain had occupied in the previous century, or that the tripolar world before the Second World War was more dangerous than the bipolar one after it.[8] All such structural flaws were held to hasten a global melee, much as an army degenerates into a band of looters once inside the gates of the city. But why did no Concert form, why did the men who returned home from Versailles in 1919 not want one as avidly as their predecessors at Vienna a century earlier? And the world was not tripolar between the wars. Its poles kept shifting in number and in weight, the variables that structural realism allows but does not account for.

As a theory, realism explained little of this world; as a prescription, it allowed isolationism and appeasement. The first invoked geopolitical necessities, the second the realities of power. E. H. Carr, one of the most celebrated of the early interwar realists, advocated encouraging Germany to expand southeastward and as late as the spring of 1939 still thought highly of the "realist" Neville Chamberlain. Later he wondered how he could have been so blind. How, indeed? Like others later, he had belittled the transformative power of belief or fanaticism in history. If international structure alone governed the behavior of states toward one another, then much of recorded history would never have taken place; and even Carr soon drew back from the implications of unbridled realism.[9]

The doctrine, for all its staying power, never reigned unchallenged. Neither did Hobbes's view of the state of nature. For centuries, political philosophers imagined a primitive humanity differently and conceived of another civilized one. Liberals came to envisage an interdependent world in which nation-states might at length overcome some of their jealousies, surrender some of their prerogatives, shed some of their weapons. In the interwar years they hoped to avert armageddon not by balancing power but by lifting the mantle of absolute sovereignty from the nation-state—the irreducible unit of the modern world and of much realist thought as well. They envisioned a system of collective security at Geneva that would frustrate any aggressor in their midst. Much confusion attended the concept—would the ostracism of world opinion suffice, or might the League's members resort to force against the transgressor, a prospect that offended many a liberal conscience? But the belief moved millions, whether they could define it or not. Marxism, in its way as optimistic as classical liberalism, predicted that the progress of capitalism would lead to the dissolution of the nation-state. It would lead instead to the dissolution of Marxism, but for now the chiliasm of the International illuminated the path to a classless and warless world for many a convert, renegade, or pilgrim.

At the end of the Great War, Woodrow Wilson proclaimed the first and Vladimir Lenin the second such genial world vision. Both saw them vanish within years, in their own lifetimes. The 1930s buried them. Disciples still carried the torches, but the world moved on. The powers that had enshrined collective security at Geneva declined to set it in motion in Manchuria; it lingered on, finally expiring before Italian and German provocations in Africa and within Europe itself. Wilson had extended the other promise of his dream, national self-determination, only to peoples of the European continent, and some of these, new minorities in new states, he left unhappier than he had found them. The liberalism of free trade and the invisible hand, from which realism would borrow the notion of actors conspiring unwittingly to create an international system greater than themselves, and which oddly echoed Marxism in predicting the erosion of states and their seawalls by the tides of commerce, disappeared in the ruins of the Great Depression.[10] The Soviet leadership soon joined the international system, to the extent that it could find one.

By the mid-1930s a wilderness of answers awaited anyone asking the world's leaders about the forces that moved them. All, of course, preferred self-preservation to extinction, but the promise, like the threat, they expressed in historical visions of all shapes and hues—as spaces and races, for the Germans and the Japanese; in the recovery of lost grandeur, for the Italians and the Hungarians; in the freedom of the seas and all that went with it, for the British in their vast empire. The Soviets, with almost as much reason as the French and the Poles, never stopped worrying about the defense of their homeland. Nor did the Americans, determined to insulate their own from the vicious traps of the Old World. Not surprisingly, such motley protagonists steered by their own diplomatic and military lights. The British and the French progressively shed the chimera of collective security but still clung to the statecraft of Richelieu, Castlereagh, and Bismarck, made of treaties and incremental gains and compromises; they conceived of a war, if one had to come, that would lose in ferocity what it would gain in duration, and spare their peoples the devastation they all too vividly imagined. Germany and the Soviet Union signed pacts and proclaimed the same moderation but privately conceived of peace as temporary, and prepared for war, when it came, as an affair of annihilation.

Neither realism nor most competing theories of international politics need dwell on such national eccentricities. The theorists excavate the grammar of international history, the historians recover its spoken languages. Realists, for example, insist that power, security, or "self-help" inspire international behavior. How shifting belief systems and foreign policies express these or any other drive is of ancillary interest at most; the founder of structural realism, Kenneth Waltz, excluded them from his theoretical project.[11] But for historians they lie front and center—plural rather than singular, transient rather than fixed, and irreducible to a universal appetite, fear, or submission to a univocal and systemic deus ex machina. From their end of the telescope, historians gaze at states large and small changing the face they present to the world, sometimes in startling ways. The twentieth century alone might mesmerize. Within one decade, the 1940s, the United States assumed a role in the world it had shunned for its entire history. Within another, the 1980s, the Soviet Union adopted a novel conception of its security that transformed its relations with its neighbors and with its principal adversary. Within a generation, well before reunification, Germany had become unrecognizable to anyone familiar with its ways in the first half of the century—once avid for a place that its own resources could not sustain, it now shrank from one they insistently invited. Japan renounced imperial conquest and the arms that had assured it. Special circumstances explain such shifts, but so do conscious acts of will, the inflection of a national story to a changed sense of purpose. American exceptionalism could as easily yield interventionism as isolationism. Germany and Japan, dropping the language of existential panic, severed national from military success. For the first time in its brief history, the Soviet Union ceased to discern only threats in the world.

Sometimes, whether they see themselves differently in the mirror or not, states undertake to transform the international system through which they see each other. They define it rather than submit to it. They did so after 1815, when European powers leagued against France placed stability before individual aggrandizement in the coming peace. They resolved to give up balancing one another, a competitive pastime that had yielded only imbalance and endemic war since 1763, and to observe instead a Concert of interlocking obligations and restraints. Not everyone profited—as the Poles and Saxons could confirm—and the system relied on two hegemonic flank powers, Britain and Russia, to moderate the others between them; but its vestigial spirit spared the Continent a war between any great powers for a generation and a general war among them for a century.[12] They did so again after 1945, when the United States, its former allies and adversaries, and the countries of the nascent European community devised another novel system of international cooperation. It resembled no other before it, but once again elevated shared over individual goals. Once again it yielded an extended peace. The Cold War alone could not induce the participants to renounce proximate for remote satisfactions so readily—they had envisaged doing so before the deep freeze set in during the late 1940s, and continued to do so when it thawed during the 1970s and ended in the 1990s. They had changed.[13]

During the interwar years the reverse happened. Every effort to transform the international system, every parley in the 1920s and early 1930s in Washington, Geneva, Genoa, Locarno, the Hague, or London, had come undone before the mid-1930s. The problems began at home. There a unique sense of internal and external vulnerability came to grip greater and lesser powers alike. It had happened before, in some Continental powers before 1914, but never had it seized so many in and out of government so simultaneously—in Europe, in North America, in East Asia. It marked a new variety of nationalism, directed less at a single oppressor or hereditary enemy than at a hostile world that manifested itself through agents at home—or within an empire—as well as abroad. Communism, immigration, capitalism, Judaism, the West, pacifism, the existential threat in all its guises— such frights, wherever they took hold and whoever exploited them, crossed borders as though with passe-partout keys, and insinuated themselves into foreign and domestic politics alike.

Globalization might explain the ubiquity of such popular fears, along with the spread of political languages intelligible to peoples once deaf to one another. The spread of democracy, liberal or not—

the widening of the political nation—might explain their impact. Both novelties appeared durably not in the twentieth but in the nineteenth century. And, as a force in international relations, the crowd did not await either to make its voice heard now and again. In the sixteenth and seventeenth centuries, when armies themselves could resemble mobs, popular fury as much as statecraft sustained the wars of religion in western and central Europe. In the eighteenth century, popular Francophobia in Britain and popular Austrophobia in France disrupted the chess games of diplomats, and in the middle of the nineteenth, Russophobia in London and Christian Orthodox fervors in Saint Petersburg drew governments into a Crimean war that some of their wiser members would have preferred to avoid. The palace heard the street, not always happily. And soon the boardroom and the newsroom as well: An entire school of German historians, promoting the *Primat der Innenpolitik*, attributes much of Wilhelmine belligerence and indeed of the crisis of the summer of 1914 to a stratagem to deflect public opinion from domestic onto foreign targets, or to appease powerful domestic lobbies that pushed heady vistas of Continental domination on compliant chancellors.[14] At Vienna in 1815 the diplomats had managed, mostly, to ignore domestic public opinion. At Versailles in 1919 they could not, even though they still sequestered themselves as though they could.

The novelty of the interwar crisis lay not in the obsolescence of cabinet diplomacy, as passé as cabinet wars; it lay in the way mass politics eventually came to work against any international engagements other than the most transparently and immediately self-serving. Avoidance or predation returned as the warlike options of peace. The pattern hardened halfway between the First and the Second World Wars, in the early 1930s, the moment this book describes. "The historian of law," the great English medievalist Frederic William Maitland said in an inaugural lecture at Cambridge in 1888, "will often have to work from the clear to the vague, from the known to the unknown."[15] He would have to begin, as it were, at the end—and the historian of the early 1930s might travel backward as well, setting out from the recorded breakdown of international conferences, moving on to the hazier realms of domestic resistance to foreign commitments, and arriving at the dark territory of national delusions.

These yielded Hitler, the flight from collective commitments, the passivity of the Western powers, Japanese defiance, the Soviet persecution mania, and much else besides. They belong to the origins of the Second World War but not to its causes, which lie in the deeds committed or omitted in the years that followed. They sprang from recent experience, most obviously the Great War and the Great Depression, but also from the more remote lore of national exploits, ordeals, or humiliations; and they bridged the gap between history lived and history made. Among Americans, war in Europe was a memory, isolation a delusion, neutrality a policy. The carriers of each declined in number even as they gained in precision of speech. Between the largely silent millions who remembered and the articulate few who governed rose the hubbub of public discourse, where national beliefs took shape and where dominant motifs emerged. Germany's victimhood, Soviet Russia as savior and pariah, Japan's lifeline in Manchuria and its millennial Asian mission, Britain's imperial sanctuary—such collective conceits figure heavily in the pages that follow, for without them no one can glimpse the mental world through which even the most pragmatic national leaders moved and encountered one another, and through which the children of the First World War became the parents of the Second.

Years later, after the war and the genocides, some historians tried to find general explanations for what had befallen the world. But many more did so for the European catastrophe of 1914 than for the much wider global conflict that erupted at intervals and in bursts between 1937 and 1941. This one seemed to federate national or regional conflicts, best understood in their own terms. Besides, the incremental spread of war across three continents paradoxically presented at first glance less of a mystery than the access of midsummer fears in the smallest of them—Europe—in 1914. Posterity could best understand the outbreaks of war in East Asia in 1937, in Europe in

1939, and in the Pacific in 1941 through the histories that lay behind them, which were diverse, controversial, only slowly accessible in the archives, and rewarding as well in ways that might not even touch on the conflicts that followed. The war laid waste much of the planet, and grand or planetary strategies, the links between one theater and another, attracted much expert attention; but the search for origins on a comparable scale lagged fitfully.[16]

Some such inquiry already preoccupied American and European leaders when they emerged from what some—not all—were calling the Second World War.[17] Implicitly or explicitly, they blamed the conflagration on the breakdown in the 1930s of liberal democracy, economic growth, international trade and investment, and a collective security system engaging all. They now conceived of each as a precondition for the others and envisioned the world they wished to remake as the schematic opposite of the one they had left behind. Not by accident, and unlike 1815, they aspired to transform domestic as much as international society. In time, peace and prosperity in the West appeared to validate their premise, unimpeachable as a guide to policy yet solipsistic as a historical argument. Yes, breakdowns had led to breakdown. It fell to historians to explain how economic stagnation led to war—it had not always done so—or how the retreat of democracy had done the same, scarcely an axiomatic sequence either; and they struggled to find answers that convincingly transcended national boundaries.

Diplomatic history proposed the Treaty of Versailles, which set satisfied against dissatisfied signatories. But long before Hitler launched his war in 1939, events had nullified almost all the clauses that Germans deemed humiliating. Why did tensions only worsen as grievances left by the Great War vanished, redressed with the consent of the victors? Economic history proposed the Depression, which helped breed right-wing nationalists in Fascist, racist, or militarist form, agitating to install aggressive regimes that pursued expansion and salvation abroad. But the Depression could not explain the autonomous staying power of such nationalisms, nor why they only intensified as some of the most resentful claimants—Japan, Germany—recovered more steadily than others from the economic depths of the early 1930s. A psychosocial history rested on the degrading effects of total war, and supposed that sixty or seventy million veterans revisited on their world the brutalization that the Great War had inflicted on them. The mass diagnosis did not explain why so many became pacifists instead, or why returning German or Italian or Russian veterans should have been more brutalized than their French or British counterparts.[18] Each national passage from peace to war was different, each followed its own path from shared conditions to individual choices. No wonder historians shied away from the search for common origins that tempted so many who pondered July 1914.

This book suggests that each path ran through national mythology, now ingrained in mass politics. Each was unique, but in the interwar years each set itself against the world in some way. Each rendered international norms and rules discretionary if not irrelevant. Another school of international relations theory, more recent than the others, might welcome the suggestion. "Anarchy," according to constructivism, "is what states make of it." It may be given ab initio, as the realists insist, but it is also malleable. It can lend itself to treatments other than amoral self-help; more cooperative arrangements can emerge among friends, less bellicose stances among enemies, according to national identities made or modified. Identity is too hydra-headed a construct to be used here, but the idea is the same: who nations think they are can determine what they want.[19]

Sometimes a contagion of resentment at national insult, indignity, or humiliation spreads among them. Grievances of all kinds rankle, and popular leaders arise to voice them. "Sounds just like today"—these, more than hazardous assimilations of a regime or party then to another today, are the unsettling echoes of the 1930s today, the sounds that unnerve. A geopolitical birthright, claimed by Japan then and by China today; an ethnic rallying cry across the borders, raised by Germany among others then and by Russia today;

a repudiation of ungrateful allies, abusers of generosity in war and in peace, by their American benefactor then and again today—plaintiffs might disappear or even exchange complaints, but the rancor still stirs.

The transnational novelties of the 1930s differed profoundly from those of today. The diffusion of power among countless state and non-state actors, and a profusion of multilateral organizations demanding more acronyms than the alphabet can provide, make the world neither multipolar like the 1930s nor unipolar like the 1990s, but "a-polar."[20] No depression paralyzes the global economy today. Aggressive dictatorial regimes and the ideological challenge presented by Communism and Fascism gave the earlier decade a unique face, while the specters of environmental crisis, nuclear proliferation, and the cyberspace jungle confer an unwelcome distinction on our own. But national panics need not arise in identical circumstances. Logically, they arise at the same time, for they both conspire and contend with each other. They join even as they pull away from one another, recanting as though with one voice the internationalism of their predecessors while recoiling at any hint of a newfound community.

In the 1930s, with embarrassment or contempt, regimes of all sorts buried the vestiges of collective security and shared norms. By the 2010s their numerous descendants were adjourning sine die a global agenda that had opened the millennium promising free trade, national self-determination, and human rights. The first again fell prey to economic nationalisms—one study found that the United States in 2019 was threatening China with tariffs approximating those of its Hawley-Smoot Act of 1930, the loudest opening shot in the trade wars that followed.[21] The second again opened a Pandora's box of subnationalisms and ethnic separatisms, prone to exploitation by neighbors promising sympathy but pursuing power. The third again engaged the international community's responsibility to protect minorities at risk from their own states, and newly and boldly entertained the right to intervene with force against the oppressors; but governments soon thought better of that.[22] The order supposed to follow the Cold War proved as fanciful as that supposed to follow the Great War, and almost as short-lived; what will follow?

No one can know, not with the nationalist regression itself so resolutely resisted, notably in Europe—but even there the disputants in each land clash over national identity and not over Continental or global problems. We do know that the spreading disorder of the 1930s culminated in the Second World War. It did not have to. The future combatants had it in their power, over the decade, to make choices and turn their national stories in other directions. They did not do so. That alone suggests a parallel with our day. Anarchy, indeed, is what states make of it.

ALL AGAINST ALL

GENEVA AND SHANGHAI

2 February 1932

The flags were out again. They hung down the sides of official buildings or fluttered discreetly on the grand automobiles that drove along the lakefront and carried delegates to opening dinner parties. Geneva, on the eve of the World Disarmament Conference, was reliving its heroic years of the mid-1920s, when the flags had even emerged from hotel windows and when for a little while the League of Nations had turned the town into the capital of a becalmed continent. Crowds cheered the peacemakers, a trio of foreign ministers arriving at the station with their shared Nobel Peace Prize—Aristide Briand from France, Austen Chamberlain from Britain, and Gustav Stresemann from Germany; visitors thronged the streets; journalists came from all over. "No more war between us!" Briand told Stresemann when he welcomed Stresemann and his country to the assembly in 1926, and film cameras conveyed their flickering images on newsreels to distant cinema audiences. The moment, crowning the agreements among the former foes at Locarno on another partly Swiss lake the year before, had augured an unfamiliar and more emollient Treaty of Versailles, one that had allowed for its own consensual and peaceful revision and that might shed its harsher provisions as passions cooled. Now, in 1932, the League had invited sixty-four nations—members and nonmembers alike—to come and make good at last on the vow of its founding covenant to pursue "the reduction of national armaments to the lowest point consistent with national safety." And most had accepted, so many that to house their proceedings a new annex of glass and concrete had gone up, next to the converted old Hotel National where the League's officials met and worked for now, and just below the park where tomorrow's gleaming white habitat was rising—the Palais des Nations.[1]

Chamberlain had left office, Stresemann was dead, Briand was dying, and recently a pall of gloom had descended over the League and its projects. "The dominant fact in the world today," the Archbishop of York told an English-speaking congregation in the Cathédrale de Saint-Pierre the night before the conference opened, "is fear." A local paper spoke of contagion. Everyone was afraid of one another.[2] Absurdly or not, the Soviets feared invasion by the capitalist powers, spearheaded by Poland, which feared another partition at the hands of the Russians and the Germans, who feared a Polish invasion of East Prussia; most of the Balkan states feared subversion or isolation by the others, and Italy feared encirclement by Yugoslavia and France, which feared German resurgence and serial betrayals by the "Anglo-Saxons"—by Britain, which feared entanglements on the Continent, and by the United States, which feared them anywhere outside of Latin America. China feared Japanese militarism; Japan feared Chinese nationalism, Soviet Communism, and Western ostracism. Weaker countries looked to the League for reassurance, but lately their anxieties had deepened. Troops from Japan's Kwantung Army had invaded Manchuria in September, and neither its government nor those of the Western powers, let alone the League Council they dominated, had been able or willing to rein them in. In May war would break out between Bolivia and Paraguay over an arid wasteland, the Chaco. The members of the League Council would listen to the recitation of events there with an air of pained surprise once again, while the American State Department pursued its own efforts through the Pan-American Union, which some League officials re-

garded as an attempt to eject them from a hemispheric sanctuary.[3]
Thirteen years earlier, Woodrow Wilson had inserted the Monroe
Doctrine into the Covenant itself. The Chaco War would go on for
three years. The specter of irrelevance stalked the twelve-year-old
League, frightening some smaller members, such as Czechoslovakia,
who expected it to defend the postwar settlements to which they too
owed their existence, and emboldening dissatisfied others such as
Hungary or Germany, who seized on any opportunity to overturn
them. Few contemplated armed aggression, yet many feared it.

The paint was drying and workmen were nailing up frames and
laying down carpet in the translucent new annex for the disarmament
conference. For now, it resembled a newly refitted ocean liner. But
bombs had started falling on Shanghai. Aircraft from Japanese carriers just off the Yangtze estuary had appeared several days earlier and
left the North Station in ruins, the district of Chapei around it ablaze,
and plumes of smoke rising high into the sky. The navy was offering
the same pretext the army had six months earlier in Manchuria—the
security of Japanese residents and property, threatened not only by
a Chinese economic boycott but by random acts of violence. The
government sat lamely by. Several thousand Japanese marines had
moved in, but fierce Chinese resistance had backed them up in the
docks and the international concessions, where occasional artillery
and machine gun fire swept the avenues and panic-stricken Chinese
refugees besieged the consulates. Truces arranged at midnight broke
down at dawn. Turmoil was spreading. Seaborne British and American troops from Hong Kong and Manila were on the way to man
the defenses and protect their compatriots. The government in Nanking appealed to the League and the powers, and rumor had it that
it might declare war, just as the world met in Geneva to renounce it.[4]

Two thousand delegates, technical experts, journalists, and well-
wishers of all sorts were preparing to converge on the Electoral Building and the Old City. Here, where cantonal elections were decided, the
League now held its annual assemblies every September, in almost
as austere a great hall as the Calvinist conventicle—the Salle de la

Réformation—where it had gathered during the 1920s. Just for today, Tuesday, February 2, the building was to host as well the opening plenary session of the disarmament conference, at three thirty. Outside, onlookers were gathering; inside, fourteen ranks of tables on the floor, galleries for journalists and spectators rising in tiers along the sides, and a presidential tribune at the far end awaited the event. Behind the setting stretched seven years of arcane military and diplomatic groundwork, now jeopardized almost overnight by the hostilities in Shanghai. Telegrams from the embattled port had poured into foreign ministries all day Monday, and this Tuesday morning League Council members and their governments had conferred in a flurry of phone calls. At midday they decided to convene the council in emergency session and delay the opening across the lake—only by an hour, but coerced by the violence they aspired to tame, in a moment of cruel and suggestive irony.[5]

There would be tanks and planes and long-range artillery, the symbolic delay reminded the disarmers, as long as there were fears. The old chicken-and-egg conundrum—whether arms bred insecurity or insecurity bred arms—hardly mattered, it further intimated, as long as trust had deserted the scene. But no—abolish the tanks and planes and heavy artillery, the believers rejoined, and you will avert the collective suicide portended in the Great War. They inverted the sequence of the skeptics, and assured them that enmities would fade once adversaries shed their weapons. So determined were they to banish national animosities from their midst and concentrate on the reduction of numerical levels—to sever if they could the political from the material—that they removed themselves from the League's embrace and with its blessing dedicated the new proximate but autonomous site to their enterprise. But rumor spread on Monday that the stout and bespectacled Soviet People's Commissar of Foreign Affairs, or foreign minister, Maxim Litvinov, who had arrived at the head of a twenty-five-member delegation, would not play. He would denounce from the podium the connivance of the League's imperialist powers with Japanese aggression, subvert the opening session, and make a mockery of the independent pursuit of arms reduction even before it was underway. So the council met preemptively but *à l'improviste*, hastily convened by a new presiding figure. Its president pro tem, the French foreign minister, was detained in Paris by ill health, and in his place in Geneva sat his colleague André Tardieu—the minister of war.[6]

More irony, more of fate's practical jokes—but this time the council acted with rare dispatch. In September, during the Manchurian crisis, it had agonized, stalemated by the intramural factiousness of its permanent members and the extramural recalcitrance of the United States. For reasons of their own, neither the British nor the Americans, commanding the two navies that might conceivably intimidate the Japanese, wished to act. Now the council's fourteen members met for an hour in the Crystal Chamber, the glass-sided former dining room of the Hotel National, watched by spectators. They quickly expressed support for the Western forces on the way to restore order in Shanghai, as though wistfully picturing the international force denied the League at its birth, and voted emergency funds for a commission already on its way to look into the conflict there. Even the Japanese delegate approved. He sat still, hesitated, and quietly gave his support to a resolution directed "against the Chinese aggressor." Laughter rippled through the spectators. The hour had fleetingly restored some of the council's prestige. "If they had only started this way back in September!" a reporter overheard one of the spectators exclaim as the session ended and they and the council members filed out and made for the conference across the lake.[7]

And in Shanghai the fighting continued. It was spreading inland. On the walls of Geneva a publicity poster for the *Journal de Genève* went up:

THE NEW PEACE CONFERENCE
Japanese Bomb Nanking[8]

Policemen in white gloves were directing the traffic, which had overrun the Old City in a search for parking places, and the approaches to the Electoral Building darkened with onlookers. Some had been waiting for hours; some doffed their hats at delegates of renown as they arrived to take their places. The bells of Saint-Pierre tolled. Geneva, used to League assemblies by now, had never seen anything like it. It was the largest world gathering since Versailles.[9]

It began by opening its doors to the journalists of the world. And they came—between five and six hundred filled the special seats set up for them along the wall. The planners had expected them not only for the opening day but for the duration across the lake. There, in the new annex, they would enjoy all kinds of amenities, including access to the meeting halls, a spacious press room, their own postal and telegraph services, and forty telephone cabins. They could broadcast from the League's new shortwave station, Radio-Nation, at nearby Prangins, to North and South America and—irony again—to China and Japan. Diplomacy had finally accepted mass politics. A century or so earlier sovereigns had sent their emissaries to confer collectively in the still palaces of Vienna, Verona, or Aix-en-Provence. More recently they had alit at Versailles or in palazzi in San Remo and Genoa. There the press lurked about the grounds, intrusive but kept at bay. Here it had entered the room, in a setting that shed in elegance what it promised in transparency.[10]

During the 1920s a cosmopolitan medley of reporters, delegates, and statesmen transfigured Calvin's sixteenth-century bastion of asceticism, especially when the assembly was in session, into the world's favorite coffeehouse. The diplomats rarely stayed in town long enough to develop that esprit de corps that so naturally segregated them when they served their governments in foreign capitals. Instead they came and went and came again, like the journalists who so often hailed them. Stresemann, when in good health, drank beer and fraternized with them at the bar of the Café Bavaria. Briand, just as convivial, enveloped in cigarette smoke, would join him downstairs in the salon of the Hotel Victoria, amid outmoded furniture of red rep, green Utrecht velvet, and discolored lace. The hotel adjoined the Salle de la Réformation, and during assemblies overflowed with typists, stenographers, League officials, and fanatics of every world cause—and with journalists, who sat up at night in the writing room behind the porter's office and played poker and chemin de fer. In the Café Bavaria, their favorite watering hole, political cartoons lined the walls, and through the clatter and chatter they conceived cabled phrases about parleys for peace and compromise resolutions. In its animation one of their number could briefly imagine that he was at the hub of events: "Here, one knew what was happening, felt the world's pulse, and listened to its heartbeat."[11]

Even when the assembly was not in session and when, as usual, nothing happened, the corridors of the Secretariat teemed with frustrated enthusiasts, clusters of aggrieved minorities, and newsmen in search of copy. Hurried employees and officials struggled past them. On this February afternoon a babel of tongues was rising as the delegates took their seats in the Electoral Building. In New York, church bells pealed in the late morning with deliberate timing: Saint Patrick's on one side of the Atlantic, Saint Peter's on the other. Four days later, on Saturday morning, speakers representing millions paraded into the hall and presented petitions to the tribune, where Arthur Henderson, the former British foreign minister and now president of the conference, welcomed them to a special session. They came from women's, veterans', and youth groups, from political parties, workingmen's unions and fraternities, from churches, pacifist movements, League of Nations associations and many more, conveying the distant clamor of civil society and the voices, so rumor had it, of two hundred million members in all—some ten percent of all the world's people. The women—so few among the delegates, so many among the spectators—predominated in the corteges. Their white armbands proclaimed PAX, their green sashes identified their countries of origin, and they came bearing petitions signed by almost six million others, so many that they had been shipped in packing cases from remote train stations, where women bearing banners had seen them off. The bundles, large and small, bound or tied with string, slowly piled up on the president's bureau. To the eyes of believers, an international public sphere, one calling the nations of the world to their senses, was dawning on the shores of Lake Geneva.[12]

But this was not so. The "public opinion of the world," as activists at Geneva that day liked to imagine it, was enjoying a transnational moment, but the union was composite, even fragmentary and episodic, made up of local voices joined in aversion to the most emblematic of their nations' ills, their weapons of war. In France the loudest sometimes came from Radicals, some of whom were pacifist but few of whom were internationalist, and Communists, who were internationalist but not pacifist, and errant political nonconformists who were neither; in Britain, from atheists and churchmen, Labourites and Conservatives, and agnostic independents and many others. Such communion was fragile within nations, doubly so among them. Disproportionately Anglo-American, echoing national contradictions over the best way to reduce armaments, often discordant, ideologically diffuse, the chorus expressed an immense sentiment—that somehow the statesmen of the world might avert a new catastrophe; but was it a new public sphere, struggling to emerge from the cocoon of the old?[13] Diversity had never inhibited the growth of new public spheres within nations and some of their colonies since the eighteenth century; it had even fostered them; but they had commanded a common space within which they might grow over time and challenge the princes of the day to adapt or disappear. That was not happening in Geneva.

There, the petitioners came more as suppliants than as rivals, invoking once again the force of numbers and "the people," but only to encourage the authorities before dispersing. And the authorities beamed; the League espoused the visitors' cause; the conference opened its doors to them. This was no international Estates General, where in 1789 a millennial French royal order had confronted on its own premises an unmanageable gathering of articulate malcontents. Most of the visitors at Geneva in February 1932 did not return, even though resolutions and petitions continued to flow in from all over the world.[14] From Britain, later that month, came offers from unarmed volunteers wishing to man a "Peace Army" to stand in an imagined

"No Man's Land" between Chinese and Japanese forces, while the conference negotiated what their presiding compatriot, Henderson, would call "a turning point in the history of the world." But the moment had come and gone. What now of the morning after? Delegates coping with their thankless and insoluble tasks on the technical commissions nursed deep misgivings as they labored to reduce by common consent the tonnage of tanks, the caliber of guns, the numbers of conscripts and volunteers. It was all, one of them wrote, a colossal act of make-believe. On behalf of France André Tardieu surprised the conference as it opened by presenting his own plan. But a senior aide working on the speech a few weeks before had reminded him that "the reality of the Conference . . . is a demagogic and theatrical reality."[15] Maneuvers to conquer public opinion would govern the conference, he informed his government. Soon reporters who had roamed the world and had come here expecting news felt disillusioned, and sometimes left the bibulous warmth of the Café Bavaria to recover their senses in the sobering night air outside.[16]

Then and later a curious delusion took hold—that at Geneva *raison d'état* and the covetous habits of sovereign nations had foiled the will of the world. "The Government delegates," a venerable *Manchester Guardian* correspondent in Geneva later wrote, "played the game of Power politics without the smallest regard for the general interest of the world and without showing the least vestige of an international spirit." The culprit, for his colleague on the *Sunday Times* of London, was national interest itself, insincerity triumphant, the League a charade and Geneva its stage. But this was not quite so either.[17] Governments came to the League not to undermine it, still less to surrender any parcel of their sovereignty to it, but to use it. Amid the wreckage of the Great War, Britain wished to avoid binding and bilateral European commitments, France to assure its status and security, the governments of lesser powers to rest their survival on some framework engaging the others as well. Collective security, a notion hospitable enough to each preoccupation, and elastic enough to allow each gloss on its meaning, commanded their assent. But at home the hour of national preference was striking, everywhere, setting off local contests for its laurels and rendering the sounds from Geneva ever more alien and exotic.

In Shanghai the smoke and gunfire obscured the warring popular factions within each side, vying to take possession of a national crusade. While the fighting was still going on, the governing Minseito party in Japan lost its majority to its rival Seiyukai, which had promised not only prosperity but victory in China. The voters reproached the outgoing government its concessions to the Chinese, its useless advances to the Americans, its show of self-effacement before the League. Demagoguery crossed the Sea of Japan from Manchuria, where General Shigeru Honjo and his officers in the Kwantung Army noisily promised to settle the vast province with the families of reservists, rid their own country of the trusts, the Mitsuis and the Mitsubishis, the financial magnates personifying the world economy, and install in Tokyo a government of the desperately poor peasant masses from which so many of their own sprang. Naval officers despised the Washington and London naval treaties, which had stunted the expansion of their fleets and to which their civilian government, in its partiality to the Western powers, had chained them. They struggled coincidentally in Shanghai to reclaim some of the prestige appropriated by the army in Manchuria. Assassinations began staining the political landscape at home, the work of secret societies operating in the shadows but handily manipulated by army and navy officers alike. On the ninth, two weeks into the microwar in Shanghai, the Minseito lost its leading figure, the former finance minister Junnosuke Inoue, to them. Three months later the decision to sign a truce and evacuate Shanghai cost Prime Minister Inukai Tsuyoshi, the head of the Mitsui bank, and other dignitaries their lives. Foreign reporters and diplomats remarked that the press uniformly condemned the murders but said little about the motives. Mainstream opinion did not need to identify with a Fascistic far right to see Manchurian land and Chinese markets as their islands' economic lifeline. With martial spirit running high, the doubters and the critics of the Shanghai operation, many of them in the business and professional classes, lowered their voices. General Sadao Araki, the minister of war, complained of them—carriers, he said, of foreign materialistic ideas—and one of their outspoken fellows, the former diplomat and author Inazo Nitobe, went into hiding.[18]

The Chinese national government, the French consul general in Shanghai reported in April, was driven by a public opinion it could not control.[19] But where *was* the Chinese national government? In the remote hinterlands, with the new Soviet Republic of China and the Communists? In Nanking, where Chiang Kai-shek and the ruling Kuomintang Party had set up the republican government that most of the world recognized? But it had moved to Loyang when Japanese bombs started falling on the Yangtze valley. Or in Canton on the coast, where a powerful secessionist faction in the Kuomintang had briefly repaired, and joined the Communists in disparaging Chiang's patriotism and even accusing him of a treasonable entente with the Japanese invaders? In September, when the Japanese had invaded Manchuria, Chiang had held back from open war, finding the moment not propitious, the imperative of domestic unity too pressing. Three months later, angry anti-Japanese crowds in Nanking forced him from office. When he returned the following month in a coalition hastily cobbled together with the Cantonese, he found he could hold back the nationalist tide no longer. This was war, and all around him the population was stirring. Unemployed workers volunteered to help build the defenses, hungry demonstrators clamored for war, newspapers published manifestos. From their mountain fastness the Communists swelled their ranks by calling on workers and students to resist the Kuomintang as well as the Japanese. And Chiang sent more troops to Shanghai. Still he would not declare war. This the Communists would do for him in April, in a propaganda coup that did not help efforts to negotiate a truce.[20]

Among both Japanese and Chinese, the most vocal champions of the nation coupled a domestic with a foreign threat. They associated one with the other, and promised to save the nation from both. Such confusions surfaced in the most varied of regimes and milieus, in popular fears as well as political power struggles. In the Soviet Union a counterrevolutionary became a foreign agent as well as a class enemy—an enemy, in Stalin's nascent regime, of the Soviet people. In Germany the Weimar Republic provoked not merely institutional nostalgia for the Wilhelmine Empire it had succeeded in 1919 but also suspicions of national betrayal. Had it not signed at Versailles and promised to "fulfill" the treaty, embraced Socialists in its coalitions, and imbibed internationalist poisons in its openings at Geneva? And Communism alone, in the eyes of its many foes, dissolved the domestic in a foreign menace. When the Nazis, for their part, chanted "Germany, awake!"—a cry both seditious and xenophobic—they were vilifying not only decadence but alterity. To the east and southeast, in the successor states to the Russian, German, Austrian, and Ottoman Empires that had collapsed in 1917 and 1918, fears for national survival induced domestic alongside diplomatic vigilance. Minorities with loyalties across the border—Sudeten Germans or Carpathian Hungarians in Czechoslovakia, Silesian Germans or Galician Ukrainians in Poland, Dobrudjan Bulgarians or Transylvanian Hungarians in Rumania, and many others—personified in the eyes of hostile natives the foreign presence among them. Political strongmen took note and articulated as doctrine what had reached their ears as sentiment. Its essence diluted by parochial or folkloric infusions, it could draw in anxious multitudes, well beyond the familiar stalking grounds of the Far Right.

Sometimes an attack on the heresies in Geneva captured the fears. The most radical critics discerned in any such alien edifice another threat to the national or racial community. Behind the occasional electoral promises of Joseph Goebbels to "smash" the League once Hitler came to power lay the Nazi detestation of the cosmopolitan, whatever its racial or institutional features. To others the mirage of perpetual peace reeked of electoral hypocrisy, a ploy that grew more brazen as each voting day neared: a French diplomat described it as a fetish with which to exploit public credulity.[21] In the United States the Hearst newspaper chain, isolationist and autarkic, wished to quarantine the League, so menacing did it seem. In October it revealed to its four or five million readers the organization's plot to "internationalize" the country by indoctrinating its young. This was the "gee-whiz journalism" that had swept the streets during the Spanish-American War, and that now spoke of disarmament as a trap, the League as a European front organization, and deliverance as simple: "There is a better way for Uncle Sam. All he has to do is return to his old traditions."[22]

Such cultural paranoia did not yet touch more temperate critics of the supranational experiment. Mainstream newspapers in Japan complained only of the League's excessively "theoretical" approach to the Manchurian problem, or of its interference, or of its Eurocentrism.[23] Many German centrists and rightists, hostile to any emanation from the Treaty of Versailles, still guardedly accepted that the League might redress the wrongs they claimed to have suffered, and that they had nothing to lose for now by setting foot within its precincts.[24] A decade earlier some eastern European nationalists had looked to the League as champion and defender of their new statehood. They still did, anxiously watching the Chinese government appeal to it against aggression by a powerful neighbor. And to its most ardent devotees, those marching up to the president's bureau at the disarmament conference in Geneva, the guiding vision of the League's Covenant had provided the vital North Star ever since the shipwreck of the Great War. The League still seemed misbegotten to some and providential to others, with many variations in between; and the events in Geneva and Shanghai seemed only to encourage all of them at once.

Shanghai was not Manchuria. The seizure of the desolate northern plains had alarmed the Soviets outside the League and some of the small members inside it. But the descent on the great cosmopolitan port city, where shells were landing on the international settlement as well as among the Chinese in the Chapei district, touched distant onlookers in Europe and North America more brusquely. Some knew the city well. One week into the fighting, Joseph Kessel, the French novelist, recollected the Hotel Astor and the Shanghai Club, where customers from all parts of the globe pressed seven and eight deep against the longest bar in the world, and waiters in white passed multicolored cocktails over their heads. He imagined machine gun fire sweeping the front of the Astor and sandbags stacked outside the endless bar, and he reflected gloomily on the contrast. This time British and American intermediaries managed to find a solution that allowed both sides to save face, but it took them almost three months. They did not know that they had only helped bring the curtain down on a dress rehearsal for a far greater conflagration that in time would erupt in the same place and engulf them along with many others.[25]

Some apprehended the news from the East with forebodings and dim apprehensions of danger to themselves. In May in Berlin, Harry Kessler, the Anglo-German diplomat and patron of the arts, heard on the radio of Prime Minister Inukai's assassination in Tokyo. Nationalistic Reichswehr generals had just forced the minister of war from office, brawling Nazi deputies had just disrupted the Reichstag, and a deranged White Russian émigré had assassinated the French president at a book fair for veterans' works in Paris—kindred omens in three capitals, Kessler feared, of some "awful explosion" to come. If only tensions could moderate—"But how?"[26]

In New York, Walter Lippmann, in his "Today and Tomorrow" column in the *Herald Tribune*, saluted the "Oriental object lesson" that Shanghai had taught Geneva. Disarmament, it had instructed the assembled nations, would come not by solemn declarations or self-denying promises, or even by the calculus of permissible weapons ratios, but by overcoming the anarchy of unlimited national sovereignties. How this was to come about Lippmann did not say, but he derived as well from the news from the East a warning to the peoples of the world about "imbecile quarrels that could be settled in a few weeks of sanity and common sense."[27]

Imbecilic, perhaps; but not so easily disposed of. Domestic strife crossbred with national conflict did not pause long for negotiation or arbitration, no matter how laborious. The wars of religion in six-teenth- and seventeenth-century Europe, mixing dynastic jealousies among princes with sectarian hatreds among their subjects, had sug-gested as much. In the 1940s bitter civil wars accompanied national resistance to invaders in most occupied countries in East Asia and Europe. In the same countries ten years earlier, the precursors were appearing, and the countries that would invade and occupy them displayed some of the same confusions between domestic and foreign foes, in ways that pushed the corteges at the disarmament conference and the delegations at the League deep into the shadows.

Amid all the confusion, amid the ferment of isolationist conceits, pacifist reveries, revolutionary chiliasm, imagined existential threats to race, nation, or class, and kindred collective delusions of the early 1930s, a front line was emerging. It ran between the champions of the native heath and the prophets of more abstract fictions surpassing the call of the clan—between the past and the future, or, more phil-osophically, between immanence and transcendence, although few would have expressed it that way. Sometimes the line ran between right and left, sometimes within them. Sometimes it ran between town and country. Perhaps it ran within each and every politically conscious soul, beginning with the most illustrious among them. Stresemann had claimed the mantle of the peacemaker as well as the entitlements of the nationalist, unsettling Germany's Eastern neigh-bors even as he reassured her Western ones, and when he died in 1929 a mass-circulation German paper, the *Lokal Anzeiger*, reminded his pan-European admirers that he had been, first and foremost, a "fanatical German." Briand, who had attached his name to an inter-national pact renouncing war, and liked to repeat that as long as he was in office there would be none, had prohibited the French army from even a tactical withdrawal at Verdun when the Germans had attacked in 1916, and now insisted that disarmament would never happen without security—French security. And the unfailingly courteous Chamberlain, the signatory of Locarno in 1925, told the delegates at Geneva two years later that "not even for this League of Nations will I destroy that smaller but older league of which my own country was the birthplace and of which it remains the center." He meant the British Empire.[28]

And before them Wilson himself had married visions of a law-abiding world to assumptions of national and racial superiority. To avoid mischief, minds might separate the wheat from the chaff, or the utopian and the spoken from the atavistic and more often unspoken; but in early February 1932 they clashed openly, and the flags in Geneva, unfurled to celebrate a world connecting, expressed as well the manifold consolations of tribalism.

1

Locust Years

Ａnd we were hungry." They were hungry as children during the war and the inflation after it, with its storm of useless money, and hungry again when economic crisis returned after 1929 and took back a brief interlude that had recalled life as it once had been, under the old rules and ways before 1914. To a young German in the autumn of 1932, of the generation born during the decade before the war, all he could remember suggested that the blessings of this world came as an accidental loan. If they ever reappeared, he did not expect them to last. Unemployed, no longer building castles in the air or dreaming of a stable job paying 200 marks a month, he and his contemporaries looked on work or the dole as a means of survival, no more. They had no faith in some liberating vocation, none in a world order that had excluded them from the ranks of the living.

Childhood impressions of gray uniforms, machine guns, helmets, trenches, and field kitchens, of marches and sieges, had escorted their unanchored youth and adulthood, and mixed military fantasies with material want. The encounter could inspire revolutionary or counter-revolutionary infatuations, or others. He wondered whether governments grasped the dangers of awakening such well-preserved images in the present age, beset by hopelessness and a climate of civil war.[1]

By 1932 the Depression, immeasurable, incomprehensible, and

without end in sight for those living through it, resembled the war. To millions who had suffered both, each had happened *to* them— they were its victims, not its villains. Reuniting with the survivors of his battalion upstairs in a tavern in Bradford in 1933, seventeen years after leaving them on the Somme, the English novelist J. B. Priestley found that a few were too poor to attend. He and the others drank to the dead, killed by fatted old men and diplomats with monocles, by story-sniffing journalists and flag-waving women. But not to the living, "who had fought for a world that did not want them, who had come back to exchange their uniforms for rags." They were victims as surely as those they had left behind, even if the faces of their perse- cutors were more obscure. "And who shall restore to them the years that the locust hath eaten?"[2]

The discontents from war and peace fitfully crossed paths as though destined to unite. In 1932 conventional wisdom already linked the Great Depression and the Great War; much learned opinion cast the second catastrophe as the somber aftereffect of the first. As to how, exactly, the cause produced the effect no one could agree—some blamed the inflation during and just after the war, others the harsh deflation that governments had imposed as a result; some, the reparations owed by Germany to its wartime enemies and the sums they owed the United States, all sovereign debts the war had left in its wake to snarl the exchanges long after it had ended; some, the rise of new producers and markets during the war and the ensu- ing glut or saturation; some, the misspending of resources on armies and navies, an addiction the former combatants stubbornly refused to shed. Soviet and Communist doctrine blamed both global par- oxysms on the same imperialist struggle for markets. In Geneva the twenty-five experts of the "Gold Delegation," first convened by the League in 1929 to explore the world's financial institutions, ascribed many of the world's monetary ills, a source of commercial paralysis and by extension of unemployment and human misery, to the war. Politicians picked up the theme.[3] In the United States, President Hoover, during his reelection campaign in October, told farmers in

Iowa and city-dwellers in Cleveland of the "stupendous inheritance of debt," the increase in standing armies, the financial debacles from an international folly now coming home to roost.[4] It was a lecture on the hustings to doubtful effect, because theories of the sort, sound or not, might persuade but hardly move his massed listeners. He wished to absolve the United States and incidentally his administration of responsibility for a depression that refused to lift. They wished for something simpler.

To identify the misfortunes of their listeners with those of the nation, contestants for power and those who already held it blamed powers beyond the border, or the enemy within, or both. They nationalized resentment. The nation itself was the victim of past war and present depression, a narrative that both ennobled and exonerated the citizens and elucidated the injustices inflicted on them. The economy, like the war, had become the affair of all, a national insult that few might understand but many suffered. In all major powers and some lesser ones, people looked to leaders for national paths to regeneration, as well as detachment or salvation from the hostile world beyond. No internationalist leader, no seeker of collective solutions to the destitution and insecurity in the world, could hope to flourish in such a climate. None did.

Victimhood began with reality. Toward the end of the 1920s a scrupulous French critic examined some three hundred firsthand French accounts of the war published by soldiers and officers. "We see dying far more frequently than killing," he wrote.[5] And for a reason: in this industrial war of long-distance guns and high-explosive shells, artillerists fired, mostly, without seeing their human targets, and men died without seeing their killers. Even in the celebratory epics that pervaded popular fiction, stage, and film and swamped the more famous pacifist dirges, victimhood merely differed: it depicted wasted heroism, noble failure, or ambiguous virtue. When the film of Roland Dorgelès's novel *The Wooden Crosses* came out in France in 1932, with its unprecedented attention to agony, critics valiantly struggled to construe its realism. The film exalted, one of them found, both the chivalry and the fighting spirit of the French, yet "the filmed story of the heroic platoon will inspire horror of war and promote world peace."[6] Such muddleheaded goodwill began and ended with the soldier's suffering.

It could also point an accusatory finger at his civilian compatriots, guilty of betraying his soldierly sacrifice. In the autumn of 1932, theatergoers in Paris and Berlin could watch the haggard dead arise from their graves in an Argonne cemetery in *Miracle at Verdun*, conceived by the Austrian playwright Hans Chlumberg. Mass resurrection scenes had become commonplace ever since Abel Gance had filmed *J'accuse* during the war itself. This time, too, the soldiers returned to find their places taken, their wives remarried, their heroics forgotten. And this time the French and Germans awakened from their sixteen-year slumber to fraternize, more clearly the victims not of each other but of their own. The critics were unimpressed. But the alienation of front from home, all too real during and after the war, could marginalize the very conscripts officially venerated as idols. The popularization of angry instant histories presenting them as cannon fodder did the rest. Some sprang from the pens of authors thought to speak with authority. Both Churchill's *World Crisis* in the 1920s and Lloyd George's memoirs the following decade, massive if flawed indictments of the generals for squandering a generation of young men, appeared in serialized or abridged versions for mass readerships.[7] Once a conscript, thrice a victim—of the enemy, of the civilian, of the general: of the war.

Why could his nation not suffer commensurate wrongs? And, especially when defeated, symbolically appropriate his lot? Hitler perfected the operation, identifying one with the other in his own person. He wished to incarnate common soldier and German nation alike, betrayed by the November criminals and their armistice as he lay blinded on his Pomeranian hospital bed in 1918. He never stopped harping on the theme. It worked. Alone among the defeated powers, Germans nourished the delusion that they had lost not the

war but the victory. In 1932 theatergoers in Mannheim, and early
the following year in Berlin, could watch Paul Joseph Cremers's *Die
Marneschlacht* present the dramatis personae of the battle that ended
the German advance in September 1914 as figures in an avoidable
tragedy. "The German people and army had won the battle of the
Marne," the playwright's program notes explained, "the German
high command . . . lost it." The play toured the country. "Bravo
Mannheim!" the theater critic of a liberal German paper cried. He
had seen the war from the depths of the trenches; now he watched the
half-godly high command fight its war onstage.[8] In the Soviet Union,
another defeated nation, the imperialist war itself stood condemned
as one more tsarist crime against the people. The Bolsheviks could
not easily lament a timely military disintegration they had actively
encouraged and that allowed them to seize power in the chaos of 1917.
But with Stalin in the early 1930s the regime justified its exactions
among the people by conjuring up the rich and advanced enemies
who had so often invaded them, to awaken the living memories of
the most recent among them, the Germans, and to promise emancipation from the danger. Late in August 1932, the official daily *Izvestia* purported to demonstrate to its readers that the tsar's regime had
conspired with the other imperialists to unleash the war in 1914. The
others, it added ominously, were still at it.[9]

The victors resented each other. Each reproached the other with
its own sacrifices. The French, who had lost almost twice as many
men as the British and more than ten times as many as the Americans,
claimed to have died for liberal civilization. But the British claimed
to have died for them as well as for a lasting peace that French intransigence methodically disrupted. In the United States the Congress
and much of the press for years had looked on the Wilsonian adventure of 1917 as a waste of lives and treasure, engineered by complicit
bankers and politicians of their own, and repaid only with ingratitude.[10] The Italians, who had lost half a million men in the Alps, had
felt cheated ever since the Versailles conference, a slight to their dead
as well as their nationhood, and among the Japanese, who had lost

very few, rising voices spoke of former allies denying them their place in the sun. Rarely can any war have yielded such embittered victors.

In September 1932, for the eighteenth anniversary of the victory on the Marne, American diplomats and French military and civilian leaders gathered at the village of Varreddes in the fields of Brie, in the heart of the endless battlegrounds northeast of Paris. They had come to unveil a twenty-two-meter-high monument, the work of a French sculptor but the gift of American donors wishing to reciprocate for the Statue of Liberty. It rose atop the soldiers' Hill 109 and dominated the surrounding landscape. Niceties and compliments filled the air. The American people, their ambassador said, would always throw their moral and, if necessary, their material weight against aggression. But he had no authority to say so—the secretary of state, Henry L. Stimson, had promised only to consult, to the consternation of isolationist orthodoxy. This was not, had never been, adequate in French eyes. Already at lunch the minister of war, Joseph Paul-Boncour, had raised the specter of German rearmament, disguised as a demand for equal treatment. The war, always the war, provided the ultima ratio. "France will not be dispossessed of her victory," he said, "or of the meaning she gave to it"—by which he could mean only security from another German invasion. Did public opinion, as the American ambassador believed along with Stimson, provide a guarantee of good relations? Prime Minister Edouard Herriot, for one, seemed to doubt it. Peace was not there for the asking, he reminded his guests, and he, the Radical, hailing from a political hearth of French pacifism, called for arms and fortifications as well. And he too returned to the French hecatombs. "We are accused of being bellicose!" he exclaimed. "Where else better than here could we evoke the cruel wounds, the wrongs suffered and only apparently repaired, of that stupid savagery which is called war?"[11]

Behind the niceties festered the resentments—by the Americans, of French refusal to disarm or pay its debts; by the French, of American refusal to resuscitate the wartime unity. The Americans and the

British quarreled over war debts, the British and French over Germany, disarmament, the revision of Versailles and much else besides. *Le Temps* reported admiringly on Herriot's speech at Vareddes. The paper evoked the great battle. It added that the French had fought it alone. The voice of the foreign ministry, the paper of the establishment, had forgotten the presence there of the British Expeditionary Force.[12]

All, victors and vanquished alike, believed they had fought defensively, for their survival or for their ideals. All believed themselves somehow wronged by the peace that followed. No war had left so abiding a sense of national insult among all who had waged it.

In 1932 the spectacle of idle plant, redundant workers, and unsold goods, endlessly repeated over most of the industrialized world, required explanation. In the winter, smokeless stacks of abandoned glassworks rose above the clearings in the Thuringian forest. The kilns were closing. Most of the six thousand workers in the villages were jobless and, after exhausting the dole, close to starvation. In the industrial heartland of the Ruhr, mountains of coal—some ten million tons, nearly a year's production—stood heaped outside the pitheads, unwanted and unused. Neither finished glass nor raw coal could find any foreign markets, depressed themselves or shuttered by high tariffs. At home the government had no money, the banks had no capital, machines had replaced humans—"Do you call that an economic system?" the owner of the glassworks in Fehrenbach asked, accusingly. In Turin and Milan, in the heart of industrial Italy, local shopkeepers and business owners blamed the plant closings and collapsing sales on a regime that, unlike its liberal predecessor, had habitually intruded into the economy. Unhappily for Fascism, they turned to the closest explanation at hand—yes, the world crisis had struck Italy, but the regime had as well. In the United States the artist Charles Sheeler had first photographed the Ford Motor Company's River Rouge plant in 1927 and 1928, to evoke its mass, power, and precision—its modernity. In 1932 he painted its

lines and light again, but the stillness and the want of a human figure seemed on this canvas more sinister, as though he had photographed the plant as a temple only to paint it as a mortuary. This too
demanded explanations, along with the unsold Japanese silk and the
surfeited granaries of the Danube basin.[13]

The regression, in 1932, bewildered more than the paralysis. In
the northeast of England men without work scrabbled for sea coal
along the shore or for fragments outside pitheads. By night in German Silesia, unemployed miners hidden behind slag heaps lowered
each other in old buckets with ropes or wires into the earth below
the dormant minefields.[14] Sometimes they descended to fifteen or
twenty meters, there to find coal for themselves for the winter, or to
sell it as they could. Wires snapped, gases ignited, territorial disputes erupted. The mine owners complained, police came, pitched
battles broke out. The men had given the language a new word, the
Armutschacht or *Notschacht*, the "poverty shaft," even as they reverted
to antique exertions and mining techniques of the iron age. In Chicago the authorities ordered nonresidents without work to leave the
city, and clearinghouses sent the swelling numbers of the destitute
and the unemployed to the Oak Forest poorhouses, to Hull House, to
the shelters. None of these could match the starkness of the Angelus
Building on South Wabash Avenue, a firetrap without heat or light,
where sixty-seven African American families took refuge, as though
returning to the dark holds of their ancestors' slave ships.[15]

By the autumn of 1932 the world's financial panics were over, but
ruin and exhaustion had set in. Since the autumn of 1929, the wreckage had piled up—trade had declined almost by two-thirds, the unemployed had risen to some twenty-five million, industrial production
had fallen by more than a quarter in Europe and almost half in North
America. In many countries, especially agricultural and raw material
exporters in the Southern Hemisphere hit by new lows in commodity
prices, national income had fallen by half. Trade barriers, controls on
capital flows, and currency instability—reactions to contraction and
then obstacles to expansion—threatened to perpetuate a vicious spi-

ral. A "boomlet" in the United States and signs of recovery in Europe brightened spirits for a while, until winter and a new round of falling indicators sobered and confused the analysts, leaving an uncertain mixture of hope and fear. At the League of Nations, experts dared not say that the worst was over.[16]

By now economists were offering so many explanations for the enduring crisis, and wrapped them in such Jesuitical subtleties, that impatient laymen began urging political leaders to jettison doctrinal baggage and act without their help.[17] If overproduction, the nemesis of corporate size and technology, had saturated supply, or under-consumption, and the priority given to investment over wages, had stifled demand, then perhaps a third party—the state—should step in and restore some balance. On the other hand, if the crisis had sprung from too much interference with market forces by govern-ments or central banks or others, including unions, then perhaps less rather than more interference would allow the business cycle to correct itself. In 1932, on both sides of the Atlantic, schools of thought competed for the attention of policy makers. Their un-derstanding of causes determined their prescriptions for recovery, which ranged from managed economies to orthodox precepts of laissez-faire, from controlled inflation with cheap money and new public spending to resolute deflation with neither. In some circles, the liberal *Observer* complained, planning was becoming an end in itself, a pleasant intellectual diversion. Ideas were in flux. Keynes and some others across the Atlantic had recently begun to advocate relieving unemployment by public spending and investment rather than by merely lowering interest rates. But they had not yet artic-ulated the full implications of permanent stagnation, of a business cycle that refused to correct itself.[18]

"I approach this whole subject," the governor general of the Bank of England confessed, "not only with ignorance but in humility."[19] More than the economists, he moved in the public eye. In the press and in the open air, others, more inexpert and so less modest, trans-lated the economists' syllogisms into the blunt idiom of politics. On the left, "underconsumption" meant that parsimonious employers and governments had failed to stimulate demand by expansive measures; "overproduction" was the excuse they concocted to tighten belts. On the right, public spending meant "bribing the electorate with its own money" by recycling higher taxes into wasteful new programs. On the left, "equilibrium" was a false God, the sanctimonious varnish of ever harsher cuts to public and private wages and social protection. On the right, "disequilibrium" meant disruption by unions of wages, by governments of credit, prices, and profits, and, by both, of the natural balance of supply and demand.[20] This was not new. The postwar squalls and storms, with their adjustment crises, swings, and shocks, had politicized economic argument. At times it had nationalized it as well. In 1923, to collect reparations payments, balance their budgets, and defend their currency, the French had occupied the Ruhr basin, and the German government responded not only with passive resistance but with hyperinflation. Chauvinism married monetary policy. But worldwide depression now durably recast economic grievance as national resentment, everywhere.

In the village of Fehrenbach in Thuringia, where the glassworks had closed, the owner blamed the new British protective tariffs, which came into effect early in 1932. With his export markets went most of his sales. He blamed the absence of capital and of credit on the French demand for reparations. No matter that the Germans had barely paid them, and that the French would soon give up on them. The mental reality excluded the other. In Falkenstein, Saxony, where the textile mills had fallen silent, half the fifteen thousand inhabitants were either unemployed or dependent on those who were. Once, in 1925, they had been 323. God was punishing the world, the local Methodist preacher told his congregants in the Zion Church. "Not the French," one of them muttered.[21]

American government interventionism, *Le Temps* objected in Paris on Armistice Day 1932, had ruined its economy and set a deplorable example for the rest of the industrialized world. Protectionism, credit policies, restraints on trade—all had left high unemployment and industrial paralysis, and the paper, a paragon of the French economic orthodoxy of the day, saw the meddlesome habits as neither Republican nor Democrat but American.[22] More commonly, French papers complained of the opposite ill—of unbridled excess in the American markets, of the *aventures* on Wall Street that had left such desolation the morning after. Even the country's French friends and admirers, who saw it as the ally of choice, viewed the operations there with alarm. "The life of America hangs, breathless, on its *Stock Exchange*," one of them wrote. And it weighed on the world, he went on. A nation that denied its citizens a glass of wine or a night of gambling yet applauded their speculative fevers. "Puzzling thought!"[23] And then the American government to a man had not stopped demanding repayment of war debts, even as it urged the French to relent on reparations from Germany. And to disarm.

Such grievances, technically solvable among dispassionate experts, resisted redress in collective sentiment. The French had agreed to slash reparations at London in 1924, at the Hague in 1929, and finally to bury them at Lausanne in the summer of 1932—to the sounds of silence in German opinion. The press and the parties had hardly noticed, the German delegation's interpreter found when he returned from Lausanne. Francophobia survived easily. When French and American negotiators worked out an agreement in 1926 to reschedule war debts, French opinion was uniformly hostile, and protesters took to the streets. In the press American opinion was more exercised in 1932, when the French had been paying their installments, than in 1926, when they had not. The Depression, the threat of a French default, a view of the war—all had conspired to arouse latent resentments that overwhelmed any rational negotiation.[24]

The Americans did not disown their Depression. When President Hoover or the Hearst press, no friends of his that autumn, both blamed the crash of 1929 on the depravities of the boom years, they joined the French moralists, and forgot that one had been secretary of commerce and the other benignly acquiescent during the heyday in question. But they denied—correctly—that the crash alone had caused the world depression, which they blamed as well on the war. By this they meant not merely the events between 1914 and 1918, but the European syndrome of profligacy and belligerence that drove them, now perpetuated in arms races and unbalanced budgets. And the chastened American wastrels of the 1920s now became victims of European malefactors, of foreign speculators trying to drain the country of its gold reserves by selling off their dollar assets. Without himself at the helm, Hoover told the crowds during his reelection campaign in the autumn of 1932, the country might have been forced off the gold standard. At the Coliseum in Des Moines, he and Mrs. Hoover sang along with the crowd, and the band in the loft played "Ioway, Ioway, that's where the tall corn grows," and millions heard him on the NBC and CBS radio networks. He had resolved, he said, to stanch the outflow of gold, and defend the currency and the country itself, "the Gibraltar of world stability, because only by holding this last fortress could we be saved from a crashing world."[25]

Empires incited jealousy in those without them, a matter overtly of economics, covertly of prestige. In November *Nichi Nichi*, one of the most influential papers in Tokyo, cited the Ottawa accords as a prime example of competitive autarky. They had conferred on Britain's products or those of its dominions a position of choice and left the others out. In the world today, the paper observed, economic measures were political. By closing the open doors, Britain left others—Germany, Italy, not least Japan—asking why she had so many outlets overseas and they so few. "Old Japan," General Sato had exclaimed in April, "thy soil is spent! Poor land! Thou art entirely exhausted and thou art barren!" He concluded that Japan's new mission was to unlock the treasures of Asia. And in the autumn King Victor Emmanuel visited the Italian colony of Eritrea on the Red Sea. Could forty-two million Italians, Foreign Minister Dino Grandi had asked the Italian Senate in June, live and prosper in a country with half the territory of France, of Spain, of Germany, without riches or raw materials, imprisoned in a sea that others controlled and that lay between the peninsula and the lands of its commerce? While they strangled the movement of goods and capital? His was a demand for colonies. Italy's vital problem, he added, was inescapably that of the world.[26]

"How much money have you?" the customs officials asked at every border crossing of the seven Danube states. They asked it of tourists, of journalists, even of diplomats. Borders had become instruments of economic survival in new ways, newly widespread existential symbols. Capital controls were spreading, and in the Danube basin travelers had to declare every penny of foreign money they carried if they hoped to leave with it. Importers in need of foreign currency could wait weeks for it, a lethal impediment to the foreign trade on which these countries, more than any other, depended. National enmities, as economically irrational as war itself, erected so many barriers in the once open territories of the Austro-Hungarian Empire that currency controls seemed predestined, the consummation of a task that political destruction had begun in 1918.[27]

In Hamburg, before passengers could board the *Monte Olivia* at her pier under the harbor lights, they waited in the *Devisenkontrolle* for inspectors to examine, as politely as possible, their handbags and wallets. Each was bound for South America but could bring only 200 marks. Outside, beyond the Zollhaus, men in green uniforms walked and searched anyone leaving the ship, lest duty-free shipboard goods—French Cognac or Egyptian cigarettes—find their way to dry land. At the Soviet border customs officials informed German travelers that a ruble was worth 2 marks and 16 pfennigs. But once in their hotel in Moscow they learned that a ruble was not a ruble, that an official rate coexisted with others, and that in crossing the border they had entered a land of money madness where nothing was what it seemed.[28]

The world had descended into monetary civil strife. Gold and foreign exchange had become agents of disorder, the carriers of a contagion contained in the 1920s by prophylactic short-term treatments. These no longer worked. International capital flows, including long- and short-term loans, investments, and movements among central banks and their sovereign governments, had slowed to a trickle; creditors demanded payment and debtors demanded relief. Once an instrument of world commerce and the visible guarantor of its rules, gold, the money without a country, negotiable by all, had now hastened its paralysis, and the dense connections among the banks through which it traveled had spread exposure, vulnerability, and panic across oceans and continents. The war had spread monetary disorder in the world, which the Depression amplified into chaos ten years later.

During the last decades of peace, the gold standard fixed currencies in terms of gold and so of each other, made them freely convertible into gold on demand, and required that central banks back their note issues with minimum gold reserve levels; it made currency manipulation politically almost impossible. In 1914 war swept the gold standard away, as the protagonists suspended the free convertibility of their currencies to protect their dwindling gold reserves. Four years later, the survivors contemplated lands whose metallic wealth had largely fled the scene, some of it to neutrals such as Holland, Spain, or Switzerland, some to distant and untouched belligerents such as Japan, the lion's share to the United States, enriched beyond measure despite its own outlays. Gold, violently redistributed by the hand of war, had left their vaults in exchange for munitions and more from the others until it had all but run out in some of them. Their inflated currencies depreciated against the gold-backed dollar and began to float uncertainly against one another. Victors and vanquished alike now peopled a monetary Tower of Babel, rising above the ruined edifice of the gold standard.[29]

By the late 1920s most had managed painfully to return to it. They even attracted newcomers in their wake, so strong was the conviction that the discipline and fixed exchange rates it imposed held the key to financial respectability and economic equilibrium. A semblance of stability reappeared. But was it even the same system? Circumstances had conspired to politicize it beyond recognition. At home, voluble interest groups—the unemployed, the employed, and the employers, borrowers and lenders, the elected and their voters—pressed central banks to expand or contract the money supply in ways deemed unseemly before the war. Abroad, sovereign debts—German reparations or interallied loans—and the thickening complicity between monetary and foreign policy rendered the neutral economic harmonies of the independent gold standard, dear to the prewar optimists, increasingly quaint. Then, when most consumers ignored the very existence of the gold standard, central bankers could relegate governments to the gallery where, according to the liberal precepts of the day, they belonged. Now, when inflation and deflation were political causes, when the gain of one central bank meant the loss of another, they could not. Gold reserves had become weapons of national policy; monetary reasoning and *raison d'état* became one.[30]

In 1931 a tidal wave of fright arose in central Europe, spread outward to northern Europe, and crossed the oceans to the United States and Japan. Investors in one country pulled out of another—if they could, before moratoria, defaults, closures, or freezes cut them off from their assets first. In the past, other central or private banks would have stepped in to help their fellows and stanch the outflow; now they could not or would not do enough. The spigots were closing. So the panic traveled across the exchanges. Economic depression, political instability, chronic fears about debts and the duration of moratoria were driving holders of national currencies to liquidate their assets and withdraw them as gold while they could, from one threatened haven after another. "The gold ingots," the French justice minister Paul Reynaud said the following spring, "flee from nest to nest, like scared hare at the first commotion." In September, unable to keep frightened investors and lenders at bay, Britain suspended the convertibility of sterling into gold, effectively devaluing it.[31] The country that had brought the gold standard to the nations of the world now led them in the flight from it. The system had collapsed again.

In its place, throughout the following year, came floating currencies again, or, in many countries still nominally fixed on the gold

standard, draconian currency and capital controls that stripped it
of any meaning. Supposed to discipline governments, it had served
some and hobbled others. Few of these could now dispense with the
national instruments of capital controls, currency manipulation, or
tariffs of one sort or another, and expose their countries and their own
future to the international rules left from more stable times. Freed
of fixed exchange rates and the need to protect their gold reserves,
they could aid exporters and expand credit. Yet many of the world's
monetary specialists struggled to find the way back from the forest
to the familiar terrain of the past. Some thought the gold standard
had assured the prewar equilibriums; others recognized that where
it operated it had more nearly expressed them, and that without removing the proliferating obstacles and threats to commerce it could
never function anyway.[32]

Such chicken-and-egg conundrums passed over the heads of most
citizens, unless they were bankers or industrialists, and the politicians who courted them. But monetary strife had added a recondite
twist to the cruder reproaches that the blighted nations flung at each
other. Already France had employed the gold reserves of the Bank
of France to bend Germany to its will, most recently in the spring of
1931 when it had discerned in Chancellor Heinrich Brüning's tactless
proposal for a customs union with Austria stealthy revisionism, the
kind of subterfuge that undid Versailles by establishing over Germany's neighbors the very dominion the treaty had refused. They
withheld further loan concessions to Austrian or German banks
until their governments scuttled the project. The weaponization of
gold provoked outrage, but it worked.[33] In September and the following year, with Britain off gold and others following, a new fault line
opened. They had left the gold standard, British journalists and politicians believed, because hysterical foreign speculators had driven
them off it, because central European banks had frozen British capital, because others had not played by the rules—because France, for
one, had hoarded its reserves with *Balzacien* avidity. The French,
still on gold, saw hypocrisy in such accusations, coming from an-

other jealous neighbor struck by economic misfortune, and regretted that Britain could not leave the gold standard without taking leave of its sanity as well. They, the Continental few not manipulating their currencies, were the ones left out in the cold. Each was a victim of the other's bad faith.[34]

As well as a medium of exchange, money was a heraldic device, the emblem of national solvency. Whether leaving gold or staying on it, governments invoked the flag as well as the exchequer. Authoritarian Poland, Fascist Italy, liberal France and the United States all spoke of the gold standard with patriotic satisfaction as long as they adhered to it; Britain, after she left it, spoke of gold leaving the pound, of a happy release from "golden fetters," of injustices she had suffered and examples she had set.[35] When they posed as Horatius at the bridge and cast the others as marauding Etruscans, national leaders remade victimhood into grandeur. With the help of the press and other interpreters, they nationalized the rancor of the Depression as surely as that of the war, and lent meaning to the incomprehensible for the unhappy survivors of both.

"At this moment of quasi-delirious folly," Toynbee found, "when the dissolution of the existing World Economic Order seemed to be at hand"—at this moment, governments had not given up on the possibilities of internationalism. They reaped the benefits of throwing off the gold standard but worked diplomatically to restore it; they armed themselves on land or sea but met to lower strategic levels and promote security with less menacing tools; they clamored to collect war debts and indemnities but devised ingenious ways to lighten them. Sometimes, in 1932, they succeeded. At the Lausanne conference in the summer the victors of the war effectively abandoned their claims to German reparations, and after it all began earnestly to prepare for a world economic conference the following year.[36]

More often, that year and the next, they raised tariff walls, imposed capital controls, issued territorial demands, set immigration quotas, signed security pacts, drafted rearmament blueprints, and

deadlocked international conferences. The mass participation that
sustained such arcane transactions expressed national emotion and
self-consciousness. It came not from the fringes but from the heartland. Otherwise leaders could have resisted it. "I came to the deliberate conclusion," the British economist Arthur Salter wrote in the
autumn of 1932, "that the greatest and most fundamental difficulty
was not an international one at all, it was the impotence of national
governments." He was reflecting on all the trade negotiations he had
sat through, and on the power of economic nationalism and sectoral
interests.[37]

As an ideal, national self-sufficiency was conquering converts in
the most varied of circles. Among economists and financial journalists in the West, international laissez-faire capitalism no longer commanded unshakeable allegiance. In the nineteenth century, free trade
in the eyes of its believers assured not only freedom and prosperity
but peace as well. By the early 1930s Keynes recanted such articles of
faith, the catechism of his youth. Experience no longer suggested, he
said, that commercial entanglement between nations brought peace
between them, or that surrender to the mercies of the free international
movement of goods and capital allowed governments to experiment
and find their different ways out of the massive crisis of capitalism.
They required freedom from outside forces, even economic isolation
if necessary. He uttered such views not as a heretic, he explained,
but to "understand the urge felt by so many countries today towards
greater national self-sufficiency." He wanted to articulate new mental
habits, including his own. Two years earlier, when a balance of payments crisis and a run on sterling drove his own country off the gold
standard, calls spread in the press for economic self-sufficiency, for
buying British and growing gardens. As with national budgets, assim-
ilated to household ones, so with monetary crises—they promoted
self-reliance and the abstention from alien dependencies.[38]

Expressed as autarky, the idea took on urgency and coercion. The
Stalinist variety, pursued at immense cost and suffering, differed as

night from day from the Keynesian—if national self-sufficiency were pursued at the cost of the human mind, the liberal economist wrote, he would sooner retreat to his old nineteenth-century ideals. But, as much as Soviet ideology under Stalin's "socialism in one country" deplored self-sufficiency in the individual, it exalted it in the collective, for military as well as economic reasons—to assure the survival of the Soviet Union.[39] In Germany, where the idea commanded little respect in the 1920s, a widening circle of geopolitical seers had concluded that the country had nothing to gain from the global economy, and that, since complete national autarky was beyond reach, the country should now seek it in a regional *Grossraumwirtschaft*, the closed economic spaces of southeastern and eastern Europe, or perhaps of all continental Europe. Only that way could they compete with the United States and Japan. And only that way, for military planners, could Germany triumph over another blockade by Western sea powers in wartime.[40]

The Nazis, who lacked any economic ideas of their own, appropriated the notion. Adapted to the goal of colonizing new lands in the east to feed the Aryan race, it emerged as *Lebensraum*. Autarky, in this variety, was to be conquered. As hostile to export dependence and integration into the global economy as the others but requiring military means that only new conquests could sustain, it promised an endless cycle of violence.[41] No cartographer ever traced the borders of *Lebensraum*. The Asian soil that Japanese militarists had already seized and the African colonies that Italian Fascists would soon demand presented more finite limits, but completed the passage of self-sufficiency, a counsel for some to withdraw, into a command for others to expand.

Without Manchuria, a Japanese observer wrote in the spring of 1932, Japan would be restless; with it, it would be "as secure as the United States is today."[42] To each his own fallacy. The territorial fallacy held that prosperity, even in this industrial age, required more land; the ecological, that nations and peoples were locked in a death struggle for finite resources. Hitler, in his unpublished second book, looked at the American conquest of continental space in the nineteenth century and beheld both a model and an existential challenge, the only way out of the Malthusian nightmare of inadequate food supplies.[43] Stalin believed that the survival of the Soviet Union required that it outproduce everyone else. In the nativist fallacy, older and more diffuse than any of the others, the survival of national identity required the exclusion or expulsion of outsiders and newcomers. In both Europe and North America, it long antedated the present unhappiness. But in the autumn of 1932, it was attaching itself to it. In September in Manhattan, where shantytowns—Hoovervilles— spread across Central Park and Morningside Heights, and a million and a half were unemployed, one of the Hearst papers demanded that "criminal and otherwise undesirable aliens" be deported without hearings: "Rid the country of this scum."[44] In early November in Paris, as All Saints' Day passed and Armistice Day approached with their seasonal fogs and lamentations, a financial weekly reflected on the wretched state of France and of Europe. It went on, as though by extension, to deplore the three million immigrants, the criminals, refugees, and unemployed of all colors who had invaded the land since the war. "November is a moment of meditation," it added, "on ourselves, on our past . . . May our Consuls ponder it."[45]

Such fallacies, marked by the same fear of decline or disappearance that the war or the Depression or both had bequeathed, could ignore or embrace one another. Nazism fused them into race panic, concentrated on the Jew. They all treated the world beyond the border as a hostile place. "Disoriented as we are," the professor in Bucharest explains in Mihail Sebastian's novel of 1934, "we will perhaps one day find the truth that returns us to the soil." The author had based him on Nae Ionescu, a leading Rumanian nationalist who like his fellows detested the alien and the cosmopolitan. His fictional alter ego believed that a foreign-funded oil refinery going up amid the Rumanian grapevines and plum trees was a "deliberate crime," an "abstraction," that Europe was a fiction, and the world monetary crisis a mere symptom of cultural disintegration. A strong currency was a symbol of strong value at any level. "Don't you get the smell of the land off me?" a student of his asks the professor's Jewish protégé, the narrator, as though of Ahasuerus. "Yes," he reflects, without answering. "Indeed I get it. And I envy you for it."[46]

TOKYO AND ROME

September and October 1932

The extraordinary session of the Imperial Diet had assembled on Tuesday, the twenty-third of August, in the Ceremony Hall of the Houses of Parliament to await the emperor's arrival. He left the palace that morning in military uniform and rode out in his carriage along with Admiral Suzuki, the imperial chamberlain, followed by a procession of cars carrying court and household dignitaries. Admiral Viscount Makoto Saito, the prime minister, received him on the porch of the House of Peers, along with the entire cabinet, and in the hall the assembled members of both houses bowed in unison as the Mikado took his throne. Saito gave him a scroll with the imperial message, which he read out in a clear voice before leaving the hall twenty minutes later, amid another display of collective obeisance.[1]

The next day three speeches followed, as always, from the prime minister, the finance minister, and the foreign minister. Only Takahashi, the finance minister, spoke at length about the economic emergency, which had driven the government to request and the emperor to convoke the extraordinary session, at the end of another one in June. At the time farmers were starving and exporters were closing their factories. Takahashi spoke of the Rice Bill, the Relief Bill, the Debt

Bill. Saito's ministry was supraparliamentary, a coalition of sorts appointed in May in the wake of yet another political assassination, and like all hybrid governments it feared its fractious partners. Only the day before, the chief manager of the Seiyukai party, for now the largest, had warned of an "outbreak of discontent" and derided the government's pointless panacea of "self-help." His party wanted more spending on relief; Takahashi wanted to hold the line. And this was his own party. A few weeks earlier *Hochi Shimbun*, a mass-circulation paper owned by the "Magazine King" of Japan and friendly to the other main party, Minseito, had leveled similar accusations—that while the countryside languished the government idled. The docility of the deputies was anything but certain.[2]

The Diet did not meet often. Normally it assembled in December, adjourned until mid-January, then met and legislated in March, sometimes amid hectic motions of impeachment and protests at violations of protocol or infractions to ceremonial rite. Along with the country's rich and varied press, it incarnated political pluralism, but at pivotal moments effective power resided elsewhere. Far from the madding crowd, at the palace, around the throne and in the Privy Council, within the army and navy high commands, among some of the great captains of finance and industry, where interests competed and views clashed, decisions emerged from a mysterious crucible of consensus.[3] That was how Saito came to office in May, summoned from retirement by a conclave of the sort and a tutelary figure from the ages. At ninety-three, Prince Saionji was the last of the wise men who had helped restore the Emperor Meiji in 1868—the last of the Genro, elders wrapped in legend, closer to the deified emperor than to the mundane Diet and its restless majority. These Saionji now ignored, and contrived by common consent to have the emperor fill the vacancy left by Inukai's assassination with the former governor general of Korea, Admiral Saito, a man without a party, old even beyond his seventy-four years, the solution that disappointed the least. Seiyukai, the governing party returned with a strong majority in February, bowed.[4] For all its fractiousness and internecine feuding, the

Diet displayed a sense of the state. In March, when it had met, Inukai had invoked urgency and asked both houses to pass his projects—about financing the operations in China and suspending the gold standard—without any debate. They did so, the peers unanimously, the commoners with a few objections, and went home after five days. But the system was intrinsically unstable. Who would fill the shoes of the Genro once Saionji was gone? The generals?[5]

The formality of elections revealed public moods to governments, and the parliamentary parties, like others elsewhere, lived by the exchange with their voters and clients of services rendered for loyalty returned. They also served the valuable function of drawing popular ire away from more sacrosanct targets. Esteem for them, as they met once again in August, had been sinking. In May, as mass-circulation papers were lamenting the loss of public faith in the political parties, Prime Minister Inukai and Baron Wakatsuki, the leader of the opposition Minseito party, declared constitutional government and its parties the ideal system for Japan. Inukai condemned its critics; three days later a handful of them assassinated him. The wide condemnation that followed rarely exonerated the parties of an unwitting complicity—the foul deed, papers seemed to say, reflected the disgust they incurred. *Yomiuri*, as though to confirm its gloomy diagnosis several days earlier, bluntly declared that the people would soon demand another form of government, unless the parties in the Diet acted to stem the rising unemployment in the capital and the provinces. *Hochi* blamed the governing Seiyukai party—Inukai's—for the ambient disenchantment with the country's form of government. The cure, in such mainstream papers, was obscure. *Jiji*, a business paper, wanted a prime minister who would restore to the parties their lost prestige. *Nichi Nichi* concluded that since the parties had ignored the interests and forfeited the confidence of the nation, it needed new men, not to "dismantle constitutional government as the Emperor Meiji had created it" but to adapt it—whatever that meant.[6]

Cautiously, if not disingenuously, *Nichi Nichi* had posed the fundamental question: Would Japan continue on the Westernizing paths first taken in 1868, to industry and parliamentary government, and pursued after 1919 by the foreign minister, Baron Kijuro Shidehara, toward the League, the treaties, and the Western markets?[7] Young men had already answered by dispatching public figures, variously affiliated but all tainted in their eyes by treasonable occidental connections—Prime Minister Osachi Hamaguchi in 1930, inside Tokyo station, the same spot where nine years earlier one of Seiyukai's founders, Prime Minister Hara Takashi, had fallen to their bullets; the Minseito leader and former finance minister Junnosuke Inoue in February 1932, as he arrived at a primary school for an election rally; Dan Takuma of the Mitsui bank in March, as he arrived at his office; and Prime Minister Inukai Tsuyoshi in May, inside his official residence as he met with a visitor, and as the assassin's confederates threw bombs at will around the capital, in broad daylight, at Seiyukai party headquarters, at the municipal police station, at the Mitsubishi bank. Some wore naval uniforms and all gave themselves up, as though to identify themselves and disclaim any designs of a coup d'état. And they left a list of demands with the police, on behalf of the destitute workers and peasants from whom they sprang: an end to the Diet and its parties, to the capitalist trusts and their profiteers, to the government and its weak-kneed foreign policy. They demanded a new regime and old values, the reign of military tradition. Later they freely confessed to starting out with more victims in mind, all of the same ilk, including Prince Saionji, too friendly to the parliamentary regime, and Baron Shidehara, too conciliatory to the Chinese.[8]

The assassins of Inoue, Dan, and Inukai had hatched their plots under the ascetic and sacerdotal aegis of Inoue Nissho, once a mercenary and a spy, now a self-anointed prophet and Buddhist priest. He was the mind, they were the arm, and in his Ketsumeidan or Blood Pledge Corps they first absorbed his teachings about the end—national renovation and the removal of corrupt and alien elites—and then contemplated the means. Political assassination had rid the country of Hara Takashi in 1921, guilty of partiality to the League of Nations and all that it signified. Now, in 1932, Inoue, who wanted cuts in the military budget, and Baron Dan, who had shipped out gold and pilfered the people, and Prime Minister Inukai, who had signed the truce and evacuated the navy from its misbegotten venture into Shanghai, joined the list of surgical victims. Foreign and domestic malfeasance seamlessly united them. Who or what should succeed them was less clear. Nissho, devoted to the emperor and his millennial cult, deplored any talk of military dictatorship or of "Fascism." But his uniformed disciples and their milieu were not all so unwilling, Western as such innovations might be.[9]

Their milieu—small, more or less secret societies with overlapping zealotries—had been expanding since about 1930. The societies had numbered twenty-five in 1927; now, in 1932, there were almost two hundred of them. They found their rank-and-file members on the naval bases and in the military academies, but also in the universities and government ministries, especially among sons inclined to blame the plight of their desperately poor families on the reign of the parties and of money. They differed; one of the largest, Kokuhonsha, owing its standing to its leader, Baron Kiichiro Hiranuma, vice president of the Privy Council, was hardly secret at all; one of the smallest, Inoue's Ketsumeidan, operated in solitude, immured in its schemes. Some, like Kokuhonsha, stopped well short of sedition and overthrow; others, like the smaller Dai Nihon Seisanto, wanted nothing more. But they talked to one another. After the May 15 incidents, police found Nissho at the house of Dai Nihon Seisanto's founder, Mitsuru Toyama, as ascetic and shadowy a fanatic, whose sole literary creation was a compendium of rules for young assassins. And differ as they might over social ideals—agrarian or industrial— and political strategies—violent or peaceful—they united in wishing to rid the country of its parties and its trusts, and restore the immemorial sacred union among emperor, warrior, and producer.[10]

A magnetic field extended their reach through the army and navy into Japanese society and across the seas. Through the Zaigo-Gunjin Kai, the Reservists' League, with its 14,000 local branches and three million former soldiers, directed by retired officers, they could spread their message to the rural population. As the Diet met at the end of August, over 100,000 farmers from distressed provinces were appealing to the emperor. Weather and the economy had conspired to destroy their crops or their markets, and hunger now stalked their villages. Schoolchildren were eating wheat bran, otherwise intended for cattle. The parents and petitioners now pleaded the indifference of the parties to their plight and invoked the coming support of local conscripts, absent and under arms but conveyed by sympathetic regimental staff officers. Within weeks of Saito's assuming office, delegations were besieging his government, and the parties, hovering in constitutional limbo, feared the nationalists' inroads among their rural supporters. They clamored all the more loudly for relief for them, inflationary or not, and behind the Seiyukai warnings of "discontent" as the Diet assembled in August lay the party's preoccupation with its own mortality.[11]

At the summit, through the high command, the societies could reach the cabinet and the court. Kokuhonsha alone included in its ranks Admiral Heihachiro Togo, the country's most decorated hero, and General Sadao Araki, the minister of war, among other military dignitaries. Through Araki the army made known in May, after Inukai's assassination, that it would not tolerate a resumption of party politics, that a government of national unity must take over, and that Parliament must submit. And Prince Saionji came to Tokyo. The army and navy ministers came from active duty or from the reserves, never from civilian pursuits; the emperor appointed them and their chiefs of staff; to the rest of the cabinet, they represented as intrusive yet as familiar a threat as the emperor's Privy Council. Nothing mutinous dishonored Araki's ultimatum, which led to the suspension of party government, the appointment of the Saito cabinet, and the governmental use of *hijoji*, "time of crisis," to define the times, before the word passed into public idiom later in the year. But with the secret societies and their sympathizers at their back, generals and admirals could join the unspoken threat of domestic rebellion to their own mounting impatience with the restraints placed on them overseas.[12]

Foreign expansion did not define the societies' cause, not yet. It emerged, when it did, from their mission to arrest Japanese decline. Both the Reservists' League and the Dai Nihon Seisanto situated Japanese economic destiny in China, at the expense of Anglo-American interests there; at the head of Kokuhonsha, Baron Hiranuma married his social programs at home to a vague but bellicose pan-Asian nationalism abroad. Others showed no interest. In the manifesto they penned and left at the police station on May 15, and in their trial the following year, the Ketsumeidan conspirators rarely spoke of other lands, other seas; some even expressed skepticism about the campaigns currently underway. For now, the crusade uniting all nationalist sects was domestic in inspiration, foreign in elaboration. But to military leaders and some of the officers under their command, only the Asian mainland promised space and security, the lifeblood of Greater Japan and incidentally of their own power and prestige as well. Sooner or later, the energies of Japanese nationalists were likely to converge on a stretch of land.[13]

As the deputies took their seats in Tokyo during the extraordinary session at the end of August, the first anniversary of the Mukden incident was fast approaching. On 18 September 1931, Japanese troops in the Kwantung Army had set off a harmless explosion on the South Manchuria Railway, blamed it on the local Chinese garrison, and occupied Mukden the next day and much of Manchuria in the following weeks. Quickly a local squabble became a wider test of wills, between officers and civilians at home, between members of the League of Nations abroad, more or less eager to hear China's complaint, keep the promise of the Covenant, and punish aggression when they could not deter it.

In theory, China ruled Manchuria; in practice, no one did. A local warlord, Zhang Xueliang, held sway in Changchun, the capital, but local brigands, sometimes indistinguishable from Chinese soldiers or destitute farmers, roamed the land, and the Russians jealously guarded their interests in the Chinese Eastern Railway to the north, sending troops in 1929 when Zhang threatened it. Along the 690-mile-long railway their soldiers had just pretended to save, the Japanese enjoyed major extraterritorial rights, conceded or imposed by treaties with Russia in 1905, China in 1915, and the Western powers in 1922. The Japanese presence was unlike any other, at once more intrusive, more extractive, and more constructive. The South Manchuria Railway ran schools, hospitals, police stations, libraries, and public utilities as well as trains; farther away, the Japanese harvested grain, mined coal and iron, manufactured steel, cut down forests for lumber; by 1931 their investments in the province exceeded those of any other foreigners except the British, amounting to over a third of the total. Were they even foreign? Manchuria, the cabinet of Prime Minister Giichi Tanaka had declared in 1927, was a special region, to be defended at all costs.[14]

Defended against whom? No one threatened to drive the Kwantung Army from its bastion—not the Soviets, who lacked the motives, nor Zhang Xueliang, who lacked the means, nor the Nationalist armies to the south, still struggling to unite the country as well as themselves under Chiang Kai-shek in Nanking. When they had neared Manchuria during the Northern Expedition in 1927 and 1928, Tanaka had sent troops to stop them in their tracks. In the summer of 1931 no invasion clouds appeared on any frontier. The boycott of Japanese goods that the Nanking government organized that summer—the ninth since 1919—did little damage to Japanese commerce in Manchuria. Agitation and disorder there rose. Chinese soldiers killed a Japanese captain, off-limits in a remote corner of the province; Chinese civilians attacked some Japanese women and children in Mukden; mounted bandits—*bazoku*—held up and ransacked a passenger train on the South Manchuria Railroad. But to police the zones under Japanese jurisdiction was one matter, to invade the vast province another. On 15 September *Jiji*, a paper for businessmen and civil servants, saw no reason for the soldiers of the Kwantung Army to resort to force.[15]

To them, the most ominous threat, one they feared more than any other, came from their own government. It yielded while they held. Shidehara, the foreign minister, wished to preserve Japan's economic position in Manchuria—that much was axiomatic; but he knew that the United States was Japan's largest silk market, that India supplied Japan with much of its cotton and pig iron, that China mattered more to Japan economically than to anyone else; he knew that since 1928 the Chinese Nationalists had convinced both Britain and the United States to phase out special treaties and extraterritorial privileges. The pragmatic diplomat wanted above all to calm the waters and negotiate. And all of the Minseito party stood behind him. To the young Turks of the Kwantung Army, to the ideologues among them and their friends in Tokyo, Manchuria promised more than food and raw materials for the home islands, much more: a site for eventual military operations against the Soviet Union to the north, enabling the same against China to the south, perhaps; the coming exemplar of Japanese spiritual renewal, certainly, with a restoration of the Imperial Way and the Shinto cults; and their gateway to liberating Asia from the West, if only they could rescue their own government from its mercenary grasp. They would settle Manchuria not as agents of capitalist trusts but as soldier-farmers, as legionnaires or janissaries on the confines of empire. An egalitarian as well as an imperial ethos pervaded their fantasy. Shidehara wanted General Shigeru Honjo, the commander of the Kwantung Army, to localize the Mukden incident. Honjo ignored him.[16]

Since then, the balance of authority had shifted steadily to the soldiers. At first the cabinet and the court tried to restrain the high command, which tried to restrain the Kwantung Army. But by the end of 1931 the cabinet was gone, along with Shidehara, replaced by a Seiyukai government more disposed to champion the campaign in Manchuria, and the general staff had overcome its initial nervousness.[17] Popular donations of all sorts were flowing to the troops in Manchuria, largesse that *Asahi*, probably the country's largest mass-circulation daily, held out as proof of unanimous support for the incursion there.[18] Valid or not, the deduction betrayed the consensual pressures of wartime. Who dared play the poorer patriot? Each outbid the other. In August, even before hostilities erupted, Seiyukai, then in opposition, had investigated and claimed to find conditions in Manchuria unacceptable, a casus belli; early in the new year, Minseito was casting aspersions on its handling of the undeclared war.[19] The army leaders could only smile on such self-effacement before their enterprise, especially with party government suspended after May. They held the line, along with the civilians, at the outright annexation of Manchuria, but the fiction they settled on early in 1932 instead—a sovereign entity called Manchukuo, reflecting the separatist aspirations of an allegedly indigenous people but under Japanese protection—served the Kwantung Army almost as well. It held the keys, it appointed the officials, it fought the bandits and the Chinese Nationalists; behind a spurious head of the new state, the deposed emperor of China Pu-Yi, and a commander masquerading for form's sake as an ambassador to him, it operated imperially and hoped at last to realize its delusions.[20]

The navy, for its part, had waged a parallel campaign against the government. Both ally and rival of the army, it shared its hostility to Shidehara diplomacy but resented its power and now its success. In 1930 Prime Minister Hamaguchi had instructed Japanese delegates at the London naval conference to accept the ratios for capital ships agreed to at Washington eight years earlier. Fiscal as well as diplomatic priorities had driven him—the same mix of monetary and occidental sensitivities that provoked army officers as it filtered through their echelons. A fierce struggle over ratification followed. Admiral Takeshi Takarabe, the navy minister who shared the prime minister's priorities and even hoped to resurrect the prewar Anglo-Japanese alliance, returned from London to the rage of patriots of the sea. One of them greeted him at Shimonoseki Station with a dagger on a platter, an invitation to hara-kiri that he declined. Assassins later took Hamaguchi's life in the same station. The unequal treaty and its constraints rankled in the years that followed. And meanwhile the army was on the march. Whatever it said, it had flouted the Nine-Power Treaty of 1922, which assured among other blessings the territorial integrity of China; why should the navy live by the limitations of the London treaty? At least the government dared not speak of renewing it when the time came in 1936. Partly for prestige, the admirals embarked on their misadventure in Shanghai early in 1932, only to have it cut short in May. And they watched as the cabinet, the Diet, and the Privy Council gave in to the army whenever it requested new credits for Manchuria. To match the army's exploits and reclaim some of its glory, the navy needed to renew its mission.[21]

Like the army at Mukden, the navy at Shanghai invoked the security of Japanese residents to justify its actions before a largely hostile world opinion.[22] Both services took to playing international opprobrium against national pride, in the press and in the councils of government. They did not need to browbeat the press; the sharper the reproaches from abroad, the more defensive it grew. The government waged its own paper war, composed its own apologia; and the soldiers and sailors developed their own.

Initially hesitant after the Mukden incident, the mainstream press soon closed ranks. Circulation as well as national honor required it. Bans on news that undermined or challenged the official version went into effect, but were difficult to enforce, and only rarely did the government have to suppress articles it deemed too critical of military or foreign policy. Most papers impugned the impartiality but not the legitimacy of the League of Nations and the commission it sent to investigate the Sino-Japanese dispute; its head, Victor Bulwer-Lytton, the second Earl of Lytton, and his four fellow investigators favored in their eyes the other side at the expense of their own. By the time they arrived in February 1932, to travel from Tokyo to Shanghai and on to Peiping and Mukden, major dailies had feared they would only inflame Chinese nationalism; by the time they left in the summer, and prepared to release their report in the autumn, the editorialists had deplored their incomprehension of Japanese motives, their vulnerability to Chinese manipulations; if only, ran the lament, the commissioners had plumbed the depths, embraced the complexities. When, at the end of 1931, the Japanese had pulled their troops back from an ephemeral neutral zone around Chinchow in southern Manchuria, newspapers had seized on rumors that the withdrawal obeyed offhand suggestions by the American secretary of state, Henry Stimson—a blow to the country's prestige, a stain on its honor. That its forces should obey a distant third party!—but the withdrawal they found inconsequential.[23]

Honor, for the government, came wrapped in law, history, and ethnicity. In the narratives it sent Geneva, the Chinese revolutionary nationalists had broken treaties, inflamed sectarian sentiment, and trampled on ethnic identities. The Kuomintang Party that Sun Yat-sen had founded and that Chiang Kai-shek inherited now fulfilled its initial raison d'être—the abrogation of the unequal treaties that the West had imposed—in a systematic violation of Japan's treaty rights in Manchuria. It had deprived the Japanese of their rights there and promoted anti-Japanese agitation as well as economic aggression— the boycott—everywhere. Was China even a sovereign state? Unable to maintain order in its own realm, racked by civil chaos, "the happy hunting ground of selfish and predatory warlords," it left Japanese nationals unprotected, save by their own troops, compelled finally to act. They, not the Chinese, had national justice on their side. The Nationalist government, if such it was, had kept up the fiction of sovereignty in Manchuria, a region peopled not by Han Chinese but by over thirty million Manchus, who now asserted with Japanese help their own claim to self-determination in the state of Manchukuo. The "explanatory notes," more stinting from Tokyo than the sustained appeals reaching Geneva from Nanking, and more condescending, read as though their exasperated authors had reached the limits of human endurance.[24]

The army and navy offered yet another variant of the national cause—pan-Asian schemes, by degree more visionary as the months went by and the prospect of League condemnation grew. In March 1932, as the press chafed at the Lytton Commission, General Araki threatened to exclude the League from East Asia if it did not mend its ways. In April he told successive meetings of Kokuhonsha that Japan need pay no heed to the League, to Russia or the United States or China, that it "must be fully prepared in the event of possible contingencies." Late in July he published an article in *Kaikosha*, an army magazine, about the Japanese mission in Asia. Manchuria and Mongolia were the gateway, he wrote, to the spread of Japan's divine civilization, and he deplored the subjection of the peoples of India, central Asia, and Siberia to white rule, as well as the Chinese stratagem of inveigling Europe and the United States into protecting it, plunged as it was into chronic chaos. A month later he was promoting a Monroe Doctrine for Asia. He assembled one hundred senior officers at his official residence to hear the recollections of a Privy Counsellor, Viscount Kentaro Kaneko, before whom President Theodore Roosevelt, a Harvard classmate, had floated just such a regional possibility, privately, after dinner at Oyster Bay some twenty-seven years earlier. The idea, as old as Japan's victory over Russia in 1905, now enjoyed the very public patronage of the minister of war.[25]

At the Diet, as it met at the end of August, the patriotism of the press, the pragmatism of the government, and the heady imperialism of the army and navy briefly collided. No predestined outcome ever governed their encounters, but by now the most audacious nationalists were enjoying the wind in their sails. To no one's surprise, Count Kosai Uchida, the foreign minister, took the occasion to recognize formally, on behalf of his government, the state of Manchukuo. He did so, he explained, because the powers had always intervened abroad to protect their nationals and their commerce—the United States in Panama and Nicaragua, he said pointedly, and almost all of them in China itself. Japan could do no less in Manchuria. Most of the press welcomed the gesture; many thought it might have come sooner. More gratuitously, the diplomat who years earlier had presided over his country's signing of the Versailles and Washington Nine-Power Treaties declared that

China would never recover its sovereignty over Manchuria. This mollified some of his critics. But not all. In the Diet the militarist Mori Kaku rose to protest Uchida's speech. He found it complacent, bureaucratic, legalistic, a tired demonstration that Japan had not violated the Nine-Power Treaty or the Kellogg-Briand Pact. Mori had led the Seiyukai delegation to Manchuria just before the Mukden incident the year before, almost justifying it in advance, and in February in Yokohama he had told his party that Japan was "fawning at the League of Nations" and undermining "the prestige of a great nation." Was the country now prepared, he asked the Diet, to face the coming shock of the world, a collision with the League, friction with the United States? Was Uchida? For the foreign minister, the creation of Manchukuo had provided a solution, an end; for Mori Kaku, it marked a beginning. Japan should turn its back on Western civilization, after slavishly miming it for sixty years, and return to Asia.[26]

Nothing was decided. The voices of militant nationalism had not drowned those of moderation. Among themselves, the nationalists dissipated their energies in plots and intrigues. In September and October, as the League prepared to release the findings of the Lytton Commission, Saito's civilian government, however unsavory to the militarists inside and outside it, seemed surprisingly secure. The economy, buoyed by a depreciating currency, government spending, and the sudden recovery of the world silk market, appeared to rebound. The army could not dislodge high officials whose moderation and misgivings it suspected, including the keeper of the privy seal and the ambassador to the United States. Others among them kept assuring the American ambassador that moderation was gaining strength, that Shidehara diplomacy would return. The diplomat from Washington detected nervousness in the air, in the speculation about the most hotheaded officers, in the emperor's brother asking an American visitor at dinner whether the United States was actively preparing for war with Japan. "Everything will turn out all right," the officials assured the ambassador—perhaps too much. Word reached his ears that the emperor himself was eager to "stop the chauvinistic war talk." Perhaps the recognition of Manchukuo had stolen the militarist thunder. No one could tell.[27]

But should the economy relapse or international ostracism isolate the country, should credibility desert the government and national defiance cast its spell, then hopes of restoring the 1920s would evaporate. Militant nationalism no longer even required such auspicious circumstances to flourish. In September General Araki told the press that if Japan had to leave the League of Nations it would create an Asian equivalent under its own aegis. The persuasion was gaining ground, improbably, in the home of Shidehara diplomacy, the Gaimusho, the Japanese foreign ministry. The same month the director of its press and information bureau, Toshio Shiratori, made Theodore Roosevelt's views his own, distending them beyond recognition. The Japanese Empire, he maintained, needed not only firm soil but zones of influence beyond, like those Britain enjoyed beyond the frontiers of India in central Asia, and the right in Asia to League mandates over peoples ill suited to sovereignty, of the sort Britain and France exercised in the Middle East and Africa. Coming from the Gaimusho, the aspirations startled. Japan had been slow to embrace the latitude in northeastern Asia that the West had tacitly conceded to it at Portsmouth in 1905 and Washington in 1922 and turn it into outright hegemony. Now "Monroeism," an American doctrine that could claim no juridical validity yet commanded the compliance of a continent and of the world, extended its appeal beyond the army, the navy, the societies linked to them, and their friends, who included Shiratori. Shidehara, when in office, had tried and failed to rid the foreign ministry of him. "We are working overtime nowadays from 8 till 6," an officer of the Japanese general staff told the American military attaché, "because we have to run two separate departments, the War Ministry and the Foreign Office."[28]

Xenophobia intermittently swept the press. In September the War Department showed its hand in them. In a fit of spy mania, newspapers told of mysterious foreigners seen at military installations or munitions plants. An officer from the American embassy had appeared at

the arsenal at Nagoya; a foreigner in his midfifties, in the company
of a Japanese posing as an insurance agent, had asked to inspect a
steel plant in Hiroshima, under contract to the navy; the sightings of
foreigners "from a certain country" accelerated; they overwhelmed
the gendarmerie. One affair escalated into an international incident.
When the National City Bank of New York asked its branch offices
in Japan to photograph shipping scenes, office buildings, and industrial sections, a war scare rippled through the press. The bank had
wanted only to compile an album displaying the happy fruits of its
own capital injections, and local publicity and postcards depicted the
same sites, but newspapers and patriotic societies all over the country alerted their compatriots to imminent bombing raids. Delegations from the societies invaded the branch's premises in Osaka, and
Japanese employees there feared for their own safety as well. Radio
stations broadcast news of American aero-naval movements in the Pacific. The War Ministry declined to comment, and the Foreign Ministry protested its powerlessness over the press, which now accused
the American ambassador of wanton interference. The storm passed;
Uchida and the foreign ministry conceded that the bank had been
blameless. But they declined to do so publicly. Later, through the
American press, their concession found its way into some Japanese
papers. The War Ministry remained silent.[29]

Beyond the articulate realm of the political sphere, with its institutions, parties, and press, a war boom was sweeping the mass media.
This too served the army, which waged a concurrent propaganda
campaign. Since the Mukden incident, publishers, film studios,
theaters, and music companies had flooded the market with tales
of martyrdom from the front, all tragic or heroic, some apocryphal,
most exalting the Japanese against the alien horde. The mainstream
press could when it chose affect balance and tolerate complexity, but
not the entertainment industry; it lived by simplifying and exaggerating, by turning news into legend. For its part the army organized
rallies and petition drives; where once it had lobbied against cuts, it
now celebrated the first anniversary of the Mukden incident to rally

the faithful and galvanize any wilting provinces into action. A sea of loyalists turned out in Tokyo.[30] So fortified, the army might even contemplate new adventures. It had diminished the government by occupying Manchuria, provoking foreign reproaches, and reaping a harvest of popularity. It was now threatening Jehol Province, just west of Manchukuo and bordering on the Great Wall. A vicious circle was in the making.

Early in September, thirty thousand people gathered at the port in Kobe to greet General Honjo's ship. He was returning as a national hero from his command of the Kwantung Army. Fireworks lit up the sky, planes flew over the harbor, and storms of "Banzai!" rose from the crowd. Public emotion, both cause and effect of the surfeit of reportages and glad tidings from Manchuria, could transfigure the living as well as the dead. Honjo's Roman entry into Tokyo capped a triumphal journey that had begun when his train had left Mukden amid scenes of fervid leave-taking. It went with the season; all month some official occasion for celebration—the signing of the official protocol between Japan and Manchukuo, the anniversary of Mukden—filled the streets and parks with the ready rejoicing of faceless multitudes.[31]

What did they make of the war in Manchuria? Was it even a war? Next to the slaughter of Japanese infantry at the siege of Port Arthur or of Mukden in 1904 and 1905, which some of them might remember, this amounted to a protracted skirmish. By the summer of 1932 the Kwantung Army was deploying less than 50,000 troops there. The first year took less than 1,000 Japanese lives, next to 14,000 in five months at Port Arthur alone. National and international publicity had transfigured the Manchurian affair into an existential struggle or a threat to world peace, but few families yet felt its sting or feared its exactions. In some remote hamlets where few newspapers were read and fewer radios heard, Manchuria was still a world away.[32] Villagers, townspeople, and businessmen variously sent money and relief parcels, answered the army's call, prayed for the soldiers, visited shrines; but no more than the rapture at war films or the crowd on the docks in Kobe did such gestures, for now, betray an artificial frenzy or a newfound expansionist fever. Even the young men who volunteered to join the Manchukuo Pacification Corps, and who found their pictures in the papers as a result, acted less radically than the few antiwar dissenters of the Left, silenced but not eradicated. Tradition and technology—consensual patriotism stimulated by mass communication—had brought the army the support it craved, use it how it might.[33]

The Diet disbanded, its emergency session over. The efforts of the Seiyukai party to bring down Finance Minister Takahashi over the inadequacy of relief had only heaped more discredit onto the parties. In the press, the major dailies supported constitutional government. But some of them warned that spectacles of the sort the lower house had just provided might hasten the advent of Fascist or dictatorial rule.[34] The temptation was growing in the political nation to blame economic, political, and diplomatic impotence on a Western turn taken years earlier—ten according to some, sixty according to others—and to follow new avenues toward a place in the sun. The rest was patriotism.

In the port of Dairen, at the tip of the Liaodong Peninsula at the southern end of Manchuria, the main streets radiating from the central park bore the names of the heroes of the Russo-Japanese War, and at its center stood a statue of the first Japanese governor of the peninsula, which had briefly become a colony in 1895. Now, in the park, high school students followed their bands and celebrated Manchukuo and victory over China. By day they waved Japanese flags; by night they carried lanterns that illuminated the red dots on white and sent the emblems billowing through the park.[35]

Several hundred miles to the north, in his capital at Changchun, renamed Hsinking to mark the new era, Pu-Yi, the last emperor of China as an infant and the first head of state of Manchukuo as an adult, set up temporary quarters in a large red-tiled European house surrounded by turreted walls. Tall, twenty-seven years old, impeccably dressed in suits from Savile Row, he lived there amid an entourage of chamberlains, functionaries, and imperial princes from the deposed court in Beijing, while a palace went up for him nearby. He spent his days receiving visitors and playing tennis, billiards, and Ping-Pong, and riding one of his twenty-nine Mongolian ponies.[36]

Another two hundred miles to the north lay Harbin, where 12,000 Russians lived and operated the Chinese Eastern Railway. The train from Changchun no longer ran at night, because of bandits and derailments, and during the day soldiers on guard with rifles and machine guns—Manchukuans on flatbeds behind the locomotives, Japanese in third-class passenger cars—traveled along with the civilians. Along the line, which ran through limitless and sometimes flooded plains, trains carrying Japanese cavalry units passed, and in the desolate stations Russian police began to appear, beside Manchukuan soldiers who sometimes carried flags as identification and took pains to distinguish themselves from deserters.

Northwest of Harbin, on the great prairies, the villages resembled one another. Mud walls and towers protected them, manned by civilians with old muzzle-loading rifles. They were defending themselves against the Japanese, against the bandits and guerrillas overrunning the land, against the Chinese troops even, whom they classified as "good" or "bad" and whose presence in any case would only attract the Japanese. The Kwantung Army had spread anarchy throughout Manchuria.[37]

And still farther north, beyond the prairies and the Amur River, lay the Siberian taiga and the Soviet Union.

Benito Mussolini rode a bay charger onto the Piazza Venezia. He wore the uniform of the Fascist militia, set off with gold epaulets and emblazoned with decorations, and a black fez with egret plumes. The leaders of the columns that had marched on Rome escorted him, enacting again the stage-managed event ten years earlier, on the twenty-eighth of October 1922. Behind them came the serried ranks of black-shirted Fascists and wounded war veterans, and overhead squadrons of military aircraft crossed the skies. Tens of thousands watched from windows, rooftops, and pavements. He cut the ribbon, he opened the new Imperial Way, he rode down it to the Colosseum, now fully visible from the piazza, past a vista of newly exhumed antiquity, of excavated forums and the eastern flank of the Capitoline Hill.[38]

For ten days piazzas up and down the peninsula had resounded with the din of commemoration. They were the arenas of the new order, its clamorous sites of worship. Here the regime met the people; here, following ceremonies improvised in the early years but already ritually kept by 1932, civil and military authorities assembled, crowds came, all paid homage to the fallen of the war and the revolution that had jointly given Italy the regime. And here the Duce spoke, sometimes in person, more often on the radio or on a giant screen, luminously projected for all to behold. Such solemnities had lately taken him to Milan, where hundreds of thousands packed the Piazza del Duomo and the neighboring streets to hear him speak from the cathedral steps, and two days before that to the balcony of the prefecture in Turin—"Show your black shirts, people of Turin"—and a week before that to the Piazza Venezia, when he had inaugurated the celebrations by telling 25,000 party hierarchs from all over the country, as though to rejoice, that the Fascist insurrection ten years earlier had been one of the bloodiest in history, before a sudden downpour drove them scattering from the open square.[39]

On the morning of the twenty-eighth, as the air force planes roared by just above Saint Peter's, Cardinal Pacelli, secretary of state of the Vatican, reassured the French ambassador about the warlike trappings of all the celebrations that month. It was all for public consumption, he explained, all to sustain mass enthusiasm. *L'Osservatore Romano*, the Vatican paper, had been measured in its coverage of the regime, cool beside the dithyrambic outpourings of the controlled press, and the ambassador was inclined to respect Pacelli's judgment.[40] Since the concordat three years earlier, relations between the Fascist state and the Catholic Church had been correct more than cordial, and perhaps the cardinal at the window in the Apostolic See recognized without regret the martial antics of a newcomer uncertain of public devotion.

No doubt; but the cultivation of imperial grandeur, of *romanità*, troubled more. The Yugoslavs, Albanians, Greeks, and British as well as the French had cause to reflect on the ambitions such nostalgia disguised. Rebellious peoples—nomadic tribesmen of Tripolitania and sectarian Senussi of Cyrenaica in Libya, and villagers in the northeastern sultanates of Italian Somalia in the Horn of Africa—had only recently suffered its sanguinary literal meaning, as yet still a menace in the making for the Amharas in their sovereign, multi-ethnic empire of Abyssinia. Empire, for the regime, signified more than an archaeological divertissement or tableau for the people; its resurrection defined the promise of Fascism itself.

Fascism had seen the day in 1919 as a challenge to the new world order as well as the old Italian one. The first, it proclaimed, had denied Italy most of the fruits promised at the conference table in London in 1915 and finally won on the battlefield at Vittorio Veneto in 1918, and the second had been too weak to reclaim them. Much of Dalmatia went to Yugoslavia, Albania remained independent, not a fragment of the Ottoman Empire or a colony of the German came Italy's way, either in the Middle East or in Africa. Somewhere in the waters of the Adriatic or the Mediterranean irredentism passed into imperialism, and the drive to restore Italian rule to Italian people graduated to an ambition to extend it to others as well. No society paralyzed by class conflict, no nation fragmented by liberal individualism or emasculated by pacifism could realize such exploits. A state that exalted unrelenting struggle and a bleak uniformity could; but to mobilize the will it had to promote the goal, ceaselessly, and display without acknowledging the circularity of Fascism. The movement emerged by associating national insult with domestic decay, and by stirring a sense of each among its followers, a simple assimilation that its imitators would adopt all over Europe and beyond.

"The Italy of Vittorio Veneto," Mussolini had declared in May

1919 in the Adriatic port of Fiume, itself withheld by the allies in one of their presumptive betrayals at Versailles, "feels the irresistible attraction of the Mediterranean which will itself open the way to Africa." By the time King Victor Emmanuel III bowed to his blood-less coup and appointed him to office in October 1922, Mussolini had spelled out his designs on seas and shores abroad in one fiery speech after another. Italy would transform the map of Europe, drive foreign powers from the Mediterranean, demolish the British Empire, return to Africa. As prime minister and as Duce he punctually called on his listeners to erase their humiliations and overturn the status quo conceived at Versailles, upheld at Geneva, and enforced by London and Paris; he became a leading revisionist statesman of the 1920s. The League itself was an Anglo-French condominium masquerad-ing as pacifist internationalism, the very pusillanimous idealism he deplored at home. "Words are truly beautiful things," Mussolini told a crowd in Florence on May 17, 1930, the same day that Aristide Bri-and, the French foreign minister, proposed a European political union, "but rifles, machine guns, ships, aircraft, and cannons are even more beautiful." He spoke from the balcony of the Palazzo Vec-chio, his words carried by loudspeakers onto the Piazza della Signo-ria and crowds chanting "empire, empire." It was, one French paper thought, the most bellicose peacetime harangue of the century.[41]

Fascism had inherited many of its overseas ambitions from earlier Nationalists; it had dreamed up neither new colonies in Africa nor an Italian dominion in the Balkans and the Mediterranean. But it had joined their pursuit to that of a new total state at home, and by taking power leant them urgency that liberal governments, even when they shared some of the Nationalists' yearnings, had wisely shunned. Fas-cism elevated impatience into policy. Well before Mussolini began turning constitutional into dictatorial power in 1925, he acted—he seized the isle of Corfu from Greece. He learned then, as he would later, of the obstacles to impetuous expansion—the British navy to the occupation of Corfu, the French army to aggression against its Yugoslav ally, most pertinently, but also the League of Nations, and the yawning disparity between dreams and means. In its first ten years Fascist Italy lacked the financial, diplomatic, and military assets to impose its will abroad. Mussolini would have to wait.[42]

Meanwhile he sought allies, now in Vienna or Budapest, now in Athens or Ankara; and throughout the decade he looked thoughtfully at Germany and its turmoil. Little came of such dalliances. And, even while rearming, he played the peacemaker on the world stage, signing the treaty of Locarno of 1925 that cast Italy alongside Britain as the gendarme of the Franco-Belgian-German borders, and the Kellogg-Briand Pact of 1928 that outlawed war, which meant as little to him as the disarmament projects at Geneva he pretended to champion. Mussolini arrived in the Libyan port of Tripoli in 1926, on board the cruiser *Cavour* and followed by her sister ship and a flotilla of lesser vessels, to speak of Italy's destinies in the empty spaces of Africa; at the first signs of British and French alarm, he assured the Senate and the world that Italian imperialism was entirely pacific. Mussolini the peacemaker gained some standing among Italy's former allies, relieved that the weakest link in their postwar order still seemed to hold and that Corfu had no sequel.[43]

Still they could not ignore the regime's intermittent outbursts in the press and in the open air. Which showed its true face, the endearments or the rebukes? With good reason, the French worried more than the British, for their postwar predominance represented all that their southern neighbor wished to overturn—the status quo in Europe and the Mediterranean. The reminders came punctually, sometimes on the occasion of a bitter anniversary. In May 1932, on the seventeenth anniversary of Italy's entry into the Great War, *Gioventú Fascista*, the official youth organ, reminded its readers again of the great swindle of Versailles. It blamed French "ingratitude, selfishness, and hostility" for their peninsula's postwar shackles, for fabricating the "monstrous caricature of a nation that is the Serbian-Croatian-Slovenian state" and starving the Italians of colonies beyond the sea—they would not, it promised, "consider themselves at peace as long as they have no lands to fructify." Nothing new distin-

guished the article, not even its contention that Italy had contributed
more than France to the victory of 1918. But its author wrote for *Il
Popolo d'Italia*, the paper that Mussolini had founded; the press commented on it or reproduced it; and the editor of *Gioventú Fascista*
was Achille Starace, the empty-headed sycophant whom Mussolini
had recently made secretary-general of the Fascist Party. The regime
could not send Dr. Jekyll abroad and keep Mr. Hyde at home, at least
not forever.[44]

The most bellicose harangue in peacetime, the French *Journal
des Débats* had called Mussolini's speech in Florence in October
1930. By a head of government, it meant; for soapbox orators in Italy and elsewhere made revanchist or aggressive speeches too. How
many chanting "empire" on the Piazza della Signoria actively welcomed the prospect of a war of conquest somewhere, how many silent
others far from Florence would follow if called? Mussolini seemed
to wonder as much when he spoke of the public as a "herd" to Emil
Ludwig, the German Carlyle, biographer of great men, in 1932. The
Duce confessed that in giving such warlike speeches in 1930 he had
only wanted "to see where the nation was, and whether, if needed,
it would follow him." The authorities hastily withdrew the advance
copies of Ludwig's *Conversations with Mussolini* from circulation in
the summer of that year and instructed the press to hold off publishing any excerpts.[45]

Mussolini's comment, unflattering to the masses and embarrassing
to himself, only acknowledged reality. Between one minority of arrant
Fascists, out in the open, and a smaller one of unseen anti-Fascists,
imprisoned on the Lipari Islands or exiled abroad, moved a dark
magma of sentiment. Here no single image of Mussolini held sway—
neither the *Duce-Condottiere*, the captain, nor the *Duce-Statista*, the
statesman, nor any single understanding of the regime, including its
historical mission at home or abroad. Shifting, unstable, imperfectly
knowable, perhaps "a-Fascist," it invited the regime's assiduous attentions and exertions—to ascertain, to coerce, but more and more,
by the early 1930s, to persuade. By then so many of the regime's once

quiet and reliable supporters in the middle classes were sharing the bread of economic adversity that it had to reconquer them, so conditional was their fidelity; and for that the instruments of repression were useless.[46]

"Everyone is tired of the Fascist order," informers reported in 1931 from Milan, and they begged the government to do something for local business. Local merchants blamed the falling prices, the tight credit, the collapse of sales, the bankruptcies, the closings on the government. Yes, the whole world was suffering, but the government had only made matters worse. From other towns came similar alarms— the lower middle classes, bedrock of the regime, were deserting it; the upper middle classes showed conspicuous indifference to any of its initiatives; here and there an unthinkable nostalgia for the old liberal state was eclipsing it. No surprise that in another great industrial city of the north, Turin, the workers should display their customary despair and ill humor; but that the rest of local society should join them caused consternation—like any repressive regime, this one fretted over its own supporters, even if the anti-Fascists greatly exaggerated the imminence of its collapse. No incipient revolt threatened it. But the economic crisis, in the most socially diverse milieus of north, south, and center, had revealed the fragility of its support.[47]

Only massive public spending, on relief and on public works, stanched the draining away of support. Among the exploits that brought the regime acceptance in the 1920s, including public order, the suppression of bolshevism, land reclamation, the accommodation with the church, and a certain standing abroad, public works ranked high; in ten years the regime spent more on such projects—on aqueducts and roads and dams—than liberal governments had in the previous sixty. Now relief, generously allocated and intelligently administered, regained for the regime much of the ground that economic stagnation had lost. It accomplished little for the economy or the finances of the new order but much for its image—charity disguised as effort, the unemployed and the beggars removed from view, the largesse of the state made known by word of mouth and touted in the press as counterpoint to the miseries of German and American democracies.[48]

Fear of revolution—in the summer of 1931 truckloads of troops patrolled the streets of Milan—and the gratification of foreign esteem did the rest. "There is a quietness and a soundness in Italian public life," the *Observer* noted in London on the eve of the tenth anniversary celebrations, "such as force themselves into contrast with the contemporary spectacle in other Central and Southeastern European countries." The *Observer* was a conservative weekly, but even left-leaning papers abroad passively withheld fire, chide the regime as they might for its secret police and its repressive ways. And it thirsted for their praise; long used to condescension or worse, Italians might now attribute their stature to its magic.[49]

Grievance diplomacy, when Mussolini waged it, had won the regime little esteem abroad and played no part in the regime's survival in popular opinion. The ambient apathy that so darkened the reports on popular opinion in the early 1930s came with material misery and lifted only with material relief. Yet this was the moment when he hardened his resolve to embark on a foreign adventure driven by imperial envy, a world-historical grievance, one he later came to believe would rouse the masses from the torpor that threatened Fascism itself. But would they follow?[50]

He need look no further than the elites around him to realize the misgivings his ambitions aroused. Among the officers of the general staff, the senior officials of the foreign ministry in the Palazzo Chigi, and the advisers to King Victor Emmanuel, caution and resistance dogged his every step. Who could not applaud his wish to avenge the defeat of Aduwa in 1896, when Abyssinian troops had defeated an Italian army and dashed hopes of a colonial empire in East Africa? Almost all shared it. But planners and diplomats alike convinced him not to even contemplate an invasion there without prior British and French consent and a semblance of security at his back. Out there, in the magma, no one had yet suffered much from any Fascist escapade abroad, and no one had yet to oppose one. But nothing suggested either that public opinion hankered after one. It would have to be prepared.[51]

Acceptance of the regime, once it had overcome the crisis of confidence between 1930 and 1932, helped make the task easier; so did *mussolinismo*, the cult of the Duce, and the devotion manifest in the 1,500 private letters that flowed into his offices every day. The regime encouraged them, just as it brought in by train or bus some of the supporters who lined the streets and packed the squares when Mussolini came to town. But they displayed a touching and authentic faith in his humane compassion for their personal lot, responding to yet another mask of his myth—that of the father figure. They wrote to express their adoration but also their distress—*se lo sapesse il Duce*, if the Duce only knew, they wrote, of the headaches local party officials or government functionaries caused them. He might help; and sometimes, with suitable publicity, he did.[52] But some foreign enterprise of his, some war, far from alleviating their daily woes, might bring new ones.

"When will you stop tormenting me with this Africa of yours?" Mussolini had grumbled to Dino Grandi in May, his arms folded, as the chamber applauded a speech in which the foreign minister had called on Italian industry to open up the continent's empty spaces. That was not how Mussolini understood the coming campaigns. In the autumn of 1932, with the tenth anniversary at hand, the logic of Fascism unfolded. Its official doctrine, published in the summer in the *Italian Encyclopedia* in time for the celebrations, signed by Mussolini but ghostwritten by Emilio Gentile, made much of war and the imperial spirit. The first "sets the seal of nobility on those peoples who have the courage to face it"; the second marked "an essential manifestation of vitality . . . of a people who, like the people of Italy, are rising again after many centuries of abasement and foreign servitude." On the twenty-eighth of October the great Exhibition of the Fascist Revolution opened in an austerely modernistic edifice on the Via Nazionale, amid trappings of Pompeian red. Fascist dignitaries took turns standing sentry in the heart of the exhibition at the sanctuary of the war dead, muskets at their sides. Several times daily the guard changed, ritually; the exhibition opened and closed with fanfares, Roman salutes, and volleys from riflemen; it celebrated Mussolini as the contemporary apotheosis of the Italian epic, so martially that the future left little to the imagination. Dino Grandi was gone, brusquely dismissed as foreign minister in the summer for his penchant for the League of Nations, itself rejected in the doctrine along with the equally shallow illusion of perpetual peace. Now Mussolini, who took over the Foreign Ministry along with the army, the navy, and the air force, could drive his agenda forward, against compromise, against Geneva. In *Gerarchia*, the Fascist periodical about current affairs, Emilio de Bono, the minister for colonies, recalled the excitement of coming ashore with the troops in Eritrea, the first of Italy's colonies, in 1885. Where were such youthful desires now? he wondered. Nowhere to be found, he complained, among neither the people nor their deputies, and he implored his readers to imagine the future of Italy in Africa— and he was not, he explained, thinking of Libya. The preparation was under way.[53]

The October commemorations called on Italian youth to redeem the promise of Fascism and along with it the country's dignity.[54] The celebrations threatened no one with war, but unmistakably consecrated a forceful variety of national regeneration. Outside the exhibition hall, beyond the parades and the pageants, a defiant tone crept into the speeches and the articles, and foreign embassies sat up and took notice. In Turin, Mussolini deplored "French hegemony" and reminded the crowd that their border town had never feared war. In Milan, on the steps of the Duomo, he recalled the French mutinies of 1917 "after bloody and unsuccessful offensives," and in Rome he gestured to the Palazzo Venezia, where Bonaparte's mother, Letizia, had died—"The same Bonaparte, sprung from the powerful race of Dante and Michelangelo . . . who never learned to speak French correctly . . . who called to arms the Italians, whom he ranked among the best soldiers in Europe." Was this to encourage the Italians who claimed Corsica as theirs? And when, in Milan, he promised not to allow the flagrant injustices of Versailles to crystallize, the Czechs and the Poles and probably anyone else with new borders to hold on to frowned. He promised, too, that in ten years all Europe would be Fascist, forgetting that in sager moments he had said that the innovation forever tied to his name was not "an article for export." The same week the head of the journalists' union echoed his condemnation of French "hegemony" in the *Corriere della Sera*, the most important daily newspaper in Milan and one of the most influential in the country. To it he added his own diagnosis of the "instinctive jealousy" that had denied Italy the international standing due "its high civilization, its 42 million people, and the glory of Vittorio Veneto."[55]

Mere words—but over time daily cultivation of national resentment, by a government monopolizing all the print and audiovisual means to do so, might harden the collective will to wrest restitution for past wrongs. In the meantime, the government quietly conceived varieties of aggression abroad, from subversion to invasion.

If Yugoslavia did not disintegrate on its own, then help was available; the prospect beckoned, as long as no other way to interfere or extend Italian influence lay at hand. In Fiume, finally ceded to Italy in 1923 in spite of its Slav majority, local authorities gave shelter and sustenance to Croatian separatists who had never accepted the Serbian predominance in the new kingdom of the south Slavs. The local Fascists housed them, translated their propaganda into Italian, protected their correspondence with other Croatians abroad; and they gave them weapons and munitions as well, with which to cross and recross the borders into Croatia and Dalmatia. In September and October 1932, from there and from the Italian enclave of Zara to the south, terrorist Ustashe tried vainly to incite local uprisings, by detonating bombs and attacking police stations in the rocky and desolate Lika Valley. Bandits roamed the mountains and provided the bulk of what support they could find. They fled—the locals to their hills, the Ustashe back to Zara and Fiume, leaving Italian military matériel behind. The Italian press reported that a Croatian national insurrection was holding an entire Serbian army in check. If only—

years later, when the German Wehrmacht had destroyed the entire kingdom, the Ustashe would rule Croatia as Italian protégés. But not this time. No more than in Macedonia in the south, where local separatist agitators enjoyed its kindnesses as well, was Italian mischief able to exploit the fragility of Yugoslavia and realize the dream of its decomposition.[56]

In July 1925, when Mussolini had instructed his minister of colonies to draw up plans to "smash" Abyssinia, he had asked that he do so quietly—if possible with British acquiescence, but, in any case, "chloroforming" the Ethiopians to the designs he was hatching. Since then studies on the ground had proceeded, envisaging Italian expeditionary forces, local Eritrean troops, air power, chemical weapons, and the prior corruption of Abyssinian feudal magnates along the borders with Eritrea and Italian Somalia. With each year Mussolini's most sanguine expectations grew, and by the celebrations of October 1932 an operational blueprint for invasion under de Bono's guidance was almost in place.[57]

The timing was not; Mussolini's ministers and advisers still insisted on the prior consent of Britain and France, and by extension the League of Nations, which in 1923 had welcomed Abyssinia—along with Liberia, one of the two fully sovereign states in Africa—into its fold. The arts of diplomacy still recommended themselves, along with the reciprocal virtues of aggressive and moderate behavior. Mussolini needed somehow to "chloroform" the European powers as well. This too would require preparation. In Turin, as he complained of French hegemony, he also spoke of a pact among Britain, France, Germany, and Italy, a kind of condominium to tranquilize Europe. But—and this he did not say—such an arrangement might also isolate France from its continental allies, especially in eastern Europe and the Balkans, and push the League itself into the shadows. The dissonance between de Bono's cruel blueprint and Mussolini's affable proposal was more apparent than real. And other options might surface; they might, perhaps, embrace Germany alone.

Then the exhibition opened; and before it closed two years later,

Mussolini was talking of another one, to celebrate the twentieth anniversary—E 42 for now—with a new city at the gates of Rome, facing the sea and set above a great new avenue parallel to that just built between Rome and Ostia.[58]

No one seemed to have noticed, but on the edges of Asia and the Mediterranean two movements were erasing the line between domestic and foreign affairs. Each rejected any hint of the cosmopolitan—of the alien at home, of internationalism abroad—and promoted the mystique of a unique nation that could tolerate neither dissent within its borders nor failure beyond them. But they had to share power, much against their will, with domestic civil or religious actors whose views and interests did not always coincide with their own. The road to undivided rule ran through unchecked expansion, so that the League and collective security, if their champions chose to uphold them, stood between them and dominion not only over others, but over their own as well.

3

BERLIN

6 November 1932

Sunday, November 6, was Election Day in Berlin, the fifth in eight months.[1] The day was gray, and the transport workers were on strike. The voters flowed through the streets and avenues on foot, hurried but indifferent. At the doors of voting stations in local halls, schools, and restaurants, pathetic men and women in sandwich boards conveyed the last appeals of their parties. They received a few marks that way.

The Nazis, in mustard brown uniforms and shoulder belts, with swastikas on their armbands, raised their forearms in rapid greeting to one another. The Socialists did the same, but with a clenched fist, like the Communists—but they pulled the elbow back, pugnaciously. The Catholics of the Center Party raised two fingers of the right hand, suggesting benediction. Around Berlin, flags hung from the windows of apartment buildings—the red hammer and sickle toward Wedding and the north of the city, swastikas toward the western neighborhoods of Steglitz and Friedenau; here the constitutional black, red, and gold of the Weimar Republic, or the three Socialist arrows, there the nationalist black, white, and red of the Wilhelmine Empire that had collapsed amid defeat and revolution in November 1918.[2]

The voters waited patiently and entered the booths to mark with

an "X" their party's lists. Every sixty thousand votes in a single con-
stituency entitled a party to send one of its members to the Reichstag, a system of proportional representation that since the birth of
the Weimar Republic in 1919 had disposed of enough goodwill to
yield governing coalitions, one after another, fourteen in all in the
first eleven years. But many had hung on without half the deputies in
the Reichstag, and since 1930 the aged president, Field Marshal Paul
von Hindenburg, recognizing the inability of any would-be chancellor to cobble together a working majority, had deployed his constitutional powers to appoint one and then another. No one expected
that today's democratic rites would cure the parties of their mutual
detestation or the parliament of its paralysis. Eighty percent of the
citizens turned out to vote, in the gray and the cold rain, without a
bus or a tram in sight—high by the standards of most democracies,
but lower than the last time, in July. They displayed little emotion
in the queues, more before the cinemas. On the publicity columns
lackluster political posters—a Nazi depiction of a skeleton in Soviet
uniform, a Nationalist caricature of Nazi and Communist partners in
crime, arm in arm—set off the bright movie bills. German and foreign
reporters made story lines out of the listless devotion to civic duty.[3]

Wahlmüdigkeit—election fatigue—was setting in. After the first
round of the presidential election in March, the second round and
the Prussian elections in April, the Reichstag elections in July, and
new ones now again in November, voters were losing hope more than
patience. They had returned old Marshal Hindenburg to the presidency, the Social Democrats in the minority to the government of
Prussia, where about two-thirds of the Reich lived, and a hung parliament to Berlin, this time with the Nazis as its largest party; but
Hindenburg had merely replaced one unpopular chancellor with
another, the Social Democrats had meekly allowed the government
of the Reich to evict them as incapable of maintaining order, and the
parliament had gone home as well, dissolved after a chaotic session in
September, to another campaign and another election. All of which
had changed nothing—neither the economic nor the political crisis,

nor the misery, nor the pervading sense of drift. Why vote again? "This," wrote a leading newspaper on the morning of the election, "is perhaps more dangerous than ever before in German history."[4]

At the end of August, Chancellor Franz von Papen had traveled to Neudeck, Hindenburg's ancestral estate in East Prussia, to foil if he could the unruly parliament imposed on him by the July election. Papen was a leader without a following, a politician without a party. This he advertised as a virtue, as the mark of the true patriot, but it only invited more of the derision that the dilettante and the debonair man of the world in him had already provoked. Some of his friends laughed at him. In press photos and newsreels he smiled and laughed, in theaters, at tennis matches, fashion shows, and racetracks—for he was a horseman, a former cavalry officer who had run steeplechases, over timber at hippodromes. George Bernard Shaw found him a mindless and contented clubman. The Catholic Center Party had disowned him as a false friend, and he made his way now thanks to Hindenburg, who saw him as more malleable than his stiff-necked predecessor, Heinrich Brüning, as close to the army, and best of all as determined to reform if not extirpate the parliamentary regime itself.[5]

At Neudeck Hindenburg received him along with three other members of the inner circle, the Camarilla, including General Kurt von Schleicher, the minister of war and ever the intriguer, Hindenburg's confidant, the "Machiavelli of postwar Germany" who had helped make Papen chancellor and might just as deliberately unmake him. Papen the landed aristocrat and Schleicher the general typified the government of the Reich, described by critics as the "Herrenklub" or "the barons," answerable more to a kinglike sovereign than to a dysfunctional parliament, ghosts of the Bismarckian empire in a moribund republic. The American ambassador remarked on their sequestration, plotting the country's future while leaving it in the dark.[6]

Weimar democracy had been languishing for two years. Elections, unlike this one, had been lively and intense, but liberal institutions had been seizing up while the economic depression stealthily destroyed millions of lives. Both Brüning and Papen had governed by emergency decrees, without parliamentary majorities, and the Reichstag had gradually ceased even to meet. Among the major parties, the Nazis and the Communists openly proclaimed their hostility to the Republic; a third, Brüning's Catholic Center Party, supported and even sustained it, but more as practice than principle, hinting at adaptability to whatever the future might bring. Brüning himself, conservative to the core along with Hindenburg, hoped that the Weimar Republic would evolve by legal means into an authoritarian state, perhaps with a restored monarchy. So did Papen. In June 1932, in his first speech as chancellor, he denounced the regime of the parties and called for the spiritual renewal of the country along "Christian, national, and social lines." This was the language of organic conservatism, and he sounded like his prewar Wilhelmine predecessors, but as he stood at attention in his black silk Sunday suit, he looked like a figure out of Alice in Wonderland. Late in August, before he dissolved the Reichstag a second time, Papen told Westphalian farmers gathered in the town hall in Münster that he, like they, was tied to soil and homeland, that the intellect could not challenge the way of this world and eternal life, and that national regeneration could come only from "an authoritative independent government" "responsible to the President and able to defend this work from disturbing party influences." When Hindenburg dissolved the Reichstag again the next month, Papen actively hoped that it would return once again tied up in knots, give up the ghost, and meekly submit to the unitary and hierarchical polity of his dreams.[7]

With its constitution and its core representative institution so maligned, the Weimar Republic might hope for salvation from its own civil servants. If its elected officials could not uphold the liberal order, perhaps its appointed ones would. But when in October the state court in Leipzig tried to reinstate the Socialists in Prussia, ousted by Papen's *coup de force* in July, it made no difference: they returned only as shadows along the road taken to a newly centralized state. Meanwhile neither the courts nor the police that served them could stem the rampant violence between Far Left and Far Right that left dead or injured Communists, Socialists, and Nazis on the streets, in meeting halls, in their homes, in the Reichstag itself. The specter of arbitrary justice stalked the young republic, whenever magistrates, some of them holdovers from the old regime, found Communist thuggery more reprehensible than the Nazi variety. Justice was weakening; by contrast, armed force—the Reichswehr—was strengthening. It had existed since 1919, in its eyes, to serve the nation more than the new regime. Steady growth, flouting the limitations imposed on it by the Treaty of Versailles, had only encouraged it to meddle in politics in ways its early founder, General Hans von Seeckt, deplored. General Schleicher and other generals had prevailed on Hindenburg to make Brüning chancellor in March 1930; they had practically imposed Schleicher as war minister on Papen in May 1932; and when in July 1932 Papen took over the government of Prussia, Schleicher's troops patrolled the streets, lest the Socialists should be foolish enough to resist. By then Schleicher too had given up on the parties and the Reichstag, and he had Hindenburg's ear. The more passive the other institutions, the more active the army.[8]

Then would another pillar of a liberal polity, a free press, uphold the cause or buckle as well? The country had about 4,700 newspapers, 147 of them in Berlin alone. Article 118 of the Constitution had guaranteed their freedom and abolished the wartime censorship, but already Brüning had begun using emergency decrees against major dailies. Papen went further and allowed the government to suspend papers guilty of attacking it in bad faith—in *böswillige verächtlichmachung*, malicious aspersion, an offense that could take legal form only in the eye of the beholder. Since then the authorities had shut down, for as long as a month, papers of the Left and Right, Nazi, Communist, and Socialist, and even the more moderate *Berliner Volkszeitung*, for sharp but hardly injurious allegations in their columns; and the government of the Reich had as well vigorously exercised its right of reply, and even instructed the wayward editors on page placement and letter size. The country's five million radio sets sat handily at Papen's disposal for major speeches, but not at his opponents', for he had banned party politics from the airwaves and so assured himself of a monopoly in time for the November election. Still, in the autumn of 1932 the press at least remained stubbornly independent, a platform crowded with critics of the government and of one another, more audible than a Reichstag that rarely met or a civil service that rarely remonstrated. Germany was not Fascist Italy or Communist Russia, the French ambassador insisted to his government, but proud to a fault of its cultural traditions, and the enslavement of the press, he believed, would insult and violate "the prestige and the independence of German thought."[9]

That press was now giving free voice to the electioneers of a failing democracy. It made for a bewildering spectacle. Swathes of the political class employed liberal institutions with the avowed aim of subverting them. The autumn campaign began absurdly, with the government trying to dissolve the parliament and the parliament trying to vote down the government. More absurdly still, the Nazis and the Communists posed as the upholders of parliamentary legitimacy. They wished to use their commanding presence on the benches of the Reichstag to destroy it and hasten the decomposition of the republic around it.[10] Meanwhile Socialists and centrists, the most authentic supporters of the parliamentary regime, defended the dissolution, hoping in the ensuing election to rid the country of a chancellor who governed without a majority. It all made no sense.

Nazis and Communists killed one another on the streets but echoed one another on the hustings or in their newspapers. In their first rally of the election, amid storm troopers, flags, and marches, the Nazis gathered in the Sportpalast to hear Hermann Goering— the president of the outgoing Reichstag—denounce the reactionary clique that governed the country, the *Baronen* who oppressed the *Volk*.[11] The National Socialist German Workers Party was reviving its earlier anticapitalist and populist affinities, and when the Communist *Rote Fahne* newspaper proclaimed its struggle to the death against capitalism and Versailles alike, it could have lifted the type off the Nazis' *Völkischer Beobachter* or *Der Angriff*. Capping their collusion, the two most determined foes of the regime joined arms in November, just before the election, to launch the Berlin transport strike. The conservative nationalists, whom the Nazis now derided as a "bourgeois mishmash," deemed their former comrades-in-arms political extremists, revolutionaries too wild to remake Germany, but not, perhaps, to play junior partners beside them in the enterprise.[12] From the other side the Socialists accused them of plotting to restore the monarchy; yet they themselves had supported Hindenburg for the presidency in April. The Catholic Center agreed to reform but not to destroy the state; but with whom? Certainly not with Papen.[13] From the small liberal parties came uncertain calls to defend the constitution. But to expel the Papen government was one matter, to replace it another. The Reich had become ungovernable.

The regime as well as the government rested on a minority. In 1920, in the republic's first parliament, the parties of the Weimar coalition, flanked to their right and left by the republic's enemies, could not cobble together enough seats for a clear majority. They never would. But they governed nonetheless, until 1930 when the coalition itself fell apart. Meanwhile the hostile forces grew or bided their time. In 1925 those on the right elected the venerable Hindenburg to the presidency. They were nationalist, populist, antirepublican, *völkisch*; and they had chosen a president who had no fondness for the republic either. Seven years later, during the elections of 1932, the Nazi surge at the polls came in the same bastions, swollen now by the victims of the economy, often dispossessed or impoverished. Among them the punitive antirepublican belief system came to rest, in a mass protest party, abetted by the Communists on the other side, who drew on the votes of the unemployed in particular. By the summer of 1932, almost two-thirds of the deputies in the Reichstag had deserted the Weimar Republic, and left marooned a democracy without enough democrats.[14]

The Nazis, the creed's final incarnation, came from all walks of life, women as well as men, blue- as well as white-collar workers, young as well as old. Their river, as one of their opponents observed in 1930 after the first electoral breakthrough in the Reichstag elections, was fed by many streams. But they displayed some predominant traits— more likely to be middle class, much more likely to be Protestant, and certain to be indifferent to the fate of liberal institutions. Their rise had begun before the onset of the Depression in 1930, in local and regional elections that saw their vote climb steadily from 1926 to 1929. In Saxony, between May of that year and June of the next, they tripled their vote. By then, with the simultaneous onset of the Great Depression and the breakup of the Weimar coalition, their national breakthrough was imminent, and the first fables about inevitability began to blight political conversations. Cheer or despair escorted them, even among the most philosophically inclined. "By 1931 I was firmly convinced that the Nazis would take the helm," Hannah Arendt later recalled. "I thought it was hopeless." But at Christmas that year Martin Heidegger happily assured his family that the Nazi movement could only grow. It was a matter, he added, of the salvation or destruction of European and Western civilization.[15]

Yet the movement's leader made an improbable prophet. Earlier in 1932 Adolf Hitler had inspired disbelief among callers setting eyes on him for the first time. The Führer startled them—he was comically commonplace, notable for his insignificance. As Dorothy Thompson of the *New York Post* made her way to meet him in the Kaiserhof Hotel in Berlin, she imagined a future dictator. Instead she came upon "the very prototype of the Little Man." He was practically faceless, she found, yet voluble, unpoised, and insecure, occasionally sounding a hysterical note, capable mostly of vague answers that sometimes degenerated into rants. In Munich he frequented the Carlton tearoom, where the author Klaus Mann, son of the great novelist, found himself one afternoon, at the next table. Across the street was the more raucous and plebeian Café Luitpold, where storm troopers gathered. Hitler sat with two of his fellows and devoured strawberry tarts, one after another, with infantile and rapacious gluttony. With his pale and bloated face, he struck Mann much as he did Thompson—as a harmless "little man" with a comical mustache, common, even base, with a hysteric's wild glance. But then Mann already hated him and all he stood for. "You wish to rule Germany?" he thought, amid the subdued music and the soft light. "You want to be a dictator—with *that* nose? You will never come to power!"[16]

The banality came with trappings as incongruous as the aspirations. During the winter Hitler had received Hubert "Red" Knickerbocker of the *New York Evening Post* in his office at the Brown House in Munich, amid an entourage of secular idols, symbols, and graven images. A swastika in the window, amid salmon-pink hangings; a portrait of Frederick the Great behind his chair, a life-size bronze head of Mussolini beside it; farther down one wall another painting of Frederick, down the other one a battle in Flanders—all conveyed grandeur and kitsch, instead of the decadent and despised expressionism of Weimar artists. On the round table in the middle of a room stood a statuette of a giant in chains: "Germany enslaved."[17]

More incongruous still, in light of the slight impression he made in private, was his crowd persona, his gift of awakening a dense mass to its own hopes and fears, as though by legerdemain or telepathy. Any thoughtful observer might wonder how all this talk of Jews, landlords, and Versailles could take in multitudes.[18] But it did, not only because his aroused countrymen could hear what they liked and turn a deaf ear to what they did not, but also because his oratory rarely committed him to any course of action, any promise other than national redemption. He would save Germany, he promised them. But from what? From bolshevism as well as finance capitalism, from the Soviet Union as well as the raptors of the West, from Weimar but not, it seemed, from the parliament the Nazis now dominated. This was no program at all. But it flattered his listeners. They, like he, were the ordinary foot soldiers in the irresistible movement that would sweep away the decadent aristocrats around the aged Hindenburg. They, like he, had earned their honor, not inherited it, he told a mass rally in the Krone Circus in Munich in September, and he gestured toward the dense columns of SA and SS. "There stands the new nobility of the Nation! The men who for 13 years have fought for the freedom of their people!"[19] His speeches that autumn mixed social resentment with chauvinism and the intoxication of predestined success. And of a power that would be theirs to keep: he wanted real power, he said over and over, not some ministerial title, and in October he told a crowd in Königsberg that once they had it they would keep it: "We will not let them steal it from us ever again."[20]

Not that his persona alone converted multitudes—the Nazis deployed a national press with tentacular provincial arms, and no scrutiny reveals any ironclad connection between local electoral triumphs and the Führer's coming to town. But party mythology exalted his messianic accomplishment in the face of a hostile and Jewish-controlled press, validating his own belief in the superior persuasive powers of speech over print; and long after he and they were gone posterity often innocently attributed his rise to the same oral magic. It helped; but a thousand variants of the same hollow message, overseen by Goebbels notwithstanding his master's skepticism, put out by local editors, and insinuated into friendly mainstream papers, helped more.[21]

The words, though vacant, concealed the unspoken project of a racial dictatorship. The swastika, adopted to signify Aryan supremacy, implied it, in an emblem announcing yet another vision of tomorrow's Germany. But others conveyed more recognizable preferences. The yellow and white of the Center Party promised a Christian state, the hammer and sickle of the Communists a soviet republic, the arrows of the Socialists a social democracy. The conservative nationalists, on whom the Nazis now heaped scorn and derision and whose rallies they broke up with cries of "Germany, awake!" decked their meeting halls in the black, white, and red of the Wilhelmine Empire.[22] How or in whose name restoration was to proceed remained obscure even to the adherents. Fourteen years earlier, defeat had posed a question about the identity of Germany. What sort of a nation was it now?[23] Neither the regime that had lost the war and fled the scene nor the one that had bowed to the victors and taken its place had credibly answered. The question was still open.

The answers embraced more than a constitution, if there was to be one. They prescribed as well German action in the world. No one called for war, but world revolution, moderate pacifism, and muscular nationalism enjoyed no other international posture in common. The Communists identified the cause of proletarian revolution in Germany with that of the Third International and the Soviet Union throughout the world. Friends of the parliamentary republic, even those with misgivings, still favored engagement—parleys—with the country's former enemies, at Geneva or elsewhere. Weimar's foes on the right made out lunacy or treachery in such dealings, and preached the urgency of strength at home and abroad, as though unity and authority demanded enmity. When a nationalist leader told his party's executive in October that since 1918 Germany had become "a colony of international socialism" he was complaining about diplomacy as well as society, about national sovereignty as well as the regime.[24] Foreign and domestic visions described a circle, the arcs passing into each other. Toward the end of the campaign a major daily complained that Germans knew nothing about foreign policy because the government told them nothing—nothing about the east, about France's allies there, about Rumanian demands, about almost anything.[25] The candidates for their part offered few specifics in the campaign, as few as in July.[26] But perhaps they did not need to: their party colors on the posters already conveyed notions of Germany among the nations, unspoken sentiments that other vehicles only disseminated again.

The conservative Right chose to revere in President Hindenburg the victor over the Russians at Tannenberg in 1914, and the architect of a mighty but short-lived eastern empire of colonies and satellites during the last year of the war. A happier outcome in the west would have established Germany as the dominant power all over central and eastern Europe.[27] Right-wing leaders no longer floated such heady vistas before voters' eyes. But they laced the aspiration to a renewed great power status, one that many Germans shared, with nostalgia and veiled militarism. In October Chancellor Papen evoked before Bavarian businessmen in Munich the "sacrum imperium" of the Holy Roman Empire. "May the invisible stream of the idea," he told them, "speed through the German provinces from the Alps to the Memel." This took his audience back beyond the *Mitteleuropa* of the war, beyond Bismarck and Frederick, to Otto and a unique medieval realm in central Europe. The relevance was obscure. He was vaguely proposing a new kind of constitution for the Reich, and arguing even less coherently that military security for Germany would improve trade. But his talk of the "Holy Empire of the Germans" lifted his listeners—who were many, for a national radio hookup was broadcasting his words—out of the impasse of the present and into a geopolitical dreamland. A nationalist paper approved. Here, it considered, were sound old traditions, here was a "politics of faith."[28]

Uniformed veterans of the Stahlhelm, the Steel Helmets, who sometimes sported the black, red, and white emblems of the Wilhelmine Empire that the Weimar Republic had replaced, spilled drunkenly out of trains, sang "Watch on the Rhine," or rallied on the Polish border.[29] When twenty thousand of them gathered in the Sportpalast in Berlin on Friday, September 2, 1932, imperial flags and regimental standards festooned the walls, and the band struck up the Sedan march, in memory of the victory over the French there sixty-one years earlier to the day. The past seemed to lie at the heart of the matter. Crown Prince William, the idle heir to his dethroned father, came, together with an honor guard and a dozen other Hohenzollerns. So did Papen, Schleicher, and most of the government. From the tribune the veterans' leader called on his comrades to complete the empire that Bismarck had founded, and when he declared that Versailles and Weimar were one and the same, all, including the crown prince in the front row, applauded vigorously. On Sunday at Templehof field, on the parade ground where Prussian kings and German emperors had passed their armies in review, 180,000 Stahlhelm marched all afternoon and into the early evening. "Do you hear the battalions' tread?" the radio announcer asked his compatriots over the Deutschlandsender, and across the border in Alsace French listeners heard it too.[30]

On Thursday, on the evening before the veterans gathered in the Sportpalast, the radical nationalists—the Nazis—had flocked to the same place in the same number. The future more than the past roused their enthusiasms; they displayed little of the others' orderly antebellum pageantry and protocol; they cheered, the conservatives applauded. Hitler delivered an empty and frenetic speech, a philippic against the government, to ovations from listeners alive to the promise of power—and Hindenburg, they heard, was almost twice as old as he. About foreign policy they heard nothing.[31]

They would hear little more about it during the campaign. What could the Nazis say that the rest of the right had not? They too wanted "German greatness," to "lift Germany above the surrounding dangers";[32] they too hated Versailles, Geneva, Moscow, Paris. Their silence implied consent. The blocks that voted for Hindenburg in 1925 and the Nazis in 1932 also voted, in between in 1929, to reject the Young Plan—by which the country's former foes rescheduled reparations payments and the French left the Rhineland.[33] Any agreement was suspect to them. A mood fixed their outlook on the present world, commanding the parties that courted them. It was harder to define what distinguished a Papen from a Hitler, a French columnist remarked, than what united them—the will to make Germany a military nation again.[34]

Hitler and Goebbels appealed to emotion, not reason; they employed the spoken more furiously than the written word, and resorted to vitriol and slander as weapons of choice. They impugned motives and character, whatever the policies. Once, after Papen's radio speech in Munich in October, Hitler almost descended to the level of substance. Papen endangered Germany, he wrote in an open letter, at the "Geneva disarmament comedy," at the Lausanne reparations conference of the summer, at all such exhibitions that sold national interests down the river.[35] The insinuation of treason traveled easily. In August, five Nazis had murdered a Polish Communist in Upper Silesia. When a special court sentenced them to death under an emergency decree that Papen's government had just promulgated against political crimes of the sort, the right erupted in indignation. But Hitler exceeded them. Papen and his government became the gravediggers of the German nation, his name drenched in the blood of the fighters for German freedom. "These people," Harry Kessler wrote in his diary when Hitler demanded the reprieve of the five condemned, "are to govern!" The sanctification of murder shocked many, but few noticed the enabling partner, xenophobia. The victim had been a Pole—and repeatedly Hitler returned to the rectitude of his killers. "I cannot understand," he told all 230 Nazi members of the Reichstag, "that because of one Polish rebel"—he was alluding to the earlier conflicts over Silesia—"five National Socialists should fall to the guillotine." He added that whoever fought for Germany had right on his side, and whoever fought against it had none. Such Manichaean tribalism reached a climax in his occasional anti-Semitic outbursts, when the distinction between the domestic and the foreign enemy vanished. Jewish bankers, Jewish newspapers, the scourge of Jewish bolshevism that had seized almost an entire continent and that threatened to submerge Germany—"Either the German people escapes the hands of the Jews or it will go to waste," he told a crowd in Essen a week before the election. Hatred was the driving force of his foreign policy, the authentic voice of Nazism.[36]

Had his publisher, his wartime comrade Max Amann, only brought out his second book when he finished it in the summer of 1928, his compatriots and the world beyond might have grasped his goals. But Amann did not, fearing that it might detract from the already poor sales of the rambling autobiography Hitler had concocted in Landsberg Prison in 1924 and published the following year, *Mein Kampf*.[37] In 1926 he had published its second volume, and in it he had already supposed that Germany must conquer its *Lebensraum* in the east and the Soviet Union, the breeding grounds of Jews and bolshevism, but he had not provided much detail.[38] Now, four years later, he warned more expansively of the Malthusian vice gripping Germany, as its population crowded its confined land, and of racial degeneration through emigration and demographic stagnation.[39] Salvation would come only in the conquest and Germanization of the east, where the Slavs were incapable of self-rule anyway, and in the war against the Jews, everywhere, but especially there, where they had loosed bolshevism upon the world.[40] But first the Germans must defeat France, an ancillary requirement that a natural alliance of interests with Britain and Italy, and perhaps also Spain and Hungary, would help realize.[41] He spoke for the first time of a distant confrontation, perhaps in a coalition again, with the people who had conquered their own continental living space in North America, and settled their superior race on its rich soil.[42] At home Germans would breed the warriors and forge their swords.[43] This was no revisionist tract, clamoring yet again for Germany's old colonies or borders, but a declaration of race war without end. It had nothing to do with Versailles, or with the way back to 1914 and some status quo ante bellum, and all to do with a blinding vision of past and future—of existential struggle and *Raumpolitik statt Grenzpolitik*, a world of peoples and spaces, not of states and borders.[44]

Outside of Amann, his close confidant Rudolf Hess, and perhaps one or two others in the inner circle, no one had read the manuscript. But he had spoken that way at times, to thousands. In July 1928, as he was finishing the manuscript, he repeated in a speech on foreign policy in Berlin much of what he had just consigned to paper—the ecological panic, territorial imperative, the enmity of France and Russia today and of the United States tomorrow. "We need power, to gain living space," he had said earlier that year, repeating a leitmotif of a worldview uncluttered by many others.[45]

So it remained, but during the electioneering of 1932 it almost vanished amid a torrent of words about the internal decomposition of the nation. Foreign policy, he repeated again and again, depended as much as economic recovery on cohesion and strength at home. Neither conferences nor commerce would determine Germany's fate, but unflinching national will, untroubled by the nation's assorted gravediggers, who had betrayed the German army in November 1918 and had clung to power ever since. National ruin had brought on

Versailles, he declared, and not the reverse; quite consistently, only a spiritually renewed *Volk* could assure the basis for a "bold foreign policy."[46]

And what might that be? He did not say. Anyone who cared to listen and remember might harvest a few hints, no more. Brute force was primordial. The white race had conquered the world through might not right, he told seven hundred businessmen in the ballroom of the Park Hotel in Dusseldorf in January. Force, the cause and not the effect of the economic ascendancy of the race, sprang from the will, and from it sprang both the defense and the propagation of the race.[47] German greatness lay with the farmers and the settlers "in the east," he told a crowd in East Prussia—perhaps meaning farther on, perhaps not.[48] "The day will come," he assured the town of Ortelsburg, set amid the Masurian lakes and forests, "when 65 million Germans will stand with you here in East Prussia and the 'so-called Corridor' will no longer exist."[49] When and how this Polish land would become German again, when and how his listeners would be reunited with their compatriots in the Reich across it to the west, he did not say—partly because he did not know, partly because warmongering made little political sense. But playing on pride and resentment did. In the Rhineland town of Rodenkirchen on the other side of the country, he vowed in the local riding arena that with the Nazis at the helm the Germans would no longer "quake before Poland," and a loudspeaker broadcast his words to listeners on the town square outside.[50] To British and Italian journalists he refloated the alliances he had conceived of years earlier, directed against their common adversary, France, or at the global menace of Soviet bolshevism. But he always circled back to German *Macht*. The Soviet Union, he told the Italian Fascist official Carlo Scorza in the Brown House in Munich, would fail to subvert a strong Germany, forcing it to turn its energies eastward, against British, American, and Japanese interests in Asia.[51] The Germans, more perhaps than any other people, he told them in Essen a week before the November election, depended for their weight in the world on their inner strength.[52]

Neither the Nazi press nor its ambulant orators had much to add.

They invoked foreign policy to flay the government, not to pledge policies of their own. During the campaign for the November election, *Völkischer Beobachter* attacked the Papen government as weak-kneed at Geneva, where it threw German rearmament to the four winds of foreign consent, inept in London, where it squandered British goodwill, and treasonous in Paris, where it pursued rapprochement and even a military alliance.[53] France was the enemy, the paper reminded its readers, the implacable foe who had occupied the Ruhr in 1923, denied Germany the right to arm itself, supported hostile powers in the east who oppressed German minorities. This was standard revisionist rhetoric, laced with occasional taunts about the importation of "negro troops" from North Africa but free of bellicose threats. About *Lebensraum* and race war in the east, the readers learned nothing, no more than from the Führer himself.

What might an intelligent voter expect the new order, once it came, to change in the conduct of the Reich abroad? To guess, Germany would rearm, and stop seeking solutions in useless parleys or parliaments abroad, and pursue autarkic or bilateral arrangements of its own. But beyond lay darkness. *Germania*, the main organ of the Center Party, thought Hitler only wished to restore Germany as a great power. Few Socialists or Communists scrutinized the warlike omens either, because few had read *Mein Kampf* or taken it seriously. One who had, Friedrich Wendel, a Socialist journalist, warned in a brochure in the spring of 1932 of Hitler's candid promise in his book to invade the Soviet Union, and found it bizarre—why divulge your plans to your enemy? But more often the Socialists pondered the sociology of the movement, or its propaganda techniques.[54]

Their cry, "Hitler means war," came later, when they were in exile in Prague. For now, they warned more of the Nazi threat to democracy than to peace. *Lebensraum* and expansionist designs to the east or west did not escape the attention of every Communist, as expressions of capitalist imperialism or class war; but mostly the party denied the Nazi movement any ideology at all.[55]

The Nazis had never held national office, and, in foreign policy, the curious had only their words to go by. In domestic matters they might look by now to local and regional experience to know more. In Thuringia—ironically enough, in Weimar—the first Nazi to hold a cabinet seat, Wilhelm Frick, had held office as minister of the interior between January 1930 and April 1931. While there, he had replaced high police officials with Nazis, forbidden jazz and other performances "glorifying . . . the Negro," introduced in schools a prayer appealing to God to deliver Germany from "betrayal and treason"— signifying, probably, the republic—and generally tried to promote Nazi conceptions of Teutonic culture. In Braunschweig another Nazi minister of the interior, Dietrich Klagges, had begun banning Social Democrats and Jews from public positions. Their experiments, condemned by some, could boast some predictive value.[56] In the early months of the Third Reich each would join in instigating state-sponsored terror, one from high office in Berlin and the other still in Braunschweig. They and others gave ground for supposing—for hoping—that with Weimar would go some basic liberties and protections, and a political party or two as well.

About the political culture something was clear, about the economy little, about war and peace even less. All came wrapped in national divinity. An ethereal message of resurrection and redemption came out of the sky, as a chartered tri-engine Junker 52 bearing the messenger descended to expectant crowds in one city after another. "Hitler over Germany," recited and depicted in the Nazi propaganda, was triply symbolic—of modernity, dominion, and messianic promise. The cult fused disparate and sometimes discordant newcomers into a mass of followers, but did nothing to enlighten them about prosaic matters of earthly governance.[57] This was deliberate, a strategic imprecision that left much to their eclectic interpretations. They could ascribe to the Führer's words the varied assurances they craved—the destruction of the Left, or of the Jews, or of Weimar, or the salvation of the German farmer, or the return of German dominance or of Germanic culture. The rest they could overlook.

Nobody voted for war. Yet Nazism reveled in it. In the brown-uniformed troopers visiting daily violence on their adversaries, the quasi-regimental standards in black, red, and white, the submission of the raised arm and the fealty of the *Heil!*, the verbal drumbeat about *Kampf*, the Führer's own and that of all Germans, the primacy of *Macht* and the maligning of every enemy—in its texts, gestures, symbols, and ceremonies, Nazism exhaled war. In March 1932, across the Rhine from Strasbourg, six hundred Nazis gathered in a restaurant to listen to a local leader. He spoke of a piece of chocolate and a rifle lying side by side on a table. The Jew would take the chocolate, the German would take the rifle. Germans were fighters and would choose Hitler.[58] In August, in Pirmasens farther north in the Palatinate, thirty thousand enthusiasts flocked from all over southern Germany to demand the return of French territory in Alsace and the Saar and in the east as well. Speakers called to compatriots across the Rhine, bands played military marches, and soldiers paraded in spiked helmets and uniforms from the Great War. Swastikas appeared in most windows, Wilhelmine colors in some; only the post office and the town hall displayed the colors of the republic.[59] In the east the Stahlhelm, uniformed and regimented, mobilized provocatively on the Polish border. Their youngest members aimed branches, as rifles, at Poland.[60] But they were a veterans' group, and the Nazis were a political movement, unlike any other in their cultivation of warlike emotions. To what end? Nazism was more mood than program, and for now the most obvious affect concealed the most obscure goal, that of race war.

Early in 1932 an American journalist talked at length with an unemployed schoolteacher, among others, in Weimar. He had joined the Nazi Party three years earlier. With Hitler, he promised Hubert "Red" Knickerbocker of the *New York Evening Post*, Germany would tear up Versailles, re-create an army of at least 600,000 men, "tell France to go to hell" with reparations and if it tried to reoccupy the Rhineland they would "throw her out," which would be easy to do because they would have Britain and Italy with them. They would take back the Polish Corridor, Upper Silesia, their colonies too. This was indistinguishable in content if not in tone from any nationalist agenda. It was indistinguishable too from the domestic agenda, for the two lay on a continuum in the Nazi worldview. Not only would the Nazis give the jobless jobs, the teacher went on; they would prohibit the Communist Party and drive the Jews out of Germany. "Hitler will make Germany for the Germans and if any foreigners want to do business here they will have to watch their step."[61] Hitler had stopped uttering such exact pledges, but his followers had not stopped hearing them. A language of force, xenophobia, and resentment united them, along with a driving goal: power. "What will you do when you get power?" Knickerbocker asked another Nazi in Berlin. "Keep it," came the reply.[62]

They would have to wait. The Nazis fared poorly at the polls on Sunday, November 6. That night, radios around Berlin began broadcasting the returns. Papen listened to them at Schleicher's residence, in his company. In a hotel bar in the west, men in tailcoats drank cocktails and listened too. Goebbels heard them come in with dismay, at home with guests. "We've suffered a major setback," he confided to his diary the next day.[63] The Nazis had lost two million votes and 4 percent of the electorate from their peak of 37 percent in July. Words—the rediscovery of pseudosocialist rhetoric—and actions—support for the Berlin transport strike—had only frightened away voters of the Right, some of whom returned to the German National People's Party (DNVP), and attracted none from the Left, who now turned in greater number to the Communists. Indignation at the crimes of the SA had not helped either. Morale in the party sank. Its coffers emptied out, and dissension seethed again over Hitler's refusals to accept anything other than the chancellorship, his "all or nothing" obduracy. The Führer appeared fallible, his cult fragile.

Political obituaries of the Nazi movement appeared at once in Germany and abroad. More than losing two million votes, the *Berliner Lokalanzeiger*, a paper of the Right, told its readers, Hitler had lost his magic. "The belief is fading," *Vossische Zeitung*, the mainstay of the liberal center, announced, "Hitler is the loser." The papers of the Left acclaimed the defeat of Fascism. The Communists claimed victory. In London the *Evening Standard* speculated on the rapid disappearance of the Nazis. In Paris dailies announced that Hitler had a bright future behind him, that his moment had come and gone, that the rats were deserting the Nazi ship. In Berlin the American chargé d'affaires was relieved. "Even the most ardent Nazi followers," he informed his government, "must realize that the much-heralded Third Reich has become a very remote possibility."[64]

In fact, little had changed. The election had only confirmed what most Socialists and Communists had failed to grasp—that in national rather than class struggle the Nazis had found their tune, and that when they reverted too stridently to social motifs, they lost their audience. Meanwhile Weimar itself remained a minority government: in the Reichstag the antirepublican deputies on the extremes still outnumbered the wilting constitutionalists between them. Hitler had lost his bid, but the Nazis remained the largest party. "Who wins?" the *Vossische Zeitung* asked on Tuesday morning, only to conclude that no one had. Papen had not: his support in the Reichstag was even weaker than before. No working coalitions were viable, and another election was out of the question. The crisis continued. Hindenburg could appoint another chancellor without a majority, another foe of Weimar. He had already done so twice. On Wednesday, the anniversary of the downfall of the empire in 1918 and of Hitler's failed beer hall putsch in 1923, Goebbels called on him at home in Munich. "A splendid man," Goebbels wrote, and outside their Brown House some Nazis rallied, standards, swastikas, and all.[65]

And in Berlin, in the stately buildings clustered around the Wilhelmstrasse, where rulers and lawgivers had governed the German Reich since Bismarck, the struggle for power continued. Steps to the north, just beyond the Brandenburg Gate, the domed Reichstag that Kaiser Wilhelm had derided as a "chatter chamber" had fallen silent. It would convene once again in a month. In the Tiergarten on the west side, General Schleicher sometimes rode for an hour in the early mornings. Papen trotted past as well, in stylish hat and equestrian bow tie. Not Hitler; he was not of their world. But whenever he emerged from his rooms in the Hotel Kaiserhof on the east side of the Wilhelmstrasse and looked out between the columns of its portico, he could behold in his line of vision straight across the avenue his end and his means, in a palace that still bore on its other facade the extinct eagles of the kings of Prussia: the Reich Chancellery.[66]

4

Moscow

7 November 1932

On Monday, November 7, the day after the election in Germany, Moscow was ablaze for the fifteenth anniversary of the Bolshevik revolution. Since Sunday, red flags, multicolored lights, bright portraits of Lenin and Stalin, and posters proclaiming production figures had lined the approaches to Red Square. Early in the morning tanks appeared on the streets, then cavalry squadrons, flags in front, armed soldiers on the sides, and after them artillerymen, border guards, and infantry. Military marches sounded. Marshal Klim Voroshilov, people's commissar for war, galloped out on a white horse from the Kremlin's Savior Gate Tower to greet them to the music of the "Internationale." For three hours they marched past on the square, joined by units from the security police, officer cadets, and many others, as tri-engine bombers droned overhead. Posters in English, French, German, and Chinese greeted the foreign press and the diplomatic corps with LONG LIVE THE REVOLUTION. On the parapets atop the new gray mausoleum housing Lenin's embalmed corpse, about twenty party and military leaders watched the avalanche roll across the square. Stalin stood in the middle, looking morose and gloomy, in a simple army coat and cap. On one side of him stood a somewhat cheerier Voroshilov, returned from his appearance below, on the other Mikhail Kalinin, the titular but powerless head of state, who stood forward, preceded by his white goatee; flanking them, the others receded in carefully graded precedence, including Premier Vyacheslav Molotov, who looked troubled, and General Semyon Budionny with his handlebar mustache, who stood stiffly with four medals on his chest. To a British journalist in the press stand far below, they resembled a row of pygmies, and he struggled to comprehend the tie that bound the dictatorship in the sky to the proletariat on the ground.[1]

Later in the morning, civilian workers gathered in clusters nearby, formed into columns, and marched out onto the square behind the soldiers. They included Stalin's wife, Nadya Alliluyeva, who marched alongside her fellow students in the Industrial Academy. Several more hours went by. Seen not from afar, from some tribune high above, but from among the serried pedestrians, such spectacles could sadden. One German worker had to be at his Moscow factory by seven, to leave by nine along with the whole workforce, amid music and song and confusion that only grew as they neared Red Square and joined a million and a half others to march past party leaders and foreign dignitaries. It ended by three. He had been standing or walking since five a.m. Weariness set in, especially among the aged. There would be a buffet at the factory, perhaps some delicacies in the shops. On the anniversary of Lenin's death, or of the Revolution, or on May Day, or on some unforeseen occasion requiring a spontaneous demonstration of popular indignation, they might have to leave work early and march. Earlier, in November 1930, some engineers had stood trial for hatching a counterrevolutionary plot to wreck the Soviet economy, and the hapless German had narrowly escaped another forced march to the center of the city to demand with banners "the shooting of the bourgeois mercenaries" and "death to the hirelings of foreign capital."[2]

Orchestrated tedium, one face that Soviet patriotism showed the world, might easily raise doubts about the sincerity of the patriots. Are the Soviet people happy? the American minister in Riga, in diminutive Latvia next door, asked his legation in August 1932. Washington maintained no diplomatic relations with Imperial Russia's successor, still a pariah among nations and much of a mystery to all of them. All of the minister's staffers answered that they did not know and could not answer, but most took pains to explain that some were happier than others—that many factory workers, rising party members, or urban youth in their Komsomol units, for example, enjoyed an altogether different lot from the "former people"— the nobles, priests, bankers, or other notables of the old regime—or recently dispossessed peasants, now numbering in the millions. One of the staffers, George Kennan, stressed in his answer that "the romance of economic development" had inspired a generation to sacrifice itself, its "comfort and nerves," to a doctrine and a cause. From them, rather than from the mass of the already discontented, he foresaw future dangers. Material contentment or economic failure alike would deprive them of a cause, and condemn the regime to eventual moral chaos.[3]

All over the world friends touted the promise and foes chronicled the savageries of the regime. In England Sidney and Beatrice Webb, Fabian Socialists who had visited the Soviet Union that year, held forth about its radiant future to visitors who called on them in their house at Passfield Corner in Hampshire. At a café in Choisy-le-Roi outside Paris, a physician and town councilor returned from his journey with tales of widespread hunger, long hours, and, to cap it all, violent Francophobia. A right-wing Parisian journalist complained in his paper of Soviet GPU security officers minding the stage-managed tours of vulnerable enthusiasts, many of them snobs, intellectuals, or aristocrats at loose ends. In New York, Communist intellectuals took their leave of each other: "Meet me on the barricades."[4]

Whether such connoisseurs applauded or deplored Soviet Communism, they remained blind in their verdicts to its emerging identity: the construction of socialism had become a form of nationalism. It endowed the homeland of the revolution with a unique mission in the world, and elevated it, as nationalisms often do, above all the others.

To grumble about hardship, corruption, inefficiency, to doubt the wisdom of the hierarchs, could yet leave the faith unshaken.

In Kharkov in the early 1930s a technical foreman, who had joined the party, as he told his father, to serve his country and advance its vast plans, usually found ways with his fellows to rationalize the chasm between slogans and results. Not all recited *Pravda*, *Izvestia*, or Stalin himself with the same slavish devotion, but most managed "to discover noble motives for seemingly ignoble behavior, and in general to fortify our common faith in a distressing period."[5] Even the stigmatized might turn to patriotism to erase their stigmata; many a "dekulakized peasant," dispossessed of whatever land or livestock he or she might once have owned, became an ardent Bolshevik.[6] In Moscow, one of them, uprooted from his native Ukraine, strove mightily to remake himself as the new *Homo sovieticus*, dreamed of joining the shock brigades building the Dnieper dam, and when he visited his exiled father in his barrack in Archangelsk felt alienated and endangered.[7] In Voronezh, where the party in 1930 had accused the Agricultural Institute of various conspiracies against the Soviet Union, a science teacher had lost faith. The charges, she thought, were absurd. But she had regained it by listening on the radio to the anniversary celebrations on November 7. And she believed the accusations against the engineers, the same that left the German specialist in Moscow skeptical. On May Day 1931 she had marched with the thousands, "merging with everybody . . . I was a drop in the sea." The Soviet Union, she reflected, had become her new home, with parade grounds for corridors. As for the various stories of sabotage and wrecking, "one must not confuse the particulars with the general."[8]

Yet opposition, in the autumn of 1932, there was, and Stalin was acutely aware of it—he was its target. The industrialization and survival of the Soviet Union, he had been repeating for three years, depended on the collectivization of agriculture, a nightmare that soon unfolded as an economic and humanitarian disaster. Resentments already simmered among rivals and purists in the party at the dictatorial powers accruing to him since 1928; the persecutions in the countryside threatened to bind the jealousies of the elect to the resistance of the wretched.

By now some ten million peasants had been driven from their homes into penal colonies, work camps, factories and cities, or vagrancy, and famine was ravaging or threatening large parts of Ukraine, Kazakhstan, the lower Volga, and the northern Caucasus. By the following year, between four and nine million had died from starvation or disease.[9] Violent resistance had greeted the campaign, and try as the authorities might to seal off the catastrophe and shut down any movement of news or of refugees out of the stricken zones, word eventually leaked out to the country and, to Stalin's fury, the world beyond. Malcolm Muggeridge, the British journalist who had watched him on the parapet of Lenin's mausoleum in November, would also watch peasants in March climbing into cattle trucks at gunpoint, their hands tied behind their backs. At every railway station in Ukraine, the Communist author Arthur Koestler, on a pilgrimage from Berlin under the aegis of the Comintern, watched crowds of peasants in rags, holding out their icons and their linens in exchange for bread. In Kharkov, then the Ukrainian capital, he made his way at the bazaar through hordes of destitute nomads who had abandoned their villages and now sold whatever candle ends they had left.[10]

Whispers of debacle also saw out the first five-year plan, the headlong industrialization that collectivization of the farms was supposed to sustain—rumors of goals not met, production figures falsified, quality degraded, of bottlenecks and shortages and breakdowns. To Koestler, Soviet industry resembled a young giant afflicted by paralysis one moment and epilepsy the next. Real wages fell to half their 1928 levels. The party blamed "wreckers," but many blamed officials, who blamed each other; and where did officialdom stop?[11] Stalin, steadily tightening his grip on the party apparatus and the government ministries, rarely appeared in public outside of May 1 or November 7, and rarely spoke or appeared in newsreels when he did.[12] But he more than anyone had signed collectivization with his name, and reports were reaching him of opposition, aimed not at the revolution or the regime but at him. Stalin had enemies.

Nothing new for him in itself, such ill will endangered political survival, when violent resistance stirred behind it in the lands of hunger and frustration simmered in the half-finished factories. Early in 1932 the Politburo, with Stalin's blessing, had relaxed some of the harshest measures in the countryside and reined in the OGPU, the security police, until thinking better of it in the summer. In August fundamentalism returned, most unmistakably with a draconian law imposing the death penalty for theft of the harvest, deemed Socialist property. That month Martemian Riutin, an old comrade whom Stalin had once helped along, organized a small cabal among bureaucrats and party members intent on overthrowing the dictator. He was, they declared in writing, the gravedigger of the revolution, the adventurist who had brought collectivization, dictatorship, and terror, and betrayed Marxism-Leninism. Naturally, their principal subject found them out, and in October the Politburo imprisoned, exiled, or expelled from the party the conspirators and some high-placed officials who had wind of their machinations but had remained silent. More plots followed in November and into the new year, unmasked again to the public as "antiparty factions" or the "Anti-Party Counterrevolutionary Group." Unlike the victims of the terror later in the decade, most of these adversaries were real, and escaped with their lives. But Stalin could never know how many sympathizers they might be hiding. A purge of the party began, a reflexive move to save the rulers from the unplanned consequences of their own misrule.[13]

"The most reactionary," *Pravda* said of the designs of Riutin's accomplices, "yet professed by any anti-Soviet group." It was announcing in early October the expulsion of twenty party members implicated in the conspiracy, including some—Alexander Slepkov the "red professor," and two of Lenin's closest fellow revolutionaries, Grigory Zinoviev and Lev Kamenev—well-known to the readers.[14] They conspired, in Stalin's eyes and those of the party apparatus he controlled, to subvert the construction of socialism and with it the Soviet Union itself. Such was the ambition of the class enemies at home and of the imperialist powers abroad. Objectively, they could not have any other. Objectively, they were one. Three years earlier, on November 7, 1929, Stalin had announced in *Pravda* that with the Great Break the last battle, to eradicate the vestiges of the moribund society that still clung to life in the countryside and in the interstices of the clandestine old regime, was at hand. But this time utopian bolshevism returned as great power nationalism. Each rekindled the other: urgently build socialism to surpass all the hostile powers; and foil the hostile powers—their agents here, their diplomacy abroad—in order to build socialism. One day the final confrontation would come.

This Stalin believed. National survival had given new meaning to the class struggle, and a martial slogan, "catch and overtake," adorned party meetings and new factory walls. In 1931 Stalin had reminded his compatriots of the historic backwardness that had so often assured the triumph of their foreign enemies. The Soviet Union must now overcome it or perish: "We are fifty to one hundred years behind advanced countries. We must cover this distance in ten years. Either we do this or they will crush us." Soviet nationalism was born.[15]

He had long seen foreign hands at work whenever Soviet domestic fortunes took a turn for the worse. He believed the intelligence reports in 1927 that blamed nationalist movements in Georgia and Ukraine, and a bomb at the party club in Leningrad, and the assassination of the Soviet envoy in Warsaw, on British mischief-making; and those in 1928 that blamed the accidents in the north Caucasus coal mines not only on bourgeois specialists but on foreign saboteurs as well; and those in 1930 that blamed falling production on an underground "industrial party" of engineers manipulated by the general staffs of a dozen nations and their co-conspirators in the Soviet planning agency, Gosplan—on sabotage on a European scale. Now, in Ukrainian recalcitrance in 1932 to forced collectivization, Stalin discerned subversion by Polish secret agents. "We may lose the Ukraine," he wrote to his deputy and head of the party central committee, Lazar Kaganovich, and added that the Polish network there was many times stronger than that of their own Communist Party.[16]

The OGPU lived by such fictions, and war scares, like that of 1927 with Britain, served handily to incite a general animus against political rivals. The press office of the Foreign Ministry had warned of foreign offensive plans that year, its director acknowledged, because "in explaining affairs to the masses extreme simplification was necessary." But the fear of foreign encirclement drove the first five-year plan as powerfully as any domestic compulsion. It was a mental reality, however crudely the regime might render it for propaganda purposes. The abiding anxieties that accompanied it, about the inadequacies of the Red Army, could not easily be allayed without the industrial capacity that modern war demanded, nor without the popular mobilization against any and all suspected of doubting its urgency. In the war against the international class enemy, the lines between foreign and domestic vanished. However preposterous the assimilation by the official imagination of stalled assembly lines and empty granaries to counterrevolution and foreign subversion, it displayed a coherence all its own. The epic project required a hostile world. One of Stalin's exiled opponents contemplated the hybrid, which he deplored, of motherland, ideology, and dictatorship. "We were defeated," he later wrote, "by Party patriotism."[17]

The Red Army commanders still fretted, but by the end of 1932 the first five-year plan had endowed the Soviet Union with the makings of a well-equipped wartime army and the foundations of a military-industrial complex second to none. This, at least, had succeeded. To have turned out 5,000 new fighter aircraft and 3,500 new light tanks in the dire conditions between 1930 and 1932, to have begun producing them and new artillery pieces from Soviet rather than pre-Soviet or foreign designs—all this fell short of the chimerical targets of the plan, but the surge of mechanization had left behind the cavalry of the Civil War a dozen years earlier and the 1920s, and the signs were everywhere.[18]

On May Day the panoply of mechanized matériel on Red Square, after a suggestively brief passage of infantry and horse-drawn units, struck the French ambassador as less than subtle. On November 7 the impression deepened. This time the cavalry made only a fleeting appearance, and the tanks, even those of foreign design, were Soviet made. The ambassador reflected that much of the weaponry, the armor in particular, was highly suited to offensive warfare. Old Russia, Stalin had also said 1931, bowed again and again to Mongolian khans, Turkish beys, Polish nobles, Japanese barons, English and French capitalists, and they could not, they must not, allow that again—they must rush the five-year plan and all that went with it; the new Soviet Union, he told the Central Committee and the Central Control Commission two years later, had the now-completed plan to thank for deterring invasion and "a bloody and unequal war."[19]

Signs of militarization abounded. Early in 1932 a lathe-manufacturing plant employing one thousand workers opened in Moscow. To one of them, the only American, it resembled a munitions factory in its layout and design, and he grasped that it could be adapted almost overnight to produce shells. At one end stood an armory, housing small arms and machine guns, and with these the workers drilled in the afternoon hours. That month an American engineer in Moscow watched fifteen of the new "tankettes" rumble through the streets. They were "whippet tanks," about six feet long and four feet high, armed with a single gun turret, and moved very swiftly. "A damned neat piece of machinery," he thought. No one had ever seen them before. That month too another American, working in a Moscow machine plant, learned that all the southern tractor plants were turning out tanks instead. At the Tractorostroy tractor plants in Moscow and Stalingrad, a Russian-born American engineer found much the same. He kept discovering departments devoted to military production closed for inspection, and stumbling over tank parts, shells, and sulfuric acid useless in ordinary production.[20]

At the Children's Village in the Park of Culture and Rest in Moscow, Red Army soldiers directed war games for young children, with assigned roles and uniforms, thick smoke, sirens, and gas masks. That summer of 1932, they mimed foreign wars and foreign spies in the village. Two English Boy Scouts infiltrated the country to join kulaks and a former White general in overthrowing the Soviet government; adults, with red flags named after Lenin, Stalin, and Voroshilov, led four hundred children on a hunt around the grounds to find them. Around the park stood grotesque effigies of capitalists, priests, drunkards, and slackers, and life-size busts of shock brigade workers. "All during the thirties," recalled an American engineer at the Magnitogorsk steel plant, built to surpass its model in Gary, Indiana, "the Russian people were at war." They fought on many fronts, of grain, chemicals, armor, and aircraft. In the main stairway of the Central House of the Red Army, a clubhouse for officers and enlisted men alike, a montage displayed ships of the world: "there" idle and rotting in American harbors, "here" steaming and full in Soviet waters. Two foreign visitors called on an editor at the *Izvestia* newspaper plant. He sat amid heaps of newspaper clippings, and in good German told them what to think of all the military training for children. Think of a woman and child in a hut in the forest, with hungry wolves closing in, he suggested. "Soviet Russia is a Socialist nation alone in the midst of a ravenous, jealous pack of capitalist nations. These nations have invaded our land once. They may do so again."[21]

Who, where, was the enemy? Like the elastic epithets "kulak" and "wrecker" at home, "imperialist power" or "capitalist power" abroad begged some further identification. This Moscow alone could provide. All foreign news came from the single official wire service, TASS, and all elucidation from the government or party press. Even news from a neighboring province had to travel through the censors and the editors in the capital before it could reach the curious citizens nearby. In 1932, France, Poland, and Rumania, *Izvestia* and *Pravda* told them and the world, were the most anti-Soviet powers. Earlier Britain had enjoyed the role, and more recently, since its inroads into Manchuria,

Japan had joined them. But throughout 1932 the Soviet Union had bent over backward to avoid provoking Japan, and the war of words it was vocally waging obliquely allowed the conciliatory diplomacy it was conducting in quiet. Behind a pacifist facade at Geneva, *Pravda* told its readers in October, France was seeking to dominate the continent and forge an anti-Soviet coalition. Rumanian court cliques with their links to "the adventurers of international imperialism" threatened peace as well. Even as the Soviet Union pursued nonaggression pacts with its neighbors and with France, the papers reminded their readers of the wrongs it had suffered at all their hands. In this they reflected the military thinking of the day. In its threat assessment in late 1932, drawn up for the coming second five-year plan, the high command saw a Polish-Rumanian coalition, supported by France, "the strongest enemy of the USSR in Europe," as the plausible scenario for the near future. But with Japan looming—a new and ominous development since the previous decade—the USSR had to prepare to wage war simultaneously in the east and the west.[22]

An enemy so abstract and indeterminate, imperialism and its national variants, could induce free-floating anxieties among a people deprived of any countervailing news or views of the world. They could at times heed the evidence of their eyes or the commands of their prejudices. When, early in 1932, convoys of trucks bearing small arms and machine guns moved through Moscow in the early hours of the morning, said to be destined ultimately for the Soviet far east, and trainloads of troops and artillery began moving east along the Trans-Siberian Railway, and volunteers for the army came forth among the miners and peasants of eastern Siberia, rumors of war took flight with no help from the press. When Stalin, no Polonophile, complained of a "narrow, common-minded mania of 'anti-Polandism'" that might obstruct a tactical rapprochement, he acknowledged a collective animus against a hereditary enemy.[23] But mostly conjecture reigned. The war scare of early 1932, which the press did nothing to encourage, provoked speculation that hostilities in the Far East would encourage the anti-Soviet Europeans to attack in the west, that it might end badly for the USSR, that the United States might go to war with Japan to defend its interests in the region, which might turn the Pacific Ocean into a hell on earth, and involve France and set off another world war, or that war with Japan would make the United States an objective Soviet ally, and discourage the Europeans from aggressive acts—at times in 1932 war talk of the sort was common; and then it passed.[24]

There would be no more war scares, advertising all the certainty of a premonition, for the rest of the decade. In place of the imminent threat settled in the eventual prospect of war, envisaged at some time and still embellished with rich conjecture. How could it be otherwise, when Marxism-Leninism taught that a final confrontation between capitalism and socialism was unavoidable, when a geography textbook of 1932 told young readers that the pope, who prayed that God would punish the Bolsheviks and destroy their five-year plan, secretly joined the capitalist and especially Catholic nations—France, Poland—in their military preparations; when the stock saying "Poland will attack us from the west" recurred with the force of inertia; and when the five-year plan itself already came in the apocalyptic trappings of an existential struggle? Whenever war came, they would be ready.[25]

In the meantime, the Soviet Union needed breathing space. Such was Stalin's assignment to the diplomats. To promote world revolution while reassuring the reactionary powers and siphoning off their capital and their technology, to pursue diplomatic recognition or nonaggression pacts while arming mightily, required feats of persuasion, set the pragmatists in the Foreign Commissariat against purists in the Comintern and the party, and posed an insoluble dilemma: had the Soviet Union entered into a period of peaceful coexistence with the capitalist world, or were the wars and the revolutions soon to resume?[26] "Socialism in one country" evaded the question for popular purposes, and preferred to the imponderables of world history the here and now of national salvation from an ominous threat. It spoke the concrete language of Soviet, especially Russian, workers, not the abstractions of cosmopolitan bourgeois intellectuals, who still prattled about revolution in China or Germany, and whose archetype Lev Bronstein, alias Leon Trotsky, now lived on Prinkipo Island in the Sea of Marmara off Istanbul, under the watchful eye of Turkish police, while Joseph Stalin sat in the Kremlin.

There, on November 8, Stalin's wife, Nadya Alliluyeva, the fervent Bolshevik who the day before had marched on Red Square, killed herself. Depression, disenchantment, or despair might plausibly have been responsible, but not appendicitis, the cause of death that *Pravda* lamely gave out two days later.[27] Reading it, a printing apprentice and GPU informer who had mingled with the crowds on the seventh now recalled Stalin's dark look atop Lenin's Mausoleum as one of foreboding.[28] The loss unsettled Stalin, and it may have deepened his paranoid conviction that his and the regime's enemies were closing in.

He and the Politburo renewed with a vengeance the assault on the suffering populations in the countryside. In the Ukraine in particular, they assured mass starvation in the coming winter. Acute malnutrition and pockets of famine had festered there since the grain requisitions in 1928 and 1929. But to refuse, now that collectivization had so manifestly miscarried, any domestic or foreign relief, to blacklist delinquent villages and collective farms for giving no grain when there was no grain to give, to renew requisitions and confiscations of everything else, to seal off the borders of the province, and to terrorize wilting party officials into compliance—to do all this, as he did over the next eight weeks, was to set about starving an entire nation.[29]

He had feared losing the Ukraine. The Bolsheviks had always feared losing the Ukraine. Ever since the peasant revolts there in 1919 and the Polish intervention the following year, the specter of separatist intellectuals, hostile peasants, and annexationist Poles had haunted them. To keep the new Soviet republic and its riches within the fold, they had conceded to it a measure of cultural and linguistic autonomy that they now resolved to suppress. They confronted, they

thought, the same league of nationalism, jacquerie, and Polish subversion all over again, and in every "kulak" their OGPU agents deported, arrested, or otherwise disposed of, they pretended to unmask
a White Guard, a foreign agent, a Petliurite—after the Ukrainian nationalist leader who in 1919 and 1920 had fought the Bolsheviks with
Polish help. To Stalin, prone to believe the very reports the agents
wanted him to, resistance to grain collection sprang from national as
much as social interests. Flanking the assault against any lingering
resistance to grain collections in the late autumn came an onslaught
on Ukrainian culture, not only in its homeland but wherever Ukrainians lived—in the Russian republic, in the Kuban and the northern
Caucasus, and beyond. Their history, language, and religion, their
identity, came under sustained attack, in a campaign that would continue for years, long after resistance to collectivization withered and
finally died in the famine of 1932–1933.[30]

Neither the five-year plan nor collectivization had begun as an
attack on the Ukrainian or any other nationality. But it eventually
devolved into one. Until then the Soviet conception of the union as
multinational and multiethnic had yielded thousands of ethnically
autonomous territorial units, large and small. The Bolsheviks, revers-
ing Tsarist efforts to Russify the empire in its last decades, intended
not only to neutralize nationalism with kindness, but also to win with
the same weapon influence and esteem among coethnics across the
frontiers in border regions. Collectivization finally doomed such enlightened self-interest in the Ukraine. There and in the north Caucasus, by the end of 1932, "Ukrainization" was held to account for the
violence of the resistance, the flow of peasants toward the Polish and
Rumanian borders instead of from them, the disintegration of party
authority, the intensification instead of the taming of nationalism.[31]
In some situations, national or ethnic particularism might threaten
rather than sustain the Soviet project; and this was one of them.

How many others might follow? Beside the Civil War and foreign
intervention of a dozen years earlier, the penumbral villains—the regime's opponents at home and assorted powers abroad—posed little

danger to it in 1932. But in the regime's mind the threat was real, especially along the borders. Today it showed the faces of Ukrainians and Poles in the west; tomorrow it might show those of Balts and Germans there as well, and Tatars in central Asia, and Koreans in East Asia, where Japan threatened subversion if not invasion. Soviet nationalism, unlike German, was neither ethnic nor racial, but almost infinitely versatile.

In the dying liberal democracy and in the nascent Communist dictatorship, the dominant sense of national mission was shifting. Should the German gain power and join the Soviet, each might threaten the other, not to mention those in between. But the ascendancy in each of a national self-image resolved domestic as much as foreign struggles; and in this, at least, the two were not alone.

5

NEW YORK

8 November 1932

O n Tuesday, one day after the anniversary on Red Square and
two days after the new elections in Germany, New York City
went to the polls, along with the rest of the country. Governor Roosevelt voted at home in Hyde Park before traveling down
to the city to await the returns at the Democratic Party headquarters
in the Biltmore Hotel. Inside, supporters choked the corridors, and
outside, excited crowds milled about until late in the night. President Hoover withdrew to his Spanish mansion on the West Coast in
Palo Alto where, four years earlier, he and friends had celebrated his
landslide victory. The returns lengthened, inexorably, state by state,
etched onto a blackboard in the great living room, and the chalk
figures stood out boldly in the indirect lighting. Presently Hoover
withdrew to his study to compose a message of congratulations to the
president-elect.[1]

In New York, long lines had waited outside the voting stations—
outside a school, a florist's, a rug shop, an art gallery, a reception
room on upper Fifth Avenue, or a barbershop in Harlem, where a
patrolman on duty sat in one of the chairs. Blue signboards hung
from lampposts, warning against loitering and electioneering in such

a privileged spot, on such a privileged day. If the voting machines with their eighteen levers—one for each office at stake, from sheriff to president—broke down, trucks with sirens wailing brought in new ones. Foreign reporters admired the order and the diversity of the American urban canvas. But voters and candidates alike grumbled at the delays and the long lines. "Disgraceful," the Democratic leader in the Bronx called them, and he blamed the Board of Elections. "You might add," he went on, "the inefficiency of the President."[2]

Hoover, who had ridden a crest of popular adulation to the White House, only to demonstrate a seemingly imperishable gift for incurring blame, now stood answerable for the wait outside polling stations in the Bronx. He had already given his name to the shantytowns, to the patched aprons and mule-drawn carts and other desperate improvisations that had darkened his last years in office.[3] Nowhere else in the world had the victims of the world depression settled on so personal a scapegoat for their country's lot; nowhere else had yesterday's icon of affluence so durably become today's byname for destitution. Such a humbling fall from grace turned incumbency from an asset into a handicap, and handed any challenger a precious advantage, if only he knew how to exploit it. And Roosevelt did—he knew how to pit his sunny promise against Hoover's grim resignation, the allure of experiment, any experiment, against tired doctrine and bankrupt orthodoxy, how to uphold the "forgotten man at the bottom of the economic pyramid" and reproach the few with the plight of the many. He knew how to run the classic campaign of opposition to the status quo. Democrats, he told 2,500 diners at a banquet in Chicago, were the party of "I will"; Republicans, of "I would have, but." His program of government was flexible, so flexible that it never stopped evolving, but when the Republicans derided his "glittering generalities" his supporters retorted that he, at least, was not promising more than he could deliver. Were they reminding the Republican incumbents of their most exuberant slogan of the 1928 campaign, "A chicken in every pot, a car in every garage"?[4]

All this bewildered the foreign press. Where was the ideology, where were the fault lines between Left and Right? At the Democratic National Convention in Chicago in June, a correspondent from the *Manchester Guardian* gazed through the glare at the political folk festival—the wheeling doves, marching bands in fur shakos, radio singers on the chairman's desk—and imagined a Gustave Doré rendering of hell. Delegates paraded, cakewalked, and snake-danced down the aisles. How did American and English politics compare, a voice asked him. "Politics?" he replied. "How should I know? So far, I have seen everything here except politics."[5]

Nine weeks before the election, a German reporter complained, he saw almost no sign of it on the streets of New York, nothing to compare to the flickering neon advertisements for cigarettes and movies. Once, as he was driving out of the city with a Republican assemblyman, boys pressed yellow and red metallic bumper stickers on them and others, stopped at red lights. "We Want Beer," they read, followed by "Hoover" or "Roosevelt." Price was negotiable. One boy set off a bidding war between drivers. But otherwise the contest was bloodless. This was, the reporter concluded, an apolitical country, quite unlike Germany and Russia.[6]

Publicity there was, French and German journalists found, even to the point of saturation, but it left them starved for controversy. Two weeks before the election, a roving German reporter came upon party activists in New York speaking and gesticulating on street corners, their messages borne by loudspeakers onto the air, and wondered in turn why the candidates avoided critical issues—the threat to American trade in Manchuria, the policy toward the Soviet Union, the war debts with former allies, the budget deficit, the sacrifices to come. Millions, a French reporter reflected the same day, watched Hoover and Roosevelt in newsreels, heard them on the radio, saw their names emblazoned on banners that stretched across streets, on storefronts and car windshields, in buttonholes and on lapels. But where, he wondered, were the open-air debates organized in the courtyards of French schools, the door-to-door canvassing in English parliamentary constituencies? And he complained, three days later, and with some exaggeration, that with the world in crisis, major fires in Germany and Japan, and ten million hungry in their own country, all they could argue about was Prohibition. To the itinerant interlopers, the election appeared as detached from reality as a sporting contest from its spectators.[7]

As though to absolve their European colleagues of hauteur or condescension, American journalists ironized in the same vein. The election was about beer, H. L. Mencken affirmed archly in his columns in the *Baltimore Sun*. Roosevelt, he wrote, showed some wear when he spoke at the Fifth Regiment Armory in Baltimore late in the campaign. The hall itself seemed somnolent, until the word "beer" brought the crowd to its feet. "That is what the crowd had come for," Mencken affirmed, "that and nothing else. Beer tomorrow. Beer this afternoon. Beer right now." The Republican convention in Chicago in the middle of June reminded John Dos Passos of the Wild West Show or Barnum and Bailey's, climaxing in the appearance through faulty lighting of the Great Engineer in the White House on-screen, as his voice poured out of loudspeakers. For Anne O'Hare McCormick, of the *New York Times*, "the typical American attitude toward politics remains that of the spectator at a professional game in which he has a large stake and no place." It was early in the campaign, but already she beheld the silent crowds, the passivity and the fortitude, the farmers shrugging their shoulders at the antiquated ballyhoo of it all. She beheld the aloofness of the downtrodden. Dos Passos had walked among it too, outside the Democratic extravaganza in Chicago at the end of June, two weeks after the effervescent mass of Republican delegates had left. The homeless and the jobless outside on West Madison Street knew nothing and cared nothing about the mass cabaret inside or the identity of a future president. "Even if they're right on West Madison Street, they're way off. Roosevelt or Hoover? It'll be the same cops."[8]

Like most historical moments later deemed pivotal, this one escaped such treatment at the time. The only manifest choice, so manifest that all, native or foreign, remarked on it, was personal. In manner and mien, the president and his challenger were polar opposites. When Hoover formally accepted the nomination in Constitution Hall in Philadelphia some six weeks after his party had offered it to him in Chicago, he spoke in a low monotone as he always did, like a robot, without gestures or emotion, as uncomfortable before a crowd as a timid expert among surging laymen. When Roosevelt broke with precedent, came in person to accept the nomination in Chicago, and traveled by plane across stormy skies from Albany to do so, he threw his head back in a challenging manner and spoke in clear and ringing tones that echoed among the rafters. To a French reporter, who had met them both in recent years, Hoover seemed an honest but querulous petty bureaucrat, cold and rigid, devoid of charm or magnetism, and marked, perhaps, by a mute bitterness at the misfortunes fate had handed him in office; Roosevelt, who had received him in his living room in Albany, as welcoming and kind, conveying both bonhomie and authority, yet betraying at times an uncertain cast of mind, vacillating and even weak. Hoover was better informed, almost captive to his expertise, while Roosevelt appealed to hope and heart, with all the photogenic and sonorous qualities so wanting in the other.[9]

The party platforms, mostly as vague and cryptic as the Democrats' stand on trade and tariffs—"A competitive tariff for revenue"—or the Republicans' on the repeal of Prohibition—referring it to the states while condemning the "evils inherent in alcohol"—and as infrequently read, did little to deepen the contrast in voters' minds. Hoover did not help by declining to campaign until the autumn. When he emerged from the White House, he blamed the Depression on the war and the world. American excesses were to blame for the crash of 1929, he allowed, without dwelling on his own antics as secretary of commerce during the exuberant years; he had reacted swiftly to restore business confidence, save the banks, protect the currency and the gold reserves from foreign depredations, and place the country on a path to recovery by 1931. Since then a contagion of bank failures and plant closings had ravaged the world, as foreign nations raised tariffs on US goods, defaulted on US loans, spent excessively on armaments, and generally ignored his sage counsel. This he could not control. "The critical assaults and dangers swept upon us from foreign countries," he told a crowd of 125,000 in Des Moines, in his home state of Iowa. "We were therefore plunged into a battle against invading forces of destruction from abroad." This time he had prevented the worst from reaching American shores. He had insulated the country from the world's troubles and prevented the disasters that would surely come if his opponent, whom he painted as a dangerous radical, ever came to power. Like the Democrats in Congress who had nominated him, the rank amateur would extravagantly expand the scope of government and demonstrate a "reckless disregard for the safety of the nation." This was no time to drop the pilot. Times might be bad, but they could be "infinitely worse."[10]

When he cast the Depression as a national emergency rather than a global misadventure, demanding activism rather than stoicism, Roosevelt hinted at a deeper ideological polarity. Already, in Albany, he had committed public funds to the relief of the unemployed in ways that Hoover resisted in Washington. Once, at the Commonwealth Club in San Francisco, he set forth a creed that owed much to the progressivism once espoused but since abandoned by his rival: the closing of the frontier and the reigning titans of a new economic oligarchy had destroyed equality of opportunity, which it now fell to the federal government to restore. But oftener than not he drew back from the unadorned meaning of his voluntarism. Unemployment relief, public works, refinanced farm mortgages, a federal presence in utilities and railroads would cost millions, but Roosevelt liked to present himself, like Hoover, as a fiscal conservative, a champion of balanced budgets, limited government, and sound money. Much to the chagrin of some of the academics in his "Brains Trust," whose prescriptions he listened to keenly, he sounded at times like his adversary. If elements of the "new deal for the American people" that he had pledged at the Democratic convention now materialized in his campaign stops across the country, many of the monetary, fiscal, and industrial experiments that would define its first incarnation the following spring did not. During the campaign and after, Rexford Tugwell, one of the principal architects of the New Deal, feared that Roosevelt's variant of it was "mild medicine. . . . It had glamour but not substance. It was not enough." Another, Adolf Berle, disagreed: Roosevelt, he later insisted, knew the gulf between dreams and possibilities, and sought to locate the common denominator of opinion in the country. "You fellows have a lot of things you want to see done," the nominee told his advisers one day. "Don't you realize that none of them *will* get done unless I'm elected?" Either way, the result was a call to restore purchasing power one day and to balance the budget the next. "Concerning what might be done about the Depression," Tugwell recorded, "there was no agreement."[11]

The New Deal, unhewn, a work in the making as it always would be, answered a political more than a doctrinal exigency during the campaign. Roosevelt was striving to define a message that might gather in the motley malcontents of the land, scattered far beyond the safe bastions of a minority party that had been out of office for all but eight of the last thirty-six years. The candidate aspired to unite ideological clans—liberals, progressives, populists, even Socialists if they could, and others who defied any label—who were viscerally at variance on particular matters of state. In courting them he often had to choose between throwing consistency to the four winds or observing the better part of valor.

On tariffs and trade, he volubly came and went and came again, only to espouse as murky an expedient as the "flexible tariff" endorsed by his adversary. Could he do otherwise, with the party split between purists on either side, with the cotton growers of the South opposed to protection, the wheat and corn belt of the Midwest strongly in favor of it, and industry divided between product lines and large and small manufacturers everywhere? As a candidate for the nomination, he had attacked the Smoot-Hawley tariff that Hoover had signed into law, and proposed instead some kind of reciprocal trade agreements; as the nominee in Chicago he attacked the tariff again, vaguely; as a campaigner he supported it in Kansas and attacked it again in Kentucky; he promised protection to farmers in Baltimore, to manufacturers in Boston. He could only beat out compromises, seeming to promise bilateral arrangements in the future that might gradually restore trade while preserving "the tariff" in the abstract. "So began," one of his disillusioned advisers complained at the end of the decade, "seven years of evasions and cross-purposes on the tariff."[12]

On money he chose to remain silent. He might have advocated experiment and inflation, notably by detaching the dollar from gold, and gladdened the backers of silver in the West and indebted farmers in the South and Midwest, revenants from the days of Greenbacks and Populists. But that would only have estranged the already untrusting moneyed interests of the Northeast, guardians, so the others thought, of the diabolical cosmopolitan metal itself. Best to avoid, at least for now, backing the Grange against Wall Street.[13]

And on foreign policy he chose to remain silent as well, as silent as the president. Outside of the tariff, a hornet's nest for Roosevelt, and the global economic depression, a limp alibi for Hoover, the two managed to ignore the world beyond. The Democratic platform had called for a "firm foreign policy" and "peace with all the world"; the Republican, for "going forward in harmony with other peoples without alliances or foreign partnerships." Neither candidate volunteered to elucidate these benign platitudes, but at least they resisted adding to them. Hoover spoke briefly in his acceptance speech about constructive engagement, and then fell silent for the rest of the campaign. Roosevelt, who spoke more often and more widely than Hoover, told the director of the Foreign Policy Association in New York in mid-October that he had made up his mind to say nothing at all about foreign affairs. The choice was strategic, one of his principal advisers later revealed, determined by the minimal level of public interest and the likelihood that by speaking out he would lose more than he would gain among undecided voters. Besides, his newly cautious views on foreign affairs were already popular in the Midwest and the West. Why risk distracting an electorate fixated on the predicament at home?[14]

Presidential elections had often relegated foreign affairs to the sidelines or banished them from the arena. In 1928, Prohibition and the Catholic religion of another New York governor, the Democratic nominee, Al Smith, had dominated the contest; in 1924, domestic prosperity had persuaded voters to "keep cool with Coolidge," a president who knew almost nothing of foreign affairs. Silence reigned, especially about Europe—let Germany soak in American loans and capital investment, the wisdom held, but let the government stay out, and stage no encore of the folly of 1917, ever. The more the American entry into the European war receded in time, the more unpopular it became. Skepticism about German villainy emerged almost as soon as the cheering had died and Versailles was on the books. None displayed it sooner than some of the veterans, aspiring writers idling in the cafés of Greenwich Village. "We believed that we had fought for an empty cause," the critic and poet Malcolm Cowley recalled, "that the Germans were no worse than the Allies, no better."[15] Europe seemed no better off than before, the French as heavily armed and intransigent as ever, and journalists and popular historians quickly shed any inhibitions about challenging the nobility of purpose and the innocence of motive in the Allies' war of 1914. Why not Mr. Wilson's of 1917 too, the *New Republic* demanded to know in 1926, and by the end of the decade the American entry, wrapped in conspiracy theories about arms manufacturers, bankers, and British propaganda, had long lost whatever inspirational power the songs at the moment had exerted.[16] The country had been "had," its generosity exploited. In all, the *Saturday Evening Post* wildly claimed in 1931, Europe had cost the United States $40 billion in less than fifteen years and had "not solved the first problem of all, which is how to live at peace with herself." The magazine probably reached six million readers. The following year the Hearst daily press, which reached almost as many, urged the government to seize the French and British West Indies as partial payment for the war debts their colonial rulers owed, heed the wisdom of the Founders, and "stay out of European affairs."[17]

Unsurprisingly, European affairs stayed out of American elections. But the renewed silence of the candidates in 1932 also concealed a double evolution underway. Hoover and his secretary of state, Henry Stimson, had been stepping away from their predecessors' doctrinaire detachment from former allies and foes alike, and from the international organizations they had set afoot, and toward varieties of soft-spoken engagement without obligation. Roosevelt had evolved in the opposite direction, away from his earlier enthusiasm for the League of Nations and for the design of a new postwar world order, to an open rejection of membership in the first and deep misgivings about the second. The two had moved unknowingly toward each other.

In January, as the election year began, Secretary Stimson, hoping to rally opposition to the Japanese seizure of Manchuria and its creation of a puppet state there, announced that the United States would not recognize any de facto situation resulting from the use of force. The doctrine, which Hoover had proposed two months earlier, required only moral disapproval of the aggressor, yet marked a departure from the late orthodoxy of political insulation from much of the world and its conflicts. In April 1932, Stimson became the first American secretary of state to cross the threshold of the League of Nations, when he briefly took a seat at the disarmament conference. He conspicuously received his foreign counterparts well away, in a secluded mansion overlooking the lake or in the Hotel des Bergues on the quay, but his entry that day provoked all the excitement of a symbolic moment.

In August, in a speech before the Council on Foreign Relations, he declared that condemnation of an aggressor was no longer a matter of choice for the sixty-two signatories of the Kellogg-Briand Pact, which had outlawed aggressive war in 1928: they were now obliged, in his eyes, to consult and somehow to act. He sought to bridge the gap between the gesture of the pact, which his country had ratified but which contained no enforcement provisions of any kind, and the demand of the League Covenant, which his country had not ratified but which did—especially Article 16, which allowed for the eventual imposition of sanctions and even of force. Stimson explored options for constraining Japan, including an arms embargo, but openly ventured no further than invoking the sanction of public opinion. Nor did Hoover, who ruled out employing American arms to help enforce peace and recoiled at economic sanctions on Japan as well, believing that the American people were in no mood to risk war for Manchuria. The United States could go no further than Stimson's urgings. But ten years earlier the Senate had effectively forbidden the secretary of state, Charles Evans Hughes, from having anything to do with Geneva, and the American minister to Switzerland had communicated with the League's secretary-general by sending messages to his private residence. Now the minister in Berne represented the country at the disarmament talks in Geneva, American envoys sat on countless League committees, and the press was accustomed to see American faces among the international officials in the old Hotel National where they worked.[18]

"An old Chinese wall policy of isolation," Roosevelt had called the emerging resistance to membership in the League in 1919, during the Versailles conference. Jettison the relic of prewar thinking, he urged, because in the new world and the crises to come the United States could not "escape an important, perhaps even a controlling voice."[19] In the 1920 election he had campaigned tirelessly as Democratic vice-presidential candidate for membership in the League, and after his loss went on speaking ardently into the early 1920s of entry and engagement, of free trade and a reasonable settlement of the debts owed to the country by its wartime allies. But as the decade advanced, as domestic well-being kept company with Europhobic bile over the late war and its ruinous sequels, the Wilsonian rather than the isolationist accents came to sound passé, the antique tones of a foolish idealism.

As he returned to Democratic politics after his illness in 1928, Roosevelt moderated his enthusiasms. He spoke of American leadership in the world, but of only cooperation with the League; of the obstacles that high American tariffs placed in the way of Europeans repaying their debts, but not of free trade; of domestic but not of foreign affairs.[20] As governor of New York for the next four years, he could fittingly say nothing more of such matters, but the new year of 1932 began with the press demanding answers of the presumptive presidential candidate. In New York, Walter Lippmann deplored his "two-faced platitudes"; in Los Angeles, William Randolph Hearst likened him to other "Wilsonites and internationalists" and called on all of them to return to the "high road of Americanism" after Wilson's "visionary policies of intermeddling in European conflicts and complications." Hearst, who had competed with Joseph Pulitzer at the turn of the century for what a British critic called the "primacy of the gutter," spoke over an NBC radio hookup of fifty stations, carried abroad by shortwave, one of the most expensive broadcasts in history. Later he demanded an open recantation from Roosevelt in return for his support.[21]

It came, in sackcloth and ashes, the following month. On the day the disarmament conference opened in Geneva, Governor Franklin Roosevelt told a crowd in Albany that he opposed American entry into the World Court and the League of Nations, which he derided as "a mere meeting place for the political discussion of strictly European national political difficulties." With these, he said, the United States wanted nothing to do. He opposed as well the cancellation of war debts, warned against entanglements in the affairs of others, and urged that "with strict adherence to the principles of Washington, we maintain our international freedom." Politics, he reminded the dismayed internationalists and League supporters among his supporters, including his wife, Eleanor, was the art of the possible. "Repent ye," ironized Idaho senator William Borah, who had led the opposition to League entry in 1919, "for the kingdom of heaven is at hand."[22]

Roosevelt had managed to repudiate collective security without embracing isolationism, and there he remained for the campaign. But his foreign policy was now indistinguishable from that of the administration he proposed to oust, complete with all its ambiguity, incoherence, and muddleheaded goodwill. He like Hoover was navigating a misty zone of involvement without commitment. The country would voice outrage at aggression in Manchuria, send the consul general in Geneva to attend League Council meetings on the matter, but do nothing to prevent or punish the aggressor, because it lacked the power and the will to challenge his fait accompli—Japanese actions spoke louder than American words. The United States would urge or coerce Europeans into disarming but do nothing to guarantee their security, while pursuing naval parity with Britain. It would "interfere everywhere and act nowhere." As a campaigner, Roosevelt did nothing to challenge the diplomacy of prolixity and passivity. Would he as president continue "to combine the mission of John the Baptist with the methods of Pontius Pilate?"[23] Only on Latin America did rays of clarity pierce the fog. Hoover had begun and Roosevelt had advocated reining in earlier armed interventions at will in the affairs of the hemisphere—the Japanese drew pointed parallels between their actions in Manchuria and those of the United States in Panama and elsewhere—and pursuing the more constructive Good Neighbor Policy. Shortly after the election, Hoover withdrew the US Marines from Nicaragua. It was a beginning. But elsewhere "nonintervention" was purely negative. Behind the scenes, Stimson had floated the possibility of force against Japan—of collective sanctions backed if needed by navies. The president would not hear of it, and his challenger would not speak of it.[24]

Roosevelt, whatever his innermost convictions, had staked his ground in order to unify his party, capture the nomination, and win the election. Hearst applauded the "genuine conservative democracy"[25] of the Democratic ticket, the liberal internationalists fell reluctantly into line, and far from New York State isolationist multitudes who had known little about its governor could lay their anxieties to rest. In November he carried all the most isolationist parts of the country, losing only four states in the Republican but also "internationalist" Northeast as well as Pennsylvania and Delaware. Only half of the electorate—52 percent—had bothered to vote, but among those who had, a clear and eclectic majority, multiclass and multiparty, rich and poor, Democratic, Republican, Socialist and independent, had given Roosevelt its support, and on his coattails his party had conquered the Congress and thirty of thirty-four governorships.[26]

He had judged the mood of his compatriots well. They had voted for action at home, not abroad—not for debt cancellation that would shift the burden of repayment from European ingrates onto their shoulders, or so they thought, nor for opening their own markets to foreign goods, nor for renewed foreign extravagances that would only deepen their disenchantment at the squandering of blood and treasure on the last one. Not everyone had felt quite this way. Pacifist leaders returning from their day in Geneva and outraged Sinophile sympathizers had agitated for an arms embargo against Japan, and the Chaco War that erupted in the spring of 1932 between Paraguay and Bolivia provoked demands for such embargoes to any and all belligerent countries. Stimson discerned in such instruments a possible punitive weapon for use against Japan. But they died in committee in Congress. And some of their most ardent promoters, unlike Stimson, conceived of the embargo as a means not to act in the world but to withdraw from it, to avoid entanglement in distant conflicts, and to bridle culpable industrial and financial interests that had drawn the country into war in 1917—they saw the embargo as isolationist. As the interregnum began, neither Hoover nor Roosevelt had heard the last of them. For now, the president-elect could rest his success on an inchoate collective sentiment of national self-sufficiency. He was not likely to violate it.[27]

Foreign observers—journalists and some diplomats—did not easily grasp that the national consensus so forged would powerfully bind the new president. Dialogue seemed second nature to this "liberal . . . cultivated, intelligent, open-minded" man; suppler and more open, less constrained politically than Hoover, he might fraternize with his beleaguered European counterparts. He might well favor reducing if not canceling war debts, some ventured, and lowering tariffs on a case-by-case, reciprocal basis. Relieved Japanese papers assumed lightly at first that he would allow more Japanese exports to America and display more goodwill toward them than Stimson ever had. From a position of political strength at home, the new president might even "help pull the world together" and avoid another war. They could not know that some of the New Dealers closest to him were economic nationalists who deplored, even more than Hoover's global diagnoses of the Depression, the new engagement abroad pursued by his secretary of state. They could not know that the candidate who would not risk his election on uncertain foreign causes would not risk his political capital or his recovery program on them either, once he assumed office the following March. They could only speculate. Three days after the election, a cartoon in the *Manchester Guardian* depicted a portrait of Wilson holding a dossier about "cooperation policy." Under it sat his old disciple Roosevelt in an armchair, and behind him assorted world leaders gathered furtively: "Shh! What do you think he's thinking?"[28]

6

PARIS AND LONDON

11 November 1932

The cheering for Roosevelt had died outside the Biltmore in New York when, on Friday, crowds in Paris and London stood in silence for Armistice Day, the fourteenth since the war had ended. They ignored the day in Berlin, where each year the anniversary only opened old wounds and where more auspicious moments to remember the dead lay at hand; Matthias Erzberger of the Center Party had signed the armistice in the Compiègne Forest in 1918 only to fall to vengeful assassins in the Black Forest in 1921. The day was meaningless in Moscow, where the entire imperialist war lay buried in official oblivion. In the United States, local ceremonies marked the occasion around the country; Indianapolis dedicated a cenotaph in World War I Plaza, veterans gave speeches all over Westchester County in New York, and Newton Baker, the secretary of war who had phoned President Wilson with the news of the signing, delivered a glowing tribute to him by his tomb in Washington National Cathedral. But in France as in Britain an entire nation stopped in sorrow, as though to disown the euphoria on the same streets and squares fourteen years earlier.[1]

Guards on parade stood at attention before the Cenotaph in London, troops with regimental standards ringed the Arc de Triomphe in Paris, and artillery salvos sounded in both capitals at eleven a.m. as the onlookers fell silent; poppies were worn, wreaths laid, last posts sounded; but otherwise the lingering day, more civilian than martial, shunned pageantry. For hours the serried crowds stretched down Whitehall and darkened Trafalgar Square, and into the late afternoon multitudes of widows, orphans, and maimed veterans made their way past the flame of the unknown soldier under the arch in Paris.[2]

Even so, many stayed away, as they always did, and later that day violence disrupted the moment of apparent French national communion. In the Latin Quarter, five thousand pacifist veterans and Socialists marched to the Pantheon, jeering at the names of wartime generals, crying "Long live peace!" "Disarm! Disarm!" and "Never again!" They carried a huge banner with the words of Jean Jaurès, the Socialist leader assassinated as war was breaking out in 1914: "Down with blind hatreds! Down with fratricidal wars!" and at the Pantheon they placed palms of peace on his tomb. From fifth-floor windows on the *place*, indignant residents waved tricolors, provoking catcalls from the marchers below. As they dispersed and moved on they collided with several hundred nationalists from the royalist *Action française*, who cried "Long live France! Long live the army!" and attacked them with canes. In the Vincennes Woods at the eastern edge of the city, ten thousand Communists assembled, sang the "Internationale," and threw stones at the police sent to break them up.[3]

The press elevated such incivilities into a war of words, waged with syllogisms instead of slogans. At times the victory became almost as divisive a memory in France as the defeat in Germany, setting the partisans of intransigence against those of conciliation. Nowhere else had the arcane and technical problem of disarmament become so inflammatory a proposition, so infallible an indication of political sensibility. On the right, *L'Echo de Paris* lamented the unseemly outbursts after the minute of silence—the pacifist enthusiasms that had undermined the country's defenses in 1914 and now threatened to disarm it again, before a Germany that had learned nothing from its defeat. On the left, the Socialists cited their election manifesto of the spring and called for the submission of international disputes to compulsory arbitration before a sovereign League of Nations. Léon Blum, the party's leader, argued that French security depended on success at Geneva, that significant disarmament now might mollify the German government, preempt its own rearmament, and pull the rug out from under Hitler. These were all hazardous postulates, resting on mistaken or unverifiable assumptions; but they enjoyed the staying power of dogma, often indifferent to evidence and to argument.[4]

This matter more than any other appeared to define political families. Much of the Left, including the Socialists and many of the Radicals, but not the Communists, swore by disarmament, reconciliation, the League of Nations, and collective security; most of the Right, by military strength, vigilance, and the pursuit of a strong and defensible border: the left bank of the Rhine. One was pacific, the other bellicose. It had not always been that way. In 1871, amid the wreckage of the Second Empire and the flames of the Paris Commune, the Left had exhorted the fainthearted with a radical democratic patriotism that called not only for equality but also for popular war against the Prussian invader. "Gambetta is war!" cried the moderate Right, to frighten away the peasantry from the adventurism of Léon Gambetta, the most popular Radical leader; together with the Center it counselled respect of the mournful fait accompli for now and a safely conservative regime to rebuild the country. A generation later, at the turn of the century, nationalism, militarism, and Germanophobia were migrating to new homes on the right, while a new universalism, sometimes Marxist or anarchist, sometimes pacifist, was winning converts on the left. The war kept the lid on their mutual antipathy, the postwar removed it: now the Left was "defeatist" and the Right "chauvinist," and in the early 1930s their invective returned with a vengeance.[5]

By then the afterglow of victory had long faded in the deepening gloom of international isolation. France feared Germany. The menace would return, the conviction ran, if not today, then tomorrow. Repeatedly, French governments had asked former wartime allies for security guarantees before they would agree to drop the country's military guard or allow Germany to expand its own. Repeatedly, Britain and the United States had declined. With the ink scarcely dry on the Treaty of Versailles, the promised security guarantee that France had extracted from them in return for abandoning ambitions on the Rhine had evaporated into thin air, never to materialize again. Serial French concessions availed little—over reparations from Germany, rescheduled in London in 1924 and again at The Hague in 1929, and finally renounced in effect at Lausanne in the summer of 1932; over the French pockets and bridgeheads on the Rhine, the last of them evacuated by 1930, five years early; over measures of disarmament, offered in 1923 and 1924 in return for security pacts. They never yielded the coalition that France never tired of trying to revive. In the east the old Russian ally, crucial to France in 1914, was now the Soviet Union, and the attempted rapprochement pursued by Edouard Herriot's center-left government eked out a nonaggression pact by November 1932; but the Chamber was not close to ratifying it, and any meaningful military convention remained conjectural at best. Instead France tried hemming Germany in with Polish, Czechoslovak, Rumanian, and Yugoslav alliances, of uncertain scope and even more uncertain value. France was isolated. For two decades before 1914, thanks to its entente with Russia and Britain, the country had discovered a sense of security unknown to it in the 1870s and 1880s. Nothing comparable consoled it now. Recent German governments, of Brüning and especially Papen, had sounded more brazen and more strident, and the Francophobic Nazis were pushing at the gates of power. What was France to do? Deter, or conciliate?[6]

Occupy Mainz, *Action française* replied from the far right, develop Franco-Belgian military cooperation, restore two-year military service and the monarchy as well. Better that than the "insanities" of Joseph Paul-Boncour, the foreign minister then traveling the rails back and forth between the Gare de Lyon in Paris and the Gare Cornavin in Geneva. "Let's liquidate war," a Socialist leader suggested instead, arm and empower the League of Nations, he went on, and incidentally balance the budget as a result. The ugliness of war itself was not at issue; even *Action française* and the rest of the saber-rattling Right proposed only to assure peace by deterring aggression. And the protagonists wasted few words on the complex proposals from technical experts far and wide to do away with offensive weapons. Something else rankled. The reversals performed on the matter by Right and Left since the Franco-Prussian War, the reciprocity of their changes of heart, suggested that a deeper discord assured their enmity; suggested, too, that they might invert their stances on war and peace again if the context so required, as indeed it would, some four or five years later.[7]

Thirty years earlier, in the Dreyfus affair, the guilt or innocence of a Jewish army officer had set order and tradition, enshrined in the nation, in its military and ecclesiastical hierarchy, against universalism and human rights, abstractions dear to many on the left and incarnated, or so they hoped, in the republic. *L'Affaire* refused to die. Postwar politics resounded with its rancorous old polemics, and when in the early 1930s the French predicament deepened, and the country tasted the bitter fruits of the victory of 1918, they reverberated again. "We've seen it all now, in their politicians' Republic," Gustave Hervé, a flag-waving nationalist, exclaimed in his paper, *La Victoire*, two weeks before Armistice Day. Léon Blum had kept up a running attack in *Le Populaire* on General Maxime Weygand, the chief of staff of the army, for holding up the government's disarmament proposals destined for Geneva. "Does he realize," Blum had asked, "that he would discredit himself before universal opinion?" And Hervé, an apostate from prewar antimilitarist socialism who had discovered nationalism during the war and Italian Fascism after it, and promoted both with the zealous penitence of the convert, had gone on to conjure up the nightmare of Weygand "sacrificed to the [Masonic] lodges and the party of social revolution." *Le Populaire* saw a "nationalist and militarist pack unleashed against Léon Blum," because the entire right-wing press had taken up the cry. Blum and Weygand had clashed before, vicariously—during the Dreyfus affair, when the lawyer and the officer had sided with fervid conviction for and against the wronged captain. Now they clashed directly, once again over the place of the army in the nation, and by extension over the place of the nation in the lives of its citizens.[8]

To follow the rift, which ran like a thread in time through recent French history, was to arrive sometimes in 1789 but more often in 1914. Royalism flourished only on the fringes, but doubts spread well beyond it over the soundness of the third republican regime to govern the country since 1792, and *Action française*, with its highbrow authors, incendiary press, and incessant agitation, was reaching the acme of its influence. The Great War, which reconciled the domestic adversaries while it lasted, revived their antagonism as soon as it ended.

Who was responsible for the war? Pierre Renouvin, the preeminent professional historian in France to have worked on the war, and the first to have done so with official archives, declared in 1931 that all the arguments abroad about blame fell on deaf ears in France. For his compatriots, he insisted, the matter was closed, hardly requiring them to furnish any proof of their pacific inclinations or of Germany's heavy culpability in the July Crisis of 1914. This was not quite so. No one blamed France alone for the outbreak of war in 1914, but many refused to blame Germany alone either. One of the classic school texts of the day, updated to include the war, declined to do so, giving a German as well as a French view and treating 1914 as a catastrophe surpassing any singular national agency.[9]

To provoke a war was one crime, to allow it another, and among the foes of militarism in the early 1930s, many recalled the patriotic effusions of the last years of peace with revulsion. Upbringing injected the young with just the right dose of poison to immunize them against the pestilence when it came, in the recollection of Jean Guéhenno, the editor of *L'Europe*, early in 1933. He had turned forty recently, and he dwelt now on the idiotic sailors' and soldiers' uniforms, the berets and rosettes he and other boys had worn on carnival days in Brittany, the dates of kings they had memorized on

weekdays, the bizarre hymns they had sung at First Communion—
"*Save Rome and France / In the name of the Sacred Heart*"—and
understood poorly if at all. The macabre hoax had prepared them
for the holocaust, for Verdun, and it filled him with an indignation
he now directed at the complacent masters of the postwar era, who
had remembered the nation but forgotten Europe. "It's still the same
night," he mused. They lived on, marked by those days as though by
an incurable wound. Impieties of the sort appalled Louis Madelin, a
member of the Académie française, a historian of France, and a cele-
brant of its victories in the war. Indifference to the nation threatened
its survival more than whatever projects Paul-Boncour was carrying
to Geneva, he warned as Armistice Day neared in 1932, because the
country would recover its weapons sooner than its soul. Its army had
rebounded from the depths before—at Orléans with Joan of Arc in
1429, at Valmy in 1792, on the Marne in 1914, and at Verdun in 1916.
Would it again, if the schools no longer inculcated patriotism? He
did not think so.[10]

For the pacifist and political philosopher Alain, conscience of the
centrist and governing Radical party, the "fury of the elites against
peace" was insatiable. But even he acknowledged that they celebrated
not war itself, but authority, and that in the same sanguinary vocation
the Left feared above all the threat to democracy and to its fundamental tenet, equality. Military thinking, Alain held, forbade thought
itself, at least among the men; but all authority was military, that of
the church and the moneyed few as well as that of the army. Comply
or die—but those forced to submit could still, must still, resist with
their minds: "the spirit must never obey." Destiny meant nation on
the extreme right, class on the extreme left, and the individual, in
some shape or form, in between, with Alain; and the existential dilemma of war and peace brought all such irreducible certitudes into
endemic and occasionally violent contradiction.[11]

"Liar!" the French nationalists shouted at the German delegate
Dr. Joseph Joos from the Center Party, as he tried to speak at the
Trocadéro palace at the end of November 1931. "Hitler! Hitler!" An

international conference of peace groups, hosted by Edouard Herriot, the Radical leader, was meeting there, two months ahead of the world disarmament conference in Geneva. Veterans, royalists, and young blue-shirted Fascists of a sort had invaded the hall. "Nonsense!" they shouted at Herriot, as he appealed to reason over "the brute forces of the world." The veterans' leader, Colonel de la Rocque, took over the podium and read a statement about "our reasons for not disarming." A thousand had gathered in the hall to hear diplomats and other figures from some thirty countries talk about disarmament, and amid the uproar and the violence on the floor the speakers at the closing session gave up. Demonstrators surged past them, smashed furniture, waved bloody handkerchiefs. The American delegate, a former ambassador to London, could scarcely speak at all, and hoots and catcalls vied with the radio transmission of a message from Senator Borah in Washington, drowned by static and its own volume. Stanzas of the "Marseillaise" and cries of "Vive la France" did the rest. "I never saw anything like that peace meeting in my life," a shaken and perspiring ambassador said as he left.[12]

That such measured pronouncements could provoke such pandemonium—Herriot himself, no stranger to the frenzies of French politics, waxed incredulous as well as indignant. "Such convulsions of rage, such outpourings of fanaticism" left him wondering what had happened to French liberalism, to French politesse. On the right the papers rejoiced. The *Echo de Paris* mocked the "internationalists of all countries and classes" and "the noisy cortèges of bearded foreigners with their rough accents of Germany and of Asia." *Le Figaro* celebrated the victory of popular common sense, of "an answer based not on ideology but on facts, on human experience," over the figments of the intellectuals, mindless apostles of leaving France defenseless.[13] For years more dispassionate critics had seen in German demands for French disarmament a transparently self-serving ploy, unacceptable without other guarantees, but this was different. The verbal antics of the nationalists had swept the issue up in gusts of populism, xenophobia, and anti-intellectualism.

Their passion had surprised Herriot. His party and his paper recalled at once the odium that had rained on the defenders of Captain
Alfred Dreyfus. This time the fever on the right, like the event itself,
went unrecorded in the more moderate French press, as though the
riot was too minor, the commentary too toxic, to touch. When voices
rose in anger in the Chamber of Deputies over the scandal of the Trocadéro, calmer heads prudently agreed to let the matter drop, and discuss it no further.[14] But an omen had crossed their sky. In July 1926,
on one of the days of panic over the plunging franc, twenty thousand
veterans had taken to the streets in Paris to protest a financial rescue
accord with Washington that they feared would ruin their country
while freeing Germany of its obligations to pay reparations. A wave of
xenophobia against tourists from lands with stronger currencies had
swept the city. Now, late in 1931, a gathering of French and foreign
peace groups had provoked another storm of recriminations about
national sovereignty and national identity. Confidence in the franc
had returned, but anxieties over national security had deepened and
were unlikely to lift; if financial insecurity returned to join them, as
it now threatened to, the prospects for domestic tranquility would
durably darken. The debris on the floor of the Trocadéro threatened
more extensive wreckage.[15]

The following March, Aristide Briand, Geneva incarnate, died
in Paris. "As long as I am alive," he had said, "there will be no war."
The critics on the right deplored the self-serving mystique of the
apostle of peace, the serial concessions that had brought France so
little and Germany so much, and the pact authored with the American secretary of state Frank Kellogg to outlaw war—"The most
hollow, sentimental, nebulous diplomatic instrument that a minister ever signed," one of them called it. But his funeral revealed the
depth of the pacifist sensibility in France and beyond. Dignitaries
from the League and each of its fifty-five member nations came; four
hearses piled with pyramids of flowers from emperors, presidents,
and kings followed the casket from the Quai d'Orsay to the Arc de
Triomphe, amid muffled sobs and cries of "La paix! Vive la paix!"

from the onlookers; later, once the procession had passed, pacifist veterans demonstrated on the Champs-Élysées. The critics on the right remained silent.[16]

Throughout the year, occasions to proclaim the contending credos punctually brought forth gusts of vehemence. As in the Trocadéro in November and on the Champs-Élysées in March, the shadow of the war loomed over each. In July, France effectively renounced its reparations from Germany: the Right saw the country robbed in Lausanne and disarmed in Geneva, the Left looked forward to the European fruits of Herriot's "victory."[17] In August, the Radical paper L'Oeuvre began publishing advance excerpts of a book about the mutinies that had shaken parts of the French army in the spring of 1917. Based on partial archives from a closed parliamentary committee of investigation, but riddled with error and exaggeration, the front-page philippics against a high command that had wantonly massacred "100,000 men" exposed the vainglory that had first provoked the mutinies and then suppressed any news about them.[18] In October, Blum and Weygand locked horns over disarmament in the press. "Yes, Blum was magnificent with Weygand," the future anthropologist Claude Lévi-Strauss wrote to his parents. He had just taken up his first teaching position in a high school in Mont-de-Marsan and was following the affair keenly. "One really gets the impression that by his talent alone, he [Blum] leads France; or rather he doesn't, except in rare circumstances."[19] And in November, Armistice Day brought both sides out again. Ahead lay the military budget, German demands at Geneva, payments due on the American war debt, now highly controversial after the loss of reparations: enough to sustain the recurring polemics well into the new year.

Civilian against military, lay against clerical, revolutionary against reactionary: aging specters still haunted the political contests, still swung elections in the era of radio and mass-circulation dailies. They had just done so, in May 1932, when antipathy, especially in *la France profonde*, to the manorial and churchly susceptibilities of the government swept it from office and returned Herriot at the head of a Radical-led, center-left majority.[20] "Party of the commoners, party of the provinces," wrote a sympathetic observer of the Radicals—hostile to the church not because of religion, but because of its partiality to the rich, and hostile to the rich, because of their proximity to power. The campaign had been quiet, the meetings decorous, the speeches predictable. Herriot had insisted on the republican and lay values of the Radicals, Premier Tardieu on the danger of socialism—"An incomplete Bolshevism"; each had accused the other of menacing the financial health of the country, now precarious as the world economic depression finally reached French factories. Three thousand candidates, at the first round, had echoed their leaders' pronouncements and then attended more assiduously to their local clients, the voters. Over nine million had come to the polls, 82 percent of the electorate—as dutiful as the German, much more so than the American.[21]

What then of the country's gloomy international predicament? Very little—not because no one cared, but because for all the tussles in the press and in public squares on Sunday afternoons, a surprising unanimity assured the assent of the political class to the only foreign policy deemed possible and practical. *Sécurité d'abord*: national security alone, the sine qua non of any agreement to jettison arms, sign pacts or alliances, or borrow or lend large sums of money, drove the agenda. To preserve the peace and protect the country from invasion meant, for 80 percent of the Chamber, rapprochement and cooperation with Germany, but only on the basis of existing treaties or adequate security guarantees. It meant too that anyone wishing to abrogate existing treaties—Versailles or any other—could do so only in Geneva or through bilateral accords, and not through threats or bluster. On this almost everyone agreed. At Briand's funeral André Tardieu, who had once, in the Chamber, derided his policy as a "dead dog floating downstream," paid tribute to his efforts to "gather the necessary conditions for a durable and guaranteed peace." Scarcely had the soil landed on Briand's coffin, *Le Temps* observed, than Tardieu, the new premier, vigorously resumed his late rival's foreign policy. Governments of all hues embraced each other's actions ecumenically: the Left evacuated the Ruhr in 1924, the Right evacuated the Rhine in 1929, in spite of the nationalists among them, and Herriot's disarmament proposals in November of 1932 broadly resembled Tardieu's in the winter, with only slightly better prospects of acceptance in Geneva or Berlin. *Briandisme* lived on, its continuity personified in the grand figure of Philippe Berthelot, the general secretary of the Foreign Ministry, who ruled the Quai d'Orsay while premiers and cabinets came and went. Even if the Socialists won the elections, the Radical *L'Oeuvre* acknowledged bluntly at the end of April, the outcome would not matter to French foreign policy.[22]

Secure in the knowledge that *Briandisme* rested on a necessity—to modify the postwar settlement enough to appease Germany but not so much as to weaken France—the deputies of the Right could sustain it with their votes while excoriating it with their invective. Over and over, Briand had dared them to show him the door; over and over, they had implored him to stay. Nothing had changed. Most deputies still knew very little about their country's dealings abroad. As the election in May had approached, a right-wing editor doubted whether even twenty out of the six hundred in the Chamber could find their way through the labyrinth of League covenants, Polish Corridors, war debts, and the rest. A fortiori their voters. Foreign affairs did not divide them—not yet; no more than their counterparts across the Rhine or the Atlantic did they pronounce themselves at elections on such matters. As long as invasion did not threaten, the renowned political analyst André Siegfried thought, they asked only to be left in peace. Meanwhile the epithets filled the air, detached from geopolitical and financial realities.[23]

By the end of 1932 these were cruelly illuminating the vanity of the country's postwar aspirations. Recriminations on both sides of the Atlantic, in the French and the American newspapers and legislatures, were rising as the December debt installment neared. The Germans were refusing to return to the disarmament conference in Geneva unless it recognized their a priori right to arm themselves with the same weapons and in the same way as anyone else, without any counterparts or preconditions. This ultimatum Sir John Simon, the British foreign secretary, seemed disposed to accept in the abstract, seeing nothing sacrosanct about the ink at Versailles, and provoking the semiofficial *Le Temps* to complain of the battle France had waged to implement the treaty ever since its signing. Meanwhile the French treasury deficit had soared ominously, just as the skirmishing over the budget began in the Chamber.[24] Short of allies and losing their gold reserves, facing an imminent shortage of young men of military age as well—the unborn from the war years, the demographic as well as the financial deficit hobbling their strategic possibilities—France began to renounce enforcement, along with the hope of containing Germany within some newly consensual international framework.

Instead a fortress mentality grew, imposed by isolation and responsive to fears. Already the first lugubrious tunnels and armored turrets of the Maginot Line were disfiguring the Franco-German border—fortifications to save precious manpower, buy time for mobilization, allow for a counteroffensive on the flanks, perhaps in Belgium, and reassure the French people and the world that the country harbored no offensive designs. The intellectual foundations were ready. The material ones were wanting, and over these reproaches flew between civilian and military authorities.[25] But the line miraculously bridged the gulf between nationalist Right and pacifist Left; for now, it mollified the first with its weaponry and the second with its defensive posture. This was the national identity—pacific, defensive, prepared—that divided the French the least. Only once the aggressor had attacked, only once France had absorbed the initial invasion, would it riposte with offensive operations. *Sécurité d'abord*—in this incarnation, as a web of forts and strongpoints, the formula transcended the clash of values, another powerful incentive to build them.

"France has done all she can to help Europe recover," Herriot told the journalists in his office at the Quai d'Orsay, which housed the premier as well as the foreign minister, one floor above him. "Now it is up to others to act." Mayor of Lyon for twenty-seven years, erudite, stocky, and jovial, he delivered bon mots, chuckled, slapped a guest or two on the knee, and embodied the rising middle classes and the Radical party on which the Third Republic had come to rest. Almost as avidly as Briand, he had pursued a new order—gone to London in 1924 to open the door to Germany's return to international society, paved the way for the Locarno agreements, abandoned reparations at Lausanne, come up with a new disarmament plan in Geneva. More than anyone, he had cultivated the British. "France can do no more," he said, but he conceded that French security relied on protecting a military superiority that Germany found intolerable. An impasse, it seemed, had been reached. Listening to him in the tapestried and heavily carpeted office, Hubert "Red" Knickerbocker of the *New York Evening Post* found him paternal and relaxed. But was he not also, in his optimism and his bonhomie, imminently passé, along with so much French voluntarism, so many French initiatives?[26]

In a café in Les Halles, Knickerbocker listened at length to Théophile, a well-traveled fifty-nine-year-old former chauffeur. The words flowed—France would neither disarm, nor pay the Americans, nor lend her remaining gold reserves, nor, it seemed, forgive or forget an invasion in 1914 for which reparations—the currency of atonement—had slowed to a trickle. Wilson's English and Hoover's German blood showed in their sympathies; now Germany had many more men under arms than France, most of them camouflaged in paramilitary political groups, including those of Hitler, a straw man for the Hohenzollerns. Théophile had not forgotten Kaiser Wilhelm, the gunboat he had sent to Agadir in 1911, the ruined cities and villages of 1918, the Rhine that France had evacuated so early in 1930, the peace benefit it never reaped. He resented America, distrusted Britain, feared Germany. His emotions, Knickerbocker thought, were the stuff of national policy.[27]

Not quite—necessity had its word as well. France no longer had the military, financial, or diplomatic means to impose its will or pursue a grand vision. The vexations and the apprehensions of a Théophile pointed the same way—to the irresolute ways of the 1930s, averse to risk, passive, apprehensive, and still looking to Britain.

Britain, on Armistice Day, escaped the political acrimony that rudely disrupted the scene across the Channel. Here and there isolated Communists contrived to shatter the two minutes of silence. In Sunderland cries of "Down with the National Government and up with the workers' republic" rang out, to the indignation of the crowd. In Newcastle an aspiring orator clambered onto the public drinking fountain as the silence began. Police quickly took them all away. In Edinburgh, where several hundred members of the National Unemployed Workers' Movement gathered, constables removed a speaker and one of his supporters, and forced them to stand hatless as soon as the field gun sounded. When it sounded again, two minutes later, they resumed their march to the local jail.[28]

These were distressed areas, where collieries, steel mills, and shipyards lay idle. But political strife of the Continental variety, or of the kind that had so frightened the middle classes during the general strike six years earlier, rarely troubled governance now. On Albion Square in Salford, a church canon, standing beside the mayor's chaplain, lamented "the war clouds that do not roll away" and "that worse enemy than that which we fought in the war, unemployment, the killer of body and of soul."[29] No one found the allusion to the politics of the day, to disarmament or the Depression, exploitative of a sacred memory, destructive of a national communion. Sometimes foreign journalists or diplomats found the ideological calm unsettling. Exaggerating freely, a German correspondent claimed in late October that the victory of the hundred-to-one horse, Pullover, at the Cambridgeshire Handicap at Newmarket excited public opinion more than the two thousand hunger marchers converging on Hyde Park the same day. This was not true. They resented, he reported as well, the foreigners who seized on every tremor of discontent to foretell upheaval and undermine the country's currency, and in this at least he had shed hyperbole. A year earlier many of the editorials had blamed foreign

mischief for the crisis that had forced the country off the gold standard. Good riddance, some of the editorials ran, to the speculators
who had drained the reserves, the foreign tongues that had talked up
the minor mutiny among the sailors at Invergordon and panicked the
investors; welcome to British civic pride, to belt tightening and self-
sufficiency. A "bankers' ramp," or international swindle, to the *Daily
Herald* on the left, an unprovoked assault from abroad to the *Financial Times* on the right—in major crises the political actors turned not
on each other but on the foreigner. And in lesser ones as well: if the
German journalist was to be believed, his British hosts were blaming
the weakening pound on the unseemly attention that he and others of
his ilk were paying to the thousands now filling up Hyde Park. Hunger marches, the *Observer* declared, as though in confirmation, were a
foreign import, a "stunt" that conveyed misimpressions abroad—after
all, the men had only to march to the nearest relief office.[30]

The financial crisis of the summer of 1931 had precipitated a national government, ostensibly a coalition under the Labour apostate
James Ramsay MacDonald, in reality a form of one-party rule, perpetuated by the massive Conservative majority returned in October with
the "Doctor's Mandate" it had requested of the voters. The French
ambassador complained of ambient apathy. He found no ideas, no
doctrines, no controversy—a Gallic or Cartesian lament in a land of
empiricists, betraying no hint of envy. The new government bored the
Parliament and the country, he found in May 1932, six months into its
tenure; a conscientious administrator, it avoided grand ideas like the
plague; no minister explained any doctrine because none could agree
on one, making for a vague, monotonous, and depressing cabinet. In
December he found the mass of the population indifferent to politics.
The government no longer basked in the prestige of its early days,
when it had relished the allure of the savior, but for now no opposition
could rouse the House or stir the country. There people cared little
about the world's problems, he concluded harshly and sweepingly,
unless, like the war debts to America, they imagined some material
impact on themselves.[31]

The government needed no doctrines. It had stumbled almost accidentally on a recipe for economic recovery—protective tariffs and cheap money—which few of its members would have endorsed when the financial crisis threw them together in August 1931. Then they thought to save the country and the currency with the orthodox medicine of deflation and austerity; none countenanced devaluation and a floating or managed currency, few openly espoused protection, and some among the Liberals still preached doctrinaire free trade. Instead they abandoned gold in extremis and devalued the pound within a month; the chancellor of the exchequer, Neville Chamberlain, introduced import duties in February and imperial preference in trade at Ottawa in August. For the rest of the decade, Britain, abjuring its nearly centennial devotion to free trade and the international gold standard alike, withdrew into a preferential sterling zone and enjoyed a bank rate at home that rarely rose above 2 percent. Conceived and pursued pragmatically, such measures still left the unemployed on a pittance, foreign producers cut off from British markets, and the imperium of the City bankers straitened.[32] They left empty warehouses by the Liverpool docks, old cotton mills up for auction in Lancashire, their owners picking up cigarette ends in the street, and silent rusting shipyards and broken-down pitmen's cottages around Newcastle upon Tyne. But they benefitted such a wide range of others that the national government could safely ignore embittered pleas to change them. Then and later economists argued over their relevance to a recovery that some saw as cyclical, but in large parts of the country, in the south especially, recovery came, visible in new chromium-plated factories of glass and concrete, rows of semidetached villas in stockbroker Tudor, and glittering picture palaces.[33]

Looking back on the interwar years a decade later, the Oxford historian E. L. Woodward recalled the same intellectual bankruptcy in political life that the French ambassador had diagnosed at the time. Men returning like himself from the war in 1918 counted for little in politics after it; everything went on as before, he thought, conducted by dated, humdrum figures offering little to choose between the socialism of the one and the conservatism of the other, and personified in the ailing leader of the national government, MacDonald, who abandoned one for the other in all but name.[34]

Perhaps; but a dominant consensus was beginning to take hold in 1932, recognizable as moderate conservatism, and boasting an intellectual pedigree as old as Edmund Burke—allergic though it was to some grand doctrinal system that might capsize its crowded vessel. Coming on the heels of a failed Labour government, it breathed hostility to socialism and all that it might mean, including threats to property and privacy, and even to organized religion. The celebration of native political culture and its aversion to universalisms allowed for compromise and expedients and easily withstood the declining incidence of social strife. "Buy British," the posters urged. "With What? The dole?" some of the first hunger marchers had scrawled onto them. But the young national government and its antique ministers enjoyed the broad support of the press, apart from the Labourite *Daily Herald* and the Liberal *Manchester Guardian*, and in spite of some Conservative muttering about the enforced cohabitation with yesterday's antichrist—the *Morning Post* at first referred to MacDonald as the "titular" prime minister. The paper carped with clairvoyance: inexorably, as MacDonald receded into cloudy, infrequent, and increasingly unintelligible speeches, the personality of the government, and the popular mood it entertained, emerged instead through the reassuring figure of the Conservative leader and president of the board of trade, the former prime minister Stanley Baldwin.[35]

He owed his success in the country to his image—that of a blunt, trustworthy, simple man, who spoke to his public in a mellow voice, as though from man to man, shunning oratorical affect and somehow turning arcane into vernacular idiom. "Good old Baldwin!" came the cordial cries as he took his morning walk down Whitehall or across Saint James's Park, ironically, for his growing authority within the House of Commons rested not on plain speaking but on the elevation of ambiguity into an art form, or of inveterate hesitancy into political moderation. Critics accused him of drift and worse—of passivity and an ostrichlike evasiveness, of "intervening as a rule only to declare his boredom with politics and his anxiety for retirement." Such aspersions, often cast in hindsight and with an interested malice, ignored his hankering for the middle way that embraced as many of his compatriots as possible, his pragmatism, and his deep aversion to intoxicating and transitory ideologies. When he had told a Welsh audience in 1927 that "men who deny their national spiritual heritage in exchange for a vague and watery cosmopolitanism become less than men" he might have posed as Burke himself. He aspired to hold not only the governing coalition but the entire country together with his genre of consensual common sense, expressed in the compromises he habitually sought to any dilemma before him—to free trade or protection, defense spending or disarmament, the dole, unions, the preservation of the empire, and Britain's relations with the rest of the world. More than anyone, he was the man of the moment.[36]

Arriving for the first time in 1932, a French journalist found Londoners indifferent to the intermittent and garbled news that reached them from the Continent. They were more easily aroused by the hieroglyphics of cricket scores, he complained, as though to echo his ambassador. "Germany was beginning to stir, and the *Morning Post* wrote an exquisite leader on the flower show"—but he too verged on caricature. News from the Continent did not regularly crowd the columns of the daily and weekly press, and left readers unruffled when it did, but leaders and opinion pieces about international affairs poured into print as often and as earnestly as anywhere across the Channel. War and peace alone gave rise to the impassioned pleas and quixotic or chimerical visions so wanting in the palaver of domestic disputes.[37]

"The pre-war generation is a generation of failures," a reverend in north Wales wrote to the secretary-general of the League of Nations in February 1932, "and if they do not wipe away the awful crime of the Great War . . . then the sooner they clear out . . . the better for us all." He was thirty-four, had served throughout the war, and now joined other volunteers for the "Peace Army" proposing to interpose themselves between Japanese and Chinese troops in East Asia.

Another joined to atone for the folly of having enlisted in the "War Army" all those years ago. Behind the agitation for peace seethed the anger at the war, an evil presence that every activist, from luminary to commoner, hoped to banish from the earth. The memory of August 1914 drove them—drove Viscount Robert Cecil, a leading proponent of disarmament and president of the 400,000-strong League of Nations Union, to devote himself to ridding the world of the fetish of the balance of power and of international anarchy, drove the Peace Army volunteers to imagine themselves standing in no man's land between trenches, as though the western front had emerged again on the Manchurian plains, and drove the signatories of mass petitions to reclaim the cause of peace from the "cold wisdom of this world." The friends and foes of disarmament, of the League and collective security, of France or Germany, argued as though haunted by 1914 and the imminent danger of its recurrence. That crisis had taken them unawares, the archbishop of Canterbury told parishioners in Kent as Armistice Day neared in 1932, but now they knew the omens, beheld the arms and fears and suspicions, and he placed on them "a great duty . . . to pray that another war may be avoided."[38]

Sentiment was united, but opinion was divided. Early in November, as France and Britain prepared to bring new disarmament proposals to Geneva, *The Times* plausibly claimed to voice the unimpeachable aspirations of the entire country—to avoid a new arms race, to abrogate Versailles and grant Germany equality in armaments, not by rearming it but by disarming the others down to its level, to redress—but never by force—the territorial grievances left by the war and the treaties that ended it. The country, the paper of the establishment had said a month earlier, sought the final reconciliation between the victors and the vanquished.[39] Amen; but how? No single prescription commanded national assent, and the polemics that any one of them set off exposed the animosities that pacifism concealed. In France the fault lines ran between those wanting more concessions to Germany and those wanting less. In Britain they proliferated, in a maze of precepts and presumptions.

Already talk in the newspapers of revising Versailles confirmed the worst fears among the French, dismissed by much of the Conservative press as retrograde and Germanophobic—"The public of this country," wrote the editor of the *Observer*, "is determined that faith shall be kept with Germany." Others preferred to speak for themselves. Papen and Schleicher, the *Manchester Guardian* concluded—accurately—wanted rearmament, nothing but rearmament, and the right not to arms equality but to superiority over its neighbors, and *The Times* conceded that militarist agitation in Germany was now undermining popular faith in the purity of German intentions. For ten years, British opinion had clung to the hope that the path to peace ran through German rehabilitation. Now the first doubts began to appear.[40]

And who should jettison which weapons? No one could agree. In November the British government was contemplating the general abolition of military aviation, to the alarm of the service ministers, some Conservative backbenchers in the House of Commons, and part of the press, including the Conservative *Daily Telegraph*. At the end of the month the *Daily Herald*, Labourite and partly owned by the Trades Union Congress, denounced a militarist plot, led by Winston Churchill within the Commons and the arms industry without, to sabotage any reductions in the fleet or in the air. For its part, the *Daily Express*, Conservative but eager to disabuse the government, paid a visit to the Paris air show and found thirty-three French military aircraft on display and only four British. The dreamers at Geneva, the paper suggested, should travel to the show as well. The Liberal press wanted more ships scuttled, planes grounded, guns destroyed, not fewer; the *News Chronicle* approved the government's proposals but wanted it to renounce its battleships as well, along the lines that the Liberal Herbert Samuel, by then out of the government, had proposed. The gesture, he said in October, might save the world.[41]

Peace was a grand idea, but was disarmament? The Conservative *Morning Post* doubted it; it blamed the crisis in the Far East on Chinese military debility, guilty of provoking the Japanese into attacking and the West into defending its hollow sovereignty. And how could the Western nations disarm in the face of a Soviet Union arming itself to the teeth? And while Germany rearmed in secret?[42] Peace knew no greater foe than the pacifist, Mussolini declared in Turin in October, and the *Yorkshire Post* invoked his words to warn readers that pacifists would now plunge Britain into a general war to help China. More often the doubters mustered a familiar species of realism to cool pacifist ardors. Wars caused arms, and not the reverse, and as long as political enmities set one nation against another, each would keep its weapons. Until Germany's eastern borders were restored, both the Conservative *Observer* and the Liberal *News Chronicle* believed, it would keep rearming, secretly or openly. The axiom, which some of the delegates and technical experts in Geneva shared, entailed removing the causes of wars before discarding their instruments—a realists' argument that Cecil rejected as unrealistic.[43] Others objected to conferences in principle. Lord Beaverbrook's mass-circulation *Daily Express*, which treated any European commitment as treasonable, complained that each parley only led to another.[44] The *Morning Post* warned that the ostrichlike ignorance of political realities at Geneva might rearm rather than disarm the world. Most alarming of all was the French fondness for binding arbitration schemes through the League Council that might draw Britain against its will into sanctions or worse against violators of an arms pact. Had not the military understandings with France that Edward Grey had entered into in 1904 drawn the country into a Continental war in 1914? David Lloyd George, one of the most vocal Germanophiles in the country, believed so, and would say so in the first volume of his war memoirs in the new year.[45]

In November matters seemed—not for the first time—to come to a head at Geneva, imposing some clarity on the words that flew at Westminster and in the country. Lucidly and convincingly, Cecil and Churchill expounded their clashing credos about war and peace. Oddly alike in their circumstances, they differed profoundly in their outlook. Both had been born into great families, into the governing class, yet deviated from the path to power with a maverick's obstinacy, scions gone astray. Lord Cecil of Chelwood, a fixture of Geneva, with his aquiline features and gentle manners, "a vulture chasing butterflies," had left the government to devote his life to disarmament and collective security. He had, it was said, one foot in the Middle Ages and the other in the League of Nations. Churchill, descended from the dukes of Marlborough, now out of office, "very brilliant and amusing but not constructive," had considered and abandoned the prospect of a national opposition party and toyed with headstrong press barons, but presented as much danger to the national government as an extinct volcano. He traveled, wrote prolifically, argued, and, still a Conservative member for Epping after the 1931 election, spoke in the House of Commons.[46]

The day after Armistice Day, Cecil spoke to a crowded gathering in the Free Trade Hall in Manchester, organized by the League of Nations Union. The new lord mayor, who introduced him, feared that the world was nearer to war than at any time since the last one, but Cecil spoke soberly. He—who had a hand in the writing of the Covenant in 1919—saw the League as a first step away from the chaos of the prewar and toward organizing peace, no more, no less. Whether armaments caused wars or not left him cold; limiting them hastened cooperation and hindered conflict; and as for Germany, let it have equal arms in principle, but not in order to rearm at will, as its most vocal militarists intermittently threatened. Then and later, Cecil displayed a sense of limits unlikely to inflame his most emotional supporters, but apt to defang his most alarmist critics. "War will go on until nations have resolved not to have war," he would say, but disarmament would increase mutual confidence if it could eliminate the danger of a sudden surprise attack, especially by air—the shadow of 1914 again, cast over the technology of 1932.[47]

"What impresses me most about them," Churchill said of the members of the League of Nations Union, "is their long suffering and inexhaustible gullibility." He was speaking in the Commons eleven days later, on the twenty-third, during the debate on the king's speech to both houses of Parliament. India, war debts to America, the World Economic Conference—all was under review, and he spoke for an hour and twenty minutes; but he spent more time on the dangers of disarmament and the "melancholy scene" at Geneva than on all else combined. Equality of military status for Germany—as though "all these bands of sturdy Teutonic youths, marching along the streets and roads of Germany, with the light in their eyes of desire to suffer for their Fatherland" only wanted equality? They wanted more than that. Every concession made had brought only fresh demands, and with its parliamentary system breaking down, with twice as many men of military age as France, with a lethal mix of territorial demands and latent power, to upend the military balance with equality schemes now was madness. So too was any plan that might bind Britain to act against its own will. By such follies the conferences in Geneva unwittingly undermined Britain's safety. He preferred an armed peace on the Continent protected by France to a war that would erupt between equally matched foes as long as the Polish Corridor, Transylvania, and the rest envenomed the air. Best to resolve those first, but uphold the borders of anxious smaller nations, and not deceive the British people with pious hopes of eternal peace. "Every time one of these plans is launched," he went on, "the poor good people of the League of Nations Union clap their hands with joy. . . . The process is apparently endless, and so is the pathetic applause."[48]

Where did the government stand? On the tenth, Baldwin had spoken in the Commons as well. "The bomber will always get through," he said. He voiced the fears of millions. That was his way and his blessing, he had long believed: "My worst enemy could never say that I do not understand the people of England." But whether to pacify the skies over the people of England by arms accords or to retaliate with bombers of their own—this he did not tell them. The prospect of destruction raining from the air seemed to render war unthinkable, and Arthur Ponsonby, the Labour leader in the House of Lords and a prominent disarmer, wrote to thank him for his speech. Into the new year Baldwin would advocate a convention at Geneva banning bombing. But since, as he acknowledged, no prohibition would hold up once war started, and since towns and cities were indefensible, bombing would provoke counterbombing "to kill more women and children more quickly than the enemy." No conclusion emerged from Baldwin's dark words, Churchill complained, and so did newspapers of different hues. If prohibitions were useless once war broke out, why bother with them at all? It seemed a counsel of despair. Readers wrote in, some to proclaim the speech an endorsement, others a dismissal, of disarmament. No one could be sure.[49]

Buffeted by crosswinds, the government struggled to find a course. Disarmament, the League's most iconic project, was popular, but so was national security. Uneasily the government celebrated both, navigating the thin line between governing and pandering. Its predecessor had behaved no differently. In January, three weeks before the disarmament conference opened, the cabinet had gloomily contemplated the alternatives—cuts unacceptable to others, cuts unacceptable to themselves, or public blame for derailing the proceedings in Geneva.[50] The problem had not changed. But the moment had— Germany had walked out of the disarmament conference and the cabinet could not agree on how to bring it back. MacDonald and Simon, the foreign secretary, feared breakdown at Geneva and a bad press at home; the service chiefs feared improvident proposals to disarm. And many feared new commitments of any kind.[51] At Locarno in 1925 Britain had agreed, along with Italy, to guarantee the Franco-German-Belgian borders against aggression; but it had remained the judge of the obligation, the arbiter of its fate. Behind all the talk about arms, peace, conventions, and safeguards lay the unspoken question about how much further it should go.

About this the Dominions too had a word to say. They weighed on the government as heavily as any claimants at home, and more than some—more than the purists of Old Labour, the forty-six survivors of the electoral massacre in 1931, who at their party conference in October declared their "unqualified hostility to the rearming of any country in any circumstances."[52] No historical grievance, no memories of

Irish dimensions, strained the loyalties of Canada, Australia, New Zealand, or South Africa, where the Boer War had receded in time; no constitutional obstacles stood in the way of concord either, not since the Statute of Westminster in 1931 had confirmed their full legislative independence. And Britain, especially Conservative Britain, looked to its empire for political and strategic cohesion: it could not defend itself or its world position alone.

But access to British markets, and the protection of their own, threatened to come between the Dominions and the mother country, unless it could sacrifice the sensitivities of its European trading partners to their own by bestowing preferential treatment on them. For this Chamberlain and Baldwin had traveled to Ottawa in the summer. For this they had sacrificed not only the goodwill that still lingered on the Continent since leaving the gold standard a year earlier, but also three Liberal ministers and one renegade Labour Lord, who all resigned at the end of September from the national government with several undersecretaries in tow, as though on the funeral pyre of free trade. Imperial cohesion required as well that nothing irreparable estrange Britain from the United States, lest any of the Dominions—Canada in particular—feel compelled to choose between them. It required conversely that nothing irreversible bind Britain to the Continent, lest imperial security suffer in its wake. Beaverbrook—a Canadian—took European pacts to task in his press for that reason. Talk of abolishing bombing or military aviation to break the impasse at Geneva furrowed the brows of service chiefs and some of their counterparts in the Dominions for the same reason. Prudence, if not timidity, reigned as the tutelary virtue over any promises to the Continent: there, at least since Locarno, Britain had sought to restore a balance of power that would spare it from having to choose sides and make even tacit demands on independent Dominions. India was another matter; the nationalist movement there grew regardless of Britain's European quandary. But new commitments on the Continent, even to safeguard a disarmament agreement, might turn a conjecture into a threat, on the subcontinent as in the Dominions: Would they once again fight for Britain in a European war? As a third roundtable conference between British and Indian leaders convened in London in November and the Indian National Congress refused to attend, such existential digressions would hardly strengthen Britain's hand. All this weighed on the national government as it contemplated the deepening turmoil across the Channel.[53]

Above all, do no harm: the coalition that claimed a doctor's mandate would take no risks. It would do nothing to undermine consensus, so novel at home, or cohesion, so uncertain among the Dominions ever since the war. European or East Asian adventurism might endanger both. The government would pursue peace and disarmament by words and gestures, security by exceptions and limitations. It would take one step toward Germany, one toward France, one toward Geneva. To do so it needed a foreign secretary able to thread the needle, to find the right formula and balance the popular with the prudent. In Sir John Simon it found a barrister, a pragmatist, a skilled tactician, a lifelong Liberal but not so doctrinaire as to break ranks with the government over protection—Simon was a realist, his lawyerly closings a strange contrast to MacDonald's increasingly mystical reveries. During the general strike in 1926, as riot swirled about the House, he rose and irrefutably demonstrated its illegality. Between 1927 and 1930 he chaired the Indian Statutory Commission, which traveled the subcontinent pursued by black flags and hostile crowds, proposed provincial representative governments but not Dominion status, amid boycotts, salt marches, civil disobedience, and roundtable conferences. But it was a step. Simon was a reasonable man. Now he turned to the European situation. In the Commons, on the eve of Armistice Day, he subscribed to Germany's right to arm itself as others did, but not to rearm at once; to a goal of general equality in armaments, but not at once either; to Britain's word at Locarno, but not to any new one. At the end of the week he took his balanced suggestions to Geneva. At least he was not going empty-handed.[54]

Baldwin, who acted as prime minister when illness kept Mac-Donald away, had been to Geneva once, for a day in 1921, while on holiday in nearby Aix-les-Bains. He never went again. Neither the League nor its enthusiasts inspired much faith in him. "There is so much I dislike in the Union propaganda," he wrote privately to Austen Chamberlain about an invitation to address the League of Nations Union, "and I should have to steer between the Scylla of cursing them and the Charybdis of mush and poppycock." He was insular to a fault. But he was no xenophobe, no Europhobe, no bored amateur in foreign affairs as his critics put out. To preserve the empire at all costs, including concessions on tariffs to the Dominions and on governance to the Indian national movement, to fight shy not of Europe, which he recognized as impossible—"Our island story is told," he allowed—but of open-ended engagements there, to disarm now if possible and rearm later if necessary—this was a diplomacy of the golden mean, conveniently ambiguous and anything but bold; but was it so out of tune with the country he effectively led? Or with the coalition he ably managed? "I think things are going well in the House," he told a friend early in 1932. "Our fellows will discuss anything which bears directly on the country's condition but are impatient of all else."[55]

Besides, his popularity lay elsewhere, in the country "among the middle multitudes who voted for Baldwin because he was Baldwin," because he promoted social pacification and had concluded a speech on industrial relations in 1925 with the words from the Anglican liturgy, "Give peace in our time, O Lord." That year he told the Swedish ambassador, a friend of his, of his tie to the English people. "I give expression, in some unaccountable way, to what the English people think. For some reason," he added with a characteristic blend of confidence and modesty, "that appeals to me and gives me strength." And when he left office in 1937, he did so as the most respected statesman in the land.[56]

For all their political and intellectual differences, Herriot and Baldwin resembled each other—each was a solid and affable provincial, a stocky, pipe-smoking personification of landed sanity, even though neither hailed from the farm, a persuasive speaker and an avid reader of the classics, a companion if not a mover of men. In office the past weighed on each of them. Without ever saying so, each wanted to return—Baldwin to a prewar "long summer afternoon of industry and empire," Herriot to a system in which his country was anchored among other great powers against the most unruly one in their midst, and could pursue its republican mission untroubled by persistent rumors of invasion. Neither conceived of any brave new world. Under the circumstances, it was mentally impossible.

7

WARSAW AND BUDAPEST

November 1932

The statue of Joseph Poniatowski stood in the heart of Warsaw, on what had once been Saxon Square. The prince had defended the city against the Russians during Tadeusz Kosciuszko's uprising in 1794, the last vain attempt to stave off the final partition and Poland's disappearance from the map of Europe. Then he had fought with Napoleon in Russia and died, a marshal of France, at the Battle of the Nations at Leipzig in 1813. On the eleventh of November 1932, the troops circled his statue and marched past the Tomb of the Unknown Soldier, under the eyes of Marshal Joseph Pilsudski, head of state in all but name. The event once again linked him to Poniatowski, Kosciuszko, and the insurrectionary tradition. He had relived it with his underground struggles against Tsarist rule before 1914, the legions he raised when war came in 1914, and the independence he claimed as it ended in 1918; he had crowned it with resurrection, *Polonia Restituta*.[1]

On Saxon Square they were not commemorating the armistice on the western front, on the eleventh hour of the eleventh day of the eleventh month, at all. In fact, the ceremonies had begun the evening before, when long processions of the faithful had converged on the Belvedere Palace, where Pilsudski lived and where he emerged under the portico to greet them, looking as always like an old wolf of the eastern forests, with his gray cloak and grizzled countenance. The prewar droop of the mustache, by contrast, and the fierce gaze recalled Vercingetorix, or perhaps some seaborne Norse raider. In 1917 the Germans had imprisoned him in the Magdeburg fortress when he had refused to lend them his legions. His captors had occupied all of Russian Poland in addition to their own, and were proposing a spurious independence, a sovereignty on sufferance of no interest to him. When he returned on the tenth of November 1918, amid chaos and urban risings, he began asserting some semblance of political control, enough that day and the next to lay the specter of anarchy, disarm the German garrison, and present his compatriots and the world with a fait accompli. The Western Allies were friendly to Polish independence but had not expected it so soon or so suddenly. Around him, by 1932, a cult had grown up. Saxon Square had been renamed after him four years earlier. The parades, speeches, religious services, the songs and emblems and crowned white eagles on the tenth and the eleventh celebrated not only the rebirth of the nation as a sovereign republic, but Joseph Pilsudski as the savior of the first and the demiurge of the second.[2]

This embittered his opponents and his rivals. Whenever this anniversary—still not a national holiday—came around, some of the most prominent among them put the country in mind of their own roles in 1918, ones they accused the cult of Pilsudski, among its other misdeeds, of energetically ignoring. That year the Western Allies were drawing maps and charting the future of Europe, and in Paris the Polish National Committee and in Washington Ignacy Paderewski, the celebrated pianist, had patiently secured a seat at the table. They had secured for Poland a place in the victorious coalition and for its rebirth the thirteenth of Wilson's fourteen points. How now could they watch in silence as glory transfigured a self-trained general released from a comfortable captivity and his disbanded legions? Especially when the disarming of the German garrison in Warsaw had begun even before Pilsudski's return, by patriots often indifferent to him? But above all, they stressed in their press, their own work had ensured that the Western armistice would work for Poland. In January, one of their leading members, General Wladyslaw Sikorski, had published an anti-German screed in the French *Revue des Deux Mondes* and pithily described the events of 1918. "With the arrival of M. Paderewski in Poznan on 27 December 1918," he wrote, "the insurrection that would liberate Greater Poland broke out." He made no mention of Pilsudski.[3]

This gave the marshal's followers their opening. "What happens within Poland does not matter," they accused their critics of believing about the events of November 11, 1918, "because in their eyes only the events in the West count." It was two days after the commemorations in 1932, and the semiofficial *Gazeta Polska* was defending the anniversary. It honored, Pilsudski's loyalists continued, the expulsion of the last of the occupiers, the Germans, by the sword; his foes dishonored it as the manipulation of an alien victory thanks to their ink, chatter, and guile in Western capitals.[4]

Both were right and wrong; the rebirth in November 1918 required both an Entente victory and domestic initiatives, however fragile. Other anniversaries remained possible as national days, including the third of May in honor of the liberal constitution of 1791, another vain attempt to place the old kingdom on a sounder footing before its neighbors finished devouring it, and the seventh of November, to mark the 1918 rising in Lublin by the Socialists, who regarded Pilsudski as one of their own but whose sectarian enthusiasm by then only embarrassed him. Polish Soldiers' Day in August was another, to remember the counterattack in 1920 when Polish forces under Pilsudski's command had routed the Soviets at the gates of Warsaw and begun their expulsion from the country. Consensual enough, the celebration stopped short of Pilsudski's paternity of the victory, much exaggerated in the eyes of his detractors. In the end November 11 set in as the semiofficial national holiday, and became an official one in 1937, two years after Pilsudski died and two years before the Polish state disappeared yet again. The calendar had suggested almost as many candidates for the day as there were political families in Poland, but a date per se did not matter. Behind the polemic over the anniversary lay a deeper question, about the identity of Poland itself.[5]

It began with the past. For part of the 1920s, Saxon Square had played home to a heap of rubble, all that was left of the five bulbous cupolas and the belfry and minaret of Alexander Nevsky Cathedral. The Russians had consecrated it there just before the war. With its gold and enamel, superb mosaics, and immense frescoes, the Orthodox *sobor* had injected a mix of the Byzantine and the modern into the heart of the Poles' Catholic capital. They had torn it down. And they had removed every ornament, every Muscovite vestige from the walls and doorways of the city. Everywhere in postwar Poland, cultural conflict had written its history on the face of public architecture. Everywhere facades and streets bore the traces of rivalry between the alien and the native, Russian domes and Polish spires, or between a recent and a remote past—the scars left by rival claims to the territory, to the land and its dead. *We were here before you*, the claims usually ran, announcing themselves, when they could, by building, naming, or destroying.[6]

In Katowice, the capital of Upper Silesia in southwestern Poland, the station, building facades, and well-paved roads embodied the German presence since 1740, when Frederick the Great had seized the province. But beyond the city center, in the suburbs and the "black country" of the mining centers, the people, like their place-names, were Polish. They had voted in a complicated plebiscite in 1921 to become so by law, after Polish insurgents had occupied the region, and now the burghers of Katowice held on as a prosperous minority in their midst. The Poles read *Polonia*, they read the *Kattowitzer Zeitung*, which was pan-Germanist and often censored. Peopled by Germanic tribes before the sixth century, then by Slavs, subject to the kings of Poland in the tenth, then fought over between them, Czechs, Austrians, and finally Prussians, Upper Silesia was a major loss to the Germans after Versailles; they had made of it a miniature Ruhr in the east, with a million people, coal, zinc, and iron ore mines, steel factories, and a maze of rail and tram lines. Neither the Czechs nor the Austrians had tried to eradicate Polish culture from the region, but the Prussians had, during their 175 years there, and now the border, a stone's throw away, confronted the memory of Germanization with the ambition of Polonization.[7]

Across it lay the parcel of the province that plebiscites and arbitration by the League of Nations had left Germany. The local Silesians led the struggle for their "severed compatriots in the Polish state" by espousing rightist nationalism or, more quietly, by preserving their own cultural heritage. In Beuthen, where some dwellings opened at the front to Germany and at the back to Poland, a museum opened in early November 1932, mobilizing documents, artifacts, art, and history to convey the Germanic identity of the divided province. The Oberschlesischen Landesmuseum did not deny the place its distant Polish past, but insisted on the more urgent call of the living present. In Katowice across the border the Poles had opened their own Silesian Museum to demonstrate the opposite, and, in the immoderate fears of even the liberal German press, "influence world opinion in favor of further Polish advances beyond their western borders."[8]

In Poznan to the northwest, German streets and architecture called up the late dominance of a German upper class and the relegation to the shadows of an irredentist Polish aristocracy. Kaiser Wilhelm II had left a colossal neo-Roman castle, with a massive keep that rose eighty meters into the air, and, in the imperial hall, two thrones resting on elephants. A sixteenth-century town hall, its loggias and towers betraying the accents of the Italian Renaissance, had come the Prussians' way after the partitions of the late eighteenth century. Around 1900 they blackened the outer facade and its frescoes depicting medieval Polish kings. They struck at other subversive threats as well, and forbade Poles from owning or erecting buildings, putting on plays, teaching the catechism in their language; and they sent Polish government employees far away, to the Rhineland on the other side of the Reich. Now the entire population of the city was Polish, and as fiercely Germanophobic as any in the country or perhaps in Europe.[9]

To the north of Poznania, in Pomerania, ran the narrow Polish province of Pomerelia, separating Germany on one side from the now-orphaned German province of East Prussia on the other. Here no plebiscite had sounded local sentiment, reflecting Wilson's wish to grant Poland its access to the sea, its "Corridor," and to right the wrong of the partitions. Most of the Germans had vanished almost overnight. A migratory horde of half a million officials, workers, and middle-class professionals, swelled by expropriations and other encouragements, had deserted the eastern marches of the old Reich. In their place, rejoining their newly enfranchised compatriots, had come an even larger influx of Poles from the mines of Westphalia and the turmoil of the east. Bromberg became Bydgoszcz, Thorn became Torun, and the ethnic topography of the land shifted once again: Slavs and Teutons had turned it too into a battleground for almost a thousand years.

But at the tip of Pomerelia, at the mouth of the Vistula River, the Free City of Danzig was all German. Its bright mercantile town houses and northern Gothic halls recalled the halcyon days of the other Hanseatic ports around the North Sea and the Baltic, Dutch or Flemish or Scandinavian, but its 250,000 inhabitants spoke German and lost no chance to proclaim their affinities. When the Red Army had reached Warsaw and the Vistula in the summer of 1920, the dockers had folded their arms rather than unload weapons and munitions destined for the beleaguered Poles. The police donned the uniforms of the German *Schupos*; the senators chose as their president—a sort of head of state and foreign minister in one—the director of the German police in Warsaw during the wartime occupation of the city. Danzigers excluded Poles from citizenship, and dismissed inefficiency or slovenliness, an inferior restaurant or a failing company, as *"polnische Wirtschaft"*—Polish shambles. To little avail, the Poles insisted that Slavic vassals of Polish dukes had founded the port in the tenth century, and only lost it for the first time to marauding Teutonic knights early in the fourteenth. Then they had regained it in the fifteenth, only to lose it along with Pomerelia and much else to Prussia in the second partition in the eighteenth. Now the Danzigers bitterly resented their detachment from the German Reich, and the bizarre, almost medieval status that Versailles and the League had conferred on their city in this age of the nation-state—free, subject neither to the German nor the Polish republic, but included within the Polish customs union and so bound to its economy. The solution satisfied no one.[10]

As though to dramatize the point, a rival port appeared: almost within sight of the architectural charms of old Danzig, the silos, elevators, and cranes of an artificial harbor rose into view. Backed by wooded hills and sheltered from the northern winds by the Hel Peninsula that jutted into the sea, Gdynia had become, by 1932, Poland's port of choice on the Baltic. Once a fishing village of 200, now a commercial hub of 45,000, it threatened Danzig with commercial obsolescence and even strangulation, much to the satisfaction of its Polish master builders. They had not forgotten 1920—they had no wish, in the event of another emergency, to rely on the kindness of the Danzigers for their supplies, still less for the leeward requirements of an infant navy. National sentiment precluded what economic logic dictated—a shared and already functional port, served by land and sea routes open to all. The tonnage moving through Danzig stagnated while that in Gdynia rose, adding a commercial to an ethnic and even a military grievance: the presence of a Polish munitions depot on the Westerplatte, a small peninsula within the harbor channel on the Vistula estuary, enraged the Danzigers and added to the woes of an already inundated League of Nations high commissioner.[11]

In the east, from Wilno to Lwów, the past still poisoned the present as much as it did from Katowice to Danzig. Around Wilno, to the northeast, the country resembled a war zone—unsurprisingly, because for the 1920s the Lithuanian government in Kaunas, unlike that in Berlin, had believed itself at war with its counterpart in Warsaw, and by the next decade the two had still not restored diplomatic or consular relations. It claimed Wilno, which the Poles had seized and annexed in 1920, as its capital, and objected vehemently to Polish recollections of the distant but prosperous union of the two peoples under the Jagiellonian dynasty, to the Polonization of their own Vilnius, whatever its predominantly Polish and Jewish, or non-Lithuanian, population, whatever the linguistic evidence of its shop signs and tombstones. Did the Poles not invoke the Virgin there as *Regina Poloniae*? Twenty kilometers away, the Lithuanian border was hermetically sealed. The rail line between Wilno and Kaunas was cut, and travel between the two countries—which did not in any case grant each other visas— required an absurd and laborious detour through Germany or Latvia. Far to the southeast Lwów still bore the traces of the fighting in 1919, when the city's Poles had fought, as they saw it, to keep it Polish, and its Ukrainians or Ruthenians to win its independence. The hostilities still spoke on leprous walls, scarred by the fusillades of that chaotic year. Once Polish kings had ruled all Ukraine. Now its eastern reaches were Soviet, but much of Galicia, with its three million Ukrainians, provided yet another province, yet another minority, in the resurrected Poland—a restive minority, roiled by separatists who now and again assassinated police officials, burned down buildings, attacked tax and post offices.[12]

So many minorities—German, Ukrainian, Byelorussian, Jewish, among others—coexisted within Poland that only two-thirds of the population considered itself Polish.[13] All had their own papers, local associations, and deputies in the Polish Parliament, and a degree of local autonomy. But they posed uncertain threats to the unity of the struggling nation. The three million Jews, varied and unevenly concentrated, posed none at all, even though relations with anti-Semitic neighbors were deteriorating swiftly in many distressed towns and cities in the 1930s. Others, incited or exploited by national patrons abroad, threatened not only the coherence but the survival of the state. The Soviets and the Czechs encouraged the Ukrainians, but the Germans, even though not the most numerous, posed the greatest existential danger, thanks to the potent brew of memory and politics in the neighboring Reich. On its own the German Volksbund merely agitated for local autonomy, especially around Katowice.[14] But in concert with greater Germany it acquired a new and more menacing mask. Not only did German papers and politicians vow never to forget their compatriots languishing under Polish rule in the most prosperous part of the country, the part they had ruled for 130 years. Many, especially on the right, condemned the accursed Polish state itself.

In 1931 General Hans von Seeckt, a nationalist deputy in the German Reichstag, declared in speech and in print that the existence of Poland—an "artificial" state—was unacceptable to Germany and the Soviet Union alike. Poland harbored designs on German territory, he believed, and was in any case intrinsically, unalterably hostile; any rapprochement, even economic, was unthinkable. Seeckt was no mere deputy. As commander in chief of the postwar German army, the Reichswehr, until 1926, he had created the core of the future German military machine, envisaging its use against the country's most proximate neighbors. Seeckt enjoyed a following. That year and the next, his slender and Polonophobic pamphlet, *Paths in German Foreign Policy*, found ample echoes in the four weighty volumes of memoirs of Prince Bernhard von Bülow, the imperial German chancellor between 1900 and 1909. In them he recalled his warning to the kaiser never to restore Poland, and he castigated his successor, Theobald von Bethmann-Hollweg, for doing so: "Next to the extravagant ultimatum to Serbia," he declared, alluding to the Austrian ultimatum in July 1914 that Germany had encouraged, "the restoration of Poland is the gravest blunder in our history"—this indeed distinguished it. The sentiment flourished on the German right. Alfred Hugenberg, the press magnate and founder and leader of the nationalist German National People's Party, had devoted his prewar and wartime energies to colonizing the eastern borderlands, and openly regarded the Poles as an inferior race, incapable of governing the land they occupied. Not everyone shared such views or welcomed such vitriolic candor; commercial milieus and two of the most important political families of the Weimar Republic, the Socialists and the Catholic Center Party, did not. But the Nazis did, enthusiastically. In their papers they claimed not just Upper Silesia and the Corridor, but the entire province of Poznan, their Posen, which was overwhelmingly Polish. In the spring of 1932, the brown-shirted SAs, briefly banned in Germany, marched in force and sang lustily in the streets of Danzig. Seeckt, Bülow, and Hugenberg were aging contemporaries, figures who had reached adulthood under the empire; but the Nazis were young, with the wind at their backs.[15]

Nowhere was the German belief in Polish aggressive designs stronger than in East Prussia, now severed from West Prussia by the Polish Corridor. The Reich had sustained the province with infusions of capital and people, but, half-surrounded as it was by protectionist Poland, its commerce had suffered. The great harbor of Königsberg had become as quiet as a churchyard, its citadel disarmed, its wharves deserted. An obsolete social order, resting on backward and inefficient landed estates, still turned the face of the Junker to the world, including the bewhiskered jowls of old Marshal Hindenburg, the president of the republic himself. Perhaps such semifeudal remnants needed a Polish threat to justify their preeminence; the borders, closed to trade, still seemed open to invasion. None came, but that did not matter.[16]

From the spring of 1932, with a mounting hue and cry, papers and parties in the province stoked fears of an invasion. The *Königsberger Allgemeine Zeitung* ran a regular page, "Defense and Homeland," instructing readers in the dangers at hand; authorities organized gas drills in towns and villages, with inhabitants taking refuge in assigned shelters as planes circled overhead; the press warned of imminent attacks, there and in Danzig as well. Early in May, warnings of ACHTUNG! appeared on billboards all over the province. They advertised a newly published cautionary account of a Polish invasion in all its villainous particulars. These did not materialize, but the author of the literary fantasy, one Lieutenant Hans Martin of the Reichswehr, a.k.a. "Nitram," claimed possession of "irrefutable documents," and his book, initially serialized in the East Prussian papers, quickly sold six thousand copies. Rumors spread that Polish soldiers disguised as civilians were spreading through the border villages. Frightened readers withdrew their savings and sent valuables to Germany for safekeeping. At length, but without any official disavowals, police took down the advertisements. All this delighted the Nazis, authors of much of the propaganda, artisans of much of the hysteria. They did well in East Prussia in the successive elections of 1932, especially among voters close to the Polish border, those most susceptible to panic and to the untiring canard that the Weimar government would do little to save them, in the very part of the province where an invading Russian army had met doom, in August 1914. Showing scant regard for toponymy but much for cultural revenge, Hindenburg, the German commander, had named the victory of Teuton over Slav after Tannenberg, the adjacent site of a decisive Teutonic defeat by Poles and Lithuanians some five centuries earlier.[17]

More lucidly than the Poles themselves, but to little avail, the liberals, centrists, and Socialists in the Reich disparaged such angst. The Polish general staff had built a railroad along the East Prussian border, and had made contingency plans to invade in the event of war? It would be surprising if it had not. Besides, just when Poland needed recognition of its borders, it had nothing to gain by violating the postwar settlements and affronting the League of Nations. Polish immigrants were colonizing East Prussia? The statistics showed the opposite; Germans, patronized by an Ostpreussische Landgesellschaft in Berlin, had come and Poles had gone—in a province of about two million there were only ten thousand of them, and perhaps a few thousand more seasonal laborers. Poland was plotting a commercial union with the province? It lacked the means to make it work.[18] The Socialist *Vorwärts* denounced the campaign to incite Germans against Poles; the Catholic Center *Germania* warned the German press against tendentious reports from the east; the liberal *Vossische Zeitung* deplored Hitler's "panic propaganda" in the East Prussian border zones. By the autumn of 1932 the war fever of the spring had subsided some, but still most of the German population refused to accept the eastern borders, and still almost any Pole, from the street to the government, feared German determination to revise them. "An abyss of aversion, fear, and distrust," concluded the Warsaw correspondent of *Vossische Zeitung*, "seems to stretch between the neighboring states"—and he, in the eyes of the French chargé d'affaires in Berlin, was one of the few German journalists who treated Poland objectively.[19]

Any German talk of a Polish invasion menace echoed that of the Soviets.[20] To Poles, both scenarios inverted the menace; both aroused memories of the partitions and of the forced Germanization and Russification that had followed a century later. This, at least, united the country. On Pilsudski or Saxon Square in midsummer 1932, several months before the November ceremonies there, 25,000 had gathered to protest German nationalism, the violation of Polish rights in Danzig, the incessant provocations; some two hundred professional, political, and religious organizations came. The Warsaw City Council passed a resolution denouncing any attempt to revise the Treaty of Versailles. In Poznan, the day before, 15,000 members of the Polish Riflemen's Association from all over the country rallied to proclaim the inviolability of frontiers. A few hotheads went off the rails—in July the former Polish consul in Königsberg called for the freeing of East Prussia—and provided much grist for the German nationalists' mill. Most Poles ignored them. But all rejected any modifications in the existing borders, especially in the Corridor, at the country's expense. To concede even a parcel of land would open the country to fragmentation and, sooner or later, disappearance from the political map. They would concede transit or customs or other rights to Germans in the Corridor, General Douglas MacArthur, the US Army chief of staff, concluded after a visit in October of 1932, but not the Corridor itself: they would rather die, he added, than part with it.[21]

There the unity ended. Did national survival require a multiethnic or an assimilationist ethos, a German or a Soviet tilt, a western or an eastern orientation? These were existential questions, and they pierced the war of words over the choice of a national holiday and Pilsudski's place within it. When the National Democrats insisted that the efforts of Roman Dmowski, their leader, and the Polish National Committee at Paris and Versailles had mattered more in 1918 than Pilsudski's return from the Magdeburg fortress, they were not merely harping on a historical quibble. From their bastion in Poznania and western Poland sprang an irreducible hostility to Germany and a Catholic, ethnically homogeneous vision of Poland. This made Poland's east into a land ripe for colonization and the Jews into an unassimilable minority. Pilsudski, a child of the Lithuanian borderlands, a bearer of the memory of the joint kingdom, shared with his followers a visceral distrust of Russian or Soviet designs and a multinational and vaguely federal vision of the resurrected state. His grand scheme of 1919 and 1920—a brotherhood, somehow dependent on Poland, of newly independent Lithuanian, Byelorussian, and Ukrainian states around the Soviet Union—ended in failure and nearly in national disaster. But his wartime legions somehow provided the model—supranational, egalitarian, incorruptible—for the postwar state, and beside Dmowski's organic and rightist vision, his own promised, even if it could not deliver, a more secular, ethnically federated polity, a commonwealth rather than a republic.

The National Democrats with their Germanophobia naturally made the Western powers and France in particular the anchor of Polish security, the salutary counterweight to Germany, renewing a long tradition of Franco-Polish alliances. Pilsudski and his followers worried about the German but concentrated on the Soviet threat; they wished daily to contain it, whatever the diplomatic or military means needed to do so. They saw little sacred about the French alliance, useful as it was. For now, neither Germany nor the Soviet Union planned to invade, mostly because neither was in any position to do so; but the hypothesis still posed the confining quandary of Polish policy, and by the autumn of 1932 a turning point was approaching.[22]

Pilsudski held power. He held it unconstitutionally, the tainted prize from his coup of 1926, and he exercised it remotely. He was a patriot, a romantic figure, a leader of men; but a democrat he was not. "You are a parliament of rogues," he had told the deputies in the Sejm from the podium, not even disguising his contempt for them and their parties. Unlike Mussolini, whom he disdained, he had no doctrine;

no one, least of all he, could define "Pilsudskism." His followers, who
hated the term "dictatorship," had gathered themselves into an amor-
phous nonparty bloc, the Sanacja, hanging not by the moral regeneration they promised the nation but by him and his prestige. His
legal opponents, from the Socialist left to the National Democrats, the
Endecja, spoke out, often and loudly, but wielded no effective power
as long as he lived. Pilsudski governed in the shadows, by mystery;
he revealed his plans to no one, spent little time in the open, left his
closest entourage as poorly informed as his widest public. He acted
by intermediaries, an occult and unpredictable force. So it was with
foreign policy.[23]

He had formed his political persona underground and in war,
practicing the arts of tactics and ruses, of strokes and counterstrokes.
He was an opportunist. And Poland was surrounded by enemies. The
French alliance of 1921 for him was an instrument, of variable utility,
that he had inherited from his predecessors. At Locarno, in 1925, a
separate bilateral treaty committed France to come to the aid of Poland if Germany attacked, but the arrangement was contingent and set
within a League framework. This Pilsudski disliked, as much as the
multilateral Locarno treaty itself, which did nothing to guarantee Poland's borders. Stresemann, one of its architects, had never accepted
them. Every French concession to Germany or British nod at talk of
revising the frontiers, every rumor afloat in Geneva about German
rearmament, raised questions about the ultimate value of collective
security and the Western powers to Poland. By 1932 Pilsudski had
come to doubt the staying power of the League-based French system
and the security it offered his country, enough not to jettison it but to
cast glances elsewhere.[24]

Throughout 1932 he found ways to remind France not to take Poland for granted. As much as realpolitik, national pride, the same
that had driven the legionnaire to speak French rather than German
to demonstrate his independence before his Austrian command in
the early years of the war, now drove the diplomacy of the statesman.
In June, authorities in Danzig protested when a Polish destroyer

steamed into the harbor of the free city, ostensibly to greet a small British squadron, in fact to precede the arrival of a German cruiser, much to the annoyance of the French. They reminded their Polish ally that such displays could only fuel revisionist propaganda and might as well endanger sorely needed French financial assistance. Later that year the French withdrew the military mission they had kept in Poland practically since the end of the war and that had crucially helped the Poles repel the Soviets in 1920. Pilsudski and his military advisers had by now found it superfluous, even patronizing, and had duly requested its departure. In its place came a new French military attaché, a colonel on the cusp of becoming a general, whom Pilsudski received with great cordiality in October. But he spoke—with the frankness he reserved for other military men and that he habitually withheld from mere civilians—of mounting doubts about French constancy. "Yes, yes, watch out for us!" he exclaimed. "France will abandon us, France will betray us! That is what they're thinking and I owed it to you to tell you."[25]

The theoretical war game that the French general staff had conceived in the autumn of 1932 would not have reassured him, had he only known of it. The scenario supposed that the Germans would attack Poland and the Italians France, and that the Poles would hold out for three or four months on their own while the French waged war in the Alps and the Mediterranean. Meanwhile the Germans would sit tight in the west behind the demilitarized Rhineland and reassure the British and the Belgians that they would respect the Locarno frontiers. The Franco-Polish alliance, in short, would protect the stronger of the two partners and leave the weaker in the lurch.[26]

As though to stress his misgivings, Pilsudski replaced his foreign minister, August Zaleski, a week later. Zaleski had never ceased advancing the convergence and the harmony between French and Polish diplomacy. For six years he had been the voice of the French alliance and of the League, a familiar face at Geneva; he had revered Briand, who had died in March. Now, in early November, he had sought and secured Poland's reelection to the League Council as a nonpermanent member, only to find that skeptics in the Polish press frowned on such constraining commitments, and that the undersecretary, Colonel Józef Beck, was to succeed him at the head of the Foreign Ministry in Wierzbowa Street.[27]

Beck, more authoritarian and energetic than the temperate Zaleski, and a closer confidant and protégé of the marshal than he, had been filling the Foreign Ministry with his own underlings while his superior was away in Geneva and Paris. His advent signified the possibility rather than the certainty of new departures in Polish foreign policy. Unlike Zaleski, he was no Francophile, a trait that newspapers on the German right immediately welcomed; unlike Pilsudski, he admired Mussolini and his regime, a partiality not missed by the Italian press either, along with his promising coolness to France; and unlike Dmowski and the National Democrats, he might, under the right conditions, countenance a limited rapprochement with Germany. Zaleski's departure, like that of Grandi from the Palazzo Chigi in July, had unmoored his country from the haven of the League, and ensured as well that its foreign policy would henceforth answer to the whims of a single and obstinate leader.[28]

At the end of the month, with minimal fanfare, the Polish government ratified a nonaggression pact with the Soviet Union. The two had already signed it the previous summer. It presented no great surprise to the world, nor any intrinsic threat to France or the French alliance—they were negotiating, at a snail's pace, their own parallel pact with the Soviet Union, and the foreign ministries in Warsaw and Paris had kept each other fully informed of their progress. For its part the Soviet Union was pursuing other such pacts with its western neighbors, and Stalin did not place much store by the Polish one. Yet the moment mattered, more than the fine print. It sent messages. Pilsudski's opportunism not only allowed him to conciliate his perennial foe in the east; it drove him to raise the value and perhaps the price of the Polish alliance to the west whenever the chance arose. In 1932 it did: with the Japanese coming ominously close in the Far East, the Soviets craved tranquility along their western borders rather than the usual antagonisms that festered there. Pilsudski seized the same chance as well to impress and even tame the Germans. And more: Poland could never trust its eastern or its western neighbor. But rather than rely on the French alliance alone for protection against them, why could it not play off when possible one against the other, perhaps balance the two, inimical to each other as they were, with evenhanded inducements or threats, and contemplate a modus vivendi with Germany as long as Poland's borders remained untouched? The political turmoil in the Reich would have to subside, and no one knew when or how that might happen. But Beck fancied such flexible options as well; and, at age thirty-eight, he would outlive the already ailing Pilsudski.[29]

With an economy starved of agricultural export markets, a large but imminently obsolescent army, and an ethnically and politically fragile union, he had a weak hand to play. Each of the country's neighbors, except for Rumania, with which Poland shared a fifty-mile border, was hostile. If war came, Germany risked losing East Prussia, the Soviet Union perhaps some more parcels of the Ukraine; but Poland risked destruction. "There is not a country in Europe with a future so precarious as Poland," wrote the *Manchester Guardian* in mid-November. It was a Liberal paper, one that objected to Polish obduracy over border revision even more than to Pilsudski's illiberal regime itself; yet it understood the stakes. "No one can say that in ten years from now Germany will not exist. But who could say, with any certainty, that in ten years from now Poland will exist?"[30]

Existential anxieties gripped all of eastern Europe; Poland was only its most populous member. Rising from the ruins of empires after 1918, the successor states fretted over the compatriots they had lost or the foreigners they had gained, and over bygone glories or rude awakenings. Hungary believed itself already dead; Yugoslavia, like Czechoslovakia, only just born; Greater Rumania, swollen thanks to the largesse of the victors at Versailles, eyed its new minorities with misgivings and its neighbors with distrust. All had erected autarkic national economies, enclosed by tariff walls that stifled the commerce that empire had once enabled; the lands along the Danube, then an imperial mosaic of trading units as well as ethnicities, now offered living demonstrations of economic as well as political nationalism. Economic boundaries had followed political ones, and the tutelary spirit of national self-determination, escorted by its blood relative, national security, had not only ignored an ethnic group here in order to embrace another there; it had helped ruin the economy of half of Europe. Was it any surprise that almost all the peoples involved should succumb to the authoritarian temptation, and imagine that order might bring what postwar disorder had denied?[31]

Four new statues, colossal and white, had gone up on the square in front of the stock exchange in Budapest—four helmeted Magyar warriors from the time of Saint Stephen, the first king of Hungary almost a millennium earlier. Each held a dying young hero, and each stood on a pedestal engraved with a point of the compass—north, for southern Slovakia, now part of Czechoslovakia; south, for the Banat, now part of Yugoslavia; east, for Transylvania, now Rumanian; and west, for the Burgenland, now Austrian. All this Hungary had lost, along with most of their non-Hungarian ethnic inhabitants and about three million Magyars as well, now subject minorities living across the borders. For centuries the Magyars, a soldier-people of the plains, had ruled over alien Slavs, Germans, or Latinate Rumanians in historic Hungary, within natural boundaries loosely formed by rivers and mountains. Now, in the truncated kingdom that remained, those had gone too. Since the Treaty of Trianon in 1920, a flag at half-mast had floated over the square, from a cast-iron pole that rested on a wounded eagle. Everywhere else official flags flew at half-mast, and everywhere, on trams and in post offices, the patriotic Credo reminded the faithful of God, justice, and the resurrection of Hungary.[32]

"You're looking at our four Alsaces," a Hungarian journalist told his French colleague. "You understand, don't you?" He did.[33] Black crepe had draped the statue of Strasbourg in its corner on the Place de la Concorde until France recovered Alsace and Lorraine in 1918.

But there the parallel faded. To renounce the lost provinces, for Hungarians, was to renounce their own historical identity, and they proclaimed more defiantly and provocatively than the French ever had their refusal to do so: "*Nem, nem, soha!*"—"No, no, never!"

In a word, revision! General MacArthur, visiting in the autumn of 1932, concluded that they more than anyone hated the map of Europe that the war had left them.[34] Unlike Poland, unlike the lands around that had gained provinces at its expense, Hungary wanted above all else to undo the iniquitous postwar treaties. Talk of rewriting the armaments or reparations clauses could unnerve the Poles or the others as the prelude to territorial revisions, but elate the Hungarians for the same reason; even the war debts that Britain and France wrangled over with the United States, which had nothing to do with Versailles or Trianon, inspired them with hope—if those could be amended or annulled, why not any other misbegotten offspring of the Great War? The French ambassador threw up his hands in despair. The Magyar, he wrote his minister, believed himself the most miserable as well as the most handsome man in the world, and he reduced every event in the world, near or far, to the everlasting "Hungarian question."[35]

On November 11, as the British and French observed Armistice Day, and the Poles celebrated their independence, 120 Rumanian runners ran a relay race to the Tomb of the Unknown Soldier in Bucharest, where they rekindled the flame with their torches. For New Year's Day that year, King Carol had bestowed the Order of Ferdinand I on all who had worked to unite the country's provinces in the late war. A politician willing to return a parcel of Transylvania to Hungary might enjoy the same reception and expect as short a future as a Hungarian counterpart unwilling to reclaim it. When the Fascist Alexandru Cuza, a Nazi sympathizer, had stood up in the Chamber a year earlier to defend "revision" in the abstract, the entire Rumanian press had denounced him.[36] This was blasphemy. In Budapest across the border, such demonstrations rankled. The eleventh of November there came and went, unobserved but not unnoticed.

It did not help that the Czechoslovaks, Yugoslavs, and Rumanians surrounding Hungary had thought to protect their newfound dimensions from its recriminations by allying themselves into a Little Entente, backed by the power and the paragon of the status quo, France. The other haunting postwar memory, the four months of a Hungarian Soviet Republic in 1919, did little for any sense of inner security either, and no leaders in eastern Europe called more urgently for a cordon sanitaire around the Soviet Union than the Hungarians. They looked for an ally; with Britain disengaged, France on the wrong side, Germany in chaos, and the Soviet Union unthinkable, they looked at Rome.

At the head of the government sat Admiral Miklos Horthy, the regent, in the old imperial palace of Gödöllő. During the war he had served as an aide-de-camp to Emperor Franz Joseph and as commander of the Austro-Hungarian navy, based in the Adriatic. In 1919 and the civil war that followed, he had helped chase the Bolsheviks away, organize a White Terror, stymie attempts at a Hapsburg restoration, and install a de facto dictatorship. Now he was a regent without a monarch, an admiral without a fleet in a country without a coast. As others waited for Hungary to rise from the ashes, he warned against Communism and waited for an heir to claim the crown of Saint Stephen.[37]

None came. Horthy had been waiting for twelve years. In August an octogenarian poet, Eugene Rakosi, acting on behalf of a "Hungarian League for the Revision of the Treaties," offered it to Lord Rothermere, the British press baron, to the outrage of the legitimist Hapsburg press. He was tempted, but soon thought better of it.[38] Meanwhile the prime ministers who served under Horthy usually exercised moderation and restraint. They counted among themselves statesmen of standing, worldly but high-minded, some of whom had served under the empire and now found themselves guiding the affairs of an impoverished relic watched over by implacable enemies. Throughout most of the 1920s Count Istvan Bethlen pursued revisionist goals by pragmatic means, including taking his country into the League of Nations on the one hand and signing a treaty of friendship with Fascist

Italy on the other. A conservative, he had kept the lid on rising Fascist movements at home, even while promoting agrarian reforms as long as they did not destroy the landowning classes from which he, like so many others in the governing elite, had sprung. His successor, Count Gyula Karolyi, was a man of government but not of the masses, a professional who had not, he claimed, left his study for sixty years. Given not to demagogic promises but to imposing order on the country's financial anarchy, he left office in October in the face of rising social and political discontent. Riding its crest came a firebrand who would dominate the country until his death in office four years later.[39]

Gyula Gömbös, racist and anti-Semitic, violently anti-Communist but just as hostile to any Hapsburg restoration, belonged to those errant officers whose moment all over central and eastern Europe came in 1918 when defeat toppled thrones and counterrevolutionary bands terrorized the Reds. He founded Magyars Aroused—the cry of "Awake" resounded in the streets of Budapest years before it did in Munich or Berlin—and soon forced his way into Parliament and the corridors of power. As a minister, Gömbös shed his insurrectionist ways but never his ambition or his aspiration to refound a Magyar state, sui generis but marrying the telltale fondness for a single party to a pledge to avenge national insult. On the eighth of October, a week after Horthy asked him to form a government, he harangued the crowd from the balcony of Parliament, thrice asking "What do you want?" and thrice hearing "The resurrection of Hungary" before finally assuming the mantle of the people: "May God bless your will and mine."[40]

Within three days he had staged more public rallies than Karolyi had in a year. Gömbös decorated his office with a portrait of Napoleon and another of Mussolini, a way of suggesting to even the most myopic visitor that before the man of yesterday and the man of today stood the man of tomorrow. Unable to do much more than his predecessors with the stagnant economy at home, and forced to contain his disruptive racial enthusiasms, he seized opportunity where hamstrung demagogues often find it—abroad.[41]

He had cheered Mussolini in 1922 and upon assuming office ten years later sent him a doting telegram. The cabinet shared his veneration, and within days pilgrimages began setting out from Budapest for Rome. An official legation arrived, bearing an album full of the signatures of the Duce's Hungarian admirers, and when it returned students sang "Giovinezza," the Fascist anthem, under the windows of the Italian embassy. The National Association of Hungarian Ladies in its turn left for Rome, followed in November by Gömbös himself. Hungary, too small to act alone, needed a kindred power; Mussolini, whatever doubts he harbored about the new Hungarian prime minister—akin to those he entertained about another agitator, Adolf Hitler—would not pass up the chance to threaten by proxy his old bête noire across the Adriatic, Yugoslavia.[42]

"We need to move," Gömbös told the upper house of the Parliament, "and to show ourselves on the international stage." He and others had come to believe that the moment was propitious, that the European order was dissolving, and when they saw Germany speak as an equal to its former foes, and induce them at Lausanne in the summer to abolish in all but name the hated reparations, and push in the autumn for the right to equality in armaments with them, they castigated the timidity of their predecessors, and resolved to make up in any way they could for lost time.[43]

Whether they had gained like Poland or lost like Hungary by the postwar treaties, the successor states preyed on one another as greater powers preyed on them. Ethnic resentments practically ensured enduring friction among neighbors; the dispossessed demanded redress from the beneficiaries, who, grand yet weak, smarted at the cross-border pull on their fractious minorities. Accusations of treason flew. Bulgaria, another of the Central Powers forced to cede land to a neighbor fortunate enough to have joined the Entente during the war, had lost some eighty villages in southern Dobrudja along the Black Sea to Rumania, which began importing Wallachian settlers from Macedonia and other lands south of the Danube. Familiar irredentist demands from Sofia, backed by a uniformly indignant press, by rallies, and even by occasional vigilante raids, provoked equally familiar counternarratives in Bucharest. The Dobrudja had always been theirs; they had held it from the Ottoman Turks and never the Bulgarians—such wars of words raged all over eastern Europe. They were insoluble, their protagonists impervious to reason or evidence, but avid for a way to seize as well as a pretext to retain high office.[44]

How could an unruly multiethnic novelty, the kingdom of Yugoslavia, resting on the precarious unity of the south Slavs, not attract invidious attentions? On its northeastern borders the Rumanians complained repeatedly about the Vojvodina, once Hungarian, now Yugoslav, but, to cap it all, left with a Rumanian minority. The government in Belgrade confiscated their lands, persecuted their churches, oppressed their schools, the Rumanians complained; they had been better off under the Hungarians.[45] On its southeastern borders quarrels of the same sort poisoned relations with the hapless Bulgarians, who had helped occupy Serbia during the war and now looked on as former subjects, especially in Macedonia, fell under Greek rule on one side and Yugoslav on the other.[46] On its southwestern border, Albanian tribesmen in the province of Kosovo looked to their countrymen in the Land of the Eagle to the south, and to their Muslim coreligionaries in the new Yugoslavia in Montenegro and Bosnia to the north. Like other non-Slavic minorities, including Hungarians, Germans, and Turks, they found themselves at odds with Yugoslav centralism almost from the beginning.[47]

And in the northeast, interwoven religious and ethnic animosities endangered the experiment from the start as well. Asked to define their religion, Bosnian peasants might answer "Serb" rather than "Orthodox," "Turk" rather than "Muslim," "Croat" rather than "Catholic." King Alexander had suspended parliamentary democracy and installed a virtual dictatorship from the old Serbian capital of Belgrade in 1929, sanctioned by a paper constitution two years later that Croatian and Dalmatian malcontents in particular viewed as legalized oppression. Federalists who saw the Yugoslav assimilationist dream as irretrievable made some headway. On the other side, Yugoslav nationalists invoked national unity to prolong the dictatorship and denounce "traitors in foreign pay." In April 1932, a new administration began exploring the road back from dictatorship to liberalism, but with a constitution that allowed only governmental candidates to stand in elections and that forbade the secret ballot, the undertaking itself was stillborn. The government fell three months later. "Yugoslavia, awake," the theme of a popular campaign that spring and summer in *Vreme*, a major Belgrade paper, invoked national survival to warn of all the centrifugal hazards of political as well as ethnic fragmentation.[48] Into this tangled web lumbered Fascist Italy.

At least the other squabbles had not attracted the active interest of third parties. The Italians, with no compatriots of their own in play, had still exploited the tensions across the Adriatic for all they were worth. From their enclaves in Fiume and Zara they had hosted and armed the Ustashe and other Croatian separatists, and they were steadily turning the kingdom of Albania into an economic colony, seeming to announce a protectorate and presage an invasion of the diminutive mountainous kingdom—which, as all knew, the Yugoslavs would regard as a casus belli. Now the Hungarians chimed in. In October their press, like the Italians', celebrated the incidents in the Lika Valley, when self-styled guerrillas and local bandits attacked police stations before taking to their heels, as a Croatian national insurrection. No one reading the accounts in Budapest or Milan would have suspected that most Croatians remained loyal if not devoted to Belgrade. Yugoslav unity, to believe such papers, hung by a thread, a case of wishful thinking but also of ethnic strife bursting its own confines, the perennial Balkan hazard since 1914 and before.[49]

It was now a generalized eastern European hazard, and never more so than when mass domestic politics drove a great power to beat the drum for its own distressed minorities compelled to live abroad. Weimar Germany was there to show that democracy, no less nationalistic than autocracy, could ill afford to moderate irredentist effusions even when temperate leaders were so inclined.

Conversely, Czechoslovakia across the border was there to show that no democracy could afford to indulge separatists in its midst. The multiethnic democracy, born like the other successor states in 1918, had resisted the authoritarian tide all over central Europe, and its press and its parties had watched since the autumn of 1930 as Nazis in Germany and the right-wing Heimwehr in Austria threatened to leave Prague, their baroque capital, as the sole democratic seat of government west of the Rhine. More than the encroaching and hostile dictatorial sea, the Czechoslovaks feared the siren calls coming across it to their many minorities. In an international crisis, mischief makers in Berlin, Vienna, and Budapest could turn their three million ethnic Germans and 800,000 Magyars to good use; and by 1932 the horizons in central Europe were darkening.[50]

They felt, more than the Poles did, the centrifugal pull of German resentment in their midst. Late in September, a court in Brno imposed sentences on seven Czech Germans from the Sudetenland ranging from one to three years for high treason. Their Volksport, or "People's Sporting" association, Nazi in all but name, and enjoying the support of the genuine article, had agitated throughout Bohemia, sometimes armed. The trial had lasted almost two months, amid noisy interjections from supporters of the accused inside the court and the pan-German press outside it, and demands from the defendants' counsel that Foreign Minister Edward Benes, Hitler, and Brüning, among others, be called to the bar. The court described the Volksport as an illegal army, akin to the Nazi SA, and deprived its officers of their nationality as well as their freedom. The verdict outraged the Czech German press, and in the Reich even the liberal papers found the charges "naive" and "absurd." One of them alleged that the Czech paragons of centralization had employed any means, including high treason, to destroy the empire that harbored them fifteen years earlier. The paper despaired of the Prague government ever respecting the sensibilities of its German minority.[51]

The government in Prague had others to mind as well. Many of the Slovaks had accepted union with the Czechs largely because they hated the Hungarians more; the peace treaties had exchanged sovereigns for them, and, now rid of their former Hungarian rulers, their nationalist party called for autonomy from the current Czech ones at the helm of the new republic. In this the irredentist Magyars in the Provincial or Land Christian Socialist Party echoed them. In the neighboring sub-Carpathian Rus', the easternmost and poorest province of the country, many Ruthenians thought of their homeland as Greater Russia or Ukraine. They wrote, if they wrote at all, in the language of the first but spoke that of the second, whose folkloric costumes they wore on horseback in local corteges and whose agents traveled the land with money in their pockets.[52]

But the three million inhabitants in the Sudetenland, clustered around the German and Austrian borders, posed the gravest threat to the republic's cohesion. As ethnic Germans, once subjects of Austria-Hungary and now citizens of a new republic carved from it, they had initially preferred recapturing the past by joining the rump state of Austria, before the blandishments of German politicians, especially on the far right, offered a more credible alternative. The Nazis in their midst vowed to unite them with the Fatherland. This the government in Prague vowed never to allow. Locarno had no more guaranteed their borders than it had those of the Poles.

Most of the Czech Germans voted for the majority parties—Social Democratic, Agrarian, or Christian Social—and until recently the Czech Ministry of the Interior had not worried about the Nazis among them. Early in the spring of 1932 it awoke to the local threat, some eighteen months after taking note of the foreign one. Some 25,000 mostly young men, its investigators concluded, had joined the paramilitary movement, met with counterparts across the border in Germany, and mouthed slogans about a "Third Reich." They envisaged not merely autonomy for Bohemia but the amalgamation of the Sudetenland with the German Reich, and local insurrections to hasten the union on its way. More alarming still, their elders in the establishment did not always disavow them. Rectors of the German universities in Bohemia interceded on behalf of arrested students, even visited them in prison; at communal elections in Karlsbad-Marienbad, their candidates took votes from the other parties. German irredentism was gaining. By the autumn of 1932, after the closings, the arrests, and the trial in Brno, the government had acted—not, as the *Frankfurter Zeitung* had it, to appease Czech nationalists but to defend its authority against brazen sedition. Prague rather than Berlin was master in its house, for now.[53]

Some summers Tomas Masaryk, the father of his country, spent time at Topolcianky Castle in Slovakia, and visited mountains and villages peopled by Slovaks, Hungarians, and some Germans; he spoke in each language, often more in moral than political terms, of the need for equity in the treatment of minorities, of the blessings of liberty, of the duties that democracy imposed.[54]

He had feared the German threat even before he had espoused the cause of Czechoslovak independence. In October 1916, as a philosopher and journalist in exile in London, he had published the first article of the first issue of *New Europe*, a weekly committed to national self-determination. In it he had warned of pan-Germanism, which would begin with the absorption of Austria-Hungary but end with the conquest of the Balkans and Turkey: a political and commercial union, a Germanic empire from the Baltic to the Persian Gulf. In September 1932 he was eighty-two, an architect of independence in 1918 and of the central Europe that, with five of ten new states on the continent, had sprung from the empire he had helped dismember. He still worried about the same threat. "The road to Baghdad," he told a French journalist in Lany Castle near Prague, where he spent most of the summer, "still runs through central Europe." So tenacious was his fear of an Austro-German condominium along the Danube, another empire in commercial clothing, that he rejected any collective arrangement that might allow or invite it, even a customs union among the now-fratricidal national economies. Bilateral arrangements were preferable, he told an American journalist that autumn. And now, in his declining years, living out his second term as president, he found the nightmare was at hand—an *Anschluss*, a customs union between Austria and Germany, the certain prelude to a political union that would encircle his country on three sides and embrace its Sudeten minority to boot. Fortunately, the French had blocked just such a project the year before; it remained a dead letter; but for how long?[55]

So Czechoslovaks, along with Poles, Rumanians, and Yugoslavs, bristled at talk of revision. They had heard it before, from the usual suspects across their borders, but recently the postwar peacemakers themselves had given signs of opening their temples to subversives, and this alarmed them deeply.

In the autumn of 1931, Senator William Borah of Idaho, the isolationist chairman of the Senate Foreign Relations Committee and a would-be presidential candidate, had called for sweeping territorial revisions to the treaties. He advocated the restoration of Hungary, the elimination of the Polish Corridor, and much else besides, without explaining how such changes might come about peacefully; fond of lecturing Europe, he also boasted of never having been there. Rejoicing and recrimination followed. Written and cabled thanks came Borah's way from Hungarian and Austro-German revisionist leagues, protests from Polish, Czech, and Rumanian statesmen. Overnight, the Warsaw correspondent of the *New York Times* reported, Borah had become the most hated man in Poland. Before the parliament in Bucharest the foreign minister applauded the protests of his Rumanian compatriots living in America and warned that the campaign for revision would result in war and "the destruction of civilized humanity."[56]

In Borah's eyes, Europe could disarm only if it first redressed all territorial grievances.[57] A year later, with the disarmament conference in Geneva alternately raising and dashing hopes, the cause of territorial revision in the east had acquired new political urgency, especially in Britain. Even the Cassandra-like Churchill, who had not stopped warning of German resurgence, espoused it in the House of Commons. "Thoroughly let it be grasped," the *Observer* laid down shortly before he did so, "that the principal cause of difficulty and

danger is not the simple Franco-German question, but the complicated Polish question." Upon "the Polish frontiers as drawn with
haste and folly in the flush of conquest" hung the peace of Europe.
The Times assured its readers of a solid consensus in British public
opinion behind peaceful territorial revision. In the 1920s, *Le Temps*,
as nearly the voice of the establishment in Paris as *The Times* in London, had often enveloped the sequelae to the postwar settlements
under a regular rubric about "the regulation of peace." Now, late
in 1932, it covered them almost daily as "the problem of war debts"
or "equality of rights in armaments." On January 2 it added a new
heading: "The projects for territorial revision." Among the new or
resurrected successor states, the drift among the former victors, like
their gullibility, confirmed their worst apprehensions. A Belgrade
paper likened their naivete to the benighted optimism of Dr. Pan-
gloss in Voltaire's *Candide*, ever sanguine—"We live in the best of all
possible worlds"—even on the way to his own hanging. Reparations
and arms equality had only paved the way for the offensive on territory now unfolding, the final frontal push assuring their mutilation
or destruction.[58]

Most worrying of all was the League of Nations itself. Irredentist
or sheltered behind legalism and the sanctity of treaties, the nationalism of the weak now eyed the League doubtfully. To the revisionists
it had always upheld an order they wished to overthrow. But even the
others, the diehards of the status quo, wondered now whether the
Covenant provided much of a rampart. Its Article 19 envisaged
the reconsideration of treaties in the light of "international conditions whose continuance might endanger the peace of the world."
This offered revisionists a tortuous but peaceful road, one that the
others might block, but only as long as France and Britain stood fast.
And what if a resort to force majeure dispensed with the League and
its protocols altogether? All year the champions of the new borders
in Europe had watched as Japanese youngbloods crossed the Manchurian plains and admirals sent naval infantry and aviation to wreck
factories and dwellings in Shanghai. They more than anyone save the

Chinese pushed the League to act, only to watch the powers hold it back. Edward Benes, the Czechoslovak foreign minister, a cofounder of his country with his mentor Masaryk, and a founder of the League as well as its most popular figure, worried aloud. He had once advocated territorial sacrifices to bring national reconciliation and a new Europe. He soon thought better of it, opposed Hungarian demands for their compatriots living in Slovakia, and dismissed as utopian the European Union imagined in 1930 by his French colleague Aristide Briand. Now, after the Japanese incursions in China, he hung in doubt about the League itself. "Simonds," he told an American journalist in 1932, "after this we can only hang on to the pieces and hope to be able to start and build again."[59]

And how much did the former Allied powers in the west even know or care about the peoples east of the Elbe? "The Governments which helped to frame the peace treaties," the *Manchester Guardian* warned in October, alluding to Yugoslavia, "cannot remain indifferent while a powder magazine is smoldering under their noses." Minds were fixed on Geneva and Manchuria, it complained, instead of the Balkans. Or of central Europe: in the 1930s some Tory backbenchers at Westminster still talked of "Czechoslovenia." Perhaps the feuding over minorities and borders reached their ears only as tribal squabbles from the marches, to be kept at arm's length, lest higher priorities and tranquility at home should suffer. Intermittent disdain, fortified by ignorance, jeopardized constructive diplomacy. "The Poles are a hopeless set of people," Lloyd George had exclaimed at Versailles, "very like the Irish . . . they have quarreled with every one of their neighbors . . . and they are going to be beaten." He believed as well that the Polish Corridor would create a new Alsace-Lorraine, in the east, and that Germans should not be made to live under Poles. Even before the ink was dry on the postwar treaty, he had pronounced with oracular conviction the two idées fixes that would muddle domestic opinion and foreign policy in Britain for the next twenty years—that Germany had justice as well as civilization on its side.[60]

By late 1932 the great fear was that France might somehow inveigle

Britain into defending the Poles. Their Corridor was preposterous. No matter that the partition of Ireland looked just as odd and answered some of the same necessities.[61] Public opinion, the mass-circulation *Daily Express* repeatedly affirmed, would never allow British soldiers or sailors to become janissaries in Polish service. Never, the *Observer* was insisting at the same time, would Britain, its Dominions, or the United States take up arms to defend "the Versailles boundaries in Eastern Europe." Would the remaining major victor of 1914, France? At Versailles its delegates had clashed with the British over their in-souciance about Poland. "It is serious," Marshal Ferdinand Foch had told them. "If Poland falls, Germany and Russia will combine. You will have a worse position than in 1914." Anxious about German ex-pansion, the French insisted then and later that the sovereignty and security of the successor states was critical to that of the entire con-tinent, a conviction that Lloyd George rejected and that Woodrow Wilson, however sympathetic to Poland, never understood—and his successors even less. But late in 1932 disenchantment in France was setting in. On the right, the press chafed at the appointment of Beck, who appeared less than Francophile; it treated the Polish-Soviet non-aggression pact as heresy and infidelity. It feared as well that the Poles might turn to Germany next. "Colonel Beck," the conservative *Les Débats* complained when he succeeded Zaleski, "has appeared of-ten to look more toward Berlin or Moscow than toward Paris." On the left, the press had never cared for Pilsudski's regime. And mean-while France was building the Maginot Line along its eastern border, a project of dubious strategic relevance to the French commitment to defend Poland. In Poland, the opposition press reprinted the French attacks, which Beck complained about to the French ambassador. Pilsudski for his part suspected the pacifist French Left of wanting to sacrifice Poland to appease Germany, and the nationalist French Right of supporting his rightist opponents among the National Dem-ocrats. The alliance held. But the skeptics were proliferating.[62]

The British public, *The Times* had assured its readers, favored ter-ritorial revision. But the same public, it also observed, did not feel "as directly concerned as the public opinion of some other countries"—in short, that the Polish Corridor or the borders of Yugoslavia were not their problem. This was true enough, unless they looked at a map. Had they forgotten that the Great War had broken out eighteen summers before in this part of the world, in a smaller country than Poland, beset with ethnic and existential worries? Or, remembering, resolved to turn their backs lest history repeat itself? The peacemakers at Versailles had been unable to reconcile ethnic and economic realities with national self-determination, or to endow the League with the strength to enforce the peace. Nations reigned. Then let them over there consume themselves if they must with their atavistic recriminations, the benevolent bystanders across the Channel mused, while we resume commerce with a strong and contented Germany. Like so many more in the Dominions and the United States, happy to enjoy their own naval and maritime security, they failed to grasp that for millions of continental Germans and Slavs, and Hungarians and Rumanians and Greeks, ethnicity was still destiny, and that any power unscrupulous enough to inflame their passions and stoke their imaginary grievances might engulf all the others in another war to dominate the continent. The leaders could only bow, even though most of them knew that to look inward now was to invite just such misadventures. They resolved to meet anyway.[63]

8

Doors Ajar

In early December, statesmen from five powers—France, Britain, the United States, Italy, and Germany—gathered at the Hotel Beau-Rivage overlooking Lake Geneva. They had come to hold parallel talks to those languishing in the disarmament conference across town. After months of cajoling and posturing, they had agreed to Prime Minister MacDonald's proposal to meet and try to revive the flagging conference, and he now received them in a small salon in the hotel, under an 1880s ceiling of birds, blue skies, and flowers, in gilded armchairs arranged around an oval inlaid table. In this gaudy setting they agreed on the eleventh to concede rights to equality in armaments to Germany, but within some framework to assure security to all. The first principle seemed to placate Germany, the second, France, and MacDonald, who had drafted the final compromise and all along been more eager to bring the French and the Germans to the salon than they had been to come, was gratified, even smug. "We have done a great work," he told one of the British delegates to the conference as he emerged.[1]

The declaration resolved nothing. It brought the Germans back to the conference, which they had left in high dudgeon in July when it would not grant them the a priori right to equality in armaments. But they now claimed that the declaration allowed them to revise their borders with Poland; the British and French claimed the opposite. Nobody quite knew what "equality in armaments" meant. In November, Sir John Simon, the British foreign secretary, had explained that it came with the rider that Germany not implement it, at least not right away. At a celebratory luncheon on the eleventh, MacDonald happily reminded his listeners that Germany had promised not to resort to armed force. Such provisos struck German and French critics as absurd. The French government saw the five-power declaration as an end point, a final theoretical compromise; the German government claimed it as a liberation from the military clauses of the Treaty of Versailles—and by implication, one more victory in the campaign to undo it. Mostly, the press was perplexed in Paris, relieved in London and New York, and grudgingly contented or, on the nationalist right, implacably hostile in Berlin. With the Germans back at the table in the new League annex in Geneva, what would happen next? No one was even close to disarming.[2]

In the early days some of the grander founders had openly derided the League and its projects. "You—you believe in it?" Clemenceau had retorted to a deputy in the Chamber who had dared mention the new organization. George (Lord) Curzon, the British foreign secretary, had described it as "a good joke"; Philippe Berthelot, the general secretary of the French Foreign Ministry and Briand's protégé, as a "sham."[3] But few did so now, and some had even changed their minds. Both the British and the French now visibly supported the League. An aura of respectability had descended on it, as they and others had grasped its less avowable uses—for the British, to assure Continental stability, vital to their imperial tranquility, and spare them Continental commitments; for the French and their eastern allies, to defend the postwar order as long as they could; for the Germans and all the revisionists, to disrupt it as soon as they could; for the others, to accede to the world stage; and for everyone, to appear on it as the apostle of peace. All now promoted disarmament in the name of world peace and haggled over it in the name of national security. It demonstrated the accessory status of the League, which greater or lesser powers would exploit if they could and bypass if they could not. And how probable was it that fifty-nine nations could bind themselves to a single arms convention that touched on the survival of each of them? The conference of 1932 delivered an answer even before it ended.[4]

Never, Bertrand Russell wrote a little later, were "men's rational convictions more opposed to war." Yet, try as they might, they could not limit the spread of its instruments. Since the autumn of 1925, when the League Council began appointing them, preparatory commissions had struggled to produce a draft convention on general disarmament before the conference convened. With acumen and for-bearance, unsung experts had applied their minds to the recondite distinctions between offensive and defensive weapons, qualitative and quantitative disarmament, long-term and short-term military potential, long- and short-service armies, civil and military aviation, and much else besides. In 1927 they held 253 sessions and produced 3,760,000 sheets of paper. The French by then had conceived of com-puting a nation's war potential as a numerical coefficient, the prod-uct of every imaginable factor—population, industry, coastline—and possibly rationing armaments that way. "Never discuss general principles with a Frenchman," Lord Cecil had instructed the Brit-ish delegation, but such was the French power of persuasion that all filled out the questionnaire they somehow persuaded the council to distribute. The Dutch claimed more armaments in light of their cli-mate and subsoil, in a document that became known as the "fogs and bogs memorandum." The Rumanians argued that national courage and military spirit, or their absence, should be included. Months, years went by. Intellectually able foreign ministers, past or present, sometimes acted as delegates, often from keenly interested smaller countries—among them the Czechoslovak Edward Benes, almost too clever to command confidence, Nicholas Politis, a Greek jurist and a professor at the Sorbonne when not a minister in Athens, and the tempestuous Nicholas Titulescu from Rumania, an agile debater and a formidable wordsmith. They worked out prodigies of conciliation and compromise, but never quite the elusive via media that might win assent to permissible levels for all.

In the end they and the others produced a document for the conference but hardly a draft, and asked the delegates to fill in the numbers, so defeated were they by the interests in play, so eager to produce a semblance of consensus instead of a confession of failure. "Technical arguments," the Spanish delegate remarked, "are only political arguments dressed up in uniform." Like the others, he came with a purpose, not as a herald with blazonry but as an envoy with political instructions. These resisted compromise, because they sprang from the real or imagined threats to national soil or identity that for now gripped so many of the participants. The delegates arrived from capital cities and border regions seething with such collective mentalities, so alien to the rational convictions dear to Bertrand Russell.[5]

"It goes without saying," a British delegate once said to his French counterpart, "that our fleet will only ever be used in the service of right." Recent history had left the maritime empire feeling safer from aggression than the continental land power, inspiring the first to favor the a priori reduction of land armaments and the revision of the Treaty of Versailles to Germany's benefit, and the second to resist both in the absence of any security guarantees. But why, the French delegate wondered, could the French army not also be employed in the service of right? Eager to ban large tanks and retain small ones, but bedeviled by definitions, Simon remarked at Geneva that he knew an elephant when he saw one. But, asked the Spanish delegate, do you know a whale when you see one? The Spaniard chaired a committee of eight smaller countries, which one of the British delegates later called "an unmitigated nuisance."[6] Multiplied among fifty-nine members, such conceits protracted the conference proceedings and reduced its pace to the slowest among them, and sometimes to a standstill.

"And, therefore, Germany demands *Gleichberechtigung*," Defense Minister Wilhelm Groener read, out loud, from a large screen behind the camera in his office. "Equality of rights," the interpreter beside him translated, looking into the camera's eye. It was January 1932, just before the conference opened in Geneva, and they were recording a talking movie message for English-speaking viewers. Later they watched a projection of the film in one of the other offices of the ministry. For the first time, the interpreter saw his own image on the screen and heard his own voice on the sound band. "Take care, Hollywood will ask you to do the next gangster movie," a friend come to watch the show warned him. Unlikely; but how often, over the next two years at Geneva, he would have to translate again into French and English the word that Groener had just flung into his darkened office in the Friedrichstrasse![7]

It was the clearest and to some the most unwelcome of any national demand, striking at the letter and the spirit of Versailles in a way world opinion could easily grasp. Part V of the treaty had limited Germany's army to 100,000 men and denied the country any offensive weapons, including tanks, heavy mobile artillery, submarines, and planes. Its preamble suggested that the draconian interdictions would "render possible the initiation of a general limitation of the armaments of all nations." Article 8 of the League Covenant called for much the same—"consistent with national safety." And the Allies had replied to German protests by promising that general disarmament would be "one of the first duties of the League of Nations." That was in 1919. This was 1932, and Britain's land army was now a shadow of its former self, that of France smaller by a quarter, and by more than a half in trained men. But the victors had still not disarmed to the German levels imposed on paper, and absent the fulfillment of the supposed promise, the Germans demanded a new convention that would abrogate Part V and restrict its arms only as it restricted theirs. What could be more just?[8]

Much opinion in the United States and in Britain and its Dominions concurred—either disarm or lift the discriminations from German necks. "I regard this claim of Germany," Sir John Simon, the British foreign secretary, told the cabinet in September 1932, "as entirely reasonable and quite irresistible." All of the revisionist states, the Italians most vocally, proclaimed their support for German equality of rights and began as well, more aggressively and sometimes more menacingly, to vent their own grievances with the League, the bailiff of their oppressors. With Grandi gone from Geneva at the end of July, General Italo Balbo, the aviator and heir apparent to Mussolini, arrived to take his place as his country's chief disarmament delegate, only to lead a brawl in the council chamber, call the League "a limited liability company under the control of England, France, and the United States," and threaten to leave the conference. The next day Mussolini told the very conservative readers of the *Morning Post* that the era of conferences was ending, just as Germany announced that it would not return to the Conference without *Gleichberechtigung*.[9]

For France, the Platonic demand camouflaged sinister material designs. Equality of rights in theory meant rearmament in practice, by a country rich with thirty million more people and two or three times its industrial potential. Without adequate security guarantees the measure would only amount to a "dupery" today, as *Le Temps* had it, and a repetition of 1870 or 1914 tomorrow, as the nationalist right warned. Neither the British nor the Americans, their only effective guarantors, ever relished the prospect or jumped at the role, leaving the French to propose at Geneva, under a government of the Right in February and of the Left in November, a League endowed with its own armed force, as well as concentric new security pacts, an arrangement that in spite of its concessions to German rights enthused the "Anglo-Saxons" even less. France's eastern allies did not doubt that *Gleichberechtigung*, Germany's ploy for rearmament, would sooner or later leave them powerless to resist territorial revision. They looked out as though from a citadel's battlements; territory was its inner bastion, reparations and armaments its defensive outworks, in the sights now of an increasingly brazen assailant. In July he had taken reparations at Lausanne while laying siege to armaments at Geneva. How long before he breached the bastion? Abstract talk of arms equality alarmed the protégés in Warsaw, Prague, and Belgrade as much as their protector in Paris. Mussolini's aggressive support for it in his speeches in October in Milan and Turin alarmed the Polish ambassador to the Vatican even more than talk of revisionism itself, he told his French counterpart, and he lamented the inability of the targets—Poland and Czechoslovakia in particular—to work together against it.[10]

Even at their most technical, the long colloquies in Geneva kept circling back to fears for national status or security. Representing his country there until December 1931, Count Johann von Bernstorff, a relic from the imperial court and prewar diplomacy, held his notes in his left hand and his lapel in his right, and repeated politely that it was the turn of the others to disarm and that Germany could no longer accept the status quo. For all his refinement and all his faith in the League and in disarmament, he was as unyielding on this as any rabble-rousing nationalist; so was his successor, Rudolf Nadolny, without the temperate habits of mind or manner. The chief French delegate for much of the time, Joseph Paul-Boncour, resembled with his silvery mane, distinctive profile, and diminutive stature a shortened Robespierre. He repeated just as tirelessly as his German counterparts, but in a famously caressing voice, in one variation or another, the fetching slogan he had conceived years earlier: "arbitration, disarmament, security." France's eastern allies in the Little Entente—Czechoslovakia, Yugoslavia, and Rumania—followed loyally.[11]

More than most, the British and American leaders articulated the popular rationale for the effort underway at Geneva—that the extravagantly destructive means of modern war in themselves endangered peace, and that their elimination or reduction provided the surest guaranty of political security and of economic recovery. This they believed—including MacDonald, the pacifist who had opposed British entry into the war in 1914, and Hoover, the Quaker who had worked miracles with Belgian war relief, and Simon, the Liberal who had resigned over the imposition of conscription in 1916 and who told the cabinet in September that failure at Geneva "might put in jeopardy peace itself."[12]

But their cause was politic as well as principled. It played to a body of opinion at home and abroad. They and others felt, as the experts did not, the hot breath of international lay opinion. In October, when Paul-Boncour was drafting yet another disarmament plan in Paris for the conference, he confessed that "international public opinion" would hold France responsible if the League's great project foundered. The same month, MacDonald asked the cabinet in London whether, to avoid blame, they ought to offer to give up whatever anyone else would—which might commit them to disarm down to German levels. Simon warned the same listeners that in the eyes of the disarmers Germany was above reproach, that if it rearmed now they would reply, "Can you be surprised at Germany's attitude, when she has been refused all reasonable treatment?" Across the Atlantic, peace activists since February had besieged the White House and touched the heart of its incumbent. In March the *Ladies' Home Journal*, the Curtis monthly with three million subscribers and more readers, presented a five-point program for peace, including the abolition of battleships, submarines, aircraft carriers, and warplanes, and the obligation for every signatory of the Kellogg-Briand Pact to impose an economic boycott on any violator. The editorial looked forward to the abolition of war itself and invoked the allegiance of "29 million mothers." Hoover chose to answer their pleas in an election year on the eve of the Republican and Democratic national conventions, when he called on all nations to rely on a "police" force and on greatly reduced armies, to eliminate many land and air armaments including tanks and bombers, and to drastically reduce many seagoing ones as well.[13]

Like so many other plans, his met initially with vocal esteem, especially among the smaller powers, and much quiet consternation at Geneva among the greater ones—it would have imposed, among other sacrifices, massive cuts in the land armies of France and her allies, and abolished the best weapon—the submarine—that smaller navies could bring to bear on American and British surface fleets, and maintained the naval ratios that the Japanese resented; but it answered the ardor of all who believed that "the overall problem was simple—should the newly acquired human command over nature be put at the service of war?"[14]

The overall problem, as experts from the preparatory commissions had long grasped but as public figures still hesitated to avow, was neither military nor technical but political. Nations armed themselves because they distrusted one another, and not the reverse, and when they labored to shed their weapons before they had tempered their animosities they labored in vain. This the public figures, including most auspiciously the Americans, were quietly coming to accept as well.

Whatever he preached in public, Hoover knew that his Republican predecessors had only agreed to the limitations in the Washington Naval Treaty of 1922 once firm diplomatic arrangements, including a nine-power treaty to assure the integrity of China, had provided a scaffolding of security. With Japan now threatening to sweep that away, Hoover and Stimson reminded it and the world that the self-denying naval limitations depended on the equally self-denying diplomatic ones. Yet, in Europe, where the United States proclaimed its indifference to the vicissitudes of power and the chessboard of the Old World, it officially and vocally prescribed disarmament on its own merits, a deus ex machina, most boldly in Hoover's plan of June 22. The American delegate, Hugh Gibson, still insisted that security was best assured by removing the fear of aggression—by removing, in short, the offensive weapons such as tanks, or mobile artillery, or poison gases that made it possible. But cautiously and much more quietly, American diplomats, led by Stimson, resigned themselves during 1932 to promoting ancillary political agreements at Geneva to save the conference from itself. They had, they knew, to act to loosen tensions between France and Germany, France and Italy, Japan and themselves, before they could sign any covenant or trust one another to disarm. And Stimson came to Geneva in April to meet with MacDonald and Brüning, and committed the United States in his speech in August to consult with others when aggression threatened, for such was the shifting nature of neutrality including that of his own country, and sent Norman Davis in December to meet with the four others in Simon's sitting room in the Beau-Rivage in Geneva. With Hoover's grudging assent, he had shed habitual sermonizing for unwonted negotiating, almost surreptitiously, rejecting French proposals for new treaties lest he alarm an isolationist public and raise the black specter of American membership in the League; but he had stepped into a forbidden province, one which Hoover and his newly elected successor viewed with deep ambivalence.[15]

The result as the new year came in was a conference celebrating good intentions aboveground and self-interest below. Britain sought to avoid not only German rearmament and a new arms race, but any new commitments. France sought to slow if not suppress German rearmament, and to entangle others in its own security. All was relative; the Italians and the Germans sought to weaken France, the Japanese to weaken the Americans, the Soviets to weaken everyone; the Americans saw in massive arms expenditures a cause of the economic depression and incidentally of its European debtors' delinquency. But from all sides came fervid pleas to disarm. No one had prepared more thoroughly for this conference than the French, and one of their most senior civil servants had reminded the defense and imminently prime minister, André Tardieu, of its "demagogic and theatrical reality" shortly before he left for Geneva.[16] To this he contributed handily once there, with proposals that had little chance of acceptance. Was the Geneva declaration of December 11 any different? Early in 1933, a year after it had opened, the conference began exploring ways to apply the newly conceded "equality of rights," and once again the primacy of politics asserted itself. In time it took the form of refusals: by the Germans, of humiliating inspections of the sort the French wanted; by the British, of bans on the military aircraft so crucial to policing the vast reaches of empire; by the Japanese, of perpetual naval inferiority; by the Italians, of naval conventions that denied them parity with the French—"No Frenchman," as Stimson later recalled, "could give parity to Italy and survive in public life." And sometimes the most grandiloquent advocates of disarmament at Geneva pursued the most far-reaching rearmament at home, where politics—the conquest of national sentiment—had a way of putting security first.[17]

Tardieu hastened to reassure the French people that the plan he had presented in Geneva hardly entrusted their defense to others. If attacked, he told them over the radio the day after he addressed the delegates at the conference, France would defend itself with any and all means at its disposal, "and this too reflects the will of the people." To Sir John Simon, the British foreign secretary, who explained to him the moral if not legal reasoning behind the German demand that others—France—disarm down to their level, Tardieu retorted that French public opinion would never accept any system that strengthened Germany even as it weakened France.[18]

In August, in his speech in Constitution Hall in Philadelphia accepting the Republican nomination, six weeks after calling on the world to disarm, Hoover insisted on an army and navy that would deny any invader access to American soil—precisely the extravagance that he deplored in the French. That summer, artillery shells, searchlights, and tracer bullets illuminated the skies over Camp Dix in New Jersey, culminating in September with submarine exercises off Sandy Hook, all to foil the fleets, planes, and men of an imagined enemy. The country's army was Lilliputian, its navy enormous. It planned never to send an expeditionary force to Europe again, but always to defend its own waters and assure its maritime communications around the world, if necessary in a climactic battle with a challenger at sea, however far and however formidable—a role that Japan had now durably taken over from Britain. War Plan Orange envisaged just such an encounter with the Imperial Navy somewhere in the western Pacific. In practice neither Hoover nor his predecessors kept the fleet at the full parities with Britain and Japan, which the Washington and London naval treaties of 1922 and 1930 allowed, partly because a parsimonious Congress withheld the monies. An expansive new administration cast off the restraints. Almost as soon as Roosevelt entered office in 1933, he demanded funds from a new

Congress to resume sustained naval construction, even as he renewed his predecessor's calls for disarmament at Geneva.[19]

In September, as the submarines prowled off the New Jersey coast, a red cavalry corps invaded from the east and occupied German Silesia as far as the right bank of the Oder. A providential blue army arrived to defend in a coming "battle of Berlin." President Hindenburg came to watch, attracting crowds of curious onlookers who followed him about in cars, on bicycles, and on foot. It took little effort to imagine the national origins of the invaders, more to grasp the prowess of the defenders. Troops arrived and left in disorder before the eyes of all, and whether blue was able to resist the pincers of red, or red to defeat blue once by some miracle its horses and makeshift tanks crossed the pontoon bridges and its men swam across the river, remained shrouded in confusion long after everyone had gone home. We already knew, a liberal paper complained, that Germany lacked the most basic modern weapons—what else lay behind our unanimous demand that others disarm?[20]

This—the most innocent formulation of *Gleichberechtigung*—the country's military and civilian leaders no longer believed likely or even desirable. They had been rearming for years, behind a facade of vulnerability and penury that they erected for credulous foreign observers and that they deployed as well to rid themselves of reparations. They had long evaded many of the military prohibitions of Versailles, by concealing a general staff behind a bureaucratically innocuous office called the Truppenamt, by making and testing planes and tanks in the Soviet Union, by secretly stockpiling smaller weapons, by amassing half-trained reservists in all but name in sporting, paramilitary, and veterans' associations, including, by the summer of 1932, half a million Stahlhelm and almost as many Nazi SAs. Such subterfuges assured them of no immediate warfighting capability. But, overseen after 1928 by a government committee that escaped all parliamentary control, the secret drive also yielded plans that in 1932 envisaged a twenty-one-division regular army within a few years, with armored brigades and two hundred aircraft. Why and for how much longer, the senior officers of the Reichswehr asked, must they operate in secrecy? They rightly believed their transgressions almost an open secret—the French threatened to reveal what the British preferred to ignore, and in September gloomy officers at the War Ministry in Paris could only cling, they thought, to a lingering edge over Germany in artillery and heavy tanks. Why, the German officers asked, could their country's delegation at the conference in Geneva not demand material and numerical parity with the others, the only kind that counted, instead of the Platonic satisfaction of *Gleichberechtigung*? And why, the French officers asked their government in turn, could it not reveal what the world preferred not to know, and expose German hypocrisy for what it was?[21]

The diplomats demurred. An immediate demand for numerical parity, the Germans felt, might betray a design for rearmament rather than disarmament. Chancellor Brüning, in the end, agreed. He feared appearing too aggressive at Geneva while reparations hung in the balance at Lausanne. And nothing, as the conference opened, seemed more righteous to the German voters. For several months, political parties, women's groups, even church groups had espoused it, the Nazis to threaten, the clerics to call for general disarmament; brochures and press articles and newspaper articles repeated what speeches had uttered; and Groener spoke to the world on talking film. The French diplomats for their part skillfully withheld the damning dossier on German rearmament from the glare of public scrutiny. They carried it about, seeing value in the threat but danger in the act of disclosure—better to apply silent pressure on the German delegates, they reasoned, than run the risk of public opprobrium for provoking them and perhaps sinking the conference. The diplomats prevailed over the officers, and came to Geneva speaking the language of sweet reason. It was all a matter of tactics.[22]

Through the weeks and months of the conference that followed, the impatience of the Reichswehr commanders mounted. With Papen and "the barons" in office in May, and General Schleicher at the War Ministry, their influence grew, while that of the diplomats waned. And Schleicher eyed the Nazis, surging in the polls, hostile to the very idea of disarmament, and a rich source of manpower for the mass of reservists that he and others intended to muster around a highly professional core army already in sight. Schleicher wanted both to co-opt and to despoil the movement. That summer, in provocative radio speeches and press interviews, he pressed German demands for rearmament, prevailed on the foreign ministry to demand armament figures giving Germany "parity with France or at least parity with Poland + Czechoslovakia," and threatened to walk out of the conference—which Papen duly agreed to do, at the end of July. "In any case—yes, in any case," Schleicher announced in September, at maneuvers in East Prussia, Germany would rearm to protect itself. "We cannot submit any longer to being treated as a second-class power." And he called on every inhabitant in East Prussia to train for the Grenzschutz, a paramilitary border force of the kind the government had never formally recognized before.[23] All this was tantamount to tearing up Part V of the Versailles Treaty if Germany did not receive immediate satisfaction, and it provoked a stiff reply from the usually obliging British; but MacDonald began hurriedly ministering to the rifts, and launched a flurry of diplomacy culminating in the five-power declaration in December that so gratified him. The German delegation returned to Geneva, old faces with new demands for new levels of new weapons.

By then the will in Germany to ignore Versailles had developed its own dynamic. It drew its strength from a compelling urge to retaliate against recent history. Some in the center, most on the right, and everyone on the far right wanted to undo not merely Versailles, but the defeat that had preceded it—not 1919, but 1918—and return the Reich to the position and the prestige it had enjoyed in 1914. The leader of the Nazis wanted more, much more, but few understood this, and he was not chancellor—not yet.

Of all the words spoken in Geneva, none encountered more skepticism than the Soviets'. They came, even though they were not members of the League, that imperialist fraternity—the victors, Lenin had said, are always pacifists. But when the disarmament conference opened in February, the Soviet foreign minister, Maxim Litvinov, came with twenty-five officials in his wake, and proposed immediate general disarmament. All laughed. He joined in. For years he had appeared at the preparatory commission meetings, to expose the hypocrisy of the League or embarrass its pontiffs with a mischievous twinkle or the antics of a knockabout comedian. In the late 1920s he and his entourage of pariahs, friendless except for Turks and Germans, were denied rooms at many local hotels, scrutinized by all, and followed inside the League buildings. Austen Chamberlain, the British foreign secretary, met him there in 1927 and confided to a journalist, "Do you think it was pleasant for me to shake the hand of the representative of men who killed the cousin of my sovereign?" The following year Litvinov made the first of his suggestions for total disarmament, and provoked a stir. Now it met with hilarity.[24]

His listeners could not know that Soviet defense expenditures far exceeded the official amounts the People's Commissariat for Military and Naval Affairs shared with the League and the conference—by half for 1931, and by three times for 1932.[25] A massive increase in military spending was under way, unseen in the public figures but manifest to foreign visitors in factories, in theaters, on Red Square.[26] War presented no ideological contradiction with Marxism-Leninism, where it lay on a continuum with peace, sooner or later fated to erupt between Communism and capitalism. In its brief history, the Soviet Union had already fought several wars—one, which it had not started, against Poland in 1920, another, which it had, against Georgia in 1921, both with the design of absorbing and bolshevizing any territories gained, and a third to recapture its Chinese Eastern Railway across northern Manchuria from the forces of Chiang Kai-shek in 1929.[27] Now, vulnerable and consumed by headlong industrialization, purges, and famine, it bent over backward to avoid another one, even as it militarized its economy with obsessive determination.

Japanese actions in Manchuria since September 1931 had shaken the Kremlin, but only accelerated a shift in investment priorities that the Politburo had already decided on in the summer of 1929. It had deflected the first five-year plan toward the instruments and the infrastructure of modern war—toward the men and the weapons that waged it, but also toward the industries that fed it, including chemicals, ferrous and nonferrous metals, and machines of all kinds. To assure not just fighting strength when the day came, but the capacity to replace and sustain it over the months and years that would follow, they envisaged an economy and civilian industry close to a war footing or easily convertible to one—and, ironically enough, the Soviet planners looked enviously at the United States. They had studied the Great War, and pondered the successes and failures of national economies, above all their own, to satisfy its voracious appetites. This too defined Stalinism, which did not greatly need Japanese aggression close to its borders to justify the five-year plans, the authority it bestowed on the Red Army, and the omnipresence of the enemies it discerned at home and abroad. But the Manchurian alarm helped—however unwelcome, it brought the international context into line with the domestic one, and unified the threat environment.[28]

Tank and aircraft production targets doubled and tripled almost overnight. By late 1932 and early 1933, as the second five-year plan came into effect, the country could boast 10,000 tanks of all kinds instead of 73 in 1927, five times as many aircraft, twice as many heavy machine guns, 150 divisions instead of 100; a fighting capability, in short, exceeding that of the French, the Germans, or the British. It surpassed them in its thinking as well—in its experiments with mechanized mobile units or tactical air power, among other revolutions latent in the Great War but not yet widely embraced. A combined arms doctrine of "deep battle" or "deep operations" was stirring almost ten years before the term "blitzkrieg" even came into use.[29]

In September 1932, one of the doctrine's principal authors, General Mikhail Tukhachevsky, deputy commissar for military and naval affairs, attended the German war games on the Oder. He came away unimpressed. But still that autumn and winter the planners fretted over the potential, the indispensable potential, of their most likely enemies. Tukhachevsky also visited the Krupp works, Rheinmetall, Junkers, and the mortar factories in the Ruhr, ostensibly peaceful enterprises for the most part, and this time he praised the prowess of his hosts. He and Revvoensoviet, the Revolutionary Military Council, wanted the next five-year plan to match not only the best armies of the capitalist world, but the most militarily productive capitalist economies as well. They wanted not only to fill the skies with 32,000 military planes at mobilization, but to turn out more aircraft of any kind than anyone else in Europe by 1937, on par with the United States at 60,000 a year, and not only to field 40,000 tanks at mobilization but to roll out many more each year from the assembly lines of the Stalingrad Tractor Plant; they wanted practically to erase in their visions the line between military and civilian, between a wartime and a peacetime economy. And Gosplan, the peacetime planning agency, complied within limits; even if the new quantum leaps did not appear in the arsenals until a few years later, around 1936, the capacity for them was taking shape.[30]

World disarmament did not take up much of the frame in their projections, nor weigh very heavily on their minds. The press savaged the proceedings at Geneva. In October, *Zaria Voskoka* called the French plan yet another ploy for hegemony over Europe and for an anti-Soviet coalition under the aegis of the League. In January, *Izvestia* repeated that each imperialist power at Geneva schemed only to disarm the other. In February, *Pravda* applauded Litvinov's renewed proposal at Geneva for general disarmament and reminded its readers in the same breath of the success of the first five-year plan, assuring the defense of the socialist fatherland against its enemies. "Continue to howl, gentlemen!" it threw at the capitalists and the social Fascists.[31] At the party Central Committee plenum in January, Marshal Klim Voroshilov, people's commissar for war, reported with diagrams at hand that the Soviet Union had overtaken others in military production. "Give this to Litvinov," Sergo Ordzhonikidze, the commissar for heavy industry, broke in, "it's suitable for Geneva." Laughter broke out.[32]

Marxism-Leninism had little time for pacifism, but did not preclude exploiting its popularity abroad.[33] Beset by the imperative need
to avoid war, Soviet diplomacy was beginning to look differently on
the League and its Western members, and the possibilities they presented. And why not also impress its good intentions on the Communist movement around the world as well as upon its own citizens?
The others were not behaving so differently.

So Litvinov had gone to Geneva in February 1932 and proposed
immediate disarmament. Salvador de Madariaga, the Spanish delegate, thought of the Russian bear and told the tale of the animals.
They had decided to disarm. The bull proposed clipping the eagle's
wings, the eagle the lion's claws, the lion the elephant's tusks, the
elephant the bull's horns; but the bear suggested instead that they all
abolish their arms, and join in a fraternal hug. And again everyone
laughed.[34]

Two days after the Geneva declaration on arms, on the evening of
December 13, a crowd gathered outside the Palais Bourbon, where
the Chamber of Deputies was meeting to debate Premier Herriot's
plea that the country honor the next installment of the American Great
War debt. It fell due on the fifteenth. Some of the evening papers proclaimed that the government would not survive. "There's always a
crowd to watch governments fall," a policeman told a reporter. "It's
like watching the lions eat their tamers." As though on script, in the
early hours of the morning, Herriot's government fell. Even deputies
swayed by his reasoning voted against him, rather than commit electoral suicide. The issue had raised national hackles. In July, France
had ceded on reparations at Lausanne, in effect canceling almost all
of Germany's sovereign debt to it. Two days earlier, it had ceded on
German rearmament at Geneva as well, at least in principle. Now it
was debt repayment to the Americans, who did not care that reparations to their wartime ally had dried up. France was isolated. Would
it next have to cede on German borders, or on a customs union with
Austria, or on the size of the Italian navy? But for now it needed a

government, for the third time this year. Next year it would again need new ones on three occasions, and even then neither the lions nor the crowds would be sated.[35]

"I will not be the one," Herriot told the Chamber, "who refuses to honor the signature of France." For over two hours he leaned with all his considerable weight on the podium, spoke to one arc of the hemicycle after another, softly as though in confidence, then solemnly or with lyrical flourishes, in a brave display of lost eloquence. Yes, France had kept faith. Yes, the Mellon-Bérenger accords of 1926 scheduling French payments, the Young Plan of 1929 rescheduling German reparations, and Hoover's own moratorium on debt payments in July 1931 had all at least tacitly linked Allied war debts and German reparations, making the payment of the first dependent on the receipt of the second; and yes, France had sacrificed at Lausanne with the understanding that new arrangements on inter-Allied debts would follow. They had not. And he knew how all in the Chamber felt—they would never forget the dead the Americans had left on their soil in the last year of the war, but next to their own 1.5 million it was a "tragic episode that did not deeply trouble the course of their history." Now the Americans would not even grant a delay. To give even more of their treasure, after so much of their blood? But what was the alternative to paying up? To do so unconditionally was out of the question. To repudiate the debt, as the Belgians just had, would damage relations with the United States for years to come and break ranks with the British. Best to submit with reservations, as the British just had, and part with 480 million francs but insist on lasting revisions to come. By implication, the December installment would become the last.[36]

No matter that Secretary Stimson had accepted the British payment but rejected similar reservations they had attached, or that expectations of the sort at Lausanne, unsigned or unfulfilled, had left France where it stood now, or that the American Congress in 1926 had refused to accept the rider that the French had attached to the Mellon-Bérenger accords—that their repayments depended in part on the recovery of their own reparations from the country that had ravaged their own during four years of war. The cause was lost in advance, in a tide of sentiment, even before Herriot stepped up to the podium. Two days earlier, when he had made the deputies' resentments his own, and chastised the American government for meddling with Germany's reparations, which did not concern it, without relenting on the French debts, which did, and reminded his listeners too that he had opposed the Mellon-Bérenger accords, they had applauded fiercely; when he had pleaded for payment this one time nonetheless, they had sat in silence. So it was at four in the morning today, as he made his final plea. His proposal, on which the government had staked its confidence, went down to defeat by 402 votes to 187. Only Herriot's Radicals and a few smaller groups had supported him, and as the cabinet marched out of the Chamber following tradition the loyal deputies shouted at the opposing benches "down with Marin-Blum," twinning the Nationalist and the Socialist leaders in a reproachful but purely partisan slogan. From its Olympian perch *Le Temps* deemed the vote a plebiscite, showing "the manifest will of the country," and even the Radical press mourned the departure of its leader more than the defeat of his motion.[37]

During the debates in the Palais Bourbon, right-wing demonstrators nearby and around the war ministry cried, "Not one cent! Not one cent!" and "Down with the debts!" If he were twenty again, Herriot had told the Chamber, he would be in the streets with them. Apart from a handful of experts, neither they nor anyone else understood the numbers or the arcane apologetics about payment and repudiation, reparations and war debts, and even informed opinion in the press happily invoked justice to debtors across the Rhine and sentiment to creditors across the Atlantic. Few noticed the sober appeal to national interest in Herriot's homage to France's word. "Gentlemen," he asked them, "at a moment when dictatorship is spreading, are you, for 480 million Francs, going to fracture the unity of liberty against dictatorship?" They needed, he said again, to pay in order to organize the defense of Europe. Herriot wanted to assure French security, which he still sought in a partnership with Britain and the United States. It did not matter. Opinion was inflamed against the United States. All blamed it for refusing to extend the Hoover moratorium, as portentous a postwar moment, *Le Temps* bizarrely judged, as the Soviet march on Warsaw in 1920 alone, because it so endangered the general settlement. The paper did not reflect that in Paris popular opinion had just refused to salvage what remained of the wartime alliance with the United States. Some looked to Monsieur Roosevelt to revive it. But not even its ghost would return.[38]

This time but no more: a balking acceptance in Britain, like full-throated refusal in France, suited almost everyone. In November and December most of the editorialists and columnists flocking to the subject preferred commonsensical analysis to the furies of national pride. Washington's notes expecting 20 million pounds sterling on December 15 defied economic rationality, the papers repeated, and served no one, least of all the United States: the operation would hurt trade, by cutting British ability to import American goods, add to America's already unusable gold reserves, erase all the benefits of the Hoover moratorium that had suspended such payments, and throw the precious Lausanne settlement into question: reparations would now reappear on the table.[39] Economists and leading writers alike repeated that huge international transfers having no basis in goods or services would hurt both debtors and creditors, would only further paralyze world commerce and finance, and that only more exports to or fewer imports from the United States could settle the debt.[40] But, faced with American obduracy, Britain could not default. Nor could it return to the old obligations it had agreed to in 1923. We will pay, the *Daily Telegraph* declared on December 9, but never again on the same bases. Most of the others said the same; so, five days later, did Neville Chamberlain, the chancellor of the exchequer. To default now, he told the House on the afternoon of the fourteenth, as the French Chamber had that morning, "would have resounded all around the world" and "administered a shock to the moral sense of our people." In any case, he said, "in these days we cannot shake ourselves free from our international connections." They would pay, but demand and expect revisions. The House cheered.[41]

Only some of the diehard Little Englanders held out. The government had liberated England's debtors, including Germany, and submitted to its American creditors, the *Daily Express* held, as usual at the expense of the groaning taxpayer. Besides, to promise to pay now and threaten to default in June amounted to the worst kind of seasonal honesty. The *Evening Standard*, unlike *The Times*, applauded the "realism" of the French Chamber. Sometimes they and others recalled the common struggle, against an enemy that had threatened the United States as well, and reproached their former ally for remembering the loan and forgetting the cause. But usually a sense of resignation set off the British papers and politicians from their French counterparts, as though honor and expedience alike bound them to meet the lingering obligations from a deal gone wrong. We will keep our word, the *News Chronicle* suggested, until our creditor realizes how badly it damages him too.[42]

Neither Anglo-Saxon equipoise nor Gallic amour propre, nor any other flimsy figments about national character, governed their reception of the American notes—only their unequal treatment by recent history. The French had lost too much for any beau geste to tempt them now. Since the war that had cost them almost twice as many men as Britain, twelve times as many as the United States, and infinitely greater devastation than either, they had conceded too much—especially this year—and received too little to bow again to an unscathed lender. And the war had until now appeared to leave Britain more secure than ever, the home islands impregnable, the distant imperial frontiers and long lines of maritime communication no longer threatened by Germany or Russia. Was it any surprise that at the end of 1932 only a British government could propose an accommodation with Washington and survive?

Washington, by then, was paralyzed. As papers on both sides of the Channel complained, and as the foreign ministries well knew, nothing could happen until Hoover had left and Roosevelt had come in—until March 4, 1933. Not much could have happened either during the recent election—that "quadrennial frenzy," as the *Manchester Guardian* called it, that prevented any informed discussion of the matter, lest ruthless electioneering deepen the ambient incomprehension. The gentlemen's agreement between Hoover and Roosevelt to avoid discussing any matter of world concern other than the tariff probably spared the country, as Walter Lippmann observed early the following year, "a gross perversion of the facts and the consolidation of ruinous commitments under the stress of partisan appeals for votes." About war debts neither Republican nor Democrat, neither party platform nor nominee, dared recommend cancellation, revision, or even reconsideration.[43]

But neither before nor after the election did the silence of the candidates about war debts discourage any others. To hear "To hell with Europe" or "Buy American," to see in cartoons a French diner, sated and mannered, not condescend to pay his bill to a menial Uncle Sam, or a governor of the Bank of England inveigle an obedient Hoover into debt cancellation, was to endure on one side of the Atlantic the same rancor betrayed by slurs about Uncle Shylock on the other.[44] To read, above all, the utterances of the uninformed was to see the war as a swindle and a generous people as its victim. Fleets of gold had left their shores for prodigal ingrates across the sea. In the heat of the moment the debts themselves almost vanished, amid recriminations about elitism, internationalism, and financial oligarchies. The Hearst papers, ardent supporters of Roosevelt, led the charge in the popular press. When "American gold was sent overseas along with the pride of American manhood," the Europeans had solemnly and treacherously promised to repay it. Now the bankers schemed with them to shift the debt onto the American taxpayers and hasten the repayment of their own private European loans. The internationalists, more distracted by Europe's troubles than their own country's, connived with foreign diplomats to the same end, led by Hoover, who aspired to "save the world" and whom the Europeans wished to see reelected. He, the papers insinuated, was un-American—"Lincoln was old-fashioned, so they say!"—and his government that of big business. When France finally defaulted, the same press implored "American- ism" to cut itself loose from any foreign entanglement, including the League, the disarmament conference, Old World politicians, and the World Court that France dominated and that American internation- alists wished to join—"A whited sepulcher, a poorly baited trap, a snare spread by the fowler." The populist rhetoric, routinely progres- sive in its aversion to the corporate elites and retrograde in its thinly veiled xenophobia, fastened like a predator onto the war debts.[45]

How now could Congress, which had the final say, justify forgoing $12 million to the electorate—to the indebted or dispossessed farm- ers, hereditary foes of bankers, to the unemployed workers clamoring for relief, and the squeezed taxpayers alarmed by cavernous federal and municipal budget deficits? The debtors must pay. In July 1932 not one of four hundred Congressmen polled about the European debts voted to revise or forgive them. The campaign was just begin- ning; during it, five of the smaller debtors—Greece, Poland, Es- tonia, Latvia, and Germany, which had some American war claims and occupation costs to settle—deferred payment. After November 8 the due dates for the British and French lions' shares loomed, and their reluctance to comply, coming on top of the recent deferrals and capped by the French default, roused American opinion to heights of indignation not reached since 1926.[46]

"I never found a single person high or low who wanted to let France off a single franc," Lord David Astor reported to Chatham House in London when he returned from the United States in January 1933. That month the French ambassador in Washington complained of a rampant Francophobia, rooted, he thought, in deep incomprehen- sion. Britain had paid in December and its stock was soaring. "Your country never stood higher in American opinion than to-day," Will Rogers, revered icon of homespun wisdom, wrote in a telegram to Lady Astor. "That is the cheapest hundred million you have ever spent. Keep on being Englishmen and quit trying to be Frenchmen and you will be at the top where you belong." Roosevelt, whom Rogers

staunchly supported, conveyed much the same suggestion to Herriot
a few months later, in April. The newly inaugurated president was
hosting the former premier at the White House, and during an intermission in a concert he leaned over to him. By refusing to pay a
mere four hundred million francs, he told Herriot, France had lost
what billions of dollars could never buy—the esteem of the American
people.[47]

Opinion was not quite so univocal as Lord Astor and his friend
Franklin Roosevelt suggested. By 1932 some economists and self-
styled internationalists in both parties had relieved the uniformity
of 1926. Then, when Newton Baker, the foremost supporter of the
League of Nations in the Democratic Party, had proposed debt revision in the interests of international order, he met with little support
and much abuse even within his own party. When forty-two professors
at Columbia proposed the same that year, they fared no better. Now,
in 1932, the cause had won some converts. Church groups proposed
to link it to arms reduction, industrial groups to trade concessions;
Al Smith, the former governor of New York and 1928 Democratic
presidential nominee, proposed a twenty-year moratorium with reductions for purchase of American exports.[48]

They argued, oftener than not, from reason rather than sentiment.
And from facts: very little gold had ever left the country during the
war; goods had, purchased by the government from farmers and industrialists and shipped to insolvent, war-torn allies on credits established with the Federal Reserve Bank. The end of the war found them
seated atop mountains not of American gold, as so many cartoons had
it, but of promissory notes. The debtors could not repay, not unless
they could generate a surplus of gold or foreign exchange by selling
more goods and services in American markets than they bought from
them—not unless they could repay as they had borrowed, in goods
and services; but steep protective tariffs had closed them out.[49] The
same Hearst papers that demanded repayment also complained
that the tariff walls, some of the highest in the world, were not high
enough.[50] As long as American banks lent sums that the Europeans,

including the Germans, could use to repay some of their sovereign debts to each other and to the United States, such truths remained hidden from lay eyes. But when the source ran dry and the transatlantic carousel stopped, as it had by 1931, even the American government bowed to the unavoidable, and Hoover decreed his moratorium on debt payments. It angered some in the depressed country, and angry they remained as it expired at the end of 1932. But, in the eyes of the author and journalist Frank Simonds—"The best-informed American about Europe," according to Premier Tardieu—the world war had been a disaster, not an investment: "the war debts are dead, like the soldiers who perished in the great struggle."[51]

Such views commanded respect in restricted academic or financial circles, especially in the US Northeast. They aroused deep suspicion elsewhere, allowing the confrontation between internationalist elites and populist or nationalist masses, already apparent elsewhere—in Japan, in Germany, even in the Soviet Union—to appear in an American guise. A few years later, under the hostile gaze of the historian Charles Beard and those he cited, debt cancellation was an article of faith among free traders, who included "almost every graduate of every Eastern University who had dipped into the fields of foreign relations or economics" and excluded "only their prospective dupes, the majority of American citizens, [who] refused to believe them." He exaggerated; Roosevelt's entourage included such graduates as well as their teachers, some of whom anathematized debt cancellation and its internationalist ether. But, as outliers, the supporters of cancellation proposed while the servants of the majority disposed. After the election Congress remained as hostile, Hoover and Roosevelt as silent, as before.[52]

"Hello, Ogden," Roosevelt said cheerily to Secretary of the Treasury Mills, his old Harvard classmate and Hudson Valley neighbor. It was two weeks after the election, and he was arriving in the Red Room of the White House, where Hoover had invited him to discuss war debts with him and Mills. At last they might say or do something. Between the incumbent and the president-elect stretched a red carpet with the great seal of the United States woven into it. Hoover displayed formidable expertise; his guest listened and broke in from time to time, and looked to the aide he had brought along, Professor Raymond Moley, a law professor at Columbia and one of the leading lights of the Brains Trust born during the campaign. All smoked nervously.[53]

Seemingly nothing much divided the two principals at first—cancellation was out of the question, settlements must arise country by country and never collectively, war debts remained unrelated to reparations; and Congress, as Hoover insisted, dominated the entire matter. He proposed then to reconstitute with Roosevelt the World War Foreign Debts Commission of 1922, which could resume negotiating payments now and into the new administration. At this Roosevelt, following Moley's ardent lead, balked. Country-by-country talks should continue, they agreed, but normal diplomatic channels sufficed. A month later, two days after the French default, and again in January, Hoover and Mills proposed more wide-ranging ways to involve the president-elect in immediate efforts to settle the war debts. Once again he declined. This was uncooperative of him, Hoover intimated to the press, and reduced him to dealing only with "situations as they arise." Roosevelt expressed surprise, and found it a "pity" that the president should resort to such statements. At one over principles, the two seemed icily at odds over methods.[54]

"It is just as well," Cordell Hull, the Democratic senator from Tennessee, said of the exchange between the two, "that President Hoover has abandoned his move to reconsider the debts. He might as well have done that from the beginning."[55] But how? Public opinion forbade it. Now, embittered but released, with a legacy to save and no office to lose, he could risk more, if only his successor would play. Roosevelt hung back; innocuous commissions hid open-ended commitments, process threatening to engage policy, another's policy, even before he assumed office. The advisers now hovering around him differed over every conceivable matter of state, including war debts, and he indulged a disconcerting penchant for agreeing with each of them. But few of them could doubt his certitude that recovery, like depression, began at home. Neither he nor they saw, as Hoover did by 1931, the country's economic woes as the side effects of the world's errant ways, including its arms and its debts. In any case, no controversial foreign distraction could compromise the domestic reflation they now pondered.[56] British and French expectations ebbed.

In 1932 and 1933 the burden of the debt installments represented between 4 and 5 percent of Britain's and only 2 percent of France's national expenditures. Chamberlain himself had spoken to the House of Commons in December of "a sum which they could not truthfully say they were unable to pay." Across the Atlantic, the defaults that began in 1932 represented just under 2 percent of the American federal expenditures, and between 4 and 5 percent in the following years.[57] Treasuries might groan, but economies barely notice such impositions; they represented 0.1 percent and 0.3 percent of the American GDP, and approximately the same of the French and British.[58] But the excess baggage, the political burden, weighed immeasurably more.

On Christmas Day, the financier Henry Morgenthau, one of Roosevelt's advisers, compared the situation to that of 1913. Europe, he told a Hearst paper, had been armed and seething, and President Wilson had resolved to concentrate his energies on domestic problems. There was every reason, he said, to expect similar priorities from Roosevelt, who faced a much more acute crisis at home. Most of the Europeans' problems were of their own making—"Your League of Nations" he wished to tell them, "has not been able to keep the peace." The United States had no intention, he added bluntly, of listening to their debt proposals. Seen from London and Paris, these were not good omens.[59]

Once again passion, through politics, had prevailed over reason. Debts resembled arms. Self-abnegating national gestures, supposed to purchase longer-term benefits as lasting perhaps as peace or prosperity, were also self-defeating, in the age of mass participation in affairs of state. The costs were too immediate, the returns too uncertain, for the tribunes of the people to champion. Some thought that the defaults by France and four smaller countries had closed the book of American altruism forever. The country, they correctly pointed out, had repeatedly stretched out and hence, because of ambient inflation and interest rates, reduced the debts. It was time to turn inward, they said less convincingly, "high time that we begin to think of insulating ourselves at the borders against the international economic conflagration."[60]

But the statesmen strenuously kept up appearances. A world economic conference was in the offing, decided on at Lausanne in July and still on the planning boards. It was to meet in London under League auspices, but no one could agree on a date, let alone an agenda. When not even bilateral agreements on a single problem— war debts—lay within the grasp of the participants, were multilateral accords on all of them likely?

The fifth annex to the Lausanne convention, which had resolved reparations, invited the League to take up in the conference every other problem that had paralyzed the world economy. Chamberlain in particular had insisted on it. After all, why restrict it to monetary policy, as some wished, when the confidence that governed it depended on removing not just reparations but debts, tariffs, quotas, and all other obstacles to the flow of goods and services? Almost at once Washington took war debts and tariffs off the table. In London and Paris, a chorus of protest greeted the proscription. "When growing protectionism is one of the fundamental causes of the crisis," *La Volonté*, a Radical paper close to Herriot, complained, "the refusal to discuss tariffs is both monstrous and childish." The preparatory committee had not even begun to meet.[61]

When its twenty-two experts did, in early November, the agenda of the conference remained shrouded in mystery. Allied debtors wanted war debts to disappear once and for all, as reparations had at Lausanne, before the conference even convened. Countries on the gold standard wanted those who had left it—Britain and others in its wake—to return, and restore some equality in terms of trade. Countries outside preferential trading zones, such as the British Empire or its sterling zone since Ottawa, or the Benelux countries, wanted easier access to them. In January the preparatory committee made these and other desiderata the basis for an agenda, for a conference tentatively scheduled for April, but the confusion deepened as the principals balked at the demands on them. In any case, since Washington would not act on war debts until after Roosevelt's inauguration, how could the conference meet in April, in London or anywhere else?[62]

In its agenda the committee had espoused, without saying so, economic liberalism. It had made worldwide recovery synonymous with the restoration of free trade, the gold standard, stable currencies protected from governmental manipulation, and the unhindered flow of capital, which sovereign debts and exchange controls, among others, made impossible. Yet the missionaries from the homelands of such creeds, Great Britain and the United States, now proved the most heterodox, the most resistant to their adoption. The compatriots of Adam Smith and Richard Cobden could not renounce their now fluctuating paper currency and their new imperial trading spaces; those of Woodrow Wilson, the third of whose fourteen points called for "the removal, so far as possible, of all economic barriers," could not knock down their steep tariff walls, and their president-elect could not promise to keep the country on the gold standard. Behind such seeming apostasy lay a fixed notion of the national interest. Britain, which since the nineteenth century had imported most of its foodstuffs and raw materials, depended on exports of manufactured goods and on shipping and other services to pay for them; once foreign markets closed their doors, it had to find others, and protect them. The United States, once described as "the largest free trade zone in the world," imported few of its primary needs, and depended less on finding and keeping foreign trade outlets, but it keenly protected its own market. In different ways, both countries now deserted abroad the economic liberalism they preached at home. For them and for others the collective problem was the same: yes, restore the circulation of goods, capital, and services around the world; but how to do so without killing the patients—themselves?[63]

As the League's own economists acknowledged early in 1933, they and others at the Bank for International Settlements, the International Chamber of Commerce, and other international bodies were not proposing any revolutionary measures or miraculous cures, only transnational ones. And the impatience with such experts and their prescriptions spread, as domestic opinion clamored for results. All the more reason for governments to succumb to autarkic temptations, whether currency or trade restrictions or forced industrialization behind protective walls in less-developed countries. The preparatory committee hardly underestimated the danger. National self-sufficiency, it warned, "would shake the whole system of international finance to its foundations, standards of living would be lowered and the social system as we know it could hardly survive."[64]

Clearly, "economic disarmament," as the committee called it, would prove no easier than the genuine article, and for the same reason: the first steps, in the absence of trust, were too dangerous, and no one was powerful or determined enough to impose a solution. In June, the French and American ambassadors in London had shared gloomy prognostications about the World Economic Conference that Prime Minister MacDonald had just suggested. Never, the Frenchman said, had international cooperation been so poor. Governments had proposed local or partial solutions, but none had dared suggest a general remedy for all. "That's because," the American ambassador, Andrew Mellon, a former secretary of the treasury, replied, "no general remedy exists."[65] The League provided a way out: governments could turn to it, invoke its ideals, and let it assume much of the work and all of the blame.

9

JAPAN CLOSES A DOOR

On the morning of December 6, 1932, the ministers of the five powers left their salon in the Hotel Beau-Rivage in Geneva and their deliberations about German arms equality and proceeded to the glass house built for the disarmament conference. There the assembly was using the capacious premises to meet in special session about the conflict in East Asia. The Europeans among them sat in the assembly with the other members; the Americans sat in the box for non-League attendees, beside the Soviet observer. They all listened in silence while representatives of several smaller powers gave their views about the report by Lord Lytton's commission of inquiry, made public that autumn. The next day they returned from the Beau-Rivage to give their own views.

Led by Dr. Benes of Czechoslovakia, the smaller powers on the sixth had called urgently for the League to accept the Lytton report's findings and condemn Japan for detaching several provinces by military force from the sovereignty of another member nation. But the next day neither Joseph Paul-Boncour nor Sir John Simon, neither Konstantin von Neurath of Germany nor Pompeo Aloisi of Italy, said anything about Japanese violations of the Covenant or the Nine-Power Treaty, or about the legitimacy of the new state of Manchukuo, or the Japanese claim to have acted in self-defense—anything about

the legality of all that had taken place in Manchuria since the Kwantung Army had staged the incident on the railroad near Mukden
in September 1931. They neither accepted nor rejected the report.
Instead they proposed to find a way out by referring the matter to
the same Committee of Nineteen that had helped end the fighting
in Shanghai in the spring. Let us be practical, Simon and the others
kept saying, let us not dwell on the past now. "Provided we can find a
practical solution, let us pass a sponge over the rest," as the Spanish
delegate parodied his plea.[1]

To the smaller powers, the past was primordial, the key to asserting the authority and the principles of the League; to the great powers it was an embarrassment. Two weeks earlier they had listened just
as silently to the Japanese and Chinese themselves argue over the
commission's report and its rendition of recent history. The League
Council had heard them in the Crystal Chamber of the old Hotel National, its fourteen members gathered around the great blue-covered
horseshoe table and gazing out the window from time to time at the
laurel tree veiled in fog. Yosuke Matsuoka of Japan had spoken all
morning, Dr. Wellington Koo of China all afternoon. No one had
ever spoken at such length there before; mercifully, the two read out
their 25,000 words in soft voices. Lord Lytton sat with the four other
members of his commission one row back and listened to both delegates invoke the recent and sometimes the distant past, the Japanese
to damn and the Chinese to bless his report. He had heard them
before. China's chronic inability to govern itself and protect foreigners and their property from banditry and spoliation was to blame;
Japan's continental depredations, the latest in a run that had started in
the sixteenth century, had to stop. The new state of Manchukuo must
stay; the new state of Manchukuo must go. The smaller powers feared
the legitimation of aggression, the great ones an appeal to principle
and the Covenant that might require action that only they could take:
sanctions or worse.[2]

In September 1931, the government of Nanking had brought the
Japanese invasion of Manchuria before the League Council, invoking

Article 11 of the Covenant, which allowed the body to find a solution to which all parties would agree. The Chinese agreed to accept arbitration, but the Japanese would not; far from withdrawing their troops to the railway zone, they sent them all the way to northern Manchuria, and in late November the council finally abandoned its conciliation efforts. The appointment of a commission of inquiry with no powers to mediate saved the Japanese face—they even suggested it themselves, after first balking at it. When it left, early in 1932, the smaller powers looked with dismay on the prospect of another long delay and on their own exclusion from its proceedings. Its five members included Lord Lytton, two other diplomats—an Italian and a German—and two generals—an American and another Briton. These were the permanent members of the council, the "great powers," without Japan but with an American instead. Neither they nor their governments had displayed any eagerness to act against Japan—to invoke, for example, Articles 15 or 16, which envisaged more formal and eventually more forceful ways of designating and punishing an aggressor than Article 11, which was mostly useful before armed conflict had erupted. No one could suppose them unduly biased against Japan—could suppose, for example, that the German member—Dr. Heinrich Schnee, the governor of East Africa before the war—nourished any animus against the colonial aspect of the Japanese project. When the commissioners journeyed home by sea and over land in September, their report finally drawn up over two weeks in Beijing, Schnee mused aloud to a reporter after leaving the Trans-Siberian Railway. Yes, it would be nice if the "two most important nations of the yellow race" could reach some understanding. But 400 million Chinese, with their bandits, Communist agitation, and ancient ways, needed to modernize—such sentiments seemed, as the Chinese might fear, to exclude them from the Covenant, and elevate the Japanese as others did into honorary Westerners.[3]

But before he and his fellow commissioners had even arrived in the Far East, Japanese bombs were falling literally on Shanghai and figuratively on Geneva, Japanese troops had overrun Manchuria and erected on its desolate plains the puppet state of Manchukuo, and the island empire had squandered much of the esteem it had earned abroad over sixty years. Far from confining the conflict, the Japanese had extended it—far beyond the railway zone, far beyond Asia. Soviet troops were massing on the Manchurian border, inciting the Japanese to bring the fighting in Shanghai to an end somehow and withdraw. The initial game of the Kwantung Army officers in January, to manipulate the foreign ministry and the navy into detonating events in Shanghai in order to deflect attention from its imminent moves north toward Harbin and the rest of Manchuria, had gone awry. It had only brought more attention, of an unwelcome kind. Meanwhile, Chinese diplomacy had ably recruited the sympathies if not the muscle of the Western powers. Only the day before, the Kuomintang's "revolutionary diplomacy" railed against the presence of these uninvited guests in their settlements, concessions, and enclaves, neocolonial vestiges of humiliation and of the unequal treaties that had forced open the country. Now it invoked the League Covenant, the Kellogg-Briand Pact outlawing war, the Washington and Nine-Power Treaties, to bind the Western powers to its stand against Japanese aggression. Chinese nationalism was shifting its animus, from west to east, and in the process the vague outline of some future anti-Japanese coalition dimly took shape.[4]

And the Lytton report, when the League made it public in October, impressed the world by its objectivity. Only the Japanese and the shadow state of Manchukuo took exception to it. Even the Soviet Union grudgingly praised it. The report blamed both sides for the conflict, acknowledged the Chinese boycott and the rampant lawlessness, but denied the Japanese claim to self-defense as well as the legitimacy of Manchukuo or its basis in majority support. It concluded trenchantly that Japan had violated its international obligations, and it called for a restoration of Chinese sovereignty over an autonomous Manchurian administration that would protect Japan's extensive and legitimate economic interests and include Japanese advisers. Manchukuo would go but the Japanese would not. Without saying so, the report dispatched the puppet but retained the puppeteers.[5] This was not the smoke screen for Japanese imperialism that some had feared, but an exemplary exercise in fact-finding from an impartial international civil service—so exemplary that it soon began to gather dust in the archives of the League in Geneva.

Behind the smaller powers' impatience in December to accept the report's findings and act on them rankled their mistrust of their mightier colleagues on the council and in the assembly. Benes of Czechoslovakia suspected the Western powers of conniving at an informal directorate within the League. He suspected them too of harboring secret sympathies for Japan, the imperial newcomer reenacting their own history of economic penetration in China backed by military power. Unwittingly, he had accepted Matsuoka's most telling argument, so telling that the Japanese delegate repeated it ad nauseam—for a century the Western powers had shown their respect for Chinese sovereignty by sending in gunboats and marines whenever they felt the urge; why could Japan not protect its own more vital interests in the same way? Such chaos reigned in China that the League could not treat it as a normal sovereign member. But thirty years and more had elapsed since the high noon of Western imperialism in China; the world had changed since. As for the argument from chaos, what, the Spanish delegate asked, were Japan's armed sorties on the mainland if not armed mutinies against its own civilian government, complete with assassinations and attempted coups?[6] He, Benes, and their friends wanted to place the report before the full assembly now, that it might act as an international body and not as the antechamber to a club of the council's permanent members.

They would have to wait. In December, the report left the council for the Committee of Nineteen before it found its way back to the assembly in February. The League had mobilized world opinion, carried out its inquiry, and kept Japan within the fold. Technically it had preserved peace, as Japan still traded and maintained diplomatic relations with all third parties. Had it only offered Lytton's solution before the dust had cleared from the explosion near Mukden, recognizing and securing Japanese interests in the area, perhaps brandishing the coercive menace of Article 16 as well, the government in Tokyo might have felt strong enough to accept. Now, after fifteen months of intermittent warfare and frustrated conciliation, it could not.[7] It had ostracism but not economic sanctions to fear—not once had the Western powers, the only ones able to enforce them, darkened their words with the threat. And Japanese public opinion, fired by patriotism and stoked by the army and navy, would not bow before the blame and shame of a foreign inquisition. Could any government minister who did so hope to survive for long?

Indignation greeted the release of the Lytton report when it was published in Japan on October 2. The error-laden translation appeared as *Report of the League of Nations Commission for the Investigation of China*, and minimized its recognition of Japanese grievances. Army and navy leaders shed all reserve, advertising the annexation of diplomatic by military preoccupations, and commented with abandon on the report. The first among them, General Sadao Araki as minister of war, derided it as a "mere book of travel," and a worthless one at that; the navy minister agreed, the War Office blamed the League for assigning blame, and the army general staff challenged its facts. The civilians followed. The muffled dissension within the cabinet after the Mukden incident now gave way to univocal declarations of outrage from the cabinet, the foreign office, even the chambers of commerce. "The report contains many things unfair to Japan," a spokesman for the Foreign Ministry said, "but nothing unfair to China." Most of all they disputed the report's finding that Manchukuo would never have come into being without the Japanese irruption onto the scene, that it had no basis in majority support, and that they were anything other than chivalrous gallants coming to the rescue of a people in distress. Both main parties dismissed the report. Dr. Kisaburo Suzuki, the former justice minister and leader of the Seiyukai party, bluntly told its annual congress in Wakayama that the report was all wrong, and his listeners passed a resolution calling on the government to pursue a purely Asian policy from then on.[8]

In the press some nuance survived, until events submerged complex truth in a tide of feeling. The report was not all wrong, *Yomiuri* acknowledged in November, even though its preconceptions and prejudices doomed it from the start. Some of the delegates at Geneva, *Jiji* reported, showed salutary signs of understanding the Japanese position, but the paper affected a proud indifference nonetheless: "In this country," it declared, "we are all convinced of being in the right, and foreign commentary whether favorable or not changes nothing to us." At such moments the press, even the most balanced, pretended to represent as well as inform the public, and even if no demonstrations had greeted the Lytton report, and no paper had plumbed the depths of collective curiosity about the esoteric document, no editor could cast the displeasure as other than uniform and undiluted.[9]

Pride did not preclude misgivings about military hotheadedness. Once the patriotic fevers of September 1931 cooled, and the war zones in Shanghai and Manchuria stabilized, voices in and out of the press, stifled since September 1931, began suggesting ways to moderate the military enthusiasms. Amid the ire of October, the *Japan Times and Mail*, without singling out the military leaders, chided the "Japanese" for ignoring a newly pacific and idealistic mentality abroad in the West. *Jiji* went further and published rumors that Minseito party leaders were eager to oust Araki, whose continued presence wrecked relations with the West and threatened the country with bankruptcy. "What Ministry brought Japan's national finances to inflation and uncertainty?" *Asahi* asked rhetorically a few days later. "Just think it over." And it too impugned Araki by name. Even less circumspectly, the outspoken Baron Gonsuke Hayashi, Master of the Emperor's Household, pronounced the Lytton report admirable, especially the chapter presenting Manchukuo as a contrivance of the Japanese army; he told friends so. When the new session of

the Diet opened at the end of December, a Seiyukai member—the
publisher of the *Japan Times and Mail*—rose to accuse the military
leaders of usurping the foreign office and commandeering the foreign policy of the nation—"A disgrace," he deemed, "to the constitutional government of Japan." The statement sent ripples through
Tokyo and Geneva, where Matsuoka took umbrage at the suggestion
that the army had marginalized diplomacy—that is, himself. Scarcely
possible a few months earlier, such outbursts sprang from a different
breed of patriotism, fearful of military adventurism and of military
rule, and still following the waning star of internationalism and Occi-
dentalism. Early in the new year *Hochi Shimbun* pointed to the folly
of Japan taking on the world, and the daily, known like *Asahi* for its
suspicion of the high command, called on the government to resume
normal relations with the Western powers.[10]

The gathering menace at Geneva soon stifled such voices again.
As in September 1931 after Mukden and in February 1932 after
Shanghai, the will to transcend the jingoism of the hour faded before
the threat of international condemnation. Over the winter weeks, as
the League Assembly's Committee of Nineteen tried and failed to
devise conciliation, and the specter of isolation stalked the country,
defiance reclaimed its cachet, and public face demanded that each
appear more Japanese than the next.

And at least as Asian—both to reproach a Western-dominated
League for its obtuseness, and to espouse even tacitly the regional
and continental role of the world's newest great power. The Seiyukai
deputy who had caused such a stir in December by speaking out in
the Diet had challenged the role of the army in Manchuria, not that
of the empire. That month, too, Kenzo Adachi, a former minister
of the interior who by deserting his Minseito party had hastened
its departure from power and deepened the disrepute of the parties
themselves, formed a new one, the Kokumin Domei, or National
League. Its thirty-three members in the Diet, mostly renegades from
Minseito like Adachi, pledged themselves to social justice and the
state control of economic interests, but also to the spirit of the Japa-

nese empire and to the elimination of obstacles to its expansion—to a Monroe Doctrine for Asia. The attentions to Asia became a way of resisting those of the West. The League Covenant could not apply to the complexities of East Asia, Count Uchida, the foreign minister, told the Diet in January. If it did, he added, the clause that allowed for regional understandings—and which cited the Monroe Doctrine as an example—should apply to Manchukuo. His words could only signify that Japan would resist anyone who tried to alter the status of the new state, the same that the Lytton report refused to recognize.[11]

The timeliness as well as the mistiness of Pan-Asianism became obvious two days later at the inaugural meeting of the "League of Asiatic Peoples" in Tokyo. The president, from the Tokyo Imperial University, began by explaining that the inability of the League of Nations to resolve the East Asian dispute, its incompetence even, demanded the alternative league they were now establishing. He did not point out that both sprang more obviously from Japan's own contradictory ambitions. Ever since the Sino-Japanese War of 1894 its leaders had tried to deny other powers a voice in regulating their dealings with China; ever since 1919 they had helped found and sustain in Geneva an organization to resolve interstate disputes. Nor did he reflect on the dubious appeal of the new league to its intended beneficiaries on the Asian mainland. Only one member in attendance at the gathering in Tokyo hailed from there—a Mr. Pao, bearing the friendly wishes of Manchukuo. And some confusion surrounded the breadth of "Asia"—it seemed to embrace China and Siam, but on the other candidates few could agree.[12] Among the audience, which included a future premier, Prince Fumimaro Konoye, as well as senior military and diplomatic officials, only the literal minded could complain. However vague the contours of Pan-Asianism, it served a punctual need—to exclude the meddlers, and root Japanese policy in a regional mission. If the doctrine legitimated ambitions that violated the Nine-Power Treaty of 1922, which guaranteed an "Open Door" into China as well as the country's sovereignty, and which Japan had ratified, so be it. The treaty had no enforcement mechanisms anyway. "You see," the executive secretary of the America-Japan Society, himself close to liberal circles, had already told the American military attaché five days after the Lytton report came out, "Manchuria is so vital to Japan that we do not like to think of treaties."[13]

At Geneva, the assembly had asked the Committee of Nineteen at the beginning of December to devise as quickly as possible a way to settle the dispute. Within a week, the committee proposed to conduct negotiations between the two parties, and to add to its participants two nonmembers of the League it regarded as crucial—the United States and the Soviet Union. It proposed as well to rely on the Lytton report for general principles and for matters of fact. It then adjourned until mid-January while the two parties considered the matter. The Japanese party responded on New Year's Day by attacking Shanhaiguan, an Inner Mongolian city where the Great Wall joined the sea. It commanded the entrance into the Chinese province of Jehol and lay on a historical invasion route from the north, only one hundred miles from the imperial city of Beijing, where the greatest of the Manchu emperors had taken their summer rest.[14]

The trouble had been brewing ever since the newly proclaimed state of Manchukuo had claimed Jehol as its own, in March 1932. To clean out a staging ground for subversive raids on their new protégé north of the wall, and to establish a buffer between it and China proper, the Japanese decided to cross the wall and overrun the province, displaying even less regard for international opinion than when they had stage-managed the incident at Mukden in September 1931. This time they complained feebly of bombs and rifle fire coming from Shanhaiguan. And this time the League was awaiting their reaction to its proposals.[15]

The collision course they were steering dismayed the internationalists among the bystanders as deeply now as before. The police broke up occasional peace protests, but within civil society, activists in the League of Nations Association still called timidly for restraint. In the Privy Council around the emperor, the venerable Prince Saionji and Count Nobuaki Makino, the former foreign secretary, fretted and regretted the passing of the Western-oriented Shidehara diplomacy that so recently had brought Japan from the cold margins into the fold of the great powers. The young emperor bristled at the insubordination of his generals and admirals. In Geneva itself, Sugimura Yotaro, an undersecretary-general and an ardent believer in the League and in collective security, labored with the secretary-general, Eric Drummond, to find a way out of the impasse.[16]

In vain—the threat of international ostracism, which the framers and the friends of the Covenant had expected would bring a recalcitrant member to its senses by frightening domestic public opinion, had instead perversely emboldened it. In the press and the parties, in the upper and lower houses of the Diet, a rare unanimity reigned, proclaiming the justice of the country's cause and fissuring only over tactics. The League had erred in supposing that Japanese opinion writers, in order to win the world body's blessing, would comply with its reading of a covenant they denied ever breaking; but they themselves had erred in assuming that the other members of the League might discard their founding compact in order to keep Japan among them.[17]

Prime Minister Saito's government could ill afford to beat against the current. It had already lasted longer than anyone had expected— eight months since Prince Saionji had cobbled it together in the wake of the assassinations in May. The falling yen and the ensuing revival of export markets had helped, restoring the trade balance as well as employment levels, but so had the government's recognition of Manchukuo in September. Both Araki and Uchida had so willed it, and the aged Saito enjoyed neither the character nor the political strength to oppose them and the presumption of the uniformed warriors looming behind. Takahashi, the finance minister, harbored misgivings about the rising cost of the adventures on the mainland, but for now he had balanced the budget and made himself as palatable to business leaders as the others had to the generals and admirals. The parties sat tamely by. This was no time to brave the public temper and strike a dissonant note, not while the drumbeats of patriotism sounded so insistently.[18]

Yet no power great or small threatened Japan militarily. The call to arms came oddly, the response more oddly still. During the Russo-Japanese War of 1904–1905, when a major power menaced the empire on land and sea, domestic resistance had been more outspoken than now.[19] Japan joined the Soviet Union and Fascist Italy, which for years had been mobilizing morally and materially against imaginary or unnamed enemies; Germany would soon follow and overtake all of them in readiness. The hour of national preference was striking, amid receptive publics and friendly climates that awaited only the ablest exploiters. It had nothing to do with security and everything to do with national imagination, the latent force now roused from dormancy by keen promoters of internal change.

To thoughtful foreign observers, the Japanese attack on Shanhaiguan, which fell to their troops on January 3, responded as well to an announcement by Maxim Litvinov, the Soviet foreign commissar, and Dr. W. W. Yen, China's chief delegate to the disarmament conference. Their countries, they had declared on December 12, were resuming diplomatic relations. The announcement revealed Chinese efforts to recruit support outside as well as inside the League, laid to rest for now rumors of an imminent pact between the Soviets and the Japanese, and deepened the isolation of the island empire, as one great power after another appeared to blackball the newest member of the club. Litvinov's reference to Chinese sovereignty over Manchuria did not sit well in Tokyo, where a spokesman for the Foreign Ministry described the news as "most unwelcome." The alliance between Chinese chaos and Soviet Communism, he said, presented "a menace not only to the peace of the Orient but to that of the entire world."[20]

The two had broken off relations in 1927, when the nationalist Kuomintang government in Nanking ended its experiment in cooperation with Communism, expelled Soviet officials, and shut down many Soviet institutions. Late in 1929, Chinese Manchurian troops loyal to Nanking tried to seize the Chinese Eastern Railway, which the Soviets had inherited from their Tsarist predecessors and half of which they still controlled. Far Eastern units of the Red Army moved in and prevailed easily in a discreet war that left the rest of the world and even the Soviet people in the dark. The commanders of the Japanese Kwantung Army that protected the South Manchuria Railway watched the rout, already determined to exclude the Kuomintang from Manchuria, ideally by a preventive occupation. Logically, they might wish to exclude the residual Soviets as well. After Mukden, in September 1931, they, like the Chinese nationalists before them, eyed the long stretch of strategic Soviet track. It ran like a ribbon across northern Manchuria from southeastern Siberia, from Chita on the Trans-Siberian Railway to the Soviet port of Vladivostok on the Sea of Japan. The Soviets needed it to enhance their communications across the difficult reaches of their Far East. The Kwantung Army needed it too, once it had set its sights on conquering a province twice as spacious as the French hexagon. Its own south Manchuria line ran only from Dairen to Harbin, where the other crossed it, forming a logistically providential T for forces on the move against Manchurian and Chinese rebels. It began seizing the eastern end of the line. In February 1932, Japanese infantry columns emerged from the frozen plains and occupied Harbin, almost as Russian a city as it was Chinese, housing the headquarters of their Chinese Eastern Railway to boot. Would a casus belli against the Chinese in 1929 incite the Soviets as powerfully against the Japanese in 1932?[21]

If geopolitics alone mattered, a resumption of the conflict over Manchuria that had ended in a catastrophic Russian defeat in 1905 might have seemed inevitable. Time had not erased the economic and strategic appeal the province held for the rival powers, and recent history had done little to assuage their reciprocal fears. The Soviets pressed in and around Manchuria, the bastion that gave access to China as well as the Sea of Japan. To its west they had installed a Bolshevik regime in Outer Mongolia; to its north and east they manned the two-thouand-mile border that curved along the Amur and Ussuri Rivers and ended at Vladivostok, within shouting distance of the Japanese Empire at Korea; to its south they had never severed their links with the Chinese Communists, now leading the cry from their fastness in Kiangsi Province against the Japanese. And inside Manchuria they had their railroad and their agents. For their part the Japanese invaders had on occasion boldly appeared on the Soviet marches. Late in 1932, hot in pursuit of a Chinese Manchurian general and his ragtag army, their troops crossed the Khingan Mountains in the extreme northwest of the province and occupied the Inner Mongolian town of Man-chou-li, just beyond Manchuria proper and on the Soviet border. There, at the end of the year, they remained, facing their former foes across the border for the first time since their war of 1904–1905. When the Japanese moved into Jehol Province early in 1933 they appeared to threaten Outer Mongolia, where commercial inroads, political intrigue, and ethnic mischief-making might subvert the Soviet dependency. Now and again, rumors of war spread. In the summer they spread around Dairen—war, they had it, was imminent or would come with winter when the Soviets would surely start one. *Nippon*, a paper close to Japanese military circles, envisaged a Japanese and Manchukuan war to recover eastern Siberia, over much of which, it recalled, the Qing dynasty had once ruled. *Pravda* saw a new provocation.[22] A second round of the earlier war was not inconceivable.

Yet each government bent over backward to avoid provoking the other and to contain the havoc wrought by hotheaded officers or zealous officials on the scene. Just as each was preaching disarmament while resolutely arming itself, each openly warned its people of the other's transgressions while pursuing conciliation behind the scenes, as though to entertain the fear of war but keep its risk at bay.

Ever since the Mukden incident, the Soviet government had displayed, as Arnold Toynbee in London put it, "invincible restraint and impenetrable reserve."[23] To the surprise of the Americans and the Europeans, it reacted first passively and then pacifically to the rampage of the Kwantung Army after Mukden. In September the Politburo pointedly passed no resolution about the incident. Not until the end of the year did Vyacheslav Molotov, the chairman of the Council of People's Commissars and technically the head of the government, deliver a speech about it, before the Central Executive Committee, and then only to deny Soviet territorial ambitions beyond its borders, and to pave the way for the nonaggression pact he proposed the same month to his Japanese counterpart. Throughout 1932 the Kremlin received intermittent warnings from its ambassador and less avowable sources in Tokyo about the more avid Japanese militarists' annexationist designs on eastern Siberia, Sakhalin Island, and the Kamchatka Peninsula. It sent reinforcements to the area, and protested each Japanese encroachment, but stubbornly resisted the Chinese efforts to draw it into the conflict and derail the nonaggression pact it continued to pursue with Japan. With Stalin's approval, it restrained Far Eastern batteries from firing on Japanese aircraft that strayed into their airspace along the Amur River, and sent back Chinese emissaries who crossed the border to ask for weapons and assistance.[24] In the autumn it accepted the arrival of a consul from Manchukuo in the Soviet Far Eastern city of Blagoveshchensk and sent six of its own into the new state on the opposite bank of the Amur River.[25] The niceties recognized de facto the Japanese puppet that the Lytton report dismissed de jure. Peace at any price, turn the other cheek—such saintly behavior on the part of so proximate a power puzzled many, including Toynbee.[26]

Military inferiority escorted by domestic upheaval had made temporary pacifists of them. The Soviet Union, with its economy in chaos and its military infrastructure still too wanting to sustain a major war with another great power, might reinforce and defend its borders, but not yet back a more ambitious policy with any credible offensive threat. Floating a nonaggression pact declared its own pacific intent and tested the other's, and throughout 1932 Soviet diplomacy had multiplied similar proposals to its European neighbors. Taken together, they might foil at least for a while the ultimate conspiracy—an offensive alliance joining Japan to any number of anti-Soviet powers on the other side of the globe. Such meekness in the face of repeated provocation in the Far East humiliated the Red Army. The more muscular response was not long in coming: the nonaggression pacts camouflaged a frenetic military buildup. In 1932 in East Asia alone, the Revolutionary Military Council created a Pacific fleet, began constructing aviation plants in Siberia, and sent in tank battalions and aircraft to Kamchatka—within range of the Japanese home islands.[27]

At home the Soviet press conveyed to its captive readership the risk but not the imminence of war, now warning, now reassuring the population. Both *Pravda* and *Izvestia* sounded the alarm about Japanese militarism at the gates of the Soviet Far East—about the anti-Soviet calumnies in Japan and Manchuria, the sabotage along the Chinese Eastern Railway by White Russian émigré hirelings, the poorly disguised ambition of the warmongers in Tokyo and the generals on the spot to extend the conflict beyond Manchuria, to the north. But almost as often they juxtaposed such alarms with perplexing tales of Japanese diplomats seemingly eager to calm relations between them, and of Japanese masses who would warm to Soviet peacemaking efforts if only they knew of them. Illustrious commissars harped on the grievances before party cadres—regretted, as Defense Commissar Voroshilov did before the assault sections of the state farms early in 1933, that the Japanese listened more to their bellicose imperialists than to their sager statesmen. Before the country, he and his colleagues claimed to cultivate the hope and arm against the danger—presciently, but also to justify themselves.[28]

At the opening session of the Central Executive Committee of the party in January 1933, Molotov read out a characteristically interminable and soporific speech, this time exalting at one point the "prudent and reasoned" Soviet policy toward Japan. But he dwelt on the danger of war, the real reason why the five-year plan had brought not success but privation. The foreigner, he explained in many more words, was responsible for the sufferings at home. And Stalin, when he addressed the same body, blamed the imperfections of the five-year plan that had just ended on the troubles in East Asia. Since 1931, he had invoked foreign warmongering to justify first the urgency of the plan, then its acceleration, and now its shortcomings. Sergo Ordzhonikidze, the heavy industry commissar, said much the same, and so did Sergei Kirov, the party secretary in Leningrad: "On the dawn on the last year of the Five-Year Plan, the fourth year [1932]," he said when he returned from the same Plenum in Moscow, "around our Soviet Union storm clouds gathered very threateningly, mainly in the East." All this was true but heavily interested; grain shipments to the hastily assembled forces in the east had worsened the famine in the west, but not caused it. The speakers had. The invocation of the foreign menace served a political purpose—to bind the people to the policies of their leaders.[29]

They—the people—had seen war scares come and go. The most recent had peaked in the late winter of 1932, with Japanese troops camped on the Soviet border at Man-chou-li, provoking contradictory reactions. Travelers from Siberia reported some panic—"No matter where you turn, you meet alarm—the expectation of catastrophe . . . the collapse of the [five-year] Plan . . . the loss of eastern Siberia." By the summer, secret police elsewhere were reporting both alarmist and skeptical views. Some thought war had already broken out somewhere, others that the authorities had invented it. It might accompany other fears rather than displace them. Schoolbooks still taught the young in 1932 that the Pope would connive with the Catholic nations, especially France and Poland, to attack them. "The Far East is giving off smoke," they said in Tula, some five thousand miles from the fire, "and the Polish-Rumanian border is in a bad way." The Japanese scare, however episodic, nourished the presumption that someday, on some frontier, the Soviet people would fight a defensive war—a state of mind the authorities did nothing to dispel.[30]

The Japanese neither accepted nor rejected the Soviet diplomatic advances. A nonaggression pact was inopportune, Inukai's government claimed early in 1932. It would weaken the Kellogg-Briand Pact outlawing war, his successor, Saito, explained in June. Not now, Foreign Minister Uchida replied in September when the Soviets renewed the offer. But he did not rule it out either.[31] And, cool though they were to a pact, the Japanese did not shrink from the small steps that often precede one in the diplomatic dance—from agreements

about fisheries in Kamchatka, about the use of the Chinese Eastern Railway, about access to Soviet oil.[32] A war of words simmered
between the War and Foreign Ministries, but this time the diplomats prevailed. When the soldiers, beginning with Araki, spoke of
confrontation, perhaps to enhance their own importance, the others spoke of conciliation. Even before Mukden, in March 1931, the
Japanese military attaché in Moscow had argued that war with the
Soviet Union was inevitable, and the moment propitious; the government dismissed his enthusiasms. In April 1932, Araki gave a bellicose
speech in Osaka—Soviet troublemaking and military preparations,
he said, would not deter the Japanese from their mission in Manchuria; the next month, Japanese diplomats abroad and in Tokyo spoke
only of détente with the Soviet Union.[33] The idea, anathema to many
officers, had won friends in the mainstream press by the autumn.[34]
To anyone clear-eyed enough to read the signals, the Soviets shrank
from conflict; this was no moment to invent one needlessly and allow
the heady imperialisms of officers gazing at Mongolia or Siberia to
run completely amok.

Then why not sign a pact? Unpalatable to officers for military reasons, the gesture troubled civilians for political ones. For long they
had inflated the subversive dangers of Communism and reaped the
domestic rewards of periodic but highly visible roundups of alien
leftist Marxists. Best not to embrace the Antichrist too openly. More
recently, since the Mukden incident, Japanese diplomats had exerted
themselves to repeat the feat and cast their country as the sole rampart against the same threat on the Asian mainland, in Soviet and
Chinese guise. The claim was dubious—the Nanking government
was at war with the Chinese Communists, and—unlike Japan—did
not even have an ambassador in Moscow, and Japanese aggression
in China, far from extirpating the Communists, was self-evidently
encouraging them. And even if Stalin and his Bolsheviks could not
openly disavow the Communist International, they had long ceased
rooting Soviet policy in its avowed mission of fomenting revolution
in the four corners of the globe. But signing a pact would make the

argument more dubious still, just as Japanese diplomats strenuously wielded it to Western journalists and at Geneva. On his way there early in December 1932, Matsuoka stopped in Moscow. The main purpose of Japanese military action in Manchuria, he told the *Manchester Guardian*, was to hold the line against Soviet infiltration, and he had not hesitated to tell his Soviet hosts so. As for a pact, he hinted that it might be possible if Soviet behavior merited—as though to place Japanese vigilance at the service of the Western world.[35]

When the Soviet Union resumed diplomatic relations with China that month, it signaled confidence that the Japanese, however displeased, would not resort to war with them. Over the next two months, as the Japanese and their Manchukuan surrogates overran Jehol Province, talk of a pact, always desultory, ceased altogether.[36] But Japan and the Soviet Union continued their awkward courtship, quietly cultivating while vociferously denouncing each other. The tensions on the border between the Soviet Union, Mongolia, and Manchukuo would degenerate six years later into skirmishes and a brief war, which by then the Red Army, with or without the Mongolian army it had trained and equipped, was strong and tactically inspired enough to win handily. For now, neither side wanted it.

The announcement from Litvinov and Yen in December signaled, as well, a long-term Soviet refusal to surrender the future of China to Japanese expansionism. Before the party plenum the following month, Stalin spoke as always of the long term, of the past and the future and historical necessity. He made plain a Marxist-Leninist aversion to premature action, before the country's military and economic organization assured it of success, and at times betrayed perhaps his ambition to regain in East Asia what the Soviets and their Tsarist predecessors had lost there. In September 1945, even after a protracted war of annihilation with Germany and the briefest of unequal conflicts with a prostrate Japan, he would not let the Soviet people forget—they had, he reminded them, a special score to settle with the Japanese.[37]

*   *   *

"As you are aware," Hoover wrote Secretary of State Stimson late in February 1933, ten days before leaving office, "I have all along been inflexibly opposed to the imposition of any kind of sanctions except purely public opinion." He was speaking of Japan, and of its confrontation with the League then coming to a head at Geneva. The imposition of military or economic sanctions would, he feared, "in the present state of mind of the Japanese people provoke the spread of the conflagration already in progress and might even involve the United States."[38]

Ambiguity had clouded the policy of nonrecognition ever since Stimson had communicated the doctrine to the Japanese and Chinese governments in January 1932. It refused to recognize states or territorial changes imposed by force but said nothing then or later about any action it might take to undo them. He appeared gingerly to associate the United States with League action against aggression, by sending an emissary to sit at a council meeting about Manchuria, appearing himself in Geneva, and envisaging "consultation" with its members and the signatories of the Kellogg-Briand Pact. There Hoover drew the line. The United States would consult in council, he told the country when he accepted the Republican nomination in August, but never resort to force to keep the peace. He saw nonrecognition as an alternative to force. Stimson was never so straightforward.[39]

The administration could not lightly acquiesce in so violent a shift in the balance of power in East Asia, not with its commercial stake in the Chinese market, a territory still to defend in the Philippines, and a domestic population before whom it liked to wave its own authorship of the Kellogg-Briand Pact outlawing war. But it could not resort to force either. After renouncing at Washington in 1922 the right to fortify its base in Manila, it scarcely possessed the naval means to engage the Japanese fleet in its own waters. The Japanese would overrun the Philippines long before any relief reached the archipelago's shores from across the Pacific. And how effective were economic sanctions, if others did not join, and a blockade was unenforceable? The Stimson doctrine provided a way to take the sting out of the

Germany views the world. *From left to right:* The world's doctor-statesmen—US president Hoover, UK prime minister Ramsay MacDonald, French premier Pierre Laval, French foreign minister Aristide Briand, British foreign secretary Arthur Henderson, and US secretary of State Stimson—look smugly at an ailing Germany: "After a thorough examination we have reached the conclusion that her condition is so serious that she can only help herself."

Germans view the world. The "world question" that Germans ask themselves: "Is this a new dawn or a new conflagration?"

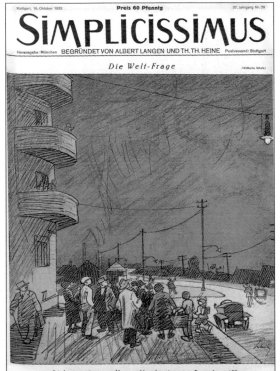

CIEL DE PRINTEMPS

(Dessin d'Abel FAIVRE.)

France views the world. Under a "spring sky": Marianne, the French Republic, shelters from a swastika, Hitler, revenge (for 1918), war debts (to the United States), treaty revision (of Versailles), the great power directory proposed by Mussolini, and disarmament (of herself).

Italy views the world. "Yesterday, today, forever!": Striding over a French serpent and an anti-fascist foreign press, past a braying Yugoslavian donkey, anti-fascist hoodlums, assorted naysayers, and a protectionist Uncle Sam, a Fascist blackshirt proclaims, "I don't give a damn!"

The Soviet Union views the world. *Top:* "Our reserves in the West . . .": workers of the "Red front" wish "long life to the USSR." *Bottom:* "And their reserves in the USSR" consist of "opportunists, saboteurs, Kulaks, former persons [Tsarist holdovers]" plotting in the shadow of Soviet industrialization.

The United States views the world.

War debts: the American creditor's view of the British debtor—and of foreign interference in US elections. Montagu Norman, the governor of the Bank of England, who sometimes traveled incognito or under an alias in the United States, funds Hoover's reelection campaign in return for promises of debt cancellation.

War debts: the British debtor's view of the American creditor.

War debts: France views its American creditor.

War debts: America
views its French debtor.

The German question: a Soviet view of the
November 1932 elections. Soviet officialdom
was still demonizing the German Social
Democrats while picturing the coming
Communist victory. "At the elections in
Germany," reads the text in the lower left,
"Communists gathered six million votes,"
while below the image, as "a specter prowls
around Europe," one "social fascist" tells
another, "It's the first time I hear this
specter has so many votes!"

The German question:
a British view
of Hitler's accession to
the chancellorship on
January 30, 1933. President
Hindenburg and Vice
Chancellor Papen bear
a new burden.

The German question: a French view. Two days after Hitler's appointment, he appears as the puppet of the conservative right and of the former chancellor Papen, who tells him, "Yes, my dear successor, that is indeed what being chancellor is." This was a common early view of Hitler's prospects.

International cooperation: a British view. As Mussolini hosts Daladier and MacDonald in Rome, a young upstart upsets their talk of peace and disarmament.

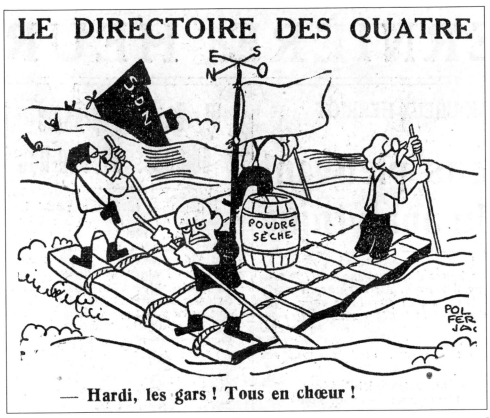

LE DIRECTOIRE DES QUATRE

— Hardi, les gars ! Tous en chœur !

International cooperation: a French view. Hitler, MacDonald, and Mussolini, survivors of the shipwreck of the League of Nations, row at cross-purposes: "At it, lads! All together!" A jaundiced view of the "Four-Power Directory," of the cartoon's title, that Mussolini was floating.

International cooperation: an American view of the World Economic Conference. On July 3, 1933, with his "bombshell" message, FDR effectively ended all hopes at the conference in London.

International cooperation: a Soviet view of the World Economic Conference. In London, Soviet foreign minister Litvinov, standing, addresses the seated representatives of the capitalist powers. In front of him, "the five-year plan has been fulfilled" and "an order for a billion dollars' worth of purchases." In front of them, dossiers labeled "crisis"; the caption reads: "IMPERIALISTS: What a large order from the USSR! Perhaps we can split it up."

A French view of Japan: "Come then to the disarmament conference," the angel of peace bids. "A moment—I've some last preparations to finish. . . ."

dilemma but not to resolve it. Both parties endorsed it. But critics likened it to Woodrow Wilson's moral posturing between 1914 and 1917 and feared the same outcome—the descent into an unwanted and unnecessary war. During the London Naval Conference in 1930, Congress had denounced and Hoover disavowed Stimson when he merely talked about a consultative pact to prevent aggression in the Mediterranean. Stimson now recalled for some Wilson's uneasy mix of neutrality and belligerency, when domestic opinion overwhelmingly cherished the first and condemned the second. Popular as far as it went, the Stimson doctrine lost its sheen whenever he or anyone else thought to implement it.[40]

This made it awkward for Stimson to push on others a policy he could not enforce himself. But push he did, and with predictable results. He sent copies of his note announcing nonrecognition to all the signatories of the 1922 Nine-Power Treaty, which had guaranteed Chinese sovereignty and territorial integrity as well as its "open door" to foreign commerce. It was a tacit invitation to the others to take some similar step, to go beyond the painfully tentative effort of the League until then. Among them Britain mattered the most. It had the imperial reach and, with the Royal Navy, the grasp to pressure the Japanese; it, unlike the United States, sat on the League Council in Geneva as a permanent member and could bring its weight to bear on others. It declined to do so.[41]

"Remarkable for its incoherence and utter futility," a senior Foreign Office official called Stimson's approach. The secretary of state, he thought, had "long been at his wits' end." In Washington, the British ambassador thought the same:

> Refusal of recognition costs nothing and to a sanctimonious government it might well appear a handy sort of chloroform wherewith to stifle the outcries of unintelligent idealists. As a form of international pressure it is, of course, perfectly futile, but in European questions the United States seems proudly and purposely resolved to be futile anyhow.

Sir John Simon, the foreign secretary, did not think much of Stimson's "flat-footed announcement," as the parliamentary undersecretary later called it, and deemed it "unnecessary" to endorse. Later Stimson tried to put some teeth into his doctrine by suggesting that the Washington Treaties of 1922 were of a piece, and that with the Nine-Power Treaty Japan had violated went the linked naval treaties of 1922 and 1930. He hinted, in so many words, at a new arms race in the Pacific, at lifting ceilings on naval construction and bans on fortifying the Philippines and Guam. Once again, he looked to the British Foreign Office for support, and once again none came. None ever did.[42]

The stony indifference in Whitehall disguised some heated arguments behind closed doors. Most exercised was the British ambassador in Tokyo, who regarded any indulgence toward China or the League as suicidal. Japan, a desperate adversary, could do great damage to British interests in East Asia, he told the Foreign Office, "if we fall afoul of her." Make no threats, avoid being dragged into a war—"If the United States likes to indulge in them, that is their affair." Officials at home did not agree. British policy obeyed imperatives other than good relations with Japan; it had, for example, its standing in the League of Nations to worry about. They found the ambassador intemperate, a troublemaker among diplomats.[43]

Their exchanges reflected a rift in British opinion. Conservative opinion, perhaps reflecting a lingering imperialism offended by successive concessions to the Chinese "antiforeign" and the Indian national movements, shied away from principled confrontation with Japan. "What Japan did in Shanghai found little support in this country," *The Times* allowed in September, "but her position in Manchuria is very different. . . . The Japanese frequently argue in their own defense that they only wish to do in Manchuria the civilizing work that Britain has accomplished in Egypt." Repeatedly, the paper, the unofficial journalistic voice of the Foreign Office, preached prudence and moderation, and the higher wisdom of "going slow." Japan, after all, had acted under great provocation. Nothing good could come of upbraiding it; neither blockade nor financial boycott would help Manchuria; the League, the paper reminded its readers early in 1933, could and should only offer advice. The admirals spoke more forcefully. They deplored any mention of sanctions, boycotts, or embargoes, convinced that they would lead to war under the worst conditions against a formidable foe. In the absence of the American navy, their own would be left to impose a blockade against an island practically immune from attack, within reach of hostages its powerful navy and army could seize—British in Hong Kong and Singapore, American in the Philippines, Dutch in Indonesia, French in Indochina, evoking premonitions of the serial debacles a decade later. The prospect had reduced Admiral Sir Sydney Fremantle, one night at Chatham House during the Shanghai crisis, to mutinous mutterings. Soldiers and sailors, he said, sacrificed their lives as a matter of duty, but to expect them "to do this in furtherance of an international object with which they might or might not agree was a very different matter." Perhaps retirement had loosened his tongue.[44]

Outrage at Japan came more easily to some liberals and leftists, to whom the Covenant signified an epochal rupture with prewar international anarchy. Manchuria had become the proving ground of the new order supposed to replace the old world of unbridled national sovereignties. The Lytton report, in the view of the *Manchester Guardian*, had to be implemented, because the authority of the Covenant, once flouted in East Asia, would decline everywhere else. But the liberal journal did not elaborate, notably about enforcement. Nor did the letters from elsewhere that began to pile up on the desk of Secretary-General Drummond in Geneva, as fifty thousand Japanese and Manchukuan troops advanced across Jehol in the dead of winter. They came in from the National Peace Council, from the Quaker Religious Society of Friends, local branches of the League of Nations Union, YWCA hostels, from the Church of Scotland and prominent academics and many others for whom international law had become a profession of faith. Some suggested an international arms embargo. Among other imperfections, this would deprive the Chinese of any arms and leave the Japanese with the many they made themselves, paving the way not for peace but for massacre. And if the American president wished to impose one, the Congress would not allow him to do so selectively. But some of the signatories expressed relief that their government was looking into the matter.[45]

Their government, true to its cultivation of consensus and avoidance of risk, searched for a way to marry the high-minded to the sure footed, and found one in a policy of passive condemnation. To support Stimson's nonrecognition without committing itself to act, it suggested in March 1932 that the members of the League collectively endorse the doctrine. The day after the assembly did so, the state of Manchukuo announced its birth. But Britain had made a gesture, especially to the smaller powers at the League. By the turn of the year, as the assembly prepared to act on the Lytton report, the message had become clear. Much to the dismay of the smaller members from all over the world, some of whom feared for their own security, Britain would speak but not act through the League.

And then France would certainly not do so either. It had few vital interests to protect in Manchuria or China, and, with colonies in Indochina, much to gain from preserving Japanese goodwill. The French right-wing press, more outspoken in its support of Japan than the British, applied its own kind of pressure on the beleaguered governments of the day. As always, domestic politics drove the dialogue: by holding up the Japanese army as the guarantor of peace and order against Chinese chaos and the spread of Bolshevism, the Right was pursuing its war of words against Radical pacifism, the adoration of the League, and genuflection before every German demand. With their armies, the paper believed, France and Japan were the only guarantors of peace in the world. By ejecting Japan, *Le Figaro* complained, the Lytton report opened the floodgates to the spread of Communism. In December, as the assembly met and asked the Committee of Nineteen to recommend a course of action, *Le Figaro* waxed dithyrambic about "Japan's preservation of peace by preparing for war." China was no normal nation, Nanking no normal government. It had duped the world, the paper concluded in the new year—the League, the Liberals, the Socialists, George Lansbury in Britain, Léon Blum in France.[46] The French government could afford to offend the Right by rallying to the defense of the Covenant, but not the Radical Center and the Left by belligerence at a moment of financial penury. And, with Germany pressing ahead on arms in Geneva, it could neither slight the authority of the League nor desert its own eastern European protégés, the outspoken backers of League action against the first great power to defy it. They feared for their security as France did for its own and presumably for theirs. So the government in Paris followed the British lead, and spoke but did not act. To "join the general will of the League" but not "take any initiative which might draw Japanese attention to us"—such became the uninspiring maxim of French policy by January; and Sir John Simon, its authors added for good measure, would probably follow no other himself.[47]

And Hoover, as he left office, laid down for Stimson the policy that *The Times* blessed as "go slow" and that Simon in Westminster and in Geneva followed without enunciating. He wanted, the outgoing president wrote, to avoid hasty action, allow time for solutions, and make it clear to the world that the United States would not support coercive measures beyond the pressure of public opinion, which he believed would ultimately triumph. The declaration alone would help—"It would, I believe, relax a considerable amount of present tension."[48]

Would his successor, Franklin Roosevelt, see it the same way? In January, in the middle of the interregnum, Stimson called on him at his home in Hyde Park and stayed for five hours. He had enjoyed a delightful lunch, he told journalists unhelpfully. Within a week, close advisers of the president-elect feared the worst. Both Rexford Tugwell and Raymond Moley, two originals of the campaign's Brains Trust, feared that he had surrendered to the "internationalism" of his guest, and committed the country and the New Deal without their knowledge to all manner of East Asian adventures. Most alarming were Stimson's indications that he expected no changes to his nonrecognition policy when the new administration took office, and

Roosevelt's the next day committing the country to uphold the sanctity of international treaties. Such platitudes seemingly rendered Moley, for one, sick at heart, and Tugwell almost as anxious. Neutrality thrown to the winds, a major war brewing in East Asia, waged perhaps by the United States and Britain against Japan—they exaggerated. And they wrongly supposed that Hoover himself might entertain any such prospects. But they were economic nationalists, convinced that the New Deal and recovery began at home and that Roosevelt, when he had declined Hoover's overtures about war debts in December, had believed as much himself. By refusing to cancel war debts, Moley later recalled, they had signified their refusal to underwrite another European war. But now? They too went to talk to Roosevelt, on January 18, in his 65th Street town house in Manhattan.[49]

Tugwell, the economist, tried to convince their host that by indulging Japan's economic imperialism he could take the wind out of the militarists' sails. The Stimson doctrine played directly into their hands, he thought, and American interests would be better served by gestures to the liberals. But it was no use. "I have always had the deepest sympathy for the Chinese," Roosevelt replied at length. "How could you expect me not to go along with Stimson on Japan?"[50]

Many years later, when Tugwell had come to reconsider some of his own views about the origins of the conflict between the United States and Japan, he came to believe that Roosevelt had already conceived of the world as polarized between peaceful freedom and aggressive dictatorship, one of which must one day surrender to the other. But Tugwell cited no word from him before or after his inauguration expressing such religious certitude, because there was no word to cite. The president-elect's invocation of the sanctity of treaties could not alone sustain so Manichaean a vision of the world or of armageddon, and no other sign came from him then, that year or the next, that confrontation with Japan must come sooner or later. With relief, Stimson had taken Roosevelt's statement to signify continuity in American policy in East Asia, and so it did—the new president upheld the doctrine of Stimson but the policy of Hoover.[51]

To act otherwise might have endangered his New Deal politically. Like his French and especially his British counterparts, he acted to reconcile two urges at large in the land, each too powerful to ignore—to blame Japan and to avoid carrying any spears for the League. In New York alone, the liberal Republican *Herald Tribune* warmly welcomed the Lytton report, while the conservative Democratic *New York American*, a Hearst paper, abhorred the League, ridiculed the report, and warned of American involvement: "Why can't we concentrate on OUR business?" The United States was not a member of the League, and need take no umbrage when Japan thumbed its nose, as the editorial cartoon in the *New York American* had it in December, at Geneva.[52] But it could always associate itself with the indignation of the world, and condemn what it could not forbid.

In December the League Assembly had asked the Committee of Nineteen under paragraph 4, Article 15, of the Covenant to submit a report and recommendations if its efforts at conciliation under paragraph 3 of the same article failed. Predictably, they did, over minimal premises for negotiations. In mid-February the Japanese delegation baldly insisted on the recognition of Manchukuo as the only basis of peace in East Asia. The next day the committee recommended in its report that the assembly adopt the Lytton report, affirm Chinese sovereignty over Manchuria, and request inter alia the withdrawal of Japanese forces to the South Manchuria Railway Zone. On the twenty-first the assembly convened to consider; two days later, the Japanese government demanded instead that Chinese forces leave the Manchukuan province of Jehol, and massed thirty thousand troops of its own to encourage them to do so.[53]

Would Japan leave the League if the assembly decided against it and adopted the committee's report? Within the cabinet, opinions were divided. Araki, the minister of war, and Uchida, the foreign minister, favored withdrawal; Prime Minister Saito and Finance Minister Takahashi hesitated. Even the Japanese delegation at Geneva was divided. Yosuke Matsuoka, the chief delegate who had toiled for six months despite his bluster to avoid just such an outcome, felt they had no choice. The others were not so sure.[54] The Japanese press, seeing the writing on the wall at Geneva, debated the question. Major daily newspapers took opposing views, equally persuasively. Since the League had no powers of enforcement, Japan need not leave it, *Jiji* argued on the nineteenth. Its resolutions were no "verdict by a super-state organization," *Asahi* added the same day—Japan should only leave if it tried to enforce them with sanctions under Article 16. And of that there was no sign. Why invite further humiliation by staying, *Nichi Nichi* asked a contrario, as continued presence would only court Article 16. If Japan feared isolation, it insisted, it ought never to have recognized Manchukuo. The sooner Japan seceded the better, for *Chugai Shogyo*, not to confront the powers but to "return—to put it plainly—to Asia in quest of peace in the orient . . . and unite Asia for the Asians." The imminence of an indictment at Geneva reopened the feuds in political opinion, among internationalists, pragmatists, and nationalists. Some lamented such squabbles, when the hour cried out for unanimity.[55]

Once again, a sense of crisis handed the nationalists their victory, and an uncertain government fell into line. The army spared no effort to organize its public and politicize patriotism. On the eighteenth and nineteenth, reservists and ex-servicemen rallied to demand that Japan leave the League. On the twenty-second, thirty thousand of them gathered in Tokyo at the Yasukuni Shrine. One of their groups carried a banner with ideographs in blood demanding withdrawal. To mark the gravity of the moment, they sent copies of their resolution to Prince Saionji, the Genro himself. By then the cabinet had decided as much anyway. It had sought and won the endorsement of the Privy Council to leave the League if the assembly adopted the resolution before it. Instructions went out to the delegation in Geneva. Public opinion had forced their hand, the foreign minister told a foreign diplomat, as though to apologize; but he, along with Araki and other cabinet ministers, had begun broadcasting to the country to explain the decision. Unanimity, the American military attaché thought, returned quickly.[56]

On the morning of the twenty-fourth the delegates to the League gathered in the assembly hall, watched by crowds in the galleries. They heard eloquent but familiar pleas from the Chinese and Japanese delegates. Dr. Yen accepted the committee's recommendation to accept the committee's report, if Japan did the same. Matsuoka declined, firmly but less belligerently than before.

Listening to him from the nonmembers' bench, the American minister in Berne grew despondent. For the first time, Hugh Wilson began to doubt the wisdom of Stimson's nonrecognition doctrine, of condemning without redressing, of making war the only sanction in international law, and of driving Japan beyond the pale into a community of the damned. He feared more for the diplomacy of the country he represented than for the integrity of the international fraternity he attended.[57] But for months world journalists of varied cloths and abilities had seized on the Manchurian debacle to announce the untimely end of the League. Believers in collective security blamed the governments, unbelievers claimed vindication. The habit had caught on in September, as the Lytton Commission handed in its report and Japan recognized Manchukuo. Gloomily, the *Sunday Times* had envisaged Japan leaving, followed by Germany, Hungary, and Italy, a prospect that the *New York Herald Tribune* feared as well, unlike the isolationist *New York American*, which contemplated it without consternation. It had already dismissed the organization as irrelevant. Twin deadlocks—over disarmament and Manchuria—cast a shadow over Geneva and conspired to deepen the doubts about the League. How, General Araki had asked when the Lytton report came out, could the League hope to resolve the dispute between Japan and China over Manchuria when it could not even resolve that between France and Germany over arms? How, French newspapers wondered as the report finally came before the assembly in February, could the League make any headway on disarmament when it had made none on Manchuria? The League's efforts to bring peace to East Asia had only discredited it in the eyes of the world, the Communist *L'Humanité* quoted approvingly from Molotov's endless speech—but then the Soviet Union, the commissar added, had never placed great hope in it.[58]

Had any of them considered that their own domestic contradictions had turned the League into an international theater of the absurd? The East Asian power that had most eagerly joined the League, Japan, now most flagrantly flouted it; the Western power that shunned it, the United States, affected for a moment the strongest inclination to uphold its mission; the two European powers that had espoused its ends most volubly, Britain and France, connived most stealthily to disable its means. The vagaries of domestic beliefs—pacifist, chauvinist, nativist, or merely patriotic—had allowed or more often commanded such official poses, in the improvisation of what is solemnly called the "national interest." So with disarmament, so with the world economy. Had the detractors or the defenders of the League tried tracing the latest impasse to its source, they might have reflected that if any new international order were ever to take root, it would have to begin there, at home.

With a muffled "No," Matsuoka voted against the motion to accept the committee's report. No one else joined him, and forty-two voted in favor. He returned briefly to the podium to announce with regret and disappointment that Japan could no longer cooperate with the League in trying to resolve the East Asian dispute. He thanked the members of the League, walked down the center of the aisle past the silent delegates, and, followed by some thirty members of his delegation, left the hall and closed the door quietly behind him.[59]

10

THE REICH UNDER FOREIGN EYES

Carnival in Berlin: On the evening of January 30, bystanders gaped from the sides of the Wilhelmplatz as Nazi storm troopers and the nationalist veterans of the Stahlhelm marched by. Many carried torches. In the entrance foyer of the Kaiserhof Hotel, the Nazi headquarters, uniformed SS formed an honor guard, and others patrolled the corridors. On the steps outside, party dignitaries gave Fascist salutes to endless columns of brown-uniformed SA. But the men on the steps were second-rate, even faceless, for Hitler was already in the Chancellery.[1]

He had entered there much as his immediate predecessors had—appointed by an aged president under no obligation to do so, after weeks of favoritism, speculation, and backstairs intrigue. The election of November 6 left Chancellor Papen further than ever from cobbling together a semblance of a parliamentary majority—he could boast only 4.5 out of 35 million votes. Early in the mornings after the election, an attaché at the French embassy would cross paths with him in the Tiergarten. Papen still rode there, in gray waistcoat, beige breeches, and white gloves, looking very English, and when, one of those evenings, he dined at the Rumanian embassy, he seemed as insouciant and worldly as ever. But his days were numbered. He had lost not only the voters but the army as well, in the person of the minister of war. General Schleicher viewed the chancellor he had helped install as disloyal and now useless, unable to cajole and deliver the Nazis into some kind of authoritarian coalition that he might direct in obscurity from the wings. Reluctantly Hindenburg accepted the resignation of his favorite, and at the beginning of December appointed Schleicher in his stead.

"I am a fanatical servant of the state," the general had told the French ambassador, as though to impress on him his Prussian bona fides.[2] But to the Germans he presented himself improbably as a peacemaker, the architect of détente with the Left, a "social general," neither a Socialist nor a capitalist, indifferent now to concepts of either a market or a planned economy. In a radio speech on December 15, he proposed work programs and relief for the unemployed, the parceling out of bankrupt estates in East Prussia to the landless, and a halt to wage reductions. Such heresies—"Agrarian bolshevism," among other epithets, greeted his words—alarmed conservatives without winning over any social democrats, and his political base, narrower even than Papen's in spite of the army behind him, continued to erode.[3] Around him the plotting began at once, orchestrated by a Papen who not only connived to oust from office the false friend who had just ousted him, but also still had the ear of Hindenburg and still occupied an official residence near the president's, in the Wilhelmstrasse; and his discreet rounds quickly came to include his own most savage critic, Adolf Hitler.

The election of November 6 had pierced the Nazis' nimbus of inexorable success, and since then, regional elections in Saxony and Thuringia had done nothing to restore it. In its place came buoyant predictions of decline and disappearance. "The National Socialist danger is past," Schleicher said, and many in the press—liberal, conservative, or further left—agreed. The year then ending had marked the rise and fall, a peak attained and a descent begun. "We are over the mountain," Thomas Mann wrote to his fellow novelist Hermann Hesse, "the summit of insanity seems behind us." And the Nazi Party appeared bankrupt, out of money as well as voters. The coffers were empty. On the Kurfürstendamm and the Unter den Linden, on other arteries of the capital, SA in faded, worn uniforms held out collection boxes stamped with swastikas, like beggars on the steps at the exit of a church service, only more insistently, more angrily.[4]

But the Nazis were still the largest party in Germany, and their leader's now-familiar refusal to enter any government he did not head, even as any without him seemed a blind alley, blocked any issue to the crisis. This delighted many Nazis, who posed as deliverers from the very paralysis, chaos, and violence they had done so much to spread. Schleicher enjoyed the allegiance of the army, Papen that of Hindenburg and his entourage, Hitler that of some twelve million voters and untold sympathizers. A Byzantine three-way power struggle began, as the former and current chancellors courted the aspiring one, and the old president, who esteemed the first, tolerated the second, and disdained the third, looked on, both acting and acted on. Between late November and the middle of January, Schleicher asked whether Hitler would enter a government under him; Papen asked whether he would consider some sort of duumvirate; Hindenburg asked whether he would head a government on condition that he find a majority in parliament. Hitler refused each. Schleicher tried to peel off schismatic Nazis, those dismayed at the Führer's "all or nothing" intransigence. He waved a vice-chancellorship and a ministerial portfolio before Gregor Strasser, to weaken the Nazis and broaden his own cabinet by the defection of their party organization chief and his following. Strasser was tempted, and a split threatened to worsen the Nazis' woes until Hitler put a stop to the incipient coup and to Strasser's political career as well, forcing him to resign his offices, his organizations to disband, his followers to recant. "I intend to wait," Hitler boldly told the senior party Gauleiters early in December, "until I am offered the post of Chancellor. That day will come—it is probably nearer than we think."[5]

It came, seven weeks later, largely thanks to Papen—so eager was the former chancellor to return to office, so confident that he and other conservatives from the cabinet and from Hindenburg's entourage could control the marginal hireling once they had engaged him. But first he would have to entice him somehow into a conservative coalition government. Hitler saw in him a conduit to Hindenburg, a sycophant who might overcome the antipathy of the "old one" to his person and his party. In January the two began to converse, in trysts in Cologne and Berlin, each conniving to make the other the dupe of his own ambition. The government they finally concocted—one that Hitler would head, as long as Papen became vice-chancellor and could fill most of the cabinet with conservatives and nationalists of his ilk—had every prospect of protracting their hostile pas de deux. But to Hindenburg it represented the united right of his dreams, a government of "national concentration," even if "that Bohemian corporal" had to head it, and to Papen, who ably fulfilled Hitler's expectations, he finally gave his assent on the twenty-third. A week of haggling and cabinet-building followed. Only two Nazis—Frick at the Interior and Goering as minister without portfolio and of the interior in Prussia—accompanied Hitler into power. Some of the conservative others were elated, openly sanguine about domesticating their Nazi chancellor. "We'll close him in," Alfred Hugenberg, the nationalist leader, assured doubters when Papen won him over with a superministry of the economy and agriculture. "I have Hindenburg's confidence," Papen said, which was true. "In two months we'll have Hitler in a corner and make him squeal," he added, which was not.[6]

Six months earlier, with the Nazis riding a crest, Hindenburg's appointment of such a government would not have surprised. Now that they were losing votes and spawning schismatics in their midst, it did. Ten days before he entered the Chancellery, Hitler had beseeched ten thousand Nazi officeholders in the Berlin Sportpalast to surpass defeatism and the setbacks of the day, to last—as though a long struggle lay before them. Inside and outside the party, rumors of an impending military coup began to fly, whisperings followed by assertions that Generals Schleicher and Kurt von Hammerstein, the chief of the Reichswehr, would seize control, disperse the Reichstag, perhaps even depose Hindenburg. They were unfounded, but Papen put them to good use to frighten and sign on the last reticent members of the new government. Hohenzollern emblems reappeared, suggesting a restoration, perhaps to cover a military dictatorship, perhaps not. On January 15, assembled dignitaries, including Hindenburg and Schleicher, celebrated the anniversary of the founding of the empire in 1871, and the imperial flag floated once again over public buildings, including the Prussian legislature, the Landtag. Foreign observers had never tired of predicting or proposing such a denouement to the afflictions of Weimar. Instead, intrigue yielded yet another presidential cabinet, as though to remind the world of the continued primacy of palace coups in the annals of political history. After Schleicher's fall, the French ambassador overheard him at lunch—sixty-eight days I've been chancellor, he was saying, and sixty-eight times I've been betrayed. He had not himself inspired great trust, but the ambassador conjectured that he had only sojourned in the Chancellery so that Hindenburg could watch him fail and then recall Papen. In place of both now stood Hitler at the window of the Chancellery, looking onto the marching torches below.[7]

Beneath the surface turbulence flowed a current of common sentiment. All the principals—Hindenburg, Schleicher, Papen, Hitler, and members of the new cabinet—wished to rid Germany one way or another of its parliament and its parties, and restore it as a military nation and a great power. One required the other, reflecting the abiding existential myth that the army high command had sown during the war—that the unarmed enemies at home, variously identified as social democrats or Jews or pacifists or internationalists, threatened the country as mortally as their armed counterparts at the front. Schleicher had hoped to dissolve and effectively suspend the new Reichstag sine die, instead of then submitting to new elections within sixty days as Papen had in the fall and as Article 25 of the Constitution required. Hindenburg saw no reason to concede to him what he had denied to Papen, who had hoped for the same. Hindenburg, like Brüning, had wanted to transform Weimar by legal means, including the expansion of presidential emergency powers, into a semiauthoritarian state. The first cabinet meeting, on the thirty-first, resounded with authoritarian alternatives to representative democracy. Hugenberg, who wanted a clean and immediate break with the moribund republic, also wanted to suppress the elected Socialist government in Prussia, that Papen had dissolved in the summer but that still met; Schwerin von Krosigk, the finance minister held over from the last governments, proposed doing away with all the Reichstag committees, the enemies of good government in his eyes; Otto Meissner, the state secretary in Hindenburg's office, proposed dissolving the Prussian Landtag. The new chancellor, for his part, had already insisted on new elections, not to save democracy but to end it—these were, he told the cabinet, to be the last elections, for the last Reichstag; Papen said the same; but that was not all that Hitler wanted.[8]

He had claimed the interior ministries of the Reich and of Prussia, where three-fifths of all Germans lived, most obviously to control the police and the coming election campaign, which they intended to win by any means necessary. "[Now] to prepare the election fight," Goebbels noted in his diary on the thirty-first. "The last one. Which we'll win hands down." This the others knew, and Hugenberg had extracted a promise from Hitler not to shake up the cabinet once the election was over. Did they reflect, though, on the Thuringian precedent from 1930? There Wilhelm Frick, who now headed the Interior Ministry, had used the same strategic post to subvert as many walks of government and society as he could. Subversion now could not await a docile Reichstag. The existing legislation, Goering complained on the first day of February, was inadequate to repress Communist "terrorism." That month, emergency decrees above and violence and intimidation below began to suppress the newspapers, break up the meetings, and detain the leaders of the Left. The Nazi terror was beginning. Hitler's conservative partners might tolerate or even applaud the spectacle, as long as it left the Right intact; but their own prospects were less secure than they thought. On the thirty-first, within hours of their appointment, Goebbels had privately identified Hugenberg,

Papen, and Franz Seldte—the Stahlhelm leader—as flawed. "They must be removed," he noted.[9]

Hitler intended to install a bleakly uniform dictatorship, an ancillary goal to that of waging a race war. On the evening of February 3, between twenty and thirty military leaders gathered at General Hammerstein's dinner table to hear the new chancellor speak of both. Konstantin von Neurath, the foreign minister, joined them. The German race faced extinction, Hitler told them, unless it purified and steeled itself for the conquest of its living space in the east. Removing the agents of decomposition—"First Marxism must be extirpated"— and rebuilding the armed forces would take seven or eight years. Only then could the army expand the living space of the German *Volk*, most probably in the east, where it was to Germanize not the people, which was biologically impossible, but the land, "because only land can be Germanized." In the meantime, he promised rearmament and more— the sovereignty of the military in its own domain, as long as it left the political task of domestic cleansing and leveling—*Gleichschaltung*—to the new Nazi authorities. He called on the assembled guests, in short, to envision a division of labor culminating in the expulsion or extermination of millions in Poland, the Baltic republics, and the Soviet Union.

He spoke soberly at first, then excitedly, gesticulating and hovering over the table. He said nothing he had not declaimed or written before, beginning with *Mein Kampf*, but during the rise to power, electoral politics and the charade of legality had silenced talk of aggression and colonization. Now, four days after becoming chancellor, he had dropped the mask before a crucial audience. Whatever the speaker's abject ignorance of history, demography, and economics, however deranged his reasoning, his listeners could only rejoice in the assurance of arms and independence. He did not even think the equality of rights in armaments won at Geneva meant anything, he told them, to an army and a country still infested with bolshevism—an indication that *Gleichschaltung* mattered more than *Gleichberechtigung*, and

Geneva not at all. Some greeted the visions of race war skeptically, perhaps not seriously; but none protested.[10]

No one else heard about it. The press reported tersely that Hitler had gone before the military leaders, but revealed none of his words, other than a brief platitude about his belief in the "critical importance of military support among the people and of the army's work."[11] This meant nothing, and readers could not know that Hitler had just taken the first step toward co-opting the armed forces. He had purchased their tacit complicity in the coming terror and their active participation in projects to come. So it would be with other crucial constituencies, fed with one hand and collared with the other. Hitler had some friends in the business world, but not as many as Papen; a banker in Cologne had arranged the first meetings between the two at his house there, and a champagne salesman by the name of Joachim von Ribbentrop had hosted the next ones at home in the pleasant Dahlem district of Berlin. Now Hitler could promise to the entire business community to destroy Communism and tame the unions. So it would be with the churches, and the political parties except for the Social Democrats, and with professional groups and many others. And so it would be with entire swaths of the population— promised work, or order, or peace, they could accept what they liked and ignore what they did not, should a deluge of propaganda ever let the crimes float to the surface. Massive rearmament could bring work, and terror could bring order, and affectation of pacific purpose, studied and sustained, could dull fears and hide the ulterior logic of war without end.

And so it would be with foreign powers, whose journalists and diplomats might report what they saw, but whose governments, especially when answerable to voters, chose to see what they wished to believe.

"Never, perhaps," the correspondent of a mass-circulation French daily, Philippe Barrès, wrote from Berlin as Hitler's cabinet was announced, "has a mere assortment of names raised so many questions." A few spoke of a historic moment, but no more than the diplomats could they explain how history had suddenly changed course. In Paris, *Le Temps* announced a turning point but not what had turned. Everywhere the appointment of "the little Austrian house painter" made front-page news, but nowhere could anyone identify how or even whether he mattered.[12]

Sometimes, especially around the German periphery, among those whose shared frontiers with Germany gave the most to fear from pan-Germanism and radical revisionism, analysis gave way to anxiety. In France, where no one could be neutral about German nationalism, papers of the Right and Left alike sensed immediate danger—the end of Weimar, perhaps a military dictatorship, a restoration of the monarchy, diplomatic crises, saber-rattling. Much of the comment bordered on diagnosis, as though of a dangerous lunatic. Barrès, who had seen the torches and heard the "Horst Wessel" that night on the Wilhelmplatz, closed his report with a thought for his son asleep in their village in Lorraine. Four weeks later *Le Temps* anxiously described a German descent into many-sided civil war, among the Nazis, the Left, and the conservative nationalists, between Berlin and the Catholic southern states, a war practically of all against all. No one found this implausible. In the middle of February, an intransigent interview that Hitler gave the *Sunday Express* in London met with universal scorn, sarcasm, and indignation across the political spectrum of the French press.[13]

Will he make trouble for us? the worry ran in central Europe, often in opposition or even seditious organs eager to browbeat their own governments. In Warsaw, the opposition *Gazeta Warszawska*, the paper of the anti-Semitic as well as Germanophobic National Democrats, feared a wave of returning Polish Jews living and working in Germany. It wished to stop them before they had even begun to leave. In another opposition paper, the *Kurjer Warszawski*, General Wladyslaw Sikorski, a former premier, and a foe of Pilsudski, feared imminent danger if Hitler stayed in power, and did not doubt that "the first blow [would] be struck against Poland," probably as a descent on Pomerania or Silesia. In Prague both *Lidové Noviny* and *Narodni Listy*, the first a friend and the other a critic of Foreign Minister Benes, warned of a new danger, to add to Hungarian revisionism and rearmament, and called for a strong army. And in Vienna the Social Democratic *Arbeiter Zeitung* also feared the belligerence of the new cabinet in Berlin, made up of "the most notorious German reactionaries." But it foresaw class rather than national war, a social conflagration all over central Europe. It stood at the antipodes of the Austrian Nazis, who, like their Czech counterparts, welcomed the new government in Berlin and with it the prospects for autonomy or assimilation.[14]

Some saw dictatorship and sounded a different alarm. In France the papers of the broad center, left or right, grasped very quickly that Hitler intended to rule alone, and that the advent of the Nazis signified the demise of human and civil liberties in Germany. Racist demagoguery, attacks on Jews and Communists—such was the future that Louise Weiss, the pan-European author and activist, foresaw in the weekly she edited, *L'Europe nouvelle*, within days of Hitler's accession to office. Across the broad center, moral indignation rather than existential fear inspired the commentary, from a defense of liberal values on the moderate right to a new front in the struggle against Fascism on the non-Communist left. "Never," the Radical *L'Oeuvre* deemed a week after Hitler's first night, "has such an assault been made in Europe on the parliamentary regime, on democracy, on peace." On peace? It did not elaborate.[15]

But often, there and farther away, correspondents and their editors shrugged, and injected into their columns a blasé tone of déjà vu. Nothing had changed, they concluded. Of this they remained convinced for weeks.

Nazism was Germanism. The danger remained the same. In France, the Germanophobic nationalist Right remained unfazed by events across the border. It saw the Prussian eagle in the Nazi swastika, the spiked helmet in the SA cap, the Wagnerian in the Aryan. "The new Germany," according to Charles Maurras, the royalist leader, was "the Germany of yesterday, of today, of tomorrow." The antics of the new chancellor obscured the ways of the old order— militarist, authoritarian, and aggressive. Papen was its creature, Hitler its puppet. Others on the political spectrum at first belittled Nazi novelty as well. "Don't be alarmed," *L'Avenir*, a paper of the moderate Right, told its readers. "Germany today is what she was yesterday. . . . Let's not be afraid. Let's guard the barriers and build our strength." Even Blum, the Socialist, made out a feudal and cor- porate order at work behind the new cabinet. But so convinced were the doctrinaires of national character that not even the onset of the Nazi terror startled them. When Hitler took power, a right-wing col- umnist wrote of "a Germanic movement towards authority"; a month later the royalist historian and columnist Jacques Bainville was still describing the Nazi regime as another authoritarian government of the Right.[16]

Circumstances hamstrung the Nazis, whatever they might be plotting. So ran one of the most common judgments of the current danger. Will Hitler make trouble for us? the worry ran, and often, in Warsaw, Prague, and Vienna, the papers reassured their readers that he would not, because he could not, that he was so constrained by circumstances that they had little to fear from any impulsive adven- ture. These days, the pro-government *Kurjer Polski* told its readers in Warsaw, politicians in Berlin had nothing to gain and everything to lose, and Hitler's talk of revising the eastern frontier was "nothing new." *Nasz Przeglad*, the Jewish paper, foresaw no great upheavals. "Hindenburg tied Hitler's hands," the semiofficial *Prager Presse* told its readers in Prague, "when he put von Papen and von Blomberg in the new cabinet. Consequently, Hitler will be unable to realize the program of the National Socialist Party." Some of the German minority newspapers concurred. In Vienna, the *Neue Freie Presse* believed that Hitler by joining a rightist coalition government had abandoned his goal of imposing National Socialism on Germany. The conservative *Reichspost* also supposed as much. "One must as- sume," it announced, "that the National Socialists have guaranteed that they will observe the Constitution." These editorial musings did not often mention the prospect of absorption by the Reich, of an *Anschluss*—oddly, for the first of the Nazi Party's twenty-five-point program threatened Austria more obviously and more imminently than Poland or Czechoslovakia: "The union of all Germans, by right of self-determination, in one Great Germany."[17]

Farther away from the Nazi threat, in Britain and the United States, anxiety could wait. Instead, one European response—detached equanimity—took its place, followed more durably by another: moral indignation. It crowned a month of confusion and speculation with a semblance of consensus—the story was too important not to report, but not important enough to set one paper against another. Other stories mattered more, and raised partisan hackles in a way this one did not. The British papers devoted many more column inches to the impending showdown between Japan and the League of Nations over Manchuria than to "this latest quip of German politics," as the *Economist* first called it. In this they resembled their American but not their French counterparts, who turned in entire columns about Berlin or Stuttgart for every paragraph about Tokyo or Geneva. And that month, in the United States, the domestic emergency deepened. As Roosevelt's inauguration neared, the country's banking system verged on collapse, and the incoming administration had no plan yet to save it.[18] How much space could the press give to yet another political crisis in Germany?

Besides, no one could agree on whether or how much it mattered. The liberal *Economist* confessed to "feelings of bewilderment and concern." But the stock markets in London and New York reacted mildly. The *New York Times* thought that Papen and Hugenberg were likely to dominate Hitler. It still thought so at the end of the month, when it likened his followers to "a gang of sophomores trying to break up the freshman dinner" and dismissed the possibility of a "Mussolini stroke" in Berlin.[19] Some welcomed Hitler's appointment, others deplored it. Party affiliations meant little. Conservative papers in Britain could be either. Lord Beaverbrook's *Daily Express*, the isolationist, anti-Communist, and "Little Englander" tabloid that would soon set records for daily newspaper circulation, heralded Hitler as the "Fascist hero" who had "smashed a military plot" and set himself against a "red wave of terror" unleashed at Moscow's orders. *The Times* welcomed Hitler's chance to show himself "something more than an orator and an agitator," because his qualities as a statesman remained a mystery, even if assuredly no one doubted his sincerity. But the *Daily Telegraph*, Tory to the bone, immediately described the new chancellor as distilling the worst reactionary and hysterical traits of German political culture. The Liberal *News Chronicle* deemed the new government "good and necessary," promising the only formula that might work; the equally Liberal *Manchester Guardian* distrusted it at once. Other papers both welcomed and deplored the news in the same issue, sometimes in the same sentence. In Chicago, the *Tribune* professed American sympathy for the youthful Nazi revolt against national decay, but fretted over anti-Semitism and Fascism.[20] At the end of the month, it still imagined seeds of greatness in Hitler's revival of national pride. In both countries readers encountered disdain and esteem, resignation and hope.

But slowly the censorship and the purges, the arrests, beatings, and killings of Jews or political opponents, the outrages that revealed a regime instead of a government, dissipated lingering confusion or naivete. In New York, *The Nation*, a month after doubting that Hitler could rule unchecked, mourned German democracy, and *Time* reported that Hitler had done more in two weeks to suppress his enemies than Mussolini had in two years. In Britain, some—in particular the *Manchester Guardian*, which worried as early as January 31 that Hitler might drive the Jews out of Germany—were quick to scan for signs of incipient terror or dictatorship, and relentless in divulging them to their readers in the following days. Others held back. In the middle of the month, *The Times* began referring to a "German 'Fascist' regime" and a "Hitlerist state," but still wondered whether the chancellor might acquire the arts of statesmanship.[21] Not until the twenty-sixth did the *Sunday Times* accept that "a full-blooded

Fascist experiment" was underway in Germany. But sooner or later, all papers gave up contesting the incontestable. Even the *Daily Express* eventually did so. It dropped the German story from its pages in February, returning to it only to publish a single panegyric to Hitler penned by a sycophantic correspondent in Berlin. But at the end of the month it acknowledged the arrival there of "an era of undiluted Fascist government." It withheld either relief or regret. A minimal consensus was emerging in both countries, one that upheld their own values but imposed no obligations on them.[22]

Where the press possessed no mind of its own, and journalists and their editors had no views, only instructions, to express, they spared their readers the head shaking and the perplexity of their confreres in more open societies. In Italy and the Soviet Union, they shed no tears over the destruction of civil liberties in Germany. In Fascist or Communist idiom, they happily described the obsolescence of the liberal capitalist order; they observed Schleicher exit and Hitler enter the Chancellery in Berlin, and Paul-Boncour leave the premiership after only six weeks and the Radical Edouard Daladier come in, in the latest round of musical chairs in Paris. The two crises, *Izvestia* explained, were actually one, "in which the economic crisis transforms itself into a political crisis." Soon the struggle between capitalists for power would evolve into one between classes. "It's the crisis of a regime," the *Piccolo* in Trieste wrote, assimilating the two republics much as *Izvestia* did.[23]

Over Hitler, the two parted ways. The Italians applauded in his advent a German renaissance and a vindication of their own Fascism, a renewal of the spirit in which Italians could only recognize their own and rejoice. Italy, the *Giornale di Sicilia* wrote in the middle of February, had become the hope of humanity. The Soviets had nothing to celebrate. Had they not long assured readers that Germany would be the first to follow the Soviet path, and since November that its Communists were rising, its Nazis spent, and that proletarian revolution would end the impasse? Twenty-three days after Stalin touted the success of the first five-year plan before the Central Committee of the Communist Party, and the press continued to dismiss the Nazi danger, Hitler came to power and the German Communists began to disappear. An awkward silence soon fell over the official organs, broken by explanations that the advent of the Nazis had only accentuated the class conflict anew, with Hitler, like Mussolini, now revealing to the masses the true face of modern capitalism.[24]

The Italian prolixity misled as much as the Soviet silence. In Rome as in Moscow, the bloodless task of analysis and assessment was proceeding elsewhere, behind the closed doors of power. There the powerful disagreed more than the unanimity of their scribes suggested, but this the readers could not know. The press served to impart to the governed what the governors wished them to know, unlike elsewhere, where it revealed them to each other. Yet the pains that Fascists and Communists took in their single-party dominions to shape public thinking revealed their respect for its power. However differently, they too needed to align national policy with national mood. Their hold on power required that each sustain the other. And meanwhile, events in Germany unfolded faster than they or anyone else could absorb.

Oddly enough, in view of their privileged perch, some of the best-informed diplomats betrayed the same perplexity as the journalists. Anxious, blasé, bewildered, or disgusted, the foreign emissaries reported to their governments as volubly and yet as guardedly as the foreign correspondents to their readers.

On February 8, at the dinner offered every year for the Berlin diplomatic corps, the French ambassador, André François-Poncet, sat opposite the new chancellor. Like so many before him, he found Hitler at close range ordinary, slightly comical, as though about to rise and sing some sentimental song; but his eyes shone, seeming to laugh fleetingly, darken suddenly, or discern some ruse or peril. He lacked self-assurance and was visibly bewildered by the stuffed shirts and diplomatic regalia around him. A village Mussolini, the ambassador concluded. After dinner, Hitler told him that he was too busy with the March elections he had just called to worry about much else, but he spoke hopefully of a Europe united against bolshevism and of good rapports with France. For that to happen, he added, the French would have to accept that a new era was beginning in Germany, a radical break with the past. When he spoke of extirpating the criminals of November 1918, his eyes burned with fanatical hatred. Then he seemed wild, unsettled. The Foreign Ministry officials seemed anxious. What do you think of him? they asked. How do you find him? And they assured the diplomats that the new chancellor was subtler and more refined than he might seem.[25]

Rather than subtlety or refinement, the ambassador had long discerned in Hitler the crude, grand certitudes of the self-taught and the half-learned, as well as the intuitive gifts of the demagogue and a craftiness unencumbered by any sense of honor or the given word. He had already reflected that Papen and the other conservatives, confident of manipulating the new chancellor, might soon fall victim to him instead. Three nights earlier, at a dinner at the British ambassador's, Papen cited Hitler's hollow utterances so often and so reverently that François-Poncet quickly surmised which of the two dominated the other.[26] His British colleague, Sir Horace Rumbold, thought much the same. Perhaps Papen might cut Hitler down to size and induce him to give up aping Mussolini, he wrote the Foreign Office, but he had not harnessed the Nazis to his wagon, as he had claimed.[27] The astute diplomats were more clairvoyant about the coming power struggle than the complacent partners of the Nazis.

But they speculated, in those early days, almost as they might about any other new coalition government; they raised no alarm, not yet discerning any break with the past, uncertain and perplexed about the future. "Alice in Wonderland," the British ambassador thought about the political scene, not for the first time. He grasped the illegality of the decrees of the first week of February, which empowered the government to ban newspapers and assemblies and lock up peace breakers, but a week later still thought the power struggle and the election to come could proceed along constitutional lines.[28]

His American counterpart, Frederic Sackett, thought the same. The Nazis, he thought, hoped "to govern by practically dictatorial methods for at least four years" by winning an outright majority in the election on March 5. But this only recalled the ambitions of Papen and Schleicher before them. Sackett did not yet grasp the incipient dictatorship, the design to sweep away the entire liberal order. Yes, they had monopolized the radio, recorded on wax records the chancellor's manifesto and repeatedly broadcast it throughout the country, suspended their opponents' newspapers, changed the electoral law. But they had done so solely to subtract votes from their coalition partners in the election campaign under way. "If the Nazis do not resort to unfair methods to keep their political opponents from the polls," he thought, they could only win by bringing abstentionists to the polls.[29] François-Poncet still thought that Hitler might lend himself to a return of the Hohenzollerns, might yet go down in history as the harbinger of a monarchical restoration.[30] Some Soviet diplomats thought Hitler would not last long anyway—the working-class movement would tame or even overthrow him.[31]

Soon, within weeks, and before the March 5 election, some of the diplomats apprehended more than a political simplification, or a passive Reichstag, or a transition to a constitutional monarchy. Rumbold began sounding the alarm. Unless the electorate regained its sanity, he wrote, or President Hindenburg recovered some respect for the Constitution, the government would undermine the very foundations of popular liberties and representative government. "If the German people abandon us in this hour," he had heard Hitler vow to the mass in the Sportpalast on February 10, "then—Heaven forgive us—we will follow the road which we feel to be necessary in order that Germany may not perish." What was this, if not a promise to keep power whatever the electorate decided?[32] In Stuttgart the American consul watched the gangs of four or five armed and uniformed Nazis swagger about the streets, especially on Sundays and holidays, and he remembered the dominical brawling during his posting to Rome a decade earlier and the Fascist rise to power. He watched houses searched, liberties suppressed, the small Württemberg parliament subverted, the officials cashiered, the citizens terrorized, all to save the land from the Bolshevik menace, and he remembered.[33] François-Poncet hesitated. Yes, the Nazis slavishly imitated the Fascists, and Mussolini had seemed to many a joke at first. But, he mused, "German fascism applies to a people who do not resemble the Italians. It will encounter more formidable resistance than Roman fascism did. . . ."[34] No one knew what to expect.

On the night of February 27, as he hosted a dinner at his embassy, the French ambassador received a note from an aide. From a window he watched the great glass dome of the Reichstag glowing. He returned to the table to share the news of the fire with his guests. One of them, the finance minister Schwerin von Krosigk, a conservative guarantor of sanity and continuity in the eyes of so many diplomats and governments, could not contain himself. "Thank God!" he exclaimed joyously.[35]

Cui bono? To whom the profit? Foreign diplomats and journalists as well as skeptical Germans immediately doubted official denunciations of a seditious plot hatched by the Communists, a Guy Fawkes–like attempt to overthrow the government.[36] It, not they, exploited the timely blaze. When Frick, the Nazi minister of the interior, proposed in the cabinet the next day to suspend civil rights and assume direct powers in all the German states, his non-Nazi colleagues—Krosigk among them—assented. Wholesale arrests of Communists followed, allowing others as well. The designation of "Marxist," an ecumenical and elastic word in Nazi parlance, embraced among others "Bolshevik," "Socialist," "Communist," "Jewish," and even "Asiatic"—the last employed by Goering's new chief of police in Berlin four days before the Reichstag fire: "I shall tolerate no plants of Asiatic origins which create unrest among the Berlin people," he told his subordinates. "I take this opportunity to warn these murderers, these political gangsters."[37]

The Reichstag had burned on Monday night; on Sunday, the

German voters went to the polls again, in massive numbers—almost 90 percent of the electorate cast ballots. Once in the booth they could mark them with the party of their choice; the election, less than free but more than sham, still carried some meaning. The Nazis had gained two million votes since their peak in July 1932, and four million more since their disappointing showing in November, and together with the votes of their coalition partners, Hugenberg's Nationalists, they now commanded an absolute majority in the Reichstag. No government had enjoyed anything of the sort since the spring of 1930. Goebbels and Goering exulted. Hugenberg himself applauded Hitler's triumph. Yet the Nazis, despite their silencing of so many opponents and their monopoly over so many instruments of mental and physical persuasion, had once again fallen short of an absolute majority. They had reached their electoral limit.[38]

In the end this did not matter. In the first elections of the Weimar Republic, in 1919, two-thirds of the voters had cast their ballots for parties friendly to it, members of the "Weimar coalition." Now, in its last elections, almost two-thirds had cast their ballots for its enemies—the Nazis, the Nationalists, and the Communists. To condemn not the imperial regime that with reckless gambles had brought defeat and disaster on Germany, but the republican successor that had tried to salvage what it could and restore stability, to blame it as well for an economic depression that any fool knew was worldwide—a doctrine approaching drivel had triumphed at the polls. Scarcely a third had voted for the republican parties, including the Center Party, now even less certain a supporter than usual. And the Communists, who though hostile to the republic would have opposed whatever the Nazis proposed, were now illegal, absent from the Reichstag. Antiparliamentary sentiment by whatever name, and all that went with it, had come to rest with the Nazis, who now exploited it to consummate, as papers of the Right recognized, the demolition of democracy by more or less democratic means.[39]

Some two weeks later, on the first day of spring, the deputies to the new Reichstag assembled in the Garrison Church for the comedy of Potsdam. All—date, site, and ceremony—gaudily proclaimed continuity and renewal. On March 21, 1871, after the victory over France, the first Reichstag of the new empire had met in Potsdam. The throne in the old church today was empty, but Wilhelmine Germany came in the person of former crown prince Wilhelm, who sat in the old imperial box, in his death's-head hussar's uniform and tall fur hat. Frederic600 Prussia was here as well, in its military capital, in the tombs of its soldier-kings. And the Third Reich was here, in the brownshirts and in Adolf Hitler. He sat in the chancel beside the bemedaled Hindenburg in a sober civilian suit, the two under the Nazi swastika and the monarchical black, white, and red, the new Germany vowing to redeem the old. Earlier the two had descended into the crypt, to bow before Frederick the Great. This too was drivel. An Austrian rabble-rouser ruling under the aegis of old Prussia? His raucous brownshirts, come to meditate among its remains? He had no intention of restoring the Hohenzollerns or anyone else. But the pretense served its purpose, that of lulling conservatives long enough to cement the Nazi grip before dispatching not only Weimar but their fantasies as well.[40]

Two days later, in the Kroll Opera House across the Königsplatz from the darkened Reichstag, the itinerant deputies, homeless since the fire three weeks earlier, convened again. This time they met to divest themselves at Hitler's behest of all but their most honorific functions, and empower the cabinet to ignore them, bypass the president, and rule by decree. The Catholic Center deputies capitulated after gaining assurances about protections for the church. The Communists were gone, into prison, hiding, or exile. Only the Social Democrats voted against the act. Ostensibly it would expire in four years, but, together with the decree that had suspended civil liberties the day after the Reichstag burned, it provided Hitler with all the legal scaffolding of a perennial dictatorship. For now the Wilhelmine colors flanked the swastika, but not for much longer; and today the chancellor stood before them in brownshirt and boots.

By then the swastikas were spreading out from the bastions of officialdom and pervading the rooms and streets of daily life, hoisted in schools, stamped onto toothpaste tubes and children's play balls, plying the listless and the stupefied with visual admonitions of a revolution in progress. To Viktor Klemperer, a professor of Romance languages in Dresden, the lawful and the familiar had vanished overnight, and he struggled to find some historical referent for the sudden breakdown. Perhaps November 1918? Or the Terror in the French Revolution? Or the pogroms of medieval Europe or Tsarist Russia? He found escape in the cinemas. Harry Kessler, the peripatetic patron of the arts and fervent critic of the Nazis, left for Paris. Friends from the French embassy in Berlin warned him not to return. He never did.[41]

All this was difficult to miss, and diplomats, even when they described the events of March differently, usually read them the same way. The French ambassador saw the ceremony in Potsdam as darkly farcical, the British ambassador as "simple, dignified, and significant." But both understood it as the final nail in the coffin of the Weimar Republic. The American ambassador as well as the British now began writing home of "revolution," resting on administrative purges of Jews and political undesirables and their progressive hounding from any kind of public office or profession, of *Gleichschaltung*—the homogenization of German society—and its elastic and ominous kin, Aryanization. This required no special insight, no more than the decree of March 31, which suppressed much provincial autonomy, leveled the assemblies of the states and peopled their officialdom more and more with Nazis and less and less with Nationalists, and centralized the administration of the Reich at its summit. But the diplomats hesitated naturally to draw a line under the dizzying transformations they witnessed, and to sketch for their governments the shape of the future. The French ambassador, a Germanist steeped in the history and literature of his host country, cast the administrative reforms in a perspective of tension between Reich and Länder stretching back to 1871. But only time would tell, he concluded prudently, whether they would succeed. And Horace Rumbold, the British ambassador, remained stubbornly ambivalent about Hitler, unwilling to shed once and for all illusory hopes that the new chancellor might moderate the excesses or rein in his wilder followers and colleagues, foremost among them Hermann Goering in Prussia.[42]

In the press, place and sometimes party governed how editors chose to print their correspondents' reports of the demise of Weimar. None doubted it, but the unanimity went no further. The Italians continued to revel in the vindication of Fascism across the Alps. The Czechoslovaks in mid-March were devoting more space in their pages to Germany than to all other foreign news combined, and often found in the surprising staying power of the Left in the March 5 election a sign that Hitler might not attain the aims "he has set his heart on." The Soviet press, whether of the party or of the government, now protested the campaign against the Communists, the scapegoating of them that followed the Reichstag fire, and Hitler's speeches—*Pravda* called him a "jester on the throne." Frederick's tomb in Potsdam symbolized for the *Giornale d'Italia* in Rome a strong Germany and an authoritarian state, for *Le Temps* in Paris the hegemonic urge that had brought catastrophe to the world in 1914. By now all, including the nationalist Right in France, had accepted that Hitler was establishing a regime that was somehow sui generis, whatever else it might be, and that it was likely to last; but the unanimity ended there.[43]

In the latter half of March, a boycott of German commerce abroad gathered steam, and a Nazi counterboycott of Jewish shops and firms, with all its attendant violence, loomed on April 1. Through the ironclad censorship, anonymous correspondents sent word, confirmed by travelers as well as the first refugees, of anti-Semitic rampages, of shops closed and homes searched, of hundreds beaten and robbed. "Hardly a day passes," the semiofficial Polish *Gazeta Polska* announced at the end of March, "without assaults by Storm Troopers and attacks on the private homes of Jews," and news services began reporting the incidents all over Germany.[44] In France, and even more in Britain and America, the newspapers reported the crimes and condemned the perpetrators. They all did so differently. April 1 marked, for *Le Temps* on its eve, the persecution of imaginary enemies, a regression to the wars of religion, and the paper ridiculed the aspiration to ethnic or racial homogeneity in any modern nation, especially that of Kant. But it injected as well a dash of national smugness when it welcomed the Anglo-Saxon awakening, at last, to the "aggressive Germanism" the French had warned of, and reminded its readers that they, at least, had overcome their conflicts and their aberrations—an oblique allusion to the passions of the Dreyfus affair a generation earlier. *The Times* deplored the violence but persisted in supposing, even after April 1, that Hitler with his calls for discipline might end it with his "unmistakable wish" to control his unruly followers. More aggressively than its two confreres in Paris and London, the *New York Times* graphically reported not only the misdeeds of the perpetrators but the passivity of the bystanders, inclined—almost like *The Times*—to write off the violence to a culpable excess of zeal. It covered the story almost daily.[45] Three establishment papers, all considered journals of record—yet the condescension of *Le Temps*, the credulity of *The Times*, and the assiduity of the *New York Times* did not exhaust the ways of conveying so stark a spectacle.

Some, like the *Sunday Times*, did not convey it at all, until at the end of the month the boycotts grew too pressing, the rising outcry too loud, for the paper to ignore. Then reflexive fears of new dangers might follow hard on the reporting of new persecutions. In France, *Le Figaro* feared another invasion from across the Rhine, this one by 500,000 German-Jewish refugees—not because they were Jews, but because they were Germans.[46] "Judea Declares War on Germany," the *Daily Express* announced in an incendiary headline a week before the anti-Semitic day in Germany on April 1. It had ignored the story all month, and now reported that "the whole of Israel throughout the world is uniting to declare an economic and financial war on Germany," in sequel to "stories of German Jew-baiting." Like *Le Figaro*, it was a nationalist paper of the Right. It was isolationist as well, hostile to unwanted newcomers at home and unwanted burdens abroad. So was the *Chicago Tribune*, but its own headline about the German boycott—"Hitler Nazis Declare War on World Jewry"—

could not differ more suggestively from that of the *Daily Express*.[47] Even the reprehensible lent itself to an abundance of readings, presaging a wilderness to come.

An implicit confusion had arisen. Until now, the champions of rapprochement with Germany, of treaty revision and economic rehabilitation, had invoked morality and international equity. Now, with the tales coming out of the Reich, the conceit, if it was to survive, required some pruning. The American press had reported widely on intimidation and terror, and sometimes on the cost to German standing abroad, but not on the implications for German reintegration into the world.[48] Already *The Times*, as earnest a proponent of German claims as ever, had explained that "the cruelties inflicted by German upon German . . . [are] primarily a matter for Germany herself."[49] But only in international law was this so. Otherwise the commotion near and far suggested that they had become a matter for many. If, cruelty notwithstanding, the cause of conciliation remained as popular as ever, then its prime movers might have to invoke expedience rather than justice, and boast their adaptability rather than their consistency. Over time they might have to admit at least to themselves that all along they had obeyed the same inner command as the fiercest antirevisionists, the staunchest upholders of the status quo—to protect their own nation.

Did anyone believe that the "cruelties" might not spill beyond the borders? That a regime so belligerent at home might be as pacific abroad, Dr. Jekyll in one and Mr. Hyde in the other? The new German regime wished its neighbors to accept as much. Ever since February 1, Hitler had posed before the world as an apostle not only of justice but of peace. He had broadcast that night to the German people, speaking at breakneck speed like a political agitator on the hustings, promising to annihilate Communism, to end misery and unemployment within four years, demanding as others had before him the just return of German lands and the disarmament of the other powers down to German levels—for here lay the only road, he clamored, to the peace he so ardently craved. American radio stations and European wire services picked up the speech, his first as chancellor. He had not changed his public tune since.[50]

Occasionally he sounded a discordant note about Poland—a demand for the Polish Corridor, all of it, in the *Sunday Express* in February, which his Foreign Ministry subsequently denied, a promise to the people of East Prussia on election eve to "fight for it to the very last." But more often, when the world was listening, he exerted himself to reassure. When he demanded of the Reichstag on March 23 that it surrender its powers to him, and promised to extirpate traitors with "barbaric ruthlessness," he also commended a new British disarmament effort at Geneva. The masquerade bought time. This was not the moment to risk confrontation with the Western powers, to provoke the French or the Poles or endanger British goodwill, not when Germany was militarily weaker than they and when the dictatorship had not yet perpetuated its hold. If foreign governments did not believe their denials of the domestic persecution, they might at least divorce it from the conduct of foreign policy. Even the liberal *Vossische Zeitung*, long a fierce critic of the Nazis and still—for another year—publishing, accepted as much. Yes, it acknowledged, the new government had aroused preoccupations among its neighbors. But diplomacy enjoyed its own sphere and its own laws, determined by interests and stubborn historical realities, and governments all over Europe had embarked on bold domestic escapades and not touched their foreign policies. Tsar and commissar, Liberal and Fascist, pursued the same national ends abroad. Had not Herriot himself, the paper asked, acknowledged the same, and pursued rapprochements with both Italy and the Soviet Union?[51]

From Foreign Minister Neurath down through the echelons, the German foreign ministry and its emissaries were pushing the same message. Well before anyone abroad had time to comment on Hitler's appointment, and well before the new chancellor had spoken to the nation and the world on the radio, Bülow, the state secretary of the Foreign Office, was instructing embassies abroad to calm the waters. Tell them, he advised on the day of Hitler's appointment, of

the new cabinet's obedience to constitutional and majority rule, of
the continuity personified by Baron von Neurath at Foreign Affairs,
Count von Krosigk at Finance, and General von Blomberg at Defense; and remind them that in Germany governments emancipated
foreign from domestic policy.[52] Foreign governments east and west
began receiving the first of the reassurances that would keep coming
their way in the following years. The day after he received Bülow's
telegram, the German ambassador in Moscow conveyed its message to an alarmed Nikolay Krestinski, the deputy Soviet commissar
for foreign affairs. Meanwhile, his colleague in London explained to
the foreign secretary that German domestic changes did not affect
foreign policy. Two days later, in Washington, the undersecretary of
state learned the same from the German ambassador, who, though
no Nazi himself, added that "as a matter of fact, the men in power,
including Hitler, had almost a pacifist mentality." Another two days
later, Neurath in Berlin did his best to allay French concerns. Surely
the French ambassador had noticed, he asked him, how measured
Hitler's pronouncements about foreign affairs had become?[53]

They had—Hitler and his ministers now posed as traditional revisionists, no more, moved by the guiding light of universal equity,
proclaimed in the open the message that diplomats conveyed to their
foreign counterparts in camera. If rupture there was, it was not with
their predecessors in office but with their own campaign rhetoric. No
one doubted that today the new German government feared war and
ostracism. The American ambassador reported that the Nazi leaders would rather disappoint their most chauvinistic followers than
fulfill their heady promises to isolate France or turn their backs on
the League of Nations or otherwise upset an already fragile international order. But tomorrow? Neither diplomats nor journalists were
disposed to believe all that officialdom told them, even if officialdom
itself, beginning with Bülow, usually did. Sometimes the spectacle
unsettled them more than the words could soothe them.[54]

Sitting in Neurath's office on February 4, the French ambassador,
François-Poncet, did not doubt the foreign minister's good inten-

tions. He doubted instead his mettle, his fitness to resist the Nazi leaders or the aggressive public sentiments that sustained them. In the weeks that followed, François-Poncet discerned both drift and danger. At the end of March, he still found himself unable to define German foreign policy, so inchoate seemed the working doctrine, so uninformed the leader. But he mused about Nazism itself. He had read *Mein Kampf.* He had noticed the allusions to the spirit and communion of 1914 in Nazi papers and Nazi utterances, heard the Francophobia in the songs of the storm troopers and the evocations of the German wars of liberation from the Napoleonic French in the previous century; and he had winced at the official indulgence. Early in March some four hundred Nazi storm troopers, some of them armed, occupied a few barracks in Kehl, on the Rhine at the edge of the German demilitarized zone, violating the Treaty of Versailles and alarming the French inhabitants across the river. The SA rowdies withdrew the next day, but official apologies came lamely; and even Neurath, it seemed to François-Poncet, had succumbed to the ambient demagoguery, and not dared in the press to advertise too profound a sense of sorrow.

Perhaps the new Reich had not implemented any of the foreign policy precepts of *Mein Kampf*—for of the unpublished second book, the ambassador knew nothing—including the reduction of France, the alliance with Britain and Italy, and the pursuit of living space in the east. But rumors reached François-Poncet's ears of Hitler's determination to Nazify German diplomacy. At the beginning of April, Alfred Rosenberg, the Nazi ideologue and diplomatic editor of the *Völkischer Beobachter*, as different from Neurath as night from day, took over a new foreign political bureau in the Nazi Party. As he did so, he expressed a special interest in the Danube basin and eastern Europe. Two weeks later, he told the Hearst press that Germany had no interest in friction with Britain or the United States. "Our attention is today directed to the East of Europe. There lie Germany's future markets." The prospect of parallel power or worse—infiltration and submersion—could not delight the career diplomats in the Wilhelmstrasse, and when

François-Poncet met with Bülow there he found him melancholy and disenchanted. The Foreign Ministry head advised him to meet with Hitler, who alone would soon drive German foreign policy. The ambassador did, a few days later, and found him as he had in February more comical than frightening in aspect, but polite and prudent, even platitudinous, unwilling to commit himself and seemingly unsure of his ground. The quandary about the German danger deepened.[55]

Most diplomats sooner or later confronted it. They could not resolve it. Like his French confrere, the British ambassador came to doubt German declarations that severed foreign from domestic policy. It took Rumbold longer, for he remained mostly silent about the matter until the end of April, when he had finally read *Mein Kampf*. None of it had yet appeared in English, and the original German struck Rumbold as turgid in style and fantastic in content. But he took it seriously, telling the Foreign Office in a long memorandum that already the Nazis had launched their campaign against the Jews, and that they spoke of peace—which he had taken at face value early in the month—only to lull their adversaries while they rearmed. He had fathomed Hitler's hegemonic ambitions, even loosely the connection between domestic and foreign drives; yet he remained ambivalent, unwilling to jettison all hope of negotiating with a leader he persisted in seeing as less radical than his followers.[56] His American counterparts, professional diplomats who had fully chronicled for their government the domestic energies of the Nazis, rarely speculated about their foreign ambitions, if any. The consul in Munich, Charles Hathaway, had as early as 1931, and again in early May 1933, when he took *Mein Kampf* seriously enough to dissect it in a long report. Three months after the Nazis took power, he repeated that the hankering for a "warlike tribal unity" and the "passionate violent German nationalism" of Hitler's book remained the key to understanding Nazism, and that the ongoing "reorganization" of Germany might logically lead it to war. But he concentrated, in his forty-five-page report, on the acts of the new government at home, and said nothing else of any threats it presented to its neighbors or others.[57] His colleague in Berlin, the vice-consul George Messersmith, warned that the Nazis were bent on war; he would never stop warning, then or years later as assistant secretary of state. Few of Hathaway's or Messersmith's colleagues joined them. The Nazis strove to avoid isolation, a senior diplomat ventured in February. They were too preoccupied with domestic matters to have any clear-cut foreign policy, another American diplomat, the delegate to the disarmament conference, concluded after meeting Hitler in April, and he declined to predict what the future might bring.[58]

No Marxist could detach foreign from domestic power struggles—class conflict, like capitalism, transcended national boundaries—but the Soviet diplomats had more prosaic and less doctrinal reasons for seeking clues to one in the other. Hitler as chancellor attacked Soviet bolshevism, blamed Communists for the Reichstag fire and banned them from public life, yet received the Soviet ambassador in mid-March, an honor until then extended only to the Italian. Nazi agents rounded up Communists and raided the offices of Soviet trade delegations, yet Neurath assured Foreign Minister Litvinov that their relations would remain unchanged. What were the Soviet diplomats in Berlin to think? A long history of depreciating the Nazi danger lay behind them and their superiors, Stalin included, in Moscow. Now their confidence began to desert them, and their ambivalence, bordering on confusion, unfolded in official news—the only news—in the press. Late in March, in *Izvestia*—which spoke not for the party but for the government—Karl Radek, a recanted Trotskyite and major foreign affairs spokesman, reminded readers of German imperialism and the draconian treaty of Brest-Litovsk, imposed on the "young Soviet republic" in 1918; and he reminded them of the eastern ambitions Hitler had expressed in *Mein Kampf*. Five days later, the same paper published an excerpt from *Täglische Rundschau*, as though to approve the German Nationalist paper's apologia, which drew a line between the struggle against Communists at home and Hitler's statesmanlike pursuit of sensible relations with the Soviet Union

abroad. Which reading of Nazism—the essentialist or the realist—
Izvestia and the People's Commissariat for Foreign Affairs behind it
endorsed remained unclear.[59]

Perhaps to dispel the confusion, the Soviet leadership had com-
missioned a critical translation of *Mein Kampf* for its own internal
perusal in the autumn of 1932. Grigory Zinoviev, a Bolshevik purist
from Lenin's inner circle, but en route in disgrace to Siberia for his
complicity in the Riutin conspiracy against Stalin, undertook the
task, perhaps to rehabilitate himself. When he had finished, by the
spring of 1933, he had dubbed *Mein Kampf* the "bible of German
fascism," set forth the centrality of race and the Judeo-Bolshevik
menace to Hitler, and insisted on the existential threat his accession
to office represented to the Soviet Union. Sobering reading for the
Politburo; but it left no trace of relieving their perplexity, and they
kept it out of the press and the public eye.[60]

If even the Soviet press could accept that a kind of realpolitik
might ignore the ideological furies that drove the Nazis at home,
then others in the West might as well. They raised the question just
as the diplomats did, sometimes before them. The Italians welcomed
another Fascist regime as another dove of peace—not only would
it promote treaty revision, it would bring to the heart of Europe a
"solid, orderly, tranquil Germany," as the *Corriere della Sera* had it,
"assured of dignity and work," and indispensable to the peace of the
continent. Elsewhere, journalists and editors freer to express themselves stopped well short of identifying a tyrannical regime with the
cause of peace. But they divorced its crimes at home from its conduct
at Geneva or anywhere else where its writ did not run. Such domestic
methods need not worry other governments, *The Times* concluded
late in March—"There is nothing yet to show that the new Chancellor
intends to be immoderate in his foreign policy." Across the Atlantic,
the *New York Times* reported as much from Berlin, even while recording anti-Semitic and other outrages almost daily.[61]

Others frowned and hesitated. "Does he bring peace or war?" the
Manchester Guardian asked, alarmed at the ominous ways Hitler

had won and celebrated power at home. Any foreign journalist con-
founding Nazism with "Prussianism" fell prey to similar doubts, for
"Prussianism" meant militarism, and militarism meant the summer
of 1914. *Germany Puts the Clock Back*, as Edgar Ansel Mowrer, the
correspondent of the *Chicago Daily News*, titled his book of February
1933; in it, he diagnosed the rise and triumph of the Nazis as just
such a regression—a revival of the Hohenzollern spirit without the
dynasty, filling a void among a "nation of natural extremists." Mowrer, the president of the Foreign Press Association in Berlin, antago-
nized the Nazis, who forced him to leave later that year, but he had
helped launch the genealogy of Nazism, an industry that thrived on
tracing the ancestry of the Third Reich to the depths of the Germanic soul or the mists of the Germanic past. A year later, Wickham
Steed, erstwhile editor of *The Times*, linked Hitler beyond racialism
to Hegel, progenitor of the "state absolute." No matter that Hitler had
never read Hegel. Others would follow, including historians. But in
1933 the more pressing memory was 1914, the same that drew shud-
ders from the editors of *Le Temps* when they reflected on the ceremony in the old Prussian shrine in Potsdam.[62]

A few in these early months had already discerned in the Nazism
of *Mein Kampf*—and not in the original twenty-five points of the party
program, which the credulous cited and Hitler ignored—a threat to
their national survival. In Lithuania a Socialist paper mistakenly
identified it as a Nazi Party pamphlet with multiple authors but signed
by Hitler, but cited it to expose the threat to the Baltic states and to
the existence of their own. The tract was danger enough. In Paris
L'Europe nouvelle, through its correspondent fresh from the torchlit
processions under the Brandenburg Gate, reminded its readers that
the Nazis had never repudiated *Mein Kampf* and that from now on
their demands for equality of arms could only mean international anarchy and the right of the strong. A few warned as well that Hitler was
of a piece, that Nazi violence was sovereign and indivisible, and that
to ask him to respect the order and peace of Europe was to "expect a
cactus bristling with needles to bear olive branches." But the foreign

project at the heart of Nazism never drew the attention that the domestic did.[63]

In Kaunas and in Paris, the few were right; but even they, and the diplomats along with them, failed to grasp that this was no ordinary nationalism. It spoke the usual language, an emancipatory and irredentist patois, its vocabulary confined to the foreign yoke—Versailles and the Communist International—and to the lot of German brethren across the borders. It inherited too the appetite of nineteenth-century nationalisms for domestic as well as foreign enemies. But *Lebensraum* never stopped there. Where it stopped no one knew, and no one ever would know, because racial diplomacy did not exist and could provide no answer. This was a nationalism that had burst its own bounds, disguised for now as conventional revisionism for conventional diplomats.

They, straining to comprehend, scanned the horizon for the known rather than the unknown. Ambassador Rumbold concluded his long cable alerting the Foreign Office to the "fantastic proposals" in *Mein Kampf* by citing Papen, who had declared in Breslau a few weeks earlier that Nazism marked above all a revolt against the Treaty of Versailles. "The Vice Chancellor," Rumbold commented, "for once spoke the unvarnished truth." He credited Hitler with erasing, at least symbolically, the humiliation of Versailles, "but only at the cost of burdening Europe with a new outbreak of nationalism." In short, he was all too familiar, however unwelcome. The American consul in Stuttgart, whose troubled sense of déjà vu in February sprang from his time in Rome a decade earlier, settled in April on a more proximate blood-relation of the Nazis around him. When they dealt with foreigners, he said, they reverted to "the cynical militarism of their predecessors of pre-Weimar days"—the Hohenzollerns, again. To the Soviets—even though Stalin early in 1934 would warn of Nazi plans to dominate the Slavs—endless race war was unimaginable. Neither Marxism-Leninism nor their own reading of European politics allowed for it. Notwithstanding Zinoviev's study—if they had read it—no more than anyone else could they identify the clues to Nazi ambitions abroad in their choice of enemies at home. They missed the continuum.[64]

Almost all the Germans missed it as well. The Nazis flattered enough of their beliefs to blind them to the latent perils. The peaceful revision of Versailles, *Gleichberechtigung* and German honor, the salvation of European civilization from Communism—for several years the sanctimonious pablum would deceive them. In 1940, looking back, Goebbels even boasted of the deception.[65] He passed over in silence the many minds so conveniently disposed to believe it. He ignored as well the myopic and the parochial in the foreign reactions. Even the most skeptical journalists and diplomats listening to him and his fellows construed the scene in their own national and ideological idioms, and spoke of Hohenzollerns, 1914, 1919, class war, national character, and all that sounded familiar. When they reported their findings to their compatriots, they set off confusion, indignation, and sometimes acrimony among them. In France, any hope of a consensus over the best way to handle the latest fit of Teutonic madness soon vanished in a new outbreak of ideological feuding. The Right, from sounding the drums of national redemption and seeing in the advent of Hitler the bitter fruit of *Briandisme* and its deplorable illusions, soon began to wonder whether the Reich might not after all provide a buffer against Soviet Communism at home and abroad. Parts of the Left, so attached to disarmament and the cause of peace, began to worry about the vulnerability of the nation. Already the Right was sounding less bellicose, the Left more so. They had begun an inversion that would only accelerate as the decade advanced, adding ideological confusion to economic stagnation and social strife. The same crossover was underway in neighboring Belgium, where a right-wing press that for years had presented Nazism as a threat to peace and security now warmed to it as a bulwark against bolshevism, and the papers of the Left, once accused of pacifism and Germanophilia, now warned of new breaches in the Versailles system. The nascent Third Reich, which had violently simplified political life within its borders, had durably snarled it beyond them; and this too helped Hitler.[66]

11

UNWILLING ACCOMPLICES

T his House will in no circumstances fight for its King and Country," read the motion before the Oxford Union on the evening of February 9, 1933, and, by a vote of 275 to 153, the students of the debating society approved it. The union had supported the national government when it took office in August 1931, but unlike the country had moved leftward, and shed much of the conservatism as well as the frivolity of its predecessors. In their day they had debated such weighty propositions as "it is better to be a knave than a fool." No one had paid much attention, until now.[1]

Dissenters invaded the union's offices and tore out the pages in the registers that recorded the vote. Indignant students in Cambridge proposed to boycott the boat race. He was only following the government's own aversion to war, one of the victors of the debate explained lamely, appearing no more inclined to fight for his motion than for his king.[2]

"'Un-British' Oxford Men. Communist Motion Stirs City," announced the *Daily Express*, which found the townspeople of Oxford alarmed and the mayor in tears, clutching his Bible. A populist streak, fusing patriotism with social resentment, ran through the paper's reporting, which continued for most of the week. A more condescending *Times* lamented the poor taste of it all, so soon after the sacrifices of the war. At least "the children's hour," with its "little clique of cranks," did not reflect the rest of the country. Communist plot or undergraduate silly season, the passage of the motion alarmed opinion, and misled some observers abroad into hoping or fearing that Britain's future leaders would never fight for anything at all.[3]

As an Oxford don recalled a few years later, they had misunderstood the insularity of a bad joke. Most of the speakers condemned war rather than patriotism, and the voters for the poorly worded motion probably registered a preference to fight for collective security, or the League of Nations, or a rational international order rather than for the symbols that had yielded the hecatombs of the late war. *The Times* might have pointed out as well that the cranks in question did not speak for all the students either, and that enlistments in the Officer Training Corps at the university began suddenly to rise.[4]

The reaction, much more than the vote, revealed the temper of the country, at once patriotic and unwarlike. The affronted patriots, for whom the vote in the union had insulted the memory of those who *had* died for king and country, had nothing to say about new foreign threats or about meeting force with force. Their strictures mentioned no Hitler; then and later both *The Times* and the *Daily Express* busily sought ways to accommodate him. The *Sunday Times* too found the students' motion tasteless. But a week earlier, six days after Hitler had become chancellor, it had rejected any new European commitments, deplored the French insistence on security, and reaffirmed its credo: "Disarmament is the thing." Later it reprieved the students, whom it deemed hostile to war but not to patriotism—which no longer demanded martial enthusiasms, and even sometimes shunned them. "Appeasement" in those days rang of enlightened self-interest, a byword for national sanity and not yet—not for six more years—for craven surrender.[5]

Neither in Britain nor anywhere else did any mass movement of foreign sympathy or support for the Third Reich develop in the early months of its life, apart from some ethnic Germans living across the borders in Austria or Czechoslovakia. Where the papers were free to publish and newsreels to project their revelations about the new regime's doings at home, displays of defiance, dread, or revulsion followed. But nowhere either did popular support for intervention or preventive war appear. Some voices, often on the right, arose to warn of a renewed German menace and of the dangers of disarmament. But the boycott of German goods and firms petered out. A hostile accommodation set in.

Abroad, Nazi ideas, such as they were, mattered very little. Few in the general public knew much about them. An abridged English-language translation of *Mein Kampf*, drastically shortened, appeared in London and Boston only in the autumn, to some interest in Britain and almost none in the United States, after an initial flurry of reviews and a spike in sales. Among the French, where the danger was closer— only the Jews drew more vituperation than them in the book—and the anxiety rifer, a short potboiler of the "Hitler according to Hitler" variety, taken from his book, appeared in Paris in the autumn as well, and a full translation the following spring—which the courts promptly confiscated because of copyright violations. French readers did not need to await Hitler's interview in *Le Matin* in November—"War would solve nothing," he told his guest—to know anything about him. Already, in 1932, a well-informed author had warned them that his was a novel mass movement, its prophet anything but the puppet of the Prussian military caste. But he too missed the sinister eastern projects foretold in *Mein Kampf*, designs that now lay disguised in pacific cant. Zinoviev's Russian translation probably did not become available to those of Stalin's circle allowed to read it until later in 1933, and to the Soviet public in any form until 1945, when its author ended his days in the bunker in Berlin. Translations in all shapes and sizes began appearing around the world, finding a million buyers by 1941— compared with ten million for the successive German editions. How many remained unread the author, happily, could not know; but even without them, in the early months of the Nazi era, news already mattered more than knowledge, and anxiety more than curiosity. Enough became known of *Mein Kampf* to grasp the radical meaning of Nazism, but as for the diplomats and the journalists, so for the reading public: How much store should they set by it?[6]

All over eastern and central Europe, the threat of invasion or subversion concentrated public fears. In Poland, the parties and their papers might differ over the immediate peril, but unanimity reigned about borders—they were sacred, to be defended at all costs. Had not the partitions begun with the Polish Corridor? Here "revision," understood in most of Europe to mean the mitigation of the offending clauses of the peace treaties, signified national extinction. Before the Belgian author and journalist Georges Simenon could utter the word in Warsaw in 1933, his hosts knew it was coming. "Never! Not the Corridor, not Vilna, not Ukraine . . . We've waited a hundred and fifty years!" Any heresy, any whisper of territorial renunciation, would doom the guilty party in that land of long memories, and any government, including Pilsudski's, that ceded to foreign pressure would fall. Political opinion differed over the Jewish protests in synagogues and outside German consulates; government supporters and anti-Semites on the right disapproved.[7] But about the German revisionist campaign, Polish opinion, so often at daggers drawn, crystallized.

In Czechoslovakia, fears mounted about repercussions of the new regime among the Czech Germans in the Sudetenland, where a local Nazi defeated leftist and moderate candidates—including a Social Democrat, from a party in the governing coalition—at a by-election in March. Yugoslavs shared the Poles' fears of a Germanic onslaught under a new flag. Half had lived under Austro-Hungarian rule, Vienna and Budapest transmitting the powerful influence of the German ally; during the war it had helped them conquer and occupy Serbia. The others, once they had wrested their independence from the Turks, had lain along the path of the *Drang nach Osten*, between Berlin, Vienna, and Baghdad. "After the Jews," a professor at the university in Belgrade told the French ambassador, "it will be the turn of the Slavs"—a sentiment echoing in Prague and Warsaw. The Yugoslavs, no keener on Latinization than Germanization, had contended as well for a decade with Italian intimidation, and feared above all the collusion of the older with the newer Fascist regime. Some, in the troubled multiethnic kingdom, had hoped that Germany might deter Italy, champion regionalism and decentralization, let be weaker neighbors in central Europe. With Weimar went their dreams.[8]

In Britain, the German ambassador found in May, opinion had reversed itself. In every circle he frequented, however inconsequential, the attitude so friendly to Germany before Hitler now recalled for him the hostile pain of the disillusioned lover. Prime Minister MacDonald had already told him much the same the month before—the great shift, he thought, had occurred in the first half of March, when he had noticed it on returning from a diplomatic trip to Rome.[9] "I don't think Hitlerism has made our people pro-French," Baldwin's confidant Thomas Jones wrote to a Canadian friend in April, "but it has made them pause and question the wisdom of confidence in Germany which had been steadily growing since the War."[10]

There and in the United States, the regime's anti-Semitic outrages, much more than its revisionism, mobilized public sentiment. Editorial opinion, almost unanimously harsh, helped. On March 27, in major American cities, a million people rallied on behalf of the German Jews, stirred by wide daily news coverage. Anti-Semites did not come, and many Jews stayed away, fearful lest raucous rallies, demonstrations, and boycotts bring reprisals on their coreligionists in Germany; but outside an overcrowded Madison Square Garden in New York 35,000 huddled shoulder to shoulder, packed the stoops of tenements, and clambered onto rooftops. Not since Election Day in November had so many filled the streets, outside the Biltmore a few blocks away, then to rejoice, now to protest: But could one sovereign state intercede in the affairs of another?[11]

At the end of February, at Huningue on the Rhine, several hundred uniformed Nazis advanced to the middle of the bridge from their side of the river, waved swastikas, and sang "Deutschland über Alles." On his side a baker set about organizing a French counter-rally until the authorities dissuaded him. Up and down Alsace and Lorraine the incidents spread. In the Moselle, annexed by Germany in 1871 and recovered by France in 1918, locals still knew German and reacted angrily to the annexationist demands reaching their eyes and ears from Nazi papers and radio broadcasts across the border.[12] At cinemas in Paris, audiences hissed and jeered when the sights and sounds of the Reich appeared on the screens. At the famous Omnia Pathé on the boulevard Montmartre, the director asked the spectators to contain their animus as newsreels showed the pomp of Potsdam—the goose-stepping troops and imperial eagles of the Reichswehr, Hindenburg with his marshal's baton, Hitler on a platform, fanfares and artillery salvos.[13] At home, the French displayed in equal measure the insecurity of their eastern and the indignation of their western allies. They feared invasion and condemned persecution. At the beginning of April, as the anti-Semitic campaign in Germany intensified, Jews began arriving at the Gare du Nord in small groups of fifty to one hundred, some to stay with friends or relatives, others in transit to Palestine or elsewhere. Protesters gathered in synagogues; the Ligue des droits de l'homme and the Ligue Internationale contre l'antisémitisme organized meetings; shopkeepers refused German goods.[14] The assimilation of German policy to Germanism, which had flourished during the war in French civil society, received a new lease on life.

The new Germany enjoyed none of the enthusiasms that the new Russia did, none of the excitement around the world that the other violent experiment in a new order and a single-party state had aroused and that stubbornly refused to die. Familiarity bred discernment—in much of Europe and North America, the newspapers revealed German and obscured Soviet realities, illuminating the first with sound reporting and obscuring the second in clouds of myth, confusion, and speculation.

The foreign correspondents who had flocked to the Soviet Union to report on the first five-year plan flinched during the winter of 1932–1933 at relaying rumors of famine, deportations, and indiscriminate executions, even if they talked of little else among themselves. In December, John Maynard Keynes advised travelers to the Soviet Union to silence their doubts. "This is the right spirit in which to visit

Russia, if one wants to enjoy oneself." And the correspondents did—the regime dusted off an antique rule from the civil war to keep them out of the stricken regions but housed them comfortably in Moscow; unable to verify the rumors at first hand, often well-disposed toward their hosts, and eager to stay, they conveniently disdained sensationalism. The *New York Times*, which reported so thoroughly on Nazi crimes, ignored the Soviet variety, and conveyed to its readers a sense of serious but well-managed economic difficulties. "Compared with other countries," its correspondent Walter Duranty reported in mid-November, "the Soviet Union has the advantage of complete internal peace." In Paris in *L'Europe nouvelle*—so alert to the new Germany—Louis Fischer alluded to the mass deportations of peasants, only to gently chide their persecutors. "The Bolsheviks must learn patience," he concluded.[15]

Not until March 1933 did Malcolm Muggeridge and Gareth Jones reveal in the *Manchester Guardian* the horrors in the Ukraine and the northern Caucasus. By then Muggeridge, who would satirize himself and the others in his novel *Winter in Moscow* a year later, had recanted the faith in the classless society of tomorrow that he had brought with him in the autumn. So had Eugene Lyons of the Associated Press, after almost four years on assignment there, resolved that month to reveal later on a speaking tour in the United States "the truth at last about Russia." Both were expelled. But neither Duranty of the *New York Times* nor Louis Fischer of *The Nation* nor other well-wishers or fellow travelers of the regime accepted the truth—accepted, for one, the reality of a man-made famine at all. Such fixation on the future made for a poor understanding of the present among their readers as well as themselves. In Paris, the celebrated author André Gide, who rarely spoke in public, felt compelled to break his silence and declare one night in March in the crowded hall of a Masonic Lodge that Hitlerism marked a regression to a detestable past, while the Soviet terror held out the "unlimited promise of the future."[16]

Had they only known—but, when it came to the Soviet Union, minds had been made up long before, and with even less information than reached them now. The Bolshevik revolution had elated many and terrified many. Over fifteen years, neither conversion nor disenchantment had greatly shifted. Perhaps, if the distant admirers had understood that the Soviet regime was killing, incarcerating, or deporting millions more of its citizens than its Nazi counterpart, they might have inverted their levels of indignation. But only if religious imitated scientific belief, and enthroned evidence in the place of dogma. Soviet Communism in its youth, in the 1920s and 1930s, could graft itself onto revolutionary traditions around the world, and conquer souls in foreign lands in a way that Nazism never could. What possible appeal could German biological racism hold for alien onlookers, even those whom it did not directly threaten?

The conundrum that would eviscerate pacifism later in the decade—how much peace to give the enemies of peace—did not yet arise. Nowhere in public did the dislike for the regime and its ways yield many demands to put an end to it by some form of force majeure. In Britain, some influential voices were calling for an end to indulgence. Lord Grey, the foreign secretary who had presided over Britain's entry into the war in 1914, and who rarely spoke out, warned his fellow Liberals of danger if Germany were as armed now as then. "The feeling has grown, apparently throughout Germany," he said in a speech to the Liberal Council, "that might is right and that all means are legitimate." Concessions without compensation had to stop; the era of Stresemann and Brüning was over.[17] "He who sups with Frederick the Great must use a long spoon," the historian E. L. Woodward reminded his readers, from All Souls College, Oxford. As dismayed as Grey at the grim spectacle of Prussianism redux, he went a step further and asked rhetorically in *The Times* whether it was safe for the pacific democracies of France and Britain "to give up their present superiority of armed force."[18] Winston Churchill went another step further and rejoiced that the Germans had no heavy artillery. "The Polish Corridor is inhabited by Poles," Austen Chamberlain, the former foreign secretary and an architect of Locarno, exclaimed. "Do you dare to put another Pole under the heel of a government like that?" In the *Evening Standard*, Papen, the vice-chancellor, protested such utterances. They do not understand the Communist menace, he complained.[19] But neither Grey, nor Woodward, nor Churchill, nor Chamberlain spoke for the government, or for majority opinion. Disarmament had lost none of its sheen, rearmament none of its odium—to suggest major military programs now, in 1933, was still politically unpalatable. *The Times*, for one, found the implication of Grey's remarks—that peace rested on German military inferiority—unwarranted. The government that spoke to the majority still couched policies in language congenial to the League of Nations, an idiom pleasing even to its opponents on the Labour left. And Cecil, at the head of a League of Nations Union still commanding some 400,000 members, still promoted the cause of disarmament and of arms equality. It did not signify any indifference to the new regime.[20]

No more in France than in Britain did the pacifists or the crusaders for disarmament fold up their tents. However angrily the voices of the Right blamed the Left for allowing German resurgence, they rarely envisaged a strong arm to end it now. Early in March, *Le Figaro* suggested reoccupying Mainz, the Rhineland town the French had evacuated in 1929, to discourage any further Nazi provocations along the river. Its fellow paper of the Right, *L'Ordre*, vaguely denounced "non-resistance" and called the pacifists warmongers for egging on Germany.[21] But aggressive action charmed almost no one. The Radical center, like the Socialist left, could be naive as well as astute. In *La République*—the paper closest to Daladier, now prime minister—Bertrand de Jouvenel, a political theorist and commentator, foresaw the course of things to come: Hitler would, he predicted, first cement his grip over the government and the military, then remilitarize the Rhineland, and then turn east. All the more need to reach an accord, he concluded oddly. Germany was rearming, the French Socialist leader Léon Blum warned in March. He had never minimized the Nazi danger. But general disarmament, he wrote then, was still the solution. Many years later, after beginning rearmament as prime minister, after war, occupation, and the rest, he regretted the aversion—his own and that of Socialists everywhere—to force in 1933. Derided as "bleating pacifists," he recalled, they should have called for a Franco-British-Polish preventive war on the new German regime. It would have prevented the much greater one of 1939.[22] But the will was wanting, and not only on the left. So was the de jure justification.[23]

In Poland, Pilsudski had aired the hypothesis in secret, but the press, which had covered the revisionism and the anti-Semitism of the new regime in Germany, never proposed the option and opposed it once it heard of it. Some supposed that the advent of so anti-Bolshevik a regime put the final nail in the coffin of the German-Soviet Rapallo pact of 1922, and rejoiced at the passing of a recurrent Polish nightmare.[24] American involvement in any interventionist scheme was out of the question.

The Germans themselves, whatever they made of their new regime, could not condemn its posture of victimhood on the world stage, any more than that of Weimar. The Nazis had savaged the regime that had wrung concession after concession from the former victors; they had condemned its pusillanimity, only to emulate its prudence. But they had won power as the party of national redemption. They could not now become the government of accommodation. In 1929 and 1930, when the Young Plan stretched out reparations until 1987 in return for the early French evacuation of the Rhineland and the departure of the allied oversight committee from Berlin, everyone knew that ending the insult to sovereignty dwarfed in significance the rescheduling of reparations they never intended to pay.[25] But the Nazis had cried surrender. They had done so again in the summer of 1932, when the allies effectively canceled reparations altogether, and again in December, when they conceded equality of rights in armaments. Such demagoguery did not cease to work for them in power. They kept alive the sense of injustice at home, however pacific their promises abroad. Versailles still rankled, among a chronically indignant population. Even while speaking against the self-immolation of the Reichstag in the Kroll Opera House on March 23, and upholding the honor of his party, the Social Democratic leader, Otto Wels, applauded Hitler's demands for German equality and recalled his own repudiation in 1919, before an international audience in Berne, of the war guilt "lie."[26] Two days before, in his speech in the Garrison Church in Potsdam, Hitler had decried the frenzy of the victors, as though nothing had happened since 1919. Something approaching unanimity persisted, even though Wels soon took to the road and to exile in Prague and Paris.

How a regime so unpopular abroad was to bring home success, how the others were to acquire from it what they needed and fend off the unwanted—how they were to cut a path through this tangle of thorns now fell to governments, as they contemplated the reports of their diplomats, the views of their press and political classes, and the emotions of their peoples.

One option, feasible in countries where official monopoly of the media could most easily leave public opinion in the dark, was a collaboration that went beyond begrudging toleration.

In the autumn of 1932 the Soviet railcars, dark green and familiar, that carried the gold from Moscow to Berlin looked like any other, but steel plates, invisible to the naked eye, armored the walls inside and protected a huge safe and its metallic cases. Sometimes these held not only gold ingots and coins, but platinum as well—two thousand kilos of "white gold." They might also bear jewelry, if any remained, from the Tsar's treasure, objets d'art, anything that would earn the credit the Soviet Union desperately needed to finance its imports and satisfy the appetites of headlong industrialization. In Moscow armed civilian officials boarded the trains, and at the border station at Indra, Latvian security police joined them. In Riga, the Latvian press reported on the trains that came through, but not until they had unloaded their precious shipments onto a German train with a European gauge, safely left the country, and rolled on to Berlin and sometimes points farther west, to the vaults and subterranean chambers of banks and commercial lending houses.[27]

Meanwhile, in German Silesia, General Tukhachevsky turned up during the September war games on the banks of the Oder, the same that Hindenburg attended. Foreign military attachés had come from elsewhere as well, seeing little, taking walks, and feasting well. But the presence of the deputy commissar for military and naval affairs, at the head of a delegation of a dozen officers including two army corps generals, made manifest the Soviet wish to renew the military conventions with Germany, beckon to Papen's government, and keep alive the possibility of joint action in case of another European war.[28]

A chronic German fear of encirclement, as old as the Wilhelmine Empire and perhaps the kingdom of Prussia, complemented a more recent Soviet phobia about a league of hostile capitalist powers, especially European. To allay the first and foil the second, a natural complicity had arisen between the two, born at Rapallo in 1922 and very much alive when Hitler entered the Chancellery in January 1933.

At Rapallo they had forged diplomatic, economic, and secret military relations. They had recognized each other, a gesture more precious to pariahs than to others, arranged to exchange Soviet raw for German finished materials, and to make and test German military equipment and train airmen far from the eyes of the guardians of Versailles. Since then, the Soviet Union had become Germany's largest export market, factories had made aircraft and poison gas, and schools had turned out tank officers and pilots.[29]

Initially their partnership had served as well to balance French predominance. But a common enemy provided a more lasting raison d'être—Poland. General Hans von Seeckt, the creator of the Reichswehr and one of the most influential strategic minds in Germany, still saw it that way as Hitler came to power. *Germany between East and West*, the brochure he published early in 1933, rested on his country's irreconcilable clash with French interests and Polish existence to make conciliating the Soviet Union a cornerstone of German policy. "Do we want to be seized upon again by two enemies?" he asked rhetorically. "Will Poland drive to the Oder?" Only a common cause with Russia could free Germany to face its eternal western enemy. "Keep the rear free!"[30] In February, the *Tägliche Rundschau* published extensive excerpts. Close to Schleicher, the army, and the Right, the paper expressed the widely shared prepossession of such milieus with Soviet and German joint hostility to Poland.[31] In September, their newspapers published photos of Hindenburg shaking hands with the Soviet officers on the Oder.[32] In this sense Hitler was atypical, but few took his full eastern territorial ambitions as seriously as his antibolshevism.

For the Soviets, the influx of German machinery, capital, and expertise stoked their five-year plan and by extension their burgeoning military infrastructure. It also, they supposed, kept their enemies at bay. Whenever Germany appeared to draw closer to France or to the western powers, as it did at Locarno in 1925, or at The Hague in 1929, when the Young Plan eased the reparations crisis, or at Paris in 1931, when Chancellor Brüning visited, the Soviets fretted, for such fraternization could only aim at them. German nationalism, the surest solvent of European concord, might help them, and partly for that reason the Soviet authorities looked on the rise of the Nazis with equanimity. They feared French hegemony or a Western coalition more than Fascism—especially if, as they naturally suspected, it tacitly encouraged Japan's antics in East Asia.[33]

Once Hitler came to power they could not dismiss, try as they might, the anti-Communist outbursts and the militarism of a new German government. Schleicher's variety, facing westward, had not unduly troubled them, but Hitler's broke new ground, and coming on top of the Japanese threat in East Asia, it gave them pause. Surely the modus vivendi, too valuable to jettison, might survive the Führer's fulminations. Seeckt had launched German-Soviet military collaboration just as he was energetically suppressing Communist revolts in 1923. Blomberg, one of the most active artisans of the partnership since his time heading the Truppenamt, the army general staff, in 1928 and 1929, was now the minister of defense. A new German military attaché had arrived at the embassy in Moscow, a Russian specialist who had guided Tukhachevsky around the maneuvers in

September.[34] But for each token of esteem came another of hostility, including Hitler's tales of the miseries visited by Marxism on the Soviet people. At the end of February, as Goering blamed Communists recently arrived from the Soviet Union for the fire that had so opportunely gutted the Reichstag, German and Soviet negotiators reached agreement on ways to reschedule the Soviet debt for German imports and ease its acute foreign exchange problem. Uncertain how to read such erratic and contrary displays, the Soviet leaders hesitated, a state of mind faithfully reflected in the ambivalent messages their press conveyed to their people. The right hand of the German government did not know what the left was doing, *Izvestia* complained in March. Sometimes the Soviet press reported the German affronts, sometimes it passed over them in tactful silence.[35]

The Soviets needed peace—of this all commissariats were certain. The Japanese alone, whom they were doing all to conciliate in the east, provided a powerful incentive to ensure calm in the west. The throes of famine, penury, revolt, and forced economic transformation left them ill suited to fight a war with anyone just now, east or west. But hardships unimaginable to others prepared the country to fight tomorrow or the day after, in Soviet groupthink. Military weakness, to Bolsheviks, was the child of economic backwardness; Stalin had justified the first five-year plan in precisely such terms in 1931, and he did so again as he stood before the Joint Central Committees of the All-Union Communist Party in January 1933. Now that the plan had run its course, in four years rather than five, he invoked military necessity more than any other to vindicate its harshness and its hastiness. No one had invaded, no one had intervened; he had cried wolf, no wolf had appeared. But the well-equipped imperialists might have been tempted at any moment, he said, and "in that event . . . we should have had . . . bloody and unequal war, for in such a war we would have been almost unarmed before the enemy." The plan, he claimed somewhat disingenuously, had made the Soviet Union militarily independent. It had laid foundations on which the next plan would build, but for now it had left the country more chaotic and vulnerable than four years earlier, driven to pacify its many adversaries.[36]

But how? About this the commissariats did not agree. Already in 1932 Soviet diplomacy had begun to emerge from sectarian seclusion and pursue pacts, détente, and even friendships on the world stage. Foreign Minister Litvinov regarded German hegemony as more menacing than French, over time, and rather than pin hopes on perpetuating Rapallo or pitting the European powers against one another he set to spinning a web that might contain Germany, keep the peace, and spare the Soviet Union. By the time Hitler took office, the Soviet Union had signed or ratified nonaggression pacts that Litvinov had crafted with five of the country's western neighbors, including Poland, and with France as well. In 1933 he pursued three others, as well as diplomatic relations with the United States, and a broader treaty defining aggression with a dozen countries that did not include Germany. With Litvinov the Soviet Union seemed to have warmed to collective security, just as the Japanese and the Germans challenged it and the League with guns or words; it seemed as well to have shed revisionism and embraced the status quo. The powers wishing to revise Versailles, Karl Radek, a party foreign affairs specialist, declared in *Pravda* in May, had themselves become a cause of war. This did not sit well with the diehards of German cooperation in Moscow, for whom the Polish problem could not be solved without it, or with those who suspected the United States and the western European powers of trying to engineer a Soviet-Japanese war, or with the Bolshevik fundamentalists, who anathematized pacts or alliances with one capitalist camp against another.[37]

The diplomatic hazards of their domestic xenophobia and foreign—as well as domestic—spy mania became apparent in March. That month, Soviet security police from the OGPU descended on the premises of the Metropolitan-Vickers Electrical Company outside Moscow and arrested four British engineers and another four Soviet employees. The raid, and even more the show trial for sabotage and espionage that followed, undermined Litvinov's efforts in London, and inflamed British and Western opinion far more than the meager reports in the Western press of mass man-made famine. *Krasnaya Zvezda*, the army paper, now resumed attacks on British foreign policy and sounded a hidebound, isolationist note. But the Soviet authorities quickly commuted the two- and three-year sentences handed down to the hapless British employees. Then and for some time to come, Litvinov's ascendant star shone over Soviet policy.[38]

World revolution could wait—such was the sense of Stalin's "socialism in one country," but its implications for foreign policy had remained obscure. Now Litvinov began to spell them out. At Geneva he declared that counterrevolution abroad would not bring armed Soviet intervention, a heretical twist to official dogma, which had always made the Red Army the instrument of world revolution. This did not sit well with the fundamentalists either; theocracies do not readily admit error. But, for now, they had to follow. The USSR was aware, *Izvestia* explained, that "people of all countries will find their own route to emancipation." Under the pressure of circumstance, the Soviet government was extending olive branches, most obviously to Poland and France. By May, *Izvestia* was giving first-page honors to the Soviet-Polish rapprochement. Never had relations between the two been better, the Polish legation and the Soviet Foreign Affairs Commissariat agreed. And the purists of the Communist International, who had long opened their temples to the revision of Versailles and the subversion of the regime in Poland, had to follow as well. Russian and German Communists were used to leaving each other with "To Warsaw!" on their lips. And now?[39]

The many German advocates of the old Soviet entente found such developments deeply troubling. Haunted by renewed fears of encirclement, they fretted that the new regime's anti-Bolshevik furies were driving the Soviets into the arms of Germany's hereditary enemies. Papers of the right and center, the only ones still publishing, raised the alarm. Twice, the old conservative Prussian *Kreuzzeitung* reminded its readers, under Catherine II and again in 1914, the French and Russians had joined against Prussia or Germany; it must not happen again. The Catholic *Germania* warned that the country was now more isolated than ever. The liberal *Vossische Zeitung* saw in the Franco-Soviet pact the culmination of the French search since Richelieu for an eastern ally. In the Wilhelmstrasse the diplomats brooded over the ruin of a dozen years' work, as the Soviet Union now befriended the makers of Versailles. "In a few months," one of them told the French ambassador, "Germany has lost 100% of the influence she had regained in the world." Officers close to Schleicher expressed fears of a Franco-Soviet military alliance to replace their own. After an anti-Bolshevik preelection rant in Königsberg, Hitler heard from industrialists and bankers, who reminded him that Russian orders represented a third of German exports and employed hundreds of thousands. Interest was challenging ideology.[40]

Compromise emerged. By the end of the year, Hitler had his way and military collaboration with the Soviet Union had ended. That autumn a dozen German officers made a last visit to Moscow. German plants closed, specialists returned home. But it mattered less now—the Reich was openly defying Versailles, no longer afraid to build its own tanks and matériel at home; and the Soviet Union too was mass-producing its weapons of war, no longer in need of the German helping hand.[41] The Cassandras who prophesied the recurrence of the national nightmare, a Franco-Soviet alliance, forgot that geopolitics lasted but regimes did not, that the anti-Communist French Right would never allow the dalliance with the Soviets to assume the proportions of the military entente with its Tsarist predecessor—that 1933 was not 1914. And, incarnated by itinerant technical specialists or not, the idea of Rapallo lived. In May, the German and Soviet foreign ministries agreed to ratify protocols of 1929 and 1931 and extend the 1922 treaty. All the papers in Berlin, Nazi or not, applauded: the *Völkischer Beobachter* called it a step toward peace; *Kreuzzeitung*, on behalf of the Stahlhelm, a welcome warning to Germanophobic Poland and intransigent France and Britain; *Vossische Zeitung*, more soberly, an act likely to lessen tension. In Moscow, TASS published the communiqué and concluded that Hitler had revived Rapallo.[42]

Hitler was reassuring the Soviets as he was everyone else. When—at the behest of the businessmen and the bankers—he received the Soviet ambassador at the end of April, he was all smiles. He dismissed a raid a few days earlier on the offices of a Soviet-German oil company in Hamburg as exceptional, an accident of circumstances, and elevated good relations with the Soviets to a high priority of his. *Der Angriff*, a mouthpiece of Goebbels's Propaganda Ministry, said much the same. The chancellor and the minister promoted commerce to salvage diplomacy and spare it any more damage from their visceral anti-Bolshevism.[43]

The compromise in the Soviet Union favored *raison d'état* and stable relations with everyone as well. Litvinov's openings to the former enemies had never required a clean break with Germany, and later in the year he told the Central Executive Committee of the party that the Soviet Union would never undertake hostilities against Germany. Stalin had never understood the openings of his foreign affairs commissar to former adversaries as exclusive of less formal understandings with the only postwar friend—without the pacts, without the publicity, amid a deafening war of words, quiet diplomacy pursued its ends. So it did with the more immediate and starker threat from Japan. In the summer, the Soviet ambassador advised caution: pursue rapprochements with Poland and France, he advised, but do not jettison Germany, if only to retain some value in the eyes of its adversaries. This was realpolitik, and the following February, at the Seventeenth Party Congress—the "Congress of Victors" over the kulaks and the others—Stalin would announce that "we have no orientation toward Germany, just as we have no orientation toward Poland or France." In the massive steel plant going up at Magnitogorsk, an American engineer found that the Soviet worker harbored no particular antipathy for the Nazis—like the press and, he might have added, like Stalin. They were figures in a hostile landscape already etched in their minds since the 1920s.[44]

Both powers were keeping their options open. They had carried out no diplomatic revolution, reversed no alliance systems. Both shied away from crisis and confrontation, with each other or anyone else; but neither discarded gainful collusion out of hand. In April 1933, the German ambassador in Moscow pleaded with his government to arrest the slide in relations with the Soviet Union, "with whom we shall sooner or later have a common border"—Seeckt and his disciples had been saying no less ever since Rapallo. Two years later the chairman of the Kiev Oblast raised a glass to German diplomats at an official reception. "And together," he proposed in his toast, "we shall be bombing Warsaw again!" The German consul thought his words meant for Berlin. Another four years later, in the summer of 1939, commercial talks again hid nonmercantile purposes. The Nazi-Soviet pact announced in August shocked the Western world. It should not have.[45]

In the early 1930s neither power expected the modus vivendi to last forever. Their calculated courtesies could not veil an unrelenting suspicion of visitors from the outer darkness, embedded in belief systems that elevated enmities at home and abroad into conditions of existence and axioms of policy. Their realpolitik served much that was unreal, including the inevitability of war with race or class demons. They endeavored to indoctrinate their people with such caricatural visions, exploiting love of nation and ignorance of the wider world. In the process, they made international relations even more anarchic, for they envisioned ending tomorrow the same equilibrium they pretended to live by today.

Another option, for weaker powers determined to resist the new Germany, was to contain or circumvent it by diplomatic means.

The Italians offered a mirror image of the Soviets—they celebrated the Nazi regime in words while holding it off in deeds. Moscow and Rome inverted each other's hypocrisy. Mussolini had never returned Hitler's veneration. He had doubted the prospects of the candidate, now he distrusted the intentions of the chancellor. He repeatedly rebuffed Hitler's requests to visit, unimpressed by the talk of a natural alliance in *Mein Kampf*, "that enormous brick which I have never been able to read." He did not succumb to its author's subsequent evocations of untroubled spheres of influence, Italian in the Mediterranean, German in eastern Europe, or his forbearance about the ethnic Germans in the Alto Adige, the southern Tyrol transferred from Austria to Italy at Versailles. Even as the Italian press applauded the coming of the Third Reich, the first skeptic in the Palazzo Venezia and other Fascists around him withheld their embrace of the new chancellor's renewed overtures.[46]

Mussolini, the founder of Fascism and Hitler's tutelary spirit, doubted his disciple's judgment. He thought the anti-Semitic campaign unwise and told him so, warning of the reaction of "world Jewry." This angered Hitler, who complained to the Italian ambassador that his Duce did not understand the global threat of Judeobolshevism, perhaps because there were so few Jews in Italy. And Mussolini saw German rearmament, a Weimar project and a Nazi obsession, for what it was—a two-edged sword. It might end French predominance, but it might also threaten Italy. A year earlier, in March 1932, he had told the Fascist Grand Council that, if done quickly, it would provide a counterweight to French and British power. But Italy could not lag far behind. It would have to rearm as quickly, "so that we can look Germany in the eyes."[47]

Above all, he worried about Austria. The idea of an *Anschluss* allowing the Reich to absorb the Germanic vestige of the old multiethnic empire had always unsettled Fascist diplomats, if only because of the Teutonic titan it would place at their Alpine gates. This was one Versailles prohibition they did not condemn, one revisionist demand they did not echo. It was also the first of the twenty-five points of the Nazi Party program. With Hitler in power, Italian resistance stiffened; Fulvio Suvich, the undersecretary of the Foreign Ministry and since Grandi's departure in the summer its effective head under Mussolini himself, feared any concession that might open the door to the unthinkable. He was a native of Trieste, a former subject of Austria-Hungary; he knew the byways of central Europe more intimately than any of his colleagues, and the avenue that Austria would provide for

German interference there. Now Mussolini had added another, more pressing reason to keep it out of German hands. Secret planning had begun for the invasion of Ethiopia, an enterprise that would allow no distractions, especially far behind them in Austria. "Our operations in Ethiopia," Mussolini told Suvich early in January, "could succeed only provided we are completely free of complications in Europe." Fascist expansion for now required that it arrest the Nazi variety, even as each regime trumpeted the virtues of the other.[48]

The surest way to protect Austria was to make it a protégé. The opportunity had arisen in May 1932 when a right-wing nationalist opposed to Communists, Nazis, and an *Anschluss*, an appealing mix to an Italian Fascist, became Austrian chancellor. Engelbert Dollfuss became, with Mussolini's active encouragement, the emerging face of Austro-Fascism; the two met as soon as he assumed office, and a year later, after he had banned the Communists and was about to ban the Nazis, sent Parliament home, and assumed quasi-dictatorial powers, they met again. Mussolini promised arms, money, and protection from Germany; he promised loyalty. Neither the pan-German Austrian Nazis nor their patrons in Berlin would give up so easily; a summer of terrorist bombing and years of fruitful subversion lay ahead; but for now Hitler would have to leave the German Christian corporatist state of Austria alone.[49]

To the south and southeast of Austria, in the Balkans and the Danube basin, Italian and German interests did not collide as frontally as in Austria, but they did not run parallel either. Mussolini still aspired to subvert Yugoslavia, loosen or dissolve the Little Entente, and spread Italian influence up and down the Danube. This served German interests as well, up to a point—to weaken France in any way possible, most neatly through detaching or smothering its allies in Prague, Belgrade, and Budapest, and to open a rich source of raw materials and a market for its manufactured exports. But beyond that it might compete with them. When the German ambassador in Rome pressed for an economic pact between the two powers in the Danube, each supporting the other, his superiors in the Foreign Ministry in the Wilhelmstrasse demurred. What can Italy do for us in eastern Europe, it asked the ambassador, and what can we do for Italy in the Mediterranean? The Austrian question rendered cooperation in the Balkans impractical. And Italy, by its clumsy great power behavior, had only strengthened the resolve of the Little Entente to resist. Best to leave economic cooperation there to private interests, the head of the ministry advised the ambassador.[50]

German policy toward the Balkans was in flux. As the Foreign Ministry instructed the ambassador in Rome that Germany had no political ambitions in the region, Alfred Rosenberg, the newly named head of the Nazi Party foreign affairs bureau, was telling a startled Rumanian ambassador in Berlin the opposite. In the event of war, he and an aide told him, the Reich needed to know whom it could count on, and Rumanian oil and foodstuffs would sustain them. They had learned the lessons of the last war. And he sketched an eastern circle of economic dependencies around Germany to include Rumania, which would have to sever all its political ties to others—to France, and the two allies in the Little Entente, presumably—in favor of an entente with Germany. Politics came first, and the economic ties that would make of Germany a trading partner in peace and a citadel in war would follow. Rosenberg, a blood-and-soil Baltic German, spoke the language of another German from outside the Reich, the Hitler of *Mein Kampf.* Through his words loomed the specter of a third restless and expansionary power, to add to Japan and Italy. Would the last allow it to spread its wings over the Danube basin? The answer would not come until three years later, when the Italian Ethiopian adventure, of which the Reich's leaders at present knew nothing, would bestow precious leverage on them, and remove the peninsular obstacle to their central European ambitions.[51]

In the meantime, Mussolini continued trying to contain the new Germany. He contemplated a triad with the Austria of Dollfuss and the newly congenial Hungary of his admirer Gömbös, an experiment that went awry when its unspoken traffics set off whispers and then rumors of war.

Since the summer of 1932 Mussolini had been donating arms to
the paramilitary Austrian Heimwehr, a member of Dollfuss's governing coalition, and shipping others to Hungary through the Hirtenberg munitions plant some twenty-five miles outside Vienna. He had
neatly managed, with Dollfuss's connivance, to violate Austrian neutrality as well as the postwar Treaties of Saint-Germain and Trianon
that had restricted the arms trade to and from the two former Central
Powers. A predictable international scandal erupted in January, when
a Socialist Austrian newspaper, the *Arbeiter Zeitung*, reported that
forty freight cars loaded with rifles and machine guns had arrived at
the Hirtenberg plant, en route from Italy to Hungary. The British and
French governments, pressed by the Little Entente to bring the matter before the League Council, but not eager to poison relations with
Italy, discreetly but firmly requested the return or destruction of the
arms in a joint note to Vienna. This the *Giornale d'Italia* promptly
leaked in Rome, betraying its government's wish for an international
incident. Indignation in Austria ensued, and glee among the Nazis
there, who brandished proof that only an *Anschluss* could save Austria from such arrogant foes across the Rhine and the Channel. The
New York Times recalled the summer of 1914, when Britain and France
faced Germany and Austria in the wake of another diplomatic incident in central Europe, with the obvious difference that this time Italy had thrown in its hand with its northern neighbor. Hungary was
preparing to make war on its neighbors, papers of the Right and Left
supposed in France. *L'Ami du Peuple* imagined that the Hungarian
army on spring maneuvers along the Yugoslav border would foment
a Croat revolt across it, and invade the country as well as Austria and
Czechoslovakia, an enterprise in which its German and Italian friends
"would not remain inactive." The French threatened to cancel loans,
as they had in 1931 when Chancellor Brüning had imprudently proposed an Austro-German customs union. But, eager to mollify both
Dollfuss and Mussolini, whose partnership, however unsavory, might
prevent an *Anschluss*, the British and French calmed the waters. They

had intended no ultimatum, they explained. Dollfuss agreed to return the arms, and never sent the defiant reply to their note that Mussolini had urged on him. The Hirtenberg affair blew over.[52] The Austro-Italian-Hungarian project lived, but Mussolini needed a less exciting way of confining even while propitiating Germany.[53]

In March he resurrected the idea of a four-power pact he had floated before the throng from the balcony in Turin in October. The idea had come to him, he claimed, when the disarmament conference had adjourned the previous summer without any progress, and involved, most controversially, a directorate of Italy, Germany, France, and Britain that would revise the peace treaties and find ways to put the principle of German arms equality into practice.[54] This might placate Germany, as well as interest Britain and magnify Italy. At the Foreign Ministry, Bülow expressed cautious approval, if only because the pact promised fewer decision makers and a less public stage for diplomacy than the League. Before the end of the month, Hitler accepted it in principle, in his first public and anodyne *tour d'horizon* of foreign policy, a reassuring speech that Foreign Minister Neurath might have given, because he and his staff had written it.[55]

But the pact might also isolate France, toward whom Mussolini now cast thoughtful glances. They were already at one over Austrian independence; French as well as British acquiescence would remove a major stumbling block to his Ethiopian adventure, when the time came. As the negotiations over the pact proceeded that spring, and the French raised objections, the contrary prospect of a thaw in relations with them also crossed his mind. They might have their uses. In July 1931 and again early in 1932, Premier Pierre Laval had suggested to him and Dino Grandi that an entente might bring them benefits— "Ethiopia, for example." Now Ethiopia loomed larger for them, the German menace for the French. No affinity for Nazi Germany drove Fascist Italy, only the pursuit of any combination that would allow it to boast at home of aggrandizing the nation abroad. Prestige—the acquisition of great power status, an ambition rooted in Italian history since the nineteenth century and now monopolized by Fascism—required no single diplomatic recipe yet, and even indicated that Mussolini decline Hitler's poisoned chalice.[56]

Poland too hankered after great power status, and fancied that it had regained and could retain it, if only it could avoid subordination or subjection to its two powerful neighbors. The newfound cordiality with the eastern of the two, solemnized in one of Litvinov's nonaggression pacts, suggested that Poland might now face down the loudly revisionist western one. For a moment it appeared tempted to, and alarmed much of Europe, until it revealed the intention to handle the new regime in Berlin not by threatening but by befriending it. Poland could bear neighbors' friendship as long as they were too weak to impose it, and by choosing it freely sent an unmistakable message about its status to Paris and Geneva—it was independent. Perhaps, too, the Soviet Union's openings to the western powers, and the Russian reentry into the international orbit, lessened the value of Poland to them. Where would the Franco-Soviet pact leave Poland, France's indispensable eastern counterweight to Germany, now that a heavier candidate seemed to come forth? It had no substitute for the French alliance, but might gain more by placating both neighbors than by relying on France to deter them.[57]

From Geneva, that winter, came unwelcome whiffs of a great power condominium that excluded Poland. Ever since the five-power declaration of December and the disarmament proposals that followed in its wake, Pilsudski and his new foreign minister, Colonel Beck, feared that the western powers were about to concede heavy arms to Germany without consulting the most likely target of their use. Even disarmed, Germany in their eyes was turning the disarmament parlay into the Trojan horse of border revision. The press—governmental and opposition—enthused. "Poland will never become a toy in anyone's hands," Beck told the foreign affairs commission of the Parliament in mid-February, in his peroration, and the German ambassador half-jokingly asked his French colleague if Beck was not complaining about the French alliance.[58]

In March, Mussolini's proposal for a four-power pact confirmed the Poles' deepest suspicions; Pilsudski recalled from Rome a newly named ambassador, Beck canceled a trip to Paris, and the press enthused again. All the pact would leave Poland, the *Gazeta Polska* exclaimed, was a jump seat at the League of Nations. He would sooner abandon the League, Beck told the French ambassador, sooner face isolation, than allow a four-power directorate under its aegis to interfere in his country's affairs. He added that Hitler had been sounding remarkably moderate lately. "It would be better," he added, "to talk things over now [with him] than after two or three years of consolidating the Hitlerite regime."[59]

In April, Pilsudski took some cabinet ministers with him to Wilno to talk over the dangers of treaty revision in Mussolini's plan, and incidentally to celebrate the fourteenth anniversary of the Polish seizure of the contested town from Lithuania. Surprise instructions had suddenly gone out all over the country for a great military parade, and ordnance and some forty thousand uniformed men along with tanks and artillery were rushed to the scene. Poland, Beck told a surprised French ambassador, was not a creation of the great powers—"She had taken Vilna, she had drawn its own frontiers in 1920."[60]

And at the beginning of May, Hitler received the Polish ambassador in Berlin. Beck had followed through on his hint to the French ambassador. Détente had come oddly, amid acrimony and saber rattling. The usual recriminations flew across the border—a provocative German memorial unveiled on one side of the Corridor, the disappearance of minority German papers from town squares on the other—but the world sat up when over one hundred Polish troops disembarked from a freighter and landed on the Westerplatte Peninsula in Danzig harbor. The agreement of 1921 had allowed a small Polish garrison there to protect munitions stores, but the new arrivals more than doubled it. Ostensibly angered by measures taken by the Danzig Senate restricting shipping to the peninsula, the Poles had vividly dispensed with diplomacy, as they had the previous June, when they had sent in the cruiser *Wicher* under similar circumstances.[61] Then as now the League Council hastily patched matters up, and the Poles drew in their horns; but then as now their *coup de force* alarmed the Germans, the French, and the British, as it was intended to. In April, the Germans watched again as synagogues, politicians, and newspapers denounced the campaign in Germany against Jews in general and Polish Jews in particular. Demonstrators took to the streets and broke the windows of the embassy in Warsaw. Pilsudski's government could easily have reined in such outbursts; it chose not to. The new German ambassador protested in person, to the prime minister on the sixth, to the foreign minister a week later. He complained of Germanophobic hysteria throughout the land, "of a kind never seen before," of German papers suppressed, theaters attacked, of Hitler burned in effigies of straw, and he blamed the complicity of officialdom and its press for the contagion—he traced a "planned action" to the Polish government itself.[62]

Yet, amid the hostilities, Beck was sending amiable signals. Just as tempers flared over the Westerplatte at the beginning of March, he hastened to oblige Hitler and allow him to fly over the Corridor on his way to East Prussia. When the German ambassador remonstrated in April, Beck twice speculated that interested parties, in Geneva and elsewhere, were scheming to poison German-Polish relations, and twice he asked his guest whether the Germans had not observed such mischief as well. These were feelers, the German ambassador concluded, and he reminded his superiors that Beck had told others he needed no intermediaries to discuss whatever he wished with the Germans. Beck had even acknowledged that no treaty was unalterable—although of course Poland's borders were. A week later the Polish ambassador was requesting a meeting with Hitler. In a classic diplomatic ploy, Beck's game, and Pilsudski's habit, mixed threats with inducements.[63]

And bluff with sincerity: In April, rumors of a Polish preventive war against Germany traveled the embassies in Warsaw. They had surfaced before, but the chatter now reached a new level, and moved on easily to neighboring lands. In Prague, President Masaryk was convinced that war was imminent. In Berlin, the foreign minister, Neurath, brought the rumors before the cabinet and urged calm, an injunction that Papen, the increasingly irrelevant vice-chancellor, ignored the next day when, in the press, he denounced talk of war as a crime against Germany. The rumors swirled about the chanceries, spoken more than written, remembered more than recorded, selectively forgotten years later when postmortem inquiries after 1945 turned their light onto the disasters of 1939 and 1940. "It is known," the British ambassador wrote from Berlin early in April, "that in France responsible people are talking of a preventive war.... There is no doubt that Poland is now being held back by France." After the war, Prime Minister Edouard Daladier, Foreign Minister Joseph Paul-Boncour, and General Maxime Weygand, chief of the general staff, remembered nothing about all the talk. But enough did—what lay behind it?[64]

If Pilsudski meant to launch a war against Germany, this was the moment. The Reich was militarily still inferior, but time was on its side, and the Reich would overtake Poland soon if allowed to violate the Versailles restrictions at will. With the December five-power declaration, the mischief-making at Geneva, and Mussolini's four-power pact, German rearmament seemed on the way, destined to accelerate legally or illegally under a government that outdid all its predecessors in nationalist vituperation. Should the Poles wait until it turned on them with newfound might, or act now? The Soviets would have no wish to intervene, just as they were seeking normalization with Poland and others and were cooling their revisionist ardors. The Soviet ambassador in Warsaw had even said so. "Poland," he told his French counterpart, "could in any case rest easily about us," and word of their neutrality had reached the ears of his German counterpart as well.[65]

Yet no one could detect any military preparations, any telltale movements or alerts. In early April, the French military attaché found that the Polish general staff would choose war now over war later but still displayed no desire for it. A month later he could find no trace of plans for an offensive war. Nothing unusual distinguished the military moves he knew of, the German ambassador reported, and no military attachés told him anything else. The entire Polish press, including the governmental press, recoiled at the idea when German papers reported Papen's mindless talk of it at the end of April. It would be a folly, they declared, that would turn the League, the French, and the world against them. And—but this they did not say—the economy, not to mention the army, might be in poor shape to embark on such an adventure, to seize East Prussia or German Silesia—and what then? Attempt the impossible, to Polonize the regions against the will of sixty or seventy million Germans who would never accept it? The German ambassador found the rumors dubious. "To distinguish truth from bluff in them," he concluded, "is difficult."[66]

To launch a war without preparing for one, while ensuring that all including the intended victim knew of it and a partly docile press opposed it—the rumors of war only continued policy by other means. Emanating from Pilsudski, occasioned by the fear of German rearmament, the rumors probably tested the mien and the mettle of the western powers and of France in particular, bound by treaty to aid Poland—but only if it became the victim of an "unprovoked attack." They advertised independence. And they swelled while the anti-German boycotts and demonstrations spread, but also just as, in mid-April, the Polish ambassador requested a meeting with Hitler. To the Führer, the prospect—as odious perhaps as that of meeting with the Soviet ambassador—offered the chance to calm the waters. He agreed. He wanted no war now. The rumors died.

At a meeting on May 2, Ambassador Alfred Wysocki and Chancellor Hitler exchanged complaints and cordialities. Each attributed the hostile climate in his country to provocations in the other. But Hitler now wore his mask of moderation. He assured his guest that he, a nationalist, understood and respected Polish nationalism—which was untrue—and could not conceive of the assimilation of another people into his own—which was true, as his predilection for more draconian methods of Germanizing the Corridor and more would demonstrate in 1939; and he, a man of peace, wanted no forceful expropriation of Poles across the border, but a peaceful solution—which was true, but only for the time being. Reluctantly, he agreed to the ambassador's suggestion of a joint communiqué. Both promised to abide by existing treaties and pursue dispassionately the resolution of common problems. A single paragraph filled with hackneyed words of good intentions, the diplomatic politesse—but it would become, eight months later, a formal nonaggression pact, the first that the Third Reich would sign, providing the reality of détente and the illusion of lasting peace between the two.[67]

And when the new regime in Berlin cemented its grip and rearmed the country, and Hitler shed his mask, and rediscovered the Corridor and Danzig—what then? Treaties might be sacred, Mussolini had said, but they were not eternal. A longer-term view by Pilsudski and his ministers, unwilling to rely on France alone, might have commanded a quest for credible military ties with their Czechoslovak neighbor and the other two members of the Little Entente, Rumania and Yugoslavia, all French allies as well. They considered it. Feelers came their way, from a Little Entente struggling both to strengthen and to enlarge itself in the face of Hitler, Mussolini, and deepening doubts about the League of Nations. In April, the Polish and Czechoslovak general staffs considered options. But too many tensions with their southern neighbors, national conceits older than statehood, too many Polish worries about regional power and status, stopped them from throwing their hat into the ring of the Little Entente.[68] Independence, an end for the nation, became a means for the government. It yielded open options and individual pacts, which lasted as long as they lasted.

Another option was to seek a protector, if one were available. The Little Entente considered inviting the Soviet Union to join. Strong historical ties bound the Yugoslavs to the Russians. The Serbs remembered their Orthodox Slav brethren from the east, who had gone to war for them in 1914, and whose monarchy they still mourned. In April, the

Yugoslav royal family inaugurated a Russia House in Belgrade, dedicated to the memory of the "Tsar-martyr Nicholas II," in one of the most beautiful buildings in the city. Churchmen, officers, and foreign dignitaries came, and when the queen entered, the band struck up "God Save the Tsar." But Russia now was Communist—some 25,000 émigrés, many of them Tsarist officers, lived in Yugoslavia—and of questionable utility should new Germanic invaders arrive again the next day. And historical reasons only alienated another member of the Little Entente. The Soviet Union refused to recognize Rumanian sovereignty over Bessarabia, the strip of Moldavia abutting the western edge of the Ukraine. The squabble posed an insuperable obstacle to a pact of the sort the Soviets had signed with their other eastern neighbors, and to any role they might play in the Little Entente.[69]

The Germanophile Rumanian king, Carol II, a Hohenzollern as infatuated with military uniforms as his relative Kaiser Wilhelm, but without his army, now nervously contemplated the embraces of the Third Reich. All politically conscious Rumanians, like their Polish counterparts, regarded their country's borders as sacred and its postwar territorial gains as untouchable. In this Carol joined them. But he and his various ministers could not always agree on the greater threat to them—was it Hungarian, Soviet, or German? The first two wanted land, the third wanted economic influence and might one day use it to redraw the map of the Danube basin. Should they, as the renowned foreign minister Titulescu, a star in the firmament of Geneva, wanted, warm to the Soviets as the Poles had? Like Pilsudski, Carol was skeptical about exclusive reliance on a visibly weakening France. But he was too capricious, too inept, and, with his dictatorial aspirations and the camarilla around his hated common-law mistress, Magda Lupescu, too unpopular to impose his whims. Madame Lupescu, "the Jewess," the "Red Queen" because of her hair, as extravagant and vain as her royal lover, drew every social and national resentment in the land on herself. One night two recently demoted officers fired shots at the windows of her salon, where she entertained the inner circle. And France, almost as historic a friend as Russia to the Serbs, still commanded much sentiment in the country, as well as the authority of a major creditor amid parlous finances and out-stretched hands. It could keep Rumania in its orbit for a while longer and ignore Carol's irritating gaffes. Once he spent an entire lunch touting the Germanic virtues of the Transylvanian Saxons to the French ambassador. "What can a government accomplish with a par-liament like yours?" he threw at the same ambassador on another oc-casion. For now, Rumania hung precariously between several power centers at home—the king and his entourage, the government, and the parliamentary parties—and as many abroad. In the wings a five-year-old Fascist Iron Guard was growing, much fonder of the Nazi than of the Wilhelmine Reich that Carol fancied. For now, the Ru-manian government could only humor the new Germany, and hope vainly in the following years to arrest the descent into economic de-pendency, and the eventual transformation of Greater Rumania into a German satellite.[70]

And Hungary, as avid to recover its landed patrimony as Rumania was to retain its own, still looked to Rome. Since coming to power in October, amid grandiloquent promises of territorial revision and national redemption, Gömbös had accomplished little, apart from a pilgrimage to the Duce in Rome. To the "100 points"—which were in fact 95—of his original program, he now added another: "Pa-tience!" But disaffection was rising, government candidates were los-ing by-elections, and hecklers were greeting Gömbös himself in the provinces. A prisoner of his promise, he might welcome the help of another anti-Communist and revisionist government, even though the Nazis had Versailles in their sights and he the Treaty of Trianon. But the prospect of an *Anschluss* with Austria threatened Hungary as directly as Italy, if not more; nothing in Hungarian eyes would then stop German progress down the Danube. By the spring it was already underway. German agents appeared at their embassy in Bu-dapest requesting its good offices and offering no other information; propagandists crisscrossed the country. In its *Voice of the Nation* the "Hungarian Hitlerite party" rode revisionist sentiment and described

the French as "the gangsters of Europe, relentless foes of the swastika, capable of befriending murderers." In the Chamber, an ethnic
German from the Hungarian Burgenland delivered a kindred tirade.
Once again, vistas of economic empire in the Danube basin wafted
about Berlin. An official in the Nazi Party's foreign affairs bureau
likened the coming dominion to other great autarkies, "such as the
British empire, France and its colonies, North America." Food and
raw materials would travel to Germany, manufactured goods from it,
across a protected zone stretching from Holland and Scandinavia to
the Danube, bringing a Valhalla of self-sufficiency in peace and above
all in war.[71]

Gömbös and his close friend and foreign minister, Koloman de
Kanya, handled this Reich ever more gingerly. Kanya was a Magyar nationalist, Germanophile, Slavophobe, and Francophobe. He
had risen through the diplomatic ranks in the Ballplatz in imperial
Vienna before the war and, already violently anti-Hapsburg, needed
no encouragement to denounce any talk of a dynastic restoration in
Vienna and to distrust Austrian motives in the region. This, along
with revisionist passion, made it easier for him to observe the silence
that prudence already dictated about the perils of a Nazi-inspired
Anschluss. He did not care to pose as Austria's defender. However
deeply he and Gömbös feared an *Anschluss*, they feared antagonizing
Germany more. They limited their rapports with Dollfuss and Austria, and in June, Gömbös accepted Hitler's invitation to visit Berlin.
On his way back through Vienna he ignored Dollfuss. Kanya told
the German ambassador how impressed his leader was by Hitler's
charm, by the dynamism of the Nazi mass movement, which he had
seen and heard in the stadium in Berlin, and by the bond between
people and regime. Not for the last time, Hitler had stage-managed
a mass rally to awe a foreign leader. The regime was there to stay,
Gömbös told the Hungarian Parliament, and before the ambassador
he waved the prospect of economic, military, and political ties. He
saw Austria, he added, through German eyes.[72]

So he told the German ambassador; but in Rome his own ambassador assured the Italian government, peeved by its Hungarian protégé's sudden sojourn in Berlin, that Gömbös and Hitler had met only to exchange greetings, to put out feelers, that economic matters predominated. Gömbös and his government needed the Italian entente, if only to share hostility to Yugoslavia and the ambition to whittle it down or dismantle it altogether. And both resented the Little Entente, Hungary for reasons of territory, Italy for reasons of status. In his speech to the Hungarian Chamber, Gömbös insisted that Italian friendship remained the cornerstone of Hungarian policy. As Germany and Italy were neither friends nor enemies, he could sup with each and not offend the other, as long as the Austrian question did not force the issue; but by trying eagerly to placate one and befriend the other he opened the same road to satellite status that his neighbor Rumania had already taken.[73]

In May, at Timisoara in western Rumania, representatives of German minorities in Czechoslovakia, Hungary, and Rumania gathered. Representatives of the German Nazi Party joined them. They urged the Rumanian Germans from the Banat and Transylvania to resist the revision of their borders, the Czechs from the Sudetenland to favor it, and the Hungarians from the Burgenland to denounce their "untenable situation" within Hungary. Already the Nazis had begun playing with national fears. They wished to reassure Rumania that German ambitions would not threaten it, to push Czechoslovakia into accommodating them, to alarm the Hungarians with the specter of the German *Drang*—to act on one or the other as circumstances demanded, dividing to rule, using the *Volksdeutsch* now as incentive, now as threat. "Hitlerism," the Rumanian ambassador in Bucharest told his French counterpart, "is like a trail of powder. If Austria goes—and all indications are that she will—the Czechoslovaks will be no more able than the Hungarians to resist . . . there will be no more Little Entente, there will be nothing but German hegemony over central and eastern Europe." He was pleading with France, with or without Italy, to do something.[74]

But France was weakening, losing the will and the ability to act without the British or the Americans; and the British and Americans had lost interest in the region, depreciated the gravity of its ills and their relevance to themselves, and forgotten that one great war had broken out here in 1914, until a second one six years later reminded them, and engulfed them again.

On February 2, one year after the disarmament conference had opened, Germany returned to Geneva to resume the general talks it had left in July. The next day, in his secret speech to the generals, Hitler told them that success at Geneva was meaningless if the *Volk* were not militarized, prepared for war. The paradox of negotiating disarmament while covertly rearming in countless ways had long antedated Hitler. But now, with the Rhineland evacuated, reparations gone, theoretical equality of rights in armaments conceded, and no rectification of the eastern borders possible without war, rearmament with guns rather than words had become the central demand of German revisionism. Geneva in 1933 became the common proving ground, the place where the military ambitions of the new regime tested the limits of the status quo powers.[75]

Rüstungsfreiheit—freedom to arm—was the goal; dissemblance, negotiation, and intermittent obstruction, the means. To recover the military standing of a great power without incurring the odium of peace breakers or saboteurs at Geneva, to reject any unequal restrictions and protect German designs from the glare of international scrutiny—on this the diplomats and the soldiers were at one, even if they sometimes quarreled over timing and tactics. Hitler and his defense minister, General Werner von Blomberg, had no long-term expectations of Geneva. Neither had any use for collective security or disarmament. Military means alone assured national security, in the eyes of the general, and *Lebensraum* itself made armament a perpetual and self-sustaining process, following the dim Darwinism that pervaded Hitler's vulgate. At the War Ministry, Schleicher before Blomberg, and Groener before Schleicher, had accepted that a treaty—Locarno—and not an army secured the western borders, unlike the eastern ones. No more—but Hitler, hand in glove by now with Blomberg, also shared the wariness of the Foreign Ministry, where Bülow feared that too energetic a rearmament might provoke preventive attacks and a war that Germany at present could not win.[76] Already the previous February, soon after the conference had opened, Blomberg had suddenly invited Lieutenant Colonel Louis Koeltz from the French delegation to his quarters in the Hotel Metropole. Koeltz, a military historian who had also served as military attaché at the French embassy in Berlin, knew something about Blomberg's milieu. "Soldiers can always arrange things among themselves," his host began, amiably, in excellent French. "Among us military men there is no animosity, no hatred toward France. It's essential that our two countries come to an understanding."[77] Now he and Hitler, warlords at home and peacemakers at Geneva, confused not only their adversaries but also their own delegates.

Should they, as Bülow at the Foreign Ministry believed, spin out proceedings by inducing the others to disarm slowly? Or should they challenge the French, who had proposed in the autumn and again in the late winter and spring that all, including Germany, be allowed short-service, lightly armed national militias only, but that France be allowed colonial troops as well? Or the British, who proposed a new plan in March that would allow the Germans as many troops as the French but deny them certain offensive weapons? The French, to say nothing of the Poles, grew more insistent every day that the two-million-strong SA, which by mid-April had incorporated the other paramilitary forces as well as the Stahlhelm, and the much smaller SS count as military effectives. Hitler's reaction, when known, sometimes surprised the delegates by its caution.[78]

They were already unpopular at Geneva. Most were not Nazis and listened gloomily to the news from home on their radios. But the Swiss newspapers carried unflattering stories about the regime, and Genevans in the streets greeted the delegates with catcalls and flung stones at their cars. Matters worsened when Reinhard Heydrich, the head of the SS security service, appeared along with two auxiliaries, one from the Stahlhelm and the other from the SA, to enlighten a committee in session about their organizations' purely civilian functions. He refused the services of a Jewish interpreter, but insisted through another that the SS existed only to protect speakers from Communist attacks, the SA only for sports, the Stahlhelm only for veterans. A malicious laugh completed most of his utterances. Later he pulled down the red, gold, and black flag of Weimar still flying above the premises of the German delegation in the Carlton Hotel, and ran up a swastika he had brought with him in his luggage. Sensation reigned in town for a few hours, until the head of the delegation took it down. Heydrich left Geneva scarlet and furious—had the delegation, with its Jewish interpreter, Weimar flag, and reactionary old members, not heard of the National Socialist revolution? Then the Nazis would clean it up.[79]

The new German regime had not made the disarmament conundrum any easier for the country's former victors. As before, the British, the Americans, and the French wished to convince their peoples and each other of their commitment to reducing the instruments as well as the risks of another war, without exposing themselves to losing it. But now they contended with a regime their peoples disliked, a novelty for the Anglo-Americans if not for the French. The deepening distrust had the perverse effect of estranging them not only from the Germans but from each other.

Moral condemnation was easier for them to formulate than to implement. Even when they shared it they could not always act on it. In March, Prime Minister MacDonald had cared enough about public indignation at the Reich to remonstrate with the German ambassador, but at the end of April he and his ministers were no closer to modifying policy as Nazism revealed itself. When Ambassador Rumbold's long telegram about *Mein Kampf* reached the Foreign Office, senior officials pondered it and Simon, the foreign secretary, circulated it to the cabinet. Rumbold had warned of the hollowness of Hitler's peace pledges, and of the dangers that his wild book announced.[80] At the Foreign Office, Robert Vansittart, the permanent undersecretary, shared Rumbold's repudiation of Berlin; so did General Arthur Temperley, the country's chief military delegate to the disarmament conference. But much of the cabinet did not. Did Rumbold himself? He would not rule out some accommodation at Geneva, a goal that ministers, Simon in particular, now elevated in urgency.[81] In France the latest prime minister, Edouard Daladier, inclined in spite of a deceptive image of toughness to relax his country's obduracy about revision and about borders; he betrayed all the confusion of the Radical and Socialist left, caught between pacifism and outrage.[82] And in the United States, President Roosevelt remained silent about the anti-Semitic campaign that had brought so many of his compatriots into the streets of New York and other cities. He wanted to keep the disarmament conference alive, to dampen any suspicion that minorities manipulated his New Deal, to avoid making new enemies inside or outside the government—like his cautious secretary of state, Cordell Hull, he would do no more than use back channels to convey concern. No anti-Semite himself, he displayed no urge now to challenge those who were, and withheld condemnation; and some Jews supported his reticence, fearing the backlash that might answer any sortie from him.[83]

Besides, disarmament and collective security—whatever it might mean when tested—were still popular in the democracies. All three governments still pursued and sometimes preached both. The moral revulsion at the new regime in Berlin provided a way to escape the kinds of arms reductions or security pacts they could not sign for other reasons, as well as blame for derailing the train at Geneva.

There, Hitler continued to conciliate, not to reach an agreement but to delay one and protract the proceedings while rearming in every way possible. Rearmament was the goal, diplomacy the subterfuge. He still held back the delegates, when they came close to a rupture with the French, the British, or the Americans over the usual apples of discord. They held center stage, if only because of their tacit threat to leave it as they had the previous summer. Where would the conference be then? In their eagerness to demonstrate pacific will, the others began falling over one another, in high but dark comedy that had shifted the initiative from those wishing to disarm to those who did not.

When the conference opened in February 1932, and again in November, the French had pressed on it their plans with much fanfare. Their intricate innovations included an international League military force and uniform short-service armies for all, dependent on security treaties and on inspection and verification, for a while, of German compliance. The first condition alarmed the British and the Americans and held no interest for the Italians; the second insulted the Germans. Only the French allies in eastern Europe supported the plan, the Poles ever more coolly. Now, in mid-March 1933, MacDonald came to Geneva again to present a British plan.

This one added concrete limits on effectives and matériel to the French plan for uniform conscript armies within Europe. Almost everyone found it objectionable; almost no one said so aloud. The Germans seemed perplexed, but withheld refusal. They balked at the denial to them of military aircraft, submarines, and heavy mobile artillery for another five years, and it did little to promise the revision they expected as a quid pro quo; but it might serve as a basis for discussion.[84] The French regretted the rearmament it allowed Germany, the complete freedom it would enjoy in five years, the sizable cuts it would make in their own men and matériel, not to mention the absence of compensatory security guarantees.[85] But no more than the Germans did they savor the role of naysayer. In Prague, Bucharest, and Belgrade, the Little Entente followed the French objections to the British plan; so did another small neighbor of the Reich, Belgium. It asked much of France, little of Britain, and conceded too much to the Germans, the Czech press complained.[86] The Americans chafed at the plan's concession of unrestricted freedom in armaments to Germany after five years. Their chief delegate, Norman Davis, told his French counterpart that France with its smaller population should enjoy a permanent superiority in military matériel.[87] The Hungarians appeared pleased that they would be allowed an army of eighty thousand men, the imprimatur on a force they had already reconstituted in violation of the peace treaties; but they disliked the ban on military aviation.[88] Only the Japanese, denied the naval parity they demanded, rejected the plan; only the Italians, who warmed to its reduction of French strength and the concession to them of naval parity with France, accepted it. Mussolini cared more about his four-power pact. In April, Pompeo Aloisi of the Italian Foreign Ministry impressed on him the urgency of a settlement at Geneva. "Well, work it out," the Duce replied. The talks went on.[89]

"I don't think an Archangel could do much at Geneva at the moment," Stanley Baldwin wrote Lord Cecil, the voice of disarmament in Britain, days before MacDonald presented his plan. "The French are in a panic, the Germans won't go to Geneva, and my unhappy colleagues are faced with an almost impossible situation. The Americans are so immersed in their own trouble as to be completely useless in international matters."[90] At the end of April, the Germans surprised the conference and themselves when their chief delegate agreed abstractly to a British provision for consultation among the great powers to identify any aggressor if the occasion arose, and to the French provision for international inspection. This pleased the French and seemingly Davis of the Americans—but the British delegate complained of his "hazy imagery" and "native obscurity," and of his wish to delay unrestricted arms freedom for ten rather than five years, presumably to please the French.[91] The problem remained the same: For German opinion, arms equality in principle meant arms equality in practice. For others' opinion, it came with conditions. Impasse set in. Yet to most American, French, and British leaders, beginning with Roosevelt, Daladier, and MacDonald, disarmament still made sense, a formula for economy as well as applause.[92] Was there no way out of this labyrinth?

Not unless the Germans suspended their drive to regain the status of a great power by military means, the British and the Americans their aversion to Continental commitments and their cultivation of global sea power, and the French their fixation on security. To square

such national obsessions with consensual disarmament at Geneva—
to square emotion with reason—yielded behavior that appeared perverse or erratic to all but themselves.

No one pursued a disarmament convention at Geneva more ardently than the American delegate, Norman Davis. Yet at times no
one could tell for whom he spoke, nor whether his government had
any position to communicate.[93] The identical problem had arisen a
year earlier, when delegates doubted the attachment of their American counterparts to the plan proposed by their own President Hoover. General MacArthur, the army chief of staff, had told his French
counterpart, General Weygand, that the president had not consulted
him about it and that he would have opposed it if he had. From Congress, from the State Department, from President Roosevelt himself,
came explanations that Davis's apparent promise to consult with other
nations when peace was threatened implied only a moral obligation,
not a surrender of any freedom of action. When Roosevelt sent his
peace message in mid-May to the fifty-four nations in the conference,
he called on all to renew their commitment to peace—and why not
abolish offensive weapons and solemnly pledge not to send armed
forces across their frontiers? He wished to breathe new life into a
moribund process. But he made no hard commitments of his own. A
few days later, Davis surprised Geneva again when he vowed that his
country would refrain from hindering actions that others might take
against a consensually designated violator of the international peace.
This appeared to undermine the country's neutrality, and once again
disavowals rained down. Horrified New Dealers around the president had long suspected Davis, "the darling of the internationalists
in both parties," as one of them called him, of distracting Roosevelt
from domestic recovery with foreign adventures and, much worse, of
leading the entire country to perdition abroad. Raymond Moley, the
president's adviser on almost everything, later likened Davis to Colonel House, the confidant who in his eyes had inveigled President
Wilson into the Great War. Voices in Congress demanded Davis's recall; the Senate thought to lay the specter of entanglement by requir-

ing the president to embargo the shipment of arms and munitions to all protagonists in an international dispute, and not merely, as an existing measure allowed, to the aggressor alone and at his own discretion. Neutrality had struck back. The president, who had authorized Davis's statement in Geneva, now gave him little support. Meanwhile he pushed naval expansion. No one in the State Department, Moley complained, could make out the president's objectives.[94]

The logic behind the French and British gyrations was not much easier to grasp. But it answered some similar motives. Like Roosevelt, neither Daladier nor MacDonald wished to see the conference fail. Neither wished to rearm at home, but neither could fall on his sword: the French, with their overseas empire, could not concede naval parity to Italy as the British asked of them, and the British, with theirs, could not dispense with aerial bombing "in outlying regions" as the French asked of *them*. Their tiffs continued. But the greatest roadblock in front of them was German, standing in the way of any convention setting down limits on effectives, weapons, and enforcement. And neither wished either to reward German intransigence, not now. Each was buffeted by popular demands for peace, security, and morality.

On May 10, as the conference labored, German students in university towns marched by torchlight to toss "un-German" books onto bonfires in public squares. In Berlin the funeral pyre of Western learning stood twelve feet square and five feet high. Crowds watched in silence. The same day, in New York, 100,000 Jews and Christian sympathizers marched from Madison Square to the Battery in protest at Nazi persecutions, cheered by huge throngs. A few hours earlier Foreign Secretary Simon had faced angry questions in the House of Commons about a recent meeting with Alfred Rosenberg. The head of the newly created "foreign political department" of the Nazi Party had come unhinged and demanded that Germany be allowed to make samples of the heavy weapons that the disarmament negotiators were struggling to abolish. A dialogue of the deaf followed. In two months, Simon warned, Nazi persecutions had cost the country all the goodwill it had gained in Britain in ten years. The Reich was saving Europe from bolshevism, Rosenberg declaimed, and shutting up Communist leaders in concentration camps only to preserve liberty. He pointed to British practices in Ireland and India. Had the foreign secretary explained to Rosenberg, an opposition member asked him in the House, that he intended to stand by France to prevent the rearmament of Germany? He received no reply.[95]

The climate was not ripe for more concessions to the one country that could save the conference. In Berlin the cinema on the Kurfürstendamm was showing *Bleeding Germany*, a film put out by the Nazi firm Tobis. An armed SS guarded the entrance; inside the brown-shirted SA band played military marches and the "Horst Wessel Lied" while the audience stood. The film showed the German victory at Sedan in 1870, the foundation of the empire, the revolution of 1918, French tanks and North African soldiers in the Ruhr in 1923. The crowd stirred. On April 20, for Hitler's forty-fourth birthday, celebrated like that of Hindenburg's the year before and of the kaiser before him, a new play opened in twenty-two different theaters about Albert Schlageter, the "martyr" who had fallen to French bullets in the Ruhr. Hitler they honored as the unknown soldier, the bearer of German pride. All day the radio exalted him and the Nazi movement. These were warlike motifs. The French Ministry of Defense believed that the SA and the Stahlhelm alone numbered 700,000 ready men, a trained reserve exceeding anything they themselves could count on, to say nothing of the 100,000 professionals in the Reichswehr, the spearhead of the coming mass army. British estimates put the same reserves at over a million.[96]

German intransigence was hardening. As Simon faced his interrogators in the House, the German delegate in Geneva renewed Rosenberg's demands. *Völkischer Beobachter*, the Nazi paper, accused France and Poland of deliberately misleading world opinion at Geneva. Germany had expected the other powers to disarm, Neurath, the German foreign minister, repeated in the *Leipziger Illustri-*

erte Zeitung the next day. They had not done so, they had negotiated in bad faith. The argument, disingenuous and beggaring belief for anyone who had seen the serried ranks of paramilitaries of all sorts in the new Germany, was not new. But for the first time, the foreign minister claimed that failure at Geneva would free his country in law and in fact from the shackles of Versailles, free it to rearm in any way it wished. Once again Hitler stepped in to calm the waters with a conciliatory speech before the Reichstag. Germany demanded equality, he repeated, but would not resort to force to revise the Treaty of Versailles. He had said the same before. At Geneva his delegate appeared to reverse course as well. But the impasse at the conference remained. All month its untiring president, Arthur Henderson, strained to see a way forward.[97]

Like the League, it was exhausting its usefulness for the Reich. Already, late in April, the French ambassador found Bülow at the Foreign Ministry in Berlin uncharacteristically rancorous about the French attachment to Geneva. He saw few prospects there. And France treated Germany as though it were a second-rate power. Bülow might, the ambassador thought, have succumbed to the ambient spirit of Nazism. In Paris, the German ambassador startled the French foreign minister by proposing matter-of-factly that they relieve the League of responsibility for European problems; Mussolini's four-power group should handle them instead. Late in May, Hitler met with the Rumanian ambassador, pushed for closer political ties, and raged at France, his guest's ally; and he told him that if the conference in Geneva adjourned without giving satisfaction, Germany would leave it and the League as well and never return—and that it would reclaim full freedom of action. In June the conference adjourned. In October, after the recess, Germany left it forever.[98]

Mount an effort, make no deal, and take no action—the Western powers had obliged their compatriots with their logical due. Not everyone was happy. On May 10, as Simon fended off questions in the Commons and protesters rallied in New York, Brigadier Temperley, the British delegate in Geneva, sounded the alarm about German rearmament and German insolence. "Are we to go forward," he asked, "as if nothing has happened?" What point was there to an arms convention if German war plans went ahead, with the Poles as their first target and the French their last? To disarm now would be madness. France, the United States, and Britain should jointly warn Germany to cease rearming and abide by Versailles. The Americans, he knew, would never join in the implied threat of force, but Germany was in no shape to fight the French army and the British fleet. They should call Hitler's bluff. The alternative, he concluded, was five years of drift followed by war. Vansittart, the undersecretary at the Foreign Office, supported his every word.[99]

But no one else did. Neither reward nor punish Germany—the unstated message of the Oxford Union debate, for anyone levelheaded enough to grasp it, was emerging as policy. Vansittart sent Temperley's memorandum to the cabinet, where it died. Baldwin and most of his colleagues still linked economic recovery to disarmament. In October, in a by-election at Fulham East, a Conservative backer of rearmament went down to heavy defeat at the hands of a militant Labour disarmer. His election proved, the victor explained, "that this country desires peace more than anything else." The Liberal *News Chronicle* agreed and the Labourite *Daily Herald* proclaimed that "rarely had a by-election carried a message so unmistakable and a meaning so plain." The following July, the cabinet cut back the spending estimates of the Defense Requirements Committee. Not for several years would rearmament begin in earnest, to accompany a policy known optimistically as appeasement. In January, Daladier's government in Paris cut 200 million francs from the defense budget and suppressed five thousand officers' commissions; in May it cut back call-ups of conscripts for the next three years. General Maxime Weygand at the high command protested volubly, to no avail. The Socialists, on whom Daladier depended, wanted him to cut more than he had already. He held the line, but the parsimony yielded an army with little offensive capability, and a diplomacy without the means of its ends—as the country's eastern allies had reason to suspect. In the United States, Roosevelt proposed cutting the minuscule 140,000-man army, an irrelevant gesture to Geneva but not to the army chief of staff, General Douglas MacArthur, who objected as vehemently as Weygand. He despised isolationism as well as pacifism. But the Americans, as Vansittart complained, "were tending to go native again."[100]

Everywhere the advent and the antics of the Nazis in Germany, far from drawing the others closer, had driven them apart. Mussolini's four-power pact had proved stillborn, welcomed by the Germans as empowering them, but for the same reason resented by the eastern Europeans and amended beyond recognition by the French. His ploy to marginalize the League fell to the same national caprices that had paralyzed it already. Each was seeking his own solution, concluding bilateral tactical agreements or shunning them altogether, playing out national conceits about destiny or victimhood, or entertaining delusions of tranquility conferred by fortified frontiers or oceanic moats and superior virtues. Provincialism was conquering cosmopolitanism in international relations, opening the way for mutually reinforcing urges in some to expand, in others to withdraw.

Japan's generals and admirals looked west, Mussolini south, Hitler east. The community of the damned that Hugh Wilson, the American minister in Berne, had feared as he listened to Matsuoka in the League Assembly at the end of February had not yet taken shape.[101] But the same mix of condemnation and inaction now greeted German ambitions and might answer those of Mussolini as well if he ever invaded Ethiopia as he intended. In April, hot on the heels of MacDonald and Simon, Goering and Papen had arrived in Rome. Not content with robbing Papen of the premiership of Prussia and adding it to his title as head of a supposedly civilian air ministry, Goering on tour stole the limelight from him as well. He strutted about the Eternal City in new uniforms he had designed himself, a coarse and meretricious intruder, and Papen returned to

Berlin affronted as well as outworn.[102] Nazism had arrived to stay, Goering signified in Rome, and he paid tribute to its Italian inspiration. Mussolini, less than eager to acknowledge paternity, held them at arm's length. For now; but Gibson's premonitions about pariahs seeking each other's company might yet come true, even if "community" exaggerated their good fellowship. And what if other countries without knowing it inhabited the doomed circle as well, including the pacific and the passive, such as his own?

———•◦•———

12

Washington Closes Another Door

When Franklin Roosevelt told the American people in his inaugural address on March 4 that they had nothing to fear but fear itself, he issued a call to confidence that Hoover had made before him and that presidents would punctually renew after him whenever the economy gave grounds for despair. But, by transforming the role of government in the next hundred days and entrusting it with a provision for human security far exceeding the right to life and property, by introducing the welfare state to America, he endowed the words with meaning, intending that this time spirits should lift.

In his address he also declared that no international economic commitments would stand in the way of domestic recovery. The emergency at home, he said, could not wait on the restoration of international trade. As a statement of priorities this seemed reasonable enough—the New Deal was emphatically a national deal, suited to a country deriving only 10 percent of its gross domestic income from foreign trade. But Roosevelt the politician also spoke the language of millions who either took no interest in the world's economic crisis or blamed it for their own. He left unstated the possibility that if the world would not matter to the New Deal, it might matter to the world—that it might impair the nation's relations with others and answer their inwardness with its own.

During the Hundred Days, as the domestic measures poured forth in an avalanche of improvised acts and agencies, the president concurrently administered a succession of shocks to any European expectations of a new harmony in relations with the United States. He detached the dollar from gold, allowing it to float on foreign exchanges and effectively devaluing it against most major currencies, withheld relief to the country's foreign debtors, left in place most of the country's high tariff walls, and embarked on a massive naval expansion program after urging others to cut costs and disarm—all while the nations of the world, his own included, readied themselves for the World Economic Conference, years in the making and scheduled to open in the Geological Museum in London on June 12.

As experimental as the New Deal, such policies followed no articulate strategy or doctrine, only a vague but resolute economic nationalism. Stripped of the competitive animus that the world depression had sharpened, they would have appeared mindless and erratic. Roosevelt, neither temperamentally nor intellectually averse to better relations with the European powers, rarely shared the visceral suspicions that so many in Congress and the press exhibited toward the Old Continent, notably toward the country's onetime allies on the western front. Perhaps he showed his more authentic self in the Good Neighbor Policy toward the countries of his own hemisphere. In it he renounced armed intervention in the Latin American republics and appeared to embrace a Monroe Doctrine that protected them from European interference but also from American heavy-handedness. In 1920, as a vice presidential candidate, he had enthused over more muscular methods, including those of Wilson, who for all his idealism had bombarded Veracruz and sent marines to Haiti and Santo Domingo. Republicans had accused Roosevelt of imperialism then, especially when he boasted of having written Haiti's constitution.[1] But he had changed, and now pursued an evolution already underway with Hoover and Stimson. Nothing so consistent or constructive distinguished his approach to the worsening crises in Europe and East Asia, which unlike those in Latin America threatened the peace of the world.

When they arrived in office neither the president nor his advisers in the Brains Trust knew what to do about the dollar or the gold standard. None knew very much about monetary theory; only one, Rexford Tugwell, was an economist, and he specialized in agriculture. From most of the candidate's utterances about a balanced budget and a sound currency, a thoughtful observer might deduce a partiality to the regimen of the gold standard, still thought by most economists to ensure both. But late in the campaign Hoover warned that his opponent would drive the currency off the gold standard, resort to greenbacks— federal banknotes not backed by gold bullion—and "fiat money," and revive the monetary nightmares of the Civil War. Neither then nor later could he know Roosevelt's intentions in the matter, because the Democratic candidate himself did not know them. He replied only by pledging his support for "sound money."[2]

But he was aware of the growing interest in controlled inflation—in devaluing the currency by detaching it from gold backing—as a way forward. Cheaper money, detached from a fixed value in gold and no longer fully convertible into it, might raise the badly depressed commodity prices from which farmers suffered cruelly, reduce their debt burden—the mortgages that had cost so many of them their farms— and, by lowering the price of American exports on foreign markets, conceivably stimulate depressed manufacturing industries. The call had come before. Ever since the greenbacks issued during the Civil War, the idea of a currency neither backed by the filthy metal nor controlled by the financiers of Wall Street or the City of London had appealed to millions whose daily livelihood depended on the value of money—which their elected representatives in Congress, per the Constitution, had sole power to mint and regulate. It had appealed, sometimes massively, to the straitened and the indebted farmers in the West and South and those who depended on them, those who hoped that a measure of inflation might wash their debt away or at least alleviate their plight. During the interregnum of 1932–1933, as the economic and banking crisis deepened, the political appeal of managing the national currency unilaterally, even at the cost of an elusive international stability, returned, especially where it mattered most—in a new Congress, among new Democrats, many from the Farm and Cotton Belts. During March and April, bills and amendments to inflate the currency or available credit, usually by reducing the gold content of the dollar and sometimes by monetizing silver, began reaching the Senate floor and the Oval Office, whose occupant, that spring, owed his presence in the White House to the same parts of the country now clamoring for monetary relief.[3]

The idea of experimenting with the value of the currency held little appeal for the orthodox guardians of sound money. To many, the idea of detaching the dollar from gold was irredeemably heretical. But around Roosevelt, who had seemed to identify his beliefs with theirs during the campaign, the orthodox were losing their primacy. His adviser Raymond Moley derided them as votaries of the twin deities of the gold standard and free trade, and partial as well to debt cancellation and other internationalist follies. Rexford Tugwell, for his part, was a keen advocate of economic voluntarism—of the economic planning that had found its theoretical pioneers in academic circles and was now making its first converts in policy-making ones. Whatever Tugwell's views on the currency—which by his own admission were unpracticed—he believed in national action to coordinate production with consumption, prices with wages, and supply with demand. Monetary experimentation and national planning seemed made for each other and for a New Deal that situated the cause of the Depression not abroad but at home, not between nations but within them, in the widening gulf between profits and wages and in related structural imbalances; and each removed national remedies from the prior restraints of the world economy.[4]

In April Senator Elmer Thomas of Oklahoma proposed an amendment to the Farm Relief Bill that would allow the president to issue greenbacks and reduce the gold content of the dollar by as much as 50 percent, among other measures to expand credit. Whether moved by such pressures or by his own inclination to experiment—"Above all, try something," he had said during his campaign for the Democratic nomination—Roosevelt resolved to act even before the Senate passed the Thomas amendment and vested him with new discretionary powers. At a press conference on the nineteenth, he severed the dollar from gold. The administration had already ordered depositors to return any gold they were hoarding, and suspended payments in it, in a successful effort to recapitalize the banks; now it made the embargo permanent and suspended the gold standard. The dollar ceased to represent 23.22 grains of fine gold and was left to find its own level on the world exchanges.[5]

Pandemonium had broken out in the White House the night before, when Roosevelt told several cabinet secretaries and staffers about his decision. "Well, this is the end of Western Civilization," the budget director, Lew Douglas, had said.[6] And, to many, the dollar signified in its integrity all that the pound had the previous century. It was no parochial medium of exchange. Confidence in its stability had reigned around the world since the end of the Great War; the United States, unlike the ruined European protagonists of the conflict, had never ceased to redeem its monetary promises in gold. It was a currency of refuge, a safer haven for investors than some unsound foreign currency. On occasion confidence had weakened, as in October 1931 and May 1932, when holders of dollars had parted with them in alarming quantities, but the government had quickly defended the currency with the aid of the country's huge gold reserves, as Hoover never tired of reminding voters. After April 20, unmoored from the vaults that had backed it for so long, it began to float against all currencies whether they were tied to gold or not.

Domestic pressures alone had prevailed. In September 1931 foreign runs on the British pound had driven it off the gold standard and left it to depreciate against foreign currencies. No imminent threat of the kind drove Roosevelt's action of 19 April; Prime Minister

MacDonald had complained of foreign manipulations, he had not. Britain had ceased to pay its balances in gold because it no longer held enough of it to meet them, and only after a bitter struggle; the United States had not. With about half the world's gold reserves that spring, the country could handily withstand any and all foreign claims on them. But could it withstand attacks from its own citizens? For two years they had withdrawn dollars because they distrusted the banks; as Roosevelt came into office, they were withdrawing gold because they distrusted the dollar. Emergency action had stanched and reversed the flow and shored up the banks, but not allayed the chronic anger over the currency. The departure from the gold standard was a matter of choice, not necessity, a British paper found, perhaps enviously—but wrongly: it was a measure of necessity at home if not abroad, driven by agricultural prices, farm foreclosures, and sporadic violence in the heartland.[7]

But the repercussions immediately spread far beyond American shores. The news startled two illustrious guests on their way to meet Roosevelt, at his invitation, for informal talks about the world and its dire economy. Prime Minister MacDonald and former prime minister Edouard Herriot were on the high seas when radio brought the news early in the morning of the twentieth. The fait accompli threw both delegations, one on board the *Berengaria* and the other on the *Ile-de-France*, into confusion, and some suggested turning back once they reached the New York piers. As Herriot remarked to one of the reporters on board, it brought everything back to square one— "To the zero point of the theorem." By this he could only mean that currency instability, to which the United States had now mightily added, lay at the heart of the differences between them, for how could they resolve war debts and tariffs, when some fixed their currencies in gold and others did not? When—the insinuation ran—those off gold could manipulate their currencies to gain an advantage in trade, while others still on it, such as his own, could not? The State Department assured the world that the United States had acted only to raise domestic price levels, which was true; diplomatically, MacDonald declared on arrival and Herriot by radio from shipboard that the essential questions remained unchanged, which was not.[8]

In Paris and in the City of London, which had not experienced such a sensation since sterling had left gold in 1931, the dollar fell.[9] There and in other capitals, as speculation persisted about American strategy to gain the upper hand in trade and other talks, foreign creditors of the United States began to fear that with the suspension of gold payments they, like domestic American bondholders, would no longer receive their interest or their principal in gold. In the United States, reciprocal fears arose about imagined retaliatory measures in Europe, including moves by the British Exchange Equalization Account to depreciate sterling and set off a currency war with the dollar.[10] While MacDonald sat with Roosevelt in the White House in front of an open fire or talked before the National Press Club of the need for cooperation or attended a state dinner as the guest of honor along with Herriot, the recriminations began to cross the Atlantic; and one afternoon, in an otherwise trivial mishap, Herriot's car bringing him back from a visit to Mount Vernon collided with a busload of local tourists.[11]

"Fluctuations of the paper dollar," *The Times* warned, "will add a powerful source of instability to an already unstable world." Like other dailies and weeklies in London, it feared a spiral of competitive devaluations. With his action, the *Economist* worried, Roosevelt had made it easier for the United States "still further to disorganize world trade" instead of helping to remove the restrictions on the free flow of goods and capital that, in the eyes of the devoutly classical, free-trader weekly, had made the operation of the international gold standard impossible. These were platitudes, ideals which the Americans themselves shared. More monetary instability, *Le Temps* agreed in Paris, was no way to improve the general economic situation.[12]

But, among the European gold bloc countries and especially in France, comments did not stop there. A tribal motif quickly enlivened this most soulless of deliberations. Whatever the reasons the United States had for letting the dollar fall, a right-wing French commentator wrote, they had little to do with the betterment of the world. He wrote defensively, the citizen of a country still on gold, forced now to watch while others sold their francs in return for it while French holders of dollars and pounds enjoyed no such option. France would lose her gold reserves. Other Continental countries such as Germany had defended themselves by imposing capital controls, embargoes in effect, remaining on the gold standard in theory but not in practice. Others, including France, had not. "Sacred egoism!" ironized one of the papers, to applaud Roosevelt for considering only his country, and to condemn Herriot and his party for serially betraying their own, this time merely by traveling to Washington.

And inflation, problematic in economics, became emblematic in politics. It was the American way, *Le Temps*—moderately conservative, unofficially the mouthpiece of the Foreign Ministry—wrote: an infatuation with inflation and an indifference to their currency periodically seized the American masses, forcing their leaders to yield and the rest of the world to tremble. Surely, *Le Figaro* asked, Roosevelt—"So patriotic, so lucid, so ordered"—could not indulge in criminal misdeeds worthy of the Bolsheviks themselves? It was further to the right. The Left was not so sure. In *Le Populaire*, Blum welcomed the death knell of the deflationary orthodoxy that Roosevelt himself had preached. But he did not espouse inflation, unless wages were indexed to prices to protect workers' purchasing power.[13] France now became the paragon of monetary pride. "Our Franc has nothing to fear," Prime Minister Daladier was telling his constituents at a banquet in Orange as Herriot arrived in Washington, "from the fluctuations of other currencies."[14] The entire world, he claimed, aspired to such stability. Behind the confident posture moved the anxiety of living memory. Between 1918 and 1926, the franc had lost four-fifths of its value, from depreciation and then devaluation. The fall had impoverished or ruined pensioners, veterans, and all who survived on low salaries or depended on yields from state bonds. A currency based on gold, in their eyes, stood between them and a recurrence of the nightmare called inflation. Daladier, at his banquet in

Orange, was speaking to them. "We have known the pain of monetary crises too well to accept their renewal," he told them. Domestic sentiment had pushed him and Roosevelt in opposite directions.

Through the shifting reactions in the press, a new fault line emerged—between Britain and the United States leading the world off gold, and France and its fellow Continentals calling the world back to it. The contrast delighted the commentators, and soon grew into audacious generalizations about Anglo-Saxon adventurism, addicted to the monetary demagoguery of credit and depreciated currencies, and the solid sense of the Old World, immunized to inflation through hard experience and the bread of adversity.[15]

Consistency had never tamed the discussion. Seven years earlier, during the troubles of the franc and before its return to the rule of the gold standard, André Tardieu, a future prime minister who knew the United States well, complained about the Americans and their secretary of commerce, Herbert Hoover. They never stopped preaching their own gospel of economic and monetary order to others, he noted, or touting the sanctity of the gold standard. But was consistency to be found anywhere else, in the spring of 1933? Among the British, disgruntled that the Americans should follow in their footsteps and walk away from the monetary discipline to which they still refused to return themselves? Among the Americans and their president, who assured reporters the day he took the country off the gold standard that he wanted the world to return to it?[16] None of this boded well for the World Economic Conference.

Try as it might, the League could never insulate a meeting about economics from political and national passions. They threatened to capsize it along with the disarmament conference. It was Geneva's worthy sister, the nationalist French historian Jacques Bainville wrote, because the conference would promote economic disarmament without identifying the political mainsprings of the trade wars. Prime Minister MacDonald himself, the moving spirit behind the London conference, fretted that it would drift as Geneva did. In Germany, pessimism or hostility predominated in the press: How could the gathering resolve economic differences without first settling the political ones at Geneva? Without granting Germany equal rights and accepting its new regime, its revolution? Besides, the papers said, people were interested by now only in defending themselves, they had tired of conferences, and doubted the shibboleth of a world economy. The skeptical Polish press, whether governmental or not, feared pressures on France to abandon Poland in London and elsewhere and the ruination of the Danube economies as well. All this took the conference far from the bloodless talk of exchanges, quotas, and capital controls.[17]

Early in the year, the League's commission of experts setting the agenda for the conference had concluded that it should tackle all the world's economic ills—barriers to trade, currency instability, unpaid war debts, and the cessation of foreign lending—concurrently. Logically, none stood apart from the others, presenting the spectacle of one uncommonly vicious circle after another. Trade could not recover until monetary exchanges were stabilized and controls on them lifted, which could not be risked until trade recovered. A freer flow of capital among countries required a freer flow of goods, and vice versa. Exchange rates affected debt payments, which in turn affected exchange rates. Practically, the conferees who would assemble in London could hope only for discreet compromises on each, to lay the groundwork for a gradual resolution over years to all. But, with each yoked to the other, a breakdown in one might entail a breakdown in the rest.

What defined success? Central European and Latin American countries relying on horizontal tariff walls to protect distressed economies had little enthusiasm for a multilateral injunction to tear them down. The new German government was resolved to husband its foreign exchange for strategic imports, to carve out a privileged economic zone in southeastern Europe with clearing agreements and other unequal pacts, and to repudiate the country's private-sector western debts—all to sustain its guiding project: rearmament. German autarky sat as oddly as any other at the conference table, even though its practitioners, whether in the Nazi Party, the Reichsbank, or the ministries, liked to blame it on the protectionism of others. How could the country repay its American debts, the Reichsbank asked, if it could not export into American markets? But it had no intention of repaying them anyway, and the return of a liberal world economic order would only make its default more difficult.[18]

In the United States, where war debts rankled, Roosevelt never sought authority from Congress to take up the matter in London. MacDonald, who represented the largest of the thirteen national debts, agreed to take it off the table there. He, like most of the twelve other debtor nations, and Roosevelt himself, hoped to lay the entire matter to rest before the conference even convened on June 12—three days before the next installment fell due. Would Britain default then, as France and others had in December? The two were far apart and no agreement with Britain was possible without the others. Nine other national missions had followed the British and the French to Washington, most hoping for a final resolution to war debts; they had left just as disappointed. The conference opened without an answer. "The less said about war debts," *The Times* had already concluded in May, "the better."[19]

As for trade barriers, the president did not yet ask Congress either for authority to alter existing tariffs. The commission of experts had proposed a temporary tariff truce, to last as long as the conference, and to this the Americans agreed. But others at first did not, including the French, who asked that those who had captured an export advantage by devaluing their currencies—meaning the British and the Americans—stabilize them, or face compensatory tariffs by those who had not. Otherwise, the French felt, they were maneuvering on quicksand. Yet a truce made sense. Free trade had disappeared from the globe. In the early months of 1933, tariffs and quotas had continued to proliferate as they had throughout 1932, and the prospect that nations assembled to arrest them might instead impose new ones on one another became too absurd for the conferees to contemplate. In May, after weeks of negotiations, eight of them agreed to a partial truce and invited the others to join. Almost all did. The moment sent a ray of hope, marked a step seldom taken in the depressed world, much to the credit of the unsung League organizers who had patiently persuaded members to take it. But the measure freezing barriers did little to remove them or attack the causes of the ill. Britain, for one, still steered by the lights of Ottawa the year before—it gave preference in its own markets to domestic producers, followed by those in the empire, followed by everyone else. It signed on to the truce belatedly and reluctantly. The Germans did so as well, appending so many reservations as to nullify the gesture. A clause allowed members to drop out after July—and before the end of the year, twenty of them had.[20]

Currency, as protectionist an instrument as any once freed from the discipline of the gold standard, also sowed the deepest dissension. Fifteen countries still on gold, led by France, wanted the twenty-five who had left it to return at once, without any protracted inquiry into the conditions behind their flight. But Britain, as Neville Chamberlain, the chancellor of the exchequer, had told businessmen at a luncheon in Birmingham late in February, would do so only when war debts had been liquidated, when domestic wholesale prices had risen, when conditions were ripe. "We cannot go back to the gold standard," he said, to the "Hear, hear" of his listeners, "until we can be satisfied that the gold standard will work." More surprisingly, Roosevelt continued to call for a return to gold as a fixed measure of exchange values—after he had abandoned it, while European dignitaries called on him in Washington, after they had left. He said so to the American people by radio on May 7, and in writing on the sixteenth to the fifty-four governments gathered at the disarmament conference in Geneva. Then, abruptly, he fell silent. The European gold bloc countries, unable to abandon gold lest they lose control of their own currencies, eager that others should return to the international standard of value it had once represented, heard no more from him. Three days before the conference opened, Daladier, before the French Chamber, renewed his call on all who had left gold to return, and 406 deputies out of the 591 on the benches in the Hemisphere gave him their support.[21]

Behind the sudden silence from Washington lay a change of heart. The gamble of April 19, it seemed, had paid off. Since its decoupling from the gold standard, the dollar had lost some 40 percent of its value; meanwhile, domestic prices had risen and interest rates had fallen, happy outcomes signifying relief for farmers and easier credit for all, as well as a price advantage for exporters. Then and later, economists argued over the seemingly restorative virtue of the president's decision, over the precise connection of cause and effect, especially when, later in the summer, domestic prices reversed themselves and began to fall again. But in May and June, as the conference approached, such comedowns for Roosevelt and his advisers lay in the future. "I saw the thrill," Moley recalled, "that increasing praise gave him." This was no time to change elixirs and return to currency stabilization.

Secretary of State Cordell Hull, leading the American delegation, sailed on May 31 aboard the *President Roosevelt*, as devout an economic liberal as any in the administration but much in the dark about the shifting priorities there. He looked forward, he told reporters before the ship sailed, to the urgent task of lowering tariffs and stabilizing currencies.[22]

Hull had attended only one conference about economic matters at the White House, and that had taken place during the interregnum. A Wilsonian internationalist to the core, he had led the free trade wing of the Democratic party during the campaign, incurring the hostility of some of the New Dealers–to-be gathered in the Brains Trust. One of them, Raymond Moley, accompanied him onto the *Roosevelt* until it sailed. Hull, a stranger to the kitchen cabinet, regarded him with suspicion. Roosevelt had placed Moley in the State Department as an assistant secretary, in practice a gray eminence, and the secretary resented the presence there of the president's ubiquitous utility man, a novice in foreign affairs. Besides, for two weeks Moley had been trying to deflate public expectations about the conference. "We shall not have," he wrote and said, "a vast new commerce on the seven seas, even after a successful Economic Conference." Now, as he sailed toward it, Hull did not grasp, and Moley had not impressed on him, that members of the delegation had been told to avoid discussing currency stabilization in London.[23]

Later Moley complained, as others had and many would for years to come, that nobody knew what Roosevelt wanted. Walter Lippmann, the journalist given the unenviable task in London of explaining the proceedings to the press, complained too. But there *The Times* had tried chivalry. "The temporary divorce of the dollar from its gold basis," its leader surmised, "may perhaps give President Roosevelt a greater opportunity of displaying his gift of leadership at the World Conference."[24]

Like the disarmament annex in Geneva, but older, the Hall of the Geological Museum in Jermyn Street provided a functional but drab setting for so cosmopolitan a host of delegates, 168 of them from 66 countries, gathered to restore prosperity as the others had to preserve peace. Stark and unadorned, its walls and pillars repainted in gray and green, the hall resembled a factory more than a site for the epochal conclave that George V and Prime Minister MacDonald announced on opening day, June 12. The sovereign and his first minister spoke from a dais through an odor of fresh paint, their voices distorted by echoes from defective loudspeakers on the pillars, as though the cause had not happily espoused the venue. Radio hookups carried the king's words to the four corners of the globe, and wireless technology cut out the echo and made him more audible in San Francisco, Buenos Aires, and Tokyo than in London. Cameras filmed the occasion for the newsreels, only to project onto the screens ranks of funereal dark tailcoats and striped trousers, speckled by an occasional Indian turban or Arab headdress.[25]

At the Dorchester Hotel, Jeanette MacDonald, the American movie brunette who had recently finished two film musicals with Maurice Chevalier, watched the German delegates to the conference come through the revolving doors. Amid the screenwriters and the stars, the racehorse owners and millionaires and maharajahs drawn to another international conference as though to a gala or an opening, they looked incongruously bureaucratic. Their leader, the minister of economics and agriculture, Alfred Hugenberg, entered the elevator beside the actress. Short and stocky, with a bushy mustache, cropped hair, and golden pince-nez, he seemed an unlikely satyr hovering by her, conceivably come to town to figure in a remake of *Blue Angel*.[26]

In London, the German delegation made no noise. It staged none of the scenes or issued any of the threats it did at the disarmament conference at Geneva. The Nazis within it were the quietest, perhaps betraying their indifference to proceedings so far from their thoughts. Hugenberg, one of the conservative ministers in the coalition, and as fanatical a nationalist as they, suddenly demanded living space for the Germans, a people defending the West against inferior breeds of humanity. He demanded colonies in Africa or closer to home, leaving unspecified any proximate destinations in eastern Europe. But he decried the work of chaos and destruction abroad in the Soviet Union. All this had nothing to do with the conference in London. *Pravda* protested the outburst in Moscow, *The Times* regretted it in London. The government in Berlin disavowed Hugenberg's declaration—it served no diplomatic purpose, and he himself no longer served any political one, once the Nazis had tightened their grip on power. Before the end of June, he was back in Germany, out of the government and gone from German political life. The German delegation resumed its passive role, a spectator among the principals.[27]

But the episode while it lasted reminded all that no agenda was sacred, and that each brought his own. The matter of German colonies belonged not here but at the League in Geneva, like any other revisionist project. Almost at once, in his opening speech, MacDonald mightily annoyed the Americans by raising the matter they had deleted from the agenda—war debts. Chamberlain did not help by raising the same vexed question at greater length two days later, and by insisting that it required settlement before currencies could be stabilized. Neither Daladier and the French nor other Europeans on gold, including the Poles, the Czechoslovaks, the Dutch, and the Belgians, helped by harping as well on currency stabilization, which the American delegation, Hull excepted, no longer wished to discuss at the conference. That left tariffs, which Hull wished to discuss but Chamberlain, the man of Ottawa and of the nascent zones of sterling and of imperial preference, did not. Litvinov for the Soviet Union derided the inability of the capitalist powers to resolve their problems but added that they might ship their surpluses over on credit to redress his country's "underconsumption"—a handy euphemism for famine. Had no one learned the lessons of Geneva, that a squaring of agendas, a minimal meeting of minds, ought to precede the opening of so multilateral a conference?[28]

Instead of speaking after MacDonald on the opening day, Hull remained silent. Roosevelt had requested that he tone down his draft, an encomium of classical free trade, part of which at least departed from his own campaign speeches. The American delegation began to appear isolated not only from the others but from its own government as well. Instructed to shun debt resolution as well as currency stabilization, prohibited from signing any agreements on tariffs and trade without congressional scrutiny, the delegation, as the *New York Herald Tribune* had it, was "empowered to extend to Europe a cordial invitation to heave to and watch President Roosevelt's smoke." Hull, when he did speak to the conference two days later, delivered an emotional philippic against economic nationalism and protectionism. Whatever amendments he had made to please the president, he had not cooled his ardor. But he offered no concrete suggestions. Where Chamberlain had made war debts and price levels the major ills, he indicted tariffs. When he left the speaker's dais amid mild applause no one was any wiser about a way forward. In administration circles in Washington, the *Baltimore Sun* said, he had become "the secret object of commiseration as the custodian of a lost cause."[29]

A week after Hull spoke, the State Department put a stop to the transoceanic incoherence. Currency stabilization, it announced on the twenty-second, "was never an affair of the delegation." The conference had placed "undue emphasis" on it. Most of the press in the gold bloc countries by then harbored no more illusions about American intentions. In their strongest member, France, papers of the right and center were already warning of America's infatuation with the "drug" of inflation and of the dangers of a universal addiction. France must resist. More than Roosevelt, the demagoguery of Congress was to blame. A few voices decried their own addiction to gold and the gold standard as ruinous, but they faded, and after the twenty-second a storm of protest drowned them out. The State Department's declaration had produced, *Le Temps* found, a deplorable impression not only in Paris but in other capitals as well. And if the conference could treat neither war debts nor exchange rates, what was the point of holding it? Since the conference began, the *Journal des Débats* complained, it encountered American intransigence over debts. It would do so again, it assured its readers, over currency.[30]

The announcement came as no surprise to the British government. Late in May, the ambassador in Washington persuaded the cabinet committee on the conference that Moley's variety of economic nationalism had prevailed over Hull's internationalism, much to the secretary's discouragement. As though to stress the point, Moley himself arrived in London on June 28.[31]

The American delegation, one of the French delegates complained, camped in its tent, incommunicado save through British intermediaries. In Belgrade, the foreign minister deplored its ways. "A first delegation arrives," he told a correspondent from the wire service Havas, off the record. "We learn it doesn't have the proper authority. Then we learn a new gentleman is on his way from Washington. We have to wait and the whole conference is suspended." At the State Department in Washington, William Phillips, the acting secretary in Hull's absence, met with the French ambassador. Domestic considerations, he explained, had induced the government to modify its earlier support for rapid currency stabilization. But the French position was so much more logical, the ambassador insisted.

If they were forced to devalue the franc, he went on, public opinion would see French national interest sacrificed to American. Phillips did not argue. He even seemed to agree. And he acknowledged that the Treasury, the Federal Reserve, and the Brains Trust did not agree among themselves.[32]

Roosevelt, vacationing on Campobello Island in New Brunswick across the Canadian border, had sent Moley not—as far as anyone could tell—to upstage Hull but to act as a "liaison officer" and affirm his views about the conference and promote unity within the American delegation. But the press did not believe this, and Moley's arrival only added to the humiliations the president had heaped on his secretary of state. Roosevelt thought of the conference as a study group, one that might conceive novel forms of international economic management, but not as the locus of short-term decisions and certainly not a court to air challenges to his domestic priorities. If the others would not cooperate with his recovery program to raise prices, he told Moley before he left, "then there's nothing to cooperate about. We can't be limited by their timidity."[33]

What was left for the representatives of the world's largest economy to talk about at the massive parley? Not war debts, forbidden by the creditor himself, who in any case had consented in Washington to accept token payments for the June 15 installment by Britain and others without branding them as defaults. Not even tariffs, about which confusion spread as the delegates contradicted one another—one day one of them endorsed and another opposed lowering them. Perhaps they ought not to talk to the press without the secretary's approval, came the suggestion, to no avail. About currency stabilization the president became increasingly dogmatic as the matter became increasingly urgent. The dollar continued to weaken, raising renewed fears of a downward spiral with sterling and signs of panic among holders of gold-based currencies. Parallel talks began not below the encased Pleistocene or Quaternary fragments of the earth's crust in the Geological Museum, but not far away, above the cavernous gold vaults of the Bank of England. There American and British central bankers and Treasury officials had early on worked out one stabilization agreement, which Roosevelt rejected, warning Hull against the "exchange stability of banker-influenced cabinets." Moley was at sea, on his way, but arrived to find they had drafted another one, which seven countries on gold, Chamberlain, most of the American delegation, and he, too, ardently hoped Roosevelt would accept. It committed all signatories only to limit monetary speculation as best they could and those from countries that had left gold to return to it at some time, at some parity. It was, Walter Lippmann thought, "a diplomatic formula of the sort to which governments resort when they are unable to make decisions." But the drafters and signers hoped that even a platonic commitment would reassure the nervous and calm the monetary waters, at least while the conference lasted.[34]

"The world will not long be lulled," Roosevelt replied from on board the *Indianapolis*, the cruiser bringing him back to Washington from Campobello, "by the specious fallacy of achieving a temporary and probably an artificial stability in foreign exchange." He derided the "old fetishes of international bankers" and reaffirmed his belief in managed currencies and in national paths to economic recovery. The acrimonious, almost hectoring tone of the letter did not endear its author to the recipients in London, but they would have been more dismayed by the abusive tone he penciled out of his original draft—by the allusion, inter alia, to "those nations which have lacked the ability or the courage to face boldly their present peril." He rejected the need for immediate stabilization and called on the conference to return forthwith to its mission and "cure fundamental economic ills."[35]

Even though the committee of experts, in its January report, had placed the restoration of the international gold standard high among the prerequisites for world economic recovery, League planners doubted the wisdom of allowing immediate currency stabilization to capsize the agenda. Their priorities dovetailed more with Roosevelt's than with many others'. And perhaps, as many began to repeat, the conference should not have met when it did, with currencies in renewed disarray following the American departure from the gold standard in April.[36]

"Could you tell us anything further about that Conference?" a reporter asked Roosevelt at a press conference at the White House four days later. "Not a blessed thing," he replied. But across the Atlantic, others could. His "bombshell" message, delivered and received as a public affront, stung the delegations in London to the quick. "Another American schoolmaster," went the refrain, and even editors who liked the content of the message disliked its tone. Chamberlain, who had worked for a compromise, drafted a motion to adjourn the conference. The French press called for their own delegates to pack up and leave. National stereotypes now flourished, among observers already fond of them. The American incoherence at London sprang not from a nation but a continent, able to indulge a governmental anarchy that would cost a European nation its existence; American exasperation at European debtors lecturing their creditor drove the country back on itself, more arrogant than ever; its experiments, its love affair with inflation and speculation, forced the hands of its Latin American satellites and endangered everyone else. Farewell to the agony of London, the angriest of them wrote, and to meddlesome American observers, farewell—nationalist schadenfreude—to the American guardianship of Europe.[37]

And welcome, ran another refrain, to the primacy of national over international economics. Fascists, leftists, Keynesians, and conservatives alike found that much to celebrate, for different motives, in Roosevelt's scuttling of the conference. The "nationally planned world of the future," the Conservative member of Parliament Leopold Amery wrote to *The Times*, could forget about setting the Humpty Dumpty of nineteenth-century economics, with its gold standard and its free trade and muddled internationalism, back together. Like the press barons Rothermere and Beaverbrook, he found the moment ripe for Britain to forge an imperial economy—a sterling zone among its Dominions, alone able to compete with the United States. Already the government, without their encouragement, was considering a conference of sterling-zone countries.[38] The Japanese *Asahi* announced the emergence of five other such blocs, of which Japan-Manchukuo was one, now that the conference had sounded the death knell of economic cooperation.[39] In Germany, where most still commented the goings-on in London as detached and disinterested spectators, some dusted off the "sane autarky" that Hugenberg's press had called for after his outburst about *Lebensraum*. Roosevelt had espoused Hitler's approach, the *Lokal Anzeiger* boasted—to bring about recovery at home, to restore domestic equilibrium without international scheming.[40] Already the Nazis were traveling the Danube basin, and *Lebensraum* seemed an oddly expansionist variety of autarky—but no matter, the debacle in London brought smiles of vindication in Berlin. Elsewhere self-sufficiency paid its last respects to cosmopolitanism. In Rome, *La Tribuna*, owned by the Banca Commerciale and the Fascist Federation of Building Owners, proposed that all sixty-six delegations at London solemnly swear never to gather again in an international conference.[41] In Brussels, *La Nation Belge*, hearing the finance minister call again for international cooperation, asked what the country had ever gained from these meetings, and whether it ought not to ignore the summons of the great powers in the future.[42] For a country the size of Belgium, such defiance could not signify an impossible isolation; but neutrality, equidistance from the country's powerful neighbors, was another matter.

Still, no delegation, least of all the American, wanted the blame for sinking the conference. Chamberlain changed his mind. The French stayed on, even if, like the other members of the gold bloc, they refused to participate in any more monetary discussions. For three more weeks the commissions examined trade and prices, subsidies and public works, commodities and commercial policies and gold in the abstract. The conference adjourned on July 27, leaving behind a sheaf of resolutions and a few pages of general principles.

Across the Atlantic, perplexity and dismay had greeted Roosevelt in the Republican and Democratic internationalist press, which, limited in readers but not in renown, might hope to sway

the establishment if not the millions. The *New York Times* found
the president's missive "ill-timed and ill-phrased," reproached him
for misleading the Europeans by conveying hope to them at Washington in April and dashing it at London in July, and doubted that
he understood how deeply the Europeans feared inflation.[43] Walter
Lippmann, in his syndicated column, deplored the spectacle of the
American delegation to London—ignorant and incoherent, disavowed
by the president who had sent it, and demoralized as a result.[44] The
Baltimore Sun, like the *New York Times*, depicted him as erratic and
inconsistent. The *New York Herald Tribune*, even before Roosevelt
sent his cable from shipboard, lamented his "economic jingoism"
and his truculent disregard of other nations, before dubbing him
after it the "great improvisator" whose own secretary of state and
whose own closest adviser, to say nothing of his compatriots at large,
knew not what he might do next.[45]

Some of this was true enough, but only four months had elapsed
since a new administration with only the vaguest of economic visions
and none at all of world leadership had arrived in Washington. And,
frown as they might at the president's indecorous and provocative
pose, his internationalist or free-trading critics acknowledged how
popular it was at home.[46] Mass-circulation tabloids or family magazines, big-city dailies, and even other establishment papers joined in
a full-throated chorus of national defiance.

The Hearst papers, which had opened the year with attacks on
"alien competition" and on world conferences of all kinds, especially those conceived in Geneva, now hailed the dawn of a new "independence day" and a "new Americanism." In cartoons, columns,
and editorials resembling proclamations more than news, they bade
good riddance to pestilence from across the seas—to foreign propaganda, debt cancellation, free trade, disarmament, foreign currency,
and much else that was wholly incompatible with the New Deal.
The country was now safe and sound.[47] The Curtis family monthly
Saturday Evening Post never rolled up its sleeves with the polemical
zeal of the Hearst street press, but it reminded its six million read-

ers that domestic prosperity drove foreign trade, and not the other way around. Home came first.[48] Large and established papers said the same. The *Los Angeles Times* sounded like its rival Hearst chain when it cheered Roosevelt for putting "defaulters such as France and her gold associates in their place"; the *Wall Street Journal* like both when it celebrated his declaration of intent to ignore the world. The message to London, it believed, "unblushingly acknowledge[d] national self-interest to be superior to hands-across-the-seas" and "at last discarded our own romantic fiction about America's sweet reasonableness towards all lesser breeds."[49] And the *New York Evening Post*, seeking an identity and trying out a temperate voice and an established eight-column look, threw in its hat anyway with the tabloids and the others. It too depicted another Independence Day; and it heralded the demise of "love everybody Americanism" and the ascendancy in its place of a proud New Deal of "prickly Americanism."[50]

To judge from appearances, this was the press Roosevelt heeded. One morning in the middle of the month, Moley returned from London to Washington, where he found Roosevelt in bed in the White House, surrounded by the morning papers. "Hello there," the president said cheerfully. "Say, have you seen the papers for the days that you were gone? My statement certainly got a grand press over here!"[51]

"If any nation wrecks the Conference," the hapless Hull had said in his speech on the fourteenth, "it will deserve the execration of mankind." The fate of generations lay in their hands, and they must not fail, MacDonald had already told the same delegates in his opening speech at the Geological Museum. "This cannot go on," he said of the world economic crisis. In April, the liberal economist Sir Walter Layton had deemed the imminent conference the most crucial since Versailles in 1919.[52]

Yet, after the conference had ended in failure, the sky did not fall. Layton, in a postmortem in *Foreign Affairs* a few months later, had to recognize as much. "So far the adjournment of the Conference," he acknowledged, "has not led to disaster. . . . Were we, then, all wrong in our prognostications?"[53] Over the months and years that followed, national economies recovered at their own paces, slowly in Britain, more impressively in Japan, haltingly in the United States, not at all in France, according to no discernible pattern, save the advantage enjoyed by countries reflating rather than deflating, and managing their own currencies instead of fixing them on gold.[54] One after another, countries still holding out and doing so gave up, until by 1936 the gold standard was no more. The breakdown of the conference had only quickened a pattern evident for years before and confirmed for years afterward—the inability of nations ever since the Great War to coordinate their economic and monetary policies in ways that a common international standard such as gold not only encouraged but required. Domestic pressures were too insistent, central banks and treasuries more exposed to them than before 1914. The world economic crisis had driven home the reality but not engendered it. And Roosevelt and the New Dealers were in no way the first to recognize or bow to it.

Layton, before the conference, suggested that the remote consequences of failure might be graver than any proximate ones. A world of open and independent economies might give way to one of closed and self-sufficient units. But the staunchest advocates of the first had already opted for the second. Britain and the United States had given up promoting a liberal world of laissez-faire, laissez-passer, and the conference only ratified their choice. They had also given up trying to promote by disarmament, deterrence, or coercion the world peace they had envisaged at Versailles and after. In the process, the wartime alliance among France, Britain, and the United States, the only one that could contain the nascent menaces in Europe and East Asia, finally fell apart. The other powers looked on. They had not only idealized self-sufficiency as autarky but resolved to conquer it—the Soviet Union at home, and Japan, Italy, and Germany abroad. London and Geneva, theaters of the same failure, presented the world with the demise of interdependence, of a wider kind than Layton had in mind.

It was a vague word. But whether it meant multilateralism or, more consequentially, the acceptance of short-term national sacrifices for longer-term collective gains, it had finally expired by the middle of 1933. In the Western democracies, much of progressive opinion welcomed collective security or free trade on the world's open seas or freedom from persecution in the abstract and deplored their violations by others. But the same opinion also shrank from defending them in practice whenever the risks or costs of commitments loomed too large. It joined others who had never shared such enthusiasms and withdrew into the familiar terrain of the known and the nation; the leaders followed. National mythologies about virtue or victimhood ennobled instincts about self-preservation or avoidance. To all the other powers, once Japan had turned away from it as well, interdependence was anathema. The leitmotif of the nation against the hostile world provided the current that passed between the regime and the people. In 1933, the largest among them, the Soviet Union, was already the most militarized. The others followed, also preaching peace as they prepared for war. In the void, there was nothing to stop them.

Over the following eight years, a trio of predatory powers—Italy, Japan, and Germany—tested the limits of a trio of passive ones—the United States, Britain, and France—and recruited for a while an opportunistic seventh, the Soviet Union, until all were eventually at war. In 1933, as the delegates left Geneva without a disarmament convention and London without a concerted approach to economic recovery, as the United States and its former allies bickered, as Germany and the Soviet Union rearmed, Japan consolidated one conquest, and Italy contemplated another—as the halls emptied and the doors closed, the specter of international anarchy walked, and postwar became prewar.

GENEVA

October 1933

Late in September, when the disarmament conference convened again, Joseph Goebbels came. He paid his respects
as minister of propaganda to the same League of Nations he
had vowed to destroy as an electioneer a year earlier. Now he moved
easily in the Geneva milieu, a smooth and agreeable practitioner of
the arts of conciliation, and as brazen a pretender that Nazism signified peace, a higher form of democracy, and the defense of the West
against bolshevism. But once a photographer showed him scowling
outside the Carlton Hotel, as though to expose the man behind the
mask.[1]

Arthur Henderson, as tireless a campaigner for disarmament as
ever, had not given up. The conference he presided in Geneva had adjourned in June, out of deference for the imminent World Economic
Conference and by necessity as well: the Germans demanded what
the others could not concede, an immediate right to the same arms
as they, if not at once in the same quantity. They could talk peace at
Geneva while rearming at home. At the Geological Museum in London, during the World Economic Conference, Henderson paced the
halls and lobbies and accosted the delegates, but none wanted to hear

about disarmament. Prime Minister MacDonald, the president of the conference, refused him a room in the building. Later that summer he visited capital after capital, ill and forlorn but undeterred by the polite indifference to his cause.[2]

When the disarmament conference reconvened in September, the climate had worsened. The militarization of German society kept pace with an intensive political and propaganda campaign by the Austrian Nazis, orchestrated from Berlin and faithful to the privileged promise of a Greater Germany. The French were proposing to investigate German rearmament, pursuant to Article 213 of the Treaty of Versailles, and to convince the world of what it already knew. The inauspicious moment galvanized the squabbling French, British, and Americans, ironically, to act before compromise eluded them and they all dispersed into the wilderness of another arms race. They still differed—over the French demand for a strong common front against German violations of Versailles, and over the kinds and numbers of weapons they might discard and Germany might eventually acquire. But they spoke as one when the German delegation shed its conciliatory guise and revealed immediate and substantial rearmament as its overriding ambition. This they could not accept. To emphasize the point, they insisted on inspections and verification. On October 14, Foreign Secretary Simon said so before the assembled delegates of the Disarmament Bureau in Geneva, even while consenting to German acquisition after several years of most of the weapons, including tanks and warplanes, that Versailles had denied it. Not long after he sat down, news came that Germany was leaving the conference. That night, over the radio, Hitler announced that it was leaving the League of Nations as well.[3]

He could not—no German nationalist could—allow foreign inspectors to discover and divulge the full extent of German rearmament. Already the Reich was enlisting recruits and turning out weapons for a fully integrated wartime army. This was no time to undermine Germany's public face by revelations of bad faith. Better to reproach the others for neither disarming nor conceding to Germany in practice the equality they had agreed to in principle in December. Better yet, to distract attention, vindicate himself, and impress world opinion by pacific protestations and by new elections, unspoiled by any opposition parties. Three weeks later, forty million Germans voted for him, and he appeared at the window of the Chancellery to acknowledge their cheers in the Wilhelmstrasse below. He had feared foreign reactions—sanctions, perhaps, or worse. None came. His gamble had paid off, the first of a sequence of winning bets that would finally end six years later when Britain and France refused to countenance his invasion of Poland.[4]

For now, another door had closed. At Geneva, the conference continued into the following year, but foreign ministers no longer attended. Civil servants came in their stead. The Japanese, expanding and modernizing their fleet in ways that effectively burst the confines of the 1922 and 1930 naval treaties, had already manifested their hostility to any new constraints. How could the Soviet Union sign a disarmament convention not signed by Japan, and how could Poland sign one not signed by the Soviet Union? And how could either, or any other nervous neighbor, even pursue arms limitation without Germany at the table? Italy turned away. Britain soon abandoned its own proposals and allowed Germany to pursue the rearmament it had already begun. The American delegate, Norman Davis, announced that disarmament was henceforth a European matter. So it was; Roosevelt would give no more speeches about Europe for several years. He suggested that Davis visit Chamonix, in the French Alps. The State Department suggested that he come home.[5]

In New York, leaders of World Peaceways unveiled the world's largest book on the bandstand in Union Square. It weighed 2,300 pounds and was to contain the signatures of all the opponents of war. The Simmons University band of Texas, known as the Cowboy Band, had brought it from the organization's headquarters at the Roosevelt Hotel. From Geneva, Henderson sent a cablegram with good wishes.[6]

And in Geneva, in the antechamber outside the Crystal Chamber in the old Hotel National where the council met, the allegorical frieze representing peace fell to the floor. Briand had unveiled it for the Third General Assembly, surrounded by delegates, in 1922. It shattered, and an attendant came by and swept up the debris.[7]

Acknowledgments

———◆·◆———

I have many friends, colleagues, and professional acquaintances to thank for helping me write this book.

Those who read and offered valuable suggestions on parts of it at some stage, or answered my own esoteric queries, include Robin Blackwood and Professors George Hall, Alice Kelikian, Shefali Misra, Antony Polonsky, Othmar Plöckinger, Govind Sreenivasan, and Bernard Wasserstein.

For help with the Italian illustrations, I wish to thank Professor Ada Gigli Marchetti and Dr. Elisa Paladino; with the German, Professors Sabine von Mering and Jonathan Petropoulos as well as Dr. Hans Zimmermann of the Herzogin Anna Amalia Bibliothek in Weimar; with the American, John Flynn, Robert Gillham, Susan Liberator, and Laura Hibbler; and with the Japanese, Professor Matthew Fraleigh.

I would like to thank April French for extensive research assistance with Soviet print and visual material and Natalie Cornett for help with several Polish articles.

Thanks are due to Brandeis University for generous support from its Theodore and Jane Norman Fund, Provost's Research Fund, and Research Circle on Democracy and Cultural Pluralism in the Department of Politics.

My greatest single debt to archivists goes to Jean-Philippe Dumas, *conservateur en chef du patrimoine*, and his colleagues at the Archives Diplomatiques in La Courneuve, for sustained help and support with their incomparable collections, made available in an ideal setting. I would also like to thank Bertrand Fonck, *conservateur en chef du patrimoine* at the Service historique de la Défense in Vincennes, and David Langbart of the Textual Records Division at the National Archives in College Park, Maryland.

I wish to thank, finally, Andrew Wylie and Hannah Townsend of the Wylie Agency for their invaluable efforts on my behalf, and at HarperCollins, my editor, Jonathan Jao, and associate editor Sarah Haugen for their skilled judgment and unfailing patience.

Notes

———•◆•———

ABBREVIATIONS USED IN THE NOTES

AA: Archiv des Auswärtigen Amts (German foreign ministry archives)
AN: Archives Nationales (France)
BNF: Bibliothèque Nationale (France)
DBFP: Documents on British Foreign Policy
DDF: Documents diplomatiques français
LNA: League of Nations Archives (Geneva)
LNU: League of Nations Union archives (UK)
MAE: Ministère des Affaires Etrangères (French foreign ministry archives)
TNA: The National Archives (UK)
USNA: National Archives and Record Administration (USA)
SHD: Service Historique de la Défense (France)

PREFACE

1. Ian Clark, *Globalization and Fragmentation: International Relations in the Twentieth Century* (Oxford: Oxford University Press, 1997), 33–39.
2. Robert Kagan, *The Jungle Grows Back: America and our Imperiled World* (New York: Knopf, 2018).
3. "Realism" as a theory of international relations differs from its application in foreign policy, where it pursues the national interests rather than the promotion of ideals or values in other states and societies.
4. A. J. P. Taylor, *The Struggle for Mastery in Europe, 1848–1918* (New York: Oxford University Press, 1971 [1954]), xix.
5. Thucydides, *History of the Peloponnesian War*, tr. Rex Warner (London: Penguin, 1972 [1954]), 1.23: "What made war inevitable was the growth of Athenian power and the fear which this caused in Sparta."

6. Arnold J. Toynbee, *Survey of International Affairs, 1936* (London: Oxford University Press, 1937), 35.

7. Jonathan Haslam, *No Virtue like Necessity: Realist Thought in International Relations since Machiavelli* (New Haven, CT: Yale University Press, 2002), chapters 1 and 2. For one view criticizing the ambiguities of the concept of balance of power, and another defending them, see Inis L. Claude, "The Balance of Power Revisited," *Review of International Studies* 15, no. 2 (1989): 77–85, and Richard Little, "Deconstructing the Balance of Power: Two Traditions of Thought," ibid., 87–100, www.jstor.org/stable/20097173.

8. Randall L. Schweller, "The Twenty Years' Crisis, 1919–1939: Why a Concert Didn't Arise," in *Bridges and Boundaries. Historians, Political Scientists, and the Study of International Relations*, eds. Colin Elman and Miriam Fendius Elman (Cambridge: Massachusetts Institute of Technology Press, 2001), 182–212; Clark, *Globalization and Fragmentation*, 67–74.

9. Kagan, *Jungle Grows Back*, 133, draws a parallel between President Obama wanting Europe to look after itself and the "realist" and isolationist Taft wanting the same in the 1930s. See also Hans J. Morgenthau, "The Mainsprings of American Foreign Policy: The National Interest vs. Moral Abstractions," *American Political Science Review* 44, no. 4 (1950): 833–54, doi:10.2307/1951286; Haslam, *No Virtue like Necessity*, 186–89; Jonathan Haslam, *The Vices of Integrity. E. H. Carr, 1892–1982* (New York: Verso, 1999), 79, 120; R. W. Davies, "Edward Hallett Carr, 1892–1982," *Proceedings of the British Academy* 69 (1983): 473–511 (483–85, 488); E. H. Carr, *The Twenty Years' Crisis* (London: Macmillan, 1961 [1939]), 219–23, 235–39, where he appears to envisage the necessary role of morality as well as power in politics and international relations, and his utopian *Conditions of Peace* (London: Macmillan, 1942), which he later called "pretty feeble."

10. Haslam, *No Virtue like Necessity*, 119, 142; Kenneth Waltz, *The Theory of International Politics* (Reading, MA: Addison-Wesley, 1979), 88–101, 117.

11. Waltz, *Theory of International Politics*, 47, 67, 69, 117, 122, says that he is concerned only with systems, and not with the interactions of units within it, which he allows can vary. But he challenges Raymond Aron's assertion that states determine the system more than they are determined by it. Cf. also Robert O. Keohane, "Theory of World Politics: Structural Realism and Beyond," in *Neorealism and Its Critics*, ed. Robert O. Keohane (New York: Columbia University Press, 1986): 158–94. Realism, he points out, cannot "deduce national interests from system structure via the rationality postulate" (190).

12. Paul Schroeder, *The Transformation of European Politics, 1763–1848* (New York: Oxford University Press, 1994).

13. Robert W. Cox, "Social Forces, States, and World Orders: Beyond International Relations Theory," in Keohane, *Neorealism and Its Critics*, 204–54, 224–25. Cox sees the new values and institutions underlying the new American hegemony emerging already in July 1933 at the London World Economic

Conference. But Roosevelt, in his famous "bombshell" message there, was still preaching fiscal conservatism, and he conceived of the New Deal in strictly national terms; see chapter 12 above. Far from bringing New Deal–style management to the world, he left London preaching fiscal conservatism; the New Deal was a nationally closed economic system.

14. Three of the most influential historians loosely included in this school include Eckart Kehr, *Schlachtflottenbau und Parteipolitik, 1894–1901* (Berlin: E. Ebering, 1930), who became posthumously famous for overturning von Ranke's *Primat der Aussenpolitik*; Fritz Fischer, whose *Griff nach der Weltmacht: Die Kriegzielpolitik des kaiserlichen Deutschland, 1914–1918* (Düsseldorf: Droste, 1961) attributed heavy responsibility for the outbreak of war in 1914 to Germany and belligerent domestic forces; and Hans-Ulrich Wehler, who in *Das Deutsche Kaiserreich, 1871–1918* (Göttingen: Vandenhoeck & Ruprecht, 1973) explained the Wilhelmine regime and the war in terms of social structure and the anachronistic political and feudal aristocracy.

15. Frederic William Maitland, *Why the History of English Law Is Not Written: An Inaugural Lecture Delivered in the Arts School at Cambridge on 13 October 1888* (London: C. J. Clay & Sons, 1888).

16. Frank McDonough, "Introduction," in *The Origins of the Second World War: An International Perspective*, ed. Frank McDonough (London and New York: Continuum, 2011), 1–13. A review of general works on the origins of the war suggests that only recently have transnational or transcontinental approaches begun to gain favor. Among the English-language works, Esmonde Robertson, ed., *The Origins of the Second World War: Historical Interpretations* (London: Macmillan, 1971) is heavily centered on the major European powers and the Taylor controversy; Richard Overy with Andrew Wheatcroft, *The Road to War* (London: Penguin, 1999 [1989]), consists of seven chapters, each devoted to one of the major powers; but with Robert Boyce and Joseph A. Maiolo, eds., *The Origins of World War Two: The Debate Continues* (London: Palgrave Macmillan, 2003) fully half the work, pp. 205–359, is devoted to such global themes as economics, ideology, and diplomacy. Only occasionally have single global origins tempted historians; a notable more recent instance is Joseph Maiolo, *Cry Havoc: How the Arms Race Drove the World to War, 1931–1941* (New York: Basic Books, 2010).

17. David Reynolds, "The Origins of Two 'World Wars': Historical Discourse and International Politics," *Journal of Contemporary History* 38, no. 1 (January 2003): 29–44.

18. Most studies of the Nazi and Fascist movements in Europe and elsewhere in 1930–33 pointed to the human consequences of the economic crisis, but in different ways; some stressed the "squeezed," frightened, or antimodern middle classes, e.g., Seymour Martin Lipset, *Political Man: The Social Basis of Politics* (Baltimore: Johns Hopkins University Press, 1981). Among Marxists, Antonio Gramsci as early as 1921 discerned both a core petty bourgeois element among the first Fascists and a secondary, landowning or

capitalist one; see, for example, the excerpts in David Beetham, *Marxists in Face of Fascism: Writings by Marxists on Fascism from the Inter-war Period* (Totowa, NJ: Barnes & Noble Books, 1984), 82–87. One of the earliest and best-known Marxist views of the role of finance or monopoly capital was Franz Neumann, *Behemoth: The Structure and Practice of National Socialism* (New York: Oxford University Press, 1944 [1942]). On brutalization, George Mosse, *Fallen Soldiers: Reshaping the Memory of the World Wars* (New York: Oxford University Press, 1990), especially chapter 8, adopted later in, e.g., Stéphane Audouin-Rouzeau and Annette Becker, *14–18: Retrouver la Guerre* (Paris: Gallimard, 2000), 47–49, and criticized in, e.g., Robert Gerwarth, *The Vanquished: Why the First World War Failed to End* (New York: Farrar, Strauss and Giroux, 2018), 12.

19. Alexander Wendt, "Constructing International Politics," *International Security* 20, no. 1 (Summer 1995): 71–81; Alexander Wendt, "Anarchy Is What States Make of It: The Social Construction of Power Politics," *International Organization* 46, no. 2 (Spring 1992): 391–425; earlier critiques of realism in, e.g., Keohane, *Neorealism and Its Critics*, and Andrew Linklater, *Beyond Realism and Marxism: Critical Theory and International Relations* (Houndmills, Basingstoke, Hampshire: Macmillan, 1990).

20. Richard Haass, *A World in Disarray* (New York: Penguin, 2017), 203–5.

21. Martin Wolf, "The US-China Conflict Challenges the World," *Financial Times*, 21 May 2019, citing a study from the Peterson Institute for International Economics.

22. Haass, *World in Disarray*, 115–17.

PROLOGUE: GENEVA AND SHANGHAI

1. "Parley on Arms to Open Today," *Chicago Daily Tribune*, 2 February 1932, p. 7; "Physionomie de la séance d'ouverture," *Le Petit Journal*, 2 February 1932, p. 1; "Physionomie de la séance d'ouverture," ibid., p. 3; "l'Organisation matérielle de la conférence," *Le Petit Parisien*, 1 February 1932, p. 1, photo of "le palais de verre"; Vernon Bartlett, *Intermission in Europe: The Life of a Journalist and Broadcaster* (New York: Oxford, 1938), 106; Major General A. C. Temperley, *The Whispering Gallery of Europe* (London: Collins, 1938), 26–28.

2. "Geneva Ready for Inaugural Session," *New York Herald Tribune*, 1 February 1932, p. 1; "La Contagion de la peur," *Journal de Genève*, 19 February 1932, p. 1.

3. Hugh R. Wilson, *Diplomat between Wars* (New York: Longmans, Green, 1941), 259–60; Salvador de Madariaga, *Morning without Noon: Memoirs* (Westmead: Heath, 1974), 255–56; Walter Lippmann, with the Council on Foreign Relations, *The United States in World Affairs: An Account of American Foreign Relations, 1932* (New York: Harper & Brothers, 1933), 62–69.

4. "Les évènements d'Extrême-Orient," *Le Matin*, 1 February 1932, p. 3; "Foreign Zone Is Shelled," *New York Times*, 30 January 1932, p. 1; "L'organisation

matérielle de la Conférence," *Le Petit Journal*, 2 February 1932, p. 3; "Le Gouvernement a décidé de déclarer la guerre au Japon," *Journal de Genève*, 31 January 1932, p. 10.

5. "La morne séance d'ouverture de la conférence du désarmement," *L'Echo de Paris*, 3 February 1932, p. 1; George Slocombe, *A Mirror to Geneva: Its Growth, Grandeur and Decay* (New York: Henry Holt, 1938), 61; "La Conférence du désarmement s'ouvre demain à 15 heures," *Le Petit Parisien*, 1 February 1932, p. 1.

6. "Le Front unique des grandes puissances au Conseil de la S.D.N.," *Le Petit Parisien*, 3 February 1932, p. 1; Henry Hertz, "A Genève, une séance brusquée du Conseil de la S.D.N.," *L'œuvre*, 3 February 1932, p. 2; "Arms Talk to Begin Despite War Clouds," *New York Times*, 1 February 1932.

7. Bartlett, *Intermission in Europe*, 93; "Peace Effort Gets Support of League," *New York Times*, 3 February 1932, p. 1.

8. *Le Matin*, 6 February 1932, p. 1 (photo).

9. "Die drei Aufgaben für Genf," *Vossische Zeitung*, 3 February 1932, p. 1; "Physionomie de la séance d'ouverture," *Le Petit Journal*, 3 February 1932, p. 1; "L'ouverture de la conférence du désarmement," *L'œuvre*, 3 February 1932, p. 2.

10. "L'organisation matérielle de la Conférence," *Le Petit Journal*, 2 February 1932, p. 3, and "Autour de la Conférence du désarmement," ibid., 3 February 1932, p. 3; "Genève, lieu de rencontre des hommes d'état du monde entier," *Le Petit Parisien*, 4 February 1932, p. 3.

11. Temperley, *Whispering Gallery*, 39; Slocombe, *Mirror to Geneva*, 46–47, 61, 206; Malcolm Muggeridge, *Chronicles of Wasted Time*, vol. 2, *The Infernal Grove* (London: Fontana, 1981 [1973]), 8–9. Muggeridge, a journalist by profession, was at the time temporarily employed at the International Labor Office in Geneva.

12. Madariaga, *Morning without Noon*, 34–35; "Bells to ring here for arms parley," *New York Herald Tribune*, 1 February 1932, p. 4, and ibid., 1 February, p. 1, photo of UK peace leaders at Victoria Station as seven packing cases full of two million signatures depart; "La journée des petitions," *Journal de Genève*, 7 February 1932, p. 10; see photo of "Geneva Hears Arms Cut Plea of 8 Million," *International Herald Tribune*, 7 February 1932, p. 1; "Arms Plea Opens with Plea to Heed Desire of Peoples," *New York Times*, 3 February 1932, p. 1 (reference to women in the audience); "Le défilé de la paix," *Le Matin*, 7 February 1932, p. 3; "Journée émouvante à Genève," *Le Petit Journal*, 7 February 1932, p. 1; Andrew Webster, "The League of Nations, Disarmament and Internationalism," in *Internationalisms: A Twentieth-Century History*, eds. Glenda Sluga and Patricia Clavin (Cambridge: Cambridge University Press, 2017), 139–69.

13. Thomas A. Davies, *The Possibilities of Transnational Activism: The Campaign for Disarmament between the Two World Wars* (Boston: Martinus Nijhoff, 2007), 114–17, 151–54, 170.

14. Davies, 131–48.

15. MAE, PA-AP166 498, Louis Aubert to Prime Minister Pierre Laval, 6 January 1932.

16. LNA, R 1871, correspondence between peace groups and Drummond regarding "Peace Army," mostly February 1932; LNA, S474, text of Henderson speech, 21 October 1932; Temperley, *Whispering Gallery*, 167–68; Maurice Vaïsse, *Sécurité d'abord: La Politique française en matière de désarmement, 9 décembre 1930–17 avril 1934* (Paris, 1981), 190–200; Muggeridge, *Infernal Grove*, 10.

17. Robert Dell, *The Geneva Racket* (London: Robert Hale Limited, 1941), 7–8; Wilson, *Diplomat between Wars*, 222; Norman Hillson, *Geneva Scene* (London: Routledge, 1936), 28. E. H. Carr attacked the naivete of such views in *The Twenty Years' Crisis* (London: Macmillan, 1961 [1939]), 17–19; Arnold J. Toynbee, ed., *Survey of International Affairs 1932* (London: Royal Institute of International Affairs, 1933), 173–92. Toynbee thought "the fitful and unco-ordinated but undoubtedly genuine world-wide public desire for the insurance of peace" had been stymied by "parochial" national governments and their "sycophantic" presses—in a sense, by the workings of democracy itself.

18. MAE, 39CPCOM 107, ambassador Tokyo to Paris, 25 February 1932 and 17 May 1932; USNA RG 165, McIlroy (military attaché, Tokyo) to War Department, 10 March 1932; cf., e.g., Pertinax in *l'Echo de Paris*, 17 May 1932, and André Viollis in *Le Petit Parisien*, 18 May 1932.

19. MAE 39CPCOM 102, ambassador Tokyo to Paris, 22 April 1932 (citing correspondence from Shanghai).

20. Robert Bickers, *Out of China: How the Chinese Ended the Era of Western Domination* (Cambridge, MA: Harvard University Press, 2017), 132–33; Christian Henriot, *Shanghai, 1927–1937: Municipal Power, Locality, and Modernization*, tr. Noël Castelino (Berkeley: University of California Press, 1993 [1991]), 65–78 (regarding public opinion in Shanghai); Donald A. Jordan, *China's Trial by Fire: The Shanghai War of 1932* (Ann Arbor: University of Michigan Press, 2001), 73–76, 78, 177, 212, 241–42.

21. Dell, *Geneva Racket*, 104; Auguste de Saint-Aulaire, *Genève contre la paix* (Paris: Plon, 1936), 7–8.

22. Joseph Ballinger (assistant professor of economics at Amherst), "Geneva Plots to Internationalize US," *New York American*, 23 October 1932, p. 2-E; ibid., "Disarming Ideas," cartoon and comment, 27 October 1932, p. 12; Thomas A. Bailey, *The Man in the Street: The Impact of American Public Opinion on Foreign Policy* (New York: Macmillan, 1948), 308.

23. See *Asahi* 4 December 1931, stating that since September the whole country had reproached the League its purely theoretical view, and *Asahi* 14 April 1932, complaining that the League treats the matter purely theoretically (both from MAE, 39CPCOM 102, press review, French embassy Tokyo to Paris, 24 December 1931 and 22 April 1932).

24. Wilhelm Deist et al., *Ursachen und Voraussetzungen des Zweiten Weltkrieges*, vol. 1 (1989 [1979]) of *Das deutsche Reich und der zweite Weltkrieg*, 9 vols. (14 vols. projected) (Freiburg: Militärgeschichtliches Forschungsamt, 1979–2014), 71–88.

25. Joseph Kessel, "Devant le plus grand bar du monde," *Le Matin*, 7 February 1932, p. 1.

26. Harry Graf Kessler, *Tagebücher, 1918–1937* (Frankfurt-am-Main: Insel, 1961), p. 666, entry for 16 May 1932.

27. Walter Lippmann, "Unity at Shanghai; the Conference at Geneva," *New York Herald Tribune*, 4 February 1932, p. 19.

28. Maurice Lair, "Stresemann," *Revue française des sciences politiques*, July–September 1939, pp. 365–92 (from BNF FOL-LN1-232-17309); "The League Assembly: Sir A. Chamberlain's Speech," *The Times*, 12 September 1927, p. 11.

1: LOCUST YEARS

1. "Jugend voll Hass und ohne Hoffnung," *Vossische Zeitung*, 1 September 1932 (a.m.), p. 1. This unsolicited account from an unemployed man in a newspaper of record bears the initials "K.B."

2. J. B. Priestley, *English Journey* (Harmondsworth, UK: Penguin, 1977 [1934]), 159–60, 165–66. Joel 2:25 reads "I will restore to you the years which the swarming locust hath eaten." Churchill, *The Gathering Storm* (vol. 1 of *The Second World War* [Boston: Houghton Mifflin, 1948–1953]) used the phrase as the title of chapter 5 to denote the lean defense expenditures in 1931–35 in the face of German rearmament; earlier it had been used against him when, as chancellor of the exchequer, he had imposed austerity to keep Britain on the gold standard; see Philip Williamson, "Baldwin's Reputation: Politics and History, 1937–1967," *The Historical Journal* 47, no. 1 (2004): 127–68, http://www.jstor.org.resources.library.brandeis.edu/stable/4091548.

3. "Preparing for the World Conference," *The Times*, 3 November 1932, p. 13; Clavin, Patricia, and Jens-Wilhelm Wessels, "Another Golden Idol? The League of Nations' Gold Delegation and the Great Depression, 1929–1932," *The International History Review* 26, no. 4 (2004): 765–95, http://www.jstor.org.resources.library.brandeis.edu/stable/4011058; MAE 75CPCOM 73, *Rapport de la délégation de l'or du comité financier de la Société des Nations* (Geneva: Société des Nations, June 1932), 17–22.

4. "Cheered in Des Moines," *New York Times*, 5 October 1932, p. 1; "Hoover's Speech at Cleveland," ibid., 16 October 1932, p. 34.

5. Jean-Norton Cru, *Témoins* (Nancy: Presses Universitaires de Nancy, 2006 [1929]), 566–67.

6. "Les croix de bois," *Le Matin*, 5 February 1932, p. 4.

7. "Wunder um Verdun," *Vossische Zeitung*, 2 September 1932, p. 2; "Miracle à Verdun," *Le Populaire*, 23 October 1932, p. 4; Brian Bond, *Britain's Two*

World Wars against Germany: Myth, Memory and the Distortion of Hindsight (Cambridge: Cambridge University Press, 2014), 43–44.

8. Paul Joseph Cremers, *Die Marneschlacht* (Bielefeld and Leipzig: Velhagen und Klasing, 1932), 12, 14; Paul Enders, entry for "Cremers" in *Neue deutsche Biographie*, vol. 3 (Berlin: Bürklein—Ditmar, 1957), 410; "Mannheimer Marneschlacht," *Vossische Zeitung*, 4 February 1933 (p.m.), pp. 6–7 (the military expert on the paper challenged the play's portrayal of characters, not its overall accuracy).

9. AN F 7 13504, Agence Havas citation of *Izvestia*, 27 August 1932.

10. Paul Jankowski, "Twenty Years of Disenchantment: The American Entry into World War I Remembered, 1917–1937," *South Central Review* 34, no. 3 (Fall 2017): 115–27.

11. "M. Herriot on Peace," *The Times*, 12 September 1932, p. 9; "Further than Stimson," *New York Times*, 13 September 1932, p. 20; "Amitié franco-américaine. La journée de la Marne," *Le Figaro*, 12 September 1932, p. 1.

12. "Bulletin du jour: Le discours de M. Herriot," and "La Marne," *Le Temps*, 12 September 1932, both p. 1.

13. H. R. Knickerbocker, *The German Crisis* (New York: Farrar & Rinehart, 1932), 72–83; Simona Colarizi, *L'opinione degli italiani sotto il regime, 1929–43* (Rome and Bari: Laterza, 1991), 83–85; Jessica Murphy, "Charles Sheeler (1883–1965)," website of the Metropolitan Museum of Art, New York City, November 2009, https://www.metmuseum.org/toah/hd/shee/hd_shee .htm; H. R. Knickerbocker, *Can Europe Recover?* (London: John Lane, 1932), 59–73.

14. Richard Hoggart, *A Local Habitation* (London: Chatto & Windus, 1988), 73 (vol. 1 of *Life and Times*, 3 vols., 1988–1992).

15. "Ost-Oberschlesische 'Armutschächte,'" *Vossische Zeitung*, 10 September 1932 (a.m.), p. 4; Edmund Wilson, *The American Earthquake: A Documentary of the Twenties and Thirties* (New York: Farrar, Straus and Giroux, 1979 [1958]), 457–62.

16. League of Nations, *World Economic Survey, 1932–3* (Geneva: League of Nations, September 1933), 11–24; Charles H. Feinstein, Peter Temin, and Gianni Toniolo, *The World Economy between the Wars*, 2nd ed. (New York and Oxford: Oxford University Press, 2008), 94 (numbers differ slightly, approximations given here).

17. "Preparing for the World Conference," *The Times*, 3 November 1932, p. 13.

18. William Stoneman, *A History of the Economic Analysis of the Great Depression in America* (New York: Garland, 1979), 36–65; Feinstein, Temin, and Toniolo, *World Economy between the Wars*, 128–34; Robert Skidelsky, *Politicians and the Slump: The Labour Government of 1929–1931* (London: Macmillan, 1967), 17, 210–15; Peter Clarke, *Hope and Glory: Britain, 1900–1990* (London: Penguin, 1996), 147–48; "Sir Oswald Mosley's Fascism," *Observer*, 2 October 1932, p. 7; Simeon Strunsky, review, *A New Deal* by Stuart Chase, *New York Times*, 3 September 1932, Book Review Section, p. 9.

19. "Preparing for the World Conference," *The Times*, 3 November 1932, p. 13.

20. *Daily Herald*, 24 October 1932, cited in MAE, 92 CPCOM 210, French embassy daily press review, 24 October 1932; "Déséquilibre," *Le Temps*, 10 September 1932, p. 1; Léon Blum, "La fausse sagesse," *Le Populaire*, 23 October 1932, p. 1.

21. Knickerbocker, *German Crisis*, 51, 72.

22. "Le rôle de l'état," *Le Temps,* 11 December 1932, p. 1.

23. Henri de Kérillis, "Une enquête en Amérique (IX): Comment wall street épuise les nerfs de l'Amérique," *L'Echo de Paris*, 31 October 1932, pp. 1–2.

24. Paul Schmidt, *Statist auf diplomatischer Bühne, 1923–1945: Erlebnisse des Chefdolmetschers im auswärtigen Amt mit den Staatsmännern Europas* (Bonn: Athenaeum-Verlag, 1950), 251; Ellen Schrecker, *The Hired Money* (New York: Arno Press, 1978), 235–39; "American Opinion of Arms Rejected," *New York Times*, 12 June 1932, p. 4.

25. Editorial, *New York American*, 11 December 1932 (argues that the cause of the Depression "was the great war, plus our national extravagance, foolishness, gambling and short-sightedness following the war"); "Cheered in Des Moincs," *New York Times*, 5 October 1932, p. 1, and "Hoover's Speech at Des Moines," ibid., p. 18.

26. *Nichi Nichi*, 19 November 1932, from MAE 39CPCOM 102, Lens (Tokyo) to Herriot, 1 December 1932, French embassy daily press review, 15–30 November 1932; see also MAE 39CPCOM 117, Martel (Tokyo) to Paul-Boncour, 1 and 13 April 1933 (closing of Indian markets to Japanese cotton); Lt.-General K. Sato, "The Future of Japan," *Japan Times*, 3 April 1932; "Grandi Urges Unity to End Depression," *New York Times*, 4 June 1932, p. 4.

27. Knickerbocker, *Can Europe Recover?*, 74–79.

28. "Devisenkontrolle auf dem Ozeandampfer," *Vossische Zeitung*, 4 October 1932 (a.m.), p. 5; Richard Lewisohn, "Diamanten-Währung," ibid., 1 November 1932 (p.m.), p. 1.

29. R. G. Hawtrey, *The Gold Standard in Theory and Practice*, 3rd ed. (London: Longmans, Green, 1933), 20, 30. Many realized the system was not as self-regulating as it seemed. See, for example, Gustav Cassel, *The Crisis in the World's Monetary System* (Oxford: Clarendon Press, 1932), 3–8; Jacques Néré, *La Crise de 1929* (Paris: Armand Colin, 1973), 7–32; Feinstein, Temin, and Toniolo, *World Economy between the Wars*, 3–5, 28–30, 35.

30. Paul Einzig, *International Gold Movements*, 2nd ed. (London: Macmillan, 1931), 1–4; Royal Institute of International Affairs, *The International Gold Problem: A Record of the Discussions of a Study Group of Members* (Oxford: Oxford University Press, 1931), 207–8 (remarks by R. G. Hawtrey); Luis I. Jácome, "Central Banking in Latin America: From the Gold Standard to the Golden Years" (International Monetary Fund, Working Paper 15/60, Monetary and Capital Markets Department, March 2015); Barry Eichengreen, *Globalizing Capital: A History of the International Monetary System*, 2nd ed. (Princeton: Princeton University Press, 2008), 6–42.

31. Richard Lewinsohn, *Financial Contagion: Lessons from the Great Depression*, trans. Peter Bild (Berlin: Richard Lewinsohn-Morus Stiftung, 2010 [1934]), chapter 3; Harold James, *The End of Globalization: Lessons from the Great Depression* (Cambridge: Harvard University Press, 2001), 53–63, 68–100; Paul Reynaud, *Mémoires*, vol. 1 (Paris: Flammarion, 1960), 338.

32. League of Nations, Gold Delegation Report (Geneva: League of Nations, 1932), chapter 4 and pp. 69–81; summary in MAE 75 CPCOM73, Conférence Economique Internationale, note of 13 June 1932; Cassel, *Crisis*, 65–70; Barry Eichengreen and Peter Temin, "The Gold Standard and the Great Depression," *Contemporary European History* 9, no. 2 (2000): 183–207.

33. Knickerbocker, *German Crisis*, 188–91; Einzig, *International Gold Movements*, 33–34; Pierre Coste, *Les Grands Marchés financiers. Paris, Londres, New-York: La Lutte pour la Suprématie* (Paris: Payot, 1932), 50–52; Robert Boyce, *The Great Interwar Crisis* (London: Palgrave Macmillan, 2009), 303–14. Writing at the time, Paul Einzig, *Behind the Scenes of International Finance* (London: Macmillan, 1932), indicted France as the single great practitioner of using gold reserves as a war chest for political goals. As Robert Boyce points out in *Great Interwar Crisis*, 272, this is a one-sided and conspiratorial fantasy.

34. Marguerite Perrot, *La Monnaie et l'Opinion Publique en France et en Angleterre de 1924 à 1936* (Paris: Cahiers de la Fondation Nationale des Sciences Politiques, 1955), 88–100; *Le Petit Journal*, 2 February 1932, p. 1, "La conférence du désarmement s'ouvre aujourd'hui à Genève": "La crise économique, qui a fait naître contre la France tant de jalousies . . ."; *Le Matin*, 8 February 1932, p. 1, "La perte de l'or entraîne-t-elle celle de la raison?"

35. See p. 28 above; see also the speeches from the Italian and Polish delegates at World Economic Conference, as transcribed in "Speeches at the Conference," *The Times*, 14 June 1933, p. 9; Perrot, *La Monnaie*, 96–103; J. M. Keynes, "Two Years off Gold: How Far Are We from Prosperity Now?" *Daily Mail*, 19 September 1933, in *Collected Writings of John Maynard Keynes*, vol. 21 (London: Macmillan, Cambridge University Press for the Royal Economic Society, 1982), 284–88; J. L. Garvin, "Laying the Ghosts," *Observer*, 18 June 1933, p. 16.

36. Arnold J. Toynbee, ed., *Survey of International Affairs, 1932* (London: Royal Institute of International Affairs, 1933), 2, 4.

37. Sir Arthur Salter, "The Future of Economic Nationalism," *Foreign Affairs* 11, no. 1 (October 1932): 9–20.

38. J. M. Keynes, "National Self-Sufficiency," in *Collected Writings*, vol. 21, 233–46 (from *New Statesman and Nation*, 8 and 15 July 1933, adapted from lecture at University College, Dublin, 19 April 1933); Perrot, *La Monnaie*, 88–95.

39. Lennart Samuelson, *Soviet Defense Industry Planning: Tukhachevskii and Military-Industrial Mobilization, 1926–1937* (Stockholm: Institute of East European Economies, 1996), 107; Jochen Hellbeck, *Revolution on My Mind: Writing a Diary under Stalin* (Cambridge, MA: Harvard University Press, 2006), 85.

40. Deist et al., *Ursachen und Voraussetzungen*, 220–25.

41. Ibid., 226–28.

42. S. Washio, *Transpacific*, 7 April 1932, cited in Sandra Wilson, *The Manchurian Crisis and Japanese Society, 1931–33* (New York: Routledge, 2002), 56–57.

43. *Hitlers Zweites Buch: Ein Dokument aus dem Jahr 1928*, Introduced with a commentary by Gerhard L. Weinberg with a preface by Hans Rothfels (Stuttgart: Deutsche Verlags-Anstalt, 1961), 127–32.

44. Isabel Butterfield, *Manhattan Tales, 1920–45* (Lewes, UK: Book Guild, 1999), 66.

45. "Novembre!," Cassandre column, *Commentaires*, 6 November 1932, p. 3.

46. Mihail Sebastian, *For Two Thousand Years*, tr. Philip Ó Ceallaigh (London: Penguin, 2016 [1934]), 20, 26, 116, 127, 130, 197, and preface by Mark Mazower.

2: TOKYO AND ROME

1. "The Diet Opened," *Japan Chronicle Weekly Edition* (Kobe), 1 September 1932, p. 276.

2. "The Special Session," *Japan Chronicle Weekly Edition* (Kobe), 25 August 1932, p. 231; "The Special Session," *Japan Chronicle Weekly Edition* (Kobe), 8 September 1932, pp. 303–4; USNA, RG 84, vol. 768, Grew (Tokyo) to State Department, 17 November 1932, report on "Newspapers in Japan"; MAE 39CPCOM 102, de Lens Tokyo to Herriot, French embassy daily press review, 1–10 August 1932, 12 August 1932.

3. "The Political Parties," *Japan Chronicle*, 15 September 1932, p. 335; MAE 39CPCOM 107, Martel (Tokyo) to Tardieu, 25 February 1932.

4. MAE 39CPCOM 107, Martel to Tardieu, 4, 24 March, 24 May 1932.

5. MAE 39CPCOM 107, Martel to MAE, 31 March 1932; TNA, FO 371/16243, Lindley (Tokyo) to FO, 26 May 1932.

6. "The Political Parties," *Japan Chronicle*, 15 September 1932, p. 335; MAE 39CPCOM 102, Martel to MAE, 27 May 1932; *Miyako*, 12 May 1932; *Yomiuri*, 12 and 17 May 1932; *Hochi*, 18 May 1932; *Jiji*, 20 May 1932; *Nichi Nichi*, 19 May 1932 (all from French embassy daily press review, 10–20 May 1932); TNA, FO 371/16243, Lindley (Tokyo) to FO, 23 June 1932.

7. W. G. Beasley, *Japanese Imperialism, 1894–1945* (New York and Oxford: Oxford University Press, 1987), 156–74; Peter Duus, "Introduction" and Alvin D. Coox, "The Kwantung Army Dimension," in *The Japanese Informal Empire in China, 1895–1937*, eds. Peter Duus, Ramon H. Myers, and Mark R. Peattie (Princeton, NJ: Princeton University Press, 1989), xi–xxix, 395–428.

8. MAE 339CPCOM 107, Martel (Tokyo) to Tardieu, 16 March, 15 May (Rengo wire service report), 17 May 1932; Stephen S. Large, "Substantiating the Nation: Terrorist Trials as Nationalist Theatre in Early Showa Japan," in *Nation and Nationalism in Japan*, ed. Sandra Wilson (New York: Routledge-Curzon, 2002), 55–68.

9. André Viollis, "Sous le masque japonais," *Le Petit Parisien*, 19 October 1932, p. 1; Stephen S. Large, "Nationalist Extremism in Early Showa Japan: Inoue Nissho and the 'Blood-Pledge Corps Incident,' 1932," *Modern Asian Studies* 35, no. 3 (July 2001): 533–64.

10. Sandra Wilson, *The Manchurian Crisis and Japanese Society, 1931–33* (New York: Routledge, 2002), 114–19; Robert A. Scalapino, *Democracy and the Party Movement in Prewar Japan: The Failure of the First Attempt* (Berkeley: University of California Press, 1975 [1953]), 361; MAE 39CPCOM 107, 23 April and 7 July 1932, Martel (Tokyo) to Tardieu; Viollis, "Sous le masque japonais"; TNA FO 371/16243, Lindley (Tokyo) to FO, 5 July 1932.

11. Auguste Raynal, "Les difficultés intérieures du gouvernement japonais," *Le Figaro*, 23 August 1932, p. 3; MAE 39CPCOM 107, Martel (Tokyo) to Tardieu, 25 May and 15 June 1932; TNA FO 371/16243, Lindley (Tokyo) to FO, 22 July 1932.

12. MAE 39CPCOM 107, Martel (Tokyo) to Tardieu, 23 April and 25 May 1932; Wilson, *Manchurian Crisis*, 62–67.

13. MAE 39CPCOM 107, Martel (Tokyo) to Tardieu, 25 May 1932; Scalapino, *Democracy and the Party Movement*, 361; Wilson, *Manchurian Crisis*, 114–19.

14. Justus D. Doenecke, ed., *The Diplomacy of Frustration: The Manchurian Crisis of 1931–1933 as Revealed in the Papers of Stanley K. Hornbeck* (Palo Alto, CA: Hoover Institution Press, 1981), 3–40. According to one account, the entire foreign community in Mukden at the time saw the Japanese attack on the town as premeditated: "Sees 'Bold Gamble' by Japanese Army," *New York Times*, 12 October 1931, p. 17; Beasley, *Japanese Imperialism*, 133–34.

15. Wilson, *Manchurian Crisis*, 170–73; MAE 39CPCOM 102, Martel (Tokyo) to Briand (Paris), 15 July 1931, French embassy daily press reviews of 1–15 June 1931, 1–15 September 1931, and 25 September 1932.

16. Pertinax, "Les Evènements de Tokio," *L'Echo de Paris*, 18 May 1932, p. 1; André Viollis, "Une gestation pénible au Japon," *Le Petit Parisien*, 19 May 1932, p.1; Coox, "Kwantung Army Dimension"; Louise Young, "Imagined Empire: The Cultural Construction of Manchukuo," in *Informal Empire*, eds. Duus, Myers, and Peattie, chapter 3; Ishihara Kanji, "A Plan to Occupy Manchuria," in *Sources of Japanese Tradition*, eds. Wm. Theodore de Bary, Carol Gluck, and Arthur Tiedemann, vol. 2, part 2, 2nd ed. (New York: Columbia University Press, 2006), 294–98.

17. Wilson, *Nation and Nationalism*, 84–89; MAE 39CPCOM 102, Briand to MAE, 25 September 1931.

18. MAE 39CPCOM 102, Briand to MAE, 24 December 1931, *Asahi*, 1 December 1931, from French embassy daily press review, 1–15 December 1931; USNA RG 84, File 891, Grew to State Department, report on Japanese press, 17 November 1932.

19. AE E 102, Briand to MAE, 25 September 1931; Wilson, *Nation and Nationalism*, 84–89.

20. Peter Duus, Ramon H. Myers, Mark R. Peattie, eds., *Japanese Wartime Empire, 1931–1945* (Princeton, NJ: Princeton University Press, 1996), 104–5, 136–70; Nakagane Katsuji, "Manchukuo and Economic Development," in *Informal Empire*, eds. Duus, Myers, and Peattie, 133–57, and Coox, "Kwantung Army" (see n. 7, 409–14).

21. Sterling Tatsuji Takeuchi, *War and Diplomacy in the Japanese Empire* (New York: Routledge, 2011 [Chicago: University of Chicago Press, 1935]), 292–97, 303–5; Duus, Myers, and Peattie, *Japanese Wartime Empire*, 206–12; MAE 39CPCOM 107, Martel (Tokyo) to Tardieu, 16 March 1932; Viollis, "Gestation pénible"; Pertinax, "Evènements de Tokio"; Donald A. Jordan, *China's Trial by Fire: The Shanghai War of 1932* (Ann Arbor: University of Michigan Press, 2001), 25–43.

22. Jordan, *Trial by Fire*, 25–43.

23. Louise Young, *Japan's Total Empire: Manchuria and the Culture of Wartime Imperialism* (Berkeley: University of California Press, 1998), 78, 101; Wilson, *Manchurian Crisis*, 37; USNA RG 84 Diplomatic posts, vol. 767 (1932), Grew (Tokyo) to state, 9 July 1932. For the League of Nations Commission, see *Asahi*, 4 December 1931, 14 April 1932; *Hochi*, 4 and 15 December 1931; *Asahi* and *Miyako*, 9 December 1931; *Chugai Shogio*, 13 April 1932; *Yomiuri*, 14 April, 12 May 1932; *Tokyo Nichi Nichi*, 29 May 1932; *Nihon*, 18 July 1932. For Chinchow, see *Tokyo Nichi Nichi* and *Chugai Shogyo*, 1 December 1932 (all from translations and *revues de presse* in MAE 39CPCOM 102).

24. LNA, R 1867, Japanese government to Secretary-General Drummond, 10 October 1931; LNA, R 1871, 2 March 1932, "Explanatory Note Communicated by the Japanese Government"; LNA, R 1869, summary of communications to Drummond 21 September–13 October 1931, showing many more Chinese than Japanese in Manchuria; "Text of Japan's Statement," *New York Times*, 7 February 1932, p. 1; "Yoshizawa Denies Break with League," *New York Times*, 22 February 1932, p. 13. The claim that the inhabitants were all Manchu and ethnically distinct from Chinese was nonsense.

25. "Araki Says Japan May Quit League," *New York Times*, 26 March 1932, p. 13; FO 371/16243, Lindley (Tokyo) to FO, 27 April 1932; "Araki Urges Japan to Block White Race," *New York Times*, 14 August 1932, p. 5; "'We Are Descendants of Gods—We Will Rule the World'—Gen. Sadao Araki," *China Weekly Review*, 20 August 1932, p. 438; MAE 39CPCOM 117, de Lens (Tokyo) to Herriot, 20 September 1932; "Monroe Doctrine. General Araki's Instinct for Propaganda," *Japan Chronicle Weekly Edition*, 1 September 1932, p. 325; "Asiatic Monroe Doctrine," *North China Herald and Supreme Court and Consular Gazette*, 21 September 1932, p. 450; John R. Murnane, "Japan's Monroe Doctrine? Re-Framing the Story of Pearl Harbor," *The History Teacher* 40, no. 4 (August 2007): 503–20; Kentaro Kaneko, "A 'Japanese Monroe Doctrine' and Manchuria," *Contemporary Japan* 1 (1932): 176–84.

26. J. O. P. Bland, *China: The Pity of It* (London: William Heinemann, 1932), 268; MAE 39CPCOM 107, Martel to Herriot, 29 June 1932, and Lens to

Herriot, 4 September 1932; Wilson, ed., *Nation and Nationalism*, 84–89; "Kaku Mori Dead," *New York Times*, 11 December 1932, p. 35; "The Attack on Mukden," *Japan Chronicle Weekly Edition*, 1 September 1932, p. 268, and "Japan and the World," p. 279; "The Special Session," *Japan Chronicle Weekly Edition*, 8 September 1932, pp. 303–4.

27. MAE 39CPCOM 107, Lens to Herriot, 14 and 25 September 1932; USNA, RG 84 Diplomatic posts, vol. 767 (1932), Grew to Stimson, n.d. (early September 1932), 8 October 1932, 21 October 1932, 18 November 1932.

28. MAE 39CPCOM 117, Lens to Herriot, 20 September 1932; USNA, RG 84 Diplomatic posts, vol. 767 (1932), Grew to Stimson, 8 October 1932; Joseph C. Grew, *Ten Years in Japan: A Contemporary Record Drawn from the Diaries and Private and Official Papers of Joseph C. Grew* (New York: Simon & Schuster, 1944), 36–37.

29. See the dossier on this affair in USNA, RG 84 Diplomatic posts, vol. 767 (1932), including City Bank of New York, "Far Eastern District Circular," 28 June 1932; *Jiji Shimpo*, 2 September 1932; *Chugai Shogyo*, 27 September 1932; *Osaka Mainichi*, 28 September 1932; Grew to Stimson, 18 September 1932 (summary of the affair); Grew, *Ten Years*, cites in extenso some of the correspondence now in the National Archives; "Japanese in Raid on American Bank," *New York Times*, 11 September 1932, p. 21.

30. Young, *Total Empire*, all of chapter 3, esp. 45–50, 55–65, 94–98; *Japan Chronicle Weekly Edition*, 29 September 1932, photo p. 441.

31. "General Honjo's Farewell," *Japan Chronicle Weekly Edition*, 8 September 1932, p. 320; "General Honjo's Triumph" and "Tokyo Cheers Honjo," *Japan Chronicle Weekly Edition*, 15 September 1932, p. 353; "Recognition Protocol Signed," *Japan Chronicle Weekly Edition*, 22 September 1932, p. 383 and "New State Rejoicings," photo p. 387; "Tokio feiert," *Vossische Zeitung*, 16 September 1932, p. 2.

32. John Embree, *Suye Mura: A Japanese Village* (Ann Arbor: Center for Japanese Studies, University of Michigan, 1995 [Chicago, 1939]), 74–78. Embree spent 1935–1936 in the village.

33. USNA, RG 165, M1216, roll 2, MID 2063-309 to 2063-348 (War Department, military intelligence), 15 June 1932, "Summary of Military Events"; idem, 17 December 1932, citing official sources, gives a figure of 1,161 dead and 2,574 wounded from 28 September 1931 to 12 December 1932. Wilson, *Manchurian Crisis*, 21, also citing official sources, gives a figure of 603 dead by mid-July 1932. Wilson, *Manchurian Crisis*, 132–39; Young, *Total Empire*, 136–40; *Japan Chronicle Weekly Edition*, 15 September 1932, p. 347, photo, "Volunteers to Defend Manchukuo."

34. TNA FO 371/16243, Lindley (Tokyo) to FO, 13 September 1932.

35. Kazuko Kuramoto, *Manchurian Legacy: Memoirs of a Japanese Colonist* (East Lansing: Michigan State University Press, 1999), 19. She does not give a date for this particular parade; the *New York Times* describes one such on 11 March 1932: "Say Tokyo Will Recognize Regime," 12 March 1932, p. 8.

36. Georges Moresthe, "Un entretien de notre envoyé spécial avec le régent Pou-Yi," *Le Petit Parisien*, 25 September 1932, p. 25.

37. Georges Moresthe, "Dans Kharbine au lendemain des inondations de la Soungari," *Le Petit Parisien*, 8 October 1932, p. 8; A. T. Steele, "Manchurian Towns Resemble Forts," *New York Times*, 3 September 1932, p. 23; USNA RG 165, M1216, roll 2, MID 2063-309 to 2063-348 (War Department, military intelligence), "Conditions in Manchuria," 19 October 1932.

38. Théodor Vaucher, "Rome a vu hier l'apothéose du fascisme," *Le Petit Parisien*, 29 October 1932, p. 3; "Fascisti Celebrate the March on Rome," *New York Times*, 29 October 1932, p. 2.

39. Emilio Gentile, *The Sacralization of Politics in Fascist Italy*, tr. Keith Botsford (Cambridge, MA: Harvard University Press, 1996), 46-52, 80-90, 125; "Mussolini Appeals to USA to Accept Lausanne," *Manchester Guardian*, 24 October 1932, p. 12; "Fascist Fete Ruined by Rome Downpour," *New York Times*, 17 October 1932, p. 9.

40. MAE 97CPCOM 269, Charles-Roux (Vatican) to Herriot, 28 October 1932 (two dispatches); in 1939 Pacelli would become Pope Pius XII.

41. Robert Mallett, *Mussolini in Ethiopia, 1919-1935* (New York: Cambridge University Press, 2015), 7-8, 11; "French Aims in Europe," *Manchester Guardian*, 19 May 1930, p. 9, and "Fiery Speech by Mussolini," p. 13; "Le "Mémorandum de M. Briand et le discours de M. Mussolini," *Journal des Débats*, 19 May 1930, p. 1.

42. The controversies over the continuities between pre-Fascist and Fascist foreign policy are reviewed inter alia in G. Bruce Strang, *On the Fiery March: Mussolini Prepares for War* (Westport, CT: Praeger, 2003), 2-11, and MacGregor Knox, *Common Destiny: Dictatorship, Foreign Policy, and War in Fascist Italy and Nazi Germany* (New York: Cambridge University Press, 2000), 113-47.

43. Dino Grandi, foreign minister from 1929-1932, saw himself as the incarnation of this policy. See *Il mio paese. Ricordi autobiografici* (Bologna: Il Mulino, 1985), 350 ff.; Knox, *Common Destiny*, 127-31 (for Mussolini's "pseudo-pacifism" and Grandi's *"peso determinante"*; Mallett, *Mussolini in Ethiopia*, 46-49; Angelo del Boca, *La Guerra d'Etiopia: L'Ultima impresa del colonialismo* (Milan: Longanesi, 2010), 65-66.

44. MAE 97CPCOM 269, French embassy Rome to Tardieu, 24 May 1932 (French translation of *Gioventù Fascista*, 20-30 May 1932, article by Lido Caiani).

45. MAE 97CPCOM 235-366-1, Dampierre (Rome) to Herriot, 7 July 1932.

46. Angelo Michele Imbriani, *Gli Italiani e il Duce: Il mito e l'imaggine di Mussolini negli ultimi anni del fascismo (1938-1943)* (Naples: Liguore, 1992), 14-15; Simona Colarizi, *L'opinione degli italiani sotto il regime, 1929-43* (Rome and Bari: Laterza, 1991), 5-7; Paul Corner, "Fascist Italy in the 1930s: Popular Opinion in the Provinces," in *Popular Opinion in Totalitarian Regimes: Fascism, Nazism, Communism*, ed. Paul Corner (Oxford: Oxford University Press, 2009), 122-46.

47. Colarizi, *Opinione*, 83–87; Paul Corner, *The Fascist Party and Popular Opinion in Mussolini's Italy* (Oxford: Oxford University Press, 2012), 183–92.

48. Corner, *Fascist Party*, 88–89.

49. "The World: Week by Week," *Observer*, 16 October 1932, p. 18; Colarizi, *Opinione*, 105.

50. Corner, *Popular Opinion*, 192, 193 n. 73.

51. Knox, *Common Destiny*, 146–47; Del Boca, *Guerra d'Etiopia*, 70.

52. Christopher Duggan, "The Internalization of the Cult of the Duce: The Evidence of Diaries and Letters," in *The Cult of the Duce: Mussolini and the Italians*, eds. Stephen Gundle, Christopher Duggan, and Giuliana Peri (Manchester, UK: Manchester University Press, 2013), 129–43.

53. Grandi, *Il mio paese*, 344; Benito Mussolini, "The Political and Social Doctrine of Fascism," *Enciclopedia Italiana* (1932; English tr. in *International Conciliation* 302 [January 1935]: 5–17), 7, 16; Gentile, *Sacralization*, 112–20; Emilio de Bono, "Ieri e oggi in colonia," *Gerarchia*, 7–8 (July–August 1932): 525–32.

54. Antonio Morena, *Mussolini's Decennale: Aura and Mythmaking in Fascist Italy* (Toronto: University of Toronto Press, 2015), 31–62.

55. BNF DOSS FOL-LN1–232 (21120, A), Mussolini dossier: "La France, L'Italie et la paix," *Journal Industrielle*, 25 October 1932; "Le discours de M. Mussolini à Turin," *Bulletin quotidien*, 25 October 1932, p. 240; "Le discours de M. Mussolini à Milan," *Bulletin quotidien*, 27 October 1932, p. 242; MAE 97CPCOM 258, Dampierre (Rome) to Herriot, 18 October 1932; MAE 97CPCOM 269, Charles-Roux (Vatican) to Herriot, 27 October 1932 (his meetings with Polish and Czech ambassadors); MAE 97CPCOM 269, Dampierre (Rome) to Herriot, 26 October 1932, enclosing excerpts in translation from articles by Aldo Vallori in *Corriere della Sera*, 22 and 23 October 1932; MAE 97CPCOM 269, Dampierre (Rome) to Herriot, general study of the Italian press, 19 December 1932, p. 99.

56. MAE 118CPCOM 161: Campagnac (French Consul, Split) to Herriot, 27 September and 25 October 1932; Boissier (French Consul, Zagreb) to Herriot, 12, 20, and 24 October 1932; Naggiar (French ambassador, Belgrade) to Herriot, 15 October 1932; Dubail (French chargé d'affaires, Belgrade) to Herriot, 10 November 1932.

57. Del Boca, *Guerra d'Etiopia*, 64–65, 70–71; Mallett, *Mussolini in Ethiopia*, 63–71.

58. Grandi, *Il mio paese*, 360.

3: BERLIN

1. It was the twelfth election in Germany in 1932: eight Länder elections, including that in Prussia, two rounds of the presidential elections in the spring, and the Reichstag elections of July and November. See *Vossische Zeitung*, 14 September 1932 (p.m.).

2. Camille Loutre, "La journée électorale," *Le Petit Parisien*, 7 November 1932, p. 1; Harry Graf Kessler, *Tagebücher, 1918–1937* (Frankfurt-am-Main: Insel, 1961), pp. 694–96, entry for 7 November 1932; "Wahlstimmung in Berlin," *Vossische Zeitung*, 7 November 1932, p. 5; AN F 7 14329, Comité Franco-allemande d'information et de documentation. Rapport de M. Ravoux, "Les élections du 6 novembre et la situation politique en Allemagne," 8 November 1932.

3. Jürgen Falter, Thomas Lindenberger, and Siegfried Schumann, *Wahlen und Abstimmungen in der Weimarer Republik* (Munich: C.H. Beck, 1986), 86, table 1.3.1.4. For figures on voting from Ravoux report, see AN F 7 14329, Ravoux report above: 79.3 percent of eligible voters turned out to vote; only three times since 1919 had that percentage been exceeded (once four months earlier, on 31 July, when 84 percent voted); *Echo de Paris*, 7 November 1932; *Vossische Zeitung*, "Wahlstimmung in Berlin," 7 November 1932, p. 5.

4. "Wahlmüdigkeit?," *Vossische Zeitung*, 1 November 1932, p. 2.

5. USNA, RG 59 862.00 vol. 84, Sackett (Berlin) to Washington, 2 September 1932; "Wettkampf um den Reichstag," *Vossische Zeitung*, 30 August 1932, p. 1; André François-Poncet, *Souvenirs d'une ambassade à Berlin, Septembre 1931–octobre 1938* (Paris: Flammarion, 1946), 42–44; Kessler, *Tagebücher*, pp. 689–90, 694–96, entries for 20 September, 7 November 1932; Georges Suarez, *Profils de Rechange* (Paris: Editions Excelsior, 1933), 223–26 (re: Papen).

6. François-Poncet, *Souvenirs*, 45–48; USNA, RG 59 862.00 vol. 84, Sackett to Washington, 2 September 1932; Hermann Pünder, *Politik in der Reichskanzlei: Aufzeichnungen aus den Jahren, 1929–1932* (Stuttgart: Deutsche Verlags-Anstalt, 1961), 144n353.

7. Wilhelm Deist et al., *Ursachen und Voraussetzungen des zweiten Weltkrieges*, vol. 1 (1989 [1979]) of *Das deutsche Reich und der zweite Weltkrieg*, 9 vols. (14 vols. projected) (Freiburg: Militärgeschichtliches Forschungsamt, 1979–2014), 71–80; "Papens Programm-Rede," *Vossische Zeitung*, 11 June 1932, p. 1; "Das grosse Wirtschaftsprogramm," *Vossische Zeitung*, 29 August 1932, p. 1, and "Die Programm-Rede des Reichskanzlers," p. 2; Richard Evans, *The Coming of the Third Reich* (London: Penguin, 2003), 275–76, 284; Volker Ullrich, *Adolf Hitler: Die Jahre des Aufstiegs*, vol. 1 (Frankfurt am Main: Fischer Verlag, 2013), 365; Pünder, *Politik in der Reichskanzlei*, 149 (8 October 1932); Kessler, *Tagebücher*, p. 671, entry for 11 June 1932 (likens Papen to an angry billy goat as well as a figure from *Alice in Wonderland*).

8. Jürgen Förster, *Die Wehrmacht im NS-Staat* (Munich: Oldenbourg, 2007), chapter 1, "Die Ausgangslage: Reichswehr zwischen Vergangenheit und Zukunft," 7; Deist, *Ursachen,* 459–74; Evans, *Coming of the Third Reich*, 250, 286.

9. Jürgen Falter, *Hitlers Wähler* (München: Verlag C. H. Beck, 1991), 327–28; "Reich Lists Newspapers," *New York Times*, 18 September 1932, p. E4 (the German press manual gave 1,814 of the country's 4,647 papers as nonpartisan, the largest single group); MAE 78CPCOM-620-22-1, Amb. André

François-Poncet to Paris, 2 November 1932 (survey of measures to control the press by the Papen administration); but cf. François-Poncet to Paris, 6 October 1932, in which he reported the government's success at instilling prudence in the press by the fears it inspired; "Reich Acts to Make the Radio Patriotic," *New York Times*, 18 September 1932, p. E3.

10. "Hitler Promises to Obtain Power," *New York Times*, 2 September 1932, p. 4.

11. "Göring gegen die Erbschleicher," *Vossische Zeitung*, 16 September 1932 (a.m.), p. 3.

12. "K.P.D. in nationalistichen Kostüm," *Vossische Zeitung*, 27 October 1932 (p.m.), p. 3; "Volksgemeinschaft aller Deutschgesinnten," *Deutsche Allgemeine Zeitung*, 18 October 1932, p. 1.

13. "Zentrum sucht Wahl-Plattform," *Vossische Zeitung*, 16 September 1932 (a.m.), p. 3.

14. Falter, *Hitlers Wähler*, 25–26, and esp. 123–25.

15. Falter, 32–34, 285–89; "What Remains? The Language Remains: A Conversation with Gunter Gauss," in *The Portable Hannah Arendt*, ed. Peter Baehr (New York: Penguin, 2000), 5–6; Othmar Plöckinger (Hg.), *Quellen und Dokumente zur Geschichte von "Mein Kampf," 1924–1945* (Stuttgart: Franz Steiner, 2016), 465–67 (letter from Martin Heidegger, 18 December 1931).

16. Dorothy Thompson, *I Saw Hitler!* (New York: Farrar and Rhinehart, 1932), 12; Klaus Mann, *Der Wendepunkt: Ein Lebensbericht* (Hamburg: Rowohlt Taschenbuch Verlag, 2006 [1952]), 346–49.

17. H. R. Knickerbocker, *The German Crisis* (New York: Farrar and Rhinehart, 1932), 228. Later, at the time of the Munich crisis in 1938, the portrait behind Hitler's desk appears to be one of Otto von Bismarck.

18. Cf., e.g., Mann, *Wendepunkt*, 345.

19. Max Domarus, ed., *Hitler: Reden und Proklamationen, 1932–1945*, vol. 1 (Munich: Süddeutscher Verlag, 1965), 134 (7 September 1932).

20. "The Great God Bluff," *New York Times*, 11 September 1932, p. E1; Domarus, *Hitler: Reden und Proklamationen*, 138 (speech of 11 October), 140 (speech of 17 October). In explaining so often why he would accept only the chancellorship, Hitler was also justifying to dismayed followers why he had refused Hindenburg's offer of the vice-chancellorship in the government he and Papen tried to form in August.

21. Othmar Plöckinger, *Reden um die Macht? Wirkung und Strategie der Reden Adolf Hitlers im Wahlkampf zu den Reichstagswahlen am 6. November 1932* (Wien: Passagen Verlag, 1999), 17–28, 154–78.

22. Cf., e.g., *Vossische Zeitung*, 8 October 1932 (abend), p. 2: "Nazi, erwache!"

23. Wolfgang Schivelbusch, *The Culture of Defeat: On National Trauma, Mourning and Recovery* (*Die Kultur der Niederlage, 2001*), tr. Jefferson Chase (London: Picador, 2004 [2003]), 240.

24. "Nicht mehr 'heil Hugenberg!,'" *Vossische Zeitung*, 7 October 1932 (a.m.), p. 3 (Dr. Quaatz, cited here, also incriminated "international capital" as abetting socialism, probably referring to the loans and ensuing German indebtedness).

25. "Notizen zur Aussenpolitik," *Vossische Zeitung*, 1 November 1932 (a.m.), p. 3.

26. Foreign observers commented on the absence of foreign affairs in the election. See, e.g., AN F7 13429, Ravoux report on lection of 6 November 1932.

27. Dominic Lieven, *The End of Tsarist Russia: The March to World War I and Revolution* (New York: Penguin, 2015), 359.

28. USNA, RG 59 862.00 vol. 84, George Gordon, chargé d'affaires, p. i., Berlin to Washington, 15 October 1932; "Unsere Meinung," *Deutsche Allgemeine Zeitung*, 13 October 1932, p. 1. Most of the press, including the right-wing press, found his constitutional proposals unclear or dangerous. See "Die Mehrheit des Herrn von Papen," *Vossische Zeitung* (p.m.), 13 October 1932, p. 3.

29. Deist et al., *Ursachen*, 41–47; Kessler, *Tagebücher*, p. 644, entry for 3 October 1930.

30. "Von Papen Is Linked with Steel Helmet," *New York Times*, 3 September 1932, p. 5; "Le vrai visage de l'Allemagne. Les casques d'acier organisent à Berlin des manifestations militaristes," *Le Quotidien*, 3 September 1932; "Le Congrès des casques d'acier suscité l'enthousiasme des berlinois," *L'Echo de Paris*, 4 September 1932, p. 1; "180.000 anciens combattants ont défilé hier en uniforme devant les gouvernants du Reich et le KronPrinz," *L'Echo de Paris*, 5 September 1932, p. 1; AN F7 13429, Directeur politique Alsace-Lorraine to Sureté générale, 5 September 1932.

31. "Hitler Promises to Obtain Power," *New York Times*, 2 September 1932, p. 4; "Hitler im Sportpalast," *Vossische Zeitung*, 2 September 1932 (a.m.), p. 3; Domarus, *Reden*, vol. 1, part 1, 132–33 (1 September 1932).

32. "Volksgemeinschaft aller Deutschgesinnten," *Deutsche Allgemeine Zeitung*, 8 October 1932, p. 1.

33 Falter, *Hitlers Wähler*, 129 25.

34. J. Le Boucher, "Vers la Restauration des Hohenzollern," *Action Française*, 26 August 1932.

35. *Hitler: Reden, Schriften, Anordnungen*, vol. 5, part 2 (New York: K. G. Saur, 1998), 45 (16 October 1932); *Deutsche Allgemeine Zeitung*, 21 October 1932, p. 1, text of Hitler's open letter of 20 October 1932.

36. Domarus, *Reden*, vol. 1, part 1, 130–31 (23 August 1932), 132 (29 August 1932), 134 (7 September 1932); Kessler, *Tagebücher*, p. 684, entry for 23 August 1932; Ullrich, *Hitler*, vol. 1, 367–68.

37. *Hitlers Zweites Buch: Ein Dokument aus dem Jahr 1928*, introduced with a commentary by Gerhard L. Weinberg and a preface by Hans Rothfels (Stuttgart: Deutsche Verlags-Anstalt, 1961), 36–37. Weinberg suggests as well that the political developments after 1928 may have rendered the book irrelevant or inappropriate.

38. For the contending views about when Hitler formed his foreign policy program, or whether he even had one, see John Hiden, "National Socialism and Foreign Policy, 1919–1933," in *The Nazi Machtergreifung*, ed. Peter Stachura (London: George Allen & Unwin, 1983), 146–61.

39. *Zweites Buch*, 83–84.

40. See *Zweites Buch*, 102–3, 163, 219–24, and 81, where Hitler sets forth for Poland precisely the policy that Himmler would apply in 1939: "Under no circumstances" annex Poland to make the Poles Germans, but either "isolate them in order to avoid corrupting the blood of [our] own people" or expel them and replace them with Germans.

41. *Zweites Buch*, 217–19.

42. *Zweites Buch*, 127–32, 217.

43. *Zweites Buch*, 106–7.

44. *Zweites Buch*, chapter 5, "Die Politik der NSDAP" and chapter 8, "Notwendigkeit der Militärmacht—Die Grenzen von 1914 kein Ziel."

45. Hitler's speech of 13 July 1928 in Berlin, from *Hitler: Reden, Schriften, Anordnungen*, vol. 3, part 1, pp. 11–21; for his speeches in May 1928 along the same lines, see introduction to *Zweites Buch* by Gerhard Weinberg, pp. 23–25.

46. Domarus, *Reden*, vol. 1, part 1, pp. 80, 84 (27 January 1932); *Hitler: Reden, Schriften, Anordnungen*, vol. 5, part 1, p. 150 (speech in Güstrow, 2 June 1932).

47. Domarus, *Reden*, vol. 1, part 1, pp. 74–75 (27 January 1932); Ullrich, *Hitler*, vol. 1, p. 326.

48. *Hitler: Reden, Schriften, Anordnungen*, vol. 5, part 1, p. 29 (speech in Elbing, 5 April 1932).

49. *Hitler: Reden, Schriften, Anordnungen*, vol. 5, part 1, p. 78 (speech in Ortelsburg, 18 April 1932).

50. *Hitler: Reden, Schriften, Anordnungen*, vol. 5, part 1, p. 130 (speech in Rodenkirchen, 24 May 1932).

51. *Hitler: Reden, Schriften, Anordnungen*, vol. 5, part 1, p. 144 ("Hitler Wants to Make Friends with Us," *Daily Sketch*, 30 May 1932) and 99–100 (interview with Carlo Scorza, 29 April 1932, published in his *Fascismo: Idea imperiale* [Rome: de Gasperis, 1933], 80–87).

52. *Hitler: Reden, Schriften, Anordnungen*, vol. 5, part 2, p. 129 (speech in Essen, 30 October 1932).

53. See, for example, the following, all from the *Völkischer Beobachter*: "Die falsche Politik der Papen Regierung in der Sicherheitsfrage," 8 September 1932, p. 3; "Die französische Antwortnote—eine vernichtende Niederlage für die deutschnationale Diplomatenkunst," 12 September 1932, p. 2; "Deutschlands Niederlage in London," 21 September 1932, p. 1; "Hat der Reichskanzler v. Papen Frankreich ein Militärbundnis angeboten?," 4 September 1932, p. 1; "Französische Quertreibereien gegen die Konferenz in London," 12 October 1932, p. 2; "Frankreich will Negertruppen durch Spanien befördern," 20 October 1932, p. 1; serial on French occupation of the Rühr, "Feind im Land," 12 September 1932 and following days.

54. Othmar Plöckinger (Hg.), *Quellen und Dokumente*, 511–28; Plöckinger, *Geschichte eines Buches: Adolf Hitlers "Mein Kampf," 1922–1945* (Munich: Institut für Zeitgeschichte/R. Oldenbourg, 2006), 363–66, 378–86.

55. Deist et al., *Ursachen und Voraussetzungen*, vol. 1, 99.

56. Knickerbocker, *German Crisis*, 99–100, 105–6.

57. Ulrich, *Hitler*, vol. 1, pp. 337–38; Ian Kershaw, *The Hitler Myth: Image and Reality in the Third Reich* (New York: Oxford University Press, 1989 [1987]), 38–42; *Völkischer Beobachter*, "Hitler über Deutschland," 27 October 1932, p. 2.

58. AN F7 13429, Comm. sp. Strasbourg to dir. pol. Alsace-Lorraine, 8 March 1932.

59. AN F7 13429, Comm. sp. Wissembourg to dir. pol. Alsace-Lorraine, 10 August 1932; Comm. sp. Sarreguemines to SG, 15 and 16 August 1932.

60. AN F7 13429, Int. to Pres. du conseil and Min. AE, 22 January 1932.

61. Knickerbocker, *German Crisis*, 93–98.

62. Knickerbocker, *German Crisis*, 47.

63. "Wahlstimmung in Berlin," *Vossische Zeitung*, 7 November 1932, p. 5; Joseph Goebbels, *Tagebücher, 1924–1945*, ed. Ralf Georg Reuth, vol. 2 (Munich: Piper, 2003 [1992]), entry for 6 November 1932. In this edition of his diaries, the entry is from that day, in the Kaiserhof in Berlin; in that of the Institut für Zeitgeschichte (*Die Tagebücher von Joseph Goebbels*, ed. Elke Fröhlich [New York: K. G. Saur, 1998–2006] Part I 1923–1941, vol. 2/III [2006]), the entry is from the next day and appears to be made in Munich; in it, Goebbels does not repeat his reflection of the day before that the results were not as bad as the pessimists had feared.

64. *Berliner Lokalanzeiger*, quoted in *Vossische Zeitung*, "Kampf oder Versöhnung?," 8 November 1932 (a.m.), p. 2; "Wer gewinnt?," ibid., p. 1; "Politisch keine Aenderung erwartet," ibid. (p.m.), p. 2; Adolf Kimmel, *Der Aufstieg des Nationalsozialismus im Spiegel der französischen Presse, 1930–1933* (Bonn: H. Bouvier, 1969), 111–13; Pertinax, "Les élections au Reichstag," *L'Echo de Paris*, 7 November 1932, p. 3; USNA, RG 59 862.00 vol. 84, Gordon to Washington, 11 November 1932.

65. "Wer gewinnt?," *Vossische Zeitung*, 8 November 1932 (p.m.), pp. 1–2; Joseph Goebbels, *Tagebücher* (IfZ version) Teil I, Band 2, entry for 9 November 1932.

66. Rüdiger Barth and Hauke Friederichs, *Die Totengräber: Der letzte Winter der Weimarer Republik* (Frankfurt am Main: Fischer, 2018), 13, 16, 20, 29.

4: MOSCOW

1. Stepan Podlubnyi, *Tagebuch aus Moskau, 1931–1939, Aus dem Russischen übersetzt und herausgegeben von Jochen Hellbeck* (Munich: Deutscher Taschenbuch Verlag, 1996), 100–2; "La capitale sovietique a été hier le théâtre d'une grande parade de l'armée rouge," *Le Petit Parisien*, 8 November 1932, p. 3; Malcolm Muggeridge, *The Green Stick*, vol. 1 (1972) of *Chronicles of Wasted Time*, 2 vols. (London: Collins, 1972–1973), 229–30; MAE 117CPCOM 925, Dejean (Moscow) to Herriot, 20 November 1932.

2. "Der Sowjetbürger muss demonstrieren," *Vossische Zeitung*, 18 September 1932, p. 2. Although the author does not date his experience of the earlier demonstration against the accused engineers, it appears to coincide in all

particulars with the trial of the "Industrial Party" of engineers in November 1930. See, e.g., the account in Eugene Lyons, *Assignment in Utopia* (New York: Harcourt, Brace, 1937), 470–76.

3. USNA, RG 59, T-1249, Robert F. Skinner, minister in Riga, to Washington, 30 July and 19 August 1932. Skinner had earlier asked Kennan to prepare a report on economic development in the USSR in which Kennan had referred to "the romance of economic development." See also David C. Engerman, "Modernization from the Other Shore: American Observers and the Costs of Soviet Economic Development," *American Historical Review* 105, no. 2 (April 2000): 383–416.

4. Muggeridge, *Green Stick*, 206–10; AN F7 13504, Comm. sp. Choisy-le-Roi to SG, 2 September 1932; Henri de Kerillis, "Voyages en Russie," *L'Echo de Paris*, 1 September 1932, p. 1; Malcolm Cowley, *The Dream of the Golden Mountains: Remembering the 1930s* (New York: Penguin, 1981 [1964]), 153.

5. Victor Kravchenko, *I Chose Freedom: The Personal and Political Life of a Soviet Official* (New Brunswick, NJ: Transaction, 1989 [1946]), 52, 60. Kravchenko defected to the United States during the Second World War, and his memoir became the occasion of a successful libel action he brought against the French Communist Party in 1949.

6. Sheila Fitzpatrick, *Everyday Stalinism: Ordinary Life in Extraordinary Times: Soviet Russia in the 1930s* (Oxford and New York: Oxford University Press, 1999), 138.

7. Podlubnyi, *Tagebuch*, 84 (27 July 1932), 97–98 (10 October 1932); Orlando Figes, *The Whisperers: Private Life in Stalin's Russia* (New York: Metropolitan Books, 2007), 141.

8. Jochen Hellbeck, *Revolution on My Mind: Writing a Diary under Stalin* (Cambridge, MA: Harvard University Press, 2006), 146–59.

9. Figes, *Whisperers*, 88, 97–98; Stephen Kotkin, *Stalin: Waiting for Hitler, 1929–1941* (New York: Penguin, 2017), 127, puts the figure for 1931–1933 at five to seven million dead with perhaps ten million nearly starving to death.

10. Muggeridge, *Green Stick*, 257; Arthur Koestler, *The Invisible Writing* (New York: Macmillan, 1954), 51, 55–56.

11. Stephen Kotkin, *Magnetic Mountain: Stalinism as a Civilization* (Berkeley: University of California Press, 1995), 53; Koestler, *Invisible Writing*, 67–68; James Harris, *The Great Fear: Stalin's Terror of the 1930s* (New York: Oxford University Press, 2016), 88–93.

12. Eugene Lyons, *Assignment in Utopia* (New York: Harcourt, Brace and Company, 1937), 265–67.

13. Harris, *Great Fear*, 102–12; Kotkin, *Stalin*, 103–5, 113; Lars T. Lih, Oleg V. Naumov, Oleg V. Khlevniuk, eds., *Stalin's Letters to Molotov, 1925–1936* (New Haven: Yale University Press, 1995), 225–26; R. W. Davies et al., eds., *The Stalin-Kaganovich Correspondence, 1931–1936* (New Haven: Yale University Press, 2003), 9–10, 104–9. See also the anonymous pamphlet *Letter*

of an Old Bolshevik: The Key to the Moscow Trials (New York: Rand School Press, 1937), about the Riutin affair.

14. *Pravda,* 11 November 1932 (from AN, F7 15304, *Bulletin périodique de la presse russe, du 8 October au 30 November 1932*), 18.

15. John Scott, *Behind the Urals: An American Worker in Russia's City of Steel* (Bloomington: Indiana University Press, 1973 [1942]), 270; excerpt from text of Stalin's speech, 4 February 1931; Jonathan Haslam, *Soviet Foreign Policy, 1930–1933: The Impact of the Depression* (London: Macmillan, 1983), 1–4.

16. Sheila Fitzpatrick, *On Stalin's Team: The Years of Living Dangerously in Soviet Politics* (Princeton, NJ: Princeton University Press, 2015), 38–39; Harris, *Great Fear,* 36–40, 93–95; David R. Stone, *Hammer and Rifle: The Militarization of the Soviet Union, 1926–1933* (Lawrence: University of Kansas Press, 2000), 64–76; Lyons, *Assignment,* 370–76; Davies et al., *Stalin-Kaganovich Correspondence,* doc. 57, Stalin to Kaganovich, 11 August 1932; Kotkin, *Stalin,* 102–3.

17. Stone, *Hammer and Rifle,* 43–53, 108–14, 118; Haslam, *Soviet Foreign Policy,* 1–4; Kotkin, *Magnetic Mountain,* 16, 29–35; Victor Serge, *Memoirs of a Revolutionary,* tr. Peter Sedgwick, George Paizis (New York: New York Review Books, 2012 [Paris, 1951]), 284.

18. Alexander Hill, *The Red Army and the Second World War* (Cambridge: Cambridge University Press, 2017), 37–41; Stone, *Hammer and Rifle,* 210–16; Lennart Samuelson, *Soviet Defense Industry Planning: Tukhachevskii and Military-Industrial Mobilization 1926–1937* (Stockholm: Institute of East European Economies, 1996), 174–79.

19. 117CPCOM 925, Dejean (Moscow) to Tardieu, 3 and 5 May 1932, and Dejean (Moscow) to Herriot, 10 November 1932; USNA, RG 59, T-1249, Skinner (Riga) to Washington, n.d., January 1933. For the 1 May 1932 demonstration on Red Square, see also Michael Gelb, ed., *An American Engineer in Stalin's Russia: The Memoirs of Zara Witkin, 1932–1934* (Berkeley and Los Angeles: University of California Press, 1992), 47–49; Hill, *Red Army,* 36 (the tankettes).

20. USNA, RG 59, T-1249, Cole (Riga) to Washington, 8 April 1932, with reports from US engineers in Soviet plants; and Robert Murphy (American Consul, Paris) to State Department, report on meeting with Alexander Wishnewsky, 16 February 1932.

21. Corliss and Margaret Lamont, *Russia Day by Day: A Travel Diary* (New York: Covici-Friede, 1933), 70–72, 92, 95–96, 149; John Scott, *Behind the Urals: An American Worker in Russia's City of Steel* (Bloomington: University of Indiana Press, 1989 [1942]), 5.

22. Koestler, *Invisible Writing,* 151; "The Provocations of the Warmongers," *Pravda,* 12 November 1932; "Sabotage of Peace," *Izvestia,* 16 October 1932; editorials in *Pravda* and *Izvestia,* 30 November 1932, on Franco-Soviet nonaggression pact; Samuelson, *Soviet Defense,* 189–93.

23. USNA, RG 59, T-1249, Cole (Riga) to Washington, 8 April 1932; Davies et al., *Stalin-Kaganovich Correspondence*, doc. 8, Stalin to Kaganovich, 30 August 1931.

24. Podlubnyi, *Tagebuch*, 97–98, entry for 10 October 1932; USNA, RG 59, T-1249, Cole (Riga) to Washington, 9 May 1932; A. V. Golubev, "'Rossiia mozhet polagat'sia lish' na samu sebia': Predstavleniia o budushchei voine v sovetskom obshchestve 1930-kh godov" ["Russia can depend on herself alone": The Soviet public's perspectives concerning a future war in the 1930s], *Otechestvennaia istoriia* no. 5 (2008): 108–27, 112. I am grateful to April French for translating this article for me.

25. Golubev, "Russia can depend on herself alone," 112–13, 118, 123.

26. Jon Jacobson, *When the Soviet Union Entered World Politics* (Berkeley and Los Angeles: University of California Press, 1994), 275–80.

27. Alan Sebag Montefiore, *Stalin: The Court of the Red Tsar* (New York: Vintage, 2003), 106–10.

28. Podlubnyi, *Tagebuch*, 102 (10 November 1932).

29. Anne Applebaum, *Red Famine: Stalin's War on Ukraine* (New York: Doubleday, 2017), 186–204, and Timothy Snyder, *Bloodlands: Europe between Hitler and Stalin* (New York: Basic Books, 2010), especially 42–46, make powerful indictments.

30. Applebaum, *Red Famine*, 205–21; Harris, *Great Fear*, 93–95, and passim: he stresses the critical role of flawed intelligence and Stalin's credulity.

31. Terry Martin, "The Origins of Soviet Ethnic Cleansing," *Journal of Modern History* 70, no. 4 (December 1998): 813–61, esp. 836–46; Terry Martin, *The Affirmative Action Empire: Nations and Nationalism in the Soviet Union, 1923–1939* (Ithaca: Cornell University Press, 2001), 281, 291–308.

5: NEW YORK

1. "Roosevelt, Buoyant, Gets Returns Here," *New York Times*, 9 November 1932, p. 9; "President Is Calm in Admitting Defeat," ibid., p. 14.

2. "Voting Jam Delays Notables at Polls," *New York Times*, 9 November 1932, p. 11; "Les scenes pittoresques de la journée électorale," *Le Petit Parisien*, 9 November 1932, p. 1; "Plus de quarante millions d'électeurs ont voté hier pour la désignation du président des Etats-unis," *Le Matin*, 9 November 1932, p. 1.

3. Donald A. Ritchie, *Electing FDR: The New Deal Campaign of 1932* (Lawrence: University Press of Kansas, 2007), 38.

4. "Crowd Cheers Appeal," *New York Times*, 4 September 1932, p. 1; text of FDR speech in Topeka, 14 September 1932, in which he described Hoover's philosophy as "Help the few; perhaps those few will be kind enough to help the many," 14 September 1932, ibid., p. 15; "President Decides to Take the Stump," ibid., 15 September 1932, p. 1; "So Far, so Good" (editorial), ibid., 17 September 1932, p. 14; text of FDR speech in Chicago, ibid., 2 October 1932, p. 33; Henri de Kérillis, "Une enquête en Amérique (14), 'Quoique Hoover ait

beaucoup progressé ces derniers jours, sa défaite est vraisemblable,'" *L'Echo de Paris*, 6 November 1932, p. 1; Pertinax, "Victoire écrasante de M. Roosevelt," ibid., 9 November 1932, p. 1.

5. Anne O'Hare McCormick, "A New Americanism Is Emerging," *New York Times*, 4 September 1932, p. SM1; "News from Abroad: Roosevelt's Bright Chances," *Manchester Guardian*, 1 July 1932, p. 14.

6. Franz von Höllering, "Die Grösste Freude," *Vossische Zeitung*, 23 September 1932, p. 9.

7. "Hoovers aussichtlose Kampf," *Vossische Zeitung*, 24 October 1932, p. 1; Henri de Kérillis, "Une enquête en Amérique (4): Comment la fée publicité remue la pâte politique," *L'Echo de Paris*, 24 October 1932, p. 1; "Une enquête en Amérique (6). La bataille de la prohibition pose des questions insolubles," ibid., 27 October 1932.

8. Marion Elizabeth Rodgers, ed., *The Impossible H. L. Mencken* (New York: Doubleday, 1991), 326–30; "Mencken Tells How Magic Word 'Beer' Brought the Cheers," *Baltimore Evening Sun*, 26 October 1932; McCormick, "New Americanism"; John Dos Passos, *In All Countries* (New York: Harcourt, Brace, 1934), 229–37.

9. MAE 18CPCOM 302, Jules Henry (chargé d'affaires Washington) to Herriot, 15 August 1932; "Family Flies to Chicago," *New York Times*, 3 July 1932, p. 1; Henri de Kérillis, "Une enquête en Amérique (3): Hoover et Roosevelt face à face," *L'Echo de Paris*, 23 October 1932, p. 1. Raymond Moley, of FDR's "Brains Trust," described Hoover as "full of information and dogmas" and "imprisoned by his knowledge" in his *After Seven Years* (New York: Harper & Brothers, 1939), 9–10.

10. "News from Abroad: Roosevelt's Bright Chances: Liberality of the Programme," *Manchester Guardian*, 1 July 1932, p. 14; "The Prohibition Plank Which Was Adopted," *New York Times*, 16 June 1932, p. 1; MAE 18CPCOM 302, Jules Henry (chargé d'affaires Washington) to Herriot, 6 October 1932; ibid., Claudel to Herriot, 17 October 1932; "Hoover's Speech at Des Moines" (full text), *New York Times*, 5 October 1932, p. 18, and "Hoover's Speech at Cleveland" (full text), *New York Times*, 16 October 1932, p. 34.

11. "Text of Governor Roosevelt's Speech at Commonwealth Club," *New York Times*, 24 September 1932, p. 6; Ritchie, *Electing FDR*, 140–41; Frank Freidel, *Franklin D. Roosevelt: The Triumph* (Boston: Little, Brown, 1956), 368–69; R. G. Tugwell, *The Brains Trust* (New York: Viking, 1968), xxiii, xxv, 94.

12. Ritchie, *Electing FDR*, 129–30, 133, 142–43; Robert Dallek, *Franklin Roosevelt and American Foreign Policy, 1932–1945* (Oxford: Oxford University Press, 1995 [1979]), 18–19; Charles A. Beard, *American Foreign Policy in the Making, 1932–1940: A Study in Responsibilities* (New Haven: Yale University Press, 1946), 102–4; Moley, *After Seven Years*, 47–52; Tugwell, *Brains Trust*, 193–96.

13. "American Public Opinion on the World Economic Conference," RIIA/8/289. Chatham House, London, 13 July 1933 (Chatham House Online Archive, 2017. Copyright © the Royal Institute of International Affairs).

14. Cordell Hull, *The Memoirs of Cordell Hull*, vol. 1 (New York: Macmillan, 1948), 150ff.; "Republican Party Platform of 1932," 14 June 1932, The American Presidency Project, http://www.presidency.ucsb.edu/ws/index.php?pid=29638; Richard Breitman and Allan J. Lichtman, *FDR and the Jews* (Cambridge: The Belknap Press of Harvard University Press, 2013), 42; Moley, *After Seven Years*, 61–62.

15. Malcolm Cowley, *Exile's Return: A Literary Odyssey of the American 1920s* (New York: Penguin, 1979 [1951]), 79.

16. Lowes Dickinson, "America's War Responsibility," *New Republic*, 28 July 1926.

17. "As others see us," *The Living Age*, January 1932, quoting Garet Garrett, "As Noble Lenders," *Saturday Evening Post*, 17 October 1931; "What the Hearst Papers Advocate No. 10," *New York American*, 1 September 1932; "It's Not a Pretty Picture, but It's True," *New York American*, 3 September 1932; William Daniel Everhart, "The American Press and World Peace" (PhD diss., University of Southern California, 1932), 12–13; Warren I. Cohen, *The American Revisionists: The Lessons of Intervention in World War I* (Chicago: University of Chicago Press, 1967), chapter 2; Paul Jankowski, "Twenty Years of Disenchantment: The American Entry into World War I Remembered," *South Central Review* 34, no. 3 (Fall 2017): 115–27.

18. Arnold J. Toynbee, ed., *Survey of International Affairs 1932* (Oxford: Oxford University Press, 1933), 270–73; "Stimson Rents House at Geneva for One Month," *New York Times*, 9 April 1932, p. 5; "Stimson Causes Excitement," ibid., 20 April 1932, p. 11; "Courage Is Seen in Stimson's Trip," ibid., 24 April 1932, p. E3; "Text of the Speech Delivered by President Hoover in Accepting Renomination," ibid., 21 August 1932, p. 4; Justus D. Doenecke, ed., *The Diplomacy of Frustration: The Manchurian Crisis of 1931–1933 as Revealed in the Papers of Stanley K. Hornbeck* (Palo Alto: Hoover Institution Press, 1981), 14, 23; Raymond Leslie Buell, Walter Millis, Frank H. Simonds, "Foreign Problems Confronting the New Administration," Foreign Policy Association, 23 February 1933, comments of Buell and Millis; Beard, *American Foreign Policy*, 111–16; Hugh R. Wilson, *Diplomat between Wars* (London: Longmans, Green, 1941), 212.

19. Frank Freidel, *Franklin D. Roosevelt: The Ordeal* (Boston: Little, Brown, 1954), 18.

20. Freidel, *Ordeal*, 72–73, 78–81, 87–89, 235; Dallek, *Roosevelt*, 11–12; Beard, *American Foreign Policy*, 60; Franklin D. Roosevelt, "Our Foreign Policy: A Democratic View," *Foreign Affairs* 6, no. 4 (July 1928): 573–86.

21. "Hearst Starts Garner Boom for Presidency," *New York Herald Tribune*, 3 January 1932, p. 1; Walter Lippmann, "Candidate Franklin Delano Roosevelt," in *Public Persons,* ed. Gilbert A. Harrison (New York: Liveright, 1976), 113–16, reprinted from *New York Herald Tribune,* 8 January 1932; Elliott Roosevelt, ed., *F.D.R. His Personal Letters, 1928–1945*, vol. 1 (New York: Duell, Sloane, and Pierce, 1950), 267n.; Thomas A. Bailey, *The Man in the Street: The Impact*

of American Public Opinion on Foreign Policy (New York: Macmillan, 1948), 308; Freidel, *Triumph*, 245–46; "Who Will Be the Next President?," *New York American*, 3 January 1932, p. 1 (text of Hearst's broadcast).

22. "Text of Roosevelt's Address," *New York Times*, 3 February 1932, p. 4; "Irony and Applause for Governor Roosevelt," ibid., 4 February 1932, p. 2; Ritchie, *Election*, 84; Freidel, *Triumph*, 249–53; "Hearst Starts Garner Boom for Presidency," *New York Herald Tribune*, 3 January 1932, p. 1.

23. Frank H. Simonds, *Can America Stay at Home?* (New York: Harper & Brothers, 1932), 313–22, 358.

24. Robert A. Divine, *The Illusion of Neutrality* (Chicago: University of Chicago Press, 1962), 25; Sandra Wilson, *The Manchurian Crisis and Japanese Society, 1931–33* (New York: Routledge, 2002), 93–96; MAE 39CPCOM 107, Lens (Tokyo) to Herriot, 4 September 1932 (Uchida speech in Diet opening, 23 August, in which he alluded to Nicaragua as well as Panama).

25. Cartoon: "Of the Jeffersonian School" and editorial welcoming House Speaker John Garner's acceptance of the vice-presidential nomination, *New York American*, 5 September 1932, p. 6.

26. Ritchie, *Election*, 157–60.

27. Divine, *Illusion*, 23–41; Thomas A. Davies, *The Possibilities of Transnational Activism: The Campaign for Disarmament between the Two World Wars* (Boston: Martinus Nijhoff, 2007), 106–9.

28. "Le succès de M. Roosevelt aux élections américaines: Les conséquences de la victoire démocrate," *Le Petit Parisien*, 10 November 1932, p. 1; "Après les élections américaines: L'attitude future des démocrates en politique étrangère," *Le Matin*, 11 November 1932, p. 1; "L'élection présidentielle aux Etats-Unis: Roosevelt l'emporte," *Le Petit Journal*, 9 November 1932, p. 1; "America and the Man," *Observer*, 6 November 1932, p. 16; MAE 39CPCOM 102, *Chugai Shogyo*, 10 November 1932, and *Asahi*, 13 November 1932, from Lens (Tokyo) to Herriot, French embassy daily press review, 1–15 November 1932; USNA RG 165, (M1216), roll 4, McIlroy (military attaché, Tokyo) to War Department, 14 November 1932; "US opposition much exaggerated," *Manchester Guardian*, 11 November 1932, p. 9; cartoon by Low, ibid., p. 10; "Ein wirklich unabhängiger Präsident," *Vossische Zeitung*, 10 November 1932 (p.m.), p. 2; Moley, *Seven Years*, 71–73, 78–79; Bernard Sternsher, "The Stimson Doctrine: F.D.R. versus Moley and Tugwell," *Pacific Historical Review* 31, no. 3 (August 1962): 281–89.

6: PARIS AND LONDON

1. "Waffenstillstands-Tag," *Vossische Zeitung*, 9 November 1932, p. 3; and "Drei Minuten Stille über England," ibid., 11 November 1932, p. 1; *New York Times*, 12 November 1932, p.1, "Unknown Soldier Honored at Finished Tomb"; "Germany Ignores the Occasion"; "Cenotaph Is Dedicated"; "Services at White Plains"; "Armistice of 1918 Recalled by Baker," ibid., all p. 6; David

Reynolds, *The Long Shadow: The Legacies of the Great War in the Twentieth Century* (New York: Norton, 2014), 205–6.

2. "King Braves a Cold Wind at the Cenotaph," *Manchester Guardian*, 12 November 1932, p. 11; "'C'est aux cris de 'vive la paix!' que Paris a commémoré hier l'anniversaire de l'armistice," *L'Oeuvre*, 12 November 1932, p. 1; "Paris Less Martial on Armistice Day," *New York Times*, 12 November 1932, p. 6.

3. "Police and Communists Clash," *New York Times*, 12 November 1932, p. 6; "Les manifestations pacifists," *Le Petit Parisien*, 12 November 1932, p. 2; "La manifestation," *Le Populaire*, 12 November 1932, p. 1; "La démonstration pacifiste du Panthéon: Après la cérémonie, les camelots du roi provoquent des bagarres," *L'Oeuvre*, 12 November 1932, p. 4; Stéphane Audoin-Rouzeau and Annette Becker, *14–18: Retrouver la Guerre* (Paris: Gallimard, 2000), 251.

4. Pertinax, "Le problème du désarmement tel qu'l se pose aujourd'hui pour la France," *L'Echo de Paris*, 26 October 1932, p. 3; "Les patriotes parisiens ont célébré hier la quatorzième anniversaire de l'armistice," ibid., 12 November 1932, p. 1; Pierre Renaudel, "La Conférence de désarmement ne doit pas échouer," *Le Populaire*, 4 November 1932, p. 1; Léon Blum, "La sécurité de la France," ibid., 16 October 1932, p. 1; Léon Blum, *Discours de Romans: Prononcé le 24 juillet 1932* (Valence: Imprimerie de la Volonté socialiste, 1932).

5. André Siegfried, *Tableau des Partis en France* (Paris: Bernard Grasset, 1930), 95–112.

6. Maurice Vaïsse, *Sécurité d'abord: La Politique française en matière de désarmement, 9 décembre 1930–17 avril 1934* (Paris: Pedone, 1981), 20, 54–64; Arno Wolfers, *Britain and France between Two Wars* (New York: Norton, 1966 [1940]), 11–20, 128–52.

7. Vincent Auriol, "Liquidons la guerre," *Le Populaire*, 13 November 1932, p. 1; AN F7 13429, report by Préfecture de Police on talk by Léon Daudet, Salle Pleyel, 6 November 1932.

8. Léon Blum, "Le scandale Weygand," *Le Populaire*, 24 October 1932, p. 1; "Le scandale Weygand" (including Hervé quotes), ibid., 26 October 1932, p. 4.

9. Antoine Prost and Jay Winter, *Penser la grande guerre: Un essai d'historiographie* (Paris: Seuil, 2004), 20–22, 54; Pierre Renouvin, "Les historiens américains et les Responsabilités de la Guerre," *Revue des Deux Mondes*, 15 April 1931; Albert Malet et Jules Isaac, *Histoire contemporaine (de 1815 à nos jours) 3e année avec la collaboration de M. Henri Bejean* (Paris: Hachette, 1935), 572–73.

10. Jean Guéhenno, *Journal d'un homme de quarante ans* (Paris, Grasset, 1934), 75–80, 82–87, 192, 233; Louis Madelin, "L'esprit national: L'armée et la nation," *L'Echo de Paris*, 9 November 1932, p. 1.

11. Alain, *Propos sur les pouvoirs* (Paris: Gallimard, 1938 [1935]), 157–62 (*propos* of 5 April 1924 and 12 July 1930); Alain, *Elements d'une doctrine radicale* (Paris: Gallimard, 1933); Siegfried, *Tableau*, 111–12.

12. "Hausschüssel gegen Joos," *Vossische Zeitung*, 28 November 1932, p. 1; "Arms Session Riot Approved in Paris," *New York Times*, 29 November 1931, p. 6; "Rioters Halt Paris Session on Disarming," *Washington Post*, 28 No-

vember 1931, p. 1; "Berlin Press Jeers at Paris Arms Row," *New York Times*, 29 November 1931, p. 6; eyewitness accounts also in Madariaga, *Morning without Noon*, 184, and Geneviève Tabouis, *Vingt ans de suspense diplomatique* (Paris: Albin Michel, 1958), 102–3.

13. "Les naufrageurs de la paix," *Le Radical*, 6 December 1931, p. 1; Georges Suarez, "Les thénardiers de la paix n'ont pas pu parler," *L'Echo de Paris*, 28 November 1931, p. 1; "Une bonne leçon," *Le Figaro*, 28 November 1931, p. 1.

14. "Les naufrageurs de la paix," *Le Radical*, 6 December 1931, p. 1; "Kein Wort des Bedauerns?," *Vossische Zeitung*, 29 November 1931, p. 1; "Berlin Press Jeers at Paris Arms Row," *New York Times*, 29 November 1931, p. 6; "Deputies in Uproar in Paris on Arms," ibid., 9 December 1931, p. 10.

15. Marguerite Perrot, *La Monnaie et l'Opinion Publique en France et en Angleterre de 1924 à 1936* (Paris: Cahiers de la Fondation Nationale des Sciences Politiques, 1955), 107–11.

16. Henri de Kérillis and Raymond Cartier, *Faisons le point* (Paris: Grasset, 1931), 100–5; "France Pays Hommage at Briand's Funeral," *New York Times*, 13 March 1932, p. 19; Geneviève Tabouis, *Vingt ans de suspense diplomatique* (Paris: Albin Michel, 1958), 109–11.

17. "La fin des illusions," *Le Figaro*, 8 July 1932, p. 1; "L'accord est fait à Lausanne," *L'Oeuvre*, 9 July 1932, p. 1.

18. Paul Allard, "Les mutineries dans l'armée francaise," *L'Oeuvre*, 25, 26, 27, 28, 31 August 1932. Allard's book was later published as *Les Dessous de la guerre révélés par les comités secrets*.

19. Claude Lévi-Strauss, *"Chers tous deux": Lettres à ses parents, 1931–1942*, ed. Monique Lévi-Strauss (Paris: Seuil, 2015), 186 (letter of 2 November 1932).

20. Charles Seignobos, "Le sens des élections françaises de 1932," *L'Année politique française et étrangère* 7, no. 3 (November 1932): 273–90.

21. Emmanuel Berl, *La Politique et les partis* (Paris: Editions Rieder, 1932), 62; "Tribune Libre: Louis Lafon, Opinions de province," *Le Temps*, 9 April 1932, p. 1; "Tribune libre: Louis Lafon, Opinions de province," ibid., 22 April 1932, p. 1; "Questions bien posées," ibid., 26 April 1932, p. 1; "M. Herriot à La Tour-du-Pin," *L'Oeuvre*, 18 April 1932, p. 1; "Dans le calme," ibid., 20 April 1932, p. 1; "M. Ed. Herriot à Avignon définit le 'radicalisme social et national,'" ibid., 25 April 1932, p. 1.

22. Marcel Ray, "Les élections françaises et la politique extérieure de la France," *L'Oeuvre*, 24 April 1932, p. 1; "France Pays Hommage at Briand's Funeral," *New York Times*, 13 March 1932, p. 19; Wladimir d'Ormesson, "Tribune libre: La politique et les politiques," *Le Temps*, 2 April 1932, p. 1; Seignobos, "Le sens des élections"; Berl, *Politique*, 148.

23. Berl, *Politique*, 147–50; Kérillis and Cartier, *Faisons le point*, 95–97; Vaïsse, *Sécurité d'abord*, 161–67; Siegfried, *Tableau*, 105.

24. "Questions extérieures: Amorce ou rapprochement?," *Le Temps*, 20 November 1932, p. 1; "Certitudes," *Le Temps*, 9 November 1932, p. 1; "Epargne et budget," *Le Temps*, 1 December 1932, p. 1.

25. Robert Allan Doughty, *The Seeds of Disaster: The Development of French Army Doctrine, 1919–1939* (Hamden, CT: Archon, 1985), 33–71; Williamson Murray, "Armored Warfare: The British, French, and German Experiences," in *Military Innovation in the Interwar Period*, eds. Williamson Murray and Allan R. Millett (Cambridge: Cambridge University Press, 1996), 6–49; Jean Doise and Maurice Vaïsse, *Diplomatie et Outil Militaire, 1871–1991* (Paris: Seuil, 1992 [1987]), 293–99; David Chuter, *Humanity's Soldier: France and International Security, 1919–2001* (Providence and Oxford: Berghahn, 1996), 115–26; SHD (Vincennes), 1 N 34, Weygand to Minister of War, 17 December 1934.

26. H. R. Knickerbocker, *Can Europe Recover?* (London: John Lane, 1932), 192–203. This book was based on interviews in Europe between August and October 1932; those in Paris appear to date from September. *Vossische Zeitung* published many in translation, including on 30 September 1932, p. 4, his interview with a chauffeur, pp. 169–80, but not that with Herriot.

27. Knickerbocker, *Can Europe Recover?*, 169–80.

28. "Prince at Edinburgh Service: Arrested Communists Made to Observe Silence," *Manchester Guardian*, 12 November 1932, p. 11, and p. 16, "Silence Broken by Communists."

29. "Salford's Act of Homage," *Manchester Guardian*, 12 November 1932, p. 13.

30. "Hundert zu Eins," *Vossische Zeitung*, 29 October 1932 (p.m.), p. 2. In fact, the press devoted more attention to the hunger march than to the Handicap. See, for example, "Unemployed march to Hyde Park," *Manchester Guardian*, 26 October 1932, p. 12, and p. 17, "The Hunger March Disorders"; ibid., 27 October, p. 3, photo, "The Cambridgeshire at Newmarket," and p. 10, "The Lancashire Hunger Marchers"; "Hunger March disorders in London," ibid., 28 October 1932, p. 9; Marguerite Perrot, *La monnaie et l'opinion publique en France et en Angleterre de 1924 à 1936* (Paris: Cahiers de la fondation nationale des sciences politiques, 1955), 96–101; "Hunger as a Stunt," *Observer*, 30 October 1932, p. 16.

31. MAE 92CPCOM 281, Fleuriau to Paris, 5 May and 8 December 1932.

32. Charles Loch Mowat, *Britain between the Wars, 1918–1940* (Chicago: University of Chicago Press, 1969 [1955]), 433–34, 458, 463; Peter Clarke, *Hope and Glory: Britain 1900–1990* (London: Penguin, 1996), 157–59; Ross McKibbin, *Parties and People: England 1914–1951* (Oxford: Oxford University Press, 2010), 87–88.

33. J. B. Priestley, *English Journey* (Harmondsworth and New York: Penguin, 1977 [1934]), 10, 232, 257, 292–93. Priestley undertook his journey in the autumn of 1933.

34. E. L. Woodward, *Short Journey* (London: Faber and Faber, 1942), 114–21, 222.

35. McKibbin, *Parties*, 90–104; Malcolm Muggeridge, *The Thirties: 1930–1940 in Great Britain* (London: Weidenfeld and Nicolson, 1989 [1940]), 106; Pierre Maillaud (Pierre Bourdan), *The English Way* (New York: Oxford University Press, 1946), 29–33, 81; MAE 92CPCOM 281, Fleuriau to Paris, 8 December 1932.

36. Maillaud, *English Way*, 79, 177; Robert C. E. Bechofer (Ephesian), *Stanley Baldwin: Manor Miracle* (New York: Greenberg, 1937), 231; Muggeridge, *Thirties*, 188–90; Phillip Williamson, *Stanley Baldwin: Conservative Leadership and National Values* (Cambridge: Cambridge University Press, 1999), 249, 252. Williamson has convincingly rehabilitated Baldwin from the damaging portrait drawn by some of his contemporaries and his first major biographer, G. M. Young, in *Stanley Baldwin* (London: Rupert Hart-Davis, 1952).

37. Maillaud, *English Way*, 32–34.

38. League of Nations Archives (Geneva): R1871, letters from the Revs. L. E. Roberts and Percival Desprès, and John Davis, 26 February 1932. The letters surviving in Geneva indicate that by 4 March some 250 had answered the call made in the press on 26 February by the dean of Canterbury, Richard "Dick" Sheppard. "A Peace Army: Unarmed Intervention Proposed," *Manchester Guardian*, 26 February 1932, letter from H. R. L. ("Dick") Sheppard; League of Nations Union archives (London School of Economics), 1/2 (MF 416), minutes of meetings of the General Council, annual meeting, 20–22 June 1933, remarks by Viscount Cecil; "The Cause of Armaments: Fear and Suspicion: The Archbishop's Appeal," *Manchester Guardian*, 7 November 1932, p. 5.

39. "Germany's Claim to Equality," *The Times*, 12 October 1932, p. 8; "Back to Disarmament," *The Times*, 4 November 1932, p. 15.

40. "To Keep or Break Faith," *Observer*, 16 October 1932, p. 18; "Chancellor's New Assertion of the Right to Rearm," *Manchester Guardian*, 9 November 1932, p. 4; *The Times*, "Back to Disarmament," 4 November 1932, p. 15.

41. References to *Daily Telegraph,* 2 and 5 November 1932; *Daily Herald*, 27 November 1932; *Daily Express,* 30 November 1932; *News Chronicle*, 5 October 1932; 18 November 1932 in French embassy daily review of British press, October (MAE 92 CPCOM 210) and November (MAE 92 CP COM 211) 1932; "Our London Correspondence. Tory Backbenchers and Disarmament," *Manchester Guardian*, 2 November 1932, p. 8.

42. *Morning Post* 3, 5, 10 October 1932; *Yorkshire Post* 25 October 1932, from MAE 92CPCOM 210, French embassy daily review of British press, October 1932.

43. "Whither Europe?," *Observer*, 9 October 1932, p. 16, and "Arms and the Nations," ibid., 30 October 1932, p. 16; *News Chronicle*, 10 October 1932, from MAE 92 CPCOM 210 French embassy daily review of British press, October 1932; Daniel Waley, *British Public Opinion and the Abyssinian War, 1935–6* (London: Temple Smith, 1975), 91–111 (League of Nations Union).

44. *Daily Express*, 5 October and 18 November 1932, from French embassy daily press review, MAE 92 CPCOM 210 and 211.

45. *Morning Post*, 10 October 1932, and for alarm at enforcement of article 16 of League Covenant, *Morning Post* and *Daily Telegraph*, 1 November 1932, all from French embassy daily review of British press, October (MAE 92 CP COM 210) and November (MAE 92 CP COM 211) 1932; David Lloyd George, *War Memoirs*, vol. 1 (Boston: Little, Brown, 1933), 48.

46. George Slocombe, *A Mirror to Geneva: Its Growth, Grandeur and Decay* (London: Jonathan Cape, 1937), 99–106; Maillaud, *English Way*, 208; Harold Nicolson, *Diaries & Letters, 1930–1939* (New York: Athenaeum, 1966), 81–82 (entry for 21 July 1931).

47. "British Disarmament Policy: Lord Cecil and Sir John Simon's Speech: 'Satisfactory, if—': A Straight Question to Germany," *Manchester Guardian*, 12 November 1932, p. 13.

48. Churchill's speech can be found in *Hansard,* Commons Sitting of 23 November 1932, series 5, vol. 271, at http://hansard.millbanksystems.com/commons/1932/nov/23/debate-on-the-address, accessed 11 May 2018.

49. Baldwin's speech can be found in *Hansard,* Commons Sitting of 10 November 1932, series 5, vol. 270, at https://api.parliament.uk/historic-hansard/commons/1932/nov/10/international-affairs; G. M. Young, *Stanley Baldwin* (London: Rupert Hart-Davis, 1952), 54; "The British Policy," *Manchester Guardian*, 12 November 1932, p. 10; "Mr. Baldwin's Speech," ibid., 17 November 1932, p. 8, and letters from Francis Acland and Nowell Smith, p. 18; *Morning Post*, 18 November 1932, from MAE 92 CP COM 211, daily press review by French embassy; Philip Williamson and Edward Baldwin, ed., *Baldwin Papers: A Conservative Statesman, 1907–1948* (Cambridge: Cambridge University Press, 2004), 303.

50. TNA Cab. 23 70, cabinet minutes of 13 January 1932, 29–30.

51. TNA Cab. 23 70, cabinet minutes of 13 January 1932, 29–30; TNA Cab. 23 72 10, cabinet minutes of 11 October 1932; TNA Cab. 224 34 10, memorandum from foreign secretary, 28 October 1932; Cab. 224 29 27, memorandum from secretary of state for air, 8 April 1932.

52. "To-day's Labour Conference: Preparing a Socialist Policy for the Next Time. Strong Stand on Disarmament," *Manchester Guardian*, 3 October 1932, p. 9.

53. André Siegfried, *England's Crisis,* tr. H. H. Hemming and Doris Hemming (New York: Harcourt, Brace, 1931), 306–7; J. A. Stevenson, "Canada's Foreign Policy," *Pacific Affairs* 7, no. 2 (June 1934): 153–62; Maillaud, *English Way*, 215–26; Brett Holman, "The Air Panic of 1935: British Press Opinion between Disarmament and Rearmament," *Journal of Contemporary History* 46, no. 2 (2011): 288–307.

54. BNF DOSS (Simon) FOL LN1–232 (18137): Georges Suarez, "Sir John Simon," *Tribune Nations*, 21 February 1935; "Silhouettes étrangères," *Revue des deux mondes* 3, 1 May 1932, pp. 129–35; Jawaharlal Nehru, *An Autobiography* (New Delhi: Penguin Books India, 2004 [1936]), 183, 201; "The Disarmament Debate: Sir John Simon on Germany's Claim to Equality," *Manchester Guardian*, 11 November 1932, p. 3.

55. Young, *Baldwin*, 29, 61–62, 68, 83, 94. Young, who based his biography on his personal acquaintance with Baldwin and on access to his papers, did not cite his sources, and Williamson has since rescued the truth about Baldwin's approach to foreign affairs from Young's treatment. Thomas Jones, *A Diary*

with Letters, 1931–1950 (New York: Oxford University Press, 1954), 28, entry for 27 February 1932.

56. Baldwin's speech can be found in *Hansard*, Sitting Commons of 6 March 1925, series 5, vol. 181, at https://api.parliament.uk/historic-hansard/commons/1925/mar/06/industrial-peace; Williamson and Baldwin, *Baldwin Papers*, 497; Philip Williamson, "Baldwin's Reputation: Politics and History, 1937–1967," *Historical Journal* 47, no. 1 (2004): 167, http://www.jstor.org.resources.library.brandeis.edu/stable/4091548.

7: WARSAW AND BUDAPEST

1. MAE 106CPCOM 322, Laroche (Warsaw) to Herriot, 16 November 1932; M. B. B. Biskupski, *Independence Day: Myth, Symbol, and the Creation of Modern Poland* (Oxford: Oxford University Press, 2012), 14.

2. Biskupski, *Independence Day*, 60–62, 75–77; Slocombe, *Mirror to Geneva: Its Growth, Grandeur, and Decay* (New York: Henry Holt, 1938), 253–54; Louis Duffort, *L'Autre Pologne* (Paris: Editions de la Revue mondiale, 1932), 234; Andrzej Garlicki, *Józef Pilsudski, 1867–1935*, ed., tr. John Coutouvidis (Aldershot, UK: Scolar Press, 1995), 82–90.

3. MAE 106CPCOM 322, Laroche (Warsaw) to Herriot, 16 November 1932, including summary with excerpts from *Gazeta Polska*, 13 November 1932; Biskupski, *Independence Day*, 43, 71–73; Heidi Hein, *Der Pilsudski-Kult und seine Bedeutung für den polnischen Staat, 1926–1939* (Marburg: Herder-Institut, 2002), 230–31; W. Sikorski, "La campagne allemande pour la révision," *Revue des deux mondes* VII, 1 January 1932, pp. 49–62.

4. MAE 106CPCOM 322, Laroche (Warsaw) to Herriot, 16 November 1932.

5. MAE 106CPCOM 322, Laroche (Warsaw) to Herriot, 16 November 1932 and Consul Katowice and Cracow to MAE, 4 May 1932; Biskupski, *Independence Day*, 77; Hein, *Pilsudski-Kult*, 234.

6. Jules Laroche, *La Pologne de Pilsudski: Souvenirs d'une ambassade, 1926–1935* (Paris: Flammarion, 1953), 21; Louis Duffort, *L'Autre Pologne*, 182.

7. Duffort, *L'Autre Pologne*, 16–40.

8. "Oberschlesiens Kulturzentrale," *Vossischer Zeitung*, 8 November 1932 (p.m.), p. 6.

9. Duffort, *L'Autre Pologne*, 143–51.

10. Frank H. Simonds, *Can Europe Keep the Peace?* (New York: Harper & Brothers, 1934 [1931, 1932]), 55–70; Duffort, *L'Autre Pologne*, 122–27; "Polish-German Friction. II. Danzig Dying. Polish Rival Fostered," *Manchester Guardian*, 15 November 1932, p. 9.

11. "Polish-German Friction," *Manchester Guardian*; Duffort, *L'Autre Pologne*, 122–27.

12. Laroche, *Pologne*, 58; Duffort, *L'Autre Pologne*, 311.

13. Peter Stachura, ed., *Poland between the Wars, 1918–1939* (London: Macmillan, 1998), 62.

14. MAE 106CPCOM 322, French consul Katowice and Cracow to MAE, 11 May 1932.

15. MAE 106CPCOM 350, de Margerie (Berlin) to MAE, 1 March 1931; MAE 106CPCOM 351, François-Poncet (Berlin) to MAE, 27 April 1932; Generaloberst von Seeckt, *Wege deutscher Aussenpolitik* (Leipzig: Von Quelle & Meyer, 1931), 16–17; Fürst von Bulow, *Denkwürdigkeiten in vier Bänden*, vol. 2 (Berlin: Ullstein, 1930), 244–46.

16. "German-Polish Friction. I. East Prussia Today," *Manchester Guardian*, 14 November 1932, p. 9; Fritz Kern, "Das Unglück des Roggenlogik," *Vossische Zeitung*, 2 November 1932 (a.m.), p. 4.

17. *Manchester Guardian, art. cit.,* see n. 16; MAE 106CPCOM 350, François-Poncet (Berlin) to MAE, 23 March 1932; MAE 106CPCOM 351, François-Poncet (Berlin) to MAE, 27 April, 26 May, 2 June 1932; "Hitlers Erfolg bei Tannenberg," *Vossische Zeitung*, 19 March 1932 (p.m.), p. 4; "Die Vergleichszahlen für morgen abend," *Vossische Zeitung*, 5 November 1932, p. 2; "Die Resultate in den Wahlkreisen," ibid., 7 November 1932, p. 2. The tabulation of results shows that in both the 31 July and 6 November elections, the NSDAP received twice as many votes as its nearest competitor, the SPD, in East Prussia, even though a loss of 112,000 votes in November made it their ninth-strongest bastion out of the thirty-five legislative constituencies, down from fifth in July.

18. MAE 106CPCOM 350, François-Poncet (Berlin) to MAE, 30 March 1932; idem, note from French embassy Berlin, 10 March 1931, with results of demographic study of East Prussia from S/Dir Relations Commerciales, requested by French consul, Königsberg.

19. MAE 106CPCOM 350, François-Poncet (Berlin) to MAE, 30 March 1932; MAE 106CPCOM 351, François-Poncet (Berlin) to MAE, 2 June 1932; MAE 106CPCOM 351, chargé d'affaires Berlin to MAE, 19 May 1932, and attachment to aide-mémoire of French embassy Warsaw, 30 May 1932. The full title of Nitrams's novel was *Achtung! Ostmarken Rundfunk! Polnische Truppen haben heute Nacht die ostpreussische Grenze überschritten.* "Hitlers Erfolg bei Tannenberg"; "Noch gibt es Brücken... Die eingefrorenen deutschpolnischen Beziehungen," *Vossische Zeitung*, 11 October 1932 (a.m.), p. 2; MAE 106CPCOM 351, Laroche (Warsaw) to MAE, 20 July 1932, and Pierre Arnal, chargé d'affaires (Berlin) to MAE, 13 October 1932.

20. See pp. 100–103.

21. MAE 106CPCOM 350, Laroche (Warsaw) to MAE, 13 July 1932 (two reports); SHD (Vincennes), GR 1 N42, note on MacArthur's visit to Weygand, 2 October 1932.

22. Stachura, *Poland between the Wars*, 59–60; Antony Polonsky, *Politics in Independent Poland, 1921–1939* (Oxford: Oxford University Press, 1972), 54–65.

23. MAE, 106CPCOM 322, Laroche (Warsaw) to Paris, 16 March 1933; Duffort, *L'autre Pologne*, 238; Eva Plach, *The Clash of Moral Nations: Cultural Politics in Pilsudski's Poland, 1926–1935* (Athens: Ohio University Press, 2006),

7, 14, 161 (sees a clash over moral visions of the nation between Pilsudski's friends and foes).

24. Laroche, *Pologne*, 16–17.

25. Laroche, *Pologne*, 106–9, 111–12; "Danzig Protests Visit of Polish Destroyer," *New York Times*, 16 June 1932, p. 4; MAE 106CPCOM 333, Laroche to MAE, 4 May 1932, note of bureau des affaires politique et commercial, 7 June 1932.

26. SHD (Vincennes), GR 1 N85, Conseil supérieur de la Guerre, dossiers on *exercise méditerranée*, 1932–1933, 5 November 1932 (plans) and 5 March 1933 (lessons).

27. Laroche, *Pologne*, 49–50, 101, 115; MAE 106CPCOM-333, Laroche to Paris, 20 September 1932.

28. MAE 106CPCOM-333, François-Poncet (Berlin) to Paris, 3 November 1932; French ambassador Rome to Paris, 9 November 1932; Laroche (Warsaw) to Paris, 3 (to Berthelot) and 5 November 1932; Laroche, *Pologne*, 116.

29. Anna M. Cienciala, "Polish Foreign Policy, 1926–1939. 'Equilibrium': Stereotype and Reality," *Polish Review* 20, no. 1 (1975): 42–57; Jonathan Haslam, *Soviet Foreign Policy, 1930–33. The Impact of the Depression* (London: Macmillan, 1983), 97–112; Jonathan Haslam, *The Soviet Union and the Struggle for Collective Security in Europe, 1933–39* (London: Macmillan, 1984), 11–16; James Harris, *The Great Fear: Stalin's Terror of the 1930s* (New York: Oxford University Press, 2016), 116–17.

30. "German-Polish Friction. III. The Way Out," *Manchester Guardian*, 16 November 1932, p. 9.

31. H. R. Knickerbocker, *Can Europe Recover?* (London: John Lane, 1932), 74–79; Simonds, *Europe*, 29–34.

32. Henri Béraud, "Au coeur grouillant de l'Europe," *Le Petit Parisien*, 21 September 1932, p. 1 (series on central Europe); Simonds, *Europe*, 81–91.

33. *Le Petit Parisien*, "Au coeur grouillant de l'Europe."

34. SHD (Vincennes), GR 1 N42, note on MacArthur's visit to Weygand, 2 October 1932.

35. MAE, 94CPCOM 109, de Vienne (Budapest) to Paris, 30 December 1932.

36. "Armistice Day in Rumania" (photo), *Manchester Guardian*, 16 November 1932, p. 12; MAE 110CPCOM 177, French embassy Bucharest to Paris, 16 December 1930.

37. Henri Béraud, "Au cœur grouillant de l'Europe," *Le Petit Parisien*, 24 September 1932, p. 1 (series on central Europe), interview with Horthy.

38. MAE 94CPCOM 108, de Vienne (Budapest) to Paris, 27 August 1932; "Story or Crown Offer Annoys Hungarians," *New York Times*, 26 August 1932, p. 4.

39. MAE 94CPCOM 108, de Vienne (Budapest) to Paris, 4 October 1932.

40. BNF DOSS FOL-LN1-232 (10564) (Documentation on Gömbös after his death in 1936), including "Les Commentaires de la Quinzaine," *Cahiers de la Quinzaine*, 15 January 1937; MAE Z 108, de Vienne (Budapest) to Paris, 4 October 1932.

41. MAE 94CPCOM 108, de Vienne (Budapest) to Paris, 4 October 1932.

42. MAE 94CPCOM 108, de Beauverger (Chargé d'affaires, Budapest) to Paris, 25 October 1932.

43. MAE 94CPCOM 108, de Beauverger (Chargé d'affaires, Budapest) to Paris, 25 October 1932.

44. MAE 110CPCOM 177, Puaux (Bucharest) to Paris, 3, 27 July, 3 October, 30 December 1930, 17 June, 17 September 1931.

45. MAE 118CPCOM 177, Dard (ambassador Belgrade) to Paris, 20 October and 5 November 1931.

46. MAE 118CPCOM 177, Dubail (chargé d'affaires Belgrade) to Paris, 10 November 1932.

47. Christian Axboe Nielsen, *Making Yugoslavs: Identity in King Aleksandar's Yugoslavia* (Toronto: University of Toronto Press, 2014), 37–39.

48. MAE 118CPCOM 177, Naggiar (ambassador Belgrade) to Paris, 6 July 1932; de Campagnac (French consul, Split) to Paris, 27 September 1932 (Dalmatians); Boissier (French consul, Zagreb) to Paris, 1 October 1932.

49. See pp. 66–67; MAE118CPCOM 177, Dubail (chargé d'affaires Belgrade) to Paris, 10 November 1932.

50. MAE 116CPCOM 101, Charles-Roux (Prague) to Briand, 1 and 4 October 1930.

51. MAE 116CPCOM 101, Leon Noel (Prague) to Herriot, 2 October 1932; "Harte Urteile im Volkssport-Prozess," *Vossische Zeitung*, 24 September 1932 (p.m.), p. 2; "Verurteilter Volkspsort," ibid., 25 September 1932, p. 3; "Nach den Spruch von Brünn," ibid., 27 September 1932 (p.m.), p. 3; "Germans Aroused as Czechs Convict Nazi Plotters," *Chicago Daily Tribune*, 25 September 1932, p. 8.

52. MAE 116CPCOM 101, Consul Bratislava report, 25 August 1932; ibid., chargé d'affaires Prague to Briand, 1 December 1930.

53. MAE 116CPCOM 101, Charles-Roux (Prague) to Briand, 11 January 1932; Charles-Roux to Tardieu, 2 and 18 April, and to Herriot, 14 June 1932.

54. MAE 116CPCOM 101, Charles-Roux (Prague) to Briand, 20 September 1930.

55. Henri Béraud, "Au coeur grouillant de l'Europe: Conversation avec le Président Masaryk," *Le Petit Parisien*, 29 September 1932, p. 1; H. R. Knickerbocker, *Can Europe Recover?* (London: John Lane, 1932), 44–59; Thomas G. Masaryk, "Pangermanism and the Eastern Question," *The New Europe* 1, no. 1 (19 October 2016): 1–19.

56. "Borah's Talk with French Reporters," *New York Times*, 24 October 1931, p. 11; "Borah Rejoices Germans," ibid., 25 October 1931, p. 24; "Borah Statement Alarms the Poles," ibid., 1 November 1931, p. 55; "Czech Assails Borah," ibid., 3 November 1931, p. 3; "Irredentists Hail Borah," ibid., 22 November 1931, p. 74; MAE 110CPCOM 177, French ambassador Bucharest to Paris, 29 November 1931; André Tardieu, *Devant l'obstacle: L'Amérique et nous* (Paris: Emile-Paul Frères, 1927), 295; Robert Lord Vansittart, *Lessons of my Life* (New York: Knopf, 1934), x (calls Borah's appointment "the worst joke in democratic history").

57. "Borah's Talk with French Reporters."

58. "Mr. Churchill and Europe," *Observer*, 27 November 1932, p. 14; "Arms and the Nation," ibid., 30 October 1932, p. 16; "Back to Disarmament," *The Times*, 4 November 1932, p. 15; *Le Temps* (examples): "Le Règlement de la paix," 2 September 1927, p. 1; "L'égalité des droits aux armements," 14 October 1932, p. 1; "Le problème des dettes de guerre," 19 December 1932, p. 1; "Les projets de révision territoriale," 2 January 1933, p. 1; "Le révisionnisme et l'opinion occidentale," *L'Echo de Belgrade*, 11 January 1933 (from MAE 118CPCOM 161, Naggiar [Belgrade] to Paris, 13 January 1933).

59. Peter Neville, *Benes and Masaryk: Czechoslovakia* (London: Haus, 2010), 93, 104–5; Frank H. Simonds, *Can Europe Keep the Peace?* (New York, 1934 [1931, 1932]), 91; Raymond Leslie Buell, Walter Millis, Frank H. Simonds, "Foreign Problems Confronting the New Administration," Foreign Policy Association, 23 February 1933; Simonds related this exchange during the question-and-answer session.

60. "Danger Signal in Eastern Europe," *Manchester Guardian*, 17 October 1932, p. 8; Neville, *Benes and Masaryk*, 21; Lloyd George, cited in Robert Boyce, *The Great Interwar Crisis and the Collapse of Globalization* (London: Palgrave Macmillan, 2009), 50–51.

61. Simonds, *Europe*, 47–55.

62. "Arms and the Nation"; *Daily Express*, 31 October 1932, from MAE 92 CPCOM 101, daily summary of British press, French embassy, October 1932; Boyce, *Interwar Crisis*, 51; MAE 106CPCOM 333, Laroche (Warsaw) to Paris, 10 November and 9 December 1932; "La demission de M. Zaleski," *Les Débats*, 4 November 1932, p. 1; Laroche, *Pologne*, 112.

63. "Back to Disarmament," *The Times*, 4 November 1932, p. 15; Simonds, *Europe*, 35–44.

8: DOORS AJAR

1. Hugh R. Wilson, *Diplomat between Wars* (New York: Longmans, Green, 1941), 274–75; Geneviève Tabouis, *Vingt ans de suspense diplomatique* (Paris: Albin Michel, 1958), 130; A. C. Temperley, *The Whispering Gallery of Europe* (London: Collins, 1938), 223.

2. Maurice Vaïsse, *Sécurité d'abord: La Politique française en matière de désarmement, 9 décembre 1930–17 avril 1934* (Paris: Pedone/Publications de la Sorbonne, 1981), 341–45; "Egalité des droits et sécurité. L'accord des cinq puissances à Genève. L'opinion allemande," *Le Temps*, 14 December 1932, p. 1; Henry de Korab, "La formule française d'égalité dans la sécurité prévaut dans l'entente réalisée à Genève," *Le Matin*, 12 December 1932, p. 1; Philippe Barrès, "L'accord de Genève encourage le Reich à pousuivre sa politique d'exigences," ibid., p. 3; "Die Botschaft aus Genf," *Vossische Zeitung*, 12 December 1932 (p.m.), p. 1.

3. Robert Dell, *The Geneva Racket* (London: Robert Hale, 1941), 29; George Slocombe, *A Mirror to Geneva: Its Growth, Grandeur and Decay* (London: Jonathan Cape, 1937), 116.

4. Edouard Réquin, *D'une guerre à l'autre (1919–1939): Souvenirs* (Paris: Charles-Lavauzelle, 1949), 174; fifty-nine nations had finally come to Geneva for the conference.

5. Bertrand Russell, "There Need Be No War: World Boycott of Aggressor State," *Sunday Referee*, 24 September 1933 (from LNA S 474, Henderson file); Temperley, *Whispering Gallery*, 48–54, 59–64, 71–75, 84, 92, 133; Réquin, *Souvenirs*, 97–103, 106–12.

6. Réquin, *Souvenirs*, 51; Salvador de Madariaga, *Morning without Noon: Memoirs* (Westmead: Saxon House, 1973), 48; Temperley, *Whispering Gallery*, 207.

7. Paul Schmidt, *Statist auf diplomatischer Bühne, 1923–1945: Erlebnisse des Chefdolmetschers im auswärtigen Amt mit den Staatsmännern Europas* (Bonn: Athenaeum, 1950), 231–32.

8. MAE PA-AP (Archives Tardieu) 166, "Réductions d'effectifs réalisés depuis la mise en vigueur du pacte," 12 February 1932.

9. TNA cab. 24/233/22, memorandum from Simon, 27 September 1932; "Row Ends Session in League's Hall," *New York Times*, 23 July 1932, p. 5; F. S. Northedge, *The League of Nations: Its Life and Times, 1920–1946* (Leicester: Leicester University Press, 1986), 126.

10. "Bulletin du jour: Le Plan d'organisation de la paix," *Le Temps*, 16 November 1932, p. 1; Frank H. Simonds, *Can Europe Keep the Peace?* (New York: Harper & Brothers, 1934 [1931, 1932]), 47–55; MAE 97CPCOM 269, Charles-Roux, French ambassador Vatican to Paris, 27 October 1932.

11. Temperley, *Whispering Gallery*, 57–58; Réquin, *Souvenirs*, 105–7, 113–15; Edward W. Bennett, *German Rearmament and the West, 1932–1933* (Princeton, NJ: Princeton University Press, 1979), 57; Slocombe, *Mirror to Geneva*, 280.

12. TNA cab. 23/72/10, cabinet minutes of 11 October 1932.

13. Thomas A. Davies, *The Possibilities of Transnational Activism: The Campaign for Disarmament between the Two World Wars* (Boston: Martinus Nijhoff, 2007), 134–35; Northedge, *League*, 113, 117; TNA cab. 23/72/10, cabinet minutes of 11 October 1932; "The Women's Program for Peace. An Editorial Letter to Miss Mary E. Woolley, at the Geneva Disarmament Conference," *Ladies' Home Journal* 49, no. 3 (March 1932): 24; MAE PA-AP 166 508, note to Tardieu about *Ladies' Home Journal*, 25 January 1932; Walter Lippmann with Council on Foreign Relations, *The United States in World Affairs: An Account of American Foreign Relations, 1932* (New York: Harper & Brothers, 1933), 237–40.

14. Arnold J. Toynbee, *Survey of International Affairs, 1932* (London: Oxford University Press, 1933), 173–92.

15. Lippmann, *World Affairs*, 227–29, 233; see above, pp. 115–18.

16. MAE PA-AP166 498, Note de M. [Louis] Aubert, 6 January 1932.

17. See Prologue; Vaïsse, *Sécurité d'abord*, 190–200; Henry Stimson, *On Active Service in Peace and War* (New York: Harper & Brothers, 1948 [1947]), 170.

18. MAE PA-AP 166 (Archives Tardieu) 508, Tardieu speech on TSF, 6 February 1932; MAE PA-AP 166 505, note on conversation between Simon and Tardieu, Geneva, 24 February 1932.

19. "Text of the Speech Delivered by President Hoover in Accepting Renomination," *New York Times*, 12 August 1932, p. 4; "The War Machine that Guards the City," ibid., 25 September 1932, p. SM 8; Lisle A. Rose, *The Breaking Storm*, vol. 2 of *Power at Sea*, 3 vols. (Columbia: University of Missouri Press, 2007), 54, 62–63, 167–68. Japan, by contrast, was building up to and even beyond its assigned limits.

20. "Manöverauftakt im Warthebogen," *Vossische Zeitung*, 19 September 1932, p. 2; "Die Manöver sind zu Ende," ibid., 22 September (p.m.), p. 2; "Manöverkritik. Die Lehren von Frankfurt," ibid., 24 September (a.m.), p. 1.

21. Bennett, *German Rearmament*, 16–18; Wilhelm Deist et al., *Ursachen und Voraussetzungen des Zweiten Weltkrieges*, vol. 1 (1989 [1979]) of *Das deutsche Reich und der zweite Weltkrieg*, 9 vols. (14 vols. projected) (Freiburg: Militärgeschichtliches Forschungsamt, 1979–2014), 41–47, 448, 459–79; Conan Fischer, *Stormtroopers: A Social, Economic, and Ideological Analysis, 1929–35* (London: George Allen & Unwin, 1983), 6; AN F7 13429, Préfecture de Police note of 16 September 1932, and see also idem, 4 February 1932 Int./SG to pres. Conseil, MAE: study by SG services of German-Soviet military collaboration since 1922; "Les armements de l'Allemagne," *Revue des deux mondes* 8 (1 February 1932): 509–44, by "une haute personnalité," in which the author, presumably from military intelligence, lays out all German rearmament, save the plans for the future army.

22. Bennett, *German Rearmament*, 53–59; MAE PA-AP 166 498 (Archives Tardieu), François-Poncet (Berlin) to Briand, 30 November 1931, and Service français de la Société des Nations, note on tactics regarding the German rearmament dossier, 21 January 1932.

23. Bennett, *German Rearmament*, 174–75, 203; André François-Poncet, *Souvenirs d'une ambassade à Berlin, septembre 1931–octobre 1938* (Paris: Flammarion, 1946), 51–52; MAE 106CPCOM 351, François-Poncet (Berlin) to AE, 7 September 1932; Deist, *Ursachen*, 479.

24. Slocombe, *Mirror to Geneva*, 203, 251–63; Temperley, *Whispering Gallery*, 75–78, 81, 119, 131–32, 188; see also French skeptical analysis of Litvinov's proposals in his speech of 11 February 1932 and Soviet proposals of 18 February 1832 in MAE PA-AP 166 508.

25. Robert W. Davies, "Soviet Military Expenditure and the Armaments Industry, 1929–1933: A Reconsideration," *Europe-Asia Studies* 45, no. 4 (1993): 577–608.

26. See p. 99.

27. P. H. Vigor, *The Soviet View of War, Peace and Neutrality* (London: Routledge, 1975), 4–6, 8–9, 23–24, 197.

28. David R. Stone, *Hammer and Rifle: The Militarization of the Soviet Union, 1926–1933* (Lawrence: University Press of Kansas, 2000), 1–12, 108–14, 124–28, 170–73; Lennart Samuelson, *Soviet Defense Industry Planning: Tukhachevskii and Military-Industrial Mobilization, 1926–1937* (Stockholm: Stockholm Institute of East European Economies, 1996), 134–52, 213n38.

29. Samuelson, *Soviet Defense*, 174–79; Alexander Hill, *The Red Army and the Second World War* (Cambridge: Cambridge University Press, 2017), 30–32.

30. Stone, *Hammer and Rifle*, 174, 184; Samuelson, *Soviet Defense*, 174–79, 187–99, 203–13, 227–46.

31. *Zaria Voskoka*, 15 October 1932, from AN F7 13504, "Bulletin périodique de la presse russe, du 8 octobre au 30 novembre 1932"; "Twilight in Geneva," *Izvestia*, 28 January 1933, and "For the Charter of Independence of Peoples," *Pravda*, 9 February 1932, both from AN F 7 13505, "Bulletin périodique de la presse russe, du 3 janvier au 12 février 1933."

32. Davies, "Soviet Military Expenditure."

33. Vigor, *Soviet View*, 16.

34. Madariaga, *Morning without Noon*, 248; Madariaga attributed the "apologue" to a "distinguished British statesman," meaning Churchill, who related the fable in a speech at Aldersbrook on 24 October 1928 (Robert Rhodes James, ed., *Winston S. Churchill: His Complete Speeches, 1897–1963*, vol. 5 [London: Chelsea House, 1974], 4520 [Aldersbrook, 24 October 1928]) but to whom Churchill owed it is unclear.

35. Tabouis, *Vingt ans*, 131.

36. "La séance," *L'Oeuvre*, 14 December 1932, pp. 1, 4; Jean-Michel Renaitour, "Ecrivains et Hommes d'Etat," *La revue diplomatique*, May 1937 (from BNF DOSS FOL-LN1–232 [11892]).

37. "Premier Loses, 402–187," *New York Times*, 14 December 1932, p. 1, and "France Consults Britain," ibid., 13 December 1932, p. 1; "La séance"; "La Journée," *L'Oeuvre*, 13 December 1932, p. 1; "Trêve nationale," *Le Temps*, 15 December 1932, p. 1.

38. "Paris soulevé contre le tribut," *L'Action française*, 14 December 1932, p. 1; "La Politique," ibid., 15 December 1932, p. 1; André Siegfried, *Tableau des Partis en France* (Paris: Bernard Grasset, 1930), 112–20; Vaïsse, *Sécurité d'abord*, 323–41; "La Journée," *L'Oeuvre*, 13 December 1932, p. 1; Tabouis, *Vingt ans*, 132; "La Chambre a surtout voté contre M. Hoover," *Le Matin*, 15 December 1932, p. 1; "L'Angleterre entre l'Amérique et l'Europe," *Le Temps*, 18 December 1932, p. 1.

39. MAE 92CPCOM-211, *presse britannique* November 1932, *Daily Herald*, *Financial Times*, 24 November 1932 (from summary).

40. "Appeal to the United States," *Manchester Guardian*, 25 November 1932, p. 8; from MAE 92CPCOM-275-2, *Bulletin périodique de la presse anglaise*, 23 November–28 December 1932: Walter Layton in *News Chronicle*, 19 December 1932; John Maynard Keynes in *Daily Mail*, 12 December 1932.

41. MAE 92CPCOM-275-2, *Bulletin périodique*; *Daily Telegraph*, 9 December 1932; "Commons and American Debt. Mr. Chamberlain's Statement," *The Times*, 15 December 1932, pp. 6–7.

42. MAE 92CPCOM-211, *presse britannique* November 1932: *Daily Express*, 29 November 1932; MAE Z-275-2, *Bulletin périodique* see n. 34, *Daily Ex-*

press, 12 December 1932, *Evening Standard*, 14 December 1932, and *News-Chronicle*, 30 November 1932; "The Fourth Note," *The Times*, 14 December 1932, p. 13.

43. "Appeal to the United States"; Lippmann, *World Affairs*, 159; James H. R. Cromwell, *The Voice of Young America* (New York: Scribner's, 1933), 12.

44. Frank H. Simonds, *The ABC of War Debts and the Seven Popular Delusions about Them* (New York: Harper & Brothers, 1933), 1–4, 52–60; "What? No civilization?," cartoon in *New York American*, 17 September 1932; "The Back-Seat Driver," cartoon in *New York American*, 15 September 1932.

45. "Debt Cancellation Scheme Reeks with Dishonesty, Deceit," *New York American*, 1 September 1932, p. 14; "If Cancellationists Have their Way," ibid., 2 September 1932, p. 12; "Norman's Visit First Step in New Offensive against U.S. Taxpayer," ibid., 10 September 1932 (financial editor), p. 14; "Lincoln Was Old-Fashioned, So They Say," ibid., 19 September 1932, p. 10; "What Is Washington Holding Back on the Cancellation Subject?," ibid., 1 October 1932, p. 12; "Letting Him Down," ibid., 14 October 1932, p. 14; "American Taxpayers Must Pay for Europe's War Debt Moratorium," ibid., 6 December 1932, p. 12; cartoon, "Cut the Rope!," ibid., 15 December 1932, p. 12; "French Default on War Debts a Final Answer to League Court Advocates," ibid., 16 December 1932, p. 14.

46. Cromwell, *Young America*, 16–17; Lippmann, *World Affairs*, 168–69; "Congress Unmoved in Stand on Debts," *New York Times*, 9 July 1932, p. 5.

47. "American Public Opinion and War Debts" (remarks by David Astor), RIIA/8/251, Royal Institute of International Affairs (Chatham House), London, 24 January 1933 (rough stenography), also available at: http://go.galegroup.com/choa/i.do?$id=GALE%7CIJFRVT663540028&v=2.1&u=chtacomp&it=r&p=CHOA&sw=w&viewtype=Manuscript 2017; MAE 18CPCOM 303, French embassy note, 2 January 1933; Tabouis, *Vingt ans*, 133.

48. Lippmann, *World Affairs*, 181–86; "Baker Urges Allies and United States to Erase War Debts," *New York Times*, 30 August 1926, p. 1; "Sees Cancellation an Issue," ibid., 1 September 1926, p. 6; "Plead for Generosity," ibid., 20 December 1926, p. 1; "Coolidge Deplores Debt Cut Talk Now," ibid., 22 December 1926, p. 1.

49. Supplement, "The War Debts," *Economist*, 12 November 1932, pp. 1–4, 13–14; Simonds, *ABC*, 1–10, 11–19.

50. See, e.g., "Nation revolts at menace of US markets glutted by foreign goods," *New York American*, 1 January 1933, p. L-4; "Hawley-Smoot Tariff Fails to Protect Home Market—Let Congress Act at Once!," ibid., 2 January 1933, editorial page; "US Needs Higher Tariff, not Lower—Alien Competition Must Be Shut Out," ibid., 3 January 1933, editorial page.

51. *Economist*, 12 November 1932, Supplement, 10; Simonds, *ABC*, 34–42, 52–60; André Tardieu, *Devant l'obstacle: L'Amérique et nous* (Paris: Emile-Paul Frères, 1927), 260–61.

52. Charles A. Beard, *American Foreign Policy in the Making, 1932–1940: A Study in Responsibilities* (New Haven, CT: Yale University Press, 1946), 121; Raymond Moley, *After Seven Years* (New York: Harper & Brothers, 1939), 69.

53. Moley, *Seven Years*, 72–73, 77.

54. Moley, 73–76, 86–90, 98–101; "Hoover Leaves War Debts to Roosevelt" and "Telegrams Are Revealed," *New York Times*, 23 December 1932, p. 1.

55. "Senate Democrats Back Debt Stand," *New York Times*, 23 December 1932, p. 2.

56. Raymond Moley, *The First New Deal* (New York: Harcourt, Brace, 1966), 37–39, and *Seven Years*, 70.

57. Boyce, 391–92; "Commons and American Debt: Mr. Chamberlain's Statement," *The Times*, 15 December 1932, pp. 6–7. I am grateful to Professor George Hall of the Brandeis University Economics Department for his help with these data, some of which are reproduced here: In 1932, a total amount of $84,446,000 was in default, while ordinary federal expenditures amounted to $4,535,147,138; in 1933, $170,550,536 was in default against ordinary federal expenditures of $3,863,544,922.

58. Data from Hall: In 1932, US net GDP amounted to $59,500,000,000, and in 1933 to $57,200,000,000. With French GDP in 1932 at approximately Frs. 380,000,000,000 (in 1938 francs), the December payment of Frs. 480,000,000—the only payment that year because of the moratorium—came to 0.1%. See also Paul Beaudry, "The French Depression in the 1930s," *Review of Economic Dynamics* 1, no. 5 (2002): 73–99, fig. 1. With British GDP in 1932 at approximately £4,320,000,000, the December payment of £20,000,000 represented about 0.4 percent. See James Mitchell and Solomon Solomou, "Monthly GDP Estimates for Interwar Britain," https://niesr.ac.uk/sites/default/files/publications/dp348.pdf (December figure annualized).

59. "Roosevelt May be Forced to Appeal to Europe's Masses, Says Morgenthau," *New York American*, 25 December 1932, p. E-3.

60. Merryle Stanley Rukeyser, "Which Way, America?," *New York American*, 21 December 1932.

61. Patricia Clavin, *Securing the World Economy: The Reinvention of the League of Nations, 1920–1946* (Oxford: Oxford University Press, 2015 [2013]), 78–83; "Lausanne Convention Full Text," *The Times*, 9 July 1932, p. 9; "The World Conference," ibid., 3 September 1932, p. 11.

62. Clavin, *Securing*, 93; "Preparing for the World Conference," *The Times*, 3 November 1932, p. 13; "March 4 and June 15," ibid., 9 January 1933, p. 13; "The Lausanne Model," ibid., 16 January 1932, p. 13; "La Conférence économique mondiale," *Le Temps*, 8 January 1933, p. 1; MAE 75CPCOM 73, Boisanger (Geneva) to Paris, report on preparatory committee meeting, 9 January 1933, and ibid., Massigli (Geneva) to Paris, 19 January 1933.

63. "Désarmement économique," *Le Temps*, 12 February 1933, p. 1; "Mr. Roosevelt Moves," *The Times*, 23 January 1933, p. 13.

64. *League of Nations World Economic Survey, 1932–33* (Geneva: League of Nations, 1933), 34–37; "The World Conference Draft Annotated Agenda

Submitted by Preparatory Commission of Experts," supplement, *Economist*, 28 January 1933, p. 2.

65. MAE 75CPCOM 73, Fleuriau (London), to Paris, 1 June 1932.

9: JAPAN CLOSES A DOOR

1. "Small Powers Ask for Check on Japan at League Meeting," *New York Times*, 7 December 1932, p. 1; "Arbitration in East Is Asked in League," ibid., 8 December 1932, p. 6; "La Vie Internationale: L'assemblée extraordinaire de la S.D.N.," *Journal de Genève*, 7 December 1932, p. 8.

2. "League Hears Clash of China and Japan," *New York Times*, 22 November 1932, p. 1; "Le problème mandchou," *Le Petit Parisien*, 22 November 1932, p. 3.

3. "Le Conseil et les évènements de Shanghai," *L'Echo de Paris*, 3 February 1932, p. 1; Raymond Leslie Buell, "The League of Nations' Record in the Sino-Japanese Dispute," *New York Times*, 27 March 1932, p. 3; Salvador de Madariaga, *Morning without Noon* (Westmead: Saxon House, 1974), 216–17; "Dr. Schnee ist zurück," *Vossische Zeitung*, 21 September 1932 (a.m.), p. 2.

4. Donald A. Jordan, *China's Trial by Fire: The Shanghai War of 1932* (Ann Arbor: University of Michigan Press, 2001), 10–23, 60–90, 163–67. Some journalists and old China hands deplored the susceptibility of the diplomats and the League to Chinese appeals, seeing naivete and wishful thinking about a country with no government. See, e.g., J. O. P. Bland, *China: The Pity of It* (London: William Heinemann, 1932).

5. Justus D. Doenecke, ed., *The Diplomacy of Frustration: The Manchurian Crisis of 1931–1933 as Revealed in the Papers of Stanley K. Hornbeck* (Stanford: Hoover Institution Press, 1981), 3–40; Walter Lippmann with Council on Foreign Relations, *The United States in World Affairs: An Account of American Foreign Relations, 1932* (New York: Harper & Brothers, 1933), appendix VII; "Says League Evades our Japanese Policy," *New York Times*, 16 October 1932, p. E4.

6. Madariaga, *Morning without Noon*, 220–23; DDF I, vol. 2, doc. 118, Massigli (Geneva) to Herriot, 17 December 1932.

7. "Progress at Geneva," *Japan Chronicle Weekly Edition* (Kobe), 26 January 1933, p. 104.

8. "Military Comment," *Japan Chronicle Weekly Edition* (Kobe), 13 October 1932, p. 483, and "A United Nation," 485–86; Ian Nish, *Japan's Struggle with Internationalism: Japan, China, and the League of Nations, 1931–3* (London: Kegan Paul International, 1993), 180–81; MAE, 39CPCOM 107, Agence Havas dispatch of 15 October 1932; USNA RG 165, (M1216), roll 4, McIlroy (military attaché, Tokyo) to War Department, 7 October 1932.

9. MAE 39CPCOM 102, French embassy daily press review, *Yomiuri*, 16 November 1932, and *Jiji*, 27 November 1932; USNA RG 165, (M1216), roll 4, McIlroy (military attaché, Tokyo) to War Department, 7 October 1932.

10. USNA, RG 84, file 444.00/1–2 Grew to Stimson, 8 October 1932, RG 84,
    file 442.00, Grew to Stimson, 21 October 1932, and RG 84, file 894.00/465,
    Grew to Stimson, 27 January 1933; USNA RG 165, (M1216), roll 4, McIlroy
    (military attaché, Tokyo) to War Department, 14 November [sic; December]
    and 30 December 1932; "Au Japon. L'opinion publique commence à craindre
    les conséquences de la folie nationaliste des gouvernants," *Le Populaire*, 3
    February 1933, p. 3, citing *Hochi Shimbun*; USNA, RG 84, vol. 768, Grew
    (Tokyo) to State Department, 17 November 1932, report on "Newspapers in
    Japan."
11. USNA RG 59 894.00, box 7301, Grew (Tokyo) to State Department, 20 Sep-
    tember 1932; USNA RG 165, (M1216), roll 4, McIlroy (military attaché, To-
    kyo) to War Department, 30 December 1932; MAE 39CPCOM 107, Martel
    (Tokyo) to Herriot, 29 June 1932, and Lens to Paul-Boncour, 23 December
    1932; "Progress at Geneva," *Japan Chronicle Weekly Edition* (Kobe), 26 Jan-
    uary 1933, p. 104, and "Japan and her Neighbours," ibid., 2 February 1933,
    pp. 141–42.
12. RG 84 diplomatic posts vol. 766, Grew (Tokyo) to State Department, 9 Feb-
    ruary 1933; "Pan-Asianism Again," *Japan Chronicle Weekly Edition*, 2 Feb-
    ruary 1933, p. 139, and "League of Asia," 162.
13. USNA RG 165, (M1216), roll 4, McIlroy (military attaché, Tokyo) to War De-
    partment, 7 October 1932. His remark came five days after the release of the
    Lytton report.
14. *League of Nations: Draft of the Report Provided for in Article 15, Paragraph
    4, of the Covenant* (Geneva, 16 February 1933), 12–14.
15. *Draft of the Report Provided for in Article 15*, 14; "Beginning again in China,"
    Japan Chronicle Weekly Edition, 12 January 1933, p. 32.
16. "Orthodoxy and Dissent," *Japan Chronicle Weekly Edition*, 2 March 1933, pp.
    283–84; Thomas W. Burkman, *Japan and the League of Nations: Empire and
    World Order, 1914–1938* (Honolulu: University of Hawaii Press, 2008), 177–90.
17. "Japan and Her Neighbours," *Japan Chronicle Weekly Edition*, 2 February
    1933, pp. 141–42.
18. See p. 48; MAE 39CPCOM 107, Lens (Tokyo) to Herriot, 25 September and
    23 November 1932; MAE 39CPCOM 108, Martel (Tokyo) to Paul-Boncour,
    17 March 1933; USNA RG 165, (M1216), roll 4, McIlroy (military attaché,
    Tokyo) to War Department, 7 October 1932.
19. *Japan Chronicle Weekly Edition*, 2 March 1933, pp. 283–84, "Orthodoxy
    and Dissent."
20. Walter Lippmann with Council on Foreign Relations, *The United States in
    World Affairs. An Account of American Foreign Relations, 1933* (New York and
    Boston: Harper & Brothers, 1934), 33; Arnold J. Toynbee, *Survey of Interna-
    tional Affairs 1932* (London: Oxford University Press, 1933), 537; "Relations
    Resumed between China and Russia," *New York Times*, 13 December 1932, p. 4.
21. Jonathan Haslam, *The Soviet Union and the Threat from the East, 1933–1941:
    Moscow, Tokyo, and the Prelude to the Pacific War* (Pittsburgh: University of

Pittsburgh Press, 1992), 1–11; Dr. A. Legendre, "Un Conflit entre Japon et Russie est-il possible?," *Le Figaro*, 27 June 1932, p. 1; Eugene Lyons, *Assignment in Utopia* (New York: Harcourt, Brace, 1937), 250–55.

22. MAE 39CPCOM 137, AE note, 28 December 1932, and Dejean (Moscow) to Paul-Boncour, 19 January 1933; MAE 39CPCOM 136, Consul Harbin to Nanking, 26 July 1932; ibid., Wilden (Beijing) to MAE, 19 August 1932; ibid., Lens (Tokyo) to MAE, 31 August 1932; *Figaro*, "Conflit," 27 June 1932.

23. Toynbee, *Survey 1932*, 533.

24. Jonathan Haslam, *Soviet Foreign Policy, 1930–33: The Impact of the Depression* (London: Macmillan, 1983), 74–83; Haslam, *Soviet Union and Threat*, 1–11, 24–30; R. W. Davies et al., eds., *The Stalin-Kaganovich Correspondence, 1931–1936* (New Haven: Yale University Press, 2003), doc. 26, Stalin to Kaganovich, 5 June 1932, and doc. 48, Kaganovich to Stalin, 17 July 1932.

25. MAE, 39CPCOM 136 Martel (Tokyo) to Tardieu, 12, 19 April, and 5 May 1932; and Payart (Moscow) to MAE, 24 September 1932; MAE 39CPCOM 137, Dejean (Moscow) to Herriot, 22 November 1932.

26. Toynbee, *Survey 1932*, 534–35.

27. Haslam, *Soviet Foreign Policy*, 74–96; David R. Stone, *Hammer and Rifle: The Militarization of the Soviet Union, 1926–1933* (Lawrence: University of Kansas Press, 2000), 184.

28. MAE 39CPCOM 136, press reports from Payart et al. (Moscow): *Izvestia*, 15, 18, 23 April, 30 May, 6 June 1932 and *Pravda*, 30 May 1932; MAE 39CPCOM 137, idem, *Pravda*, 13 December 1932; Dejean (Moscow) to Paul-Boncour, 28 February 1933.

29. MAE 39CPCOM 137, French ambassador (Moscow) to Paul-Boncour, 25 January 1933; USNA RG 59, T-1249, roll 5, Skimmer (Riga) to State Department, 20 January and 24 March 1933; Stone, *Hammer and Rifle*, 204–9; see p. 98.

30. A. V. Golubev, *"Esli mir obrushitsia na nashu Respubliku...": Sovestkoe obshchestvo i vneshniaia ugroza v 1920–1940-e gg.* ["If the world descends on our Republic...": Soviet society and the external threat, 1920s–1940s] (Moscow: Kuchkovo pole, 2008), 141–45. I am grateful to April French for identifying and translating parts of this work for me.

31. MAE 39CPCOM 137, MAE note 28 December 1932; MAE 39CPCOM 136, Havas dispatch from Tokyo, 2 June 1932.

32. MAE 39CPCOM 137, Lens (Tokyo) to Paul-Boncour, 23 October 1932; MAE 39CPCOM 136, Martel (Tokyo) to Tardieu, 12 April and 30 May 1932.

33. MAE 39CPCOM 136, Martel (Tokyo) to Tardieu, 22 and 30 May 1932; TNA FO 371/16243, Lindley (Tokyo) to FO, 27 April 1932; Haslam, *Soviet Foreign Policy*, 80–81.

34. MAE 39CPCOM 137, Lens (Tokyo) to Paul-Boncour, 23 October 1932.

35. William Martin, "Le Japon est-il l'ennemi des Soviets?," *Journal de Genève*, 27 October 1932; "Japan's Delegate at Geneva," *Manchester Guardian*, 7 December 1932, p. 13; Toynbee, *Survey 1932*, 535.

36. MAE 39CPCOM 137, Dejean (Moscow) to Paul-Boncour, 19 January 1933; ibid., Lens (Tokyo) to Paul-Boncour, 19 January 1933; MAE 39CPCOM 137, Martel (Tokyo) to Paul-Boncour, 17 March 1933.

37. MAE 39CPCOM 137, Lens (Tokyo) to Paul-Boncour, 19 January 1933; Haslam, *Soviet Union and Threat*, 2–3.

38. USNA RG 59 894.00, Hoover to Stimson, 24 February 1933.

39. See pp. 115–16; Frank H. Simonds, *Can America Stay at Home?* (New York and London: Harper & Brothers, 1932), 280–83.

40. Simonds, *Can America*, 253, 313–32; Raymond Leslie Buell, Walter Millis, Frank H. Simonds, "Foreign Problems Confronting the New Administration," Foreign Policy Association, 23 February 1933, remarks by Millis.

41. Toynbee, *Survey 1932*, 540–58.

42. TNA FO 370/16151, note by Wellesley, 23 February 1932; TNA FO 371/15874, Lindsay (Washington) to FO, 21 January 1932; Robert Vansittart, *The Mist Procession* (London: Hutchinson, 1958), 437; Toynbee, *Survey*, 550–52.

43. TNA FO 371/16163, Lindley (Tokyo) to FO, 11 March 1932, and FO comments.

44. Toynbee, *Survey 1932*, 523–24, 527n.; "Manchukuo," *The Times*, 16 September 1932, p. 13; "Public Opinion and the Lytton Report," ibid., 15 October 1932, p. 15; "The League and Manchuria" ibid., 23 November 1932, p. 13; "Manchukuo and Geneva," ibid., 17 January 1933, p. 13; "The Shanghai Crisis: Record of a Discussion at Chatham House, 22nd February 1932," *International Affairs* 11, no. 2 (March 1932): 153–79, remarks by Fremantle.

45. "The Lytton Report," *Manchester Guardian*, 3 October 1932, p. 8; LNA, R3609, file of letters to Secretary-General, January–March 1933; Toynbee, *Survey 1932*, 552.

46. "La France isolée," *Le Figaro*, 5 December 1933, p. 3; "Où sont les garanties de la paix?," ibid., 7 December 1932, p. 1; "La solution du problème mandchoue et chinois," ibid., 9 December 1932, p. 1; "Le conflit sino-japonais. Une heure critique pour la SDN," ibid., 10 January 1933, p. 1; "La leçon de l'extrême-orient," ibid., 21 January 1933.

47. DDF, I, vol. 2, doc. 183, "Note du service français de la S.D.N. Le conflit sino-japonais," Paris, 10 January 1933.

48. USNA RG 59 894.00, Hoover to Stimson, 24 February 1933.

49. "Roosevelt Hears Views of Stimson on Foreign Policy," *New York Times*, 10 January 1933, p. 1; "Firm on Recognition," ibid., 17 January 1933, p. 1; "Roosevelt Reveals Policy in Far East," ibid., 18 January 1933, p. 1; Henry L. Stimson and McGeorge Bundy, *On Active Service in Peace and War* (New York: Harper & Brothers, 1947, 1948), 297; Raymond Moley, *After Seven Years* (New York: Harper & Brothers, 1939), 94–95; see pp. 115–16.

50. Rexford G. Tugwell, "Franklin D. Roosevelt on the Verge of the Presidency," *The Antioch Review* 16, no. 1 (Spring 1956): 46–79.

51. Rexford G. Tugwell, *The Democratic Roosevelt: A Biography of Franklin D. Roosevelt* (Garden City, NY: Doubleday, 1957), 346; Henry L. Stimson, *The Far Eastern Crisis: Recollection and Observations* (New York: Harper

& Brothers for Council on Foreign Relations, 1936), 226; Charles A. Beard, *American Foreign Policy in the Making, 1932–1940: A Study in Responsibilities* (New Haven, CT: Yale University Press, 1946), 133–44; Bernard Sternsher, "The Stimson Doctrine: F.D.R. versus Moley and Tugwell," *Pacific Historical Review* 31, no. 3 (August 1962): 281–89.

52. "As Japan hears the Verdict," *New York Herald Tribune*, 6 September 1932, p. 14; "Japan's Request for Time," ibid., 10 September 1932, p. 8; "March of Events. Muscovite and Mongolian," *New York American*, 10 September 1932, p. E-1; "Delaying the Performance" (cartoon and comment, editorial page), ibid., 2 December 1932; editorial page cartoon, ibid., 12 December 1932.

53. *League of Nations: Draft of the Report*, pp. 14–15; Lippmann, *World Affairs 1933*, 37–38; "30,000 Japanese Attack," *New York Times*, 24 February 1933, p. 1, and "Tokyo Ultimatum Threatens Force," p. 5.

54. USNA RG 165, (M1216), roll 4, McIlroy (military attaché, Tokyo) to War Department, 24 February 1933; Nish, *Japan's Struggle*, 189–94, 209–10.

55. MAE 39CPCOM 102, de Lens to Paul-Boncour, 7 March 1933, French embassy daily press review, 19 February 1933–7 March 1933: *Asahi*, 19 February, *Nichi Nichi* 19 and 21 February, *Fukuoka Nichi Nichi* 21 February, *Chugai Shogyo* 23 February.

56. USNA RG 165, (M1216), roll 4, McIlroy (military attaché, Tokyo) to War Department, 24 February 1933.

57. Hugh R. Wilson, *Diplomat between Wars* (London: Longmans, Green, 1941), 280.

58. Wickham Steed, "German Armaments? Menace or Opportunity?," *Sunday Times*, 11 September 1932, p. 14; "Hoddo of 13th Year Threatens League of Nations," *New York American*, 11 September 1932, p. 11; "Arms and the Germans," *New York Herald Tribune*, 2 September 1932, p. 4, and "Geneva Is Upset by Prospect of Armament Race," ibid., 14 September 1932, p. 8; USNA RG 59 862.00 vol. 84, Edge (Paris) to Stimson, 14 February 1932; "Un discours de Molotov sur la situation international du pays du socialism," *L'Humanité*, 25 January 1933, p. 3.

59. "Advisory Body Is Formed," *New York Times*, 25 February 1933, p. 1; Paul Schmidt, *Statist auf diplomatischer Bühne 1923–1945, Erlebnisse des Chefdolmetschers im auswärtigen amt mit den Staatsmännern Europas* (Bonn: Athenaeum-Verlag, 1950), 252–53. Schmidt recalled that the assembly president, Paul Hymans of Belgium, immediately suspended the session, to deprive the Japanese gesture of any symbolic character. The AP newsreel does not capture it.

10: THE REICH UNDER FOREIGN EYES

1. Harry Graf Kessler, *Tagebücher, 1918–1937: Politik, Kunst und Gesellschaft der zwanziger Jahre* (Frankfurt-am-Main: Insel Verlag, 1962 [1961]), 703–4, entry for 30 January 1933.

2. Armand Bérard, *Au temps du danger allemand*, vol. 1 of *Un ambassadeur se souvient*, 5 vols. (Paris: Plon, 1976–1982), 162–63, 164, 166.

3. Volker Ullrich, *Adolf Hitler: Die Jahre des Aufstiegs* (Frankfurt: S. Fischer, 2013), 378, 392–94; Bérard, *Ambassadeur*, 174; André François-Poncet, *Souvenirs d'une ambassade à Berlin, septembre 1931-octobre 1938* (Paris: Flammarion, 1946), 64–66.

4. Ullrich, *Hitler*, 384–85; Bérard, *Ambassadeur*, 171.

5. J. Noakes and G. Pridham, eds., *Nazism, 1919–1945: A Documentary Reader*, vol. 1 (Exeter: University of Exeter Press, 1998–2001 [1983–1998]), 110–13; Ullrich, *Hitler*, 378–84.

6. Ullrich, 401, 407, 412.

7. Ullrich, 399–400, 408–9; Noakes and Pridham, *Nazism*, 1:129n.; Bérard, *Ambassadeur*, 173. See also, e.g., Jacques Bainville, "Les Hohenzollern et Hitler," *L'Action française*, 26 November 1931, p. 1; MAE 78CPCOM 676, French ambassador Madrid to Paris, 3 August 1932 (summarizing predictions in Spanish press); François-Poncet, *Souvenirs*, 64.

8. Pierre Jardin, *Aux racines du mal: 1918 le déni de la défaite* (Paris: Tallandier, 2005); Ralf Georg Reuth, ed., *Joseph Goebbels, Tagebücher 1897–1945*, vol. 2 (Munich: Piper, 1995), entry for 10 December 1932, n.; AA, Serie C: "1933–1937 Das dritte Reich: die ersten Jahre," Band 1, 30 January–15 May 1933, doc. 3, minutes of cabinet 31 January 1933.

9. Goebbels, *Tagebücher*, entries for 30 and 31 January 1933; AA, Serie C, Band 1, doc. 7, minutes of cabinet 1 February 1933; for Frick's actions in Thuringia, see p. 86; Richard Evans, *The Coming of the Third Reich* (Penguin: New York, 2003), 317–21.

10. Andreas Wirsching, "'Man kann nur Boden germanisieren': Eine neue Quelle zu Hitlers rede vor den Spitzen der Reichswehr am 3. Februar 1933," *Vierteljahrshefte für Zeitgeshichte* 49 (2002): 516–50. Some historians have questioned whether Hitler's remarks, recorded only in the notes of participants (like the later Hossbach memorandum of 1937), can or should be taken literally. See, e.g., Ian Kershaw, *Hitler*, vol. 1, *Hubris, 1889–1993* (New York: Norton, 1998), 442, who suggests that his audience could take them as a metaphor for "expansion" more vaguely. Wirsching provides the text of an anonymous copy of a record of the talk, obtained by the German Communist Party (KPD) within days and sent to Moscow, where it remained until it became public in 2001. If, as seems certain, Hitler was trying to assure himself of the loyalty of the army, the project of race war in the east would hardly be conducive.

11. "Hitler vor der Reichswehr," *Vossische Zeitung*, 5 February 1933, p. 2.

12. Philippe Barrès, "Hitler est nommé chancelier du reich et M. von Papen, vice-chancelier," *Le Matin*, 31 January 1933, p. 1; "Bulletin du jour: Le cabinet Hitler en Allemagne," *Le Temps*, 31 January 1933, p. 1.

13. Barrès, *Le Matin*, 31 January 1933; "La crise politique en Allemagne," *Le Temps*, 27 February 1933, p. 1; USNA, RG 59.862 vol. 84, Walter Edge (Paris) to Stimson, 14 February 1933.

14. USNA RG 59.862 vol. 84, F. L. Belin (Warsaw) to Stimson, 8 February 1933 and G. B. Stockton (Vienna) to Stimson, 2 February 1933; MAE 116CPCOM 94, Leon Noël (Prague) to Paul-Boncour, 5 February 1933.

15. Adolf Kimmel, *Der Aufstieg des Nationalsozialismus im Spiegel der französischen Presse, 1930–1933* (Bonn: H. Bouvier, 1969), 144–56; "Le chancelier Hitler" (unsigned editorial), *L'Europe nouvelle*, 4 February 1933, p. 1; "En présence de Hitler et de l'ex-Kronprinz" (unsigned editorial), *L'Oeuvre*, 6 February 1933, p. 1.

16. Kimmel, *Aufstieg*, 138–40, 142–44, 152–56; Charles Maurras, "La Politique. Eternelle Allemagne," *Action Française*, 7 February 1933, p. 1, and J. B. [Jacques Bainville], "Un million de voix gagnées par Hitler," ibid., 5 February 1933, p. 1; "Choucroute et Macaroni," *L'Avenir*, 5 February 1933, p. 1; Léon Blum, "Hitler au pouvoir," *Le Populaire*, 9 February 1933; Pertinax, "Hitler, Chancelier du reich," *L'Echo de Paris*, 31 January 1933.

17. MAE, 78CPCOM 676, Laroche (Warsaw) to Paris, 8 February 1933 (press summary); USNA RG 59.862 vol. 84, F.L. Belin (Warsaw) to Stimson, 8 February 1933; S. Pinkney Tuck (Prague) to Stimson, 3 February 1933; G. B. Stockton (Vienna) to Stimson, 2 February 1933.

18. "Hitler in the Saddle," *Economist*, 4 February 1933, p. 224; Sebastian Edwards, *American Default: The Untold Story of FDR, the Supreme Court, and the Battle over Gold* (Princeton, NJ: Princeton University Press, 2018), 20.

19. "Hitler in the Saddle"; "Hitler News Fails to Stir Wall Street," *New York Times*, 31 January 1933, p. 3; "Another German election," ibid., 2 February 1933, p. 16; "The German Contest," ibid., 26 February 1933, p. E4; "Hugenberg-Giant Shadow over Hitler," ibid., 26 February 1933, p. SM 7.

20. MAE 92 CP COM 213, French embassy London to Paris, 31 January 1933 (*News-Chronicle* and *Daily Telegraph*); "Herr Hitler in Office," *The Times*, 31 January 1933, p. 11; "Dissolution in Germany," ibid., 3 February 1933, p. 11; "Hitler Smashes Military Plot. Fascist Hero Forms Cabinet," *Daily Express*, 31 January 1933, p. 1; "Red Wave of Terror," ibid., 1 February 1933, p. 2; "Hitler," *Manchester Guardian*, 31 January 1933, p. 8, and "The First Day," ibid., 1 February 1933, p. 8.

21. "Hitler in Power," *The Nation*, 8 February 1933, p. 137, and "Hitler Wins," ibid., 15 February 1933, p. 277; "Scared to Death," *Time*, 27 February 1933, p. 15 (from Michael Zalampas, *Adolf Hitler and the Third Reich in American Magazines, 1923–1939* [Bowling Green, OH: Bowling Green State University Popular Press, 1989], 26, 28, 26n.114, and 28n.3); "Hitler in the Saddle," *Economist*, 4 February 1933, p. 224; "Hitler," *Manchester Guardian*, 31 January 1933, p. 8; "German 'Fascist' Regime," *The Times*, 15 February 1933, p. 12; "A Hitlerist state," 16 February 1933, p. 12, and 17 February 1933, p. 13, "Chancellor Hitler."

22. "Germany To-Day: Dangers Within and Without," *Sunday Times*, 26 February 1933, p. 16; D. Sefton Delmer, "Germany's 21-Day Chancellor," *Daily Express*, 22 February 1933, p. 10; "Liberty Officially Abolished All over

Germany," ibid., 28 February 1933, p. 1. In the second half of February, *The Times* reported almost daily on the political violence in Germany.

23. *Izvestia*, 30 January 1933, from MAE, *Bulletin périodique de la presse russe*, 226, 3 January–12 February 1933; USNA, RG 59.862 vol. 84, French Consul Trieste and Fiume to Paul-Boncour, 1 February 1933.

24. MAE, 97CPCOM 235-366-1, French Consul Palermo to Paul-Boncour, 14 February 1933; MAE 97CPCOM-258, French ambassador Rome to Paul-Boncour; USNA, RG 59.862 vol. 84, Garrett (Rome) to Stimson, 1 February 1933; *Pravda*, 19 November 1932, "In an Impasse," from MAE, 117 CPCOM 918, *Bulletin périodique de la presse russe*, no 224, 8 October–30 November 1932; Jonathan Haslam, *Soviet Foreign Policy, 1930–33: The Impact of the Depression* (London: Macmillan, 1983), 113–18.

25. AN 462 AP 14, handwritten notes by André François-Poncet, 9 February 1933.

26. Ibid.; DDF, I, vol. 2, no. 264, François-Poncet to Paul-Boncour, 5 February 1933, and no. 275, François-Poncet to Paul-Boncour, 8 February 1933; François-Poncet, *Souvenirs*, 85.

27. DBFP, II, vol. 4, no. 238, Rumbold to Simon, 7 February 1933.

28. Detlev Clemens, *Herr Hitler in Germany. Wahrnehmungen und Deutungen der Nationalsozialismus in Grossbritannien 1920 bis 1939* (Göttingen and Zurich: German Historical Institute: Vandenboeck & Ruprecht, 1996), 253–56.

29. USNA, RG 59.862, vol. 84, Sackett (Berlin) to Stimson, 7 February 1933.

30. DDF, I, vol. 2, no. 275, François-Poncet to Paul-Boncour, 8 February 1933.

31. Jonathan Haslam, *The Soviet Union and the Struggle for Collective Security in Europe, 1933–39* (London: Macmillan, 1984), 9; DDF, I, vol. 2, no. 289, François-Poncet to Paul-Boncour, 11 February 1933 (conversation with Soviet diplomats).

32. DBFP, II, vol. 4, no. 243, Rumbold to Simon, 22 February 1933, and 240, Rumbold to Simon, 14 February 1933.

33. USNA, RG 59.862 vol. 84, Leon Dominian, American Consul General in charge, Stuttgart, to Stimson, 21 February 1933.

34. DDF, I, vol. 2, no. 378, François-Poncet to Paul-Boncour, 7 March 1933.

35. François-Poncet, *Souvenirs*, 92.

36. See, e.g., DDF, no. 351, 1, vol. 2, François-Poncet to Paul-Boncour, 28 February 1933; Kessler, *Tagebücher*, pp. 709–11, entry for 28 February 1933.

37. Noakes and Pridham, *Nazism*, 1:141–42; "News from Abroad. Storm Troopers as Police," *Manchester Guardian,* 25 February 1933, pp. 13, 18.

38. A. J. Nicholls, *Weimar and the Rise of Hitler* (New York: St. Martin's Press, 1991 [1968]), 116; Jürgen W. Falter, *Hitlers Wähler* (Munich: Verlag C.H. Beck, 1991), 38–41; cf. Goebbels, *Tagebücher 2*, entry for 5 March 1933; "Die Perspektiven," *Vossische Zeitung*, 7 March 1933, p. 1.

39. Falter, *Wähler*, 25 (table), 40; *Vossische Zeitung*, "Perspektiven," 7 March 1933, citing *Deutsche Allegemeine Zeitung* and *Kreuzzeitung*.

40. "Potsdam Spirit Hailed," *New York Times*, 22 March 1933, p. 1; MAE 78CPCOM 676, François-Poncet to Paul-Boncour, 22 March 1933; François-Poncet, *Souvenirs*, 103.

41. "L'apothéose d'Hitler" (photo), *Le Petit Parisien*, 22 March 1933; Victor Klemperer, *Ich will Zeugnis ablegen bis zum letzten: Tagebücher, 1933–1934* (Berlin 2006 [1995]), entries for 10, 22, 30 March 1933; Kessler, *Tagebücher*, 712, entry for 18 March 1933.

42. Clemens, *Herr Hitler in Germany*, 299–301; cf., e.g., DBFP, II, vol. 5, doc. 22, Rumbold to Simon, 5 April 1933; FRUS, 1933, vol. 2, Sackett to Hull, 21 March 1933; MAE 78CPCOM 676, François-Poncet to Paul-Boncour, 22 March and 4 April 1933.

43. USNA, RG 59.862 vol. 84, J. Webb Benton (Prague) to Hull, 14 March 1933; ibid., *Il Giornale d'Italia*, 4 March 1933, p. 1, "Dal Teatro di Weimar alla Chiesa di Potsdam" (from Garrett, Rome, to Hull, 10 March 1933); MAE 117 CPCOM 985, François-Poncet to Paul-Boncour, 11 March 1933 (Soviet press reports); "Bulletin du jour: La reunion du Reichstag allemande," *Le Temps*, 22 March 1933, p. 1.

44. *Gazeta Warszawska*, 30 March 1933, and wire service review, both from MAE, *Bulletin périodique de la presse polonaise*, 231, 24 March–30 April 1933.

45. "Régression," *Le Temps*, 30 March 1933, p. 1, and "Bulletin du jour: Le chaos politique en Allemagne," ibid., 2 April 1933, p. 1; "Nazi Discipline," *The Times*, 9 March 1933, p. 11; "Reprisals in Germany," ibid., 11 March 1933, p. 9; "Violence in Germany," ibid., 17 March 1933, p. 13; "According to Plan," ibid., 3 April 1913, p. 15; "German Fugitives Tell of Atrocities," *New York Times*, 20 March 1933, p. 1; "Half Million Jews Affected by Hitler Furor in Germany," ibid., 26 March 1933, p. 4; Richard Breitman, Allan J. Lichtman, *FDR and the Jews* (Cambridge, MA: Harvard University Press, 2013), 55.

46. "British Jews and Germany," *Sunday Times*, 26 March 1933, p. 17; "En face d'une invasion allemande," *Le Figaro*, 2 April 1933, p. 1.

47. "Judea Declares War on Germany," *Daily Express*, 24 March 1933, p. 1; "Hitler Nazis Declare War on World Jewry," *Chicago (Daily) Tribune*, 31 March 1933, p. 1.

48. Cf., e.g., "Nazis Want Peace while they Effect Internal Reforms," *New York Times*, 7 March 1933, p. 1; MAE 78CPCOM-676 10 March 1933, French Ambassador Washington to Paris (press review).

49. "The Spirit of Potsdam," *The Times*, 22 March 1933, p. 15.

50. "Cabinet Made the Issue," *New York Times*, 2 February 1933, p. 1.

51. "Hitler Reassures East Prussians," *New York Times*, 5 March 1933, p. 20; "Hitler and the Corridor," *Manchester Guardian*, 14 February 133, p. 13; "Dictatorship Bill Passed in Germany," ibid., 23 March 1933, p. 11, and "Hitler's Reichstag Speech: Statement of Foreign Policy," p. 14; "Herriots Bumerang," *Vossische Zeitung*, 10 February 1933, p. 1; DDF, I, vol. 2, doc. 282, François-Poncet to Paul-Boncour, 10 February 1933.

52. AA, C, vol. 1, doc. 1, 30 January 1933, *Runderlass* from Bülow.

53. AA, C, vol. 1, doc. 6, Dirksen (Moscow) to Bülow, 31 January 1933; DBFP, II, vol. 4, no. 232, Simon to Rumbold, 31 January 1933; USNA, RG 59.862 vol. 84, memorandum by W. R. Castle, 2 February 1933; DDF, I, vol. 2, doc. 260, François-Poncet to Paul-Boncour, 4 February 1933.

54. USNA, RG 59.862 vol. 84, Sackett to Stimson, 20 February 1933.

55. DDF, I, vol. 2, François-Poncet to Paul-Boncour: doc. 260, 4 February 1933, doc. 275, 8 February 1933, doc. 413, 15 March 1933; ibid., vol. 3, François-Poncet to Paul-Boncour, doc. 70, 30 March 1933, doc. 92, 5 April 1933, doc. 105, 8 April 1933; François-Poncet, *Souvenirs*, 141–44, where he adds somewhat to the account of his meeting with Hitler that he gave in his cable at the time; USNA RG 59 762.00 Box 4346, Berlin to Washington, 19 April 1933 (Rosenberg).

56. DBFP, II, vol. 5, doc. 23, Rumbold to Simon, 7 April 1933 and doc. 36, Rumbold to Simon, 26 April 1933; Clemens, *Herr Hitler in Germany*, 293–94.

57. USNA, RG 59, file 862.00/3013, Charles Hathaway, Munich, to George Gordon, chargé d'affaires, Berlin, 13 May 1933, pp. 22, 33, 44–45.

58. FRUS, 1933, vol. 2, Klieforth (Berlin) to Stimson, 20 February 1933, and Norman Davis via Gordon (Berlin) to Hull, 9 April 1933; Othmar Plöckinger, *Geschichte eines Buches: Adolf Hitlers "Mein Kampf," 1922–1945* (Munich: Institut für Zeitgeschichte/R. Oldenbourg, 2006), 489, 496; Cordell Hull, *The Memoirs of Cordell Hull*, vol. 1 (New York: Macmillan, 1948), 235–45.

59. MAE, 117 CPCOM 985, Dejean (Moscow) to Paul-Boncour, 10, 22, 27 March 1933; ibid., François-Poncet to Paul-Boncour, 8, 11, 16, 27 March 1933.

60. "Die Bibel der deutschen Faschisten," in *Schlüsseldokumente zur internationalen Rezeption von "Mein Kampf*," ed. Othmar Plöckinger (Stuttgart: Franz Steiner, 2016), 11–74. In 1939, on the eve of the Nazi-Soviet pact, Stalin sent his inner circle—many of those from 1932 had disappeared—the work to read, but how many did so and how many took it seriously this time as well is unclear: Stephen Kotkin, *Stalin*, vol. 2 (New York: Penguin, 2017), 681–82.

61. "Fascismo," *Corriere della sera*, 7 March 1933, p. 1 (clipping from USNA, RG 59.862 vol. 84, Garrett to Stimson, 10 March 1933); "The Spirit of Potsdam," *The Times*, 22 March 1933, p. 15; "Nazis Want Peace While They Effect Internal Reforms," *New York Times*, 7 March 1933, p. 1.

62. "Hitlerism," *Manchester Guardian*, 22 March 1933, p. 10; Edgar Ansel Mowrer, *Germany Puts the Clock Back* (London: Bodley Head, 1933), 40–50, 326; Wickham Steed, *The Meaning of Hitlerism* (London: Nisbet, 1934), 52–55. In *The Course of German History: A Survey of the Development of Germany since 1815* (London: H. Hamilton, 1945), A. J. P. Taylor linked the foreign policy of the Third Reich to the "bad" forces in German history, before he propounded the opposite in *The Origins of the Second World War* (London: H. Hamilton, 1961); *Le Temps*, 22 March 1933, p. 1, "Bulletin du jour: La reunion du Reichstag allemande."

63. USNA, RG 59.862 vol. 84, Stafford (Kaunas) to Stimson, 22 February 1933, citing *Lietuvios Zinios*, 14 February 1933; Paul Ravoux, "En Allemagne: En

l'an I du troisième reich," *L'Europe nouvelle*, 11 February 1933, p. 1; USNA, RG 59.862 vol. 84, Edge (Paris) to Stimson, 9 February 1933, citing "Les élections allemandes: Le triomphe d'Hitler"; "Et maintenant?," *L'Avenir*, 2 February 1933, p. 1; *Le Figaro*, 6 March 1933, p. 1.

64. DBFP, II, vol. 5, doc. 36, Rumbold to Simon, 26 April 1933; FRUS, 1933, vol. 2, Dominian (Stuttgart) to Hull, 4 April 1933; Plöckinger, *Geschichte eines Buches*, 524–29; Karl Radek, in *Izvestia* 22 March 1933, accused the Germans of seeking to enslave the USSR and of regarding the Slavs as an inferior race, but this was not the dominant Soviet line, at the time ambivalent and even confused. See, e.g., MAE 117 CPCOM 985, Dejean to Paul-Boncour, 4 April 1933.

65. Wilhelm Deist et al., *Ursachen und Voraussetzungen des Zweiten Weltkrieges*, vol. 1 (1989 [1979]) of *Das deutsche Reich und der zweite Weltkrieg*, 9 vols. (14 vols. projected) (Freiburg: Militärgeschichtliches Forschungsamt, 1979–2014), 133.

66. USNA, RG 59.862 vol. 84, Walter Edge (Paris) to Sackett, 1 February and 9 February 1933 (press summaries); "Hitler chancelier," *Journal des Débats*, 31 January 1933, p. 1; "Un avertissement prophétique," *Figaro*, 9 February 1933, p. 1; Edouard Herriot, "Retour au calme," *Ere nouvelle*, 9 February 1933, p. 1; MAE Z 676, Corbin (Brussels) to Paris, 16 and 23 February 1933.

11: UNWILLING ACCOMPLICES

1. "The Children's Hour," *The Times*, 13 February 1933, p. 13.

2. MAE 92CPCOM-281, Fleuriau (London) to Paul-Boncour, 22 February 1933.

3. "'Un-British' Oxford Men: Communist Motion Stirs City," *Daily Express*, 13 February 1932, p. 11; *The Times*, "Children's Hour"; E. L. Woodward, *Short Journey* (London: Faber and Faber, 1942), 182–83.

4. Woodward, 182–83.

5. "Britain and Europe," *Sunday Times*, 5 February 1933, p. 14; "The Universities: Oxford Pacifists' Petty Triumph," ibid., 12 February 1933, p. 20; "Men, Women, and Memories," ibid., 19 February 1933, p. 13; Robert Lord Vansittart, *The Mist Procession* (London: Hutchinson, 1958), 430.

6. James J. Barnes and Patience P. Barnes, *Hitler's Mein Kampf in Britain and America: A Publishing History, 1930–39* (Cambridge: Cambridge University Press, 1980), 16, 78; Sven Felix Kellerhoff, *"Mein Kampf": Die Karriere eines deutsches Buches* (Stuttgart: Klett-Cotta, 2015), 268–70, 276–80, 287; Antoine Vitkine, *Mein Kampf: Histoire d'un livre* (Paris: Flammarion, 2009), 97–100, 115–28; "Une conversation avec Adolf Hitler," *Le Matin*, 22 November 1933, p. 1; Othmar Plöckinger, *Geschichte eines Buches: Adolf Hitlers "Mein Kampf," 1922–1945* (Munich: Institut für Zeitgeschichte/R. Oldenbourg, 2006), 461–97, 513–14, 520–24, 549–55. The full, original translation did not become available to the Russian public until after the dissolution of the USSR, Stephen Kotkin, *Stalin*, vol. 2 (New York: Penguin, 2017), 681 n243.

7. MAE 106CPCOM 334, Laroche (Warsaw) to Paul-Boncour, 24 February and 4 April 1933; Georges Simenon, *Mes apprentissages: Reportages, 1931–1946* (Paris: Omnibus, 2001), 782; cf., e.g., *Gazeta Polska* (governmental) 4 April 1933, and *Gazeta Warszawska*, both from MAE, *Bulletin périodique de la presse polonaise*, 231, 24 March–30 April 1933.

8. USNA RG 59 862.00 vol. 84, J. Webb Benton (Prague) to Hull, 27 March 1933; DDF, I, vol. 3, doc. 100, Naggiar (Belgrade) to Paul-Boncour, 6 April 1933.

9. AA, C, I, doc. 152, Hoesch to AA, 12 April 1933; Harry Graf Kessler, *Tagebücher, 1918–1937: Politik, Kunst und Gesellschaft der zwanziger Jahre* (Frankfurt-am-Main: Insel Verlag, 1962 [1961]), 715–17, entry for 5 May 1933.

10. Thomas Jones, *A Diary with Letters, 1931–1950* (New York: Oxford University Press, 1954), 107–8 (29 April 1933).

11. Richard Breitman, Allan J. Lichtman, *FDR and the Jews* (Cambridge, MA: Harvard University Press, 2013), 53–56; "35,000 Jam Streets outside the Garden," *New York Times*, 28 March 1933, p. 1.

12. AN F 7 13430, report from préfecture Haut-Rhin, 21 February 1933; ibid., report from contrôleur-général Strasbourg, 24 February 1933; ibid., reports from commissaires spéciaux, Wissemburg and Lautenburg, 2 March 1933; Préfet Moselle to Daladier, 23 March 1933.

13. AN F 7 13430, préfecture de police note, 25 March 1933; USNA RG 59 862.00 vol. 84, Warrington Dawson (Paris) to Hull, 21 March 1933.

14. AN F 7 13430, préfecture de police note, 27 March 1933; "De nombreux Juifs d'Allemagne arrivent en France," *L'Oeuvre*, 1 April 1933, p. 2; "Le mouvement de protestation contre les menées antisémites d'Allemagne," ibid., 2 April 1933, p. 2.

15. Eugene Lyons, *Assignment in Utopia* (New York: Harcourt, Brace, 1937), 281–82, 397–401, 572–80; "Soviets in 16th Year Calm and Hopeful," *New York Times*, 13 November 1932, p. E4; Keynes in *New Statesman*, 10 December 1932, p. 770, cited in Jonathan Haslam, *Soviet Foreign Policy, 1930–33: The Impact of the Depression* (London: Macmillan 1983), 112; Louis Fischer, "Nouveaux aspects de l'URSS," *L'Europe nouvelle*, 25 February 1933, p. 1.

16. "The Soviet and the Peasantry" series by "a correspondent in Russia" (Malcolm Muggeridge), *Manchester Guardian*, 25 March 1933, p. 13; 27 March 1933, p. 9; and 28 March 1933, p. 9. See also "Famine in Russia" (interview with Gareth Jones), ibid., 30 March 1933, p. 12; David C. Engerman, "Modernization from the Other Shore: American Observers and the Costs of Soviet Economic Development," *American Historical Review* 105, no. 2 (April 2000): 383–416; Malcolm Muggeridge, *The Green Stick*, vol. 1 of *Chronicles of Wasted Times* (London: Fontana, 1981 [1973]), chapter 5, esp. 256–60, and Muggeridge, *Winter in Moscow* (Thirsk: Stratus, 2003 [1934]); "Andre Gide contre le fascisme," *L'Oeuvre*, 21 March 1933, p. 2.

17. "The Problem of Revision," *The Times*, 29 April 1933, p. 15; MAE 92 CP COM 312, Fleuriau (London) to Paul-Boncour, 29 April 1933.

18. "Germany Today: The Nationalist Movement," letter from E. L. Woodward, *The Times*, 27 March 1933, p. 8.

19. Edward W. Bennett, *German Rearmament and the West, 1932–1933* (Princeton, NJ: Princeton University Press, 1979), 377–78; MAE 117 CPCOM 985, Fleuriau (London) to Paul-Boncour, 16 May 1933.

20. "The Problem of Revision," *The Times*, 29 April 1933, p. 15; Maurice Cowling, *The Impact of Hitler: British Politics and British Policy, 1933–1940* (Cambridge: Cambridge University Press, 1975), 7, 18, 19–20; Helen McCarthy, *The British People and the League of Nations: Democracy, Citizenship, and Internationalism, c. 1918–1945* (Manchester: Manchester University Press, 2011), 4, 8–9.

21. Lucien Souchon, "L'affaire de Kehl. Ce n'est qu'un commencement," *Le Figaro*, 11 March 1933, p. 1; Emile Buré, "Scandale a Genève!," *L'Ordre*, 19 February 1933, p. 1; "De l'abstrait au concret," ibid., 18 February 1933, p. 1; "Toujours dans le marasme!," ibid., 15 February 1933.

22. Bertrand de Jouvenel, "Mort de l'Allemagne démocratique," *La République*, 11 March 1933, p. 1, and "Quand l'Allemagne bout," ibid., 16 February 1933, p. 1; Léon Blum, "Le réarmement de l'Allemagne et le désarmement général," *Le Populaire*, 12 March 1933, p. 1; *Le Figaro*, 27 December 1951, p. 1; "La déposition de Léon Blum devant la Commission sur les évènements de 1933 à 1945," cited in Wacław Jędrzejewicz, "The Polish Plan for a 'Preventive War' against Germany in 1933," *Polish Review* 11, no. 1 (Winter 1966): 62–91, n. 61.

23. Extensive German violations of the arms restrictions of Versailles (clause 213) did not carry provisions for immediate sanctions. Initiation of war by France would also have violated the terms of Locarno and deprived it of British support.

24. MAE, *Bulletin périodique de la presse polonaise,* 230 (9 February–23 March 1933), 231 (24 March–30 April 1933), and 232 (1 May–10 June 1933); for the end of Rapallo, see ibid., 231; *Illustrowany Kurjer Codzienny,* 29 March 1933, and *Czas,* 28 March 1933.

25. Fritz Kern, "Vier Jahre Staatskrise," *Vossische Zeitung,* 19 October 1932 (a.m.), p. 4.

26. USNA RG 59 862.00 vol. 84, Gordon to Hull, 27 March 1933.

27. "Wie Russlands Gold nach Westen rollt. 500 Millionen in Zwei Jahren," *Vossische Zeitung,* 6 October 1932 (p.m.).

28. MAE, 117CPCOM 985, containing note from Sûreté Générale to Herriot, 28 September 1932; ibid., François-Poncet to Herriot, 4 October 1932, Arnal (chargé d'affaires, Berlin) to Herriot, 20 October 1932, and General Renondeau (military attaché, Berlin) to Ministry of War, 25 October 1932.

29. Aleksandr M. Nekrich, *Pariahs, Partners, Predators: German-Soviet Relations, 1922–1941,* ed. and tr. Gregory L. Freeze (New York: Columbia University Press, 1997), 1–12.

30. Generaloberst von Seeckt, *Deutschland zwischen West und Ost* (Hamburg: Hanseatische Verlagsanstalt, 1933), 31, 45.

31. MAE 117CPCOM 985, François-Poncet to Paul-Boncour, 1 and 8 March 1933.

32. MAE 117CPCOM 985, François-Poncet to Paul-Boncour, 4 October 1932.

33. Jonathan Haslam, *Soviet Foreign Policy, 1930–33: The Impact of the Depression* (London: Macmillan, 1983), 7–9, 55–57, 97–106.

34. MAE 117CPCOM 986, François-Poncet (Berlin) to Paul-Boncour, 8 February and 1 March 1933; Dejean (Moscow) to Paul-Boncour, 1 February 1933.

35. See, e.g., "Hitler Denounces Democratic Foes," *New York Times*, 3 March 1933, p. 5; MAE 117CPCOM 986, French embassy Moscow, "Note sur les rapports germano-sovietiques," and Dejean to Paul-Boncour, 14, 27, 29–30 March 1933 (Tass cables and *Izvestia*); MAE 117CPCOM 985, French embassy Moscow to MAE, 3 March 1933.

36. USNA RG 59, T-1249, roll 5, Robert Skinner (Riga) to Stimson, 20 January 1933 ("wolf" comment and Stalin speech); roll 6, Felix Cole (Riga) to Hull, 24 March and 16 June 1933 (January plenary session); Haslam, *Soviet Foreign Policy 1930–1933*, 4–6.

37. MAE 117CP COM 960, Payart (chargé d'affaires Moscow) to Paul-Boncour, 10 May and 2 June 1933; Jonathan Haslam, *The Soviet Union and the Struggle for Collective Security in Europe, 1933–39* (London: Macmillan, 1984), 1–26; Jonathan Haslam, *The Soviet Union and the Threat from the East, 1933–1941: Moscow, Tokyo, and the Prelude to the Pacific War* (Pittsburgh: University of Pittsburgh Press, 1992), 11–27.

38. "Soviet Police Seize 4 Britons in Raids," *New York Times*, 13 March 1933, p. 7; MAE 117CP COM 960, Dejean (Moscow) to Paul-Boncour, 16 April 1933; Muggeridge, *Green Stick*, 260–61.

39. MAE 117CP COM 960, Dejean (Moscow) to Paul-Boncour, 12 February 1933; Payart to Paul-Boncour, 2 June 1933.

40. MAE 117 CPCOM 985, François-Poncet to Paul-Boncour, 1 March and 5 April 1933; press notes from French embassy, Berlin, 3 March and 12 April 1933; MAE 117CP COM 960, François-Poncet to Paul-Boncour, 11 July 1933; "Russland in Aktion," *Vossische Zeitung*, 9 July 1933, p. 4.

41. Nekrich, *Partners and Pariahs*, 40–50, 63–70.

42. MAE 117 CPCOM 985, François-Poncet (Berlin) to Paul-Boncour, 29 April, 3 and 6 May 1933; Dejean (Moscow) to Paul-Boncour, 6 May 1933; "Berliner Vertrag Verlängert," *Vossische Zeitung*, 6 May 1933, p. 4.

43. MAE 117 CPCOM 985, François-Poncet (Berlin) to Paul-Boncour, 16 March, 29 April, and 3 May 1933.

44. Nekrich, *Partners and Pariahs*, 65–101; John Scott, *Behind the Urals: An American Worker in Russia's City of Steel* (Bloomington: Indiana University Press, 1973 [1942]), 113; cf. A. V. Golubev, *"Esli mir obrushitsia na nashu Respubliku . . .": Sovestkoe obshchestvo i vneshniaia ugroza v 1920–1940-e gg.* ["If the world descends on our Republic . . .": Soviet society and the external threat, 1920s–1940s] (Moscow: Kuchkovo pole, 2008), 268: "To a great extent, images of the external world created by Soviet caricature of the 1920s and 1930s . . . defined the foreign-policy stereotypes of a significant portion

of the Soviet society of those years." I am grateful to April French for identifying and translating parts of this work for me.

45. Golubev, 40–43, 65–70.
46. Santi Corvaja, *Hitler and Mussolini: The Secret Meetings*, tr. R. L. Miller (New York: Enigma, 2001), 7–9; Robert Mallett, *Mussolini in Ethiopia, 1919–1935* (New York: Cambridge University Press, 2015), 42–46.
47. Corvaja, *Hitler and Mussolini*, 171–78; Nicholas Farrell, *Mussolini: A New Life* (London: Weidenfeld & Nicolson, 2003), 243, 246.
48. Mallett, *Mussolini*, 75–76; Corvaja, *Hitler and Mussolini*, 26.
49. John T. Lauridsen, *Nazism and the Radical Right in Austria, 1918–1934*, tr. Michael Wolfe (Copenhagen: Museum Tusculanum Press, 2007), 251–52; Arnold J. Toynbee, *Survey of International Affairs 1933* (London: Oxford University Press, 1934), 192–93, writing early in 1934, before the assassination of Dollfuss, described him as a new Austrian nationalist, and the Heimwehren in his coalition as "counter National Socialists."
50. AA, C, I, doc. 12, Hassell to AA, 6 February 1933, 14, Neurath to Hassell, 7 February 1933, doc. 27, Köpke to Hassell, 20 February 1933, doc. 35, Hassell to AA, 23 February 1933, doc. 51, Hassell to AA, 6 March 1933, doc. 64, Hassell to AA, 8 March 1933.
51. MAE 110CPCOM 178, François-Poncet (Berlin) to Paul-Boncour, 21 June 1933.
52. Laurisden, *Austria*, 251; *Le Temps*, 20, 21, and "L'affaire des armes de Hirtenberg," 22 February 1933, p. 1; "Big arms shipment to Hungary alleged and denied in Austria," *New York Times*, 10 January 1933, p. 10; "Shift by Austria laid to Mussolini," ibid., 21 February 1933, p. 4; "Austria abandons sharp arms note," ibid., 22 February 1933, p. 8; *Documents on German Foreign Policy, 1918–1945*, 14 vols. (Washington, DC: US Government Printing Office, 1949–1983), series C, 1933–1937, vol. 1, January 30–October 14, 1933, doc. 81, Circular of German Foreign Ministry, 13 March 1933 (Hirtenberg affair); USNA RG 59 862.00 vol. 84, Edge (Paris) to Stimson, 14 February 1932.
53. The three-power agreement was eventually signed on 17 March 1934.
54. BNF, Banque DOSS FOL-LN1–232 (21120, A), *Bulletin Quotidien* 12 June 1933, giving Mussolini's speech to the Senate on 7 June announcing the initialing of the pact.
55. DDF, I, vol. 3: François-Poncet (Berlin) to Paul-Boncour: doc. 15, 30 March 1933; doc. 70, 30 March 1933 (AA official confirms Foreign Ministry authorship of the speech, except for commercial passages).
56. Edward W. Bennett, *German Rearmament*, 367, 373–79; Angelo del Boca, *La Guerra d'Etiopia: L'Ultima impresa del colonialismo* (Milan: Longanesi, 2010), 49–51; Mallett, *Mussolini*, 50.
57. See, on the last Polish fear, Toynbee, *Survey 1933*, 185.
58. See pp. 163–65; MAE 106CPCOM-334, Laroche (Warsaw) to Paul-Boncour, 21 February 1933; DDF, I, vol. 3, doc. 91, d'Arbonneau (Warsaw) to Daladier, 5 April 1933.

59. DDF, I, vol. 3, doc. 24, Laroche (Warsaw) to Paul-Boncour, 21 March 1933, and doc. 87, Laroche to Paul-Boncour, 5 April 1933; Jules Laroche, *La Pologne de Pilsudski: Souvenirs d'une ambassade, 1926–1935* (Paris: Flammarion, 1953), 122–23.

60. "Anti-revision Pact Denied in Warsaw," *New York Times*, 26 April 1933, p. 8; MAE 106CPCOM-334, Laroche (Warsaw) to Paul-Boncour, 22 April 1933; Laroche, *Souvenirs*, 125; AA C, I, doc. 180, Moltke (Warsaw) to AA, 23 April 1933 (reporting 30,000 men in Vilna).

61. "Deutsche Kultur in Polnischen Land," *Vossische Zeitung*, 14 April 1933, p. 4; Toynbee, *Survey 1933*, 186–87; Laroche, *Souvenirs*, 107, 120; "Poles Fear Nazi Raid for Arms at Danzig," *New York Times*, 7 March 1933, p. 16.

62. AA C, I, doc. 167, Moltke (Warsaw) to AA, 19 April 1933 (meetings 6 and 12 April), and *Aufzeichnung* (minute), 12 April 1933; "Polish Jews' Protest," *The Times*, 24 April 1933, p. 11.

63. BNF Banque DOSS FOL-LN1-232 (21120, A), *Bulletin Quotidien*, 12 June 1933, Mussolini's speech to the Senate on 7 June; Laroche, *Souvenirs*, 121; AA, doc. 168, *Aufzeichnung* by Hey, Berlin, 20 April 1933.

64. Wacław Jędrzejewicz, "The Polish Plan for a 'Preventive War' against Germany in 1933," *Polish Review* 11, no. 1 (Winter 1966): 62–91, and Jameson W. Crocket, "The Polish Blitz, More than a Mere Footnote to History: Poland and Preventive War with Germany, 1933," *Diplomacy and Statecraft* 20, no. 4 (November 2009): 561–79 review accounts before and after the war of this controversial episode; AA, C, I, doc. 180, Moltke (Warsaw) to AA, 23 April 1933; ibid., doc. 183, Moltke to AA, 25 April 1933; ibid., doc. 184, Koch (Prague) to AA, 25 April 1933; DBFP, second series, vol. 5 (London: HMSO, 1933), no. 23, Rumbold (Berlin) to Simon, 7 April 1933; Jędrzejewicz, "Polish Plan," 74–75, 76; "Verbrecherische Kriegsgerüchte," *Vossische Zeitung*, 27 April 1933, p. 1.

65. AA, C, I, doc. 180, Moltke (Warsaw) to AA, 23 April 1933; MAE, 106CPCOM 334, Laroche (Warsaw) to Paul-Boncour, 4 April 1933.

66. AA, C, I, doc. 180, Moltke (Warsaw) to AA, 23 April 1933; AA, C, I, doc. 183, Moltke to AA, 25 April 1933; DDF, I, vol. 3, doc. 238, Laroche (Warsaw) to Paul-Boncour, 4 May 1933, n.1; Laroche, *Souvenirs*, 127.

67. AA, C, I, doc. 201, memorandum by von Neurath (who attended the meeting), 2 May 1933; DDF, I, vol. 3, doc. 238, Laroche (Warsaw) to Paul-Boncour, 4 May 1933.

68. DDF, I, vol. 3, doc. 91, d'Arbonneau, military attaché (Warsaw) to Daladier, 5 April 1933; MAE 106CPCOM-334, Laroche (Warsaw) to Paul-Boncour, 21 February, 6, 22 March, 1 June 1933.

69. MAE 118CPCOM 960, French ambassador Belgrade to Paul-Boncour, 25 April 1933.

70. MAE 110CPCOM-170, Puaux (Bucharest) to Briand, 19 September and 18 October 1931, and to Herriot, 30 June 1932, and to Paul-Boncour, 21 January 1933; MAE 110CPCOM-177, Puaux to Briand, 16 March, 29 June, 4 July,

30 November 1931; MAE 110CPCOM 178, Puaux to Paul-Boncour, 17 April 1933; Keith Hitchins, *Rumania 1866–1947* (Oxford: Oxford University Press, 1994), 437–38.

71. Toynbee, *Survey 1933*, 193–94; MAE 94CPCOM-109, de Vienne (Budapest) to Paul-Boncour, 17 May and 16 June 1933; for a near-contemporary account of Germanophile sentiment in Hungary, see C. A. Macartney, "Hungary and the Present Crisis," *International Affairs (Royal Institute of International Affairs 1931–1939)* 17, no. 6 (1938): 749–68, doi:10.2307/3019411.

72. MAE 94CPCOM-109, de Vienne (Budapest) to Paul-Boncour, 7 May 1933; AA, C, I, 2, von Schoen (Budapest) to AA, 21 June 1933; MAE 94CPCOM-109, de Vienne (Budapest) to Paul-Boncour, 16 June 1933.

73. AA, C, I, 2, von Hassell (Rome) to AA, 30 June 1933; Toynbee, *Survey 1933*, 195, 206.

74. DDF, I, vol. 3, doc. 397, de Vienne (Budapest) to Paul-Boncour, 16 June 1933; ibid., doc. 290, de Vienne (Budapest) to Paul-Boncour, 17 May 1933.

75. Wilhelm Deist et al., *Ursachen und Voraussetzungen des Zweiten Weltkrieges*, vol. 1 (1989 [1979]) of *Das deutsche Reich und der zweite Weltkrieg*, 9 vols. (14 vols. projected) (Freiburg: Militärgeschichtliches Forschungsamt, 1979–2014), 463–79; see pp. 193–94.

76. Deist, *Ursachen* und *Vorraussetzungen*, 634; Bennett, *German Rearmament*, 330, 348.

77. MAE PA-AP 166 505 (Archives Tardieu), memorandum by Lt.-Col. Louis Koeltz of his meeting with Blomberg, 20 February 1932.

78. Bennett, *German Rearmament*, 329–30, 362–63; Conan Fischer, *Stormtroopers: A Social, Economic, and Ideological Analysis, 1929–35* (London: George Allen & Unwin, 1983), 6.

79. Paul Schmidt, *Statist auf diplomatischer Bühne 1923–1945, Erlebnisse des Chefdolmetschers im auswärtigen Amt mit den Staatsmännern Europas* (Bonn: Athenäum, 1950), 261–63.

80. See chapter 10, p. 270.

81. Detlev Clemens, *Herr Hitler in Germany: Wahrnehmung und Deutungen des Nationalsozialismus in Grossbritannien, 1920 bis 1939* (Göttingen and Zurich: German Historical Institute, Vandenboeck & Ruprecht: 1996), 286–89; DBFP, second series, vol. 5, doc. 127, Cadogan (Geneva) to Leeper, 10 May 1933, enclosing Temperley memo, and n. 1 (Vansittart's support and distribution to cabinet), 16 May.

82. Maurice Vaïsse, *Sécurité d'abord: La Politique française en matière de désarmement, 9 décembre 1930–17 avril 1934* (Paris: Pedone/Publications de la Sorbonne, 1981), 360–65.

83. Breitman and Lichtman, *FDR and the Jews*, 58–66.

84. Bennett, *German Rearmament*, 385–86; Vaïsse, *Sécurité*, 390–99; MAE 75CPCOM 537, François-Poncet (Berlin) to Paris, 17, 18, 19 March 1933, and Massigli (Geneva) to Paris, 17 March 1933.

85. MAE 75CPCOM 537, Massigli (Geneva) to US delegates, 18 March 1933.

86. MAE 75CPCOM 537: Noël (Prague) to Paris, 17 March 1933; Massigli (Geneva) to Paris, 18 March 1933 and to US delegation in Geneva, 18 March 1933; Joseph Paul-Boncour to Paris, 19 March 1933; Corbin (Brussels) to Paris, 21 March 1933.

87. Walter Lippmann with Council on Foreign Relations, *The United States in World Affairs: An Account of American Foreign Relations, 1933* (New York: Harper & Brothers, 1934), 54–63; MAE 75CPCOM 537, note of Direction politique about Massigli conversation with Davis, 7 April 1933.

88. MAE 75CPCOM 538, military attaché Budapest to Paris, 1 May 1933.

89. Vaïsse, *Sécurité*, 390–99; MAE 75CPCOM 537, Jouvenel (Rome) to Paris, 25 April 1933.

90. Philip Williamson and Edward Baldwin, ed., *Baldwin Papers: A Conservative Statesman, 1907–1948* (Cambridge: Cambridge University Press, 2004), Baldwin to Cecil, 12 March 1933.

91. DBFP, second series, vol. 5, doc. 88, Patterson (Geneva) to Simon, 25 April 1933; DDF, I, vol. 3, doc. 197, Note de la délégation française à la conférence du désarmement, 27 April 1933.

92. Lippmann, *United States 1933*, 65.

93. DBFP, second series, vol. 5, Patterson (Geneva) to Simon, 27 April 1933.

94. "Our Stand on Consultation," *New York Times*, 11 May 1933, p. 11; "Italy Yields Point at Arms Parley," ibid., 11 May 1933, p. 11; "Security Pledged only on Set Terms," ibid., 6 May 1933, p. 3; "Recall of Davis Urged in Senate," ibid., 26 May 1933; Raymond Moley, *After Seven Years* (New York: Harper & Brothers, 1939), 90–94, 163–64, 319; Cordell Hull, *The Memoirs of Cordell Hull*, vol. 1 (New York: Macmillan, 1948), 227–28; Frank H. Simonds, *America Faces the Next War* (New York: Harper & Brothers, 1933), xvi–xvii, 71–79; Charles A. Beard, *American Foreign Policy in the Making, 1932–1940: A Study in Responsibilities* (New Haven, CT: Yale University Press, 1946), 123–30; SHD (Vincennes) GR 1 N42 , note on MacArthur meeting with Weygand, 2 October 1932.

95. "Nazi Book Burning Fails to Stir Berlin," *New York Times*, 11 May 1933, p. 1; "100,000 March Here in Protest over Nazi Policies," ibid.; "Simon and Hitler Envoy in Angry Session," ibid.; "House of Commons: Herr Rosenberg's Visit," *The Times*, 11 May 1933, p. 7; DBFP, second series, vol. 5, doc. 118, Simon to Rumbold, 8 May 1933, and 138, Simon to Rumbold, 11 May 1933.

96. Armand Bérard, *Un ambassadeur se souvient* (Paris: Plon, 1976), 194–95; DDF, I, vol. 3, doc. 143, François-Poncet (Berlin) to Paul-Boncour, 19 April 1933; ibid., doc. 122, Daladier to Paul-Boncour; DBFP, second series, vol. 5, doc. 127, Cadogan (Geneva) to Leeper, 10 May 1933. The number of SA was even higher; see pp. 193–94.

97. DBFP, second series, vol. 5, doc. 124, Patterson (Geneva) to Simon, 10 May 1933; MAE 75CPCOM 538, François-Poncet (Berlin) to Paris, 11 May 1933; DDF, I, vol. 3, doc. 239, Massigli (Geneva) to Paul-Boncour, 4 May 1933; ibid., doc. 263, François-Poncet (Berlin) to Paul-Boncour, 11 May 1933.

98. DDF, I, vol. 3, doc. 145, François-Poncet to Paul-Boncour, 20 April 1933; ibid., doc. 185, Paul-Boncour to de Jouvenel, 26 April 1933; ibid., doc. 332, François-Poncet (Berlin) to Paul-Boncour, 30 May 1933.

99. DBFP, second series, vol. 5, doc. 127, Cadogan (Geneva) to Leeper, 10 May 1933, enclosing Temperley memo.

100. "The Lesson of Fulham," *News Chronicle*, 27 October 1933; "Fulham's Victor Asks for Five More Peace Verdicts," *Daily Herald*, 30 October 1933; Vansittart, *Mist Procession*, 478, 481; Vaïsse, *Sécurité d'abord*, 65–70; Edouard Réquin, *D'une guerre à l'autre (1919–1939): Souvenirs* (Paris: Charles Lavauzelle, 1949), 179–83; Robert Dallek, *Franklin D. Roosevelt and American Foreign Policy, 1932–1945* (New York: Oxford University Press, 1995 [1979]), 35–36; Hull, *Memoirs*, 222–27.

101. See p. 241.

102. Bérard, *Ambassadeur*, 192.

12: WASHINGTON CLOSES ANOTHER DOOR

1. Frank Freidel, *Franklin D. Roosevelt: The Ordeal* (Boston: Little, Brown, 1954), 78–81, 135–37, 235.

2. Sebastian Edwards, *American Default: The Untold Story of FDR, the Supreme Court, and the Battle over Gold* (Princeton, NJ: Princeton University Press, 2018), 13–20; "Hoover Attack Sweeping," *New York Times*, 1 November 1932, p. 1.

3. Chatham House Archives, RIIA/8/289, "American Public Opinion on the World Economic Conference," discussion at Chatham House, London, 13 July 1933; Edwards, *American Default*, 51–53; Walter Lippmann with Council on Foreign Relations, *The United States in World Affairs. An Account of American Foreign Relations, 1932* (New York: Harper & Brothers, 1933), 72–73.

4. Raymond Moley, *After Seven Years* (New York: Harper & Brothers, 1939), 121; R. G. Tugwell, *The Brains Trust* (New York: Viking, 1968), appendix: "Proposal for an Economic Council"; Edwards, *Default*, 7.

5. Edwards, *American Default*; Lippmann, *Survey 1933*, 74; "Roosevelt Demands 'National Income' be Redistributed," *New York Times,* 23 May 1932, p. 1.

6. Moley, *Seven Years*, 160.

7. "London and Washington. Our Budget and their Currency," *Sunday Times* (London), 23 April 1933, p. 16.

8. Edwards, *Default*, 80–81; "French Cabinet and Currency" and "Anglo-American Talks in Full Swing," *Sunday Times*, 23 April 1932, p. 17; "M. Herriot devant la situation créée par l'abandon du dollar-or," *Le Petit Parisien*, 21 April 1933, p. 1.

9. "City Chatter: Dollar Decision's Effect on Stock Markets," *Sunday Times*, 23 April 1933, p. 2.

10. Lippmann, *Survey 1933*, 76–80; Edwards, *Default*, 68–69.

11. "Anglo-American Talks in Full Swing," *Sunday Times*, 23 April 1932, p. 17; "Les Entretiens Franco-Anglais-Américains de Washington. L'automobile de M. Herriot entre en Collision avec un Car," *Le Petit Journal*, 25 April 1933; "Les Conversations de Washington: La Journée de M. Herriot," ibid., 26 April 1933, p. 1.

12. "America off Gold," *The Times*, 21 April 1933, p. 13; "The Fall of the Dollar," *Economist*, 22 April 1933, pp. 849–50; "La crise du dollar et les entretiens de Washington," *Le Temps*, 21 April 1933, p. 1.

13. Jacques Bainville, "Confusion et inquiétude," *Action Française*, 27 April 1933, p. 1; "La bataille monétaire," *Le Figaro*, 22 April 1933, p. 1, and "La Politique: La Leçon de l'oncle Sam," ibid., 23 April 1933, p. 1; "Le dollar," *Le Temps*, 22 April 1933, p. 1; Léon Blum, "Une révolution en amérique," *Le Populaire*, 22 April 1933, p. 1.

14. "M. Daladier, dans un grand discours à Orange, fait applaudir la politique française," *L'Oeuvre*, 24 April 1933, pp. 1, 4 (full text in MAE 75CPCOM 74, Relations Commerciales [Paris] to Washington embassy, 24 April 1933).

15. See, e.g., "La politique: La cour des miracles," *Le Figaro*, 15 June 1933, p. 1; Lucien Romier, "L'échec de la conférence de Londres est moins dangereux pour la France que pour d'autres nations," *Le Petit Parisien*, 5 July 1933, p. 1; Pertinax, "La conférence de Londres," *Echo de Paris*, 7 July 1933, p. 1.

16. André Tardieu, *Devant l'obstacle: L'Amérique et nous* (Paris: Emile-Paul Frères, 1927), 282–88; Robert Dallek, *Franklin D. Roosevelt and American Foreign Policy, 1932–1945* (Oxford: Oxford University Press, 1995 [1979]), 37–38.

17. "Le désarmement économique," *Action Française*, 21 January 1933, p. 1; MAE, 75CPCOM74, Fleuriau (London) to Paul-Boncour, 9 May 1933; ibid., François-Poncet to Berlin, 12, 13, 14 June 1933; MAE 75CPCOM75, Laroche (Warsaw) to Paul-Boncour, 28 June 1933.

18. Adam Tooze, *The Wages of Destruction: The Making and Breaking of the Nazi Economy* (New York: Penguin, 2008 [2006]), 41, 51; Patricia Clavin, *Securing the World Economy: The Reinvention of the League of Nations, 1920–1946* (Oxford: Oxford University Press, 2015 [2013]), 104–5 and n64.

19. Clavin, *Securing the World Economy*, 106–7; Lippmann, *Survey 1933*, 104–5; "The World Conference," *The Times*, 10 May 1933, p. 15.

20. Lippmann, *Survey 1933*, 101; Clavin, *Securing*, 102–3, 114; DDF, I, vol. 3, doc. 258, "Note de la Direction des Relations Commerciales" (MAE), 9 May 1933; "The Tariff Truce," *The Times*, 15 May 1933, p. 15, and "Trade Agreements," ibid., 19 May 1933, p. 15.

21. "World Economic Conference," *The Times*, 27 February 1933, p. 6; Lippmann, *Survey 1933*, 121–22, 125–26; "Bulletin du Jour: Le discours de M. Daladier," *Le Temps*, 11 June 1933, p. 1.

22. Clavin, *Securing*, 107; "Hull, Sailing, Hopes for Lower Tariffs," *New York Times*, 31 May 1933, p. 3; Moley, *Seven Years*, 207.

23. Cordell Hull, *The Memoirs of Cordell Hull*, vol. 1 (New York: Macmillan, 1948), 161, 198, 204–5; Tugwell, *Brains Trust*, 475–76.

24. Moley, *Seven Years*, 217; Lippmann, *Survey 1933*, 125–29; "America off Gold," *The Times*, 21 April 1933, p. 13; Cavin, *Securing*, 120.

25. Paul Schmidt, *Statist auf diplomatischer Bühne, 1923–1945, Erlebnisse des Chefdolmetschers im auswärtigen Amt mit den Staatsmännern Europas* (Bonn: Athenaeum-Verlag, 1950), 267; "Georges V a solenellement inauguré la conférence économique mondiale," *Le Petit Parisien*, 13 June 1933, p. 1; "Quick Settlement Asked," *New York Times*, 13 June 1932, p. 1; "The King's Speech," *The Times*, 13 June 1933, p. 9.

26. Schmidt, 265–67.

27. Schmidt, 265; "Bid by Hugenberg for Prestige Seen," *New York Times*, 18 June 1933, p. 22; "Dr. Hugenberg's Note Criticized in London," ibid., 19 June 1933, p. 2; "Soviet Is Angered by Hugenberg Aim," ibid., 20 June 1933, p. 4; "Les délégués du Reich suggèrent qu'un empire colonial soit restitué à l'Allemagne," *Le Petit Parisien*, 17 June 1933, p. 3.

28. "Le Discours de M. MacDonald et le Problème des Dettes," *Le Petit Parisien*, 13 June 1933, p. 1; "M. Daladier a exposé le point de vue français," ibid., 14 June 1933, and "La séance de l'après-midi," p. 3; "Les chefs des délégations apportent à la tribune les thèses de leurs pays," ibid., 15 June 1933.

29. Moley, *Seven Years*, 227; "Barriers to Trade Assailed by Hull," *New York Times*, 15 June 1933, p. 3; "The King's Speech," *The Times*, 13 June 1933, p. 9, and "US Views on the Conference," p. 10.

30. Lippmann, *Survey 1933*, 129; "L'Europe et l'Amérique," *Le Journal des Débats*, 15 June 1933, p. 1, and "Les Illusions de la Conférence," 18 June 1933; "Bulletin du Jour: Les Etats-Unis et la Conférence de Londres," *Le Temps*, 24 June 1933, p. 1.

31. TNA, T 188/71, cabinet committee on the conference, May 1933, including telegram from Lindsay (Washington), 24 May 1933.

32. MAE 75CPCOM 75, Coulondre (London) to Paul-Boncour, 30 June 1933; charge d'affaires Belgrade to Paul-Boncour, 1 July 1933; Laboulaye (Washington) to Paul-Boncour, 30 June 1933.

33. Moley, *Seven Years*, 236, 240.

34. Moley, *Seven Years*, 233, 239n.29; Clavin, *Securing*, 118–20; Lippmann, *Survey 1933*, 132.

35. FDR Presidential Library, Significant Documents Collection, FDR 9-A box 156, draft of message of 3 July 1933.

36. Clavin, *Securing*, 120; Walter Layton, "After the World Economic Conference," *Foreign Affairs* 12, no. 1 (October 1933): 20–29.

37. FDR Presidential Library, Presidential Press Conferences, series 1, transcripts, no. 32, 7 July 1932 (asked again, Roosevelt acknowledged neutrally that some nations at London might still talk about monetary matters); "London Gets Message," *New York Times*, 4 July 1933, p. 1; Walter Lippmann,

"Today and Tomorrow: High and Mighty Language," *Los Angeles Times*, 5 July 1933, p. A4; *Le Petit Parisien*, 5 July 1933, p. 1; Romier, "L'échec de la Conférence de Londres est moins dangereux pour la France que pour d'autres nations"; Pertinax, "La conférence de Londres," *Echo de Paris*, 7 July 1933, p. 1; *Ami du Peuple*, 7 July 1933, p. 1.

38. Leopold Amery, "Work Left for the Conference," *The Times*, 8 July 1933, p. 13; MAE 75CPCOM76, Corbin (London) to Paul-Boncour, 24 July 1933.

39. *Asahi*, n.d. cited in "An International Anarchy," *Japan Weekly Chronicle*, 20 July 1933, p. 74.

40. MAE, 75CPCOM75, François-Poncet (Berlin) to Paul-Boncour, 4, 5, 7 July 1933.

41. MAE 75CPCOM 75, de Jouvenel (Rome) to Paul-Boncour, 4 July 1933; details on La Tribuna in MAE 97 CPCOM 366–1, long report on Italian press from Dampierre, Rome, to Paul-Boncour, 19 December 1932.

42. MAE 74CPCOM 75, French ambassador (Brussels) to Paul-Boncour, 6 July 1933.

43. "Salvage Operations," *New York Times*, 5 July 1933, p. 18; "Foreign Exchange," ibid., 6 July, p. 20.

44. Walter Lippmann, "Today and Tomorrow: High and Mighty Language," 5 July 1933, in *New York Herald Tribune*, *Los Angeles Times*, etc.

45. "Economic Jingoism," *New York Herald Tribune*, 1 July 1933, p. 8; ibid., 5 July 1933, "French Press Bitterly Assails Roosevelt Role" and "Roosevelt's Currency Program Still Puzzles Capital Observers," both p. 7; ibid., 5 July 1933, "The Great Improvisator," p. 10; MAE 75CPCOM 75, Laboulaye (Washington) to Paul-Boncour, 2, 4, 6 July 1933.

46. MAE 75CPCOM 75, Laboulaye to Paris, 4 July 1933.

47. "The Reactionary Parley," *New York American*, 1 July 1933, p. 10; "The New Independence Day" (cartoon), ibid., 4 July 1933, p. 10; "Pest Swatting Time" (cartoon), ibid., 5 July 1933, p. 12; "Safe and Sound" (cartoon), ibid., 6 July 1933, p. 12; "New Americanism," ibid., 7 July 1933, p. 12.

48. "This Thing of Trade," *Saturday Evening Post* 206, no. 1 (1 July 1933): 5–10; "Volunteers for Industrial Death," ibid. 206, no. 2 (8 July 1933): 8–10.

49. "The Conference Totters," *Los Angeles Times*, 5 July 1933, p. A4; "Realism for London," *Wall Street Journal*, 6 July 1933, p. 6.

50. "Independence Day—1933" (cartoon), *New York Evening Post* (previously and later the *New York Post*), 6 July 1933, p. 8, and "New Americanism," ibid., 3 July 1933, p. 8.

51. Moley, *Seven Years*, 270.

52. "Opening of the Conference," *The Times*, 13 June 1933, p. 9, and "The Afternoon Session," ibid., 15 June 1933, p. 9; Sir Walter Layton, "The Tasks of the World Economic Conference," *Foreign Affairs* 11, 3 (April 1933): 406–19.

53. Layton, "After the World Economic Conference," *Foreign Affairs* 12, 1 (October 1933): 20–29.

54. Charles H. Feinstein, Peter Temin, and Gianni Toniolo, *The World Economy between the Wars* (New York: Oxford University Press, 2008), 165–67.

EPILOGUE: GENEVA

1. Robert Dell, *The Geneva Racket* (London: Robert Hale, 1941), 104; Paul Schmidt, *Statist auf diplomatischer Bühne, 1923–1945, Erlebnisse des Chefdolmetschers im auswärtigen amt mit den Staatsmännern Europas* (Bonn, 1950), 277–81; the famous photo was taken by Alfred Eisenstaedt, who described the circumstances in *Eisenstaedt on Eisenstaedt: A Self-Portrait* (New York: Abbeville Press, 1985), 60–61.
2. Major General A. C. Temperley, *The Whispering Gallery of Europe* (London: Collins, 1938), 252; Hugh R. Wilson, *Diplomat between Wars* (London: Longmans, Green, 1941), 263.
3. Temperley, *Whispering Gallery*, 254–56; Edward W. Bennett, *German Rearmament and the West, 1932–1933* (Princeton, NJ: Princeton University Press, 1979), 471–74; Maurice Vaïsse, *Sécurité d'abord: La Politique française en matière de désarmement, 9 décembre 1930–17 avril 1934* (Paris: Pedone/Publications de la Sorbonne, 1981), 462–68; Salvador de Madariaga, *Morning without Noon: Memoirs* (Westmead: Saxon House, 1973), 277; Norman Hillson, *Geneva Scene* (London: Routledge, 1936), 170–78.
4. Bennett, *German Rearmament*, 475–80, 485–90; "Hitler Smiles at Ovations Given by Festive Crowds," *New York Times*, 13 November 1933, p. 1.
5. Dell, *Geneva Racket*, 104–5; Vaïsse, *Sécurité*, 469–73; MAE, E 117, Martel (Tokyo) to Paul-Boncour, 19 June 1933.
6. "2,330-Pound Book of Peace Unveiled," *New York Times*, 17 October 1933, p. 19.
7. Geneviève Tabouis, *Vingt Ans de "Suspense," Diplomatique* (Paris: Albin Michel, 1958), 160.

Bibliography

I. PRIMARY PUBLISHED MATERIALS

A. Official Publications

Documents Diplomatiques Français, 1932–1939
Series I, vol. 2, 15 November 1932–17 March 1933. Paris: Imprimerie Nationale, 1966.
Series I, vol. 3, 17 March–15 July 1933. Paris: Imprimerie Nationale, 1967.
Documents on British Foreign Policy, 1919–1939
2nd Series, vol. 4, 1932–1933. London: MMSO, 1950.
2nd Series, vol. 5, 1933. London: HMSO.
Foreign Relations of the United States, 1933. Vol. 2. Washington, DC: Department of State, 1948.
Documents on German Foreign Policy, 1918–1945. Series C, 1933–1937, vol. 1. Washington, DC: US Government Printing Office, 1949–1983 (14 vols.).
Akten zur Deutschen Auswärtigen Politik 1918–1945 aus dem Archiv des Auswärtigen Amts, Series C: 1933–1937 Das dritte Reich: Die ersten Jahre. Vol. 1, part 1 (30 January–15 May 1933) and part 2 (16 May–14 October 1933). Göttingen: Vandenhoeck und Ruprecht, 1971.
League of Nations. *Appeal by the Chinese Government: Report of the Commission of Inquiry*. Geneva, 1 October 1932.
———. *Draft of the Report Provided for in Article 15, Paragraph 4, of the Covenant*. Geneva, 16 February 1933.
———. *World Economic Survey, 1932–3*. Geneva, September 1933.
———. *Rapport de la délégation de l'or du comité financier de la Société des Nations*. Geneva: Société des Nations, June 1932.

Ministère des Affaires Etrangères (Paris):

Bulletin périodique de la presse anglaise, 339, 23 November–28 December 1932.
———, 230, 9 February–23 March 1933.
———, 231, 24 March–30 April 1933.
Bulletin périodique de la presse russe, 224, 8 octobre–30 novembre 1932.
———, 226, 3 janvier–12 février 1933.

B. Other Published Collections

Domarus, Max, ed. *Hitler: Reden und Proklamationen, 1932–1945.* Vol. 1. Munich: Süddeutscher Verlag, 1965.

Hitler: Reden, Schriften, Anordnungen. Vol. 5, parts 1, 2. New York: K. G. Saur, 1998.

Noakes, J., and G. Pridham, eds. *Nazism, 1919–1945: A Documentary Reader.* Vol. 1. Exeter: University of Exeter Press, 1998–2001 (1983–1998).

Plöckinger, Othmar, ed. *Quellen und Dokumente zur Geschichte von "Mein Kampf," 1924–1945.* Stuttgart: Franz Steiner, 2016.

———. *Schlüsseldokumente zur international Rezeption von "Mein Kampf."* Stuttgart: Franz Steiner, 2016.

Bibliothèque Nationale (Paris) DOSS Dossiers of News Cuttings

FOL-LN1–232–10564: Gyula Gömbös.
FOL-LN1–232–11892: Edouard Herriot.
FOL LN1–232–18137: John Simon.
FOL-LN1–232–21120 A: Benito Mussolini.
FOL-LN1–232–17309: Austen Chamberlain.

C. Newspapers and Periodicals

China: *China Weekly Review, North China Herald and Supreme Court and Consular Gazette.*

France: *L'Avenir, Commentaires, Les Débats, L'Echo de Paris, Ere nouvelle, L'Europe nouvelle, Le Figaro, L'Humanité, Journal des Débats, Le Petit Journal, Le Petit Parisien, Le Populaire, Le Matin, L'Oeuvre, L'Ordre, La République, Le Temps.*

Germany: *Deutsche Allgemeine Zeitung, Kreuzzeitung, Völkischer Beobachter, Vossische Zeitung.*

Great Britain: *Daily Express, Daily Herald, Daily Mail, Daily Telegraph, Economist, Evening Standard, Financial Times, Manchester Guardian, Morning Post, New Statesman, News Chronicle, Observer, Sunday Referee, Sunday Times, The Times, Yorkshire Post.*

Italy: *Il Giornale d'Italia, Corriere della Sera.*

Japan: *Asahi* (Tokyo or Osaka), *Chugai Shogyo, Fukuoka Nichi Nichi, Hochi, Japan Times, Japan Chronicle Weekly Edition, Jiji, Jiji Shimpo, Miyako, Yomiuri, Osaka Mainichi.*

Poland: *Gazeta Polska, Gazeta Warszawska.*

Soviet Union: *Izvestia, Pravda, Zaria Voskoka.*

Switzerland: *Journal de Genève.*

Yugoslavia: *L'Echo de Belgrade.*

USA: *Baltimore Evening Sun, Chicago Daily Tribune, International Herald Tribune, Ladies' Home Journal, The Nation, New York American, New York Evening Post, New York Herald Tribune, New Republic, Saturday Evening Post, Time.*

D. Memoirs, Diaries, and Letters

Bartlett, Vernon. *Intermission in Europe: The Life of a Journalist and Broadcaster.* New York: Oxford, 1938.

Bérard, Armand. *Au temps du danger allemand.* Vol. 1 of *Un ambassadeur se souvient.* Paris: Plon, 1976–1982 (5 vols.).

Bülow, Bernhard Fürst von. *Denkwürdigkeiten in vier Bänden.* Vol. 2. Berlin: Ullstein, 1930.

Butterfield, Isabel. *Manhattan Tales, 1920–45.* Lewes, UK: Book Guild, 1999.

Churchill, W. S. *The Gathering Storm.* Vol. 1 of *The Second World War.* Boston: Houghton Mifflin, 1948–1953 (6 vols.).

Cowley, Malcolm. *The Dream of the Golden Mountains: Remembering the 1930s.* New York: Penguin, 1981 (1964).

Davies, R. W., et al., eds. *The Stalin-Kaganovich Correspondence, 1931–1936.* New Haven, CT: Yale University Press, 2003.

Eisenstaedt, Alfred. *Eisenstaedt on Eisenstaedt: A Self-Portrait.* New York: Abbeville Press, 1985.

François-Poncet, André. *Souvenirs d'une ambassade à Berlin, septembre 1931–octobre 1938.* Paris: Flammarion, 1946.

Gelb, Michael, ed. *An American Engineer in Stalin's Russia: The Memoirs of Zara Witkin, 1932–1934.* Berkeley: University of California Press, 1992.

Goebbels, Joseph. *Tagebücher, 1924–1945.* Vol. 2. Edited by Ralf Georg Reuth. Munich: Piper, 2003 (1992).

———. *Die Tagebücher von Joseph Goebbels.* Part I, 1923–1941, vol. 2/III. Edited by Elke Fröhlich. New York: K. G. Saur, 1998–2006.

Grandi, Dino. *Il mio paese: Ricordi autobiografici.* Bologna: Il Mulino, 1985.

Grew, Joseph C. *Ten Years in Japan: A Contemporary Record Drawn from the Diaries and Private and Official Papers of Joseph C. Grew.* New York: Simon & Schuster, 1944.

Guéhenno, Jean. *Journal d'un homme de quarante ans.* Paris: Grasset, 1934.

Hoggart, Richard. *A Local Habitation.* Vol. 1 of *Life and Times.* London: Chatto & Windus, 1988–1992 (3 vols.).

Hull, Cordell. *The Memoirs of Cordell Hull.* Vol. 1. New York: Macmillan, 1948.

James, Robert Rhodes, ed. *Winston S. Churchill: His Complete Speeches, 1897–1963.* Vol. 5. London: Chelsea House, 1974.

Jones, Thomas. *A Diary with Letters, 1931–1950.* New York: Oxford University Press, 1954.

Kessler, Harry Graf. *Tagebücher, 1918–1937.* Frankfurt-am-Main: Insel, 1961.

Klemperer, Victor. *Ich will Zeugnis ablegen bis zum letzten: Tagebücher, 1933–1934.* Berlin: Aufbau Verlag, 2006 (1995).

Koestler, Arthur. *The Invisible Writing: An Autobiography.* New York: Macmillan, 1954.

Kravchenko, Victor. *I Chose Freedom: The Personal and Political Life of a Soviet Official.* New Brunswick, NJ: Transaction, 1989 (1946).

Kuramoto, Kazuko. *Manchurian Legacy: Memoirs of a Japanese Colonist.* East Lansing: Michigan State University Press, 1999.

Lamont, Corliss, and Margaret Lamont. *Russia Day by Day: A Travel Diary*. New York: Covici-Friede, 1933.

Laroche, Jules. *La Pologne de Pilsudski: Souvenirs d'une ambassade, 1926–1935*. Paris: Flammarion, 1953.

Lévi-Strauss, Claude. *"Chers tous deux": Lettres à ses parents, 1931–1942*. Edited by Monique Lévi-Strauss. Paris: Seuil, 2015.

Lih, Lars T., Oleg V. Naumov, and Oleg V. Khlevniuk, eds. *Stalin's Letters to Molotov, 1925–1936*. New Haven, CT: Yale University Press, 1995.

Lloyd George, David. *War Memoirs*. Vol. 1. Boston: Little, Brown, 1933.

Lyons, Eugene. *Assignment in Utopia*. New York: Harcourt, Brace, 1937.

Madariaga, Salvador de. *Morning without Noon: Memoirs*. Westmead: Heath, 1974.

Mann, Klaus. *Der Wendepunkt: Ein Lebensbericht*. Hamburg: Rowohlt Taschenbuch Verlag, 2006 (1952).

Moley, Raymond. *After Seven Years*. New York: Harper & Brothers, 1939.

Muggeridge, Malcolm. *The Green Stick*. Vol. 1 of *Chronicles of Wasted Time*. London: Collins, 1972–1973 (2 vols.).

———. *The Infernal Grove*. Vol. 2 of *Chronicles of Wasted Time*. London: Fontana, 1981 (1973).

Nehru, Jawaharlal. *An Autobiography*. New Delhi: Penguin Books India, 2004 (1936).

Nicolson, Harold. *Diaries & Letters, 1930–1939*. New York: Athenaeum, 1966.

Podlubnyi, Stepan. *Tagebuch aus Moskau, 1931–1939, Aus dem Russischen übersetzt und herausgegeben von Jochen Hellbeck*. Munich: Deutscher Taschenbuch Verlag, 1996.

Réquin, Edouard. *D'une guerre à l'autre (1919–1939): Souvenirs*. Paris: Charles-Lavauzelle, 1949.

Roosevelt, Elliott, ed. *F.D.R.: His Personal Letters, 1928–1945*. Vol. 1. New York: Duell, Sloane, and Pierce, 1950.

Rose, Lisle A. *The Breaking Storm*. Vol. 2 of *Power at Sea*. Columbia: University of Missouri Press, 2007 (3 vols.).

Schmidt, Paul. *Statist auf diplomatischer Bühne, 1923–1945: Erlebnisse des Chefdolmetschers im auswärtigen Amt mit den Staatsmännern Europas*. Bonn: Athenaeum-Verlag, 1950.

Scott, John. *Behind the Urals: An American Worker in Russia's City of Steel*. Bloomington: Indiana University Press, 1973 (1942).

Serge, Victor. *Memoirs of a Revolutionary*. Translated by Peter Sedgwick and George Paizis. New York: New York Review Books, 2012 (1951).

Simenon, Georges. *Mes apprentissages: Reportages, 1931–1946*. Paris: Omnibus, 2001.

Stimson, Henry L. *On Active Service in Peace and War*. New York: Harper & Brothers, 1948 (1947).

———. *The Far Eastern Crisis: Recollection and Observations*. New York: Harper & Brothers for Council on Foreign Relations, 1936.

Temperley, Arthur C. *The Whispering Gallery of Europe*. London: Collins, 1938.

Tugwell, R. G. *The Brains Trust*. New York: Viking, 1968.

———. "Franklin D. Roosevelt on the Verge of the Presidency." *The Antioch Review* 16, no. 1 (Spring 1956): 46–79.

Vansittart, Robert Lord. *Lessons of My Life.* New York: Knopf, 1934.

———. *The Mist Procession.* London: Hutchinson, 1958.

Williamson, Philip, and Edward Baldwin, eds. *Baldwin Papers: A Conservative Statesman, 1907–1948.* Cambridge: Cambridge University Press, 2004.

Wilson, Hugh R. *Diplomat between Wars.* New York: Longmans, Green, 1941.

Woodward, E. L. *Short Journey.* London: Faber and Faber, 1942.

E. Contemporary Comment and Analysis (Ex-Press)

Alain. *Elements d'une doctrine radicale.* Paris: Gallimard, 1933.

———. *Propos sur les pouvoirs.* Paris: Gallimard, 1938 (1935).

"American Public Opinion on the World Economic Conference." Discussion at Chatham House, London, 13 July 1933. Chatham House Archives, RIIA/8/289.

Anonymous ["Une haute personnalité"]. "Les armements de l'Allemagne." *Revue des deux mondes* 8 (1 February 1932): 509–44.

Anonymous. *Letter of an Old Bolshevik: The Key to the Moscow Trials.* New York: Rand School Press, 1937.

Bechofer, Robert C. E. [Ephesian]. *Stanley Baldwin: Manor Miracle.* New York: Greenberg, 1937.

Berl, Emmanuel. *La Politique et les partis.* Paris: Editions Rieder, 1932.

Bland, J. O. P. *China: The Pity of It.* London: William Heinemann, 1932.

Blum, Léon. *Discours de Romans: Prononcé le 24 juillet 1932.* Valence: Imprimerie de la Volonté socialiste, 1932.

Buell, Raymond Leslie, Walter Millis, and Frank H. Simonds. "Foreign Problems Confronting the New Administration." Foreign Policy Association, 23 February 1933. Comments of Buell and Millis.

Cassel, Gustav. *The Crisis in the World's Monetary System.* Oxford: Clarendon Press, 1932.

Coste, Pierre. *Les Grands Marchés financiers. Paris, Londres, New-York: La Lutte pour la Suprématie.* Paris: Payot, 1932.

Cromwell, James H. R. *The Voice of Young America.* New York: Scribner's, 1933.

Cru, Jean-Norton. *Témoins.* Nancy: Presses Universitaires de Nancy, 2006 (1929).

de Bono, Emilio. "Ieri e oggi in colonia." *Gerarchia,* 7–8 (July–August 1932): 525–32.

Dell, Robert. *The Geneva Racket, 1920–1939.* London: Robert Hale Limited, 1941.

Dos Passos, John. *In All Countries.* New York: Harcourt, Brace, 1934.

Duffort, Louis. *L'Autre Pologne.* Paris: Editions de la Revue mondiale, 1932.

Einzig, Paul. *International Gold Movements.* 2nd ed. London: Macmillan, 1931.

———. *Behind the Scenes of International Finance.* London: Macmillan, 1932.

Embree, John. *Suye Mura: A Japanese Village.* Ann Arbor: Center for Japanese Studies, University of Michigan, 1995 (Chicago, 1939).

Everhart, William Daniel. "The American Press and World Peace." PhD dissertation, University of Southern California, Los Angeles, 1932.

Hawtrey, R. G. *The Gold Standard in Theory and Practice.* 3rd ed. London: Longmans, Green, 1933.

Hillson, Norman. *Geneva Scene.* London: Routledge, 1936.

Hitlers Zweites Buch: Ein Dokument aus dem Jahr 1928. Introduced with a commentary by Gerhard L. Weinberg, with a preface by Hans Rothfels. Stuttgart: Deutsche Verlags-Anstalt, 1961.

Ishiwara, Kanji. "A Plan to Occupy Manchuria." In *Sources of Japanese Tradition*, edited by Wm. Theodore de Bary, Carol Gluck, and Arthur Tiedemann, vol. 2, part 2, pp. 294–98. 2nd ed. New York: Columbia University Press, 2006.

Kentaro, Kaneko. "A 'Japanese Monroe Doctrine' and Manchuria." *Contemporary Japan* 1 (1932): 176–84.

Kérillis, Henri de, and Raymond Cartier. *Faisons le point.* Paris: Grasset, 1931.

Keynes, J. M. "National Self-Sufficiency." In *Collected Writings of John Maynard Keynes*, vol. 21, pp. 233–46. London: Macmillan, Cambridge University Press for the Royal Economic Society, 1982.

———. "Two Years off Gold: How Far Are We from Prosperity Now?" In *Collected Writings of John Maynard Keynes*, vol. 21, pp. 284–88. London: Macmillan, Cambridge University Press for the Royal Economic Society, 1982.

Knickerbocker, H. R. *Can Europe Recover?* London: John Lane, 1932.

———. *The German Crisis.* New York: Farrar & Rinehart, 1932.

Lair, Maurice. "Stresemann." *Revue française des sciences politiques*, July–September 1939, pp. 365–92.

Layton, Sir Walter. "After the World Economic Conference." *Foreign Affairs* 12, no. 1 (October 1933): 20–29.

———. "The Tasks of the World Economic Conference." *Foreign Affairs* 11, no. 3 (April 1933): 406–19.

Lewinsohn, Richard. *Financial Contagion: Lessons from the Great Depression.* Translated by Peter Bild. Berlin: Richard Lewinsohn-Morus Stiftung, 2010 (1934).

Lippmann, Walter, with the Council on Foreign Relations. *The United States in World Affairs: An Account of American Foreign Relations, 1932.* New York: Harper & Brothers, 1933.

———. *The United States in World Affairs: An Account of American Foreign Relations, 1933.* New York: Harper & Brothers, 1934.

Maillaud, Pierre [Pierre Bourdan]. *The English Way.* New York: Oxford University Press, 1946.

Malet, Albert, and Jules Isaac. *Histoire contemporaine (de 1815 à nos jours) 3e année avec la collaboration de M. Henri Bejean.* Paris: Hachette, 1935.

Masaryk, Thomas G. "Pangermanism and the Eastern Question." *The New Europe* 1, no. 1 (19 October 2016): 1–19.

Mussolini, Benito. "The Political and Social Doctrine of Fascism." In *Enciclopedia Italiana*, 1932. English translation in *International Conciliation* 302 (January 1935): 5–17.

Priestley, J. B. *English Journey.* Harmondsworth, UK: Penguin, 1977 (1934).

Renouvin, Pierre. "Les historiens américains et les Responsabilités de la Guerre." *Revue des Deux Mondes*, 15 April 1931.

Rodgers, Marion Elizabeth, ed. *The Impossible H. L. Mencken*. New York: Doubleday, 1991.

Roosevelt, Franklin D. "Our Foreign Policy: A Democratic View." *Foreign Affairs* 6, no. 4 (July 1928).

Royal Institute of International Affairs. *The International Gold Problem: A Record of the Discussions of a Study Group of Members*. Oxford: Oxford University Press, 1931.

Salter, Arthur, Sir. "The Future of Economic Nationalism." *Foreign Affairs* 11, no. 1 (October 1932): 9–20.

Scorza, Carlo. *Fascismo: Idea imperiale*. Rome: De Gasperis, 1933.

Seeckt, Hans von. *Deutschland zwischen West und Ost*. Hamburg: Hanseatische Verlagsanstalt, 1933.

———. *Wege deutscher Aussenpolitik*. Leipzig: Von Quelle & Meyer, 1931.

Seignobos, Charles. "Le sens des élections françaises de 1932." *L'Année politique française et étrangère* 7, no. 3 (November 1932): 273–90.

"The Shanghai Crisis: Record of a Discussion at Chatham House, 22nd February 1932." *International Affairs* 11, no. 2 (March 1932): 153–79.

Siegfried, André. *England's Crisis*. Translated by H. H. Hemming and Doris Hemming. New York: Harcourt, Brace, 1931.

———. *Tableau des Partis en France*. Paris: Bernard Grasset, 1930.

Sikorski, W. "La campagne allemande pour la révision." *Revue des deux mondes* 7, no. 1 (1 January 1932): 49–62.

Simonds, Frank H. *The ABC of War Debts and the Seven Popular Delusions about Them*. New York: Harper & Brothers, 1933.

———. *America Faces the Next War*. New York: Harper & Brothers, 1933.

———. *Can America Stay at Home?* New York: Harper & Brothers, 1932.

Slocombe, George. *A Mirror to Geneva: Its Growth, Grandeur and Decay*. New York: Henry Holt, 1938.

Steed, Wickham. *The Meaning of Hitlerism*. London: Nisbet, 1934.

Stevenson, J. A. "Canada's Foreign Policy." *Pacific Affairs* 7, no. 2 (June 1934): 153–62.

Suarez, Georges. *Profils de Rechange*. Paris: Editions Excelsior, 1933.

Tabouis, Geneviève. *Vingt ans de suspense diplomatique*. Paris: Albin Michel, 1958.

Tardieu, André. *Devant l'obstacle: L'Amérique et nous*. Paris: Emile-Paul Frères, 1927.

Thompson, Dorothy. *I Saw Hitler!* New York: Farrar and Rhinehart, 1932.

Toynbee, Arnold J., ed. *Survey of International Affairs, 1932*. London: Royal Institute of International Affairs, 1933.

———. *Survey of International Affairs, 1936*. London: Oxford University Press, 1937.

Wilson, Edmund. *The American Earthquake: A Documentary of the Twenties and Thirties*. New York: Farrar, Straus and Giroux, 1979 (1958).

Wolfers, Arno. *Britain and France between Two Wars.* New York: Norton, 1966 (1940).

F. Literature, Film, and Drama

Blutendes Deutschland. Directed by Johannes Haüssler. Nazi propaganda film, 1933.

Cremers, Paul Joseph. *Die Marneschlacht* (play). Bielefeld and Leipzig: Velhagen und Klasing, 1932.

Das Wunder um Verdun (Miracle at Verdun). Directed by Hans Chlumberg. 1930. Play produced in Paris, 1932.

Johst, Hanns. *Schlageter.* Play dedicated to Hitler and first performed on his forty-fourth birthday, 20 April 1933.

Les Croix de bois (Wooden Crosses). Directed by Raymond Bernard. 1932. Film based on the novel of the same title by Roland Dorgelès (1919).

Sebastien, Mihail. *For Two Thousand Years.* Translated by Philip Ó Ceallaigh. London: Penguin, 2016 (1934).

II. PRIMARY UNPUBLISHED MATERIALS (ARCHIVES)

A. France

Archives du ministere de l'Europe et des affaires etrangeres (Site de Paris-La Courneuve)

Correspondence politique et commerciale, 1919-1939

18CPCOM 302 USA (correspondance générale politique, juin 1931–octobre 1932).

18CPCOM 303 USA (correspondance générale politique, novembre 1932–décembre 1933).

39 CPCOM 102 Japon (presse, novembre 1930–avril 1933).

39 CPCOM 107 Japon (politique intérieure, 1932).

39CPCOM 108 (microfilm P/16983) Japon (politique intérieure, 1933–1934).

39 CPCOM 117 Japon (politique extérieure, 1932–1934).

39 CPCOM 136 Japon (relations avec URSS, avril–septembre 1932).

39CPCOM 137 Japon (relations avec l'URSS, octobre 1932–avril 1933).

75CPCOM 73 Conférence économique internationale (juin 1932–avril 1933).

75CPCOM 74 Conférence économique internationale (avril–juin 1933).

75CPCOM 75 Conférence économique internationale (22 juin–7 juillet 1933).

75CPCOM 76 Conférence économique internationale (13 juin–31 décembre 1933).

75CPCOM 537 Conférence du désarmement (mars–avril 1933).

75CPCOM 538 Conférence du désarmement (1–15 mai 1933).

78CPCOM 676 (microfilm P/16687) Allemagne (politique intérieure, septembre 1932–juin 1933).

78CPCOM-620-22-1 Allemagne (presse, septembre 1932–mai 1933).

92 CPCOM 210 Grande-Bretagne (presse, octobre 1932).

92CPCOM 211 Grande-Bretagne (presse, novembre 1932).

92CPCOM 213 Grande-Bretagne (presse, janvier 1933).

92CPCOM 182 Grande-Bretagne (presse, 1930–1936).

92CPCOM 262 Grande Bretagne (politique intérieure, dossier général, 1932–1933).

92 CPCOM 270 Grande Bretagne (politique extérieure, 27 octobre 1930–30 août 1934).

94CPCOM 108 Hongrie (politique intérieure, octobre 1931–octobre 1932).

94CPCOM 109 Hongrie (politique intérieure, novembre 1932–juillet 1934).

97CPCOM-258 Italie (politique intérieure, 1932–1936).

97 CPCOM 269 Italie (politique extérieure, 1932–1935).

97CPCOM 235–366–1 Italie (presse, 1932–1935).

106CPCOM 322 Pologne (politique intérieure, avril 1932–avril 1934).

106CPCOM 333 Pologne (affaires extérieures, 1930–1932).

106CPCOM 334 Pologne (affaires extérieures, janvier 1933–janvier 1934).

106CPCOM 350 Pologne (relations avec l'Allemagne, janvier 1931–mars 1932).

106CPCOM 351 Pologne (relations avec l'Allemagne, avril–décembre 1932).

110CPCOM 170 Roumanie (politique intérieure, 1 mai 1931–31 mars 1933).

110CPCOM 177 Roumanie (politique extérieure, 1 janvier 1930–31 décembre 1932).

110CPCOM 178 Roumanie (politique extérieure, 1 janvier 1933–mai 1934).

116CPCOM 94 Tchécoslovaquie (presse 1930–1935).

116CPCOM 101 Tchécoslovaquie (politique intérieure, 1930–1935).

117CPCOM 925 URSS (armée, mai 1932–1935–1940).

117CP COM 960 URSS (politique extérieure, mai 1932–décembre 1933).

117 CPCOM 985 Relations entre l'URSS et l'Allemagne (juin 1932–mai 1933).

117CPCOM 986 Relations entre l'URSS et Allemagne (juin 1933–avril 1934).

118CPCOM 161 Yougoslavie (politique intérieure, juillet 1932–février 1933).

118CPCOM 177 Yougoslavie (politique extérieure, 1932–1933).

Archives Nationales (Pierrefitte-Sur-Seine, France).

Série F7 (police-renseignements généraux)

F7 13429 Allemagne 1932.

F7 13430 Allemagne 1933.

F7 13504 USSR 1932.

Archives François-Poncet

462 AP 14 (ambassade de France, 1931–1939).

Archives Tardieu

PA-AP 166 498 Conférence du désarmement, novembre 1931–janvier 1932.

PA-AP 166 505 Conférence du désarmement, 12–29 février 1932.

PA-AP 166 508 Conférence de désarmement, janvier–février 1932.

Service Historique de la Défense (Vincennes, France)

1 N 34 Conseil supérieur de la guerre, 1934.
GR 1 N42 (Etat major Weygand, 1930–1935).
GR 1 N85 (Exercises combines, 1932–1933).

B. Great Britain

The National Archives (Kew, Richmond, Surrey, UK)

Foreign Office Correspondence

FO 371/16243: Political—far eastern, Japan (1932).
FO 370/16151: Political—far eastern, general (mostly Shanghai crisis, 1932).
FO 371/16163: Political—far eastern, China (1932).

Cabinet

T 188/71: Cabinet committee on world economic conference, May 1933.
Cab. 24/233/22: Memorandum to cabinet from foreign secretary, September 1932.
Cab. 23/72/10: Cabinet minutes, 11 October 1932.

C. United States

National Archives and Records Administration (College Park, Maryland)

General Records of the Department of State

RG 59.862, vol. 84: Germany, internal affairs, 1932–1933, or box.
RG 59 762.00: Germany, external affairs.
RG 59 T-1249 (microfilm): Soviet Union internal affairs, 1930–1939.

Roll 1, 1932–1933

RG 84 vols. 84, 93, 765–768: Japan Legation and Consular Posts, 1932–1933.
RG 165: Records of the War Department General and Special Staffs (microfilm).
M1216: Correspondence of military intelligence on conditions in Japan, 1918–1941
    (31 rolls).
Roll 2: 1932–1933

FDR Presidential Library (Hyde Park, NY)

Significant Documents Collection, FDR 9-A box 156 (draft of message of 3 July
    1933).

D. League of Nations Archives (Geneva)

R 1869: Sino-Japanese dispute, 1931–1933.
R 1871: Sino-Japanese dispute, 1932.
R 3609: Sino-Japanese dispute, 1933.
S 474: Arthur Henderson, 1931–1933.

III. SECONDARY PUBLISHED WORKS

Applebaum, Anne. *Red Famine: Stalin's War on Ukraine.* New York: Doubleday, 2017.

Audouin-Rouzeau, Stéphane, and Annette Becker. *14–18: Retrouver la guerre.* Paris: Gallimard, 2000.

Bailey, Thomas A. *The Man in the Street: The Impact of American Public Opinion on Foreign Policy.* New York: Macmillan, 1948.

Barth, Rüdiger, and Hauke Friederichs. *Die Totengräber: Der letzte Winter der Weimarer Republik.* Frankfurt: Fischer, 2018.

Beard, Charles A. *American Foreign Policy in the Making, 1932–1940: A Study in Responsibilities.* New Haven, CT: Yale University Press, 1946.

Beasley, W. G. *Japanese Imperialism, 1894–1945.* New York: Oxford University Press, 1987.

Beaudry, Paul. "The French Depression in the 1930s." *Review of Economic Dynamics* 1, no. 5 (2002): 73–99.

Beetham, David. *Marxists in Face of Fascism: Writings by Marxists on Fascism from the Inter-war Period.* Totowa, NJ: Barnes & Noble Books, 1984.

Bennett, Edward W. *German Rearmament and the West, 1932–1933.* Princeton, NJ: Princeton University Press, 1979.

Bickers, Robert. *Out of China: How the Chinese Ended the Era of Western Domination.* Cambridge, MA: Harvard University Press, 2017.

Biskupski, M. B. B. *Independence Day: Myth, Symbol, and the Creation of Modern Poland.* Oxford: Oxford University Press, 2012.

Bond, Brian. *Britain's Two World Wars against Germany: Myth, Memory and the Distortion of Hindsight.* Cambridge: Cambridge University Press, 2014.

Boyce, Robert. *The Great Interwar Crisis.* London: Palgrave Macmillan, 2009.

Boyce, Robert, and Joseph A. Maiolo, eds. *The Origins of World War Two: The Debate Continues.* London: Palgrave Macmillan, 2003.

Breitman, Richard, and Allan J. Lichtman. *FDR and the Jews.* Cambridge, MA: The Belknap Press of Harvard University Press, 2013.

Burkman, Thomas W. *Japan and the League of Nations: Empire and World Order, 1914–1938.* Honolulu: University of Hawaii Press, 2008.

Carr, E. H. *Conditions of Peace.* London: Macmillan, 1942.

———. *The Twenty Years' Crisis.* London: Macmillan, 1961 (1939).

Chuter, David. *Humanity's Soldier: France and International Security, 1919–2001.* Providence and Oxford: Berghahn, 1996.

Cienciala, Anna M. "Polish Foreign Policy, 1926–1939. 'Equilibrium': Stereotype and Reality." *Polish Review* 20, no. 1 (1975): 42–57.

Clark, Ian. *Globalization and Fragmentation: International Relations in the Twentieth Century.* Oxford: Oxford University Press, 1997.

Clarke, Peter. *Hope and Glory: Britain 1900–1990.* London: Penguin, 1996.

Claude, Inis L. "The Balance of Power Revisited." *Review of International Studies* 15, no. 2 (1989): 77–85.

Clavin, Patricia. *Securing the World Economy: The Reinvention of the League of Nations, 1920–1946.* Oxford: Oxford University Press, 2015 (2013).

Clavin, Patricia, and Jens-Wilhelm Wessels. "Another Golden Idol? The League of Nations' Gold Delegation and the Great Depression, 1929–1932." *The International History Review* 26, no. 4 (2004): 765–95.

Clemens, Detlev. *Herr Hitler in Germany: Wahrnehmung jund Deutungen des Nationalsozialismus in Grossbritannien 1920 bis 1939.* Göttingen: Vandenhoeck & Ruprecht, 1996.

Cohen, Warren I. *The American Revisionists: The Lessons of Intervention in World War I.* Chicago: University of Chicago Press, 1967.

Colarizi, Simona. *L'opinione degli italiani sotto il regime, 1929–43.* Rome and Bari: Laterza, 1991.

Coox, Alvin D. "The Kwantung Army Dimension." In *The Japanese Informal Empire in China, 1895–1937,* edited by Peter Duus, Ramon H. Myers, and Mark R. Peattie, 395–428. Princeton, NJ: Princeton University Press, 1989.

Corner, Paul. "Fascist Italy in the 1930s: Popular Opinion in the Provinces." In *Popular Opinion in Totalitarian Regimes: Fascism, Nazism, Communism,* edited by Paul Corner, 122–46. Oxford: Oxford University Press, 2009.

———. *The Fascist Party and Popular Opinion in Mussolini's Italy.* Oxford: Oxford University Press, 2012.

Corvaja, Santi. *Hitler and Mussolini: The Secret Meetings.* Translated by R. L. Miller. New York: Enigma, 2001.

Cowley, Malcolm. *Exile's Return: A Literary Odyssey of the American 1920s.* New York: Penguin, 1979 (1951).

Cowling, Maurice. *The Impact of Hitler: British Politics and British Policy, 1933–1940.* Cambridge: Cambridge University Press, 1975.

Cox, Robert W. "Social Forces, States, and World Orders: Beyond International Relations Theory." In *Neorealism and Its Critics,* edited by Robert O. Keohane. New York: Columbia University Press, 1986.

Crocket, Jameson W. "The Polish Blitz, More than a Mere Footnote to History: Poland and Preventive War with Germany, 1933." *Diplomacy and Statecraft* 20, no. 4 (November 2009): 561–79.

Dallek, Robert. *Franklin Roosevelt and American Foreign Policy, 1932–1945.* Oxford: Oxford University Press, 1995 (1979).

Davies, R. W. "Edward Hallett Carr, 1892–1982." *Proceedings of the British Academy* 69 (1983): 473–511.

———. "Soviet Military Expenditure and the Armaments Industry, 1929–1933: A Reconsideration." *Europe-Asia Studies* 45, no. 4 (1993): 577–608.

Davies, Thomas R. *The Possibilities of Transnational Activism: The Campaign for Disarmament between the Two World Wars*. Boston: Martinus Nijhoff, 2007.

Deist, Wilhelm, et al. *Ursachen und Voraussetzungen des Zweiten Weltkrieges*. Vol. 1 of *Das deutsche Reich und der zweite Weltkrieg*. Freiburg: Militärgeschichtliches Forschungsamt, 1979–2014 (9 vols.; 14 vols. projected).

del Boca, Angelo. *La Guerra d'Etiopia: L'Ultima impresa del colonialismo*. Milan: Longanesi, 2010.

Divine, Robert A. *The Illusion of Neutrality*. Chicago: University of Chicago Press, 1962.

Doenecke, Justus D., ed. *The Diplomacy of Frustration: The Manchurian Crisis of 1931–1933 as Revealed in the Papers of Stanley K. Hornbeck*. Palo Alto, CA: Hoover Institution Press, 1981.

Doughty, Robert Allan. *The Seeds of Disaster: The Development of French Army Doctrine, 1919–1939*. Hamden, CT: Archon, 1985.

Duggan, Christopher. "The Internalization of the Cult of the Duce: The Evidence of Diaries and Letters." In *The Cult of the Duce: Mussolini and the Italians*, edited by Stephen Gundle, Christopher Duggan, and Giuliana Peri, 129–43. Manchester, UK: Manchester University Press, 2013.

Duus, Peter. "Introduction." In *The Japanese Informal Empire in China, 1895–1937*, edited by Peter Duus, Ramon H. Myers, and Mark R. Peattie, xi–xxix. Princeton, NJ: Princeton University Press, 1989.

Edwards, Sebastien. *American Default: The Untold Story of FDR, the Supreme Court, and the Battle over Gold*. Princeton, NJ: Princeton University Press, 2018.

Eichengreen, Barry. *Globalizing Capital. A History of the International Monetary System*. 2nd ed. Princeton, NJ: Princeton University Press, 2008.

Eichengreen, Barry, and Peter Temin. "The Gold Standard and the Great Depression." *Contemporary European History* 9, no. 2 (2000): 183–207.

Enders, Paul. "Cremers" [Paul Joseph]. In *Neue deutsche Biographie*. Berlin: Bürklein-Ditmar, 1957.

Engerman, David C. "Modernization from the Other Shore: American Observers and the Costs of Soviet Economic Development." *American Historical Review* 105, no. 2 (April 2000): 383–416.

Evans, Richard. *The Coming of the Third Reich*. London: Penguin, 2003.

Falter, Jürgen. *Hitlers Wähler*. Munich: Verlag C. H. Beck, 1991.

Farrell, Nicholas. *Mussolini: A New Life*. London: Weidenfeld & Nicolson, 2003.

Feinstein, Charles H., Peter Temin, and Gianni Toniolo. *The World Economy between the Wars*. 2nd ed. New York: Oxford University Press, 2008.

Figes, Orlando. *The Whisperers: Private Life in Stalin's Russia*. New York: Metropolitan Books, 2007.

Fischer, Conan. *Stormtroopers: A Social, Economic, and Ideological Analysis, 1929–35*. London: George Allen & Unwin, 1983.

Fischer, Fritz. *Griff nach der Weltmacht: Die Kriegzielpolitik des kaiserlichen Deutschland, 1914–1918*. Düsseldorf: Droste, 1961.

Fitzpatrick, Sheila. *Everyday Stalinism: Ordinary Life in Extraordinary Times: Soviet Russia in the 1930s*. New York: Oxford University Press, 1999.

Fitzpatrick, Sheila. *On Stalin's Team: The Years of Living Dangerously in Soviet Politics*. Princeton, NJ: Princeton University Press, 2015.

Förster, Jürgen. *Die Wehrmacht im NS-Staat*. Munich: Oldenbourg, 2007.

Freidel, Frank. *Franklin D. Roosevelt: The Ordeal*. Boston: Little, Brown, 1954.

———. *Franklin D. Roosevelt: The Triumph*. Boston: Little, Brown, 1956.

Garlicki, Andrzej. *Józef Piłsudski, 1867–1935*. Edited and translated by John Coutouvidis. Aldershot, UK: Scolar Press, 1995.

Gauss, Gunter. "'What Remains? The Language Remains.' A Conversation with Gunter Gauss." In *The Portable Hannah Arendt*, edited by Peter Baehr, 5–6. New York: Penguin, 2000.

Gentile, Emilio. *The Sacralization of Politics in Fascist Italy*. Translated by Keith Botsford. Cambridge, MA: Harvard University Press, 1996.

Gerwarth, Robert. *The Vanquished: Why the First World War Failed to End*. New York: Farrar, Straus and Giroux, 2018.

Golubev, A. V. "'Rossiia mozhet polagat'sia lish' na samu sebia': Predstavleniia o budushchei voine v sovetskom obshchestve 1930-kh godov" ["Russia can depend on herself alone": The Soviet public's perspectives concerning a future war in the 1930s]. *Otechestvennaia istoriia* no. 5 (2008): 108–27.

———. *"Esli mir obrushitsia na nashu Respubliku . . .": Sovestkoe obshchestvo i vneshniaia ugroza v 1920–1940-e gg.* ["If the world descends on our Republic . . .": Soviet society and the external threat, 1920s–1940s]. Moscow: Kuchkovo pole, 2008.

Haas, Richard. *A World in Disarray: American Foreign Policy and the Crisis of the Old Order*. New York: Penguin, 2017.

Harris, James. *The Great Fear: Stalin's Terror of the 1930s*. New York: Oxford University Press, 2016.

Haslam, Jonathan. *No Virtue like Necessity: Realist Thought in International Relations since Machiavelli*. New Haven, CT: Yale University Press, 2002.

———. *Soviet Foreign Policy, 1930–1933: The Impact of the Depression*. London: Macmillan, 1983.

———. *The Soviet Union and the Struggle for Collective Security in Europe, 1933–39*. London: Macmillan, 1984.

———. *The Soviet Union and the Threat from the East, 1933–1941: Moscow, Tokyo, and the Prelude to the Pacific War*. Pittsburgh: University of Pittsburgh Press, 1992.

———. *The Vices of Integrity: E. H. Carr, 1892–1982*. New York: Verso, 1999.

Hein, Heidi. *Der Piłsudski-Kult und seine Bedeutung für den polnischen Staat, 1926–1939*. Marburg: Herder-Institut, 2002.

Hellbeck, Jochen. *Revolution on My Mind: Writing a Diary under Stalin*. Cambridge, MA: Harvard University Press, 2006.

Henriot, Christian. *Shanghai, 1927–1937: Municipal Power, Locality, and Modernization*. Translated by Noël Castelino. Berkeley: University of California Press, 1993 (1991).

Hiden, John. "National Socialism and Foreign Policy, 1919–1933." In *The Nazi Machtergreifung*, edited by Peter Stachura, 146–61. London: George Allen & Unwin, 1983.

Hill, Alexander. *The Red Army and the Second World War*. Cambridge: Cambridge University Press, 2017.

Hitchins, Keith. *Rumania, 1866–1947*. Oxford: Oxford University Press, 1994.

Holman, Brett. "The Air Panic of 1935: British Press Opinion between Disarmament and Rearmament." *Journal of Contemporary History* 46, no. 2 (2011): 288–307.

Imbriani, Angelo Michele. *Gli Italiani e il Duce: Il mito e l'imaggine di Mussolini negli ultimi anni del fascismo (1938–1943)*. Naples: Liguore, 1992.

Jacobson, Jon. *When the Soviet Union Entered World Politics*. Berkeley: University of California Press, 1994.

Jácome, Luis I. "Central Banking in Latin America: From the Gold Standard to the Golden Years." International Monetary Fund, working paper 15/60, Monetary and Capital Markets Department, March 2015.

James, Harold. *The End of Globalization: Lessons from the Great Depression*. Cambridge: Harvard University Press, 2001.

Jankowski, Paul. "Twenty Years of Disenchantment: The American Entry into World War I Remembered, 1917–1937." *South Central Review* 34, no. 3 (Fall 2017): 115–27.

Jardin, Pierre. *Aux racines du mal: 1918 le déni de la défaite*. Paris: Tallandier, 2005.

Jędrzejewicz, Wacław. "The Polish Plan for a 'Preventive War' against Germany in 1933." *Polish Review* 11, no. 1 (Winter 1966): 62–91.

Jordan, Donald A. *China's Trial by Fire: The Shanghai War of 1932*. Ann Arbor: University of Michigan Press, 2001.

Kagan, Robert. *The Jungle Grows Back: America and Our Imperiled World*. New York: Knopf, 2018.

Kehr, Eckhart. *Schlachtflottenbau und Parteipolitik, 1894–1901*. Berlin: E. Ebering, 1930.

Kellerhoff, Sven Fellix. *"Mein Kampf": Die Karriere eines deutsches Buches*. Stuttgart: Klett-Cotta, 2015.

Keohane, Robert O. "Theory of World Politics: Structural Realism and Beyond." In *Neorealism and Its Critics*, edited by Robert O. Keohane, 158–94. New York: Columbia University Press, 1986.

Kershaw, Ian. *Hitler*. Vol. 1, *Hubris, 1889–1893*. New York: Norton, 1998.

———. *The Hitler Myth: Image and Reality in the Third Reich*. New York: Oxford University Press, 1989 (1987).

Kimmel, Adolf. *Der Aufstieg des Nationalsozialismus im Spiegel der französischen Presse, 1930–1933*. Bonn: H. Bouvier, 1969.

Knox, MacGregor. *Common Destiny: Dictatorship, Foreign Policy, and War in Fascist Italy and Nazi Germany*. New York: Cambridge University Press, 2000.

Kotkin, Stephen. *Magnetic Mountain: Stalinism as a Civilization*. Berkeley: University of California Press, 1995.

———. *Stalin*. Vol. 2. New York: Penguin, 2017.

Large, Stephen S. "Nationalist Extremism in Early Showa Japan: Inoue Nissho and the 'Blood-Pledge Corps Incident,' 1932." *Modern Asian Studies* 35, no. 3 (July 2001): 533–64.

———. "Substantiating the Nation: Terrorist Trials as Nationalist Theatre in Early Showa Japan." In *Nation and Nationalism in Japan*, edited by Sandra Wilson, 55–68. New York: Routledge Curzon, 2002.

Lauridsen, John T. *Nazism and the Radical Right in Austria, 1918–1934*. Translated by Michael Wolfe. Copenhagen: Museum Tusculanum Press, 2007.

Lieven, Dominic. *The End of Tsarist Russia: The March to World War I and Revolution*. New York: Penguin, 2015.

Linklater, Andrew. *Beyond Realism and Marxism: Critical Theory and International Relations*. Basingstoke: Macmillan, 1990.

Lipset, Seymour Martin. *Political Man: The Social Basis of Politics*. Baltimore: Johns Hopkins University Press, 1981.

Little, Richard. "Deconstructing the Balance of Power: Two Traditions of Thought." *Review of International Studies* 15, no. 2 (1989): 87–100.

Macartney, C. A. "Hungary and the Present Crisis." *International Affairs* (Royal Institute of International Affairs, 1931–1939) 17, no. 6 (1938): 749–68.

Maiolo, Joseph. *Cry Havoc: How the Arms Race Drove the World to War, 1931–1941*. New York: Basic Books, 2010.

Maitland, Frederick William. *Why the History of English Law Is not Written: An Inaugural Lecture Delivered in the Arts School at Cambridge on 13 October 1888*. London: C. J. Clay & Sons, 1888.

Mallett, Robert. *Mussolini in Ethiopia, 1919–1935*. New York: Cambridge University Press, 2015.

Martin, Terry. *The Affirmative Action Empire: Nations and Nationalism in the Soviet Union, 1923–1939*. Ithaca, NY: Cornell University Press, 2001.

———. "The Origins of Soviet Ethnic Cleansing." *Journal of Modern History* 70, no. 4 (December 1998): 813–61. See especially pp. 836–46.

Matsusaka, Y. Tak. "Managing Occupied Manchuria, 1931–1934." In *Japanese Wartime Empire, 1931–1945*, edited by Peter Duus, Ramon H. Myers, and Mark R. Peattie, 97–135. Princeton, NJ: Princeton University Press, 1996.

McCarthy, Helen. *The British People and the League of Nations: Democracy, Citizenship, and Internationalism, c. 1918–1945*. Manchester: Manchester University Press, 2011.

McDonough, Frank. "Introduction." In *The Origins of the Second World War: An International Perspective*, edited by Frank McDonough. New York: Continuum, 2011.

McKibbin, Ross. *Parties and People: England, 1914–1951*. Oxford: Oxford University Press, 2010.

Moley, Raymond. *The First New Deal*. New York: Harcourt, Brace, 1966.

Montefiore, Simon Sebag. *Stalin: The Court of the Red Tsar*. New York: Vintage, 2003.

Morena, Antonio. *Mussolini's Decennale: Aura and Mythmaking in Fascist Italy.* Toronto: University of Toronto Press, 2015.

Morgenthau, Hans J. "The Mainsprings of American Foreign Policy: The National Interest vs. Moral Abstractions." *American Political Science Review* 44, no. 4 (1950): 833–54.

Mosse, George. *Fallen Soldiers: Reshaping the Memory of the World Wars.* New York: Oxford University Press, 1990.

Mowat, Charles Loch. *Britain between the Wars, 1918–1940.* Chicago: University of Chicago Press, 1969 (1955).

Murnane, John R. "Japan's Monroe Doctrine? Re-Framing the Story of Pearl Harbor." *The History Teacher* 40, no. 4 (August 2007): 503–20.

Murphy, Jessica. "Charles Sheeler (1883–1965)." Website of the Metropolitan Museum of Art, New York City, November 2009, https://www.metmuseum.org /toah/hd/shee/hd_shee.htm.

Murray, Williamson. "Armored Warfare: The British, French, and German Experiences." In *Military Innovation in the Interwar Period*, edited by Williamson Murray and Allan R. Millett, 6–49. Cambridge: Cambridge University Press, 1996.

Myers, Ramon H. "Creating a Modern Enclave: The Economic Integration of Japan, Manchuria, and North China, 1932–1945." In *Japanese Wartime Empire, 1931–1945*, edited by Peter Duus, Ramon H. Myers, and Mark R. Peattie, 136–70. Princeton, NJ: Princeton University Press, 1996.

Nekrich, Aleksandr M. *Pariahs, Partners, Predators: German-Soviet Relations, 1922–1941.* Edited and translated by Gregory L. Freeze. New York: Columbia University Press, 1997.

Néré, Jacques. *La Crise de 1929.* Paris: Armand Colin, 1973.

Neumann, Franz. *Behemoth: The Structure and Practice of National Socialism.* New York: Oxford University Press, 1944 (1942).

Neville, Peter. *Benes and Masaryk: Czechoslovakia.* London: Haus, 2010.

Nicholls, A. J. *Weimar and the Rise of Hitler.* New York: St. Martin's Press, 1991 (1968).

Nielsen, Christina Axboe. *Making Yugoslavs: Identity in King Aleksandar's Yugoslavia.* Toronto: University of Toronto Press, 2014.

Nish, Ian. *Japan's Struggle with Internationalism: Japan, China, and the League of Nations, 1931–3.* London: Kegan Paul International, 1993.

Northedge, F. S. *The League of Nations: Its Life and Times, 1920–1946.* Leicester: Leicester University Press, 1986.

Perrot, Marguerite. *La Monnaie et l'Opinion Publique en France et en Angleterre de 1924 à 1936.* Paris: Cahiers de la Fondation Nationale des Sciences Politiques, 1955.

Plach, Eva. *The Clash of Moral Nation: Cultural Politics in Pilsudski's Poland, 1926–1935.* Athens: Ohio University Press, 2006.

Plöckinger, Othmar. *Geschichte eines Buches: Adolf Hitlers "Mein Kampf," 1922–1945.* Munich: Institut für Zeithgeschichte/R. Oldenbourg, 2006.

———. *Reden um die Macht? Wirkung und Strategie der Reden Adolf Hitlers im*

Wahlkampf zu den Reichstagswahlen am 6. November 1932. Wien: Passagen Verlag, 1999.

Polonsky, Antony. *Politics in Independent Poland, 1921–1939*. Oxford: Oxford University Press, 1972.

Pünder, Hermann. *Politik in der Reichskanzlei: Aufzeichnungen aus den Jahren, 1929–1932*. Stuttgart: Deutsche Verlags-Anstalt, 1961.

Reynolds, David. *The Long Shadow: The Legacies of the Great War in the Twentieth Century*. New York: Norton, 2014.

———. "The Origins of Two 'World Wars': Historical Discourse and International Politics." *Journal of Contemporary History* 38, no. 1 (January 2003): 29–44.

Ritchie, Donald A. *Electing FDR: The New Deal Campaign of 1932*. Lawrence: University Press of Kansas, 2007.

Robertson, Esmonde, ed. *The Origins of the Second World War: Historical Interpretations*. London: Macmillan, 1971.

Samuelson, Lennart. *Soviet Defense Industry Planning: Tukhachevskii and Military-Industrial Mobilization, 1926–1937*. Stockholm: Institute of East European Economies, 1996.

Scalapino, Robert A. *Democracy and the Party Movement in Prewar Japan: The Failure of the First Attempt*. Berkeley: University of California Press, 1975 (1953).

Schivelbusch, Wolfgang. *The Culture of Defeat: On National Trauma, Mourning and Recovery*. Translated by Jefferson Chase. London: Picador, 2004 (2001).

Schrecker, Ellen. *The Hired Money: The French Debt to the United States, 1917–1929*. New York: Arno Press, 1978.

Schroeder, Paul. *The Transformation of European Politics, 1763–1848*. New York: Oxford University Press, 1994.

Schweller, Randall L. "The Twenty Years' Crisis, 1919–1939: Why a Concert Didn't Arise." In *Bridges and Boundaries: Historians, Political Scientists, and the Study of International Relations*, edited by Colin Elman and Miriam Fendius Elman, 182–212. Cambridge: Massachusetts Institute of Technology Press, 2001.

Skidelsky, Robert. *Politicians and the Slump: The Labour Government of 1929–1931*. London: Macmillan, 1967.

Snyder, Timothy. *Bloodlands: Europe between Hitler and Stalin*. New York: Basic Books, 2010.

Stachura, Peter, ed. *Poland between the Wars, 1918–1939*. London: Macmillan, 1998.

Sternsher, Bernard. "The Stimson Doctrine: F.D.R. versus Moley and Tugwell." *Pacific Historical Review* 31, no. 3 (August 1962): 281–89.

Stone, David R. *Hammer and Rifle: The Militarization of the Soviet Union, 1926–1933*. Lawrence: University of Kansas Press, 2000.

Stoneman, William. *A History of the Economic Analysis of the Great Depression in America*. New York: Garland, 1979.

Strang, G. Bruce. *On the Fiery March: Mussolini Prepares for War*. Westport, CT: Praeger, 2003.

Takeuchi, Sterling Tatsuji. *War and Diplomacy in the Japanese Empire*. New York: Routledge, 2011 (1935).

Taylor, A. J. P. *The Course of German History: A Survey of the Development of Germany since 1815.* London: H. Hamilton, 1945.

———. *The Origins of the Second World War.* London: H. Hamilton, 1961.

———. *The Struggle for Mastery in Europe, 1848–1918.* New York: Oxford University Press, 1971 (1954).

Thucydides. *History of the Peloponnesian War.* Translated by Rex Warner. London: Penguin, 1972 (1954).

Tooze, Adam. *The Wages of Destruction: The Making and Breaking of the Nazi Economy.* New York: Penguin, 2008 (2006).

Tugwell, Rexford G. *The Democratic Roosevelt: A Biography of Franklin D. Roosevelt.* Garden City, NY: Doubleday, 1957.

Ullrich, Volker. *Adolf Hitler: Die Jahre des Aufstiegs.* Vol. 1. Frankfurt: Fischer Verlag, 2013.

Vaïsse, Maurice. *Sécurité d'abord: La Politique française en matière de désarmement, 9 décembre 1930–17 avril 1934.* Paris: Pedone, 1981.

Vigor, P. H. *The Soviet View of War, Peace and Neutrality.* London: Routledge, 1975.

Vitkine, Antoine. *Mein Kampf: Histoire d'un livre.* Paris: Flammarion, 2009.

Waley, Daniel. *British Public Opinion and the Abyssinian War, 1935–6.* London: Temple Smith, 1975.

Waltz, Kenneth Neal. *Theory of International Politics.* New York: Random House, 1979.

Webster, Andrew. "The League of Nations, Disarmament and Internationalism." In *Internationalisms: A Twentieth-Century History*, edited by Glenda Sluga and Patricia Clavin. Cambridge: Cambridge University Press, 2017.

Wehler, Hans-Ullrich. *Das Deutsche Kaiserreich, 1871–1918.* Göttingen: Vandenhoeck & Ruprecht, 1973.

Wendt, Alexander. "Anarchy Is What States Make of It: The Social Construction of Power Politics." *International Organization* 46, no. 2 (Spring 1992): 391–425.

———. "Constructing International Politics." *International Security* 20, no. 1 (Summer 1995): 71–81.

Williamson, Philip. "Baldwin's Reputation: Politics and History, 1937–1967." *Historical Journal* 47, no. 1 (2004): 127–68.

———. *Stanley Baldwin: Conservative Leadership and National Values.* Cambridge: Cambridge University Press, 1999.

Wilson, Sandra. *The Manchurian Crisis and Japanese Society, 1931–33.* New York: Routledge, 2002.

Wirsching, Andreas. "'Man kann nur Boden germanisieren': Eine neue Quelle zu Hitlers rede vor den Spitzen der Reichswehr am 3. Februar 1933." *Vierteljahrshefte für Zeitgeschichte* 49 (2002): 516–50.

Young, G. M. *Stanley Baldwin.* London: Rupert Hart-Davis, 1952.

Young, Louise. *Japan's Total Empire: Manchuria and the Culture of Wartime Imperialism.* Berkeley: University of California Press, 1998.

Zalampas, Michael. *Adolf Hitler and the Third Reich in American Magazines, 1923–1939.* Bowling Green, OH: Bowling Green State University Popular Press, 1989.

Index

About the Author

PAUL JANKOWSKI is the Ray Ginger Professor of History at Brandeis University. He grew up in Geneva, New York, and Paris, and attended international schools before taking undergraduate and graduate degrees at Balliol College, Oxford. He is the author of several books, including most recently *Verdun: The Longest Battle of the Great War*. He currently researches the disintegration of the world order in the era between the world wars, and lives in Cambridge, Massachusetts.